Football and Social Sciences in Brazil

Sérgio Settani Giglio · Marcelo Weishaupt Proni
Editors

Football and Social Sciences in Brazil

Editors
Sérgio Settani Giglio 🆔
School of Physical Education
University of Campinas
Campinas, São Paulo, Brazil

Marcelo Weishaupt Proni
Institute of Economics
University of Campinas
Campinas, São Paulo, Brazil

ISBN 978-3-030-84688-6   ISBN 978-3-030-84686-2 (eBook)
https://doi.org/10.1007/978-3-030-84686-2

Jointly published with Editora da Unicamp, Campinas.
Original Portuguese edition published by Editora da Unicamp, Campinas, Brazil, 2020.
1st edition: © Editora da Unicamp and the authors 2020

This Springer imprint is published by the registered company Springer Nature Switzerland AG
The registered company address is: Gewerbestrasse 11, 6330 Cham, Switzerland

Contents

1   **Football as a Multifaceted Object of Academic Studies in Brazil** ...   1
Sérgio Settani Giglio and Marcelo Weishaupt Proni

Part I   Politics and History

2   **Football and Politics** 13
Luiz Carlos Ribeiro

3   **"My Concern Was to Play Football": Relations Between
Football and Dictatorship** 31
Sérgio Settani Giglio

4   **The Political Dimension of "*Futebol-Arte*"** 49
José Paulo Florenzano

5   **1982 World Cup: Democratic Winds in Spain and Brazil** 65
Alvaro Vicente do Cabo

6   **Brazilian Football and History** 85
João Manuel Casquinha Malaia Santos

7   **Myths, Football and National Identity (1930–1983)** 97
Denaldo Alchorne de Souza

8   **Order and Progress on the Grandstands: Sports Journalism
and the Genesis of Uniformed Football Fans During
the Political Regime of the Estado Novo (1937–1945)** 113
Bernardo Buarque de Hollanda and Aníbal Chaim

Part II   Sociology and Anthropology

9   **Sport and Society in the Writings of Roberto DaMatta** 133
Alexandre Fernandez Vaz

10 Neymar, Football and the Formation of a Neoliberal Culture 149
    Michel Nicolau Netto and Sávio Cavalcante

11 A Modernity that is not Complete? Ideas and Interpretations
    About Brazilian Football 173
    Juliano de Souza and Wanderley Marchi Júnior

12 FIFA, BRICS, and the Soft Power Discourse: Analysis
    of the World Cup in South Africa, Brazil, and Russia 193
    Marco Bettine

13 Football and Anthropology in Brazil 205
    Arlei Sander Damo

14 An Ethnographic Game of Fluid Categories of Analysis 227
    Enrico Spaggiari

15 Garrincha, Pelé and Maradona: The *Sporting Sacred* in Times
    of Football Icon Veneration 243
    Luiz Henrique de Toledo

16 When Does the World Cup 2014 Event Start and End? 263
    Martin Curi

Part III Other Areas

17 Football and Communication Studies in Brazil: Fences
    and Crossroads of an Indisciplinary Field 281
    Édison Gastaldo

18 Sport and the Media in Brazil: Vices and Virtues of a Secular
    Marriage 291
    José Carlos Marques

19 World Cups' Geography: Urban Brazil in 1950 307
    Gilmar Mascarenhas

20 Stadiums and Arenas as Privileged Lenses to Capture
    Changes in Urban Space 321
    Fernando da Costa Ferreira

21 The Football Industry in Brazil 335
    Marcelo Weishaupt Proni

22 The Controversy Over the Introduction of the VAR in Brazil 373
    Sérgio Settani Giglio and Marcelo Weishaupt Proni

Part IV Transversal Themes

23 Life Projects, Women and Football 397
    Osmar Moreira de Souza Júnior and Heloisa Helena Baldy dos Reis

24 Brazil is *Hexa*: Marta's Sporting Career 413
Cláudia Samuel Kessler and Silvana Vilodre Goellner

**25 Gender Expressions and the Multiple Practices of Football
in Brazil** 429
Wagner Xavier de Camargo

26 Football, Violence, and Democratic Politics in Brazil 443
Heloisa Helena Baldy dos Reis and Mariana Zuaneti Martins

**27 Narratives About Football Hooliganism in Brazil:
(De)constructing the Label "Violent Supporter"** 457
Felipe Tavares Paes Lopes

28 The Experience of Cheering in (So-Called) "Modern Football" 471
Silvio Ricardo da Silva and Priscila Augusta Ferreira Campos

29 Brazilian Racism in Football 489
Bruno Otávio de Lacerda Abrahão
and Antonio Jorge Gonçalves Soares

**30 "This is a Reality": The Racism Narrated by Black Characters
in Brazilian Football** 507
Marcel Diego Tonini

Index 527

Chapter 1
Football as a Multifaceted Object of Academic Studies in Brazil

Sérgio Settani Giglio and Marcelo Weishaupt Proni

Construction of the Field of Study

On July 5, 1982, almost everyone stopped in Brazil to watch the national team play. The Brazilian team would face Italy in the World Cup, in Spain. The expectation was that the team, formed by excellent players, would win the men's football world championship for the fourth time. After two disappointments, in 1974 and 1978, most people had the expectation that the nation would win again and be admired. But, as everyone knows, the title was not won because the football gods are capricious. And, on that day, almost everyone in Brazil was saddened and frustrated.

This date has gone down in Brazilian football history: the defeat of "art football" against "pragmatic football". Even though they did not win the championship, the team coached by Telê Santana is remembered as a team that played beautifully and delighted the fans. The lesson remains: the beauty of collective and creative work is perpetuated. This lesson is an inspiration for the present book.

At that time, football had timidly entered the academic field. The dissertation of Simoni Lahud Guedes (*O futebol brasileiro: Instituição zero*—concluded in 1977) and that of Ricardo Augusto Benzaquen de Araújo (*Os gênios da pelota: Um estudo do futebol como profissão* 2014 concluded in 1980), both in the Postgraduate Program in Anthropology of the National Museum of the Federal University of Rio de Janeiro, prove that this field of research was in formation in the country. However, this only consolidated in the following decade. Brazilian universities, until then, did not pay attention to a subject that, generally, was not taken seriously. There was a certain strangeness. Besides physical education professionals, only journalists were allowed

S. S. Giglio (✉) · M. W. Proni
University of Campinas, Campinas, Brazil
e-mail: ssgiglio@unicamp.br

M. W. Proni
e-mail: mwproni@unicamp.br

© The Author(s), under exclusive license to Springer Nature Switzerland AG 2021
S. S. Giglio and M. W. Proni (eds.), *Football and Social Sciences in Brazil*,
https://doi.org/10.1007/978-3-030-84686-2_1

to talk about football. Even scholars of national literature gave little importance to the theme.

But this strangeness started to be overcome little by little. In 1981, Joel Rufino dos Santos published the book *História política do futebol brasileiro*. In an attempt at periodization, he divided the history of football in Brazil into four periods, the last of which (after the 1970 World Cup victory) was marked by a "Brazilian football crisis". Issues related to football were beginning, in a still tenuous way, to receive attention in the academic environment.

The defeat of the national team in the World Cup reinforced the opinion that a crisis in Brazilian football was under way. In addition, the disaster in Barcelona made explicit dilemmas that disturbed Brazilian society, at that complicated juncture, because of the recurrent tension between reason and passion, between pragmatism and art. In fact, that team played so well, imposed itself in front of the opponents, provided spectacles, enchanted the international press. Was there a lack of pragmatism?

The year 1982 can be considered a landmark. The publication of two seminal books boosted the study of football in the Social Sciences. The book *Universo do futebol*, organized by Roberto DaMatta, brought together three other researchers (Luiz Felipe Baêta Neves, Simoni Lahud Guedes and Arno Vogel) to debate football. Simultaneously, *Futebol e cultura: Coletânea de estudos,* a book organized by José Carlos Sebe Bom Meihy and José Sebastião Witter (with the participation of several researchers), brought new readings on the theme.

In 1983, the House of Representatives promoted a cycle of debates to discuss the panorama of Brazilian sports and, in particular, the economic and political problems of professional football. The "Brazilian soccer crisis" was also becoming a topic of discussion in national politics. The end of the military regime and the re-democratization of the country stimulated analyses on the interface between football and politics. In 1984, the book *Futebol: ideologia do poder* (written by Roberto Ramos) was published. Then, in 1985, the book *Esporte e poder* (organized by Gilda Korff Dieguez) was published.

In the 1990s, studies about football spread in the field of Social Sciences. The legitimization of football as an object of academic research brought countless possibilities to be experienced in several areas of knowledge (it was no longer restricted to History, Sociology and Anthropology, much less Physical Education), especially at graduation level. Study groups and research centers emerged gathering those interested in studying new themes. Several theoretical approaches were tested, scientific analysis methodologies were applied, new interpretations gained density, academic congresses opened space for new researchers. Therefore, the academic production grew, but was still relatively modest if compared to the later period. In parallel, the country's main media outlets started advocating neoliberal reforms for the modernization of Brazilian society in that decade. And a new sporting legislation was approved, primarily to reorder the profession of football player and to drive the transformation of football clubs into commercial companies (Proni, 2000).

In the 2000s, research funding increased and the dissemination of knowledge became easier. Studies on leisure and sports gained prestige in the university environment. Football could no longer be treated as a minor subject. In this context, the academic production on football expanded both from a quantitative and qualitative point of view (Alabarces, 2004; Giglio & Spaggiari, 2010; Silva et al., 2009; Toledo, 2001). The publication of books and articles in specialized journals, the creation of courses, and the holding of seminars built bridges for dialogues and new spaces for the debate of ideas. And a regional deconcentration of academic production was the result of the creation of study groups throughout the country.

The movement toward the expansion of research lines related to football (within the Social Sciences) was consolidated in the 2010s; at the same time, the dialogue between researchers with distinct perspectives intensified (Campos and Alfonsi, 2014; Curi, 2015). The more structured research groups sought to strengthen the multidisciplinary nature of their studies. This period marks the "sports decade" in Brazil (Spaggiari et al., 2016), when the country hosted several mega sporting events. This fact influenced the academic interest and directed many researches to understand the impact of hosting these mega-events.

On July 8, 2014, almost everyone stopped in Brazil to watch the national team play the World Cup semifinal. The arena was crowded, the city was buzzing. Many fans had the expectation that the Brazilian players could be champions. However, the German team had a more convincing campaign, and Neymar's injury in the previous match was a harbinger that the football gods were not on our side. After two disappointments, in 2006 and 2010, another defeat would not be so frustrating. Now Brazil didn'–t need to win another World Cup to be admired. But, as everyone knows, the team coached by Luiz Felipe Scolari suffered an unforgettable humiliation: 71. Germany gave a perfect lesson on how to play football. And, that day, many Brazilians were anaesthetized and revolted.

The 2014 World Cup did not cause an inflexion in the studies about football in Brazil, but the return of the debate about the "Brazilian football crisis" has renewed the interest in understanding the interfaces with Politics, Economics, Education, and social movements. Undoubtedly, the "crisis" was deeper outside the field of play, and the national conjuncture was much more complex and difficult to explain. The following year, a Parliamentary Inquiry Commission (CPI) was established in National Congress to investigate possible crimes involving the Brazilian Football Confederation (CBF) and the World Cup Organizing Committee. At that time, the impeachment of the President Dilma Rousseff was under discussion. Once again, the power relations in the world of football were similar to those seen in other spheres of society.

Currently, a great diversity of approaches and an increasing number of cross-cutting thematic studies can be observed. Therefore, a survey of the broad relevant academic production on football in Brazil (covering the various fields of Social Sciences in the recent period) would be a very exhaustive task. It is important to emphasize that football is recognized today as a multifaceted object of study, constituted by multiple intertwined social relationships, whose understanding requires the contribution of several areas of knowledge.

In short, three generations of researchers helped build a field of academic studies on football within the Social Sciences. The first generation emerged in the late 1970s and early 1980s. They are the pioneers, who took it upon themselves to insert football among the subjects to be studied in Science Academy. The second generation corresponds to a rather heterogeneous group that carried out doctoral research in the 1990s. In different ways, they produced a fundamental impulse and established theoretical references (mainly published in books or in academic journals) that began to guide studies on football in several areas of knowledge. And the third generation emerged in the 2000s, contributing to a huge leap in scientific production. This generation had the Internet as a great ally to research international publications and to find sources of information and documents virtually unexplored by previous generations.

Purpose and Structure of the Book

This collection of articles seeks to portray the multiplicity of approaches that currently constitute the field of research on football in Brazil. The book brings together researchers with diverse academic backgrounds, representing some of the diversity found in different universities in the country. Studies from eight areas of knowledge are included. Besides, there are several transversal themes. Obviously, it would not be possible to include here all the relevant themes analyzed in recent years regarding football in Brazil. Some areas of knowledge are under-represented, while others (Administration, Law, Literature, Psychology) could not even be contemplated.

The book is divided into four parts. The first two parts are dedicated to the "classic" areas, in which the best known research lines are concentrated: Politics and History, Sociology and Anthropology. The third part covers four other areas: Communication, Geography, Economy, and Physical Education. The last part prioritizes four transversal themes: gender, violence, fans, and racism.

Part 1—Politics and History—has seven chapters.

Chapter 2, by Luiz Carlos Ribeiro, discusses the conceptual relationship between football and Politics from a historical perspective, highlighting not only the growing use of football by government authorities, but the very constitution of a political dimension in the universe of football.

In the sequence, Chap. 3, by Sérgio Settani Giglio, explores the intentional attempt to maintain a separation between the world of football and the sphere of Politics in the popular imagination, taking as a reference the discourses recorded in interviews conducted with male Brazilian football players who competed in the 1968 Olympic Games.

In turn, the Chap. 4, written by José Paulo Florenzano, expands the debate on the prevailing discourse in Brazilian society beyond the aesthetic dimension of football. The author shows the way in which the expression "futebol-arte" (meaning the preference for the "beautiful game") was appropriated and re-signified in political terms by rebel players, becoming a decisive instrument to combat the scientific-military matrix seen in Brazilian clubs.

Alvaro Vicente do Cabo, author of Chap. 5, explains that the 1982 World Cup contributed to celebrate democracy in Spain and that at that moment democratic discourses were under construction in Brazil. He analyzes the way the sports press referred to the mega event, highlighting the expectations surrounding the Brazilian national football team and the optimism with the re-democratization of the country.

Chapter 6, by João Manuel Casquinha Malaia Santos, shows possible paths for the construction of studies that may contribute to historical research and to the field of historiography. The chapter's objective is to offer subsidies for a reflection on the challenges and specificities of historical research in the field of football.

Chapter 7, by Denaldo Alchorne de Souza, analyzes how football became very popular and how different representations of the sport and of national identity were produced in the period between the first Vargas government (1930–1945) and the military regime (1964–1985). The intention is to understand how football was symbolically used by different social actors in the construction of national identity in Brazil.

Bernardo Buarque de Hollanda and Aníbal Chaim, authors of Chap. 8, make a historical reconstitution of the emergence of the first model of supporters club in Brazil, highlighting the disciplinarian and elitist discourse of the newspaper *A Gazeta Esportiva,* in São Paulo.

Part 2—Sociology and Anthropology—has eight chapters.

Chapter 9 by Alexandre Fernandez Vaz, analyzes the theoretical proposal of Roberto DaMatta, one of the precursors of studies on football in Brazil, pointing out the potential and the limits of its original approach.

Chapter 10, by Michel Nicolau Netto and Sávio Cavalcante, takes football as a privileged social space to understand the economic and cultural logic of capitalism. The authors deal with the characteristics of the process of commodification of football spectacle and investigate the career trajectory of the player Neymar Jr. to analyze how the dogmas of neoliberal discourse—merit, effort, and competition—are rooted in football culture.

Juliano de Souza and Wanderley Marchi Júnior, in Chap. 11, examine the discourses about the modernizing process of Brazilian football that took European football as a model and highlight the feedback between theory and common sense in the construction of an interpretation that explains the recurrent search for modernization having as reference the awareness of backwardness and the idea of trajectory deviation.

In turn, Chap. 12, by Marco Bettine, discusses the strategic interest of the federal government in three developing countries—South Africa, Brazil, and Russia—in hosting the World Cup as a way of expanding "soft power".

Chapter 13, by Arlei Sander Damo, emphasizes the contribution of anthropological studies to the understanding of football as a social and cultural fact. In particular, the chapter explains that the principle of diversity (one of the structuring pillars of Anthropology) helped build the category "futebóis".

In addition, Enrico Spaggiari presents a balance of anthropological production guided by contemporary categories of analysis in chap. 14. He emphasizes the inseparability between the production of theoretical knowledge and empirical research, as well as the necessary connection between subject and object.

The chapter written by Luiz Henrique de Toledo—Chap. 15—weaves approximations between the Anthropology of sporting practices and the Anthropology of art, taking as reference the production and destruction of idols.

Completing this part, Chap. 16—chapter by Martin Curi—uses an ethnographic approach to observe changes in state and non-state institutions in Brazil and Germany related to the 2014 World Cup. The aim is to examine the symbolic power of the mega event and to question the notion of "legacy" used to assess the impacts and consequences of this mega event.

Part 3—Other Areas—has six chapters.

Chapter 17, written by Édison Gastaldo, aims to explore some elements of the intersection between the sphere of Communication and the world of football, highlighting the tenuous disciplinary boundaries that structure this academic field, as well as some theoretical and methodological paths that allow establishing connections with other areas of knowledge.

As a complement, Chap. 18, by José Carlos Marques, analyzes the particularities of the coverage of football spectacles carried out by the sports media in Brazil, in a historical retrospective. The author emphasizes the consequences of the existence of a marriage of interests: sporting events fill spaces in the coverage of daily newspapers, radio channels, and television networks; and such sports media expand demand, enable the diffusion of these events, and publicize sponsors.

Gilmar Mascarenhas' approach, in Chap. 19, is based on the assumption that understanding how football was structured in large cities helps to comprehend certain geographical phenomena. The chapter's objective is to analyze the construction and renovation of stadiums in Brazil's largest cities in the first half of the twentieth century, and to verify how the 1950 World Cup reinforced the transition to an urban mass culture in Brazil.

Fernando da Costa Ferreira, author of Chap. 20, also shows the importance of studies developed in the field of Geography of sports. He emphasizes the need for a critical view about the attempts to impose a mercantilist logic that intends to manage contemporary stadiums (arenas)—and other areas of the city—as if they were elitist consumption spaces reserved for a restricted portion of the population.

In the sequence, Chap. 21, by Marcelo W. Proni, proposes an interpretation on the economic development of Brazilian football based on the financial performance of the national elite clubs in the period 2003–2019. The observed trends indicate similarities with the football industry in Europe, especially in the increasing asymmetry of financial power among clubs. But Brazil remains in a subordinate place in these global value chains.

To complete, in Chap. 22, Sérgio S. Giglio and Marcelo W. Proni present the debate generated by the controversial adoption of Video Assistant Referee in Brazilian football. They mention some examples of controversial use of VAR and confront the opinions of athletes, coaches, referees, managers, and journalists, seeking to highlight the positive and negative impacts of this technological innovation on the production of football spectacle.

Part 4—Transversal Themes—has eight chapters.

Osmar Moreira de Souza Júnior and Heloisa Helena Baldy dos Reis, authors of Chap. 23, discuss the personal and collective "projects" of women who dreamed of success in football and of women who built a professional career in this milieu. They point out that the women's football players career in Brazil is usually interspersed with narrow "fields of possibilities" and marked by various obstacles.

In Chap. 24, by Cláudia Kessler and Silvana Goellner, also analyzes the adversities faced by women to build a career in professional football in Brazil. The chapter takes as reference the football biography of Marta, who was attracted to play in Sweden and in the USA, where women's football is valued and well structured.

Chapter 25, by Wagner Xavier de Camargo, invites the reader to look at the various practices carried out outside the realm of institutionalized football (prioritized by the media), where expressions of "masculinity" are concentrated. Reflecting on gender relations, the author shows the forms of prejudice that involve social representation when football is practiced by people who identify themselves as "LGBTI+".

Chapter 26, by Heloisa Baldy dos Reis and Mariana Zuaneti Martins, denies the idea that football is a sphere separated from everyday social relations. The authors argue that the recurring violence among supporters' groups contradicts institutionalized forms of democratic participation in public spaces. And they explain that football can be a vehicle for claiming citizenship, but it also can serve to reproduce politically conservative discourses.

The guiding question of the chapter by Felipe Tavares Paes Lopes—Chap. 27—is quite clear. The text explains the conventions about which behaviors are violent and argue that the stigmatization of supporters' groups has the purpose of legitimizing their control, disqualifying their demands and minimizing their importance to the spectacle.

Silvio Ricardo da Silva and Priscila Augusta Ferreira Campos, in Chap. 28, analyze the planned modernization of football stadiums (their transformation into multi-purpose arenas) and the consequences for the ways of "cheering" inside these modern arenas. They make a comparison between the treatment offered to supporters by a Spanish club (Levante) and a Brazilian club (Cruzeiro).

Chapter 29, by Bruno Otavio de Lacerda Abrahão and Antonio Jorge Gonçalves Soares, discusses the coexistence of two contradictory movements (inclusion and exclusion) with regard to racial relations in Brazilian football, which is understood as a space that reproduces the ambivalence of socially constructed representations about the "black race" in Brazil.

Finally, Chap. 30, by Marcel Diego Tonini, examines representations of racism in football from oral history interviews with five well-known characters (former athlete, coach, referee, manager, and journalist), revealing the daily presence of prejudice and discrimination, which continue to be reproduced in contemporary Brazil.

The varied approaches and different interpretations brought together in this book seek to provide an overview of the fertile academic debate that has stimulated the renewal of scientific research on football in Brazil. In recent years, the interaction among study groups and the discussion of innovative ideas have been essential for the production and dissemination of new insights, and have favored the establishment of bonds of friendship reinforced by mutual admiration. It is often necessary to diverge from classical interpretations to develop critical thinking. It is often necessary to know how to dialogue without the pretension of establishing consensus. It is often necessary empathy and otherness to understand the multiple meanings of football.

The chapters that make up each part of the book are not homogeneous. Some provide a broad view of the predominant theoretical approach in studies about football in the respective area of knowledge. Others seek to contemplate more specific aspects or deepen the reflection on polemic themes. There was no concern with standardizing the methodological approach or the line of argumentation. The authors had total freedom to define the guiding question, the analysis strategy, and the writing style of their chapter.

Together, the four parts provide a kaleidoscopic view of the field of studies on football in the Social Sciences in Brazil. This understanding can be reached in different ways. Obviously, reading the chapters does not need to follow the proposed sequence. The most important thing, as the poet said, is the journey. There may be several points of departure and arrival. Various nexuses of meaning can be discovered when one transits from one approach to another, crossing various areas of knowledge. The plurality of perspectives and the non-linear flow of questions stimulate the reader to reject unidimensional explanations of his or her favorite themes.

The combination of varied lines of theoretical interpretation with diverse types of applied research can contribute to a comprehensive understanding of interconnected cultural phenomena, which are embedded in a complex changing society. In this sense, it is important to stimulate interest for a multidisciplinary vision, which establishes dialogues between the areas of knowledge. Extrapolating, perhaps it is plausible to understand football as a hologram that allows countless analyses of different facets of Brazilian society.

References

Alabarces, P. (2004). Veinte años de Ciencias Sociales y deporte en América Latina: Un balance, una agenda. *Revista Brasileira de Informação Bibliográfica em Ciências Sociais, 1*(58), 159–180. http://anpocs.com/index.php/bib-en-2/bib-58/567-veinte-anos-de-ciencias-sociales-y-deporte-em-america-latina-um-balance-uma-agenda/file

Araújo, R. A. B. (1980). *Os gênios da pelota: Um estudo do futebol como profissão* (Master's Dissertation in Social Anthropology), Museu Nacional, Universidade Federal do Rio de Janeiro.

Campos, F., & Alfonsi, D. (Orgs.) (2014). *Futebol objeto das Ciências Humanas*. São Paulo: Leya.

Curi, M. (Ed.) (2015). *Soccer in Brazil*. Roudlege.

DaMatta, R., et al. (1982). *Universo do futebol: Esporte e sociedade brasileira*. Pinakotheke.

Dieguez, G. K. (Org.) (1985). *Esporte e poder*. Petrópolis: Vozes.

Giglio, S. S., & Spaggiari, E. (2010). A produção das Ciências Humanas sobre futebol no Brasil: Um panorama (1990–2009). *Revista de História*, (163), 293–350. https://doi.org/10.11606/issn.2316-9141.v0i163p293-350

Guedes, S. L. (1977). *O futebol brasileiro: Instituição zero* (Master's Dissertation in Social Anthropology). Museu Nacional, Universidade Federal do Rio de Janeiro.

Meihy, J. C. S. B., & Witter, J. S. (Orgs.) (1982). *Futebol e cultura: Coletânea de estudos.* São Paulo: Imprensa Oficial, Arquivo do Estado.

Proni, M. W. (2000). *A metamorfose do futebol.* Campinas: IE-Unicamp. https://www.eco.unicamp. br/colecao-geral/a-metamorfose-do-futebol

Ramos, R. (1984). *Futebol: ideologia do poder.* Petrópolis: Vozes.

Santos, J. R. (1981). *História política do futebol brasileiro.* São Paulo: Brasiliense.

Silva, S. R., Nicácio, L. G., Campos, P. A. F., & Melo, M. A. (2009). *Levantamento da produção sobre o futebol nas Ciências Humanas e Sociais de 1980 a 2007.* Belo Horizonte: Escola de Educação Física, Fisioterapia e Terapia Ocupacional, UFMG.

Sppagiari, E., Machado, G. M. C., & Giglio, S. S. (Eds.) (2016). *Entre Jogos e Copas: Reflexões de uma década esportiva.* São Paulo: Intermeios; FAPESP.

Toledo, L. H. (2001). Futebol e teoria social: Aspectos da produção científica brasileira (1982–2002). *Revista Brasileira de Informação Bibliográfica em Ciências Sociais,* (52), 133–165. https://ludopedio.org.br/biblioteca/futebol-e-teoria-social-aspectos-da-producao-cientifica-brasileira-1982-2002/

Part I
Politics and History

Chapter 2
Football and Politics

Luiz Carlos Ribeiro

Introduction

Currently, both in academic studies and in common sense, football and politics are seen as distinct fields, almost always one denying the other. Although we recognize this distinction, in no way can we interpret these fields as antinomian. Trying to understand the differences, the proximities, in short, the historical and conceptual relationships between these two configurations, is the goal of this chapter.

Starting with its scope, politics is inherent to the human being par excellence; it is found in Man intrinsically. There is no individual without politics, even when he isolates himself. After all, Man is first of all a political animal, as Aristotle stated in his masterpiece *Politics*.

On the other hand, football is a particular and recent historical experience. Individuals get involved with it by spontaneous, not necessarily conscious, adherence.

Thus, given this hierarchy of values, the most correct approach to such a relationship is to ask: Is football politics?

This concern is not a mere theoretical exercise, but leads us to a better understanding of what we understand of football as a social and political practice and, at the limit, what we mean by politics. Based on this, the initial answer is yes, football is politics. However, this untimely answer may reduce everything to nothing or, in other words, if everything is politics, nothing is politics. Football is politics, but they are distinct bodies.

Both football and politics have their experiences, concrete and conceptual, historically constructed. They are experiences and concepts that have been forged as strategies of affirmation, and, invariably, denying one another has been fundamental to the understanding of football. In other words, football, in order to legitimize itself as a social practice, has needed to deny politics, to distance itself from it, imagining it could erect itself as a field of its own. Despite the success of this strategy, football has

L. C. Ribeiro (✉)
Federal University of Paraná, Curitiba, Brazil

not detached itself from Politics (Alcaide Hernández, 2009). Likewise, the political field has denied football as a political phenomenon. This denial, common among both educated and ordinary people, does not, however, undo this intertwining. In the limit, it means to say that football, to legitimize itself as an autonomous social phenomenon, has needed to deny politics. It is in this *political place of neutrality* that it is recognized and that it affirms itself. That is why we must inquire about this relationship.

Respecting the hierarchy of terms, we must begin by asking ourselves about politics.

What is Politics

The term originates from the Greek *politikós*, derived from *polis*, and designates all that refers to the governance of the common good of individuals. Comprehensively, it refers to the public space and the good of citizens. The term has gained meaning and expanded from the definitions that Aristotle (382–322 b.c.) formulated in his book *Politics*.

Considered the first treatise on the State and the forms of government, the book defined politics simply as "art or science of government" (Bobbio, 1998, p. 954). Among the modern writers, the Aristotelian understanding has continued, always referring politics to public power, in its role of ordering and ensuring governability among citizens.

Thus, politics, as a way to ensure public order, is intrinsic to power. As Bobbio states, "political power belongs to the category of power of Man over another man" and can express itself in multiple ways, "as a relationship between rulers and ruled, between sovereign and subjects, between State and citizens, between authority and obedience, etc." (Bobbio, 1998, p. 955).

Political scientist Serge Hurtig (1966, p. 74), maps the trajectory of the concept, from its enclosure in the State to its opening to social relations, but always attached to the idea of constituted power:

> Traditionally, political science has been interested exclusively in the State, in the various types of State, in the relations between the State and the citizens. It has been enriched by the study of institutions and the forces that act upon the State. Nowadays, we can define it more broadly as *a perspective of investigation that privileges the phenomena of authority, power and domination.* (our translation)

In other words, although political science is "more directly concerned with the State, public life, institutions, and forces" as sites of politics, in general, the meaning of politics must encompass the "political aspects of all social phenomena", even if its relationship to the State or public life does not come through with evidence (Hurtig, 1966, p. 75).

We see from this reading that, despite the recognition that the conception of politics opens up beyond the State and its influences, there are still resistances. This is what we define as a structural and essentialist view of categories such as State, power, and politics.

Historically, the knowledge about politics has treated it as a science of power and State governance, crystallizing an imaginary about what is outside this core as something apolitical, pre-political or proto-political. Politics has received a structured concept and acquired a status of superior value—centralized in the State—referring all other experiences to the ephemeral or peripheral.

It was only since the second half of the twentieth century that we have seen a process of reconfiguration, both political and scientific, of the understanding of these categories. Several factors have contributed to this, and in this space we will only list them: the apogee and crisis of the social welfare enlightenment project; the Marxism crisis, and the idea of class struggle and revolution; the political and theoretical movement of decolonization; the emergence of new social and cultural movements, such as May 68, feminism, the struggle against apartheid.

Those events have promoted a displacement of concepts, previously structured and self-explanatory. A radical critique of those mega theorems has been developed. From then on, State, power and politics have ceased to be seen as static categories and began to be analysed from their singular experiences. Knowledge ceased to be monolithic and became polysemic. Now, before speaking of politics as essence, it is necessary to exercise a certain genealogy of the word, both in conceptual and historical terms.

We start to think politics in its positivity, that is, what has effectively been said and experienced, in all its complexity. We avoid defining politics as a natural reality, a substance with universal and unique characteristics; on the contrary, it is a social prac-tice historically constituted. And the effort of historical understanding of politics is not enough. It is necessary not to start from a pre-established theoretical assumption, because it would end up ruining the whole exercise of empirical analysis.

The harmony between State, power and politics ceases to be natural and a sufficient explanation, and becomes a problem.

Genealogical studies of power, such as those carried out by Foucault, have produced an important displacement in relation to political science, which until then limited research on power to the State: What seems evident is the existence of forms of exercising power that are different from the State, articulated to it in different ways and which are indispensable even for its support and effective action (Machado, 1979).

State politics is an order that responds to a common good, but it is, ultimately, an order produced in the weaving of social relations of power dispute. Politics is exercised through a complex network of micro powers, integrated or not into the State, a distinction hitherto considered irrelevant by traditional political science (Machado, 1979, p. XII).

Differently, the proposal is to understand politics as a complex system of powers. Politics is not found exclusively in the State, but in a relationship that goes beyond and complements it.

There is not, therefore, in a binary and static manner, a superior and central politics—the State—and peripheral subcultures, such as, for example, football, seen as pre-political or even devoid of politics.

What one methodologically intends is to rebel against the idea that the State would be the central and sole organ of power, or that the complex network of powers would be a mere extension of the State, what would mean destroying the specificity of the powers that the singular analysis intends to focus on (Machado, 1979).

The fear of hegemonic politics, including political science, to recognize the autonomy of this singular knowledge occurs because the subjectivity of these micro powers can put the order and the common good in check. The fear is that the autonomy of local knowledge may weaken the established order supposedly represented by a single entity, the State. Depoliticizing football, for example, is an effort to protect against the insurgencies of political subfields. In this sense, strictly speaking, politics does not exist; what we find are practices or power relations.

The way to face this tension is not simply to state that football is politics or that everything is politics. What is required here is a genealogical essay of this specific knowledge. It is only in this empirical description that one can speak of the relationship between power and politics, as Roberto Machado (1979, p. XXI) observes:

> All knowledge, whether scientific or ideological, can only exist from political conditions that are the conditions for the formation of both the subject and the domains of knowledge. The investigation of knowledge should not refer to a subject of knowledge that would be its origin, but to the power relations that constitute it. There is no neutral knowledge. All knowledge is political. And that is not because it falls within the net of the State, is appropriated by it, and is used by the State as an instrument of domination, thus losing its central nucleus, but because all knowledge has its genesis in power relations. (our translation)

Briefly, politics is not a thing or a unique knowledge, which opposes other knowledge and social practices. It can only be investigated in the complex relation of powers, the State being one of them. It is wrong to discuss football as politics, taking as a starting point the theorem that is based on what politics is to the State, defining everything else as peripheral.

Differently, we should exercise the genealogy of this relationship, from the experience of the sports field itself.

Football as Politics

We should do the same exercise by asking: What is football? Football is, par excellence, a modern social and sporting practice. As we know it, it is the fruit of the traditions invented at the end of the nineteenth century, with its cradle in Victorian England, which symbolized the apogee of capitalism and of the bourgeois classes. Within this context, sporting activities had become a tradition among the middle bourgeois classes, composed by traders, liberal professionals and young students of English public schools. It was a practice that was strengthened in the body of a complex culture of bourgeois class distinction. Needing to distinguish themselves from the upper bourgeois classes and nobility and, above all, from the proletarian masses, the emerging British middle class developed a series of customs of social distinction, among others the practice of sports, such as football (Hobsbawm, 1997, p. 296).

Summing up, modern football was born as a political action of class, of occupation of free time. Consciously or unconsciously, this attitude emerged as a policy of political distinction and affirmation of class. Football was a physical activity practiced on Saturday afternoons and Sundays, and it took place among work, neighbourhood or school friends, inside or outside their social clubs. Participation was so discriminatory that following the rules of the game and controlling violence were signs of honour and civility. To practice only among peers was a way, through exclusion, to alienate sport from the tensions present in society. From this comes the defence of sports only as entertainment, detachment, amateurism and fair play.

Amateurism was considered an affirmation of the athlete's detachment from any type of interest other than exclusively the practice of sports, as well as the demonstration of moral capacity to perform a combat respecting the rules that defined it.

In this understanding, the precept of disinterested game and the denial of ideological connotation, recurrent in class tensions, are evident. It is a sportive speech that intends to exist in a depoliticized field, alienated from any interest other than exclusively the compliance with the specific rules of the game. It is this detachment that legitimated the specificity of its practice and fed, among the Victorian English, the "myth of autonomy" (Allison, cited in Taylor, 2006, p. 94). The principle of honour therefore required the game to be played by individuals capable of civilized respect for the rules. The foundations of balance, solidarity and fair play, central to modern sport, thus presupposed a sociocultural equity.

Thus, the elements of specificity and autonomy of the athletic field were established. As individuals who should play among themselves were, in principle, socially equal, recognized the rules and practiced the sport under the moral condition of respecting those rules, there was no need for external intervention to the sportive system. The sport, based on those values, was understood as capable of self-regulating, thus legitimating its autonomy.

It was a view of the world inspired by the spirit of modern Olympism, which assumed a friendly competition and an atmosphere of fraternity and world peace (Gameros, 2010, p. 226).

However, it is important to remember that the idea of restoring this "Olympic spirit"—the first modern Olympics took place in 1896, in Athens—arose in a moment when international relations were tense, occurring from imperialist rivalries in the global market to specific disputes in Europe, such as the bloody Franco-Prussian war (1870–1871). The discourse of the apolitical character of sport was produced, therefore, as a way to relax tensions—a discourse that interested both the traditional political field and the incipient modern sport, eager to authenticate itself.

There is no naivety or masking of principles in these assumptions, but an ideological conviction aimed at formulating the autonomy of the sports field. The ideological sense of distinction is intrinsic and expresses some class consciousness among its formulators. In fact, the basis of sport autonomy was exactly that of moral and cultural distinction, i.e. social and political.

Thus, as a form of occupation of the free time of the bourgeois, modern sport has been born as a political affirmation of class; alienation as a cultural and political strategy of distancing; therefore, a manifest class consciousness.

Early Days of Modern Football

With intensity, those sport practices have very quickly broken the class circle and socialized in the urban scenario, in the figure of clubs. The so-called traditional sports, generally of peasant or artisan origin, practiced in wasteland spaces and with less social control, tended to disappear or to be urbanized. The football club, with its headquarters, regulations and board of directors, is one of these re-significations.

The paradox is that, simultaneously to this exercise of political power by the bourgeois classes, a process of massification and parliamentarization of the European society took place in the capitalist society (Hobsbawm, 1997), in a process of dilution of class boundaries and constitution of mass politics.

In describing this cultural behaviour of the middle classes, Hobsbawm (1997, p. 297) identifies a moment when the segregated practice of football is transformed into a diffused proletarian mass culture, as he describes (our translation):

> At first developed as an amateur, character-shaping sport by the middle classes in private high school, [football] was quickly (1885) proletarianised and thus professionalized. [...]
>
> With professionalization, most of the philanthropic and moralizing figures of the national elite moved away, leaving the administration of the clubs in the hands of local merchants and other dignitaries, who sustained a curious caricature of the class relations of industrial capitalism, as employers of a predominantly labour force, attracted to industry by high wages, the opportunity for extra earnings before retirement (charitable departures), but, above all, by the opportunity to acquire prestige.

Thus, the process of professionalization of football, due to the recruitment of players among the "skilled workers", is what would have transformed this sport modality into a popular and mass culture. The adoption of sports, especially soccer, as a mass proletarian cult is confusing, recognized the English historian (Hobsbawm, 1997, p. 296).

The growth of the middle and working classes demanded new regulations of social control. The social distinction as an original force of the sportive field has proved itself to be fragile and provisional. Sports, as well as schools, have needed to be disseminated, both by the demand of the poorest as well as a mechanism of normalization. In schools, factories and clubs, more and more sports, and particularly football, have been both demanded as leisure and, after the establishment of sportive rules of discipline, used as a factor of self-control of violence (Elias & Dunning, 1992). As Dietschy and Holt (2013, p. 93) explain:

Those codified collective games spread quickly among factory workers, for whom new social conditions had created a demand for limited-duration sporting activities and entertainment available indoors. Starting in cities, modern sports - football, rugby, tennis, hockey, athletics, cycling, and handball - spread rapidly to smaller towns and rural areas, driving out traditional games and increasingly taking the place of the gymnastic forms of physical culture developed in Sweden and Germany in the nineteenth century. (our translation)

By socialization, what was distinction became *mimesis*. By the end of the nineteenth century, football in England was already a popular sport and threatened the culture of amateurism. In countries like Germany and France, despite the significant presence of the working classes (in the 1920s and 1930s, a third of athletes were of working-class origin), the process of professionalization was much slower. The constant war conflicts linked, in this country, the practice of sport to militarization and national honour, associating professionalism—even among the working class—with the idea of lack of patriotism (Eisenberg, 1999). The moral and political refusal of professionalization preserved for some time amateurism as a distinctive class effort in those countries.

At this juncture of the apex of capitalist expansion, a phenomenon controversial to liberal logic had developed: the formation of the nation-State and nationalist feeling. If, on one hand, the capitalist market claimed the loosening of barriers to facilitate commercial expansion, paradoxically it was necessary to build a structure that would bring some security to the internal and external interests of capital. This structure was the modern national State. Then, the phenomenon of introjection of a feeling of national belonging in individuals took place. It was a movement that should be founded on cultural and moral values that consolidated the affective involvement around the common imaginary in defence of the State and the Nation.

Unlike what happened with gymnastics and other forms of sporting practices, in the European experience of the late nineteenth century and the early years of the twentieth century, football was not a central element in the formation of national belonging. Nationalism, recognized as the "realm of emotions and irrationality" (Guibernau, 1997, p. 154) had, in that period, a less intense affective bond with football. And the explanations for this behaviour are in the words of Hobsbawm, quoted above. In other words, at that time, football was marked by the logic of the market and feelings of club belonging. Proletarianization, professionalization and private administration in clubs and governing entities, to a certain extent, separated football from the moral and civilizing spirit of amateurism that founded nationalism. This form of development ended up distancing football from the immediate interests of the State and consolidating, therefore, its organizational autonomy, which fed even more the myth of self-sufficiency. A situation that corresponds to the liberal State proposal—typical of the late nineteenth century and early twentieth century—of minimal intervention in civil society and private interests (Taylor, 2006, p. 100).

Thus, if the State was, par excellence, the place of politics, the distancing from it has reinforced the imaginary of football as a non-place of politics. This distancing has in no way depoliticized the sport. The dispute for power has been done in another way, in civil society, as a private entity, but always as politics.

Table 2.1 Main national football federations created until 1904

1862—Association Football
1873—Scottish Fitbaa Association
1880—Irish Football Association
1886—Football Association of Wales (Wales)
1889—Dansk Boldspil Union (DBU) (Denmark)
1889—Royal Dutch Football Association (Netherlands)
1891—New Zealand Football
1892—South *Africa* National Football Team
1893—Asociación del Fútbol Argentino (Argentine Football Association)
1895—Swiss Football Association (ASF)
1895—Union Royale Belge des Sociétés de Football Association
1895—Federación de Fútbol de Chile
1897—Australian Football league
1898—Italian Football Federation
1900—German Football Association
1900—Uruguayan Football Association
1904—Svenska Fotbollförbundet (SvFF) (Sweden)

It was this distancing, legitimized by the liberal policy of distinction between the State and civil society, especially in England, that characterized the formation of structured football clubs. Not coincidentally, it was in Great Britain that the first formal football clubs and the first national football federation, the Football Association, emerged in 1863. Very quickly clubs proliferated. The formation of national associations in Europe, Latin America, Africa and elsewhere was a direct result (see Table 2.1).

Despite the existence of this network, the creation of the Fédération Internationale de Football Association (FIFA) on 21 May 1904 in Paris was attended by only seven representations as founding members: France, through the Union des Sociétés Françaises de Sports Athlétiques (USFSA); Belgium, with the Union Belge des Sociétés de Sports (UBSSA); Denmark, with the Dansk Boldspil Union (DBU); the Netherlands, with the Nederlandsche Voetbal Bond (NVB); Sweden, with the Svenska Bollspells Förbundet (SBF); and Switzerland, through the Association Suisse de Football (ASF). Spain was represented by a representative of the newly founded (1902) Real Madrid Club de Fútbol.

It is important to notice the absence of the English in this movement, who were known in general politics by a certain isolation, and because they opposed the professionalization processes that had been occurring in football.

Despite the occurrence of some international matches, such as England *x* Scotland, in 1872, England *x* Wales, in 1873, France *x* Germany in 1899, it was after the creation of FIFA that this practice became more recurrent, starting with the Belgium *x* France match, on the occasion of the entity's foundation (Dietschy et al., 2006, p. 13).

It was from the participation in the Olympic Games that football gained international stature. There was no representation at the first Olympics, in 1896, and in the following ones, 1900 and 1904, soccer was only represented by amateur clubs, although the IOC-International Olympic Committee later awarded medals to the winning teams. More organized in terms of national teams, and strictly amateurish, the 1908 (in London), 1912 (in Stockholm) and, above all, 1924 (in Paris) participations of national soccer teams began to gain relevance in the international sports environment even though war conflicts and tensions between European nations hindered both the development of national championships and the holding of international matches (Dietschy et al., 2006). It is clear that, with the purpose of "regulating and developing international football", FIFA emerged as an initiative of people and entities from civil society and distanced from the State, as was proper of the liberal conjuncture. And, in keeping with the Olympic spirit of fair play, FIFA made its case as an international federation based on "sporting diplomacy", a sporting sentiment that shared universal human rights with the liberal principles of the invisible hand of the market, combining commercial interests, nationalism and entertainment. Football, through its governing body, built for itself a symbolic capital more firmly established than the League of Nations, an entity created in 1919 with the purpose of rebuilding world peace.

This football-State relationship only changed after World War I, especially in the 1920s and subsequent years.

The Totalitarian Years

This framework of distance between football and the State, which concealed the political involvement of the sport, dissolved after World War I. The Great War and the depression that followed meant the exhaustion of liberal democracy, which partly explains the failure of the League of Nations. What remained of the autonomy of civil society was rubble, forging a centralized political power with claims to the absolute.

In this context of authoritarian and totalitarian regimes, restrictions to the freedoms of sporting entities were processed and started to be politically framed, whether to meet centralization or to lend legitimacy to the regimes. The civil society started to act no longer by the specific will of the classes, social groups or parties, but by the collective interest dictated by the authoritarian state.

In the perspective of self-affirmation as authority, the State increased its interest in relation to manifestations of popular roots, such as football, in the same proportion as its warmongering. As Hobsbawm (1990, p. 170) states, it is difficult not to recognize this element of anti-war in the first international football matches organized on the European continent. In the interwar period, says the historian, international sport became an expression of national struggle, with sportsmen representing their states or nations, fundamental expressions of their imagined communities. The individual, even the one who only cheers, becomes the very symbol of his nation.

It was at that moment that the totalitarian nation-State "discovered" football and tried to put it at the service of the national interest. But the "myth of autonomy" remained, since the idea to be passed on was that football would not be serving private interests, but national sovereignty. The dissimulation of football and politics remained, but it gained nationalist colours that it did not have until then.

It is interesting to notice how much of the historiography reinforces the exceptional character and the distortion of the social function of football, by stating that this sport would be losing its spontaneity, becoming a political agent at the service of a particular interest and distancing itself from the apolitical pleasure of the game.

When the subject is football and politics, this literature invariably refers to the "political use" that authoritarian regimes would have made of football. They end up ratifying that football has a neutral, depoliticized nature that authoritarian regimes would take advantage of.

But the fact is that the successful organization of three sequential world cups (1930, 1934 and 1938) marked not only the independence of football from other sports, especially Olympic sports, but also consecrated football as a popular sport, and that was in the political interest of the sport's leaders.

At this time, dictators showed an interest in associating their governments with the popular and successful image of football, as is evident in the case of Mussolini's Italy, which won the 1934 World Cup (held in Italy), the gold medal at the 1936 Olympics (held in Berlin) and was twice champion in the 1938 World Cup (held in France).

Because of this use of football by authoritarian governments, most academic studies consider the transformation of football into politics as manipulation and exception, to the extent that the idea was given that sport agents were in a purity zone, devoid of any political or ideological interests, and that they were touched, from outside and from above, by political agents. Thus, when literature deals with the relation between football and politics, it invariably does so in the context of authoritarian regimes (Bolz, 2008). So, academic analysis misses the opportunity to discuss the fact that the alluded denial of politics is, in fact, a disguised way of doing politics. According to this approach, football would only become politically visible when manipulated—an explanation that reiterates the assumption of football as a non-place of politics—which ends up hiding the possibility of agents of the sporting environment having relations of exchange of interests and even of political and financial benefits with authoritarian regimes.

The Post-45 Conjuncture

In the post-World War II political conjuncture, the world experienced the division of societies into two blocks. This division occurred both in relation to the ideologies of the so-called Cold War (capitalist *versus* socialist) and in relation to the differences between the "West" (meaning developed industrial societies) and the "rest of the world". The concentration of capital in structurally developed countries and the emergence of new countries, with decolonization, reconfigured the international political framework, increasing the discourses of criticism of the orthodoxy of the capitalist market.

Obviously, the world of football did not go unscathed by this process. The number of countries that joined FIFA increased, which only made it more difficult to manage the institution.

The 1950 World Cup was held in Brazil for convenience, given that Europe was still suffering from the impact of the war and many countries were in crisis. Noteworthy is the absence of Germany, which not only went through the crisis of separation from its territory but had also been banned by FIFA due to Nazi atrocities. There are few studies that address this impediment, but two aspects can explain this action: the low interest of German leaders in participating in a World Cup at that time and FIFA's proximity to international diplomacy, then under the hegemony of the allied countries. In other words, Germany's ban was not an autonomous sporting decision by FIFA (Hüser, 2010).

In another context, that of the dictatorships in Latin America, football and political tension takes on a peculiar scenario. The region experienced right-wing dictatorial periods, as was the case of Paraguay (1954–1986), Brazil (1964–1985), Bolivia (1964–1983), Uruguay (1973–1985), Chile (1973–1990) and Argentina (1966–1973 and 1976–1983).

The political climate involving the Brazilian team in the 1970 World Cup, held in Mexico, when the country won its third championship, has been well studied. Brazil was going through the "years of lead", characterized by the regime's violence, and at the same time relied on populist actions seeking to legitimize itself in the society. The winning soccer was one of these instruments (Chaim, 2014; Guazzelli, 2010; Marczal, 2011).

In Latin America, other experiences were recorded, such as, for instance, in the 1974 and 1978 World Cups, when the climate of the cold war revealed a paradoxical situation, to say the least, in the diplomatic field of football. In 1973, during the qualifying matches for the 1974 World Cup, to be held in Germany, the Union of Soviet Socialist Republics (USSR) and Chile were to face each other in a play-off. The first match was held in Russia and ended in a 1–1 draw. In the second match, the USSR, citing moral and ethical issues, requested that the match be held outside Chile. In this South American country, a right-wing dictatorship had just been implanted, overthrowing the socialist and Russian ally Salvador Allende. Faced with the refusal of FIFA, the Soviets communicated that they refused to play in the Julio Martínez Prádanos National Stadium, as it was used by the dictatorial regime of Augusto Pinochet, perhaps one of the most violent in Latin America, as a prison and torture camp. Officially the match was held, but only the Chilean team took the field. The game was started, there was some touching between the Chilean players and "Camacho" Valdés shot towards the opponent's goal, which was obviously empty. The referee then declared the match ended and the Soviet Union was disqualified.

A similar environment occurred in the 1978 World Cup held in Argentina, but the reaction was quite different. At the time of the World Cup, Argentina was living under a strong dictatorship, ruled by a military junta led by army general Jorge Rafael Videla. As in the Chilean case, the Argentine authoritarian regime was also accused of violating human rights, also using a football stadium to imprison political prisoners—precisely the Monumental de Nuñez Stadium, of the River Plate in Buenos Aires, which would host the World Cup matches. Half a mile away was the Escuela de Mecánica de la Armada, which was used as a torture centre, as we read in this account published in the Spanish magazine *Cambio 16* in 1978 (cited in Marczal, 2016, p. 225):

> For almost two years, the Escuela de Mecánica de la Armada has been one of the most sophisticated torture centres in the country. There - according to several testimonies collected by international human rights organisations - the original method in group torture is practised, among others: a political prisoner is placed alive on an endless butcher's saw and cut from the groin to the head, in front of his companions, or mutilated at the wrists or ankles. There you can still find human beings reduced to a weight of 40 kilos after long torture sessions, and kept alive - though psychically shattered - by a team of medical experts, assures the Boycott World Cup Committee, according to direct testimony. It is only a handful of the 12,000 to 17,000 political prisoners who populate the prisons and concentration camps, a figure that gives Argentina the World Cup in terms of human rights violations. (our translation)

The repercussion of the violation of human rights was so great that the Argentinean political exiles created in Paris, with the collaboration of left-wing organizations and parties, in 1977, the Comité de Boycott au Mondial de Football en Argentine (C.O.B.A.). The basic purpose of the movement was to boycott the World Cup, as a form of protest against the violation of human rights in that country, as recorded in this document of the movement (cited in Ribeiro, 2013, our translation):

> Behind the World Cup, concentration camps
>
> On June 1st the eleventh football World Cup officially opens in Argentina. Soon, television and the press will relay to us from Argentina only football images and an idyllic vision of the reality that the Argentinean people live.
>
> From now on, the mainstream press will accentuate this issue, seeking to minimize the broad current of indignation, which is manifest in France, of all those who, together with the C.O.B.A., and the 120,000 signatures calling for a boycott, refuse to allow football to be played in the concentration camps.
>
> For behind the screen, the reality in Argentina is:
>
> • A military dictatorship responsible for 8,000 murders, 10,000 imprisonments and 15,000 "disappearances";
>
> • But also a people who fight and who will know how to show it during the "World of the military"; […]
>
> Solidarity with the Argentine people.
>
> Against repression in Argentina.
>
> Against Giscard's support for the Videla junta.
>
> No football between concentration camps.
>
> Boycott of the Argentine dictatorship.

It is noteworthy, in this case, that the Soviet Union openly supported the staging of the World Cup in Argentina, an apparently contradictory attitude in relation to that adopted in the case of the game in Chile in 1973. The fact is that the Communist Parties (CPs) linked to Moscow turned a blind eye to the atrocities of Videla's regime. The Argentine CP disputed the hegemony with the extreme left, especially with the Movimiento Peronista Montonero, and, like the Communist International, defended that the military regime in Argentina had a nationalist character and that, if there were any human rights lapses, these should be investigated locally; thus, they felt comfortable defending the World Cup in the country (Ribeiro, 2013).

In a declaration published on November 18, 1977, in *L'Humanité*, the official organ of the French Communist Party, the then general secretary of the party, Georges Marchais, declared himself frontally opposed to the boycott (idem, ibidem):

> If the next football World Cup were in South Africa, I would say no. But when you raise the issue of human rights in certain countries, I think you have to be more careful, because you run the risk, both East and West, of not going to any country.
>
> That is why I defend the idea that France should go to Argentina. I would add the argument that the sportsman is a citizen like any other; he must use all means to defend freedom, wherever it is in danger. If we estimate that this is the case in Argentina, fine, let's defend liberties there as any other place!

Two other factors weighed on this stance of the Soviet Union and the CPs: most unionized workers, the political base of the Communist Parties, were passionate about soccer and opposed the boycott; also, as the USSR would host the 1980 Olympic Games, it was feared that the success of a boycott of the World Cup, for the defence of human rights, would have repercussions two years later in the Moscow Olympics.

Ironically, the Russians ended up not participating in the 1978 World Cup, this time because they were eliminated in the qualifying round. They didn't even get the chance to play in a play-off, as they had done in the previous World Cup.

The Context of Globalization

The structural changes in capitalism, from the 1980/1990s, have also marked the political life of football. Among several aspects, we would like to highlight two moments: the national engagement in the conjuncture of a globalized football, taking the examples of Brazil and France, and the analysis of the speech of FIFA president Gianni Infantino, held at the G20 summit in December 2018.

The profound changes caused by the flexibilization of markets—the so-called neoliberalism—still impact the global economy. The main effect of this measure was the loosening of existing barriers, both in the financial field, in the circulation of goods and in the flow of people. This has caused a fragmented reconfiguration of the nation-state, and it is no longer possible to speak of a single model of state and nation. The most common model adopted is the so-called minimal State, which refers to reforms implemented mainly in societies where a balanced model of inclusion and social welfare had existed for decades. The global flexibilization of the market has put the effectiveness of the welfare State in check, since it has introduced within these societies both the deterritorialization of capital and a mass of subjects willing to accept more fragile labour agreements than those that local workers had historically acquired. We are talking about immigrants, one of the most visible faces of globalization. In the sports field, this dynamics imposed to the clubs and to the governing bodies a huge remodelling, a fact already well analysed by the literature (Boniface, 2006; Proni, 2000; Ribeiro, 2007).

National sporting identities have rearranged themselves, as we can observe in two distinct examples, Brazil and France. Distinct examples, but that express a common field of changes to which I refer. In Brazil, the national identity produced in the intellectual and ideological field empties itself. I am referring to the invented traditions of the national character, from the writings of a Gilberto Freyre or a Nelson Rodrigues, who mythified the *flamboyant* mulatism of a Garrincha as the essence of the Brazilian man.

For more than a century, political thought in Brazil had been engaged in the ideological project of explaining and overcoming our recalcitrant origins and recasting the people and the nation. For those intellectuals, it was a commitment, a mission that they attributed to themselves, since they took as a presupposition the incapacity of the people to acquire a sovereign national consciousness. Inventing and reinventing the nation had become a true obsession of the intellectual and political elites, as we can see from the victories of the "canary" national team in the 1958, 1962, and 1970 World Cups.

From 1980/1990 on, the great circulation of Brazilian players in the global market has weakened a possible national identity fixation. Brazil experienced, then, a process of denationalization of the Brazilian national team, at the same time that the clubs started to rehearse some professionalization and spectacularization of their stadiums, disengaging themselves from the traditional passionate fans.

This is a trend that is not restricted to the sporting identity, but to the Brazilian society as a whole. This movement has imposed on the social sciences a trajectory of disengagement with the national. The main idea is no longer to build the nation, but to insert itself with competence in the global market. Today, if Brazil loses a World Cup, Brazilians will not feel humiliated or like mongrels, if they ever effectively felt that way.

France travels on this common ground, but its experience is differentiated. Through different historical processes, Brazil and France have in common the fact that they are countries with a strong presence of immigrants. The difference is that the French national tradition is much older. It goes back to the conjuncture of the end of the eighteenth century, while in Brazil nationalism began to constitute itself at the end of the nineteenth century and was founded on an uncomfortable ethnic miscegenation. In the twentieth century, the century of football as a national culture, while Brazil had founded its nation on the mythical figure of the mestizo, France had already consolidated as a "people" the image of the white European and showed little emotional interest in the national football team.

It is only with the team's most recent victories, in particular the 1998 and 2018 World Cups, and the greater internationalization of its top clubs—Paris Saint Germain in particular—that French people's interest in football has grown. However, it is an interest that coexists with uncomfortable ethnic issues.

From the 1930 World Cup in Uruguay to the 2018 World Cup in Russia, the history of the French football team cannot be understood without the multiple contributions of emigrants from various parts of Europe and the world (West Indies, Guyana, Oceania and Indian Ocean, Maghreb, Black Africa and South America): from Michel Platini (Italian descendant born in France) and Zinédine Zidane (dual nationality, France and Algeria) to Kylian Mbappé (dual nationality, France and Cameroon). For example, two-thirds of the 2018 French team were descendants of immigrants or from former French colonies, which is still a cause for criticism, especially at a time when right-wing nationalism based on certain xenophobia is on the rise in France.

Summing up, if in Brazil internationalization has promoted a disengagement in relation to football as a national identity, in France this same cosmopolitization has made this sport more competitive, thus increasing the national passion for football. But, unlike Brazil, a country used to the ethnic mix in football, in France it remains a highly uncomfortable factor.

Another example for this genealogical essay of ours on football and politics is FIFA president's speech on December 2018 at the G20 summit, which had a suggestive title: "The power of football" (Infantino, 2018, December 1). The G20 is a summit that brings together the leaders of the globe's major economies and was formed in 1999 to address the financial crisis that the world was facing. Regarding the strangeness caused by the FIFA President's presence at the G20 meeting, Infantino explained that he was there as "a simple citizen of the world" but had clearly attended to announce a "new FIFA", a "reliable partner, from now and for the future" (idem, ibdem).

It is evident, therefore, the FIFA's interest in updating its terrible image, a result of the scandals involving its main leaders. Remember that the main criticisms and accusations against the entity did not come from the sports world, but from public and civil institutions, such as the American courts and the influential European newspapers.

It draws attention, in the Infantino's speech, the subjective strategy of placing football as an agent of social transformation. After clarifying that he is not naïve in believing that sports can change the world, Infantino stated that he is convinced that football can be a powerful tool to promote ethical values and to make the world a better place, that is, a more prosperous, more educated, more egalitarian and, perhaps, more peaceful place (Infantino, 2018, December 1).

By asserting himself as a citizen of the world and treating football as his own subject, Infantino plays the game of neutrality attributed to this sport. The person speaking (an ordinary citizen) and the subject of the speech (football) are devoid of any particular interest, because it is a narrative that aims at the balance and universal peace among men.

Infantino seeks to spread a message of hope: football is more than a game, it is a beneficial force that unites nations, breaks down borders and builds bridges between cultures. He says that football is a unique tool with the potential to help address some of the major challenges of modern society, because it is played in all countries and by all people, regardless of age, gender, or religion. Also, because it can teach ethical values: fair play, respect, inclusion, trust, teamwork, and responsibility.

Again, the protagonist is not FIFA, but football. It is football that teaches positive values, promotes inclusion and unity among peoples. Football is a promoter of sustainable economic growth, high education, health, and gender equality.

Concluding Remarks

What we have proposed here is a genealogical exercise of the relation between football and politics. Our intention is to exercise the Foucauldian method of ascendency (Machado, 1979, p. XIII), which, ultimately, means to start reading a particular social practice from its peculiarities. It is a method that seeks to avoid the study of these practices through self-explanatory models, understanding that they bury and hide the specificities of the object studied more than reveal them.

Due to an ideological and political tradition, the social sciences have linked politics to the power of the polis, of organized society, of which the State is the main subject. The social sciences, by tradition and history, legitimize the state as the privileged place of the common good and the will of all.

It has taken the political, ideological, and intellectual shifts of the post-World War II era to change this stance. It was when the social sciences made an effort to detach themselves from the idea of the State as *God ex machina* and opened up in a friendly way, recognizing subcultures also as places of power. Politics is now not found in a single place and statically. It can only be understood in power relations. This is the motto we propose to understand the meaning of politics in football.

That is what we tried to do by taking some moments, from arbitrary cuttings, from the beginnings of football in the late nineteenth century to the recent pronouncement of the FIFA President.

What we have seen makes us comfortable to affirm that politics is present both in football and in the state. And this situation can only be understood as relational.

This does not take away the weight of football's dissimulation as politics, present both in the discourse of agents of political institutions—such as the State—and in the discourse of those from the sports field, as we saw in Infantino's speech, when he defined himself as a simple citizen and omitted the political and especially economic interests of the agencies that control football. The mythification of football as a neutral, apolitical place is one of the most effective strategies to make politics.

References

Alcaide Hernández, F. (2009). *Fútbol: Fenómeno de fenómenos*. Leo.

Bobbio, N. (1998). Política. In N. Bobbio, N. Matteucci, & G. Pasquino (Eds.), *Dicionário de Política*, (Vol. 2, pp. 954–962). 11ª ed. Brasília: UNB.

Bolz, D. (2008). *Les arènes totalitaires. Hitler, Mussolini et les jeux du stade*. Paris: CNRS Éditions.

Boniface, P. (2006). *Football et mondialisation*. Armand Colin.

Chaim, A. (2014). *A bola e o chumbo: Futebol e política nos anos de chumbo da ditatura militar brasileira* (Doctoral Thesis, Faculdade de Filosofia, Letras e Ciências Humanas), USP, São Paulo, Brasil. https://www.teses.usp.br/teses/disponiveis/8/8131/tde-02042014-095412/pt-br.php

Dietschy, P., & Holt, R. (2013). História dos esportes na França e na Grã-bretanha: agendas nacionais e perspectivas europeias. *Recorde: Revista de História do Esporte, 6*(1), 91–104. https://revistas.ufrj.br/index.php/Recorde/article/view/666

Dietschy, P., Gastaud, Y., & Mourlane, S. (2006). *Histoire politique des coupes de monde de football*. Vuibert.

Eisenberg, C. (1999). Histoire du football professionnel en Allemagne. *Les Cahiers de L'INSEP, 25*, 163–188. https://www.persee.fr/doc/insep_1241-0691_1999_num_25_1_1467

Elias, N., & Dunning, E. (1992). *A busca da excitação*. Lisboa: Difel.

Gameros, M. (2010). La otra diplomacia: El fútbol y la política. In S. Martínez (Ed.), *Fútbol-espectáculo, cultura y sociedad* (pp. 225–240). Afínita Editorial; Universidad Iberoamericana.

Guazzelli, C. (2010). Futebol em tempos de ditadura: o Rio Grande contra o Brasil. *Aurora: Revista de Arte, Mídia e Política, 4*(9), 84–102. https://revistas.pucsp.br/index.php/aurora/article/view/3756

Guibernau, M. (1997). *O estado nacional e o nacionalismo no século XX*. Rio de Janeiro: Jorge Zahar Editor.

Hobsbawm, E. (1990). *Nações e nacionalismo desde 1870*. Paz e Terra.

Hobsbawm, E. (1997). A produção em massa de tradições. In: E. Hobsbawm, & T. Ranger (Ed), *A invenção das tradições*. 2ª ed. Rio de Janeiro: Paz e Terra.

Hurtig, S. (1966). Introdução à sociologia política. *Análise Social, 4*(13), 74–107. http://analiseso cial.ics.ul.pt/documentos/1224166005W9wXA0xp2Ux23DU8.pdf

Hüser, D. (2010). Sport et Politique: De la difficile quête d'autonomie du football sarrois entre 1945 et 1956. In U. Pfeil (Ed.), *Football et identité en France et en Allemagne* (pp. 65–83). Villeneuve d'Ascq, France: Presses Universitaires du Septentrion. https://books.openedition.org/septentrion/44598

Infantino, G. (2018, December 1). The power of football. [Keynote speech at the G20 Leaders' plenary session, FIFA President at G20 summit 2018], Argentina. https://resources.fifa.com/image/upload/keynote-speech-of-fifa-president-gianni-infantino-at-g20-summit.pdf?cloudid=gum06wkig0qvkb8pk7rg

Machado, R. (1979). Introdução. In: Foucault, M. *Microfísica do poder*. Rio de Janeiro: Edições Graal.

Marczal, E. (2011). *"O caneco é nosso"*: futebol, política e imprensa entre 1969 e 1970. (Dissertation, Master''s Degree in History, Department of Human Sciences, Letters and Arts), Federal University of Paraná, Curitiba.

Marczal, E. (2016). *Qué otra cosa puede festejar?* Paixão política nas narrativas sobre a Copa do Mundo de Futebol na Argentina (1975–1978). Doctoral Thesis. Programa de Pós-Graduação em História. Federal University of Paraná, Curitiba. https://acervodigital.ufpr.br/handle/1884/26466

Proni, M. W. (2000). *A metamorfose do futebol*. Campinas, SP: IE.UNICAMP. https://www.eco.unicamp.br/colecao-geral/a-metamorfose-do-futebol

Ribeiro, L. (Ed.) (2007). *Futebol e globalização*. Jundiaí: Ed. Fontoura.

Ribeiro, L. (2013). Futebol e ditadura na América Latina: a experiência do C.O.B.A. (Anais do Simpósio Nacional de História, XXVIII). ANPUH, Natal, Brasil. http://www.snh2013.anpuh.org/resources/anais/27/1364915151_ARQUIVO_FuteboleditadunaAmericaLatina,Ribeiro_1_.pdf

Taylor, M. (2006). Football et culture politique en Grande-Bretagne. In Y. Gastaud, & S. Mourlane (Eds.), *Le football dans nos sociétés. Une culture populaire, 1914–1998* (pp. 94–118). Paris: Éditions Autrement.

Chapter 3
"My Concern Was to Play Football": Relations Between Football and Dictatorship

Sérgio Settani Giglio

The choice of Mexico City to host the 1968 Olympic Games presented the world with some news: for the first time in the history of this sporting event, an edition would be held in Latin America, and for the first time in a Spanish-speaking country. This choice, which generated a series of criticisms to the International Olympic Committee (IOC), had as central argument that the altitude would influence the competitors' performance. Beyond uncertainties and speculations that arose with the altitude of Mexico City, it can be stated that this edition represents the end of a great Olympic cycle. As pointed out by the filmmaker Ugo Giorgetti in his documentary *Mexico 1968: The last free Olympics* (Giorgetti, 2013), this would be the last time the climate of free transit within the Olympic Village would be present, especially after the 1972 Munich Olympic Games, when there was the attack on the Israeli delegation. Besides, the political demonstrations that took place in athletics in this edition would be widely controlled. Although this dimension of "free Olympics" is partly true, it should be noted that it was in this 1968 edition that there was a surveillance of women's bodies regarding the use of doping substances. This control, which triggered moral issues, put women's body in evidence and, therefore, under observation. Any woman who had any body evidence that could be questioned about the expected standard of someone of this gender, such as hair growth, thickening of the voice, breast reduction, very developed muscles, amenorrhea, became suspected of doping and, in addition, her gender and sexual identity was questioned (Silveira & Vaz, 2014, p. 455).

In Brazil, the military dictatorship was at its peak. In 1968, the institutional act (AI-5) represented the greatest symbol of repression during this period of Brazilian history. The Brazilian social context was marked, in the late 1960s, by two fundamental aspects: the student movement and the workers' strikes (Antunes & Ridenti, 2007).

S. S. Giglio (✉)
University of Campinas, Campinas, Brazil
e-mail: ssgiglio@unicamp.br

© The Author(s), under exclusive license to Springer Nature Switzerland AG 2021   31
S. S. Giglio and M. W. Proni (eds.), *Football and Social Sciences in Brazil*,
https://doi.org/10.1007/978-3-030-84686-2_3

It is, therefore, in the interface and in the search for dialogue between some events that occurred in Mexico and Brazil in 1968 that we find elements to understand, in a broader way, the context in which the Brazilian soccer athletes, who competed in this Olympic edition, were inserted.

To open this dialogue, I used, as research sources, the periodicals *Jornal dos Sports, O Estado de S. Paulo,* and *Folha de S. Paulo,* official IOC documents and interviews conducted with nine Brazilian soccer athletes.

This text is structured to contemplate this relationship. Thus, in the first part I present the debate about soccer as the opium of the people. Next, I present some facts that impacted the Olympic Games in Mexico, and then discuss the Brazilian context of 1968. Finally, based on Bourdieu's concept of *habitus,* I seek to interpret how the narratives of the Brazilian Olympic football athletes belong to a certain place when analyzing the national sport.

Is Football the Opium of the People?

I do not start from the structuring idea that has been consolidated in Brazilian academic studies that football is alienating, working as the "opium of the people." The anthropologist Roberto DaMatta (1982a,1982b) deconstructed this argument more than 30 years ago, when he proposed to think the sport/society key without dichotomizing it. Those who still defend it argue that the main purpose of such sport would be to deviate the population's attention from society's most basic problems. During the years of military dictatorship, as Oliveira (2009, p. 389) points out, some people understood that football would be able to calm the spirits, to cool the controversial impulses, to channel the youthful energy that intended to question the prevailing order.

Although this view has become widespread over the years, it is possible to state that it does not hold, insofar as football is not something apart from society. On the contrary, soccer and society are interrelated and therefore cannot be in opposition. According to DaMatta, this idea was formed because the elite was not interested in what belonged to the people—football, carnival, and gambling—and these activities were therefore considered less serious. Considering football as a privileged access to understand Brazil, the author completely refutes the idea of thinking of football in opposition to society. As part of society, football provides important elements for its understanding. Those who understand soccer as a way to distract people from reality consider that its protagonists, that is, the players, would consequently be alienated, to the extent that their interest would exclusively be turned to playing football. Therein lies an important component of alienation, that of not being interested in anything else. This perspective does not include the possibility of the player having any public opinion about something outside the world of football. It is common sense the idea that a football player should just play football, not taking a position on other issues or giving opinions, because this may make them losing their concentration on what really matters, which is to play and have a good athletic performance.

Therefore, in order to understand the disputes present in this sportive field, it is necessary to follow some paths that may assist in the identification of the place of the Brazilian Olympic football players (Bourdieu, 1983). The 1968 Olympic Games took place between two World Cups that were antagonistic to the national team in terms of results. They followed the early defeat in the 1966 World Cup, in England, and preceded the triumph of the 1970 World Cup, also held in Mexico. Among the disputes that can be considered, there was, for sure, the search for Brazilian hegemony in world football. Although there was a discourse in Brazil that the country would become an Olympic power (Oliveira, 2009, 2012), Olympic football occupied a smaller space in this dynamic (Giglio, 2013).

The soccer field, in turn, was immersed in these disputes, constituting a privileged field. On the one hand, there was the interest of the State in appropriating football and spreading its ideology, its discourse that the country was doing well and would be great. And, in order to be great, Brazil should appear alongside developed countries, with sport being the most effective shortcut to do so. On the other hand, those dissatisfied with the military regime found in the voice of some players, such as Afonsinho and Reinaldo, a channel of expression. Therefore, sport comprised one of the many intervention plans of the military to achieve their political objectives (Couto, 2014; Oliveira, 2009; Florenzano, 1998).

It is necessary to break with the argument that players are alienated in order to denaturalize the discourses and, consequently, understand the particularities of what Bourdieu (1996, 2003, 2004; Bourdieu & Chartier, 2017) called *habitus*. Therefore, by taking the *habitus* as a central concept of analysis, we will be able to interpret that athletes compose a restricted space, cut by their own logics—the sports field—and that works beyond a mere conditioning. The challenge that is established is to understand how the discourses are constructed, shared, and validated within the same logic. To this end, it is necessary to refute the condition that players are alienated by nature.

In the discourses of the football universe, whether in its internal dimension or in its surroundings (Wisnik, 2008), there is a hegemonic logic that consolidates itself from the validation of the status quo, and not from its rupture. Validating the discourse instead of breaking it may be an individual position, but when thought of in a relational and dialogical way with the environment in which the Brazilian athletes lived, one can more easily understand that there was a shared collective vision, and to position oneself in a contrary way would mean being in evidence not for the football skills, but for the way of thinking. And that, by the way, might not be interesting, even more so when you think of players who wanted to become professionals, to consolidate themselves, and who did not have the support of the structure that composes football. Somehow, as the title of this chapter points out, Brazilian players agreed that they were only there to play football. Before moving on, we must understand the political context of the 1968 Olympic Games.

The Olympic Games in Mexico

Under the slogan "Mexico, yes. No Olympics," Mexican students took advantage of the visibility of the Games to protest against the government regarding the education of the country, especially for better teaching conditions at the Autonomous University of Mexico (Unam), for democratic reforms in the university and in the Mexican society. As an action to prevent the students' demonstration, the Mexican Secretary of Education "decided to suspend classes throughout the country during the competition" (Cripa, 2011).

What underlies the conflict between the students and the Mexican government is a symbolic dispute over the use of images. The Institutional Revolutionary Party (*Partido Revolucionario Institucional*—PRI) was in power, a single party that controlled, for example, the press, and that insisted on attacking the student movement based on the hypothesis that there was a communist boycott aiming to prevent the 1968 Olympic Games (Troncoso, 2013).

Before the Games, there was a lot of tension in Mexico, mainly due to the fact that the then president of the country, Gustavo Díaz Ordáz, powerless in the face of students' protests, called the claims "illegitimate." Moreover, the ruler saw the Olympic Games as an opportunity for the government to internationally show the achievements of the Mexican revolution and the modernity of Mexico City (Miskulin, 2008).

The fact is that it took some months to reach the Tlatelolco massacre, which took place in October, considered the apex of the confrontations between students and the State. While the former were in search of the legitimization of the defense of the power of the law, the latter materialized through police repression. From July 22 to October 2 marches were registered, and in a good part of them, there was great police repression. The greater the repression, the greater the number of participants in the demonstrations. According to Troncoso (2013, p. 91), the rector of Unam exercised an important leadership role at that moment:

> This is the performance of Javier Barros Sierra, rector of Unam, who, a few hours after the attack on San Ildefonso, unfurled the flag at half-mast in the college town and led the first march organized by the university and the students of the Polytechnic, which allowed the CNH (*Consejo Nacional de Huelga* or National Strike Council) to emerge as the national leadership body and sole interlocutor with the government. (our translation).

The peaceful protest organized by Sierra, according to Troncoso, allowed the mobilization to gain a space in the government-controlled press, working as a kind of truce; for the first time, a student march was reported without the critical connotation of government bulletins.

The march on August 27 gathered 300,000 people, peacefully. After the student leader Socrates Campos Lemus' aggressive speech, suggesting a student guard to demand a public debate with Días Ordáz, the army dispersed the participants and retook the square. This action marked the government's offensive against the protests. For Troncoso (2013, p. 98), the intention was to project an image different from that presented by the students:

The figure of the president was exalted by the legalist workers, defined as "authentic" representatives of the people – and to rescue the national flag, in contrast to the "agitating" students
and unionists and their illegitimate use of a red and black strike banner. (our translation)

On September 13, the "silent march" took place. Without shouts or slogans, about 250,000 people made what is considered today the most important symbolic act of the movement and that best represents the defense and civic claim of the rule of law (Troncoso, 2013, p. 101). Six days later, there was the occupation of the college town by the army. The tensions that had begun in July were nearing an end. But at that moment, how the conflicts would end was unknown. The more the clashes widened and reconfigured themselves in their form of violence and abuse of the police force, the closer the opening day of the Olympic Games was getting.

Ten days before the Games started, there was a serious confrontation between the Mexican army and the demonstrators who were protesting against the Ordáz government in the Tres Culturas square, in Tlatelolco, Mexico City. The students' criticism was mainly related to the amount spent on the event in a country where many families were experiencing all sorts of needs (Brewster and Brewster, 2009).

The confrontation was a premeditated action by the army, considering that the military were careful to evict the residents of the houses in the vicinity of the square in order to "avoid victims among the civilians."

The Mexican army indiscriminately shot at all the people who were in the Tres Culturas square at 6 p.m. local time today [October 2], when about 15,000 students from the National Polytechnic Institute were holding a public demonstration against the government of Días Ordáz. Seven students were killed and dozens were wounded. The young people gathered peacefully, under tense surveillance by the police who flew over the place in helicopters ("Movimento faz ameaça," 1968, October 10, p. 23).

The conflicts experienced in Mexico in the months preceding the Olympic Games were marked by the truculent action of the police and made explicit the violence, the repression—as an alternative to dialogue—the importance of military efforts to control and maintain order threatened by protesters and, finally, a defense of nationalist ideology that would find in this sporting event the peak of its visibility.

Among the experienced violence, there was also the fourth presidential speech, in which Díaz Ordáz announced the erasure of the student rebellion from the historical memory of the following years and interpreted its origins under the premises of international plot and conspiracy (Troncoso, 2013, p. 106).

In face of the situation of the country, there was the question of whether the Games would really take place, a doubt that was quickly resolved with the statement given by Avery Brundage, president of the IOC: "There is only one authoritative source to say whether the Games will be held or not. And that source is me. I am the only official source and only I can give an order to cancel the Games or not" ("Comitê Olímpico confirma os Jogos do México," 1968, October 4, p. 19, our translation). In the arm wrestling that placed the people and the Mexican government in opposing trenches, Brundage was skillful in conducting the episode in order to show his power. He used the tragedy to reinforce his decision-making role and to show how authoritarian he could be in the face of any threat.

However, days after these statements given by Brundage, there were still rumors about the possibility of canceling the Games. The IOC stance, historically adopted, was to deny that the Olympic Games involved political issues, acting as if there was no relation between the student demonstrations and the event that would happen in a few days in Mexico. Nevertheless, there was no way to fail to mention certain aspects ("Crise no México tumultua as Olimpíadas," 1968, October 4, p. 5):

> The spokesman made it clear that the IOC does not wish to meddle in the internal politics of Mexico, but at the same time reminded that the Mexican Olympic Committee, organizer of the Games, has a duty to ensure the safety of visiting athletes and officials. The spokesman added that "when people are killed in the street it is clear that the organizers cannot offer guarantees." (our translation)

However, despite this positioning, the fact that nothing was damaged in the Olympic Village and that none of the athletes who were in Mexico City were affected by the protests, confirmed that the Games schedule was going to be met. According to Brundage ("Comitê Olímpico confirma os Jogos do México," 1968, October 4, p. 19):

> We conferred with the Mexican authorities and were assured that nothing would interfere with [sic] the peaceful entry of the Olympic torch into the stadium on the 12th, nor with [sic] the competition that will follow the ceremony. As guests of Mexico, we have full confidence that the Mexican people, universally known for their sportsmanship and generous hospitality, will join participants and spectators in celebrating the Games in a true oasis from a troubled world. Mexico City is a gigantic metropolis of more than six million inhabitants, and no demonstration or act of violence has ever been directed against the Olympic Games. Consequently, the Mexican Games, a friendly gathering of young people from all over the world in a friendly competition, will continue as planned. (our translation)

The IOC maintained its stance of not changing the preestablished schedule of the Mexico Games despite the fact that the conflicts happened ten days before the beginning of the event. What perhaps Brundage and the other IOC members did not expect, or did not want to publicly admit, was that there was the risk of some kind of demonstration inside the Olympic Games itself. For them, the protest movement of the American athletes had been dissipated when the IOC decided to cancel the invitation to South Africa to participate in the Mexico Games.

The Tlatelolco massacre obviously resonated among the four thousand athletes already present in Mexico at that moment. However, after discussing the matter, they chose not to speak out. As for how the debate between them took place, there are no known reports. There was a generic manifestation of some American athletes, approving the decision of the IOC to hold the Olympic Games: "The athletes who were heard demonstrated to be more concerned about winning medals than discussing the student demonstrations that shake this city" ("Olimpíada: Crise chegou à ONU," 1968, October 5, p.3).

The posture of the competitors presented in the report can lead us to an analysis that the athletes are really alienated, that they are not concerned about issues other than their personal interests. The exercise we must do is to situate these athletes within a relational and disputes-related context. It is in this field that I want to highlight how much the silence says not about the case in question, but about the sportive structure and its own dynamics, capable of preventing manifestations contrary to the IOC president. It should be noted that the IOC president at that moment was the North American Avery Brundage, the only one to date to break with the European hegemony of the presidents of the entity (Giglio, 2013; Giglio & Rubio, 2017).

The Games would show that at least some athletes could take a critical stance, which was evidenced when two Americans, Jimmy Kines and Charlie Greene, in the 100-meter dash, refused to receive their medals from the IOC president: "we made no official request; we asked who would deliver them. We were told it would be Brundage. We made no comment, but we did not smile either. I think they understood us" ("Negros boicotam Brundage," 1968, October 16, p. 19). The medals were handed over by the British Marquess of Exeter.

This attitude served to warn Brundage to the possibility that other protests could arise at any moment, although it was impossible to guess how they would take place. However, when the athletes Tommie Smith and John Carlos, also from the USA, stepped onto the podium to receive their medals the IOC president could see what form the new protest would take ("Negros fazem seu protesto," 1968, October 18, p. 17):

> Raising their clenched fists wrapped in black gloves, wearing black socks also on their bare feet and without looking at the flag of the United States of America, Tommie Smith and John Carlos, the two black winners of the 200-meter dash, expressed their racial protest, during the medal ceremony to which they were entitled yesterday in the Olympic Village. The Australian (white) Peter Norman, second place in the competition, supported the demonstration of the two Americans by wearing a "Black Power" insignia with the inscription "Olympic Project for Human Rights." (our translation)

The attitude of the two athletes generated different reactions among the audience. While some supported, others booed the behavior of Smith and Carlos who, during the execution of the American anthem, kept the protest gesture: "at first, the attitude was not understood. The clenched fist represented the union of all blacks. The black socks expressed the identification with the movement of racial protest, as the Olympic athletes always wear white socks in competitions" ("Negros fazem seu protesto," 1968, October 18, p. 17). After these episodes, it was difficult to separate sports from politics.

The Relationship Between Football and the Military Dictatorship in Brazil from the Players' Narratives

1968 is considered the year of greatest repression of the military regime in relation to the rights of expression of the Brazilian society. The Institutional Act no. 5 (AI-5), promulgated on December 13 of that year, granted the government broad powers: "In other words: the regime gave itself the legal right to persecute the opposition" (Magalhães, 2010, p. 99, our translation).

The connection between sports and politics could be more-explicitly perceived in that same December 1968, when, days before the enactment of AI-5, an audience by President Costa e Silva was granted to a committee of the Brazilian Sports Confederation (CBD), at the Planalto Palace. The participants of this meeting were CBD President João Havelange, national team manager Paulo Machado de Carvalho, CBD director Brigadier Jerônimo Bastos, and congressmen Paulo Planet Buarque and Milton Galdeano. Costa e Silva's message was clear and direct: "We must win the World Cup by any means necessary," and added: "Brazil cannot lose the 1970 World Cup. We have to win it through discipline, lots of training, hierarchy, and patriotism" ("Costa exige a Copa de 70," 1968, December 4, p. 3).

Before we approach the aforementioned peak of the repression of the military dictatorship, we will try to understand how was the long path traveled by the Brazilian society in 1968, a path that had begun with the coup of 1964. As I pointed out at the beginning of this chapter, the year 1968 was marked by the student movement and the workers' strikes. According to Antunes and Ridenti (2007), among the claims of the student movement were: free public education; reform in higher education aimed at improving its quality and democratically enabling student participation in decisions; more funds for research; and the end of the dictatorship established four years ago, which had curtailed the freedom of Brazilians.

We can state that the violent events that illustrated the scene of several Brazilian cities in this period were due to the difficulties of dialogue between some social sectors and the government. If, as we have seen in the case of Mexico, the government adopted violence as a form of repression, in Brazil it was no different and resulted in the death of many people.

It is within this scenario that the students started occupying the police pages of printed newspapers. In March 1968, when youngsters gathered in the *Calabouço* restaurant, a student cafeteria located in the city of Rio de Janeiro, to organize a protest, the place was invaded and culminated with the death of the student Edson Luís Lima Souto. According to Elio Gaspari (2002, p. 278), since 1964, it was the first time that a corpse appeared in the confrontations between the dictatorship and the students.

Edson's death became a trigger for the population's dissatisfaction to manifest itself in the streets. That is how the metalworkers' strike in Contagem (state of Minas Gerais) took place in April. The movement gathered strength and reached other industries, mobilizing a large number of people: from 1200 workers on strike at the beginning, this number quickly increased to 16,000 strikers (Gaspari, 2002).

A few months after these episodes, after some protests were held, the *Passeata dos cem mil* [The March of the One Hundred Thousand] took place in June. Organized by students, the incisive speech by student Vladimir Palmeira, president of the Metropolitan Union of Students (*União Metropolitana dos Estudantes*—UME), mobilized the city of Rio de Janeiro against the way the police used violence to show their strength in the face of demonstrations.

As it had happened in Mexico City in October, in Brazil there were also constant protests and conflicts with the police in 1968. The confrontation between students from the Mackenzie Presbyterian University and the Faculty of Philosophy,

Languages and Human Sciences of the University of São Paulo (USP), in the state of São Paulo, resulted in the death of the young José Carlos Guimarães and left 11 other people injured. This conflict, which began when students from Mackenzie, belonging to the Command for Hunting Communists (*Comando de Caça aos Comunistas—* CCC), tried to prevent those from USP from disclosing the Congress of the National Union of Students (*União Nacional dos Estudantes—*UNE), became known as "The Battle of Maria Antônia"—an allusion to the name of the street where the two schools were located—and was marked by extreme police violence. On the other hand, 1968 also witnessed the death of five police officers (Gaspari, 2002).

Incidents continued to happen. A demonstration in Cinelândia, in the State of Rio de Janeiro, left four people injured, and there was also the dismantling of the UNE Congress in Ibiúna (State of São Paulo), which ended with all the students arrested by soldiers from the Public Force and police officers from the Department of Political and Social Order (*Departamento de Ordem Política e Social—*Dops). Two days later, Brazil lost 1–0 to Spain in the opening game of the Olympic football tournament.

The narratives presented here are the result of interviews conducted for the project "Olympic Memories by Olympic Athletes," coordinated by Professor Katia Rubio; many of them were also conducted by me during my doctorate program (Giglio, 2013). The interviewed athletes who competed in the 1968 Olympic Games were: Hamilton Chance Rubio, Daniel Euclides Moreno, Lauro de Mello, Ademir Ueta (China), Manoel Maria Barbosa dos Santos, Miguel Ferreira de Almeida, Sebastião Carlos da Silva (Tião), Arnaldo de Mattos, and Antonio Pedro de Jesus (Toninho).[1]

I highlight some points of the narratives regarding the Mexico Olympic Games that, to some extent, dialogue with the collective dimension of the narratives presented so far, which is to think the relationship between sport and politics based on a certain regularity and some consensus. Some points are dissonant. It is in this scenario that I introduce the concept of *habitus*, developed by Bourdieu (1996, 2003, 2004; Bourdieu & Chartier, 2017), specifically when he states that it can be apprehended "empirically in the form of regularities associated with a socially structured milieu […]" (Bourdieu, 2003, p. 53). According to Bourdieu, this idea of regularity would be the way in which the "structured structures" would work as "structuring structures," and could be "regulated and regular" without being conditioned to the obedience of rules.

Among the consonant points explored from the life history of Brazilian soccer athletes, I highlight the absence of analysis and questioning regarding the political period Brazil was undergoing in 1968 and the years before. Nor does any mention of the Tlatelolco massacre appear in their speeches. The political dimension appears in the interviewees' speech in a peripheral, almost imperceptible way. "I was young and did not have political awareness" or "we did not suffer any kind of intervention in football in this period" are some of the sentences that are repeated and that I intend to explore next.

---

[1] Of all the interviews, I was not present only in the one carried out with Toninho.

One of the first responses given when asked to reflect on the relationship between football and the military dictatorship in Brazil concerned the use of the Brazilian Air Force (*Força Aérea Brasileira*—FAB) plane to travel to Mexico. This was the first and only connection they said they had identified between both things.

The reports of the athletes highlight the dimension of the adventure they had with the Brazilian participation in this Olympic edition. The flight of the FAB, in a cargo aircraft, is emphasized in the interviewees' narratives—for Lauro, "we flew in that winged Kombi"—and the epic stops for refueling set the tone for the adventure, as pointed out by Tião. At that time, the Brazilian basketball team was going through a period of great achievements. It had been world champion in 1959 and 1963, a fact that provided a differentiated treatment to the athletes of that modality. In Tião's words, "they arrived by plane whereas we arrived 21 hours later."

The player Moreno recalled the classification of football for the Games and the uncertainty that the athletes experienced as to whether or not the delegation would participate in the event, given the lack of funds. To the reasons for this uncertainty, the player Toninho added the abandonment and lack of support to football athletes. On the political moment, he stated: "I do not remember it very well, I do not remember it."

The fact that they traveled on a FAB plane allowed the Brazilian athletes to follow *in loco* the presentations of the sports that continued in the competition after the elimination of Brazilian football. If the flight had been chartered, at the end of the football competition, or after the team had been eliminated, they would have had to return. As there was no other alternative, the Brazilian athletes stayed the whole time in the Olympic Village, thus being able to follow the other competitions. Regarding the integration with athletes from other sports, Tião reported that the football players had a lot of friendship with the volleyball players: "we got along very well with the water polo players as well. We had even watched Servílio, who was robbed of that medal." The return trip was also highlighted in the narratives as a great adventure. Among the many stops, when the plane landed in Belo Horizonte, athletes from São Paulo decided to return by bus because, as reported by Ademir Ueta, the aircraft had broken down.

For the player Arnaldo de Mattos, there was no pressure on the players to become champions. At that time, Brazil was already two-time world football champion (1958–1962), whereas Olympic football had never won any medals. About the dictatorship, his recollection corroborates the image of football players' detachment from political issues. According to him, "we did not realize it, we played football, we did not even know what was dictatorship and what was not, we had no idea."

Miguel's speech about how the Olympic football athletes understood the period of military dictatorship in Brazil was incisive and direct: "one did not even know what was that." And he also questioned the dimension of the dictatorship:

> This business, I never had any problem with it, this is something very, very... It was the height of the dictatorship for how many people? The country with 90 million people, it is kind of obscure to even discuss this. We are going to take the focus off the interview. But we did not disturb anything.

The sentence "take the focus off the interview" was the signal not to talk about it. By disagreeing with the raised issue and indicating an end point to the question, while demonstrating dissatisfaction with the approach, Miguel showed that he would not be able to present more precise arguments to defend his position. Strengthening Miguel's line of thought, the player Lauro thus expressed himself:

> We did not have much political notion, we did not even know what was happening. I know that regarding work, it was a very good time for me, the dictatorship. There came [sic] times of galloping inflation, we had to mark prices daily or almost daily. But it was a very good time to work, everyone needed employees to work in companies everywhere, and there was not this violence of nowadays, we did not even think of bank robberies that time. So there was a good side of the dictatorship, but it had a very bad side too; once I heard a person, when the dictatorship ended and democracy began, there was a time when there was a lot of unemployment and I met a guy who said "I did not know that democracy was [a time] for starving," he could not get a job. So, you know, it changed a lot in this aspect and today I have political awareness, democracy is the best thing for the country, although our politicians, you know, there is nothing to say about it.

Although Lauro points out positive and negative aspects of the time of the military dictatorship in Brazil, the fact that he emphasizes that at the end of the authoritarian period there was a lot of unemployment, and that this did not happen during the military regime, allows us to interpret that he has a thought aligned with, and not critical of, the period of military dictatorship in the country.

Following this line of argument, the player Manoel Maria stated: "I did not care about that, my concern was to play football. I was actually living a dream." Tião assured that there was no military interference in the participation of football in the Olympic Games: "but, really, we were not pressured, we were not there was nothing. I think that in football in fact, the athletes who participated [in the Games], at least in the case of football, the people I saw [there], I never heard anything of it, you know?"

For Hamilton Rubio, there was no pressure, no call from the President of the Republic to pressure the head of the delegation, nor any external interference. According to him, there was too much freedom, and if there had been more control, the players would probably have obtained a better result. So, he reported:

> We had total freedom, you know? So much so that freedom sometimes gets in the way, you know? That is what happened, that got in the way, that is what I just told you. If there had been a little more [control], a tougher head of the delegation, things would have gone better for us.

As we can observe, in Hamilton's understanding, there was a lack of some type of control that would certainly produce a greater concentration for football athletes. The fascination produced by the excess of freedom would have generated, as a consequence, the disqualification of the team. The risk of this type of analysis is the conclusion that the presence of control devices is indispensable for the exercise of a work focused on objectives.

For Tião, some factors influenced the participation of football players in that Olympic edition. He mentioned a certain lack of knowledge about what that moment represented:

We did not even know the value of soccer and the value of the Olympics, because of our age, you know? We had no incentive, we did not know what the Olympics were, and we were just "in our prime". So, what happened? People got to know that the girls stayed at the entrance of the Olympic Village. And it was crowded. There were Mustang cars, only first-world cars, we had never seen any cars there. And we would be like, two players with their backs to show we were athletes, and one, hitchhiking. So, we [...] football got bored.

In fact, the condition of being young is frequently used to justify the lack of involvement with the political dimension of collective life:

Oh, I had no notion; first, we were not interested in anything, the young people in my case were not going to be interested in that. Our business was to play football and nothing else, we did not want to direct anything or govern anything or anarchize anything. The mentality of a sportsman is different, the guy who practices sports, that what I say: "do you want your son, a boy, not to be a delinquent? Make him do sports," because sports do not give time for you to do anything, you will arrive home exhausted and go right to your bed so you can sleep, this is the advice I give to those who have children.

His discourse reproduces, as we can see, the idealized vision of sport as a savior. The lack of political interest is justified with the argument that they were there "to play football and nothing else." The "nothing else," deep down, represents everything that football cannot absorb. In other words, everything that is not absorbed by the world of football is disregarded.

The argument that the focus was on football can be understood to the extent that it is known that the Olympic Games represented the opportunity that everyone sought within the football scenario. The reality they lived was, somehow, precarious. At the same time that the restriction imposed by amateurism was the condition that allowed them to participate in these Games, it was also the limiter of a more immediate professionalization (Giglio, 2013, 2018). They would only compete in the Olympic Games if their condition of amateur was kept; therefore, they would have to wait some more time to become professional, a condition that certainly generated dubious perceptions of the process in which they were involved. They were close to be professional players and, at the same time, there was a barrier to be overcome, the Olympic Games. By being deemed as amateurs, they could not become professionals, and this impediment created the necessary condition so that they would not question anything. It was their future at stake, what they were not yet, but what they wanted to be. Being part of the Brazilian national team could be the way to get a good contract, which, however, was not consolidated for most Brazilian Olympic players of the 1960s and 1970s.

Besides, as Lauro points out, in his case (and in the case of many amateur athletes) there was an off-the-record agreement signed with Palmeira.[2] In his words: "I signed an off-the-record agreement there, blank, at that time everybody did that, and that agreement, if I did well in football, they would fill it out the way they wanted; if I did not do well, they would tear it up and throw it away."

Ademir Ueta also highlighted this condition mentioned by Lauro. He explained that because the amateur athletes were minors, it was their father or mother (or a

---

[2] Sociedade Esportiva Palmeiras is a football club from São Paulo city, Brazil.

close relative) who signed their contracts. This type of action conditioned them to the club. If they changed teams, the club that held the signed contract on a blank sheet could fill it in any way it wanted and request the player's return. The condition of being bound to a club by a blank contract was, in fact, a strong impediment for athletes to any questioning.

Distant from this scenario, there was a player who ten years earlier had actively participated in Brazil's victory in the first World Cup, in 1958. This star could occupy a differentiated space in relation to the national Olympic football players. Edison Arantes do Nascimento, known as Pelé, enjoyed a different status on the soccer scenario, not only for his quality, but also for his participation in the Swedish Cup at the age of 17. His place in football was very different from most of the athletes who were in the Olympic team. Besides, as highlighted by Souza (2018, p. 2010), Pelé was seen as an athlete role model:

> The Brazilian State of the military period agreed with the interpretation given by the great commercial press. Pelé symbolized the ideal Brazilian. He was professional, methodical in training, he rigorously followed his obligations to the club. He did not make statements that questioned the hierarchy of the *sportive field* or the Brazilian society. He was cordial and had a morally-acceptable behavior. He was a myth that needed to be praised, framed, and preserved. (our translation)

The distance and, at the same time, the proximity of this dimension that Pelé emanated put the Brazilian Olympic football players in an uncomfortable condition, to say the least. If Pelé did not even take a stand, how could they question the structure of soccer? If Pelé, who had so much football *capital*, did not do it, how could they do it? How could they talk about the political aspects of football? Pelé's lack of positioning corroborates what Oliveira (2009, p. 398) states about the sport:

> Its political dimension seems to have been linked to the proclaimed sportive mentality, which presupposed an education for discipline, of strong moralizing nature, aimed at the development of a work *ethos*, as it could form individuals of action, in addition to a perspective of treating sport as an end in itself, which is what high-performance sport presupposes. (our translation)

Still on Pelé's figure, it is necessary to clarify that, besides not taking a stand, he also did not distance himself from the uses that the military dictatorship made of sportive achievements. It was like that after scoring his 1000th goal, in 1969, against Vasco da Gama team, in Maracanã Stadium, when he was received by President Médici, who decorated him. As Magalhães (2010, p. 66) reports, "Pelé was received by the president in Brasília, and received won a national medal for merit and the title of commander. The athlete also paraded through the streets of the capital in an open car and became a commemorative stamp" (our translation).

This is a fundamental interpretative key for us to understand the lack of political positioning of the Brazilian Olympic football athletes. If the sport has an end in itself, there is no room for other possibilities beyond the use of the body, of the movement. According to this line of reasoning, it would not be up to the athletes to express themselves about issues other than those addressing the purpose to which they were bound, i.e., the game. Before moving on, we must hear the argument of the player Tostão (2016, p. 50), three-time World Cup champion in 1970, on this issue:

> Some extremists criticize the players for not having rebelled against the dictatorship, as if we were political activists and had to abandon the national team. We were all young, dreamers, ambitious, committed to our careers, and eager to be world champions. Nothing could be more human. In addition, I neither had the knowledge of the importance of that moment in Brazilian history nor the citizen awareness that I have today. (our translation)

Tostão's argument, to a certain extent, corroborates the view shared by the interviewed players. The common point is the fact that they were young. Being young, here, becomes synonymous with not having political awareness. In Tostão's words, only "political activists" would have rebelled against the dictatorship. This view needs to be distanced from the discourses, because it produces, in tow, an idea that only politically engaged people could speak out against something. As Tostão claims, today he has a "citizen awareness" that he did not have at the time.

The lack of political positioning cannot, as aforementioned, be understood in isolation. Being young, not being interested in such issues and/or not being aware of what was happening at that moment under the Brazilian military dictatorship—all this reinforces the argument that football is alienating. Nevertheless, it is necessary to think of football as part of a broader structure that, as Bourdieu (1983) points out, has its own logic.

The challenge is, therefore, to understand why athletes who position themselves are the exception. By explaining his concept of *habitus*, a system that, according to Bourdieu, has several properties, he provides us with elements to understand this question (Bourdieu & Chartier, 2017, p. 58):

> It is important to remember that agents have a history, that they are the product of a collective history, and that, in particular categories of thought, categories of judgment, schemes of perception, value systems etc., are the product of the embodiment of social structures. (our translation)

From this perspective, Tostão's position helps us to interpret the speeches of the Olympic players of the 1968 Brazilian team: there was ambition and interest in investing in their own careers. At no time the Brazilian athletes said they dreamed of winning the gold medal; what they wanted, as I have already pointed out, was to become professional players. And, even though they were young, they knew that, in the dynamic of reproduction of the social order and of the sportive field in which they were inserted, any questioning of the hierarchy imposed by the disciplinary structure of soccer could represent an obstacle for them to achieve what they wanted.

Bourdieu himself emphasizes that the *habitus* cannot always be taken as a destination, as if it was something predetermined and immutable. On the contrary, it is constantly subjected to experiences and thus transformed by these experiences (Bourdieu & Chartier, 2017, p. 62). Regarding fate, he points out that, as a probability, the social destiny linked to a life condition can confirm the *habitus*. To understand the *habitus*, we cannot deprive it of its complexity and its dynamics; after all, as the author states, it is the *habitus* that somehow constitutes the situation, and it is the situation that constitutes the *habitus* (Bourdieu & Chartier, 2017, p. 63).

Dissociating sport from politics, although this is a problematic separation, works as a modus operandi to validate the idea that, being separated, one should not talk about the relation between both. Separating them is the most efficient way to deny this inexorable connection, and also to enable the distance to produce the emptying of meaning, resulting in sport depoliticization.

Final Considerations

The discourse of denial, by the IOC, of the existence of a strong relationship between sports and politics was nothing more than a way to keep any possibility of protest away from the Olympic Games. However, each edition of the event increased the number of involved people, the public present at the stadiums, and the television audience. As the Olympic movement expanded and the Games started attracting thousands of people, the spotlight turned to the event, which became a privileged space for political action and minority protests. The International Olympic Committee, still not knowing how to deal with the political exposure that the Olympic Games attracted, sought to take measures that would guarantee its select group the power and control of the event according to its principles and rules.

If, as Bourdieu states, it is in the relationship with a given situation that *habitus* produces something (Bourdieu & Chartier, 2017, p. 62), it is similar to a spring, but a trigger is required, we can understand that, in the world of football, the relationships established between players and agents that compose the football scenario—such as coaches, fans, the press, managers, and other clubs—establish a circular exchange of experiences, which allows us to take players as a category of analysis. And, from this category, we can access the *habitus* produced by the experiences, which, in the case explored here, confirms the search for separation between sport and politics.

If we support Bourdieu's argument concerning the *habitus*, established by the duality dynamics between experience and transformation, we will realize the permanence of the *habitus* itself, which will lead us to think how much it impacts the collectivity. The understanding that it is possible for the agents of the field (players, coaches, managers, journalists) to break with the "barrier" that the *habitus* somehow produces in the sportive field has to be developed by what Bourdieu called "sense of the game" (Bourdieu, 2004).

The expression "sense of the game" carries infinite possibilities of action when facing situations/experiences. Thus, even being a player, it is possible to understand the political dynamics of football. The difficulty is of another nature, which is to understand that the origin of the *habitus*—acquired long before entering the world of football—confirms the rule rather than breaks with it. As a result, the maintenance of this status quo has produced in Brazilian Olympic football athletes the separation between football and politics.

References

Antunes, R., & Ridenti, M. (2007). Operários e estudantes contra a ditadura: 1968 no Brasil. *Mediações: Revista de Ciências Sociais, 12*(2), 78–89. https://doi.org/10.5433/2176-6665.200 7v12n2p78

Bourdieu, P. (1983). *Questões de sociologia*. Marco Zero.

Bourdieu, P. (1996). *Razões práticas: Sobre a teoria da ação*. Campinas: Papirus.

Bourdieu, P. (2003). Esboço de uma Teoria da Prática. In R. Ortiz (Ed.), *A sociologia de Pierre Bourdieu*. São Paulo: Olho d'Água.

Bourdieu, P. (2004). *Coisas ditas*. São Paulo. Brasiliense.

Bourdieu, P., & Chartier, R. (2017). *O sociólogo e o historiador*. Belo Horizonte: Autêntica Editora.

Brewster, K., & Brewster, C. (2009). The mexican student movement of 1968: An Olympic perspective. *The International Journal of the History of Sport, 26*(6), 814–839.

Comitê Olímpico confirma os Jogos do México. (1968, October 4). *O Estado de S. Paulo*, p. 19.

Costa exige a Copa de 70. (1968, December 4). *Jornal dos Sports*, p. 3.

Couto, E. F. (2014). *Da ditadura à ditadura: Uma história do futebol brasileiro (1930–1978)*. Niterói: Editora da UFF.

Cripa, I. A. (2011). O massacre dos estudantes na cidade do México em 1968: o poeta Octavio Paz e a história política. *Revista Eletrônica da ANPHLAC*, (11), 40–58. https://doi.org/10.46752/anp hlac.11.2011.1280

Crise no México tumultua as Olimpíadas. (1968, October 4). *Jornal dos Sports*, p.5.

DaMatta, R. (1982a). *Universo do futebol: Esporte e sociedade brasileira*. Pinakotheke.

DaMatta, R. (1982b). Futebol: Ópio do povo x drama de justiça social. *Novos Estudos CEBRAP, 1*(4), 54–60. http://novosestudos.com.br/produto/edicao-04/

Florenzano, J. P. (1998). Afonsinho e Edmundo: a rebeldia no futebol brasileiro. São Paulo: Musa Editora.

Gaspari, E. (2002). A ditadura envergonhada. São Paulo: Companhia das Letras.

Giglio, S. S. (2013). COI x FIFA: a história política do futebol nos Jogos Olímpicos. (Doctoral Thesis in Sciences), School of Physical Education and Sports, University of São Paulo, São Paulo, Brasil. http://www.teses.usp.br/teses/disponiveis/39/39133/tde-21012014-133735/

Giglio, S. S. (2018). *A história política do futebol olímpico (1894–1988)*. São Paulo: Intermeios; FAPESP.

Giglio, S. S.; & Rubio, K. (2017). A hegemonia europeia no Comitê Olímpico Internacional. *Revista Brasileira de Educação Física e Esporte, 31*(1), 291–305. https://doi.org/10.11606/1807-550920 1700010291

Giorgetti, U. (2013). *1968: a última Olimpíada livre*. [DVD]. São Paulo, Brasil: Canal Azul.

Magalhães, L. G. (2010). *Histórias do futebol*. São Paulo: Arquivo Público do Estado.

Miskulin, S. C. (2008). As repercussões do movimento estudantil de 1968 no México. *Anais Eletrônicos do VIII Encontro Internacional da ANPHLAC*, Vitória, Brasil. http://antigo.anphlac. org/sites/default/files/silvia_miskulin.pdf

Movimento faz ameaça. (1968, October 10). *O Estado de S. Paulo*, p. 23.

Negros boicotam Brundage. (1968, October 16). *O Estado de S. Paulo*, p. 19.

Negros fazem seu protesto. (1968, October 18). *O Estado de S. Paulo*, p. 17.

Olimpíada: Crise chegou à ONU. (1968, October 5). *Jornal dos Sports*, p. 3.

Oliveira, M. A. T. (2009). O esporte brasileiro em tempos de exceção: sob a égide da ditadura (1964–1985). In M. Del Priore, & V. A. Melo (Orgs.), *História do esporte no Brasil: do Império aos dias atuais* (pp. 387–416). São Paulo: Editora UNESP.

Oliveira, M. A. T. (2012). Esporte e política na ditadura militar brasileira: a criação de um pertencimento nacional esportivo. *Movimento, 18*(4), 155–174. https://doi.org/10.22456/1982-8918.32108

Poniatowska, E. (1971). *La noche de Tlatelolco*: testemonios de historia oral. Cidade do México: Edições Era.

Silveira, V. T., & Vaz, A. F. (2014). Doping e controle de feminilidade no esporte. *Cadernos Pagu*, (42), 447–475. https://periodicos.sbu.unicamp.br/ojs/index.php/cadpagu/article/view/8645129

Souza, D. A. (2018). *Pra frente, Brasil! Do Maracanazo aos mitos de Pelé e Garrincha, a dialética da ordem e da desordem (1950–1983)*. São Paulo: Intermeios.

Tostão (2016). *Tempos vividos, sonhados e perdidos: Um olhar sobre o futebol*. São Paulo: Companhia das Letras.

Troncoso, A. C. (2013). Memória e representações: a fotografia e o movimento estudantil de 1968 no México. *Revista Brasileira de História, 33*(65), 85–109. https://www.redalyc.org/articulo.oa?id=26327840004

Wisnik, J. M. (2008). *Veneno remédio: o futebol e o Brasil*. São Paulo: Companhia das Letras.

Chapter 4
The Political Dimension of *"Futebol-Arte"*

José Paulo Florenzano

The militarization process advanced in several sports arenas in Brazil in the early 1970s. A quick glance at the city of Recife, State of Pernambuco, might be enough to demonstrate it. Indeed, the city's main clubs competed among themselves to adopt authoritarian measures. At Náutico, Major Alves had just taken over the physical preparation on the recommendation of Coach Nelson Lucena, also a major in the Army. Without wasting any time, right in the first contact with the team, he communicated the imposition of the new training regime in "two shifts." (Náutico contrata preparador por recomendação de Lucena, 1972, February 12). At Sport, Chiquinho was expelled in the match against Central, a club from Caruaru, resulting in a fine of 20% on the player's wages because, as the manager of the red-and-black team emphasized, "we do not tolerate indiscipline" (Wilson e Osmar podem ter vez contra Corais, 1972, February 27). At Santa Cruz, coach Evaristo de Macedo had in his hands a "dossier" containing a detailed description of each athlete's behavior, whose public and private life was scrutinized "under all aspects, including moral," a crucial criterion to determine his permanence or dismissal from the team (Evaristo quer amistoso na próxima semana, 1972, January 13).

The imposition of physical preparation as a central value on the clubs' production systems walked *pari passu* with the establishment of authoritarianism as the natural order of things. The convergent processes of political repression, athletic excess, and medicalization of human existence defined the militarized matrix main contours—an analysis tool developed by us in a previous article (Florenzano, 2014), from the conceptual apparatus proposed by the anthropologist Damo (2007). Established in the context of the third World Cup, it circumscribed a new evaluative field and implied a characteristic subjection mode. It also included instances of control, surveillance mechanisms and interventions of a normalizing nature that sought to fix the behavior of the player-soldier based on the military *ethos,* as eloquently revealed in the agenda read by captain Cláudio Coutinho, at the headquarters of Brazilian

J. P. Florenzano (✉)
Pontfical Catholic University of São Paulo, São Paulo, Brazil

© The Author(s), under exclusive license to Springer Nature Switzerland AG 2021 49
S. S. Giglio and M. W. Proni (eds.), *Football and Social Sciences in Brazil*,
https://doi.org/10.1007/978-3-030-84686-2_4

football: "We use tactics we learned in the Army because there are many similarities among commanding a football team, a platoon or a regiment, e.g., organization, discipline, understanding, and cooperation." (Trajano, 1978, May, our translation).

The implementation of the militarized matrix, despite the admittedly martial character imposed on the football practice, showed the false promise of reconciling science and art by bringing them together in a harmonious and painless way. Legitimized by the three-time champion achievement, it was gradually adopted in sports associations where, however, it immediately had to face the resistance struggle waged by professional athletes. Nevertheless, for the researchers Marco Salvador and Antonio Soares, it was a matter of the permanence of a romantic vision of resistance to progress, a backwardness barricade lifted by the "myth" of the *futebol-arte* (Salvador & Soares, 2009, p. 68). Well, specifically regarding the category of professional athletes, we may state that the resistance issue requires an explanatory model more attentive to the correlative character of discursive and non-discursive practices in the field of sport. Instead of the view adopted by the authors, i.e., that of a pure and neutral science, placed toward progress, we should investigate how the types of knowledge, power techniques, and forms of subjectivity are intertwined in the government of athletes (Foucault, 1998).

From this perspective, the issue of resistance acquires a new intelligibility, revealing itself not as a result of "prejudice" or ignorance, but as the art of not allowing oneself to be led and governed by the normalization practices. It was for no other reason that rebellion came to be included in the domain of abnormality, codified as a new genre of moral madness (Florenzano, 1998).

The idea of *futebol-arte*, contrary to what is commonly believed, does not have a univocal sense, present in a supposed regularity of meaning, fixed, and immovable, intended to reiterate indefinitely the same set of statements about the style of play, innate talent, or national identity (Gilson, 1994; Souza, 1996). According to the accurate analysis of the anthropologist Toledo (2004), it should not be perceived as a homogeneous, consensual form-representation, free from contradictions. Especially in the context of the civilian-military regime, it sheltered a fierce dispute regarding the meaning of the game, the way of playing, and the player preparation, integrating into the vocabulary through which the multiplicity of confrontations that covered the field of sport was expressed. Therefore, we need to follow the displacements undertaken by the notion of *futebol-arte* to distinguish the semantic uses that it entailed, identify the struggles and clashes waged taken to establish its meaning or, on the contrary, to keep it permanently inconstant and open.

If, on one hand, it constituted an instrument of reification of borders (us/them), naturalization of differences (white/black), and reproduction of stereotyped representations about Brazil, on the other hand, it looked like as a point of resistance and escape route for dissident athletes who wanted to become autonomous, through the practices of freedom. Under this perspective, we place ourselves to undertake the problematization of the *futebol-arte* category.

Revolutionary Capital

In the early 1970s, a civilians and military elite squad took on the noble mission of disseminating the scientific methodology of "modern" football in the sports clubs (Seja um craque sem gastar muito, 1971, February 26). Among its members were the physical trainers Admildo Chirol and Carlos Alberto Parreira, the lieutenant Raul Carlesso and the captains João Bonetti and Cláudio Coutinho. Occupying strategic positions in the field of sport, this elite squad was notably present both in the Brazilian national team and in the main teams of the country. Besides taking care of the physical preparation, the members of the group were also in charge of the technical direction and administrative supervision, revealing the great influence they had obtained after the 1970 World Cup. With the declared objective of replicating the model established by the Brazilian national team, many agents of the authoritarian modernization, such as Colonel Floriano Peixoto, from Corinthians, and Major Mário Doernt, from Grêmio, proposed the confinement in the training center for the injured athletes; the surveillance of the team during vacation period; the barracks discipline in football clubs (Florenzano, 2014). The ordinance issued by Sport's management eloquently illustrates how much the refusal of the imperative of physical force was classified by the command hierarchy as an infringing conduct: "The player who is injured, as of today, will be put away in the training center until his fully recovery. In case of non-compliance of the athlete, there will be a fine, as determined by the law" (Linha dura começa hoje a vigorar no Leão da Ilha, 1972, May 10, our translation).

Those constraining practices, however, gave rise to numerous strategies of confrontation by professional players, such as open confrontation with the ruling class, judicial claims for a free pass, and veiled sabotage of the exercise of power. The resistance struggle against militarization, in turn, would be fought in the name of *futebol-arte*. Indeed, the expression *futebol-arte* was claimed, appropriated, and reframed in political terms by the rebel generation of the seventies, becoming an important weapon in the battle against the hegemonic model. Afonso Celso Garcia Reis, Paulo César Lima, and Nei Conceição, a few names who represented the protest movement, expressed their refusal to authoritarianism in the team management and their resistance to the athletic excess adopted by clubs, taking a divergent stance in relation to the evolutionary line drawn in football by the knowledge-power regime that colonized it. Certainly, they were not the only ones in the aforementioned historical context to demonstrate a non-compliant conduct. Paulinho, for example, a young winger from Bonsucesso, in Rio de Janeiro suburbs, defended the thesis that "football is skill, not strength" (Meu sonho é o Flamengo, 1972, August 25). This proposition echoed the manifesto that the plethora of dissident players, spread across the four corners of the country, drafted in the early 1970s against the truth speech about football-strength (Florenzano, 2009).

We use the expression "football-strength" not as a common sense, but as a category of analysis, thus defined from the work of Foucault (1987): "A conception guided by the imperative of physical strength, instead of the individual dexterity requirement; it is based on the idea that the team's strength resides in the composition of the players as an efficient and adjusted machine—a gear driven by a power that aims to increase the athlete's body strength, in economic terms of utility, and to decrease these same strengths, in political terms of obedience" (Florenzano, 2009, p. 33, our translation).

Indeed, we need to rescue the historical content of the political battle driven by the rebellious in order to shift the center of gravity of the analysis and epistemologically unlock the discussion about *futebol-arte*, usually restricted to the aesthetic dimension of the beautiful game and the symbolic construction of the imagined community. Not that these issues are not important, on the contrary. Criticism of the innate style of play and the deconstruction of naturalized representations of national identity are two of the main theoretical contributions of sports anthropology to the football study area (Guedes, 2014; Toledo, 2002). However, it seems to be a mistake to ignore the political dimension itself, which also characterizes and distinguishes *futebol-arte*.

In this sense, it is convenient to give the word to the athletes who claimed it with the explicit goal of questioning the effects of truth propagated by the militarized matrix implanted in the clubs' production apparatus. Let us pay attention to the reflection of Nei Conceição, former midfielder of Botafogo: "Football is not a lung, it is an art; and an artist cannot be methodical. Football is not about physical strength, it is played with thought power; not for those who want to, but for those who know how" (Futebol é para quem sabe, 1973, August 10, our translation).

Not even the possibility of Cláudio Coutinho's arrival at Botafogo, who was at that time a military supervisor, and the return of the physical trainer Admildo Chirol, intimidated the rebellious player of Botafogo. As Nei Conceição pointed out: "Discipline may become a little stricter, but that will not change my position regarding physical preparation." However, before continuing with the analysis, we should answer the following question: What was exactly the athlete's position regarding physical preparation? Obviously, the idea was not to remove it from the training centers, nor to underestimate the importance it had for the professional practice. The confrontation aimed to problematize the central place it had experienced in the clubs since the mid-1960s, when, due to the failure of the Brazilian national team in the World Cup in England, sports agents' discourses converged to the imperative need of producing the modern player, a historical urgency that the implementation of the power device sought to meet in order to make Brazilian football competitive again.

In this sense, Nei Conceição' statement expressed, above all, the refusal to submit to the athletic excess implied by the new way of playing, sacrificing, on the other hand, the analytical capacity and the political autonomy involved in the sportive activity. The historical content on the struggles of the protest movement reveals, therefore, the resistance to the biological reductionism imposed on the professional athlete at the training centers. The questioning was not only restricted to the repressive practices, but it also included the set of polymorphic mechanisms of power, activated to ensure the normalization in course, starting with the confinement regime, whose strictness perfectly matched the military spirit in force at the time. Sérgio Carneiro Redes, playmaker at Fortaleza, anticipated in almost a decade Sócrates' nonconformism with the disciplinary institution that forced the players to remain confined for several days "with nothing to do" (As máximas do Serginho, 1973, August 28).

It was surely a coincidence that Nei Conceição and Sérgio Redes ended up on board of "Trem da Alegria" (Joy Train), a team idealized in the mid-1970s by the player Afonsinho to keep alive the political dream of football as a form of art. This is a reference to Garrincha, whose way of playing made people happy and cheerful. Through the iron "trails," the rebel player traced an escape line from authoritarian modernization, challenging athletic excess, the power of the norm and the hierarchical discipline, constitutive aspects of the militarized matrix, present in varying degrees and in peculiar forms in sports associations. Instead of following the tracks through which the process of increasing medicalization of the athlete's life advanced, interpreted by body and soul specialists as a sign of progress, the "Trem da Alegria" went through a transversal time in order to unveil, in the historical horizon, a new social configuration of the game, no longer anchored on the notion of strength, but on the idea of art.

However, we should ask ourselves whether the dreamlike journey was effectively open to all those interested in achieving the political utopia of *futebol-arte*. Therefore, to answer this question, it is appropriate to return to the reflections of Botafogo's central midfielder, especially to the event where he concluded the manifesto, saying that football "is for those who have the knowledge, not for those who wish." At first glance, this assertion seems to introduce an exclusion criterion, saving seats only for those who were part of the "ball" aristocracy, while the others had to get off at the nearest station, that is, in the harsh reality reserved for passengers without football capital, which is precisely the case of the striker Dario: "Boy, you can't play. Go and find a job" (Dario está à venda, 1973, January 19). That was the advice Gentil Cardoso, Campo Grande's coach at the time, gave to Dario when the center forward was looking to build his reputation at the football world. Luckily, his advice was ignored. The "clumsy" boy, whom people "laughed" at, did not give up and returned to the squad from the suburbs of Rio de Janeiro, when he got the longed-for chance with the new coach, Gradim. Analogous to the character of "The Old Man and the Sea," Dario used to fight tooth and nail. He did not miss the rare opportunity offered to him, although he was still struggling "against the fate of permanent defeat" that never left him. However, like the simple fisherman in Ernest Hemingway's work (2003), he carried inscribed on his chest the motto a man can be destroyed, but never defeated. Years later, already established as a center forward at Atlético Mineiro Club, he would express his eternal gratitude for the old master Gradim: "You had the courage to persevere with me at a time when I used to train for a plate of food" (Aragão, 1972, October 23; Homenagem do Dadá a Gradim, 1972, November 10).

However, the obstinacy and fearlessness of the player who ran for a plate of food were not the main targets of Nei Conceição's criticism. "Everyone has the right" to their professional practice, stressed the "black-and-white" midfielder, adding that on the "football train" there was room for everyone (Futebol é pra quem sabe, 1973, August 10). Then, how can we explain the apparently excluding clause contained in the rebellion's manifesto? The supposed contradiction is broken in the framework of existing relations in the field of sport. By defending the thesis that football is "for those who have the knowledge, not for those who wish," Nei Conceição questioned the axiom inscribed at the entrance of the training centers, where it was increasingly taught that the profession of athlete, henceforth, was reserved to those who wanted it, provided that the desire, obviously, coincided with the norm established by the military-scientific matrix. The gift/talent, by itself, no longer ensured anyone a place in the sun. Confiscated by the sport sciences, it now went through a "polishing" work aimed to limit the useless excesses, banish the counterproductive twists and turns and eliminate the pernicious vices to sports efficiency, acquired in the neighborhood championships, in the suburban leagues, or in the amateur tournaments. The discontinuity between the popular spaces of the game and the disciplinary field in which the professional practice was transfigured established a distance impossible to be bridged without the help of scientific methods. The normative character of knowledge required for the high-performance production defined the correct way to play, as well as the political anatomy of the body necessary to perform it.

Before the implementation of the power device in the field of sport, which occurred in the mid-1960s, a line of continuity prevailed between the popular spaces of football and the clubs' training centers. After we won the third championship, the rupture established by the sports sciences disqualified the minor, local, and handcrafted knowledge, acquired in the areas surrounding the production apparatus of the modern player. The position occupied by the body and soul specialists demanded, as a prerequisite, the expropriation of knowledge accumulated over time by football players, a comprehensive process that involved the correct way to play, the right position on the field, the way of performing the role assigned by the coaching staff, the proper way to eat, the convenient time to sleep, and the healthy way to entertain themselves in their free time, in accordance with the demands of a lifestyle that could not jeopardize the investment made to extract high performance from each "piece" available on the pitch. Therefore, it was necessary to subdue, disqualify, and downgrade the knowledge of the athletes so that the knowledge of the physical trainers, the sports physicians, and the technical directors, considered superior, scientific, and true, could establish a new economy of power (Foucault, 1999).

However, it is not about the simple seizure of practical knowledge acquired in the fields. It is about something much broader, deeper, and more drastic regarding the power relations in professional football. We refer to the political knowledge involved in the self-constitution of the player as masters, in the organization of the team by athletes themselves, or, in general, in the freedom practices that make up the "revolutionary capital" (Fanon, 2005) of Brazilian football. Far from being exhausted in rebellion acts, tactics of sabotage or rearguard combat waged against the militarization process, the revolutionary capital accumulated in the course of a long tradition of autonomy emerged in concrete experiences of self-government, both individual and collective, elaborated in the form of self-management, cooperatives or countless variations of participatory democracy instituted by several groups of athletes in the inventive framework of the Republic of Football (Florenzano, 2009). There is no doubt that the "Trem da Alegria" was inserted in this historical framework, highlighting the political talent of the Brazilian player. However, besides that, it brings us to a question that seems appropriate to the discussion at hand. We can formulate it in the following terms: Was the revolutionary capital perhaps characterized as a particular property of a certain segment of the professional athletes' category?

Otherwise, let us see. Perhaps with the exception of Nei Conceição, all the other athletes mentioned above, Paulinho, Serginho, and Afonsinho, were, at the time, in higher education and belonged to the middle class. Including now Nei Conceição, we can identify them, based on the racial classification system, as belonging to the whites' category. So, let us rephrase the question: Did *futebol-arte* appear to be a romantic explanation of socially privileged professional athletes belonging to the dominant racial group and freed from the material embarrassment of having to run for a plate of food? Maybe it was more than a simple coincidence the fact that middle-class, white, university-educated players positioned themselves in favor of a football alternative to the hegemonic model. However, without necessarily dismissing the nexuses pointed out by the referred hypothesis, it seems licit to postulate the thesis according to which the intransigent defense of art transcended the aforementioned social group, putting down deep roots in the popular strata from which the vast majority of professional athletes came. In this regard, it is enough to mention the critique by the former Bangu defender, Zózimo, to the impoverishment of body techniques, that entailed the replacement of "*futebol-arte*" by "football-lung": "Today, a defense player who wants to carry the ball from his area, as I used to do, has two choices: He will either be immediately replaced or will receive a violent attack from the adversary. Unfortunately, that's the way the game is played nowadays" (De graça, sim senhor, 1973, August 24, our translation).

In other words, the poor, the blacks, and the athletes without higher education also cultivated the principle that subverted the conceptual limits of sport as an essentially physical activity, regulated by body and soul specialists. Let us avoid, therefore, the simplifications that consist, on one hand, in correlating poverty, blackness, and lack of schooling with *futebol-arte*, and, on the other, in associating this conception of game with a minority of whites, privileged and college-educated, divorced from the competitive reality of the game.

The cultural richness of *futebol-arte* was unveiled precisely in the interlocution that it engendered, on and off the pitch, among social classes, racial groups, religious creeds, and other variables that coexisted in the field of sport, not always harmoniously. "Armandinhos" (players with no combativeness) and "mascarados" (deceptive players), "caçadores de canela" (violent defender) and "cabeça de bagre" (players with no intelligence), "limpadores de área" (relentless defender) and "sheriffs," "trombadores" (players with physical strength) and "pipoqueiros" (coward players), crazy "crioulos" and proud "crioulos." The Portuguese word "crioulo" does not correspond to either the pejorative "nigger" nor the affirmative "black." Strictly speaking, it maintains a certain ambivalence, depending on the context in which it is employed. The plurality of characters that composed the rich gallery of Brazilian football eloquently attested to the tensions that permeated the playing field.[1] They were polarized, however, around the player who ran for a plate of food and the player who built a career as a work of art. These two symbolic categories, in turn,

---

[1] For the expression "cabeça-de-bagre," see "Linha dura no Náutico" (1973, November 9); For the expression "proud crioulo," see "A lenta morte dos anti-heróis" (1973, February 9); For the term "caçadores de canela," see "Um segundo para o gol" (1973, October 5).

had as counterpoint, respectively, the athlete who played with *raça* and the player who acted wearing a "mask." The Portuguese word "raça" means bravery, courage, determination, but it also dubiously refers to an ethnic group. The simultaneity with which these two figures acquired prominence at the moment when a new football matrix was being implemented. By coercive means, it is no mere coincidence. The extreme and opposite positions they came to represent in the sportive field translated the multiple effects of a power discourse that attached football practice to the domain of science, classifying those who insisted on cultivating the art of indocility in the stigmatized category of the problem-player. Thus, we should now focus on a more detailed analysis of the binary opposition between "raça" and "mask."

Raça and Mask

The first thing that draws our attention when we reread the news coverage of the period immediately after the 1970 World Cup is the omnipresence of the word *raça* in reports and articles about football. Any feat—a team's victory, title-winning, or even the simple performance of an athlete—was invariably authenticated by the term *raça* (É Corinthians sim! Time bom e de raça, 1970, November 20). And yet, its appearance in the football lexicon was nothing new, on the contrary, it dated back to the 1950 World Cup. It evoked, then, the distinctive feature of the Uruguayan champions, at the same time prescribing the form of action that should be mimicked by Brazilian players, if they wished to achieve, in international competitions, the same success as their rivals. Twenty years on from the *Maracanã* tragedy, when the two teams met again in a World Cup, the result showed that the hard lesson had been learned. Thanks to the ingenuity of the journalist João Saldanha, coach of the Brazilian national team during the qualifying games, the representation of the "Canarinhos" had been replaced by the image of predators, more consistent with the imperative of masculinity prevailing in the football universe (As Feras amansam o Leão da Rainha, 1970, June 12).

The redefinition of the symbology that involved our athletes, however, did not imply the suppression of the identity of "artists" that accompanied them, but rather established with it the ideal balance for achieving sporting success. However, once the epic adventure had been sealed on the Mexican pitches, the ludic animal entered into an autophagy process, with the ferocious half devouring the artistic half of the hybrid being that had enchanted the global audience. Indeed, in complete contrast to the celebration of the beautiful game displayed during the third-championship campaign, the reopening of regional competitions in the country unveiled the open option of Brazilian national teams for defensive systems, with a significant increase of violent moves among professionals. Last but not least, it exposed the idolatry of individual and collective performance based not on the principle of art, but on the imperative of *raça* (Chega de classe, 1973, August 31). The overwhelming strength with which this slogan was imposed on the Brazilian pitches allows us to distinguish an unresolved issue in Guadalajara triumph.

Indeed, it was as if the 3–1 victory over the Uruguayans had not been enough to quench their thirst for revenge and exorcise the ghost of 1950. In order to heal the wound and move on, it had become essential, moreover, to appropriate the way the faithful enemies played in order to overcome them also in terms of *raça*. Hence, the second point that draws our attention in the period following the third-championship victory is the constant presence of Uruguayan athletes in *Placar* magazine, pontificating with moral authority the attributes necessary for the practice of authentic football. First of all, we should be clear about the premise on which the whole discussion was based: "We are always eleven men on the pitch," taught Luis Ubiña, right back of the "Celeste Olimpica" (Luís Ignácio Ubiña, 1972, July 7). "In Uruguay we have a rule," added Pablo Forlan, São Paulo right back, "don't let anyone get past you twice because, on the third, he will hit you on your face" (Forlan, the Kung Fu, 1974, January 25). If the symbolic violence of dribbling turned the dribbled into a football clown, the defender's physical violence, by contrast, brings into question the dribbler's masculinity. The mutual challenge that entangled the forward and the defender surfaced in the comments of Paraná, a left-winger who also played for São Paulo: "Sometimes I hit before I get hit" to let him know that "I'm going to play that way." Hence, from hunting he became a hunter, showing the inversion as a trophy: "They may say I'm violent," highlighted Paraná, "but no one can say I'm a coward" (Aprendi com papai, 1973, September 21). Paraná was a left-winger who was part of the Brazilian national team in the 1966 World Cup in England. Nothing made him more upset than seeing a player panicked in front of his adversary: "When I see a kid who's scared, I get a bit mad with rage. I tell them that if they're going out there to run away from the fight, they'd better stay at home, taking care of the kitchen, helping their mothers. Football is a game for men and cannot be learned at school" (Aprendi com papai, 1973, September 21, our translation).

The game view expressed by the intrepid athlete of São Paulo takes us to the core of the question we have been approaching. Taking into account the overlapping of the three terms distinguished by the analysis, namely "pipoqueiro," "armandinho," and "mascarado," we can state that the coward player was hidden behind the mask, and this, in turn, was symbolically situated in a feminine space. It was as if male football involved an internal bipartition organized on the basis of virility. Those who had *raça* were situated in the space of normality represented by the male player; those who hid their identity behind the mask ended up classified in a space where the distinction between the masculine and the feminine was blurred. However, if from an endogenous perspective Brazilian football revealed an unsuspected dichotomy, from an exogenous perspective, that is the South American rivals, it appeared as a single and undivided whole made up by fearful, i.e., skilled but coward players whose playing style incorporated characteristics associated with the female universe. Seen in this light, one could say that the *futebol-arte* emerged as a logical scandal, as long as it introduced the disjunction between being an athlete and being a macho, the only possibility foreseen and accepted by the football symbolic structure, considered in the broader configuration in which the South American rivalry unfolded (Clastres, 2003).

By the way, the virility guardians were never tired of propagating the "truth" that football could only be played by men, a warning directed not exactly at women, whose participation in the professional circuit was not even considered by them, but also at athletes who did not show the insignia of genuine masculinity on the field. In this context, Obdulio Varela, in an interview for *Placar* magazine, evoked the unsuccessful experience of Didi, the inventor of the "Folha Seca" (this expression means "dry leave" and refers to a dry leave falling from a tree), as a coach in Argentina, reiterating the dogma of football-*raça*: "Didi wanted to turn River Plate into a beautiful game team, but he did not realize that the beautiful game is only good for those who see it. Beautifulness does not win games. To win you need fight and stamina. You need eleven men on the field" (Obdulio Jacinto Varela, o caudillo, 1972, May 19).

It was as if, for the legendary captain of the Celeste Olímpica, time had stopped at the final whistle at Maracanã, thus making it clear how much Uruguayan football had become a prisoner of the myth he had helped to build in the epic conquest of the World Cup in Brazil. Victory was ultimately a question of virility, which, in turn, had to be asserted in all circumstances, especially when it came to defeat: "They say that if the Uruguayan can't win the ball, he wins the fight," bragged Pablo Forlan (Até a morte, 1972, May 26). Since he had been transferred to São Paulo from Penarol in the early 1970s, Forlan was in a unique position to draw parallels between the two ways of playing, identifying the key factor that set them apart: "football here is more touch-and-go; over there it's about fighting." Thus, the new generations reproduced the mythical letter of football-*raça*, which stated that the game should be "played to the death" (Luís Ignácio Ubiña, 1972, July 7). Indifferent to the setbacks caused by historical events, the Uruguayan athletes, who appeared on the pages of *Placar* magazine, kept intact the explanatory scheme in which they reigned supreme thanks to their congenital bravery: "Everyone is afraid of our stamina" (Pobre Celeste, 1972, July 14).

Well, it is not surprising to see the exponents of the Uruguayan way of playing, so to speak, clinging to a mythical belief at the time when the Celeste Olímpica was embittered by the decadence of a football once considered unbeatable. However, it seems a terrible paradox to realize, at the moment of full hegemony of Brazilian football, the sorrow with which many agents of the sport aimed not only to incorporate the stamina attributed to the rivals, but, above all, to erect it in the cornerstone of the game practiced in the country. How do explain it? It is time to gather the various threads outlined throughout the analysis in order to clearly formulate our hypothesis.

It seems to us that playing with *raça* crystallized a way of playing that intertwined the hunger of athletes from the working classes who ran for a plate of food; the strength of the bodies produced as war machines in the training centers; and the identity of the macho player cultivated in the male universe of football, whose archetype was the Uruguayan warrior. Situated at the point of confluence of these three aspects, the aforementioned style allowed the implementation of the possibilities created by sports science, multiplying the athlete's presence on the field and raising the team's playing pace, leaving on the defensive all those who, for one reason or another, did not fit into the normalization process.

Driven by the power device implanted in the field of sport to increase the body productive forces, playing with *raça* brought to light all the ambiguity contained in the value system of *futebol-arte*, which, in turn, was conveniently exploited by the South American rivals through a lame syllogism, whose premises were chained up as follows: men do not tremble in football; Brazilians tremble in front of their opponents; therefore, Brazilians do not act like men (Pelé: "eu tricampeão," 1971, August 20). Internalized in the form of a latent malaise, the conclusion of the virility syllogism implied the transgressive identity of *futebol-arte*. The resulting tensions were reflected in the discourse produced within the country itself.

Indeed, parallel to our exaltation of the body swing, the dance, and the ballet dancer player, we came across the internal criticism of the masked player who wiggles on the field, excessively fondles the ball and dodges body-to-body inter-action (Admirável Cruzeiro novo, 1972, October 27). The allusions involving the masculinity of the national athlete thus became additional reasons to resize the mani-festation space granted to a playstyle considered effeminate, portrayed as outdated, seen as dysfunctional to the dynamics of modern football, based on the speed of movement, speed of passing the ball, objectivity of the plays. Whether for racial, sexual, or scientific reasons, playing with *raça* was increasingly imposed as the manly, correct and effective way to act, in accordance with a heterogeneous set of representations amalgamated in the norm of the macho player.

Initially linked to popular teams, notably Flamengo, in Rio de Janeiro, and Corinthians, in São Paulo, the rule in question expanded to other associations in the country, driven by the Olympic Celeste mythical feat in the 1950 World Cup.[2] To double the resistance of the recalcitrant players, besides the repressive practices of the authoritarian period, and training pedagogy of the scientific era, there was also the indispensable collaboration of the "masked athlete," who was put on the field to morally coerce those who were reluctant to submit to the principles of football-*raça*. In this way, the power device rehabilitated a decadent character, who was forgotten in some corner of the stage, giving him an unexpected prominence. For sure, a difficult mission for which the assistance of supporting actors was necessary, for instance the "firuleiro" (circus player), charged with the more specific task of inhibiting any excesses when the "jugglers" handled the ball, a censorship determined in the name of sportive efficacy. Indeed, in the entry of the *Brazilian Football Dictionary*, "firula" was defined as "difficult play," made with "great technique," but that did not meet any "practical result," being commonly performed "to please the fans" (Dicionário de futebol, 1972, January 14). However, the expansion of the semantic field orga-nized around the masked athlete produced harmful consequences to the tradition of

---

[2] In his column "Bola na Lagoa…," published on May 24, 1949, in the Sports Newspaper Jornal dos Sports, journalist Pedro Nunes alluded to "a beautiful victory of race" of Flamengo, considered by him a victory "markedly rubro-negra." Mário Filho, however, when commenting on the victory of the Rio de Janeiro team over England's Arsenal, in a long article of May 31, 1949, published in the same periodical, did not resort to the expression to characterize the distinctive trait of the eubro-negro: "Flamengo is a club that is different from the others," he said, a difference that resided in the "strength of will" (as cited by Florenzano, 2020, our translation).

Brazilian football autonomy. The defender position would not go unscathed by the impoverishment of body techniques that the alluded diffusion entailed.

Before someone objects that this analysis incurs in a romantic view of things, let us remember that the qualities associated with the lineage represented by Domingos da Guia—the pass precision during the start of the match and the ability to organize the game from the line of defense—account for an important part of the football revolution attributed to Barcelona during the turn of twentieth to the twenty-first century. The transformation carried out in Brazil in the last quarter of the last century stunted as "firula" the technically accurate play, causing embarrassment to the responsible player, especially if he acted as a defender. In order to have a vague notion of the symbolic violence that the insinuation of masked player implied to those who were found to be in that position, it is enough for us to quote the reaction of Luís Pereira, the defender of Palmeiras, in face of the rumors that considered him as a member of the cursed confraternity: "Do you know what I'm going to do with the first guy who says that to my face, whoever he is? I will punch him in the nose, as hard as I can" (Fase 3: Tapar os vazamentos, 1974, April 26, our translation).

There was no choice for the athlete classified in the infamous category, except defending himself in the court of norma. During the militarization of Brazilian football, not a few were embarrassed for sitting in the dock. Enéas, for instance, a young striker of Portuguesa de Desportos, received, right at the beginning of his career, the accusation of being "masked," invoking in his own defense the simple argument that he only practiced "inventiveness." Considering himself also a "skilled player," he refuted critics who accused him of being "slow," a serious anomaly in the context of "football-speed." Aside from his technical weaknesses, the masked athlete also revealed psychological problems. At least, that was what Dino Sani said (O garoto Enéas, 1973, August 3). In an effort to clear Falcão from the suspicion of being part of the accursed group, the coach of the Internacional explained to those interested that the social pathology, in reality, only affected "emotionally unbalanced players" (O voo do Falcão, 1973, September 28). That was a general relief for the admirers of the young promise of the Internacional! The issue, however, was not free of sexual connotations. Coach João Avelino, nonconformist with the performance of CEUB, the club representing the city of Brasília in the National Championship, went beyond criticism for what he considered to be a squad of masked players: "I warn you: whoever wants to wiggle, shall get a transvestite and go dance at João Caetano Theater" (Avelino calls the whole CEUB to the lines, 1973, October 5, our translation).

The player who wore a mask entered the stage of Brazilian football to contrast with the norm represented by the player who acted with *raça*. While the latter attested to the manly masculinity required for performing the profession, the former introduced in the field of sport an element of disturbance of the symbolic order that was desired to be built based on the identity of the macho player. The binary opposition established between the two categories was expressed in several levels of contrast: technical, moral, and sexual. An athlete could be judged as masked under one criterion or another, or even by the sum of all of them. Thus, for example, Jorge Mendonça, Bangu's forward, had barely arrived in Recife in 1973, bringing in his suitcase the refined football acquired in the fields of Rio de Janeiro's countryside, and soon found himself "accused of masking" (Linha dura no Náutico, 1973, November 9). Although he was only nineteen, he claimed to have learned many lessons. The most important of them was to take possession of the ball from midfield, rather than planting himself between the defenders of the opposing team. "Keeping your back to the area, carelessly, is to give a chance to 'shin hunters' like Assis and Moisés" (Um segundo para o gol, 1973, October 5, our translation). The harsh law enforced by Rio's "sheriffs" had forced him to play in midfield, a move partly responsible for the epithet "pipoqueiro" acquired years later at Palmeiras. The negative meaning of Jorge Mendonça's back movement was made clear in the words of Vitória striker, Carlos André de Lima, self-designated "trombador": "There's no ugly face capable of turning me into an 'armandinho,' as I see when violence happens" (André, o machão, 1974, April 12).

The kinship relations among the "pipoqueiro," the "firuleiro" and the "armandinho" were clearly established for the actors in the field of sport. On the other hand, no one questioned the blood ties between the "sheriff," the "caçador de canela" and the "trombador," to whom, however, were added the "perna de pau" (player with no skills), the "cabeça de bagre," and the "bode cego" (player lost on the field), unwelcome members of an extended family (Dario falou e fez, 1973, August 31). Conceptually constructed in the grandstands by anonymous fans, forged in the newsrooms by sports journalists, created in various configurations by athletes of all kinds, these symbolic categories were articulated around the polarity constituted by playing with *raça* and playing with art, making up two opposing semantic fields. Each of them, in turn, could be divided into a positive and a negative sphere, according to the observer's point of view. In this sense, whatever for some was defined as art, for others appeared as "mask" and, conversely, where many saw stamina, many glimpsed violence.

As the anthropologist Sahlins (2004, p. 307) points out, perceptions, far from being immaculate, depend on the cultural categories activated by historical agents in specific contexts. Likewise, we can assert that allegorical characters of Brazilian football were not axiologically neutral, but, instead, they participated in clashes fought on ground, symbolizing art, *raça*, violence, and mask. Here, however, we should make an important caveat.

If, in the scheme outlined above, the binary codification established a contrastive relationship between the player who fought for a plate of food and the player who built his career as a work of art, this should not lead us to ignore the existence of a wide range of possible combinations that disarticulated the elements commonly used to categorize the two sociological types identified by the analysis. They often got mixed, cohabiting the same team, or even merged into a single character capable of bringing together *raça* and art in the same play style, or sometimes in a particular match. Thus, for example, Paulo César Lima, labeled by the São Paulo press as "pipoqueiro," was evaluated by the newspaper *Jornal do Brasil* as the "main figure" in Flamengo's victory over Náutico, in Recife, in the scope of Brazilian Championship. As reported: "This time he was not only an elegant and skillful player," but he also acted with "fighting spirit," "winning almost all battles" (Atuações, 1972, November 30, our translation).

But in physical disputes fought in the militarization field, the opponents of *futebol-arte* often got the better of the opposition. They did not wear masks but wore boots and the *raça* they exhibited on the pitch was manufactured in the clubs' production facilities. Little by little, they began to occupy spaces and reduce the scope for action of those who did not correspond to the code prescribed by the militarized matrix. Carlos Froner, Grêmio's coach and an Army captain, described, in concise and didactic terms, the vision of the game he implied: football was defined as a "battle," the team was organized as a "troop" and the athletes became "soldiers" (O retorno ao passado, 1973, September 21). We do not need to turn to the rebellion exponents to register the desertions of the military model. Gérson, three-time champion in Mexico, warned of the mistakes caused by the warlike vision of the game, evoking, at the same time, the notion that served him as a critical reference (Gérson: o futebol e todos os seus segredos, 1972, February 2, our translation): "Nowadays, we feel, especially after they invented that so-called football-strength, that the weak player is losing his place. They are giving more importance to the tank, to the sprawler. But there is still a place for the *futebol-arte*."

Conclusion

Futebol-arte, as we have tried to expose throughout the text, seemed to be a much more unstable and fruitful notion than we are usually willing to acknowledge. Pierced by conflicts and antagonisms in the field of sport, appropriated and reframed by the rebellious generation, this notion would end up being used as a combat weapon in the fight against the militarized matrix. The repressive practices, however, would prove to be unproductive for the power relations, reason why they were relegated to the condition of last option in the strategy of athletes' subjection. The "hostel-prison" of Portuguesa de Desportos Club, set up in the *Canindé* facilities for the recovery of "injured players," illustrates the failed exercise of power (Os 7 assuntos da grande crise da Portuguesa", 1976, October 8).

The militarized matrix, indeed, constituted a peculiar configuration of football-strength in Brazil, compatible with the authoritarian environment prevailing in the 1960s. However, while repressive excess was gradually abandoned, athletic excess, on the other hand, remained more than ever an imperative in the clubs' production apparatuses. Football conceived as art represented the questioning of both the militarized matrix and the historical device within which it had been implanted. In this sense, we can affirm that it exhibited in the field a complex and heterogeneous network of ideas. Some, in fact, loaded with lyrical notes, often led to incongruities, while others, however, provided alternative ways of organizing the team, such as, for example, the "group of hippies" at Botafogo (where Paulo César was playing at that time), at Corinthians Democracy (where Sócrates was playing at that time) or even the "Trem da Alegria" (where Afonsinho, the "prophet of a new order," was playing at that time) (Florenzano, 1998, 2009).

Certainly, these "ludic utopias" (Wisnik, 2008) did not dispense with either physical preparation or sports medicine, but they subjected them to a different evaluative sieve, placing at the center of the football scenario, instead of the hypertrophy of the body, the undefined exercise of autonomy. In this sense, *futebol-arte* is extremely far from being an outdated, exhausted theme, a mere memory of a romantic past buried by the triumphal advance of sports science. It still echoes the tackling fought by the rebellious movement.

References

A lenta morte dos anti-heróis. (1973, February 9). *Placar,* (152).
Admirável Cruzeiro novo. (1972, October 27). *Placar,* (137).
Aprendi com papai. (1973, September 21). *Placar,* (184).
Aragão, L. (1972, October 23). No pé da conversa. *Diário de Pernambuco.*
As Feras amansam o Leão da Rainha. (1970, June 12). *Placar,* (13).
As máximas do Serginho (1973, September 28). *Placar,* (185).
Até a morte. (1972, May 26). *Placar,* (115).
Atuações. (1972, November 11). *Jornal do Brasil.*
Avelino calls the whole CEUB to the lines. (1973, October 5). *Placar,* (186).
Chega de classe. (1973, August 31). *Placar,* (181).
Clastres, P. (2003). *A sociedade contra o Estado: pesquisas de Antropologia Política.* Cosac & Naify.
Damo, A. S. (2007). *Do dom à profissão: a formação de futebolistas no Brasil e na França.* São Paulo: Hucitec.
Dario está à venda. (1973, January 19). *Placar,* (149).
Dario falou e fez. (1973, August 31). *Placar,* (181).
De graça, sim senhor. (1973, August 24). *Placar,* (180).
Dicionário de futebol. (1972, January 14). *Placar,* (96).
É Corinthians sim! Time bom e de raça. (1970, November 20). *Placar,* (36).
Evaristo quer amistoso na próxima semana. (1972, January 13). *Diário de Pernambuco.*
Fanon, F. (2005). *Os condenados da terra.* Editora da Universidade Federal de Juiz de Fora.
Fase 3: Tapar os vazamentos. (1974, April 26). *Placar,* (184).
Florenzano, J. P. (1998). *Afonsinho e Edmundo: a rebeldia no futebol brasileiro.* Musa Editora.
Florenzano, J. P. (2009). *A Democracia Corinthiana: práticas de liberdade no futebol brasileiro.* Educ/Fapesp.
Florenzano, J. P. (2014). Dictatorship, re-democratisation, and Brazilian football in the 1970s and 1980s. In P. Fontes, & B. B. Hollanda, *The country of football: Politics, popular culture, and the beautiful game in Brazil.* Hurst & Company.
Florenzano, J. P. (2020). A dimensão política do futebol-arte. In S. S. Giglio, & M. W. Proni (Orgs.), *O futebol nas ciências humanas no Brasil* (pp. 80–96). Editora da Unicamp.
Fonseca, M. A. (2012). *Michel Foucault e o direito* (2nd ed.). Editora Saraiva.
Forlan, the Kung Fu. (1974, January 25). *Placar,* (201).
Foucault, M. (1987). *Vigiar e punir: Nascimento da prisão* (10th ed.). Vozes.
Foucault, M. (1998). *História da sexualidade 2: O uso dos prazeres* (8th ed.). Graal.
Foucault, M. (1999). *Em defesa da sociedade. Curso no Collège de France (1975–1976).* Martins Fontes.

Foucault, M. (2014). *Do governo dos vivos. Curso no Collège de France (1979–1980)*. Martins Fontes.

Futebol é para quem sabe (1973, August 10). *Placar*, (178).

Gérson: o futebol e todos os seus segredos. (1972, February 20). *Jornal dos Sports*.

Gilson, G. (1994). O drama do "futebol-arte": o debate sobre a Seleção nos anos 70. *Revista Brasileira de Ciências Sociais*, (25), 100–109. http://www.anpocs.com/images/stories/RBCS/25/rbcs25_10.pdf

Guedes, S. L. (2014). A produção das diferenças na produção dos "estilos de jogo" no futebol: a propósito de um texto fundador. In B. B. Hollanda, & L. G. Burlamaqui (Eds.), *Desvendando o jogo: nova luz sobre o futebol*. Editora da Universidade Federal Fluminense.

Hemingway, E. (2003). *O velho e o mar*. O Globo; Folha de S. Paulo.

Homenagem do Dadá a Gradim. (1972, November 10). *Placar*, (139).

Linha dura começa hoje a vigorar no Leão da Ilha. (1972, May 10). *Diário de Pernambuco*.

Linha dura no Náutico. (1973, November 9). *Placar*, (191).

Luís Ignácio Ubiña. (1972, July 7). *Placar*, (121).

Meu sonho é o Flamengo. (1972, August 25). *Placar*, (128).

Náutico contrata preparador por recomendação de Lucena. (1972, February 12). *Diário de Pernambuco*.

Obdulio Jacinto Varela, o caudillo. (1972, May 19). *Placar*, (114).

O garoto Enéas. (1973, August 3). *Placar*, (177).

O retorno ao passado. (1973, September 21). *Placar*, (184).

O voo do Falcão. (1973, September 28). *Placar*, (185).

Os 7 assuntos da grande crise da Portuguesa. (1976, October 8). *Estado de S. Paulo*.

Pelé: "eu tricampeão". (1971, August 20). *Placar*, (75).

Pobre Celeste. (1972, July 14). *Placar*, (122).

Sahlins, M. (2004). *Cultura na prática*. Editora UFRJ.

Salvador, M. A. S., & Soares, A. J. G. (2009). *A memória da Copa de 70: esquecimentos e lembranças do futebol na construção da identidade nacional*. Autores Associados.

Seja um craque sem gastar muito. (1971, February 26). *Placar*, (50).

Souza, M. A. (1996). *A "nação em chuteiras": raça e masculinidade no futebol brasileiro*. (Master's Dissertation in Social Anthropology), Universidade de Brasília. http://dan.unb.br/images/doc/Serie207empdf.pdf

Toledo, L. (2004). Pelé: os mil corpos de um rei. In J. Garganta, J. Oliveira, & M. Murad (Eds.), *Futebol de muitas cores e sabores. Reflexões em torno do desporto mais popular do mundo*. Porto: Universidade do Porto, Campo das Letras.

Toledo, L. H. (2002). *Lógicas no futebol*. Hucitec, Fapesp, São Paulo.

Trajano, J. (1978, May). Ordinário, chute! *Revista Repórter*.

Um segundo para o gol. (1973, October 5). *Placar*, (186).

Wilson e Osmar podem ter vez contra Corais. (1972, February 27). *Diário de Pernambuco*.

Wisnik, J. M. (2008). *Veneno remédio: o futebol e o Brasil*. Companhia das Letras, São Paulo.

Chapter 5
1982 World Cup: Democratic Winds in Spain and Brazil

Alvaro Vicente do Cabo

Introduction

In 1978, when Argentina held the World Cup, that country was ruled by an extremely authoritarian military junta, which imposed a dictatorship under the name of Process of National Reorganization, while Spain, one of the countries participating in the tournament and which would host the following World Cup, was going through a period of democratic transition.

The Spanish dictatorship had ended with the death of General Francisco Franco in 1975, and King Juan Carlos I took power as head of state. This emergency situation was legally sanctioned with the promulgation of a constitution drafted by democratically elected representatives in December of that year, as highlighted by the historian Juan Simón (2012a, 2012b) in two analyses regarding the tournament. In his words (Simón, 2012b, p. 4):

> The Spain 82 project will be developed in one of the periods of greatest political and social transformations that the country will experience. The country's political transition process will supposedly move toward a new phase of political transition of recovery of the democratic political system together with the different institutions that represent it, while also bringing about the need to incorporate Spain into the European integration process, which will have as a reference what will be known as European Union. (our translation)

The fact that the 1982 World Cup was held in a European country that was consolidating itself as a democratic nation after decades of authoritarian regime, whose legislative elections held that year would be won by the socialists,[1] also contributes to reflect on the Brazilian political situation; the country was still ruled by the military but was undergoing a complex historical conjuncture of re-democratization.

---

[1] During the tournament, the Spanish Prime Minister was still Leopoldo Calvo Sotelo, but the Spanish Socialist Obrero Party (PSOE) was gaining momentum in the streets to a landslide victory in the October legislative elections that brought Prime Minister Felipe Gonzalez to power.

A. V. do Cabo (✉)
Candido Mendes University, Rio de Janeiro, Brazil

© The Author(s), under exclusive license to Springer Nature Switzerland AG 2021
S. S. Giglio and M. W. Proni (eds.), *Football and Social Sciences in Brazil*,
https://doi.org/10.1007/978-3-030-84686-2_5

In Brazil, the dictatorial regime was moving toward a gradual political opening under the government of General João Baptista Figueiredo, who paradoxically went so far as to state: "It's to open it up. Whoever doesn't want it to open, I'll arrest and break them".[2]

The nationalism mood surrounding the "little canary" national team,[3] which presented a showy football according to the specialized media, seemed to mirror a generalized optimism concerning the political and social transformations experienced in that period of democratic transition.

The campaign for the legislative elections and the choice of the state governors, a milder censorship, the logic of consumption around the event, the marketing on the character "Pachecão", which appeared in the magazine *Pasquim,* were elements of social mobilization connected with the new political reality that was coming.

Regarding the association of the event with consumption, one may observe that this is part of the very international process of spectacularism and commodification of the "World Cup" sporting tournament, a fact that intensified as of 1974, the beginning of João Havelange's management as FIFA president.

It is emblematic that, in 1982, the number of teams in the final phase increased from 16 to 24 and that, in eight years in power, the Brazilian president established several economic partnerships with multinational companies such as Adidas, Coca-Cola and Kodak, as highlighted by Simón (2012a).

This chapter aims first to describe the political and economic context of the organization of the World Cup held in Spain and then analyze, based on two Brazilian media vehicles (*Jornal do Brasil* and *Placar*), the relationship between the expectations around the Brazilian national football team and the political conjuncture of re-democratization in the country.

The Spanish Cup: In Search of a National and Democratic Image

In 1966, when Spain was ratified to host the then distant 1982 World Cup, Francoism was entering its last decade and the country was experiencing a period of economic development, political openness, and modernization of society, according to Tussel (2010).

This indication, which had previously been raised at the congress held by FIFA on the occasion of the 1964 Olympic Games in Tokyo, was part of a project of General Francisco Franco regime:

---

[2] This was said on October 15, 1978, according to information obtained from the site of the O Globo collection. Available at: <acervo.oglobo.globo.com/frases/e-para-abrir-mesmo-quem-quiser-que-na-na-abra-eu-prendo-arrebento-noo-tenha-duvidas-9047371>. Accessed Sept. 20, 2018.

[3] The term "canarinho" [little canary] refers to the colors of the uniform of the national team, having as reference the typical bird of the Brazilian fauna and the traditional yellow shirt of the team.

The marathon to have our country hosting the major international football competition and one of the main sporting events, along with the Olympic Games, is irremediably inserted in a long-lasting political process that had occurred in sports, and especially football as one of its major propaganda tools. Politics and sports were hand in hand in the Franco period, even if not always with the success expected from the government. The regime will manage to convert sports into a state issue, mainly through the Traditionalist Spanish Falange Party (FET), turning it at the same time into an essential element for ideological propaganda and the framing of youth in the values that Franco's dictatorship imposed. (Simón, 2012a, pp. 19–20 our translation)

Football was already an extremely popular sport, being one of the main leisure options for Spaniards since the 1950s. In the 1960s, despite the state interventionist nature of the Franco dictatorship in sports, according to Tussel, the body in charge, which became the National Sports Delegation, acquired a certain autonomy in relation to the dictatorial regime:

In the 1950s, sports, and especially football, became one of the Spanish people's great entertainments. Physical education has been introduced in the Spanish educational system in the 1940s. Regarding the popularity of football, it is worth noting that the newspaper *Marca*, focused predominantly, but not exclusively on it, had a circulation of 350,000 copies, becoming since then the best-selling newspaper. The organization of sports after the civil war depended on the General Secretariat of the Movement and only from the 1960s the National Sports Delegation acted with a certain autonomy in relation to the political power. (Tussel, 2010, p. 186) (our translation)

Spain hosted the final round of the Euro Cup in 1964, becoming champion after beating the Soviet Union 2-1 at the Estadio Santiago Bernabéu, four years after being disqualified from the European tournament for having refused to face the Soviets. According to Tussel (2010, p. 186), in the face of dictator Franco, who celebrated Spain's success as if it were a military triumph, the country would win its first title of international expression, which remained the only one until the victorious generation of the twenty-first century,[4] and accredited itself to postulate the organization of a world championship two years later.

The victory and the political situation can be described as follows (Cabo, 2020). Spain had just shone in the quarterfinals after beating the Republic of Ireland by a crushing 7-1 and was chosen to host the final round. This was conditional on accepting the participation of the Soviet team. In 1960, Spain had been disqualified after General Franco denied them permission to play against the USSR. Four years of political disagreements fell by the wayside when football was put in the spotlight. The USSR earned their way into the final after defeating Denmark 3-0 in Barcelona with goals from Valentin Ivanov and Viktor Ponedelnik, who had been champions in 1960. In the other semi-final, an extra-time goal by F. C. Real Madrid, Amancio gave Spain a 2-1 victory over Hungary. The Spanish team included midfielder Luis Suárez, who by then had already won the European Club Championship with F. C. Internazionale Milano, and who brought his veteran experience to a young Spain. In

---

[4] Spain's most successful generation in football were two-time European champion in 2008 and 2012 and world champion at the 2010 World Cup in South Africa. Previously, only the 1964 European championship had been a significant achievement.

the final match at Santiago Bernabéu, it took just six minutes for Suárez to send a pinpoint cross into the net, which Jesús Pereda headed home. Galimzian Khusainov soon equalized for the Soviets, but a memorable header six minutes from time gave Spain the win and the title.

If the Spanish national team did not achieve great international prestige in the second half of the twentieth century, the country's top teams, by contrast, had become major icons of world football since the 1940s. Real Madrid, for example, constantly associated with the Franco regime due to the leadership of president Santiago Bernabéu[5] and the association of various government ministers, had legendary players such as the Hungarian Puskas and the Argentinian Di Stéfano.[6] Barcelona had great economic power due to the large number of members and had symbolically become the great Catalan rival of Real Madrid; Atlético Bilbao represented the Basque minority, and Atlético de Madrid, which had merged with Atlético de Aviación de la Aeronáutica, incorporated many military personnel into the team and had its image associated with the barracks.

Despite the specificities of each one, the fact is that all Spanish teams suffered, until 1967, state intervention and the influence of the nationalist discourse of the regime in the period called by Tussel the apogee, that is, from 1951 to 1965:

> State political intervention reached even in the football clubs themselves: every team had to have at least two Falangists, a norm that did not disappear until 1967. Nationalism not only affected the need to suppress the English names of the clubs' teams, but also the absence of foreigners during the 1960s. Due to censorship, the language of the sports press became Castilian-like and, at times acquired an epic tone. Club presidents were originally appointed by national delegates. (Tussel, 2010, p. 187) (our translation)

Following the advent of television in the country in 1956, there was a strengthening of the popularity of sports and the massification of sports shows in the 1960s and 1970s. According to Carr and Fusi (p. 168), in a few years the social and regional diffusion of television grew a lot, being the only cultural medium not affected by the different cultural openings of the regime, thanks mainly to the monopoly of the state-owned TVE and to the large amount of money in advertising. While in 1960 only 1% of the Spanish homes had TV sets, in 1977, 90% of households had them.

> Live broadcasts reinforced the popularity of sports spectacles: those and the successes of a talented sportsman, Manuel Santana, produced the spectacular spread of tennis from 1964-1965. However, the basic structures of sports and its social role remained the same: a system based on attracting a few professional superstars, scarce state support and abusive nationalist exploitation of the successes of Spanish sportsmen and women. Television – and tourism

---

[5] Santiago Bernabéu Yeste (1895–1978) was a striker for Real Madrid in the early decades of the twentieth century, fought during the Spanish Civil War in the Franco troops and then became president of the club from 1943 to 1978. He was a businessman and a treasury official and was one of the main people responsible for the club's rise from the late 1940s and the team's association with the *Falangistas*. Information taken from Tussel, 2010, and available at: <en.wikipedia.org/wiki/santiago_bernab%c3%a9u> and <inbedwithmaradona.com/journal/2012/9/5/the-inviolable-santiago-bernabeu.html>.

[6] Alfredo Di Stéfano is considered one of the greatest Argentine players of all time, being one of the greatest idols and top scorers of Real Madrid, where he played from 1953 until 1964.

– also maintained interest in bullfighting, an industry in decline and corrupted in the 1960s and 1970s. (Carr & Fusi, 1979, p. 169) (our translation)

The death of General Franco in November 1975, after 39 years in power, completely changed the political conjuncture in which the country was inserted when it was chosen to host the 1982 World Cup. Francoism had already been in decadence since 1966, but the death of the "Leader of Spain" represented the last straw in the process of transformations that had begun in the period known as Late Francoism.

The organization of the event, which had been postulated at the height of Franco's authoritarian nationalism, took place in the period of democratic transition, in which diverse political disputes, new liberal interests, and the peculiar monarchical presence embodied in the important figure of Juan Carlos I were flourishing.

Curiously, Juan Carlos I had been chosen and appointed in 1969 by the dictator Franco himself as his successor, to the detriment of his father, Juan. In 1974, during Franco's illness, Juan Carlos took over as interim president, but Franco returned to office and died in power, a fact that is metaphorically compared by Carr and Fusi (1979, p. 260) to Gabriel García Márquez's classic book *The Autumn of the Patriarch*.

According to Tussel, the king played a decisive role in the period following Franco's death, mediating distinct interests and harmonizing conflicts, as well as making considered and important decisions for the democratic transformation of the country. About Juan Carlos I, the author states:

> King's protagonism was clear from the beginning. He was asked to make the rupture as absolute monarch to lead in a democracy; however, more than govern, what he did was indicate. He was described as the engine of change, and another historical work focused on his figure was entitled "The Change Pilot". Indeed, it was up to him to cut the Gordian knot of the political situation at the end of 1975, through two decisive appointments – that of Fernández Miranda as president of the *Cortes* and that of Suarez as president of the government – and, in addition, he served as a protective shield against military meddling. He did not intervene further, so that he could be described as a constitutional monarch before there was a constitution. He did not even want to play a leading role in drafting it, and on the day the text was approved, he made sure that it had been legalized. To the extent that one can simplify by establishing a kind of priority among the individual protagonists of the transition, one could well say that Don Juan Carlos was the first, although it cannot even remotely be claimed that he was the one who carried it out. (Tussel, 2010, p. 281) (our translation)

Moreover, during the transition period, Spain was in a context of electoral restructuring that culminated with the approval of a new constitution in October 1978. For Tussel (2010, pp. 302–303), the drafting of the Spanish Magna Carta was the result of an immense legislative effort that, for the first time in the country's history, represented a broad political consensus, with rare exceptions—which did not resonate with the broader sectors of the population—between extreme right-wing and extreme left-wing parties.

However, according to Simón (2012a), despite the intense political and social transformations that Spain was going through, this was not the most appropriate time to hold a spectacularized international event such as the football World Cups. The country was undergoing economic difficulties, needed major modernization and infrastructure works and was in a situation of political instability. The very image of a young democratic nation could be damaged if the tournament were a failure.

Undoubtedly, it was not the ideal context to carry out an event with the international repercussion of a World Cup; an event that transcended the merely sporting and required a global
project that would have to incorporate, to be successful, the remodeling of communications, infrastructure, the hotel network, etc. To show to the outside world the new image of
a country that was trying to make up for lost time in a hurry, amid a process of political
normalization that would have to overcome great difficulties. The process of elaboration
and planning of the World Cup was inserted in the historical period known as democratic
transition, or post-Franco transition, which comprised 1975-1982. Just over three months
after the forty-year-old Dino Zoff lifted the World Cup at the Santiago Bernabéu stadium, the
Spanish Socialist Workers Party, led by Felipe González, would impose an overwhelming
majority of votes in the October elections, opening a new historical moment in Spanish life
that would not end until the victory of the Popular Party in 1996. (Simón, 2012a, p. 22) (our
translation)

However, the tournament became a milestone in the social mobilizations of the
transition period. Regardless of whether it was a previous project, whose origin could
be associated with the attempt to use sports as a propaganda tool for Francoism,
the new political context ended up influencing a re-signification of that historical
possibility, according to Simón himself.

According to Palácio and Cascajosa (2013), football is an important tool for
mobilizing public space and political participation, and the democratic transition
period was intensely marked by the return of popular demonstrations, especially
protests and strikes:

As a starting point of our analysis, we must note that public space is a central element for
Spanish sociability, which tends to favor, due to the climate, its frequent use in multiple
activities that, instead of being forms of leisure, are examples of collective rituals: football
as the most popular sport, *verbenas* [traditional popular festivals], pilgrimages and religious
processions... despite its limited democratic experience, these factors have favored for public
space to also be a tool for political participation. (Palácio & Cascajosa, 2013 apud Mestman
& Varela, 2013, p. 241) (our translation)

The organization of the 1982 World Cup turned out to be an opportunity for the
Spanish nation to show the world that it was moving away from its authoritarian past
and modernizing itself. Liberal economic interests also contributed to the project
being incorporated into the collective imagination. The holding of the event came to
occupy a symbolic space in the current discourse of renewal.

Football once again functioned as "operator of nationality",[7] but in Spain, unlike
in the tournament held in Argentina (Cabo, 2018) four years earlier, it was the democratic and liberal voices that took advantage of the social mobilization existing around
the sport's popularity to try to coin the idea of integration.

As Bobbio (2013, p. 45) points out, the "reciprocal nexus between liberalism and
democracy is possible because both have a common starting point: the individual.
Both rest on an individualistic conception of society". In this sense, the proposed
idea of national integration is also linked to political and economic interests that
benefit specific groups within an individualistic logic.

---

[7] *Operator of nationality* is a concept developed by the Argentine sociologist Alabarces (2002) to
explain that football acts as a vector that strengthens the narrative of national identity.

However, according to Simón, this social expectation would turn to disenchantment as a result of the tournament's economic failure and the sporting underachievement of the local team known as the "Fury" in 1982:

> The level of politicization of public life and of cultural manifestations, among which, due to its condition of mass spectacle, football will play a leading role, will significantly increase, which will be reflected in factors such as the increase in the reading rate of citizens, the appearance of new magazines and newspapers, along with a wide identification and interest of young people in the political process. Social mobilization that will also have its subsequent phase of disenchantment, and that can be found in the very process of promotion, organization and development of Spain-82, in the initial identification of the World Cup as a unique opportunity to be able to show the world a new Spain, closer to Europe and away from the Franco past, and the subsequent disappointment when proving that the overflowing hopes deposited in this event, especially at the sporting and economic level, had not been achieved to the extent claimed by the Spanish society. (Simón, 2012a, pp. 24–25) (our translation)

Despite the disappointment with the "legacy" of the tournament, according to Simón, in the period of democratic transition the Spanish sporting culture itself was undergoing transformation. Claims for a greater appreciation of sports were coming from diverse social sectors. And even before the Cup, especially after the 1979 municipal elections, sports had already become an important issue on the political agenda, and the very staging of the tournament had become a matter of public debate.

The Higher Sports Council (CSD), created in 1977 as an autonomous body of the Ministry of Culture and Education, had the function of decentralizing the control of practices and investments in sports, promoting sports activities throughout the country, and tackling the archaic structure arising from the state interventionism of the Franco period.

Moreover, in 1980, the General Law of Physical Culture and Sports was sanctioned, with the purpose of providing more resources for investments in sports, in addition to enabling greater supervision and transparency in the management of public resources for sports, including in the CSD itself.

> The intense transformation of the country's sporting culture allowed the CSD to declare to the media, a month before the start of the World Cup, that more than seven thousand sports facilities had been built between 1980 and May 1982. The left-wing and nationalist parties defended the idea that the money should be given directly to the municipalities and autonomous communities, while the CSD was in favor of allocating a large part of the budget to the different federations. The CSD's lack of transparency had led the socialists to criticize the alleged waste of public funds, marginalizing the municipalities to the detriment of the provisions that emanated from the General Law 3/1980 on Physical Culture and Sports. (Simón, 2012a, p. 36) (our translation)

Regardless of the constitutional reorganization and the supposed modifications in the "sports culture", the country was going through a period of serious economic crisis with high inflation and unemployment rates and a sharp decline in industrial and agricultural activities.

The accomplishing of the tournament was thus seen as a possibility of generating employment opportunities and stimulating tourist activity, as well as attracting foreign exchange earnings for the country.

The clubs that would host the tournament were encouraged to remodel their stadiums and meet the requirements of FIFA and the Royal Organizing Committee of the World Cup (RCOM), which had been presided over since October 9, 1978, by Raimundo Saporta, a former Real Madrid manager and loyal squire of Santiago Bernabéu; despite receiving public loans, these clubs ended up spending a lot of money and increasing their debts.

In the historical context of the democratic transition period—political instability, economic crisis, and challenging to the prevailing conservative sports structure itself—it is worth asking how the RCOM managed to finance the event.

Following the logic of organizing world football tournaments, developed during the management of the Brazilian João Havelange, the holding of the World Cup in Spain was inserted in the intrinsic process of spectacularism and commodification of modern sports.

According to Melo Filho, a lawyer specialized in sports law:

> It is notorious the progressive commodification of sports that went from leisure to business (sports business), causing the replacement of the Olympic philosophy that the important is to compete for the maxim that the important is to profit. We all know the industry of sports show which gathers static advertising, sponsorship in the competition uniforms, licensing of the clubs' products, marketing of sports brands, investments of companies in clubs and sports facilities, partnerships of clubs with companies, etc. These are the ingredients which evidence the degree of commodification reached by sports, and it is undeniable that the commercial interests play nowadays a predominant role in the sports sphere, resulting in a complex network of business and even deals around the sports. (Melo Filho, 2002, p. 41) (our translation)

In this sense, according to Simón (2012a), there were three basic pillars for financing the 1982 World Cup: ticket sales, television rights, marketing, and advertising.

Regarding tickets and travel packages for the tournament, there was a monopoly by a consortium of companies called Mundiespaña, consisting of four large travel agencies (WagonLits Viagens, Viajes Ecuador, Viajes Meliá and Viajes Marsans).

Concerning television rights, an agreement was reached in March 1979 between a Spanish delegation of RCOM and the Royal Spanish Football Federation (RFEF) members and the then chairman of FIFA's organizing committee, Hermann Neurberger, which provided some 39 million Swiss francs, far exceeding the 24 million paid to the Argentinians in the previous tournament.

The issue of broadcasting the matches was extremely important both for FIFA and the country's image on the international scene. A major overhaul was required in the infrastructure of the Spanish Radio and Television (RTVE), which ended up receiving most of the investments and being one of the only positive aspects that remained for the Spanish society, according to Simón:

> At the same time, the World Cup in Spain will also force our country to promote basic infrastructure reforms in order to reduce distances with nearby European countries. The deep transformation of RTVE will allow changing the structures of the public channel, managing to give the largest television coverage of a World Cup in its entire history. The World Cup will be a success in relation to television broadcasting, marking a clear turning point in the future of sports presence on the small screen. (Simón, 2012b, p. 15) (our translation)

The marketing of products associated with the World Cup, like the charismatic mascot "Naranjito", through t-shirts, key rings, caps, etc., and the raising of high advertising resources with various multinational companies, contributed greatly to the raising of capital for the tournament.

While externally the company West Nally, accredited by FIFA, was in charge of marketing the World Cup merchandise, internally a company was created exclusively to market such merchandise. Ibermundial 82 had exclusivity to grant licenses or any other type of rights, and according to Simón (2012a, p. 15) in September 1981 it had already managed to market its products with more than 80 large companies, among them multinationals such as Coca-Cola, Canon, Gillete and Fuji.

In this context of articulating liberal investments, the Spanish government managed to enable the basic resources required to hold the event, despite several suspicions of misappropriation of funds and the referred indebtedness of major Spanish clubs such as Real Madrid, for instance, which was the association that spent most on the remodeling of the Santiago Bernabéu stadium.

Once the economic question was solved, the great fear of the organizers was the possibility of terrorist attacks by separatist groups that had become more frequent during the period of democratic transition, despite the policy of "autonomies" (Simón, 2012a, p. 29) consecrated in 1979 for the Basques, Catalans and, later, inhabitants of Galicia.

The biggest threat came from the Basque group Euskadi ta Azkatasuna (ETA), which in English means "Basque Homeland and Freedom". It was created in 1959 in the context of the national liberation struggles in Cuba, Algeria, and Vietnam. In the 1970s, when it defined itself as a Basque socialist national liberation movement, it regularly carried out clandestine attacks, according to Carr and Fusi (1979, p. 211).

According to Simón, the concern for security during the tournament was quite high, and a strict military security scheme was drawn up for the teams, fans and tourists, known as "Plan Naranja 82" [82 Orange Plan].

> At the same time, from the last stage of Francoism until the beginning of the 1980s, Spain lived through the harshest period of ETA's terrorism; the bloody years of lead caused the death of 337 people during the time of the government of the *Unión Centro Democrática* (UCD). The great fear of all the members of RCOM was that ETA would decide to take advantage of the World Cup to carry out some of the attacks to which, unfortunately, the Spanish society had become accustomed. A plan against possible terrorist attacks was put into action, the "Plan Naranja 82", with which the Ministry of the Interior tried to guarantee security thanks to the 35 thousand members of the state security forces in charge of protecting the players, delegations, and fans. The surveillance of the hotels, the teams, the control of their movements, the stadiums, and their accesses, as well as the entertainment venues and the protection of the citizens themselves were fundamentally affected, in order to try to prevent any eventuality that could occur during those days. (Simón, 2012b, p. 5) (our translation)

Despite the widespread apprehension, the extreme security surrounding the teams—especially the Spanish team, which had six Basque players who were league champions for Real Sociedad—[8] and the constant polemics on the subject in the

---

[8] Real Sociedad is a team from the city of San Sebastian; for many years, most of the team's players should be Basque.

media in the years leading up to the Cup, the tournament ended up being played under normal security conditions. It is not possible to say whether it was the "Plan Naranja 82" that worked or whether the members of ETA decided to establish a truce for the duration of the championship, but the fact is that no serious attacks were recorded during the event. Thus, the holding of the 1982 World Cup was already inserted in the new liberal spectacularism logic, accompanying the initial transformations around mega sporting events, which occurred mainly as of the end of the 1970s, with the advent of television broadcasting and the participation of many multinational companies and generating many profits for the "modern" FIFA management presided by João Havelange.

According to the geographer Gilmar Mascarenhas, taking into consideration the society of the spectacle, of the simulacrum, of the representations,

> Football is inserted in this movement as a spectacle promoted and fed in line with large capitalist interests.
>
> Being the World Cup the apex moment of football-spectacle, it could not be exempt from the mechanisms and interests that shape the spectacular production of football. In the last two decades, it is remarkable the process of transformation of this event in terms of spatiality. (Mascarenhas, 2014, p. 213) (our translation)

However, according to Simón (2012a), for the Spaniards the organization of the tournament would have represented a disappointment since, besides the national team's failure, the supposed economic and social return that would occur with the stimulation of tourism and job generation did not become a reality; the fact is that, after the World Cup, Spanish football went through a deep crisis, stemming from the large investments made by the main clubs that turned into high debts.

The victory of Felipe González of the Spanish Socialist Workers Party (PSOE) in October 1982 renewed the political hopes of the left in the country and mobilized a large part of society against the liberal transformations adopted. Spain was entering a new period in its history; the transition from the Franco dictatorship had been completed with the election of a socialist ruler. The hosting of the World Cup, however, does not seem to have contributed in any actual way to the construction of a new democratic national image.

The Euphoria with the "Re-democratization" National Team

The euphoria surrounding the Brazilian team coached by Telê Santana, who have come to be known as the "national team of the opening period"—a metaphor for the period of political transition from military dictatorship to re-democratization—heightens the climate of euphoria and excitement ahead of their tournament debut in Spain.

Paradoxically, the commander of this "democratic team" was a politically conservative and centralizing man. Despite Telê's great popularity, for some specialists, like the columnist Sandro Moreyra, from *Jornal do Brasil,* he was authoritarian and stubborn. In his column "Bola dividida", the journalist stated:

Telê always gave the impression of being a thoughtful and calm person. That's how we know him from the times he was a Fluminense player, a skinny but efficient false right winger. He was the "thread of hope", dear to the *tricolores* [Fluminense supporters], to whom he gave many joys. Later, as coach of Atlético Mineiro, Telê continued to be the same calm, quiet, intelligent, and accountable man. His work at Atlético was excellent, projecting, among others, stars such as Reinaldo and Toninho Cerezzo.

Called to the national team, Telê was surprising at first, showing dislike for press interviews. He even had friction with radio people. At the time, he seemed nervous, insecure, and introverted. Then he changed. The successes in the *Mundialito*, the European tour and the qualification of the national team for the Spanish Cup made Telê a different person. No longer insecure, but aware of what he had come to represent as the most important figure in Brazilian football. He often used this power lightly, without taking into account the consequences of his attitudes. His outdated political positions, the perhaps unconsciously reactionary statements he disseminated – after all, he comes from a traditional family from the state of Minas Gerais. But the public condemnation he made of Reinaldo, denouncing his lifestyle, his political admirations – Reinaldo is a fan of Lula – caused as much harm to the player as the lack of meniscus in his knees. It was unfair and even cruel. Nothing in keeping with the old Telê.

That's why it's feared that at this moment, when he needs to make a final decision about the national team – and the fate of our football in the World Cup will depend on it – Telê will reveal himself to be intransigent, insisting on sustaining points of view that everyone sees and feels are flawed and harmful to the team's performance. That would be disastrous. (Jornal do Brasil, 1982a, 1982b, 1982c, 1982d, 1982e, May 23, p. 9) (our translation)

In the same issue, João Saldanha, in his traditional column (Jornal do Brasil, 1982a, 1982b, 1982c, 1982d, 1982e, p. 9), also criticized Telê Santana, stating that it was essential that he defined the team soon. But, despite the isolated questionings found in some *JB* chronicles, especially after the draw with Switzerland in a friendly match, the expectation and euphoria in the country before the tournament predominated in both *Jornal do Brasil* and *Placar*.[9] One month before Brazil's first match in the Cup, which would be against the USSR, *Placar* published an emblematic article entitled "O dia em que o Brasil vai parar diante da tevê" [The day Brazil will stop in front of the TV]:

Billions of kilowatts of additional electricity will be spent over the 90 minutes that the match lasts, to power the millions of TVs and radios that at that moment will be synchronized on the game. In that hour and a half, countless extra hectolitres of alcoholic beverages will be consumed, as will countless tranquilizers. (Placar, 1982a, 1982b, 1982c, 1982d, p. 14) (our translation)

The spectacularism of the event, with the growth of advertisements, the intense consumption of shirts with the mascot "Naranjito", the board game "Escrete", created by Chico Buarque de Hollanda, Penalty football shoes, Kodak films, whose poster boy was Telê himself, and the huge sale of TV sets of different brands, symbolized a conjuncture of identification with the national team and excitement for the

---

[9] Articles from *Placar* magazine during the 1982 World Cup were also used as sources of analysis for the article "1978 and 1982 World Cups: Placar's national perspectives from the Brazilian team" (Cabo, 2014).

Brazilian participation in the event. A large part of the population, including political personalities, was anxious for the tournament to begin.

> Whether previously prepared or not, the truth is that almost no one will miss the World Cup. and that includes even the nation's highest ruler. President João Figueiredo has already warned his ministry and advisors that on the days of the national team's matches he will not dispatch or receive anyone. The new routine at the Planalto Palace will begin on the 14th, when the president will close his office at the end of the last morning dispatch, which normally takes place shortly after noon. After that, Figueiredo will leave the venue and go to Granja do Torto, his official residence, from where he will only leave the following morning…
>
> Other executive heads will follow the president's example and disconnect from state matters to tune in on the World Cup. In Bahia, governor Antônio Carlos Magalhães has already had a big screen installed at the Palácio de Ondina, and warned that he will not dispatch on afternoons when Telê's team is on the field…
>
> And you do not have to be a fanatical football fan for that. Even the austere Golbery do Couto e Silva, former head of the Executive Office and considered the architect of the political opening of Figueiredo's government, will set aside some time to watch Zico and his gang's moves against the USSR on the 14th. He will be at his farm, in the Goiás municipality of Luzitânia, next to his wife Esmeralda, a fanatical supporter of Fluminense and the Brazilian national team. But Golbery, with some coyness, claims that he will look at the "television" only in the most important moments. Most of the time, he says, he will spend trying to read a book. He will hardly succeed. (Placar, 1982a, 1982b, 1982c, 1982d, p. 12–14) (our translation)

General Figueiredo was present at the last friendly match of the Brazilian team before leaving for Europe, when they thrashed Eire 7-0. At the opening of another great stadium,[10] Parque do Sabiá, in Uberlândia, the nation's "commander" was received by governor Francelino Pereira and honored by CBF president Giulite Coutinho, receiving a commemorative plaque with the following words: "To his Excellency, Mr. President João Figueiredo, with the gratitude of Brazilian football".

Speaking to the audience that followed the farewell of the "canarinho" team, the president said, in a nationalistic tone, that he exalted the greatness of Brazilian football and the unity of the country (Jornal do Brasil, 1982a, 1982b, 1982c, 1982d, 1982e, May 28, p. 2, our translation):

> Mr. Governor,
>
> My dear Giulite Coutinho,
>
> Gentlemen in charge,
>
> Committee members,
>
> Dear players:
>
> Once again, Brazil is competing in a World Cup. Brazil has always been there and three times it has come as champion; if it did not come other times, it was not because our football was

---

[10] It is notorious that, during the period of military dictatorship, several grandiose stadiums were built as propaganda of the military regime itself and as an element of the National Integration Plan (PIN). Some examples are the "Vivaldão" in Manaus (1970), the "Arruda" in Pernambuco (1972), the "Castelão" in Fortaleza (1973), the "Serra Dourada" in Goiânia (1975) and the "Mangueirão" in Belém (1978). More information is available at <trivela.uol.com.br/da-criacao-brasileirao-a-os-ele fantes-brancos-como-o-futebol-entrou-plano-de-integracao-nacional/>. Accessed Dec. 10, /2014.

inferior or because we lacked preparation, but because of circumstances that only happen in sports or because God on that day was not as Brazilian as He always was. We were not happy, but we always left the mark of our football in foreign lands. We lost once on Brazilian soil in circumstances that we all know. We are not lacking in football, we've got the technical ability and we've got the grit, but we must not forget that the other teams will be preparing too. And they all want to beat Brazilian football. So, each and every one of us, the fans who stay here, following every move of our athletes, down to the last one of the players who will be on the bench, must be convinced that it is not possible for the spirit of the opposition to cancel out our skill, our technique and our physical preparation. And I am sure that you will make such a set that each dangerous opponent, each game should mean the last battle. We have to win them all. I trust you. Thank you very much.

Besides the optimistic expectations of the President of the Republic regarding the Brazilian team, the hopes of several other important personalities of that historical conjuncture were highlighted in *Placar* magazine (our translation): "The World Cup mobilizes all the stars of the Brazilian constellation. Besides the 22 who will fight directly for the title in the Spanish fields, countless others will remain in Brazil no less tense, waiting for victory. Cheering, superstition, and prayer are just some of the many ways of taking part in a World Cup". Among these "stars" listed by the magazine, I would like to highlight a few who made controversial or at least curious statements (Placar, 1982a, 1982b, 1982c, 1982d, May 14, p. 16–18, our translation):

- I intend to watch all the games and drink a lot of beer. PT [Workers Party] will have no programming on the days of the national team's games because we like football. Contrary to popular belief, football doesn't alienate. People already know that a world title does not fill bellies. (Lula – President of PT)

- In no way I will stop participating in this national plebiscite. This moment of union surpasses all forms of democratic evaluation of the popular desires. Victory in the World Cup will be the opportunity for the re-democratization of the country. (Alceu Amoroso Lima – writer and Catholic leader)

- If Indians participated in the World Cup, I would even watch. It would be very funny. Since they are not participating, I am worried about what might happen in the Malvinas. I'm for Brazil, but I won't go out of my routine. I won't watch television or listen to the radio. (Orlando Villas-Bôas – indigenist scholar)

- I know that football numbs people, but my male side loves football. I'm going to cheer a lot, despite the harm that winning the title might bring to the country. But, after all, it's with the national team that the country improves its image abroad. (Rogéria – transvestite)

- The World Cup is an instant of appeasement of spirits, a unique moment in the life of people. For us Brazilians, it is the ecumenical hour of national life, and the unification of all around the goal of victory. The Cup unifies, consolidates, and strengthens the spirit of national unity. Wherever I am, I will stop to watch the games and cheer on TV. (Tancredo Neves – politician)

- I think that this time, unlike the last two World Cups, the coach is respecting the creativity of the Brazilian player. Telê has restored the moves and improvisation to our football. (Jorge Amado, writer and novelist)

- Match days are days of celebration, of unity among Brazilians. The archbishop of São Paulo has the same history as the men on the streets, he has already participated in pick-up games. That is why I have already asked my Sister secretary to arrange the appointments so that I do not disturb anyone or be disturbed during the games. Brazil needs our support and prayers. (Dom Paulo Evaristo Arns – Cardinal of São Paulo)

- I won't watch the World Cup, I won't watch the national team, I won't watch football. Indians have more important things to deal with. The Indians are worried with the land, hunger, survival. The World Cup and football are ways for the government to distract the people. Juruna is going to campaign for Congressman. Juruna is not demagogic. He just doesn't like football. (Mário Juruna – Indian chief and federal representative candidate for PDT [Democratic Labor Party])

- I don't know if at game time it will be myself, *Pantaleão* or *Coalhada* in front of the TV, because my working rhythm is intense. (Chico Anísio – comedian)

Despite the caricatured nature of some statements, they mirror important debates on the relationship between football and the nation that were taking place at that historical moment. The very present discussion in the period about football as the opium of the people or an element of integration can be perceived among those who vehemently defend football, such as Lula, Tancredo Neves, Alceu Amoroso Lima, and Cardinal Dom Paulo Evaristo Arns, or in negative comments such as those of the Indian chief Juruna or the transvestite Rogéria. The issue of the playing style of Brazilian football is raised by Jorge Amado, and the presence of TV is perceived in the comments of Chico Anísio and Orlando Villas-Bôas.

The explicit optimism and the national commotion can also be observed in the editorial of *Placar* No. 623, signed by Juca Kfouri "Porque se pode confiar no nosso futebol" (Why we can trust our football), in which the Brazilian Football Confederation (CBF) is praised,[11] the national championship that had just ended and was called the Golden Cup is exalted and the Brazilian football that would hypothetically be on the way to the tetra is "venerated" (Placar, 1982a, 1982b, 1982c, 1982d, April 30, p. 3, our translation):

The truth is undeniable. Since the founding of CBF football has reached a new stage...

The Golden Cup, for example, came to an end surrounded by the greatest euphoria. First, because Flamengo and Grêmio deserved it. The world champion got it simply for having the best team in the world, pardon the redundancy...

That's why *Placar* invests, transforms, moves on.

Our confidence in the tetra is unshakeable, but, much more importantly, if by the natural contingencies of football, Telê and our national team do not get there, even then it wouldn't be a catastrophe.

Brazilian football is already mature and so are we. [our emphasis]

Furthermore, the claim of a supposed maturity by the committed journalist and editor of the magazine, in my opinion, has a symbolic perspective in which both football and the Brazilian people would be ready for conquests in the sports and political spheres.

There were very few dissenting voices in relation to the euphoric environment. One of the exceptions was the instigating chronicle of the section "opening the

---

[11] In my opinion, CBF, created in 1979 in a historical context of political opening and with a private nature, represented at that moment progress in the management model of Brazilian football in comparison with the previous organization politically centralized in CBD and that was highly criticized by *Placar* magazine itself during the 1978 World Cup, due to a possible authoritarian posture. The journalist Juca Kfouri, currently a vehement critic of CBF, probably also had this view at that historical conjuncture, which would explain the praise.

Game", by Roberto Drummond—which a posteriori seemed more a prediction of defeat in the Sarriá stadium,—entitled "nobody criticizes the selection. This is quite a bad sign". The text incisively questions the exacerbated optimism, also establishing reflections on the relationship of the event with the practices of capitalist consumption and evoking the humorous character "Zé da Galera", by Jô Soares, as the "voice of wisdom". The importance of the media in the propagation of euphoria is also signaled. The entire text is worth reproducing (Placar, 1982a, 1982b, 1982c, 1982d, April 23, p. 30–31, our translation):

> You arrive in any corner of Brazil and everyone is on a woohoo, celebrating right away.
>
> You walk into a bar, from the Amazon to Minas Gerais to Santa Catarina, and everyone is celebrating in anticipation.
>
> You turn on the radio and are bombarded not only by jingles and ads that sell tires, shampoos, banks, chewing gum, soft drinks, etc. You are also bombarded by super-patriotic announcers and commentators who invoke Our Lady of Aparecida, talk about the green seas of our homeland and swear that we are already the world champions in Spain.
>
> You turn on the television and it is the same bombardment.
>
> You open the newspapers and there is the same euphoria, the same party, the same optimistic bombardment, on the basis of we have already won, we have already won...
>
> Nobody criticizes the Brazilian team, among other reasons (including its undeniable qualities) because it is, today, the biggest advertising selling point in Brazil.
>
> Fine! I'm not against sales, after all we live in a consumer's society.
>
> From the point of view of Brazilian football, the woohoo is tremendously damaging, it creates illusions and victories before the hour, which makes the boat turn.
>
> In fact, every time we leave here singing victories, we come back defeated, or worse, we come back as moral champions, which is perhaps a greater sadness...
>
> But in all the hoopla, here comes a sensible one. This is Zé da Galera, a character played by Jô Soares. Every Monday night in the program "Viva o Gordo", Zé da Galera uses a phone booth to send messages to Telê criticizing him. The message, almost a slogan uttered by Zé da Galera, is the same as Pelé's:
>
> - Telê, the national team needs to play with *pontas* [right and left wings]...
>
> Dear reader, be aware: Zé da Galera is the voice of wisdom.

The famous slogan "Bota ponta, Telê!" would be the main popular criticism to the coach, but it was disseminated in a caricatured and relaxed way. In an article about a "press conference" with the coach in a bar in Copacabana, a reference to this expression is made in the title ("Use a left or right wing! It is the scream of the fans"), but what predominates is the party atmosphere (Jornal do Brasil, 1982a, 1982b, 1982c, 1982d, 1982e, May 29, p. 5, our translation):

> - This expression was heard more than once yesterday, at 11:30 a.m., on the Atlantic Avenue, in front of the Atlantic Tavern, during the interview of coach Telê Santana, who gave an unusual movement to the place.
>
> The movement was already greater than normal even before the interview, but at the tables on the sidewalk of the restaurant, only a group of German tourists were having fun drinking and chatting; when Telê came down from his apartment, the Germans applauded, in which they were accompanied by some Brazilians...

At the end of the interview, Telê was highly applauded by reporters when, still seated at the table, he asked the waiter for a draft beer.

- Cigarette is forbidden, but a beer is allowed occasionally.

A party that is also described in Zico's farewell, in an event with friends and family in Quintino, in the last day off before the departure to Europe. The article "O adeus da torcida a Zico com balão e tudo" (Zico's fans say farewell with balloons and everything else) (Jornal do Brasil, 1982a, 1982b, 1982c, 1982d, 1982e, May 30, p. 6) shows the atmosphere of euphoria and expectation with the success of the "canarinho" team, which, according to Sandro Moreyra, would be the great favorite in computer predictions and in the London betting parlors (Jornal do Brasil, 1982a, 1982b, 1982c, 1982d, 1982e, May 30, p. 9).

On the Flamengo idol and the new formation of the Brazilian midfield, with Falcão, tested during the friendly match against Eire, João Saldanha would claim, also triggering the victorious memory of 1970:

> One day I was asked if I would put Zico on the 1970 national team. I replied without blinking an eye. They insisted: where? In whose place? I replied, 'I don't know, but I'd find a place for him anyway. Just [like] Falcão is a player for any price and any place. He came to add to the Brazilian team, and in those final 20 minutes, when Cerezzo came on, I confess I thought Falcão would come off, but I was pleasantly impressed with the development and the series of moves made by the good ones. (Jornal do Brasil, 1982a, 1982b, 1982c, 1982d, 1982e, May 30, p. 9) (our translation)

According to most of the writers of the analyzed printed media, Brazil was favored also because the other teams were going through many internal and even external problems, as in the cases of Argentina and England. In his column "Bola dividida", from *Jornal do Brasil*, Sandro Moreyra reviewed our major opponents:

> Among the more accredited opponents, the situation is not much different. The Italians, for example, continue in their endless discussions, with more internal gaps than Vasco da Gama in an election year. The French have their biggest star Platini sold to Italian football and the other star, Six, playing in Germany, factors that weaken their team. The Germans, who should not scare us because we always beat them, have some important players injured, without knowing whether they will be able to play the World Cup, and we still have the English and Argentines involved in this stupid Falklands war, naturally much more concerned with the tragic consequences that increase every day than with their football. (Jornal do Brasil, May 28, 1982a, 1982b, 1982c, 1982d, 1982e, p. 5) (our translation)

It is important to highlight the mention of the Falklands War, a military conflict that eventually influenced the end of the Argentine dictatorship and that, according to the chronicler, could have negative repercussions on the behavior of Argentines and English.[12]

Paradoxically, the host team was not considered one of the favorites by the Brazilian press, although its irregular campaign has greatly frustrated the expectations of the Spaniards. It is possible, however, to identify a certain tacit complicity

---

[12] Argentina's surrender occurred one day after the national team (world champion in 1978) lost their opening match against Belgium in Barcelona. A few days later, on June 16, the General Leopoldo Galtieri resigned from the presidency.

with the political and social transformations that were taking place in the host country, as in the article "Espanha: Democracia em campo" [Spain: Democracy in the football field], signed by Alberto Dines, which reads:

> What happens to re-democratized Spain – has it lost interest in football or has it lost its passion? Spain has democratized, distributed its passions, spread its heat created options for devotion and enthusiasm. If before football, the Spanish people had put their fanaticism into the bullfights, disconcerting its power of vibration, now with a country that is absolutely open, clubism has been replaced by partisanship and other isms.
>
> In Spain, let us not forget, still under Franco's regime, neighbourhood communities (our neighbourhood associations) began where the willingness to "cheer" is directed to the primary issue – survival. with democratization, the problem of regional autonomies arose which, in the Basque Country or here in Catalonia, absorbs great charges of emotion and commitment.
>
> Football is important here, so important that the clubs play a social role (look at Barcelona with 120,000 members). But there are no public stadiums – in other words, there is no power or state interference, either to stimulate or to manage the sport.
>
> Curiously, by one of those paradoxes that political scientists could best explain, our national team has been giving lessons in democracy. The egregious football we present, the personal virtuosity harmonized by extremely simple and intelligent tactics is, indeed, a liberal and liberated school, a combination of individual and collective, physical and cerebral. Foot and heel. We are practicing a physiocratic football whose motto could well be *laisser-faire, laisser-jouer,* whose patriarchs are many and, among them, one cannot fail to mention João Saldanha. (Placar, 1982a, 1982b, 1982c, 1982d, June 9, p. 3.) (our translation)

In this text it is possible to identify the appreciation by the journalist of several supposed changes that would be happening in Spain from its democratization process: distribution of passions, development of party and community feelings, social function of clubs and absence of state interference are aspects presented as positive by the article, which also highlights the complex issue of regional autonomies in the country.

Moreover, in the same text, Dines inserts the Brazilian "joy-football" as a metaphor for democracy, freedom and liberalism, symbolically employing an adaptation of the expression coined by the French physiocratic economist François Quesnay *laissez-faire, laissez-passer* to exalt the supposed liberating character of football practiced by the national team.

In this sense, even with the defeat against Italy represented in several articles as a great tragedy,[13] the discourse around the 1982 team transcends the pitches and the supposed genuinely Brazilian style of play, reverberating the political sphere with the exaltation, by some journalists, of principles such as freedom, collective play with respect for individualities, joy, etc.

General João Figueiredo and other members of the government, right after Brazil's elimination against Italy, were featured both in the cover of *Jornal do Brasil* and in its

---

[13] The tragic character of the defeat in 1982 is analyzed from a heroic perspective, unlike other eliminations in Cups, in the interesting article by Leda Costa entitled "1982: Lágrimas de uma geração de ouro" [1982: Tears from a golden generation], one of the few academic texts on that World Cup (Costa, 2014).

sports supplement, all in solidarity with the team and without necessarily associating the team with the dictatorial regime:

> Strong spirits. Other Cups will come! With these words President João Figueiredo concluded the 48-word telegram sent yesterday to the president of CBF, Giulite Coutinho, after the defeat of the Brazilian team to Italy that eliminated it from the World Cup. The text was released by the spokesman of the Planalto Palace Carlos Attila at 6 pm.
>
> In another telegram addressed to coach Telê Santana, the Vice-President of the Republic, Aureliano Chaves, expressed his applause to him, the technical commission and each of his players "for the much they have accomplished praising our best sporting traditions". Ministers Delfim Netto, of Planning, and Camilo Pena, of Industry and Commerce, met yesterday, after the game, to discuss the new increase in the price of sugar for the consumer.
>
> Right after the Brazil-Italy match, General João Figueiredo, according to his advisors, left to his quarters at Granja do Torto, refusing to make any comment on the elimination of the Brazilian team. Only late in the afternoon did the Planalto spokesman disseminated, through the Empresa Brasileira de Notícias (EBN), his telegram to the CBF president, which reads as follows: "Please convey to the players and technical commission my words of understanding and solidarity. I know that everyone did what they could in search of victory. The failure against Italy does not take away the merit of the good campaign they have accomplished". (Jornal do Brasil, 1982a, 1982b, 1982c, 1982d, 1982e, July 6, p. 2) (our translation)

In the excerpts selected above, it is possible to identify again the involvement of the last military president with the 1982 national team, as well as that of the Vice-President himself, the engineer Aureliano Chaves, who was then a member of the PDS [Democratic Social Party] and would have exalted in a nationalist way the supposed "Brazilian sporting traditions". It is also worth noting that the important decision to readjust once again the price of sugar, in a country that was going through a serious economic crisis, was only taken in a meeting after the match.

That said, it is important to emphasize that, regardless any possible criticism to the line-up of some players, to the tactical scheme, to a possible stubbornness of coach Telê Santana, from a social-political perspective, what I could notice in several analyzed reports was an identification with the 1982 team both by journalists who were critical of the still dictatorial regime and by members of the military government and public authorities, without directly associating that team to the political regime in force.

In this sense, the euphoria surrounding the Brazilian "canarinho" team seemed to me to symbolically unite dissenting public voices around the showy football, thus enhancing the symbolic perspective of real integration of the country. Not even the early elimination, before reaching the semi-finals, in the worst sporting result of a national team since 1966, was able to shake the renewing aura of the team among journalists and in the official government discourse.

Conclusion

The purpose of this chapter was to develop questions on the 1982 World Cup held in Spain from a historiographical perspective both in terms of the contextualization of the sporting event and of the media political agenda of the Brazilian printed press analyzed.

In the first section, I tried to analyze, based on a specific bibliography, the context in which the event took place, prioritizing political, social, and economic issues and using mainly the work of Juan Simón to better understand the historical context and the relationship of the tournament with the transformations that Spain had been going through since the end of the Franco dictatorship.

Next, I focused on the analysis of articles from two Brazilian press vehicles, *Jornal do Brasil* (newspaper) and *Placar* (magazine). I worked with the hypothesis of popular euphoria around the Brazilian team as a symbolic representative of political re-democratization and of a supposed return to the "genuine" Brazilian football.

In this sense, I sought, from the perspective of René Rémond's New Political History, to approach the relationship between a democratic imaginary and the development of the 1982 World Cup both in the host country and in Brazil, using different references and stimulating different views on the relations between politics and football in this spectacularized sporting event.

Thus, I hope to have contributed to new research and approaches being developed on an unforgettable edition of the World Cup that, despite being quite important in the collective imaginary of Brazilians, has few academic studies in our country.

References

Alabarces, P. (2002). *Fútbol y patria: El fútbol y las narrativas de la Nación en la Argentina*. Prometeo Libros, Buenos Aires.

Bobbio, N. (2013). *Liberalismo e democracia*. Brasiliense.

Cabo, A. V. (2014). Copas do Mundo de 1978 e 1982: Olhares nacionais da revista Placar a partir da seleção brasileira. *Tempos Gerais*, (6), 27–46. https://ufsj.edu.br/portal2-repositorio/File/temposgerais/9_ARTIGO_COPAS.pdf

Cabo, A. V. (2018). *Argentina/78: Uma Copa do Mundo política, popular e polêmica*. Appris.

Cabo, A. V. (2020). Copa do Mundo de 1982: ventos democráticos na Espanha e no Brasil. In S. S. Giglio, & M. W. Proni (Orgs.), *O futebol nas ciências humanas no Brasil* (pp. 97–120). Editora da Unicamp.

Carr, J. P., & Fusi, R. (1979). *España, de la dictadura a la democracia*. Editorial Planeta.

Costa, L. (2014). 1982: Lágrimas de uma geração de ouro. In R. Helal & A. Cabo (Eds.), *Copas do Mundo: Comunicação e identidade cultural no país do futebol* (pp. 165–194). Eduerj.

Jornal do Brasil (1982a, May 23). *Sports section.*

Jornal do Brasil (1982b, May 28). *Sports section.*

Jornal do Brasil (1982c, May 29). *Sports section.*

Jornal do Brasil (1982d, May 30). *Sports section.*

Jornal do Brasil (1982e, July 6). *Sports section.*

Mascarenhas, G. (2014). *Entradas e bandeiras: A conquista do Brasil pelo futebol*. Eduerj.

Melo Filho, A. (2002). Diretrizes para nova legislação desportiva. *Revista Brasileira de Direito Desportivo*, (2), 41–48. https://ibdd.com.br/2o-volume/

Mestman, M., & Varela, M. (2013). *Masas, pueblo, multitud en cine y televisión*. Eudeba, Buenos Aires.

Palácio, M., & Cascajosa, C. (2013). España: el espacio público desde la transición democrática a los êxitos deportivos. In M. Mestman, & M. Varela (Eds.), *Masas, pueblo, multitud en cine y televisión*. Eudeba.

Revista Placar. Editora Abril. São Paulo. (1982a, April 23). (622).

Placar. (1982b, April 30). (623).

Placar. (1982c, May 14). (625).

Placar, (1982d, June 9). (633).

Simón, J. A. (2012). *España 82—La historia de nuestro Mundial*. T e B Editores.

Simón, J. A. (2012b). El mundial de fútbol de 1982: escaparate de la nueva democracia española. *Materiales para la Historia del Deporte*, (10), 1–15. http://polired.upm.es/index.php/materiales_historia_deporte/article/view/4152

Tussel, J. (2010). *Dictadura franquista y democracia*. Crítica.

Chapter 6
Brazilian Football and History

João Manuel Casquinha Malaia Santos

Introduction

This chapter aims to be a first approach for those who want to research about Brazilian football.[1] First of all, we need to think about the relations between football history with the research in history at all. If the reader is thinking of writing something related to the history of football, he should keep in mind a first basic question: historical research aims at understanding a phenomenon that occurred in the past in its entirety. It is very important to take some care when writing a history. There is a specific field of knowledge, which has existed for many years and has been perfecting the best methods for this purpose. There is even a specific training program responsible for helping those who wish to write histories to use the best tools and to understand the extent of the responsibility involved in writing about the past of social experiences.

Therefore, it becomes indispensable to read some handbooks of this specific area of knowledge, history. A very simple book, but a classic on history, such as "The Historian's Craft" (Bloch, 1977), originally published in 1949, is a good start for those who wish to enter this type of study. But it is not the only one. There are many history methodology books that can be useful and will be indicated as suggestions at the end of this chapter.

These are works that help to understand the specificities of historical research and which provide tools to be used to write history. This will certainly help the researcher not to make mistakes that are common to those who are willing to discuss the past without knowing the appropriate tools to access it.

Football is a popular and mediatized phenomenon in Brazil. Brazilian football histories comes to the knowledge of the general public usually via media professionals, who are not researchers. These stories are based on a major theoretical

---

[1] Soccer for native American readers.

J. M. C. M. Santos (✉)
Federal University of Santa Maria, Santa Maria, Brazil

framework, brought to light by a famous Brazilian journalist, Mario Filho, the same man that gives the official name to the most famous Brazilian pitch in the world, the Maracanã stadium. Mario Filho (2021) originally published "The black man in Brazilian soccer" in 1947, a book that incorporated Gilberto Freyre's concept about the advantages that the racial integration had on Brazilian society and, in some ways, provided the formation of a less racist society.

The success of black football players in Brazil was used to prove that Freyre's thesis was right. That's why Gilberto Freyre wrote the preface for the first edition of the book. Mario Filho's book sold a lot and this kind of approach was largely used by journalists in writing Brazilian football histories from that time on. Because authors are known by a high number of people that enjoys football, usually these stories sell a lot in bookstores and are largely incorporated by mass media when they approach the Brazilian football past.

But, when Brazilian football past started to play a more important role as an object for historical research, the Freyrean approach is slowing being contested. Research in universities is revealing something substantive about football as a social, political, economic and cultural phenomenon. And this is what historical research proposes to do, insofar as it has the perception that understanding the various issues surrounding football's past is fundamental for a better understanding of society itself.

This chapter, actually an introductory text, seeks to stimulate the reader to reflect on the specificities of historical research, and especially in researching Brazilian football's past. Some reflections are general ones and can be used in any approach to the past for historical research. The idea is to contribute not only to those who start in historical research itself, but also for those who need to make only a brief introduction to the theme. The precautions are equally important.

The text is divided into five parts. In the first part, we will address some characteristics of historical research. Then, we will offer some steps for the researcher to have contact with the academic production in Brazilian football and be able to work with a basic point of historical research, which is historiography. The next part will introduce the researcher to the so-called fields of history, raising, albeit in an introductory way, some important methodological issues. In the fourth stage, we will present, by way of example, two possible approaches for investigations into Brazilian football's past. We will first analyze the history that focuses on certain characters and then the history of associations or organizations. Finally, in the fifth and last stage, we will present some reflections about football history could play a relevant role in the field of historical research.

Historical Research

Marc Bloch, the French author mentioned above, was one of the most important historians of the twentieth century. In the late 1920s, together with another French historian, Lucien Febvre, he founded one of the most significant History scientific journals, which became popularly known as the *Annales*. This journal was very important because it helped to consolidate remarkable transformations in historical methods and in approaching history as a specific field of knowledge.

For the researchers grouped around the *Annales*, there was not a single history, that is, there was not "the" history of someone or something. For them, those who narrate history have their points of view, their preferences, which makes them emphasize one fact more than another. Differently of historians at that time, who claimed to be writing the truth of facts and "definitive" histories, *Annales* historians were concerned with making relationships with researchers in the other social sciences and showing that what they were writing was not "the" history, but "a" history.

And why is this *Annales* issue present here? Because it helps us to make a first reflection when we propose to write about the past of any phenomenon (including football): we will be writing "a" history and not "the" history. We should always be wary of those who show themselves as the owners of the truth of the past, writers of the so-called definitive histories.

It is obvious that when we decide to write about the past, we must assume the commitment to narrate things close to the way they happened, or with a high standard of verisimilitude. But, as we have said, each person has a preference for certain issues and will end up giving more emphasis to them in the course of his or her research and writing. The important thing is to make this clear to the reader. If I have a liberal vision and I am going to approach a certain theme from this angle, I must warn my reader about it. In the same way, if I have a Marxist view of the historical process, my reader should be aware of this, and it is up to me to clarify it. As I have done in this chapter: I have shown that, when I write history, I share Bloch's and Febvre's conception that I write "a" history and not "the" history, and that I do not claim to write a definitive version of the past.

Historical research is not a mere narrative of the past; it raises important questions for our understanding of society. It is always about a phenomenon that happened in the past (thus related to *time*), in a certain place (thus related to *space*), and from a certain vision of society (thus related to a *problem*). Febvre (1982) even challenged that without a problem, there is no history.

Thus, we can already think of two initial questions for our research on football history. The first is that we must be aware that we are writing our version of the past. The second is that this history must be written based on the tripod "time, space and problem". But there are other relevant specificities of this field of knowledge.

First of all, it is necessary to know where the historian gets his information from. The material used by the historian to support his stories is called sources. Each and every remnant of the past left by human beings constitutes a historical source. Sources, however, must also be problematized.

It is important to reveal in our research what sources we use, where they can be found, how they were produced, in what form they are archived and what their limitations are. Something common in research on the Brazilian football past is the use of sports press sources. Many times, the researcher has access to an old newspaper, reads a certain news that he finds interesting for his work and uncritically includes it in his text.

Let us imagine the following situation, absolutely common in the sports press: a sports columnist, supporter of team *A,* writes a text about team *B.* Since I, as a researcher, have this information, it is essential that my reader is also aware of this, so that he does not run the risk of taking the word of that columnist as truth, when it was written with partiality. It is essential to problematize that sports columnists are often supporters of certain teams. This is important in relation to the record of a particular phenomenon in football. When we write about football past, a mass cultural phenomenon that moves passions and crowds, this issue is particularly complicated.

Despite the countless particularities of a historical research that could be placed here, I decided to leave on record only one last and important warning, which by the way was made a long time ago, in 1942, by Lucien Febvre. This author said that the greatest sin an historian can commit is that of anachronism, a kind of chronological error that greatly compromises the credibility of any historical research. And research on football history is no exception.

For example, when we refer to football, we are talking about a sport that was born in the UK in the second half of the nineteenth century. It is a sport played on a field with specific measurements and its own rules, such as having 11 players on each side and only one player from each side being allowed to hold the ball with his hands, but only within a defined area. Other leisure practices carried out before that period and in other locations are not football. Therefore, when we talk about football history, we are not talking about the *kemari,* the *episquiro,* the *soule,* or the Florentine *calcio.* These are leisure practices carried out in times prior to the emergence of the modality we are analyzing here. Although some of them are very similar to football, to say that they are part of its history is to commit anachronism, the mistake that Febvre pointed out as the historian's greatest sin.

In football there are rules, federations, clubs, fans, stadiums, competitions (local, regional, national, and international). Are there similarities between football and these other recreational practices mentioned? Yes, of course. But there are also characteristics that are unique to this sport. For this reason, I insist once again, football must be studied within its specificity in *time* and *space.* And always on the basis of a *problem.*

Having read some introductory texts on the nature of historical research, it is up to the researcher to take a second important step. We need to know better this field of investigation, to deepen our knowledge of what is being researched in this area. This is what we shall now discuss.

Getting to Know the Field

After having had a first contact with the fundamental principles of historical research ("a" history versus "the" history; problem-history; anachronism; and the issue of sources), it is up to us to analyze what kind of research about Brazilian football's past we could develop in order to contribute to the understanding of the society as a whole, which is, I believe, the major objective of any social research. We can no longer say, as 20 or 30 years ago, that research on this subject is scarce, to the extent that currently there are numerous quality works on the subject.

It is essential for any researcher to conduct a broad survey of what has already been published in his or her area of interest. In relation to Brazilian football specifically, an exhaustive investigation of what has already been published shows that there are countless themes that can still be investigated, as well as several fields of research to be explored. It also shows where it is possible to start building a research theme that has not been analyzed so far or on which a deeper reflection is deemed necessary. The task of knowing what has been or had been researched in the field of football history does not fail to constitute a historiographical work, to the extent that historiography is precisely a kind of history of what has already been done on historical research.

Santos and Drumond (2013) published an article that proposed to analyze some of the most important reflections on Brazilian football history, since the beginning of the twentieth century, until some of the main researches published in the 2000s. They showed how the Freyrean theoretical approach was basis for the most important authors that wrote about Brazilian football past, since the Mario Filho's book. Another important article, which in a way complements the previous one, is the one by Giglio and Spaggiari (2010) on the production of the human sciences about football in Brazil between 1990 and 2009. These two works represent a good starting point for those who intend to begin Brazilian football historical research.

The fact is that today there is a vast academic and literary production about Brazilian football past. To know better about these production, a visit to the theses and dissertations Web site of the Coordenação de Aperfeiçoamento de Pessoal de Nível Superior (CAPES)[2] quite interesting. This Web site is a digital repository of theses and dissertations defended in Brazil, maintained by the Brazilian federal government. A survey conducted in this Web site, in March 2021, with the word "football", only for the area of History, resulted in 120 master's dissertations and 43 doctoral theses. Moreover, these dissertations and theses were mostly defended in universities of excellence in the country, such as the Universidade de São Paulo (18), the Pontifícia Universidade Católica de São Paulo (16), the Universidade Federal do Paraná (15), the Universidade Federaldo Rio de Janeiro (15) and the Universidade Federal Fluminense (9). Such numbers show that research on aspects of football's past has a relative space in the academic environment and that it becomes increasingly important to know these works before starting new investigations.

Another important step is to search for scientific articles on the history of football in Brazilian research Web sites such as Scielo, Portal de Periódicos Capes or Google Scholar, which can show the "state of the art" in the main scientific publications in the country. There are also scientific journals specialized in the history of sports, both in Brazil and abroad. I cite here the most important Brazilian journal in this field of research, *Recorde: Revista de História do Esporte*, published since 2008, with two issues per year. A survey in this journal only about articles that contained the word "football" in the title, until the 2019 edition, revealed a total of 53 articles related to the football past. Another national publication that can help in the search for research on

---

[2] Available at: https://catalogodeteses.capes.gov.br/catalogo-teses/#!/.

the history of football is the journal *Fulia/UFMG*, a publication organized since 2016 by the research group Fulia—Núcleo de Estudos sobre Futebol, Linguagem e Artes, from the Faculdade de Letras—Universidade Federal de Minas Gerais. *Fulia/UFMG* is not specialized in history, but it publishes texts about football past.

There are foreign journals specialized in sports history, such as the *Journal of Sport History* (published since 1974) and the *International Journal of the History of Sport* (published since 1984), in which articles on Brazilian football can also be found. In addition to researching in scientific journals, another possibility is to look for papers published in annals of events, the main one being the Brazilian Historical Association (ANPUH) meetings, which takes place every two years since 2003 and promotes a specific thematic symposium on the history of sport. In the *Annals of the XXX national symposium of history* (2019), for example, there are 14 papers on the history of football. The number is higher than the two previous events (2017 and 2015), in which nine papers on the theme were published in the *Annals* of each one.

Besides these more traditional researches, the popularization of academic content on football historical research also happens through blogs and Web sites. There are several initiatives of this nature coordinated by researchers from various universities in the country. I cite here two examples that I consider of the highest quality and that may show excellent research paths for those who intend to start in this field of investigation. The first of them is the blog "História(s) do Sport",[3] an initiative of the group Sport: Laboratório de História do Esporte e do Lazer (UFRJ), the same group that publishes the *Recorde* journal. The blog brings together texts by several researchers, both on sport and leisure, obviously counting on many interesting texts about football's past.

The second example is the largest academic portal on football in Brazil, Ludopédio.[4] This Web site concentrates the largest number of football researchers in the country's human sciences. It also intends to be a great space for the dissemination of research groups, dissertations, theses, articles, and books. All about football. Therefore, it is of great value to visit Ludopédio, read the texts that have been published there and enter through it to know a countless number of possibilities about research in football history.

All this laborious search will help us to "know the field", or the possibilities of historical research to be done, providing greater security for those who start researching the history of football. Let us now approach some possibilities of writing history in its so-called different fields, also noting certain precautions that must be taken in relation to historical research itself.

---

[3] Available at: https://historiadoesporte.wordpress.com/.

[4] Available at: https://www.ludopedio.org.br.

What to Write and How to Write

In order to start researching football history, we must keep in mind in which field of historical research the work will be inserted. Those who seek to conduct historical research must delve into the specific methodology of this field of knowledge. The methodological procedures of the historian are the ones that make his research can be clearly demonstrated. And different methods can be used to construct the text, such as those of comparative history, the elaboration of biographies, prosopography, oral history, microhistory, and many others. For this, it is also important to read books that aim to reflect on the methodology of history.

There are some good readings for those who are starting out in historical research. These are simple, introductory texts that aim to put the reader in touch with different approaches to history, such as social history, economic history, politics, culture, and other increasingly diverse fields. Research in football history can concentrate a large universe of questions. There are countless football characters and phenomena that can be investigated. We can write histories of organizations, such as clubs, fans, federations, confederations, leagues, sponsoring companies or media outlets involved with football. Furthermore, we can write about the past of the State's relations with all these organizations or of the sport's relations with the most diverse social, economic, political, or cultural issues.

We can also write the history of people or groups of people connected to football, such as players, fans, club managers, club employees, referees, street vendors who hang around stadiums, businessmen, journalists. There is also the possibility of using football as a means to observe transformations in the cities, such as the construction of stadiums and the urban impact of this type of venture, or the changes made in the organization of means of transport in order to move thousands of people to football stadiums.

There is also the possibility of studying certain competitions in particular, seeking to show the history of both major disputes and popular competitions important for the dissemination of the practice of football among less affluent sections of the population. One can also develop a study of gender relations in the past of football practice, management and fans; or of discriminatory procedures such as racism, homophobia, machismo, misogyny in the various spheres of this modality. This is just a small sample of the possibilities of studies on football history that can be explored.

The important thing is to be clear about the problem to be investigated and to know the best way to approach it, that is, the best way to write your history. As we said before, the sources are the historian's material; for this reason, it is extremely important to reflect on them.

Here I cite three introductory works on historical research in general. These are books such as "The pursuit of History" (Tosh, 2015), "Going to the sources" (Brundage, 2017), and "Doing History" (Donnely & Norton, 2011). These books present the possibilities of working with various types of sources, such as documentary, archaeological, printed, oral, biographical, and audiovisual sources. They address other types of sources, such as photography, literature, wills and inventories, criminal proceedings, parish and civil registers, archives of repressive regimes, letters, speeches and pronouncements, personal diaries, and sources for cultural heritage.

Another important issue is that we need to have a problem in historical research. And that is why we historians need to work with appropriated theoretical framework. As I have already noted, the reader has to be aware of our theoretical choices. And those choices need to have a straight connection to our research theme. For this procedure, I recommend some works on the sociology of sport, like the "Routledge Handbook of the Sociology of Sport" (Giulianotti, 2015). In this book, we have approaches to sport within different theoretical perspectives based on different authors like Marx, Elias, Bourdieau and different kinds of analyses such as anthropological, economical, philosophical and so on.

We can search for more precise approaches to sport and there are a variety of works on sport that can help us historians to observe football's past through some specific lens. Just to point out some examples, we have some important articles and books on sport and Marxism (Young, 1986; Carrigton & McDonald, 2009), sport and postcolonialism (Bale & Cronin, 2003), sports and racism (Nauright & Wiggins, 2015; Spracklen & Long, 2010), sports and homophobia (Cashmore & Cleland, 2014) and so on. All these works, although the focus on sports in general, have important issues on football. They provide lens for observing football and for us, historians, to analyze football's past under these perspectives.

We realize, then, through these basic reflections, that writing a history of football, based on a problem located in time and space, within a specific field of history, requires quite an intense previous work, which is not limited to knowing what to research, knowing and reading works already done on the subject, observing basic precepts of historical research, or understanding that one should research a problem-history: it is necessary to search a varied number of sources and analyze them critically.

Some Possibilities

Some examples of possibilities for studies on football's past experiences have already been mentioned above. The idea now is to reflect on some of the themes that may bear good fruits for future researches. The goal here is to offer some suggestions of themes that still deserve more attention, especially in relation to Brazilian football.

The large amount of academic production, generated in different regions of the country, shows us that much work has already been developed, and it is interesting that new research dialogues with these studies. I highlight here only two possibilities of approaching the theme: stories of football characters and stories of organizations or associations that somehow have greater or lesser connection with this sport.

We can choose to write about the countless characters in football, be they players, managers, fans, coaches, referees, businessmen, journalists, club employees or even state employees involved with football (from the president of the republic to the policeman who does the stadium security). There is also the possibility of writing stories of people who work on the margins of football, such as street vendors, car keepers, etc.

As already mentioned, the important thing is that the stories of these characters always start from a problem that is contextualized in time and space, and that leads us to a better understanding of society. Writing about a character's past is always a complicated task; it requires deep historical research with methods appropriate to the reconstruction of his or her life and the use of precise sources.

In most cases, works that focus on the past of a particular personage make use of microhistory and categories such as life history, understood as a research technique that aims to provide empirical grounds for studies. It is important to be familiar with classic works carried out using these methods, such as Levi's (1988) who applied this variation of time scale to reconstruct the life of an exorcist priest in a small Italian village in the seventeenth century.

By investigating, deeply and intensively, the life of this priest, Levi ended up reconstructing a range of events in the life of the population of the small village of Piedmont. The historian had in mind that his research should show not only the dynamics of the facts that could be more easily observed, because they were more visible; his aim was to draw attention to the web of relationships between individuals in the village that took place in accordance with their respective social positions and their individual and group resources, their options and their uncertainties.

This type of approach shows us how fruitful it can be to follow the life trajectory of characters in football history on a microscopic scale. Researching the past of these individuals' relationships with other individuals and groups can reveal important connections and general dynamics of football that often escape the more general view.

It is not only about reconstructing a biography or praising certain achievements of characters connected to the world of football, as it is commonly found. Most works about football called biographical are concerned only with the person himself and not with the extensive range of relationships that he built throughout his life, revealing important issues for the dynamics of this sport as a social phenomenon. In addition, few biographies are concerned with using the life trajectory of his biography to understand more deeply the society as a whole. One of the most common mistakes found in bookstores when we look for biographical works can be noticed right from the titles of the works. Many of them are presented as "the biography", or "the true story", or "the definitive biography", or "authorized biography", or even "the only biography". In this way, the authors place themselves as carriers of a single possible history, disregarding the multiple possibilities of writing different narratives, from other points of view, from other sources and other theoretical approaches.

One of the great gaps to be explored by research on football is the life trajectory of black figures in this sport in its early years in Brazil. Post-abolition analyses in Brazil are among the fastest growing fields of study in our historiography; following the trajectory of the first black Brazilian football players in the 1910s and 1920s would certainly fit into this field; most of these players did not have their histories reconstructed from a perspective that sought to understand how the black population lived in the first years after the abolition of the slavery regime in 1888. These and other experiences, such as the role of women (as players, managers, fans, referees, journalists) in the history of this sport still need to be studied in depth.

With regard to the second possibility, writing histories of football-related organizations or associations, this is also a task that requires specific procedures. We must not forget that organizations are made up of people. Therefore, writing histories of organizations is also writing histories of people.

However, these people have a common goal, which is to come together around an organization or association in some way connected with football. We are talking not only about football clubs, from the largest to the smallest, but also federations, confederations, associations of players, coaches and referees, supporters, media companies covering that sport, sponsoring companies, etc.

The analysis of organizations or associations can be approached from different angles. If the proposal is to study the power relations that take place between organizations, the focus should fall more on political history. If the aim is to analyze the dynamics of economic relations between organizations or associations, the focus will certainly be on economic history. But once again it is important to emphasize that organizations and associations should be analyzed based on a problem and situated within their historicity in time and space.

Stories of large or small organizations and associations always have a profound impact on society. It is not necessary to tell the whole story of the organization or association; it is enough to establish a time frame that is justified according to the importance of the phenomenon we intend to analyze. Nor is it necessary to write only the stories of big football clubs; small clubs have great local importance, and it is interesting to analyze, in their temporality, the impacts they cause in their city or region.

Moreover, these are not only club stories. Histories of federations may highlight important processes, such as the monopolization of entertainment markets. Fan club histories may indicate the formation of urban identities among young people in the cities. Histories of players' unions may reveal important class struggles between players and managers. Media histories may reveal the exaltation of certain clubs and the erasure of others.

Beyond the stories of people, organizations or associations linked to football, there are still countless possibilities of historical approaches to this sport. We can write stories about specific events, about rivalries, about the various forms of prejudice existing in football, about identity discourses and a huge range of phenomena.

The Last Pass

Research in football history can become a great challenge, provided we look at it that way. One of the objectives of this chapter is to stimulate researchers to develop works about aspects of football's past that can really contribute to a wider historiographical debate. For that, it is necessary to know the historiographical production and delve into the historicity of the phenomena.

As it was previously shown, although the theme "football" is not new in the historiographical production, both in Brazil and abroad, it is still far from occupying a really significant position in the field of historical research. It is, therefore, the responsibility of all those who dedicate themselves to write about the past of this phenomenon to keep in mind the importance of raising it to better levels in the academy.

We have already seen the importance of the search for sources that can help us reconstitute rigorously football's past. This search is laborious, requiring visits to archives and libraries, the handling of very old papers, the expense of wearing gloves and masks, time spent in reading all the collected material, often without being able to find what was necessary. Furthermore, documentation on football clubs, fans, federations or sponsoring companies, when they exist, are difficult to access and are hardly organized.

Because of these issues, it is not uncommon for football historians are in Brazil to use mostly periodicals, such as newspapers and magazines, as sources. This early twentieth-century press material is relatively well archived and many printed materials are available in databases such as Biblioteca's Nacional Hemeroteca Digital Brasileira. In this portal, there is a huge number of newspapers and magazines from all Brazilian states and a rich material to be used as a source for historical research. Football histories cannot, however, have only periodicals as a source. As much as different newspapers are used, it is important to diversify the sources, visit archives, insist with clubs, use other types of sources, such as oral history. One must be creative in searching for traces of the past that help to tell the story: a study on the history of violence in football may use criminal proceedings as a source; a study that seeks to show the elitist origin of groups that ran football in the past may use *post-mortem* inventories of these people to attest to their assets when they died.

All fields of historical research have their specific difficulties in obtaining sources. It would be no different with football, a phenomenon that moves millions of people, immense amounts of money, which is able to take a boy from extreme poverty to world stardom, or a football club president to the president of a nation. We need to give due attention to the history of such an important phenomenon and face its research as the great challenge it actually represents.

References

Bale, J., & Cronin, M. (Eds.). (2003). *Sport and postcolonialism*. Berg.
Brundage, A. (2017). *Going to the sources: A guide to historical research and writing*. John Wiley & Sons.
Bloch, M. (1977). *The historian's craft*. Manchester University Press.
Carrington, B., & McDonald, I. (Eds.). (2009). *Marxism, cultural studies and sport*. Routledge.
Cashmore, E., & Cleland, J. (Eds.). (2014). *Football's dark side: Corruption, homophobia, violence, and racism in the beautiful game*. Palgrave Macmillan.

Donnely, M., & Norton, C. (2011). *Doing history*. Routledge.

Febvre, L. (1982). *The problem of unbelief in the sixteenth century: The religion of Rabelais*. Harvard University Press.

Filho, M. (2021). *Black man in Brazilian soccer*. (J. A. Draper, Trans.). The University of North Carolina Press. (Original book published in 1947).

Giglio, S. S., & Spaggiari, E. (2010). A produção das Ciências Humanas sobre futebol no Brasil: um panorama (1990–2009). *Revista de História*, (163), 293–350. https://doi.org/10.11606/issn.2316-9141.v0i163p293-350

Guiulianotti, R. (Ed.). (2015). *Routledge handbook of the sociology of sport*. Routledge.

Levi, G. (1988). *Inheriting power: The story of an exorcist*. (L. G. Cochrane, Trans.). University of Chicago Press.

Nauright, J., & Wiggins, D. (2015). *Routledge handbook of sport, race, and ethnicity*. Routledge.

Santos, J. M. C. M., & Drumond, M. (2013). The construction of soccer stories in Brazil (1922 to 2000): Some remarks. *Tempo, 19*(34), 19–31. https://doi.org/10.5533/TEM-1980-542X-201317 3403

Spraklen, K., & Long, J. (2010). *Sport and challenges to racism*. Palgrave Macmillan.

Tosh, J. (2015). *The pursuit of history: Aims, methods, and new directions in the study of history*. Routledge.

Young, T. R. (1986). The sociology of sport: Structural marxist and cultural marxist approaches. *Sociological Perspectives, 29*(1), 3–28. https://doi.org/10.2307/1388940

Chapter 7
Myths, Football and National Identity (1930–1983)

Denaldo Alchorne de Souza

In Europe, the debate around the importance of sports with political-ideological purposes was already taking place since the end of the First World War. Countries such as England, France, Italy and Germany were already using sporting activities as a form of expression of national struggle, with sportspeople representing their states or nations. Football, in particular, was an effective medium for inculcating national sentiments due to the ease with which even political or public individuals of lesser expression in society could identify with the nation. The fan also participated in the spectacle, often interfering decisively in the final result. When the national team played, the imaginary community of millions seemed even more real in the form of a team of eleven people with a name. The individual, even the one who only cheered, became the very symbol of his nation (Hobsbawm, 1990, p. 171).

The Brazilian State did not remain passive before this sporting phenomenon and since the early twentieth century, rulers sought to approach this phenomenon (Pereira, 2000). During the First Vargas Government (1930–1945), controlling this sporting practice became one of the priorities of the groups that held power (Souza, 2008). In 1950, the Maracanã stadium inauguration was inserted in a political project that sought to build an image of Brazil as an enterprising, victorious and successful country (Moura, 1998). In 1958, 1962 and 1970, Presidents of the Republic Juscelino Kubitschek, João Goulart and Emílio Garrastazu Médici, respectively, actively participated in the tributes paid to the world champion players (Souza, 2018). In those years, the interrelation between football and political interests was maintained through the construction of discourses that sought to associate football to the projects of the groups that were in power.

Besides the State, other social actors—among them, the great commercial press—elaborated discourses of "Brazil" and of the "Brazilian people" that were intended to be built through football. Several sports periodicals emerged in major cities, such as *Jornal dos Sports*, in Rio de Janeiro, and *A Gazeta Esportiva*, in São Paulo. The

D. A. de Souza (✉)
Fluminense Federal Institute, Rio de Janeiro, Brazil

invention of sports journalism ran parallel to the invention of professional football. In a way, when "rewriting" an event, the press created the sporting spectacle, produced the demand for it (Lopes, 1994, p. 82) and created a vision of "nation" more appropriate to its interests. A good example is the chronicle below, authored by journalist Mário Filho[1]:

> Because in football there was no longer even the slightest glimmer of racism. All the clubs with their mulattos and their blacks. A black man scores a goal, there come the whites hugging him, kissing him. The goal is scored by a white man, the mulattos, the blacks, hug and kiss the white man. Whoever is in the general area, in the stands, in the numbered seat, belongs to the same crowd. The passion of the people had to be like the people, of all colours, of all social conditions. The black equal to the white, the poor equal to the rich. The rich pay more, buy a numbered seat, don't need to get to the stadium at dawn, go later. He stays in the shade, doesn't get the sun on his head, but he cannot cheer more than the poor, nor be happier in victory, nor more unfortunate in defeat. (Rodrigues Filho, 1946, September 21, p. 12)

What we can observe in the discourses produced both by the different groups that were in power between the 1930s and the 1970s and by the mainstream commercial press in the same period is that a common aspect unified them: the emphasis on the idea of discipline. The state and the press, despite constructing multiple visions of "Brazil" and of the "Brazilian people", saw discipline as football's positive contribution to the consolidation of the nation. A common theoretical inspiration was sociologist Gilberto Freyre. Writing about football, he made the following comment:

> We Brazilians have nothing to be ashamed of, when it comes to our style of playing football that gives too much expression to the exploits of individual heroes or dancers. What we need is to reconcile this individualism with discipline, without which the effort of a group degrades, after all, into anarchic hysteria. (Freyre, 1955, June 25, p. 22)

The above analysis certainly interprets that football was used by the rulers and the mainstream commercial press with the aim of building an ideology of national identity that sought to cement the social differentiations and unite everyone in the aggrandizement of the nation. But was this green-yellow hegemony[2] based on football only a construction of the State and the mainstream press, and from above? Did the other segments of society not also participate in this elaboration?

We can understand nations and national identities as dual phenomena, basically constructed from above, but which cannot be understood without being analyzed from below, that is, in terms of the assumptions, hopes, needs, aspirations, and interests of common people, who are not necessarily national and even less nationalist. However, this view from below, that is, the nation as seen not by governments, spokespersons or activists of nationalist movements, but by the common people who are the object

---

[1] Mário Rodrigues Filho was one of the most important sports journalists in Brazil. He was known by everyone by the simplified version of his name: Mário Filho. That was how he sponsored and publicized the most different sporting events and that was how he signed his articles and books. After his death (1966), as a tribute, Maracanã Stadium received his name, also in the simple variant.

[2] "Yellow-green" is a commonly used compound word, as something that is very nationalistic, regarding Brazil.

of their action and propaganda, is extremely difficult to discover (Hobsbawm, 1990, p. 20).

How, then, can we detect opposing initiatives and contributions that have sought to resist the dominant ideology or set limits to it? In the case of football, how did the working class,[3] or at least a significant part of it, receive the ideology of national identity via football? Did it passively accept the idealizations constructed by the State and the great press, as if they were "tabula rasas"? Or did it try to elaborate alternative answers that would resize, recreate and modify the green-yellow hegemony?

A way to overcome this difficulty would be in the study of popular myths of that period linked to football, trying to find out what they represented for certain social groups. Myth is not necessarily a falsified or invented story; it is, rather, a story that becomes significant to the extent that it amplifies the meaning of an individual event, transforming it into the symbolic and narrative formalization of the self-representations shared by a culture (Portelli, 1998, pp. 120–121).

And what we can see is that the myths created by football have not always represented what the ruling class and governments would like them to. To restrict ourselves to a few examples, in the 1930s and 1940s, the most popular player in Brazil was Leônidas da Silva, the "Black Diamond". For some, he was more popular than President Getúlio Vargas himself. During the 1938 World Cup, held in France, Leônidas became the main player of the national team. More than that, he was the player with the most popular identification.

But, after all, who was Leonidas? Why did ordinary people identify with him and even want to help him? Of humble origins, black, starting his career at Bonsucesso, a suburban team in Rio de Janeiro, Leônidas had everything to be the prototype of the Brazilian man idealized by the First Vargas Government. But reality was different. Accused of not respecting an agreement with América Football Club that he had signed on three separate occasions, of stealing a necklace of beads during his team's excursion to São Paulo, as well as being called a bad professional for not liking to train or for pretending to be injured in order to earn more money by giving lectures or opening stores, Leônidas was not the most plausible figure to represent Vargas' ideal of the "new man".

For the ideologues of the period, the figure of the "new man" stood out; the models of the rascal and the subversive were supposedly neutralized in favor of an idealization of the Brazilian citizen as hardworking and, preferably, black (Gomes, 1994). In the specific case of professional football, Brazilian players were considered immature and ignorant; uncontrolled, unstable in their nervous system, subject to instincts and passions. The Europeans, on the other hand, were idealized as controlled, educated, cultured and, for that reason, self-controlled people. Therefore, Brazilian players

---

[3] "Working class" is understood here as the result of a broader process in which such historical subjects become workers in the "class struggle". Class is a relation, not a thing. People see themselves in a society structured in a certain way, they endure exploitation, they identify who the "we" of the antagonistic interests are, they struggle around these same "we" and, in the course of such a process of struggle, they discover themselves as a class, thus coming to make the discovery of their class consciousness. Class and class consciousness are always the last and not the first stage of an actual historical process (Thompson, 1998, p.13–85).

needed to be educated and guided, and such function would be performed by no less than the elite who ran the country's sports, under the State's supervision (Souza, 2008, pp. 81–99). For ideologues such as João Lyra Filho, the leader needed to adopt a paternal and kindly style with his athletes. For this to be feasible, however, it was necessary that the players accepted this "educational practice". Thus, the "irresponsible" football players would only be useful to the nation if they were "educated"—read controlled—by a literate and civilized inner elite:

> Do not blame the psychological preparation of Brazilian players, even in the shadow of the anthem or the flag, for an evil that has its roots in the formation and endures in the organic and functional state of our people. Only the spirit's power of evasion, when densely cultivated, is capable of attenuating the effects of chronic evils. (Lyra, 1941, p. 18)

For this author, control should not only be exercised during matches, but also in the players' daily life, in their own private life. Without the "education" given by the managers, the irrational aspects would remain in the football player. Thus, the rebellious star, the rascal, the one who did not accept being "educated" by this elite, who questioned their values or who did not allowed the control of his personal life was seen as a threat to the good of the whole team, of the whole team and, why not, of the whole nation.

Leônidas da Silva represented an ethic totally different from the official one. If we compare his profile to that of another great player of the era, Domingos da Guia, we will draw a contrasting picture. Of humble origin and black like Leônidas, Domingos was polite, hardworking—very hardworking—and discreet. Differentiating himself in everything from the "Black Diamond", he was seen as a black gentleman, a perfect model of what the First Vargas Government wanted to idealize. However, despite all the respect people had for Domingos, their sympathy was directed toward Leônidas, who was marginalized like him, who was called a nigger and a brat when he did something "wrong", who, despite being directly responsible for many victories of his club, Flamengo, was, of the rubro-negro squad, the player who earned the least. And yet it was Leônidas who often took a seat at the Café Rio Branco, in the heart of downtown Rio de Janeiro, and brought the humble fans together. When it came time to choose their favorite player, the fans had no doubts: it was Leonidas. To show their gratitude to their idol, his admirers even bought packs and packs of cigarettes to give him the prize of the Magnolia Cigarette Contest, a car.

With the 1938 World Cup, the player became a true national hero. And, if the team lost, it wasn't Leônidas' fault but the Brazilian team's; after all, the "Black Diamond" had been the top scorer of the competition and didn't play in the team's only defeat, against the Italians. Upon arriving in Rio de Janeiro, the marines had to hide him to escape the crowd. The fans wanted to touch Leonidas, hug him, get his autograph, carry him on their shoulders. It was the least they could do to thank the hero who made Brazilian football be revered all over the world (Souza, 2008, pp. 117–144).

The sympathy for Leônidas was not only due to his identification with the fans, but also to the vision of Brazilianness he shared with them, in which the ideals of happiness and justice were quite different from the official ones, not found in the world of work, as in the governmental version, but in the world of leisure and social coexistence. When, from 1930 on, an entire political-ideological strategy centered on promoting the value of work and discipline began to take shape, part of the workers began to associate this "new world" offered by the rulers with oppression and displeasure. No matter how hard they worked, the results were always the same: lack of money, lack of housing, scarcity of food, much disrespect and little pleasure. For the workers, the myth of Leonidas represented the opposite. It was transgression to the prevailing order, for not accepting the values and discipline imposed from above, but it was also the hope of rebuilding a better Brazil, identified with leisure and joy (Souza, 2008, pp. 128–140).

Leônidas was definitely not a good example for the authorities. On June 16, 1941, the "Black Diamond" was suspended from the Metropolitan Football Federation and on July 26 of the same year, he was sentenced to prison by the Military Justice under the allegation of having produced a false certificate of reservist. He was imprisoned for eight months.

During his time in prison, Leônidas was replaced on the Flamengo team by Pirilo, a center forward from Rio Grande do Sul who played for Uruguay's Peñarol. A prolific goalscorer, Pirilo arrived at the Gavea club under enormous pressure, with the responsibility of trying to make the fans forget their biggest idol, an almost impossible mission, since every Flamengo fan was in love with Leonidas. Pirilo became the top scorer in the championship with 40 goals, a record. Flamengo president Gustavo de Carvalho seemed to have received a "gift from heaven". It was everything he wanted. After all, imagined Gustavo de Carvalho, Pirilo scored more goals than the "Black Diamond". Big mistake: The fans didn't give a damn about that. The sportive press showed the relationship that Flamenguistas had with the substitute of Leonidas:

> During those eight months, the fans couldn't get the name of Leonidas out of their mouths. His picture hardly appeared in the newspapers, instead Pirilo scored goals in all Flamengo's matches, forty goals in a championship, never had Leonidas scored so many goals in any championship. Pirilo could beat records for goals, it was no use. The fans didn't keep track of the goals Pirilo scored, they kept track of the ones he didn't score, the goals that Leonidas would have scored. The more Pirilo played, the more the fans missed Leonidas. (Rodrigues Filho, 1947, pp. 289–290)

Poor Pirilo!

Fans missed the "Black Diamond". He was the one in prison, suffering who knew what kind of repression. Leônidas' life in Vila Militar, however, was quite different from what the fans could imagine. The player had become an attraction; he was constantly surrounded by soldiers, who asked for his autograph or wanted to play alongside him. On the day he won his freedom—March 24, 1942—Leônidas was given a farewell lunch in gratitude offered by Vila Militar's officers.

After serving his sentence, Leônidas signed a contract with São Paulo Futebol Clube. Despite the prison, the criticism from the press, sports managers and rulers, when the "Black Diamond" arrived in the São Paulo capital the atmosphere was festive. On that day—April 10, 1942—almost ten thousand people stood vigil in front of the train station to welcome him and carry him on their shoulders.

The myth of the hero is representative of fundamental issues of the collectivity; thus, a deep investigation about its construction, its role and its meaning becomes essential to the understanding of a society. Therefore, framing Leonidas as a myth is not due to a simple individual decision. He in fact possessed characteristics that corresponded to some kind of pre-existing longing. Leonidas symbolized a whole collectivity that identified with him and transformed him into a model of behavior for the conduct of men and conferred meaning and value to their own existences (Eliade, 1992, p. 87).

The same can be said for the myths of Pelé and Garrincha. Exactly twenty years after Leonidas had excelled on the French pitch, the national team would once again compete for a world title, this time on Swedish soil. The Brazilians won the World Cup and two heroes—Pelé and Garrincha—became symbols of a generation, in a kind of synthesis of the various representations of national identity that coexisted in the same context.

Pelé symbolized like no one else the ideal of the Brazilian forged in the second half of the twentieth century. In a country with a centuries-old slave-owning past, with an undeclared, hypocritical, and often underestimated racism and a black population in much lower economic conditions than the average national population, the emergence of a black hero, who was proud to be black and who stood out before all the other athletes—Brazilians or not, black or not—represented a true abolition of social slavery.

The ideas of Freyre, that Brazil was a "racial democracy" without racial prejudice, and of the sociologist Florestan Fernandes, that it was possible, in a country undergoing industrialization, the economic and social ascension of workers, and specifically of blacks, had reached common sense and were shared by broad segments of Brazilian society at that time. However, one thing was missing for such hegemony to be consolidated: a proof of coherence. Doubts persisted: How could Brazil be a "racial democracy" if the social and economic differences between whites and non-whites were gigantic? How was social and economic ascension possible in an industrialized Brazil, if in those same industrial cities economic and racial inequalities were even greater?

It was in this context that the myth came in. Pelé was the proof of these theories; the confirmation that blacks could fight for their own life project without suffering prejudice. Pelé showed that, in an increasingly urbanized and industrialized society, it was possible for a black man to ascend socially and economically. After all, he had become very rich and had conquered greater social recognition than any other player of the past or the present. However, to reach this point, it was necessary to behave coherently and have a set of qualities that would make this ascension possible. And Pelé had it. He was an exemplary professional, had an impeccable behavior and trained hard; he was not a spendthrift and did not spend his salary on games of chance. He was an enterprising person, who cared about the future. He was a family boy; he never forgot his closest relatives; he always praised his father and mother. In short, Pelé was a fighter who suffered, fought, and won. He came from a humble cradle, felt the "hardness" of life when he was a child, shined shoes on the street, saw his parents fighting all his life to raise him and support his brothers, but not because of that did he make money the reason for all his actions. He played football because he liked it. And Pelé was, above all, a patriot who was always ready to exalt Brazil and to give his services to the national team. He did not intend to leave the country, despite all the great proposals he was receiving from abroad (Souza, 2018, pp. 113–130).

Pelé was the explanation that was missing, he was the search for "order" so desired by the workers, allowing to give meaning to the act of being Brazilian (Shils, 1992, pp. 394–398). Despite being poor, a boy, living in the countryside, and being black, he had managed to become Pelé because he had organized his life in search of a defined goal. The world might have placed several obstacles in his path, but with persistence, order, and a morally correct posture, he managed to overcome the difficulties.

It is worth noting that, for the workers, the "world of order" highlighted by the myth of Pelé was not the same "world of order" thought by the State and the large commercial press. In both there was the notion of union, obedience and hierarchy. But for the state and the press, these notions were irremediably linked to the disciplining of Brazil and Brazilians as a way to achieve social, economic and technological development. As for the workers, these notions embraced, above all, a moral code of behavior. For them, Pelé was successful because he was a good son, a correct boy, did not drink, did not smoke, was hardworking and obedient. And, therefore, Pelé was a model of behavior for those humble people who suffered with insecurity, poverty and prejudice (Souza, 2018, pp. 113–130).

However, such models of "Brazilian" were multifaceted. The popularity and prestige of Garrincha, at the same time that Pelé was emerging, were indications of this. Unlike "King Pelé", "King Mané" represented a style of football that was considered undisciplined to the point of dribbling around an entire opposing team, without aiming to score a goal. Off the field, Mané dated, hunted birds, frequented bars and played "pelada" (an informal football game). He was also admired for the solidarity with which he treated his "equals"; for not having abandoned his friends; for continuing to live or visit Pau Grande, the locality where he had been raised; for being close to the fans; and, most of all, for keeping a life style associated to the symbols considered of a plebeian culture (Thompson, 1998, p. 19). An example of Garrincha's behavior occurred at the end of 1958. The player decided to help the star Angelita Martinez to promote the carnival parade "Mané Garrincha". The lyrics read (Castro et al., 1959, February 21, p. 21, our translation):

Mané Garrincha, Mané Garrincha,
To this day my chest expands.
Mané who shone there in Sweden,
Mané who was born in Pau Grande.
It's not just coffee,
That we have to sell.
Dribble, dribble, Mané,
For the whole world to see.

"Mané Garrincha" was one of the biggest hits of the 1959 Rio carnival. The player not only helped Angelita turn the song into a hit, but also had a romantic relationship with her, although he was married to Nair. The press of the time did not usually report explicitly on the players' extramarital affairs, which were not few, but the popular quickly understood what was going on between the star and the starlet. The verse "Mané que nasceu em Pau Grande" (Mané who was born in Pau Grande) enabled a phallic interpretation.[4] The song was threatened with censorship, which only increased its success. The music was recorded on disk at the Rádio Nacional, on the program of César de Alencar, and the inspectors of the censorship service stayed on the wire. No one in the auditorium sang "Mané Garrincha" misrepresenting it. And the song passed the test.

Garrincha, despite being married, lived a freedom without guilt in relation to sex. In the eyes of his fans, mainly men, it was as if he had found the very door to paradise (Souza, 2018, pp. 131–148).

In popular comic culture, the material and bodily element is always positivized. Hence the images of the body, of drinking, of food, of the satisfaction of natural needs and of sex life. The representative of the material and bodily principle is neither the isolated biological being nor the selfish bourgeois individual, but the people, a people which in its evolution has constantly grown and renewed itself. That is why the element of bodily and material life is so magnificent, infinite and exaggerated, this exaggeration being positive and affirmative. Thus, its central images are fertility, sex, growth and superabundance, which correspond to the principle of feast, banquet, joy (Bakhtin, 2010, p. 17).

This luxuriant characterization of Garrincha always accompanied him. He had a very strong connection with "the better side of life", with the ludic, with the world of leisure and pleasure. He was always in Pau Grande drinking, hunting birds and fishing. He never left his friends Pincel and Swing, who became constant characters in his adventures narrated·by the press. In Rio, he was always present at parties, carnival balls or bars, usually accompanied by his "girlfriends". And, despite being famous, he kept a simple and unostentatious behavior.

If Pelé was the order, the sense, Garrincha was the pleasure, the passion. But despite being opposites, the myths were not antagonistic, but complementary. It was as if the Brazilian workers had built a bridge between the two extremes, the "world of order" and the "world of pleasure". On this bridge, there were no borders or tolls. They could go from one pole to the other, according to their interests and needs, and as often as they wanted. And the interesting thing was that the extremes of this bridge were flexible and fluid. Often at one end they could get what they were looking for at the other end. They could find pleasure, informality and chaos in the "world of order". And they could find meaning, respect and harmony in the "world of pleasure" (Candido, 1993, pp. 36–37).

In the initial period of development of these popular myths, more or less between the 1958 World Cup and the beginning of 1963, the workers did not necessarily think that the myth of Pelé was antagonistic to the world of leisure, pleasure and even lust, as is clear from the lyrics of the carnival song "Sem mulata é fogo", which said (Galeno, 1963, p. 20, our translation):

---

[4] The literal translation of "Pau Grande" is "Big Stick".

Where is the little brunette
Who was a queen
Of my carnival?
Where is the little blonde,
Very white,
Of the crystal eyes?
Where did our mulatto girl end up
When did she come in with your game?
No blonde and no brunette
People go by,
But without a mulatto girl it's fire!...
Without a mulatto girl you can't get up.
It's a golden team without Mané
And without a mulatto girl you can't get up.
It's a golden team without Pelé
And without a mulatto girl you can't get up.

A world without mulatto women would be like a national team without Garrincha and Pelé. For the workers, the myths of Pelé and Garrincha were not antagonistic; they were complementary and flexible. As the myth of Pelé often visited the world of pleasure and disorder, that of Garrincha could also slip into the opposite world. In the 1962 World Cup, in Chile, it was Garrincha who took the lead, giving order and meaning to the Brazilian team that won the competition.

The myths of Pelé and Garrincha were not static. Order could be present in the world of pleasure and lust. Likewise, disorder could organize and give meaning to a project of greater importance. The apparently hierarchical world revealed itself as essentially subverted when the extremes touched.

Therefore, order and disorder are two aspects of the same phenomenon: that of the Brazilian identity forged by the working class. When we state that the myths of Pelé and Garrincha were, between 1958 and 1963, opposites and complements, we mean that they could be understood as two extreme poles, yet fluid and malleable, of the same road called Brazilian identity. It was on this road, loaded with hopes, desires, interests, fears and insecurities, that Brazilians traveled their lives, based on the circumstances they were experiencing. The workers were bearers of this macunaimic characteristic,[5] for they were able to approach one of the two extremes without necessarily abandoning the opposite side, as the carnival march "Reis do futebol" well showed (Matos & Martucci, 1963, back cover, our translation):

If I was King Pelé
Or King Mané,
I played football
Only among women.

---

[5] Allusion to the main character in the novel *Macunaíma, o herói sem nenhum caráter* (1928), by Mário de Andrade.

It was all women,
Woman, woman, woman.
I passed
With Gina and Bardot.
I dribbled Sofia
To show my worth.
I was having a olé,

Olé, olé, olé.

"King Pelé" and "King Mané": It was these two popular myths that Brazilian workers revered as carnival rulers of the kingdom called "Brazil".

With all this importance, the myths of Pelé and Garrincha became objects of symbolic struggles between different social actors who sought to frame (and/or silence) them to their worldviews and Brazilian identity.

For a large part of the press, such as Mário Filho and the journalist Thomaz Mazzoni, who best represented not the real nation, but the nation that was intended to be built, was Pelé. It was in Pelé that they saw all the characteristics considered ideal of a player who pretended to be the symbol of a nation: He was skillful, had a Brazilian style of playing, had a poor background, was black, and, most of all, was hardworking and disciplined. When it came time to choose the best player not from Brazil, not from those who were still playing, but from the history of the sport, Mazzoni had no doubt, he predicted: Pelé had all the characteristics of the great stars of the past such as Meazza, Puskás and Leandro Andrade. Pelé was the synthesis, he was "football in shorthand". Imagine when Pelé, "God willing, reaches ten or more years in his fabulous career? What a hard work it will be to make statistics of his achievements?" (Mazzoni, 1961, p. 188).

However, in 1962, at the World Cup in Chile, "King Pelé" was injured. Meanwhile, Mané dribbled. Dribbled and won the title of two-time world champion. Garrincha, more than the main player of the national team, was "half of the team": He organized plays, crossed and scored goals. When he returned to Brazil, the tributes focused on him to the detriment of the rest of the team. If Pelé was the "king", Garrincha was now the "king of kings", a title displayed on the banner hanging at the headquarters of his club, Botafogo Futebol e Regatas. How to explain the popularity of an undisciplined man like Garrincha if Brazilians already had a "king"? To reframe them, Mário Filho took up his pencil and wrote, in addition to his sports chronicles, the books *Copa do Mundo, 62* (1962), *Viagem em torno de Pelé* (1963) and, later, the second edition of *O negro no futebol brasileiro* (1964). For the journalist, the explanation was simple: If Garrincha had been called "king", it was because Garrincha had played like Pelé. Garrincha had been Pelé in 1962. But all it took was for Pelé to come back. He came back more "king" than ever. According to him: "Pelé was the king. Never has an idol been better chosen. Or a king to reign in football. The difference between Pelé and Garrincha. Pelé grabbed the crown and put it on his head. Not to show it off: so that nobody would take it off. Garrincha neither" (Rodrigues Filho, 1964, p. 397).

Something similar occurred with the ideologists who worked for the Military Dictatorship (1964–1985). A good example is Otávio Costa, appointed by President Médici to head the Assessoria Especial de Relações Públicas (AERP); there, he sought to broaden the concepts presented by Gilberto Freyre and Mário Filho, of "Brazilianness" and "discipline", adding a "modern" and "technological" bias. Through football, and especially through the performance of the Brazilian team in the 1970 World Cup, held in Mexico, such notions could be consolidated, by unifying the mestizo abilities of the Brazilian player and the acquisition of the most modern techniques of physical education and sports medicine aiming at disciplining the athlete's body. However, for that to happen, it was necessary to frame its main symbol: Pelé.

The team hoped to win the definitive possession of the Jules Rimet Cup in Mexico. It was the first Cup in which the matches were broadcast live on Brazilian television. The squad was made up of players with their hair cut in barrack style, the physical preparation technology was being coordinated by military personnel, the head of the delegation was Brigadier Major Jerônimo Bastos and security was in charge of Major Ipiranga dos Guaranis. Once the sporting achievement was consolidated, the government exploited the title in every possible way, seeking to link football with the "unity of the nation" and with the economic euphoria Brazilians were experiencing. Both in films commissioned by the government and in posters, newspapers, radio and television, the figure of Pelé was recurrent. He was more than a player; he was the great hero of a campaign; he was the greatest symbol of a nation that was intended to be built by associating tradition to modernity.

The myth of Pelé was going through a process of resignification. The constant framing by the great commercial press and the State imposed a linear narrative of success. Moreover, they were narratives based almost exclusively on his professional aspects. Private life was progressively obscured. Few reports of the period highlighted Pelé's family life with his wife Rosemeri and children. The identity contradictions of the myth were not problematized: the few references about his business life, the silence about his extramarital life, the inexistence of sufferings and tragedies. One could hardly see the presence of friends enjoying some kind of leisure. The narratives were restricted to commenting on his sportive achievements. And to prove that Pelé was the greatest in the world, there were always many numbers, many goals, many titles, many statistical data. And when they tried to explain how he had achieved all those records, the answer was always the same: a lot of work, dedication, discipline, physical preparation and effort. This style of reporting became commonplace.

The discourse of Pelé as a mythical signifier and organizer of the "Brazilian being", as Mário Filho used to do, still existed; however, now on a more abstract level. Pelé was still the myth that made it possible for workers to stop being "mongrels". Only that, at that moment, he was no longer supported by his daily life, by his contact with his family members. He was an exiled myth, without concreteness, not experienced, without justification (Pollak, 1989, p. 9).

If, with the myth of Pelé, the way found by the State and the great commercial press was his framing, the opposite happened with the myth of Garrincha. After all, his characteristics were too irreconcilable with the official ideology. If the State and the press couldn't frame the myth of Garrincha, then they began to highlight not his playful and solidary side, but his dark, decadent side, full of personal scandals. His extramarital affairs, the children out of wedlock, the separation from his wife Nair, with whom he had eight daughters, the relationship with the singer Elza Soares, the athlete's physical decline, the financial difficulties, the naivety with which he managed his professional life, the sports sunset, the oblivion and, finally, the alcoholism (Souza, 2018, pp. 260–278).

They tried to silence the myth of Garrincha or associate him with values loaded with negativity. But, despite the attempts, the workers didn't forget him. On January 20, 1983, Garrincha died in a hospital in Rio de Janeiro, victim of extensive lesions in the liver and pancreas caused by excessive consumption of alcohol. When they learned of his death, the workers were the first to pay their respects to their hero. A hero who had lived like them, who had suffered the same prejudices and who appreciated the same values associated with the good side of life, the good side of being Brazilian.

The wake, organized by the singer Agnaldo Timóteo, took place at the Maracanã stadium. The fans, outraged, looked for culprits. Many harshly criticized the absence of comrades from the glory days, and especially criticized Pelé—a hero with exactly the opposite destiny. The insults were countless.

On the following day, the body was taken to the village of Pau Grande, where the star was born and raised and where he would now celebrate his funeral mass. From the chapel of Pau Grande, the body was taken to the nearby cemetery of Inhomirim. Thousands of workers went there. Humble people, dressed in simple clothes, who picked flowers on the flowerbeds to revere the popular myth. They interrupted their appointments, took the suburban trains, the public buses or any other form of transportation and headed to the village to pay a last tribute to the star. Among the several posters and banners carried by the popular, one of them said: "I came back, here is my place" (Souza, 2018, p. 272).

The workers were realizing what some historians of religion call the "religious experience of autochthony", when people feel they are "people of the place". And this feeling of cosmic structure goes far beyond family and ancestral solidarity (Eliade, 1992, p. 118). I could also add that this identification is not with the village of Pau Grande. This "feeling of place" refers to all the villages spread throughout Brazil, in the little squares, in the bars, in the suburbs, in the favelas and on the plantations, spaces where the people managed to create a common custom of solidarity and simplicity. In these places, it is only possible to have fun and suffer viscerally and collectively. The separation between public and private is fluid. Formality is nonexistent. And the disciplining of life is never welcome. It is these workers, coming from the various poor villages scattered around the country, who have gone to pay a last tribute to the one they saw as a model.

At the cemetery, more riots and protests: It was necessary to pay a fee of a little over 4 thousand cruzeiros to be given authorization for the burial. Agnaldo Timóteo faced the situation and paid the amount. There was no place for so many people. About ten thousand people were in the place. New problems arose; actually, not so new: old acquaintances, people and military police had a disagreement. The police tried to avoid the great influx of public to the cemetery, isolating the area. However, in a more creative move, just like Garrincha did with his opponents' schemes and tactics, the people dodged the police by entering through a low cemetery wall.

There were people on graves, hanging from trees or on the roofs of nearby houses. The sacrifice was great. Because of the intense heat, some fainted with suspected heatstroke. Several statues and crosses that were on graves were knocked down. Some of those present were even trampled in the tumult. The people tried to carry the coffin, but the police did not allow it. At the moment of the burial, the grave had to be widened in haste, with the help of the gravediggers' picks, because the coffin was too big for the size of the space. More commotion: Police and people, now allied, used even their hands to enlarge the hole. Finally the coffin was lowered into the grave, among people singing the national anthem and others, frustrated with the tragic fate of their idol, vented their emotions by cursing Pelé.

The insults and curses to Pelé were a constant during the wake, the funeral procession, and the funeral: "al, al, al, Pelé is a rascal!" On the other hand, the greetings to Mané were simple: "king, king, king, Garrincha is our king!" Another constant was the national anthem, always present, at the wake in Maracanã, the mass in the chapel in Pau Grande and the burial in the small cemetery in Inhomirim. They shouted "Garrincha" and "Brazil" with the same strength and emotion with which they shouted, before, the victories of the Brazilian team in World Cups (Souza, 2018, pp. 273–274).

It was a concrete burial, but also symbolic, in which the main characteristics of popular action were present. The counter theater of the workers accompanying the mortal remains of their hero through the suburbs of Rio, the allegorization of the procession by means of banners and posters, the national anthem being sung, showing the identification of the myth with the Brazilian nation. The anonymous popular outburst, after the silencing imposed for years, the swearing against models of "Brazil" and "Brazilian people" imposed by other social actors. The quick direct action in occupying public spaces in the wake, the funeral procession, the chapel in Pau Grande and the cemetery in Inhomirim, the anonymous graffiti spread throughout the city and the suburbs of Rio de Janeiro. And, finally, the burial: the hero returning to his people, returning to his land. The grave being dug by humble people, with their own hands. It was a tribute that the simple worker paid to the one who had been an exemplary model of Brazilian (Souza, 2018, pp. 269–272).

* * *

National identity was associated here with a process of hegemony construction. To prevail, it has to be renewed, recreated, defended and modified. But it can also suffer resistance and alterations. In this "tug-of-war" defined and limited by the dominant class, there will always be the possibility of workers forging a space of creation, appropriation and resistance in relation to the values imposed from above (Thompson, 1998, p. 20). In the period under analysis, if, on one hand, the State and the great commercial press saw discipline as a positive contribution of sports to the consolidation of the Brazilian nation; on the other hand, we could see, through the analysis of popular myths of the period, that a significant part of the workers evaluated negatively the disciplinary worldview. They preferred to appreciate aspects of football and of national identity that affirmed notions associated with order and justice, but also with pleasure, solidarity and joy.

National identity is a representation that carries varied meanings, disputed by different groups that organize themselves to take possession of the most appropriate meaning for their group and its legitimating effects. The projects of nation and national identity are always plural. No matter how much a given group may hold economic and political prominence over others, it will never be the only one to provide an answer to its most vital questions. Other social actors will also forge different meanings about what they consider a nation, a people or any other subject.

References

Bakhtin, M. (2010). *A cultura popular na Idade Média e no Renascimento: o contexto de François Rabelais*. Hucitec.
Candido, A. (1993). Dialética da malandragem. In A. Candido, *O discurso e a cidade* (pp. 19–54). Duas Cidades.
Castro, J., Baptista, W., & Macedo, N. (1959). Mané Garrincha. *Revista Do Rádio, 492*, 21.
Eliade, M. (1992). *O sagrado e o profano: a essência das religiões*. Martins Fontes.
Freyre, G. (1955, June 25). Ainda a propósito do futebol brasileiro. *O Cruzeiro, 27*(37), 22.
Galeno, R. (1963). Sem mulata é fogo. *O Samba. Parada de Sucessos: Carnaval* [magazine supplement], *6*(26), 20.
Gomes, A. C. (1994). *A invenção do trabalhismo*. Relume-Dumará.
Hobsbawm, E. (1990). *Nações e nacionalismo desde 1780*. Paz e Terra.
Lopes, J. S. L. (1994). A vitória do futebol que incorporou a pelada: A invenção do jornalismo esportivo e a entrada dos negros no futebol brasileiro. *Revista USP*, (22), 64–83. https://doi.org/10.11606/issn.2316-9036.v0i22p64-83.
Lyra Filho, J. (1941). *A função social dos desportos* [Unpublished manuscript]. Ministério de Educação e Saúde.
Matos, J., & Martucci, E. (1963). Reis do futebol. *A Modinha Popular: Carnaval, 2*(9), back cover.
Mazzoni, T. (1961). Pelé e os outros. In E. A. Nascimento, *Eu sou Pelé* (pp. 187–191). Francisco Alves.
Moura, G. A. (1998). *O Rio corre para o Maracanã*. Ed. FGV.
Pereira, L. A. M. (2000). *Footballmania: Uma história social do futebol no Rio de Janeiro (1902–1938)*. Nova Fronteira.
Pollak, M. (1989). Memória, esquecimento, silêncio. *Estudos Históricos, 2*(3), 3–15. https://bibliotecadigital.fgv.br/ojs/index.php/reh/article/view/2278/1417.
Portelli, A. (1998). O massacre de Civitella Val di Chiana. In M. Ferreira, & J. Amado (Eds.), *Usos e abusos da história oral* (pp. 103–130). Ed. FGV.
Rodrigues Filho, M. (1946, September 21). Da primeira fila: O negro no football brasileiro (66). *O Globo* (p. 12).
Rodrigues Filho, M. (1947). *O negro no foot-ball brasileiro*. Pongetti.
Rodrigues Filho, M. (1964). *O negro no futebol brasileiro* (2nd ed.). Civilização Brasileira.
Shils, E. (1992). *Centro e periferia*. (J. H. de Freitas, Trans.). Difel.
Souza, D. A. (2008). *O Brasil entra em campo! Construções e reconstruções da identidade nacional no Brasil (1930-1947)*. Annablume.

Souza, D. A. (2018). *Pra frente, Brasil! Do Maracanazo aos mitos de Pelé e Garrincha, a dialética da ordem e da desordem (1950-1983)*. Intermeios.

Thompson, E. P. (1998). *Costumes em comum: estudos sobre a cultura popular tradicional*. Companhia das Letras.

Chapter 8
Order and Progress on the Grandstands: Sports Journalism and the Genesis of Uniformed Football Fans During the Political Regime of the Estado Novo (1937–1945)

Bernardo Buarque de Hollanda and Aníbal Chaim

This chapter discusses the first model of "uniformed fans"—hereafter UFs—in Brazil, forged in the city of São Paulo in the early 1940s, having as background the third phase of the so-called Vargas era (Chaim, 2018). The historical period, known as "Estado Novo" [New State] period (1937–1945), emerged from a coup given by President Vargas himself, after a provisional government (1930–1934) and a constitutional interregnum (1934–1937). Directly linked to the clubs of their choice, the supporters associations that were formed in this context had a specific performance and mission to fulfill in the stands.

The guidelines for configurating game cheers, by adopting musical bands in the stands of São Paulo stadiums, are related, in turn, to the fan contests conceived and promoted by newspapers of the time, particularly those established in the regulations of the weekly newspaper *A Gazeta Esportiva* is directed by the chronicler Thomaz Mazzoni (1900–1975) and published on Mondays since December 24, 1928.

With 16 pages on average, the supplement was linked to the evening newspaper *A Gazeta*, owned by director-owner Cásper Líbero (1883–1943), and began circulating as a separate daily from October 10, 1947, being discontinued in print only in 2001, when it began to be broadcast on an Internet Web site (Toledo, 2012).

A Gazeta was considered one of the most modern newspapers in Latin America at the time, following the world standards of newspaper companies, with the acquisition of machinery, trichrome, color photoengraving, and printing that reached 120 thousand copies (Hime, 2005). In the intergroup contests, the requirements for electing the "best supporters" involved what the developers and judges understood as discipline, fair play, respect for the opposing team's supporters, and cordiality, among other terms of the time. Such criteria, along with technical aspects such as evaluating

B. B. de Hollanda (✉) · A. Chaim
Getulio Vargas Foundation, Rio de Janeiro, Brazil

the number of uniformed supporters, the sound volume of the musical band, and the size of the mosaics, determined who the winning supporters would be.

By consulting the periodicals of the period, we notice that the newspaper was not only the creator and sponsor of this type of contest—there were others, such as the election of the "most beloved" club of São Paulo, by readers' votes (*A Gazeta Esportiva*, 1943h, September 23, p. 3)—, but also the evaluator of the fans' performances, through a jury body defined by the newspaper. This allowed to shape and direct the behavior of the evaluated groups according to the values and interests that suited the media.

Gathered under the denomination "organized"—the most common term in the Rio de Janeiro press—and "uniformed"—the most common characterization employed by the São Paulo newspapers—, the segments of supporters became protagonists and participants of the sporting spectacle, which was definitively professionalized throughout the 1940s, on the condition of being shaped in the manner prescribed by the contest organizers, indicating their attachment and conformity to the sporting ideology proclaimed by the Estado Novo regime.

We aim to show how the model of football associations that emerged in the wake of the Estado Novo, a historical period with wide scope in historiography (Oliveira et al., 1982)—a historiographical object that extends to physical education (Parada, 2009) and football in Brazil during that regime (Negreiros, 1998; Souza, 2008)—, was congruent with the sporting ideals coined by João Lyra Filho (1906–1988).

This character, originally linked to the Botafogo club, was a sports chronicler and the jurist responsible for instituting and presiding over the National Sports Council (CND, hereafter), a key body of the time, implemented in 1941 (see Fig. 8.1). As an entity subordinated to the Ministry of Education and Public Health, known under the acronym *MES,* the CND started to centralize, verticalize, and control all instances of the country's sports policy, taking over clubs, associations, leagues, federations, and confederations.

Within football and sports audiences in particular, its stadiums were increasingly larger and more imposing, being able to do justice to the demand for popularization and professionalization of this sport (Leite Lopes, 1994). One could say that the uniformed fans linked to the clubs, encouraged by the managers and emulated by the sports press, whose mercantilist nature was aligned with the corporativist logic that distinguished the Vargas government from the 1930 revolution, were in line with the operational unity of this football system.

One of its most obvious dimensions was the unitary and, so to speak, *corporate* character underlying it. Similar to the corporate trade union structure, ruled by the principle of a single trade union organized according to professional categories, football at the time instituted one—and only one—fan club, which in turn was led by a single leader. This individual led the territory of the stands and was recognized as a reference both by supporters and club managers and even by the police, with whom he used to collaborate and contribute to prevent riots (Hollanda, 2008). Given this purpose, we divided the present chapter into three sections. In the first, we present João Lyra Filho's writings, published in 1941, on sports crowds and the beneficial role of collective music in controlling the masses. The second section focus on the

Fig. 8.1 Seated, jurist João Lyra Filho (left) and Minister Gustavo Capanema (front), during the installation of the National Sports Council (CND), on 7/7/1941. *Source* FGV-CPDoc

work of sports chronicler Thomaz Mazzoni and show how, by being affiliated to the Estado Novo's centralized soccer project, the editor-in-chief of *A Gazeta Esportiva* encouraged the presence of uniformed fans in the stands of São Paulo stadiums in the early 1940s. In the third and last part, we develop, based on journalistic reports from that period, how fan club competitions were implemented and how the leadership of these groupings gains importance in conducting these first intergroup competitions.

The Spirit of Sports Laws: João Lyra Filho, the CND, and Professional Football

João Lyra Filho was a jurist from Paraiba, living in Rio de Janeiro; a professor who would become rector of the Guanabara State University in the 1960s. During the Estado Novo period, he was a trusted friend of Gustavo Capanema (1900–1985), influential minister of education and health who directed the *MES* during the Getúlio Vargas government, from 1934 to 1945. A fact rarely emphasized by football historiography is that Lyra Filho, at the head of the CND, was the one who provided subsidies not only for sports legislation, but also for idealizing the model of the first uniformed football fans in Brazil. Such model would be materialized in São Paulo, by the enthusiastic initiative of *A Gazeta Esportiva*, amid the creation of physical education colleges in the country.

Lyra Filho, author of dozens of books on sports law, understood that the passion of football fans should be the object of attention of the authorities. It was a matter to be taken very seriously, under penalty of causing harmful effects to public order, to professional football, and to the State, the one in charge of intervening in sports and building sports venues as of 1940. The milestone of this cycle of public sports venues was the inauguration of the Pacaembu municipal stadium, considered a "São Paulo monument" to football, capable of holding up to 70 thousand spectators:

> When crowds gather in sporting spectacles, they find a moment of evasion, capable of stripping them of even their own instinct, imposing on the State the duty to regulate their social manifestations, through educational processes, that do not distort the sense of the guidelines it proposes. (Lyra Filho, 1941, p. 11) (our translation)

Lyra Filho raises the concern about the federal government's role of observing the behavior of crowds in professional football matches in the country. The president of the CND understood that targeted action by the State on this issue could prevent the recurrence of disturbances in stadiums and ensure that the expected public order with the gathering of thousands of club fans would prevail.

Since football is a spectacle that produces collective emotions, the state had a direct interest in observing its effects. According to Lyra Filho, government representatives should be concerned about the threats to discipline that weighed on the sporting audiences:

> The gesture is the vehicle of collective emotion. The state is interested in regulating the meaning of this gesture, in disciplining the emotions it [the gesture] produces, so that it may serve as a stimulus to the energies necessary to life and not as a negative force. (Lyra Filho, 1941, p. 5, our translation)

As his contemporary, maestro Heitor Villa-Lobos (1887–1959), promoter of civic ceremonies—youth, children, and school—, Lyra Filho understood the pedagogical and virtuous role of music, expressed through choral singing, choirs, and their sonority. His pedagogy infused spirits with a calming propensity, with cohesive effects not only on children and young people, but also on this type of football aficionado. With distinct focuses, both Villa-Lobos and Lyra Filho believed in the moral and civic renewal of the masses through music. Lyra Filho, in particular, posited that promoting music among sporting audiences could produce a calming, ordering, and, consequently, disciplining effect on spectators. He believed in the "beneficial influence of music as a resource capable of calming and rectifying in the minds of the people the inspirations of instinct, soul, and spirit" (Lyra Filho, 1941, p. 49, our translation). In his opinion, the efficiency to control the manifestations of the masses, whose disruptive potential has been the target of fear in the long history of humanity, according to the acute reflection of Bulgarian writer Elias Canetti (Canetti, 1995), involved incorporating the virtues of music. Musical entertainment should therefore be regularly adopted in sports venues:

> In the half-time of sporting spectacles, music is a break for the soul, which is not counterfeited, which expands, which opens itself to the suggestion of calm, of contentment, of the enveloping enchantment of the spirit. ...] to undo the provocations of instinct, to attenuate the force of the waves that crash in language and in the manifestations of the explosive, the indignant, the rebellious, susceptible of generalizing morbid states of passion, music is the prestige that sweetens, softens, enraptures, makes the soul rise to the projection where it can embrace for the good. ...] this is why we would admit the necessity of adding to sporting spectacles the concourse of music, which shakes the nerves, lightens the charged atmospheres, which fills with frenzy the terrified anxieties in prelude to revolts, conflicts and riots. (Lyra Filho, 1941, p. 11) (our translation)

The quote above comes from a book-conference published in 1941, the same year the CND was created, in which the author made considerations about the role of music in stadiums.

According to the bachelor's conception, head of the most important sports entity of the period, the state needed to set up a corporate structure also in the football stands, by creating what he entitled the "crowd leaders." Drawing on the analogy with classical music and the performing arts, these leaders would function similarly to a conductor before the orchestra. They would be an authority figure among the fans, able to coordinate and channel the activities of the audience during a match.

The leader, a charismatic being by principle, would have the role of moralizing and containing the passions of the crowd attending the sporting spectacles, avoiding chaos and leading it to a uniform behavior. This arrangement is better developed in the following passage by Lyra Filho: "The gathered crowd, exploding in uniform manifestation, contained by the feeling of discipline, would give beauty and life to the spectacles, besides order" (Lyra Filho, 1941, p. 12, our translation).

Based on the above, we observe that music would operate inside stadiums of ever larger proportions, built in huge structures of reinforced concrete, as a framing element for the masses. The responsible grouping would gravitate around fan-leaders, a character endowed with charisma and charged with the mission of providing disciplined and "uniform" support to the club of their preference.

> On one side, at the leader's signal, a partisan crowd, letting itself be carried away by the rhythm of the same gestures, the same palpitations, the same manifestations in favor of its club. In retaliation, on the other side, the same picture, setting up a fan's fight, each of the currents disputing to be the most rightful, most precise, most alive, in the way of imagining and defining the honest victory of one fan over the other. (Lyra Filho, 1941, p. 12) (our translation)

The adoption of musical instruments would give "assistance" (Toledo, 2000) to the shared gestures and convergent manifestations. Lyra Filho assumed that the efficient action of a leader would lead to a uniformed behavior of the audience until then spontaneously gathered. This would produce a virtuous circle, with an orderly and dilated chain reaction. The project would suit the purposes of the state, since with this figure whose role would be to coordinate the great collectivities in sports spectacles, the government could exert some degree of influence over these masses.

Lyra Filho's goal was that each group of fans, representing their respective clubs, would be identified by a leader. Through a mimicking process, during professional football matches, these supporters, ruled by a leader and galvanized by collective music, would face each other in the stands as the players in the field. He proposed to extend to the stands the criteria of "fair play," with its format of loyalty and discipline applied to the game.

The project consisted, therefore, in submitting fans to the authorities responsible for the spectacle and promoting a popular manifestation that, if efficiently conducted, could become even more beautiful and showy than the football match itself. For such, this manifestation should be cordial and regulated, so its first objective is to ensure the fans' discipline in supporting the club and, secondly, to achieve a sporting victory on the field. Having seen above how the Estado Novo project was outlined to conform the crowds in sports, the next topic discusses how, based on the principles of discipline conceived by the CND president in 1941, sports journalism of that decade will be a key mediator in creating a model of supporters congruent with those same disciplinary devices.

Body & Soul of Sports: Thomaz Mazzoni and The Ideology of the Estado Novo

Lyra Filho's propositions are inscribed in the context of a dictatorial regime—the Estado Novo. By the symbolism of burning state flags, Varga's Estado Novo suspended the guarantees of the 1934 Constitution, prevented the elections planned for the next four years (1938), and instituted a discretionary period of almost a decade in Brazil, in the mid of a world convulsed by the Second World War (1939–1945).

A few months before the publication of the propaedeutic book *A função social dos desportos*, the first of a series of books on anthropology, sociology, and sports law in the country, a prolific work that would last until the 1970s, the Vargas government had already launched legislation whose intent was to direct the political content of the artistic, cultural, and sports manifestations held on Brazilian soil.

Such legislation was enacted with Decree-Law No. 1,915 (issued on December 27, 1939), responsible for establishing the Department of Press and Propaganda (DIP). This Decree-Law attributed to the DIP (presided over by Lourival Fontes) the role of "censoring theater, cinema, recreational, and sports functions of any nature" (Decree-Law No. 1939, Article 2, paragraph b).

During the Estado Novo, the censorship agency extended its repressive actions (Fausto, 2006) to the communication and entertainment systems, with the support of police chief Filinto Müller, a notorious integralist sympathizer. Repression ranged from prohibiting the content of carnival marches to vetoing news from sectors of the mainstream press, with the invasion of the editorial staff of newspapers such as the traditional *O Estado de S. Paulo* and the exile of its owner, Júlio de Mesquita.

The DIP was the main vehicle for the publicity and propagandistic affirmation (Capelato, 1998) of the Estado Novo values. To achieve this end, it subsidized newspapers, made posters, spread its doctrine in primers, disseminated its image in newsreels, and used radio broadcasts, such as the daily official program *"Hora do Brasil,"* which put into contact, without intermediaries, the head of the nation, and the mass of the population.

On the international level, despite its nationalist rhetoric, the period cultivated the precepts of the "good neighbor policy" with the USA, by the artistic and cultural dissemination of Brazil's image abroad, and, correspondingly, the assimilation of US mass culture, recognized in the emblematic "American way of life," amplified in the imagery of comic books and Hollywood films that arrived in the country. In this period, the regime oscillated between flirtations with the Axis countries, supporters of Nazi-fascism, and policies of alignment with Pan-Americanism, promoting a march to the Brazilian West, reissued by technicians, ideologists, and bureaucrats of the Estado Novo, to populate the Brazilian Midwest (Pandolfi, 1999).

Regarding football, it was during the Estado Novo that the Brazilian national team achieved international visibility and projected the country's image, thanks in particular to its captivating performance in the 1938 World Cup in France. The nation wanted to present itself in an organic and united manner, bringing together, in the world of football, players and officials, just as, in the world of work, workers and industrialists cooperated. In 1938, the national team finished third in the World Cup, a feat that was much celebrated in the country. Of black and working class origin, Leônidas da Silva, a Flamengo player who would later be transferred to São Paulo in 1942, was the top scorer in the World Cup and acclaimed as a national idol. According to historian Boris Fausto:

> Although Getúlio did not like football, he and his entourage were aware of the popular enthusiasm for this sport and mass spectacle. Thus, Brazil's presence in the 1938 World Cup was emphasized in radios, newspapers and magazines, and Lourival Fontes, who would be responsible for creating the DIP the following year, was chosen president of the delegation that went to France. Getúlio received the players before their departure for Europe, reminding them that "their mission is not only sportive in nature, but involves the fulfillment of a civic duty". (Fausto, 2006, p. 126) (our translation)

Historian Melina Pardini states that the national interest in the World Cup caused the DIP to install loudspeakers in various locations in Rio de Janeiro to follow the games, adding:

> During this championship, the Department of Press and Propaganda (DIP) linked the figure of Getúlio Vargas to national football as a way to create a sympathetic aura to the government, valuing football victories as if they were victories of the nation itself. In this context, the president's daughter, Alzira Vargas, was the godmother of the Brazilian team during the 1938 World Cup, sending several motivational telegrams to the team. (Pardini, 2009, p. 30) (our translation)

Almost two years after creating the DIP, more precisely in April 1941, through Decree No. 3,199,[1] the discretionary government created the CND, an entity whose

---

[1] Original text of decree-law 3,199 of 1941. Available at <www2.camara.leg.br/legin/fed/declei/1940-1949/decreto-lei-3199-14-abril-1941-413238-publicacaooriginal-1-pe.html>.

role was to organize the practice of sports events in the Brazilian territory, aligning them with the interests of its state. As historian Hilário Franco Jr. argues, its legislative and bureaucratic apparatus was:

> Linked to the Ministry of Education, it subordinated the CBD and regional federations and had the power to supervise, regulate and organize all sports in the country. Its goals were sports modernization and its use for the regime's legitimacy. Or rather, sports modernization for what seemed to be the modernization of the state and society. (Franco Jr., 2007, p. 81) (our translation)

In its text, Decree No. 3,199 provided for the exercise of control and the strategy of state intervention over the organization and logistics of sporting events to be held in the national territory, but also pointed to the censorship of the sports press itself. The possibility of the sports press also undergoing the sieve of state representatives suggested the end of editorial autonomy, a significant limitation to the daily newspapers' freedom of communication. This was thus a concrete concern of most sectors of the Brazilian sports media, except for Thomaz Mazzoni, who, in the same year the CND was created, published a book in tune with the ideals of the Estado Novo.

Author of a series of sports almanacs, football novels, and books on the history of football in Brazil, Mazzoni, carried out a sort of doctrinal work to corroborate the Vargas regime (Silva, 2010). One of his milestones was the release of the book *O esporte a serviço da pátria (Sport at the service of the nation)*, which gained prominence for the content of the criticism directed at the amateur mentality and lack of organization of several segments of the sports world. According to Mazzoni, players were always focused on personal interests to the detriment of the collective spirit and ended up confusing the public with the private.

In the following excerpt, the object of criticism is his fellow journalists:

> To this [press], exclusively to this [press], belongs the double degeneration of the sporting spirit of our people through so many years of poisoning the sports public mood, fully contaminating it with factious passion, far, far from the true sports virtues. This has been the work of criminal irresponsibility, to the detriment of our sporting youth, to the total harm of the sporting ideal and cause of Brazil! (Mazzoni, 1941, p. 89) (our translation)

Mazzoni was editor-in-chief of *A Gazeta Esportiva*, the sports newspaper with the largest circulation in the city of São Paulo. Appearing in the late 1920s, it circulated weekly until 1947 as an insert of *A Gazeta*, periodical owned by businessman Cásper Líbero. The latter, initially opposed to the 1930 revolution, participating in the 1932 Constitutionalist revolution, would soon align himself with the Vargas era *establishment*.

Of nationalist inclination, owner of a journalistic complex that combined radio and newspaper, Líbero had good transit with politicians, club managers, and the CBD itself. From the late 1940s, *A Gazeta Esportiva* would be sold autonomously, although still under Thomaz Mazzoni's direction, after Cásper Líbero died in August 1943 in a plane crash.

An Italian emigrant, Mazzoni was openly in favor of state control over sports, inspired in turn by the sports management model implemented by Mussolini in Italy. The journalist understood the practice of sports as an element of moral formation of the fans, as did Cásper Líbero, who emphasized the press' power of influence "over crowds, directing them, guiding them," which led him to create sports competitions such as the São Silvestre race, among others (Hime, 2005).

Mazzoni's ideal in favor of sports morality led him to go beyond the pages of the newspaper and produce a series of apologetic books on the intervening role of the state in the sports environment. In 1939, for example, he published *Problemas e aspectos do nosso futebol,* in which he pointed out the deficiencies of the national football structure and recommended a set of corrective measures. His most recurrent criticism concerned the lack of a national vision and the persistence of the club spirit.

For this editor and chronicler, who used to sign his texts with the pseudonym *Olimpicus,* "clubism"—precisely the lack of a broader vision—consisted of the partial or factious position cultivated by most Brazilian sports leaders. Besides partiality, Mazzoni also addressed the sensationalism practiced by a significant portion of his colleagues in the sports press.

In Mazzoni's perspective, harmony in sports, compromised by certain undisciplined and sectarian attitudes, should be regulated not only by *governing bodies*—CBD and state federations—, but also by the media, especially newspapers and radio. In *O esporte a serviço da pátria,* the journalist outlines the following diagnosis:

> The cursed trinity of Brazilian sports has been composed by dissension, indiscipline and *clubismo.* [...] since the birth of sports in Brazil, its history is full of chapters of dissension, consequence of poor spirit of association and degenerated discipline. Eliminating the split is a very simple mission, since being official and recognized only one entity, for each modality, no other split will be possible in the future, for petty personal issues or for the clubs' ambition. Outside each official entity, no activity will be allowed. Thus, the dissension valve, guilty of so many evils for Brazilian sports, is automatically closed. (Mazzoni, 1941, pp. 27–28) (our translation)

Mazzoni's enthusiasm for the creation of a National Sports Council and for the censorship of sports press media becomes understandable in light of the following passage:

> With this new achievement of the government [reference to the creation of the CND], Brazil will be proud to be the first nation in South America to give sports an official function [...] It is easy to understand what it represents for Brazilian sports to be integrated into the laws and the spirit of the Estado Novo. It shall be placed at the service of the Homeland, that's all! [...] The clubs shall obey, not command. The entities must discipline, direct and guide the respective sports; the selected managers must be servants of the collectivity, they will be administrators and technicians, not simple lay politicians. Hierarchy, discipline, order, idealism, responsibility, and competence, this is what shall ensure the officialization for the national sport. (Mazzoni, 1941, pp. 16–17) (our translation)

The convergence of Mazzoni's ideals with the principles advocated by the Estado Novo contributed for A Gazeta Esportiva to end up becoming an informal official vehicle for the Brazilian sports press in the first half of the 1940s. More precisely, in March 1943, following the guidelines defended by João Lyra Filho in his 1941 book, the newspaper sponsored the first "Fan Contest," whose proposal was to highlight the fans' performance in the stadiums, since they too could put themselves at the "service of the Homeland."

During the beginning of the 1943 Paulista championship, the newspaper published the rules of the competition between uniformed fans and the scoring criteria. At the end of the tournament, the Paulista Football Federation would be responsible for proclaiming the champion fan club, by a total of five criteria assessed per match, each consisting of different points: "discipline," "enthusiasm," "chorus and organization," "harmony and originality," and "number of components."

Once discussed the relation between the ideology of the Estado Novo and the thought of editor-in-chief Thomaz Mazzoni, this third and most important part of this chapter will focus on how the proposed competition was materialized and how this project consolidated the presence of uniformed fans in the city of São Paulo from 1943 on.

A Gazeta Esportiva and the Promotion of São Paulo's Uniformed Fans

Football in the 1940s was already professionalized in Brazil and attracted to the stadiums thousands of "assistants"—term used in the early twentieth century to refer to fans (Malaia, 2011)—from all social strata. But the UFs at the time were mostly composed of members of the respective social clubs. The first known fan club is Grêmio São-Paulino, founded in 1939 and renamed the following year Torcida Uniformizada do São Paulo (Tusp).

The uniformed supporter's profile indicates the majority composition of the club members, a social filter for participating in this type of association. Tusp's founders, for instance, were benefactor Manoel Raymundo Paes de Almeida and lieutenant—later general and vice-governor of the state of São Paulo—Porfírio da Paz (Viveiros, 2010). Another important leader was Laudo Natel, who would become a prominent businessman and politician, state governor, and an active figure in building the Cícero Pompeu de Toledo stadium, the popular *Morumbi,* between the 1950s and 1970s.

According to Manoel Raymundo Paes de Almeida's recollections, Tusp's membership profile was:

> Polite people, who wore a white shirt, with the SPFC emblem with the inscription "Grêmio São-Paulino." They made shows and allegories that served as attraction for the matches. And when the players entered the field, they were greeted with confetti and serpentine streamers. Today this no longer exists, only fights, discussions, aggressions. (Viveiros, 2010, p. 119) (our translation)

The excerpt above makes it clear that these supporters associations fit the guidelines outlined by Lyra Filho in his 1941 booklet. As we have pondered in another opportunity, regarding the leaderships established in the stands with the emergence of the uniformed fans (UFs):

> The leader stood out in the stands by their seriousness and commitment, a regular and traditional figure in the matches, with an ability to communicate and a leadership considered innate, recognized by the fans, officials and the police in coordinating the encouragement to the players. (Hollanda, 2008, p. 103) (our translation)

This recognition of the leaders by police officers, officials, and other supporters is evidence of the framing role played by them in the early 1940s. An example of the propaganda made by the newspaper *A Gazeta Esportiva* about the UFs, in their capacity as promoters of good behavior by fans in the stands, can be found in an article written about the Corinthians' UF. On that occasion, the newspaper interviewed its leader, known by the popular nickname Tantã:

> Uniformed fans add a touch of beauty and elegance to our football. They decorate the fields, contribute to the education of supporters, and are useful organizations for the clubs. [...] In the brave Corinthians group, respect for discipline must be strictly cultivated. A single gesture incompatible with its purpose will cause its member to be suspended or excluded. (*A Gazeta Esportiva*, 1941, November 1, p. 10) (our translation)

Tantã said in 1941 that "elegance" and "discipline" were key elements for a member's permanence in the association's ranks. The report also stated that this leadership had no tolerance for bad behavior among members.

His figure helps us understand the structure of an organized fan club in the 1940s: as a *leader of* Corinthians fans, Tantã was a member of the club, a factor that set him apart from the mass of fans in the stands. His mission was to set an example and motivate the fans, i.e., all those who went to the stadiums, even if they had no official ties with the club, a fact that had become increasingly common during the amateur period in the 1920s.

Besides being a reference to the thousands of fans gathered in the stadiums, Tantã was also responsible for ensuring the "good behavior" of the hundreds of members affiliated to his fan club, having the authority to exclude any fan-members caught in misconduct or indiscipline.

Anthropologist Luiz Henrique de Toledo states that in the 1940s, not only the leaders, but most of the members of the uniformed supporters' groups in the city of São Paulo—the audience to which chronicler Thomaz Mazzoni was addressing—could be profiled as follows: "middle-class youths, mostly members of the clubs themselves, whose supporters' activities added to the interests and aspirations of the directors of the referred sports associations" (Toledo, 2000, p. 251).

Fan associations were charged with setting the example of "good cheering" at all times, following the cordiality and reciprocity conventions of the time. Just as players exchanged banners on the pitch, rival leaders greeted each other in the stands. In some matches, the flags of the clubs involved in the game were exchanged; this could happen before or during the match, as a way to show fair play and sportsmanship also in the stands.

An example of the "good cheering," as expected by the journalists of *A Gazeta Esportiva* and by ideologues of the Vargas regime, occurs on May 23, 1943. The newspaper's photographic record appears the next day, with images of Palmeiras and Corinthians fans on a day of confrontation between the two teams at the Pacaembu stadium. The photograph printed by *Gazeta* shows the mosaic prepared by the Corinthians' uniformed supporters, with reference to the letter "P"—Palmeirense— in honor of their opponent; while the Palmeiras' uniformed supporters wielded dozens of individual flags with the opponent club's symbol.

Besides an extraordinary event, the fraternization among fans with club rivalry was greatly cultivated in this phase. Cordial actions involved the exchange of clubs' symbols and signs, which were intensified during the "best fan club" contest promoted by *A Gazeta Esportiva* and *Rádio Gazeta*, during the 1943 Paulista championship. On these occasions, the best evaluated fan associations were awarded prizes and their respective leaders received medals. The friendly relations between the groups were reported in the newspaper, but the greatest repercussion occurred when supporters expressed their enthusiasm for nationalist values and the nation's president.

On April 14, 1943, *A Gazeta Esportiva* reported that São Paulo supporters had taken portraits of Getúlio Vargas to Pacaembu to honor the president on the occasion of his birthday. Shortly after, on May 3, 1943, in the wake of the Labor Day celebrations, whose commemorative ritual was held in São Januário and Pacaembu, involving a complex rite of official ceremonies, speeches by authorities and parades of sportsmen on the field—uniformed and symmetrically arranged—, a newspaper article shows that the Corinthians supporters also took portraits of Getúlio Vargas to the stadium.

Along with the tribute to the head of the nation and the Labor Day festivities—a commemorative calendar in which the Estado Novo announced benefits to workers, such as the minimum wage and the expansion of the rights guaranteed in the labor legislation—the images published by the newspapers also show a tribute to Cásper Líbero, founder and owner of *A Gazeta Esportiva*.

The most evident characteristic in the behavior of uniformed supporters was the mission of "sports ideals" bearers, as formulated by the Vargas regime and disseminated by sports journalism. Fights between fan associations of rival clubs were not usually reported nor did they seem to be a concern of the police or organizers of football competitions. Not rarely, a UF could attend a match not played by its team, only to make a valid appearance for the Duel of Fans promoted by *Gazeta* in São Paulo city.

On June 19, 1943, for example, a match played at Pacaembu between São Paulo and Palmeiras—the latter had just changed its name, until then Palestra Itália, as it was forced to become nationalized after Brazil entered World War II against Germany and Italy—registered a paying attendance of over 60 thousand people. Besides the uniformed supporters of São Paulo and Palmeiras, chroniclers noted the presence of Corinthians fans in the stadium.

Despite the absence of their team on the field, Corinthians fans displayed a mosaic with the Brazilian flag in the stands. Such participation was unprecedented and positively surprised *A Gazeta Esportiva* evaluators, who awarded the Corinthians fans with the victory in that day's contest.

São Paulo's uniformed fans thus acted as an auxiliary agent for the promotion of order in sports venues. With the resources at their disposal and the role assigned to them, the associations promoted the exaltation of football and, going further, endorsed the cult of the homeland and the figure of its president.

This model proved so successful that it was reproduced in then federal capital, Rio de Janeiro. There is still controversy over the chronological primacy of fan clubs, with

Cariocas and Paulistas claiming pioneer status in these groupings and contests. We have records, for instance, of a "duel of supporters" already in the year 1936, during the final of the carioca championship, played at the Laranjeiras stadium, between Flamengo and Fluminense supporters.

Regardless of the controversy surrounding the chronology, Mário Filho (1908–1966), owner of *Jornal dos Sports*, stripped the journalistic parochialism that opposed Cariocas to Paulistas and began exalting the beauty and virtuosity of Paulista uniformed fans. Commenting in the newspaper editorial on the civic festivities of the Labor Day, in 1943, in Pacaembu, he stated:

> The two fans [Corinthians and São Paulo, in this case] stand out. Pacaembu was all packed [...] that crowd that literally filled its premises, gaining an even more pronounced color with the outstanding performance, full of good humor and original numbers, of the two uniformed fans. (*Jornal dos Sports*, 1943, May 3, p. 2) (our translation)

In reading the sources, we observe that the newly emerged uniformed fans under the Estado Novo were, on one hand, an extension of the management of the clubs to which they were affiliated; on the other, they consisted in the materialization of a state-journalistic project that aimed to produce certain specific social effects in professional football.

Although conflicts between fan associations of rival clubs were not an issue for the state or for match organizers in the early 1940s, this does not mean that stadiums were spaces immune to such problems. Since the early days of football, acts of hostility, hooliganism, and disturbances among fans, characterized by the press as "sururus" and "charivaris," have been recorded. In this period, however, uniformed fans were not held accountable for such acts and these so-called uncivilized attitudes took place among supporters not affiliated to these groups.

On the contrary, the UFs were the protagonists of "good behavior," to be grasped and emulated by the mass of non-uniformed fans. There were difficulties in gaining supporters in the general public. In certain situations, UFs became the target of threats by ordinary fans, who used anonymity to intimidate uniformed fans, even those of their team. This is how A Gazeta Esportiva reported the suspension of the activities of Palmeiras' uniformed supporters during the 1943 Paulista championship:

> We learned that the alviverde's board of directors decided to temporarily suspend the activities of the uniformed fans in the 1943 championship, due to the lack of guarantees. But how? Yes, for lack of guarantees! The informants told us that after a few games, several individuals stand around the supporter group, or in front of it, and start insulting its members with swear words, or else they direct unwanted jokes at the girls who also wear the alviverde uniform. We were also told that during the Corinthians x Palmeiras prelude, held during the São Paulo City Cup, one of the leaders tried to reprimand one of those undesirables and was almost victim of aggression by the same individual. The uniformed fans have given a very special coloring to this golden phase our football is going through, and it is even unbelievable that the praise they are receiving for having done so is the one Palmeiras received. Our police authorities need to take strong measures to protect our uniformed fans by placing some police officers at their disposal. These should be placed next to the isolation cordons to act when necessary. We believe that in this way the braves will not dare try to destroy a great achievement of our football. (*A Gazeta Esportiva*, 1943g, July 12, p. 7) (our translation)

The threat non-affiliated fans made to a fan leader recognized by the *A Gazeta Esportiva*, legitimized by the club and, indirectly, by the state itself, called into question the entire vertical structure formulated by João Lyra, Thomaz Mazzoni, and the other collaborators of the regime. The disorderly fan's attitude affronted the hierarchy and the police security system designed for sports venues by the state and endorsed by the sports press.

As a result, Thomaz Mazzoni directly addressed the "official authorities of our football" and demanded that they offer guarantees to the integrity of the Palmeirense leader during his team's matches. *A Gazeta Esportiva* demanded both public and sports authorities to ensure that this figure—the leader—was respected in the territory of the stands.

The narrative allows us to assume that, in case of riot, this would tend to happen outside the spatial boundaries allocated for UFs in the stands, usually bounded by an isolation cordon, where only those wearing the group's stylized uniform could enter. Such situation is evidenced during the first fan tournament promoted by A Gazeta Esportiva. In passages of the news on the topic, it is clear that the attitude of the UFs was not extended to all the public present.

For this reason, on June 26, 1943, Thomaz Mazzoni signs an editorial entitled "Torcedores!," in which he criticizes the passionate aficionados, full of parochialism and "clubismo." In his opinion, they did not understand true sportsmanship and let themselves be dominated by instinctive impulses, to the detriment of a measured, rational behavior: "vindictive, passionate, they harm the spectacle." (*A Gazeta Esportiva*, 1943f, June 26, p. 2).

It is easy to notice the similarity between this discourse and that of Lyra Filho in *A função social dos desportos*. Although without explaining and naming the reference, the sequence of Mazzoni's argument recalls that of Lyra Filho, then president of the CND:

> However, what has improved this personal fanaticism somewhat are the uniformed fans, which bring the members tether in a large group under the control of balanced and more responsible people, and under the direct action of the board of directors. [...] in this group, there is no room for a taste for misconduct. (*A Gazeta Esportiva*, 1943f, June 26, p. 2) (our translation)

The football uniformed supporters in the city of São Paulo, precursors of an institutional model and of a behavior pattern in Brazilian stadiums, embodied thus what the press, managers, police, and the State deemed to be good supporters or, if taken in their singular collectivity, a "good crowd." The members of the São Paulo UFs were required to command the mass of fans who flocked to watch the professional football spectacle.

The set of fans, including the "passionate" and "vindictive" ones, underwent a series of guidelines and lessons, such as, for example, how the music should be produced, which slogans should be chanted, how choreographic gestures should be performed. The leaders' pedagogical role was, therefore, to teach the attending mass the ways of cheering considered appropriate to the newly instituted professional order and to the grandiosity of the newly built public stadiums.

Conclusion

Based on the above, this chapter aimed to discuss the first moments of the uniformed football fans configuration in Brazil, examining episodes still little known by the general public and even by the academia. The case chosen here was that of the São Paulo uniformed supporters, encouraged to participate in stadiums in the 1940s, under the altruistic slogans of discipline and order, dear to the Estado Novo regime. Through a selection of primary and secondary sources, with extracts from books and journalistic reports from the 1940s, besides the interlocution with pre-existing academic works, we sought to show the emergence of these groups.

By articulating a series of authors and characters, we sought to identify the basic principles with which public power entities and private press agencies encouraged the collective presence of fans in the country's new stadiums, built under the aegis of patriotism and monumentality, in the wake of the professionalization of Brazilian football, between the late 1930s and early 1940s.

This articulation highlighted the existing mediations on at least three planes, which overlap in the three sections of the chapter: (i) the *national*, through the writings of the National Sports Council (CND) president on the importance of musically animating the supporters in stadiums, deemed the most effective means of promoting cohesion and avoiding disturbances in sports venues; (ii) the *journalistic*, based on the publications of sports chronicler Thomaz Mazzoni, herald of the application of the Estado Novo ideals to professional football, issuing his daily opinions in books and in the pages of his newspaper; and (iii) the *supporter*, through information on the performance of the uniformed supporters' leaders in Pacaembu, during the year 1943, when the newspaper *A Gazeta Esportiva* sponsored the first contest among fan associations, entities that had emerged in the city four years earlier, in 1939, with the creation of the Grêmio São-Paulino.

Thus outlined, this articulation shows the existence of relations not usually made explicit by their actors, such as the indirect link between Lyra Filho and the editor of *A Gazeta Esportiva*, or the convergences between the Estado Novo ideals and the pacifying performance of the leaders in the stadiums. Such mediations allow us to understand the context of the time and, correspondingly, elucidate why football supporters took on this ordered configuration in its initial moment.

The connections established based on the selected sources thus contribute to a less Manichean and essentialist understanding, currently dominant when it comes to addressing the delicate issue of organized fan clubs and their relationship with the phenomenon of violence in stadiums. Beyond the reifying stereotypes, this still recent past allows us to perceive the dynamism of the history of these associations and how, in their origins, to the surprise of many contemporaries, their role was precisely related to preventing violent actions in the stands.

If History—as Cicero puts it—is "the teacher of life," perhaps it is also worth paying attention to the Brazilian historical lesson in understanding organized fan clubs. Their trajectory may well serve as an example to those who, as a rule, stigmatize social groups that seem strange to them. Unlike those who insist in stereotyping fans as "barbarians," "vandals," and "bums," we go against a social science that is satisfied with biological and pathological explanations. Beyond an atavistic "evil of origin," we advocate, instead, for sociological and historiographical readings capable of illuminating human beings in their circumstances, amid the dynamics of the complex networks of sociability that constitutes modern public spaces.

References

Canetti, E. (1995). *Massa e poder*. Companhia das Letras.
Capelato, M. H. (1998). *Multidões em cena: Propaganda política no varguismo e no peronismo*. Papirus.
Chaim, A. R. M. (2018). *Futebol, corações e mentes: Os torcedores na perspectiva do Estado*. (Doctoral dissertation in Political Science), Universidade de São Paulo (USP), Brazil. https://teses.usp.br/teses/disponiveis/8/8131/tde-06122018-121608/pt-br.php.
Fausto, B. (2006). *Getúlio Vargas: O poder e o sorriso*. Companhia das Letras.
Franco, H., Jr. (2007). *A dança dos deuses: futebol, sociedade, cultura*. Companhia das Letras.
Hime, G. (2005). Cásper Líbero: O empresário que criou a primeira escola de jornalismo. In J. M. Melo (Ed), *Imprensa brasileira: personagens que fizeram história*. Imprensa Oficial.
Hollanda, B. B. B. (2008). *O clube como vontade e representação: O jornalismo esportivo e a formação das torcidas organizadas de futebol do Rio de Janeiro (1967–1988)* (Doctoral dissertation in History, PUC, Rio de Janeiro, Brazil). https://ludopedio.com.br/biblioteca/o-clube-como-vontade-e-representacao/.
Leite Lopes, J. S. (1994). A vitória do futebol que incorporou a pelada: Mário Filho e a entrada dos negros no futebol. *Revista USP*, (22), 64–83. https://doi.org/10.11606/issn.2316-9036.v0i22p64-83.
Lyra Filho, J. (1941). *A função social dos desportos*. Rio de Janeiro (Unpublished manuscript).
Malaia, J. (2011). Torcer, torcedores, torcedoras, torcida (bras.): 1910–1950. In B. B. B. Hollanda, et al. (Eds.), *A torcida brasileira*. 7 Letras, Rio de Janeiro.
Mazonni, T. (1941). *O esporte a serviço da pátria*. n.e.
Negreiros, P. J. L. C. (1998). A nação entra em campo: futebol nos anos 1930 e 1940 (Doctoral dissertation in History, PUC, São Paulo, Brazil). https://sapientia.pucsp.br/handle/handle/13003.
Oliveira, L., Velloso, M. P., & Gomes, A. C. (1982). *Estado Novo: Ideologia e poder*. FGV Editora.
Pandolfi, D. (Ed.). (1999). *Repensando o Estado Novo*. FGV Editora.
Parada, M. (2009). *Educando corpos e criando a nação: Cerimônias cívicas e práticas disciplinares no Estado Novo*. Apicuri.
Pardini, M. N. M. (2009). *A narrativa da ordem e a voz da multidão: O futebol na imprensa durante o Estado Novo* (Master's thesis in History). Universidade de São Paulo (USP), Brazil. https://www.teses.usp.br/teses/disponiveis/8/8138/tde-04022010-130259/publico/MELINA_MIRANDA_PARDINI.pdf.
Silva, R. S. (2010). *O esporte a serviço da pátria: Thomaz Mazzoni e os primórdios do jornalismo esportivo (1928–1941)* (Undergraduate Monograph in History). PUC, Rio de Janeiro, Brazil. https://doi.org/10.17771/PUCRio.acad.16254.
Souza, D. A. (2008). *O Brasil entra em campo! Construções e reconstruções da identidade nacional (1930–1947)*. Annablume.
Toledo, L. H. (2000). *Lógicas no futebol: Dimensões simbólicas de um esporte nacional* (Doctoral Thesis in Social Anthropology). Universidade de São Paulo (USP), Brazil. https://repositorio.usp.br/item/001078825.

Toledo, L. H. (2012). A cidade e o jornal: A Gazeta Esportiva e os sentidos da modernidade na São Paulo da primeira metade do século XX. In B. B. B. Hollanda, & V. A. Melo (Orgs.), *O esporte na imprensa e a imprensa esportiva no Brasil*. 7 Letras, Rio de Janeiro.

Viveiros, R. (2010). *Laudo Natel, um bandeirante*. Imprensa Oficial.

Sources

A Gazeta Esportiva. (1941, November 1).

A Gazeta Esportiva. (1943f, June 26).

A Gazeta Esportiva. (1943g, July 12).

A Gazeta Esportiva. (1943h, September 23).

Decreto Lei No. 1,915 (1939, December 27). *Cria o Departamento de Imprensa e Propaganda e dá outras providências*. https://www2.camara.leg.br/legin/fed/declei/1930-1939/decreto-lei-1915-27-dezembro-1939-411881-publicacaooriginal-1-pe.html.

Jornal dos Sports. (1943, May 3).

Part II
Sociology and Anthropology

Chapter 9
Sport and Society in the Writings of Roberto DaMatta

Alexandre Fernandez Vaz

A Theory of Brazil

> Just as it happens with a match of the Brazilian team
> [that allows us to feel our continuity as a group],
> where we see, feel, shout and speak as "Brazil"
> in the immense reifying ruse that is the football game.
> (DaMatta, 1979, our translation)

If, in Brazil, part of the field of physical education/sport sciences was dedicated, in the 1980s and 1990s, to elaborate critical discourses on sport, in the registration of social sciences, it was possible to observe, in the same period and shortly before, a surprising theoretical elaboration that passed in the opposite direction. It is the work of the anthropologist Roberto Damatta, who, if he was not the first social scientist to deal with football in Brazil, certainly represented the most important impulse for this theme to become an object to be researched by the humanities.

DaMatta's analysis of football is not self-sufficient, on the contrary. Since the 1970s, the anthropologist has been developing an analytical body that seeks to understand the "Brazilian dilemma", or, in other words, "what makes brazil, Brazil". From this perspective, the role played by football finds a privileged place. Against the left wings critics on sport, DaMatta attributes to football a positivity value, linked to its character as a "democratic experience" and as a "producer of unity and national identity", something that he says, can hardly be observed in other spheres of Brazilian life.

This attempt to reflect on Brazil with its own conceptual instruments is part of a modern Brazilian intellectual tradition, which includes some classic authors of our thought, such as Sérgio Buarque de Holanda, Gilberto Freyre, Caio Prado, Celso

A. F. Vaz (✉)
Federal University of Santa Catarina, Florianópolis, Brazil

© The Author(s), under exclusive license to Springer Nature Switzerland AG 2021
S. S. Giglio and M. W. Proni (eds.), *Football and Social Sciences in Brazil*,
https://doi.org/10.1007/978-3-030-84686-2_9

133

Furtado, Antonio Candido and Florestan Fernandes, as well as a younger generation, which includes, among others, Darcy Ribeiro, Marilena Chaui and Roberto Schwarz. There is in all of them, keeping in mind the differences in their respective intellectual projects, a concern to develop, to a greater or lesser extent, a theory of Brazil that dialogue with the great classics of Western thought, but that does so clearly and consciously from the point of view of the ghetto. It is thus considered that the geopolitical distinction between center and ghetto is still alive, in spite of—or precisely because of—the constant and continuous process of globalization. Some of these authors seek to escape the analytical key that faces the ghetto as backwardness, driven by a dialectic that sees modernization processes as mutually determined in each singularity; others demarcate the civilizatory lag that the nation would have in relation to the metropolises of the northern hemisphere.

DaMatta proposes a sociology/anthropology that aims to understand Brazilian society trough its reverse, evoquing themes that, at least until the late 1970s, had been despised by "official" sociology. In this way, carnival, football, gambling, popular festivals and military parades (!) would present "a way of being of Brazil".

For DaMatta, football in Brazil, instead of being the "opium of the people", is a drama of "social justice",[1] a progressive and modernizing phenomenon, democratic in its realization. He argues that football is one of the few social practices in the country that can be recognized in its full realization, in which the rules are transparent and of wide domain. Politics and economics, for example, are highly volatile spheres, whose operating rules few people know—fields destined for the "experts". In contrast, everyone knows what is going on in the football game, where merit, after all, is what counts.

Football, so DaMatta, constitutes an experience in which the degrees of kinship or friendship do not matter, but the technical quality; there is no individual favoring by financial condition, but chances for everyone to show their skills. A social experience in which, when rules are broken, it is easy to check, and in which the possible of taking part of it is real, as the case of the action of fans in a match.[2]

DaMatta's reflections contrast, as already said, with the critical analyses of sport developed by the European New Left in the 1960s and 1970s, widely disseminated in Brazil, especially in vulgar and not very rigorous versions from a theoretical point of view.[3] On the other hand, they move toward, according to the author, some of the assumptions of the figure-based sociology of Norbert Elias, especially in his analyses of football.

---

[1] The title of one of his major works on the subject is precisely this: "Football: Opium of the people or drama of social justice?" (DaMatta, 1986, pp. 101–120).

[2] Note that the organized fans have today a form of action that goes beyond the moment of the game itself, since they exert enormous pressure on managers, players and coaching staff.

[3] In general, it was the works of Bracht (1986, 1989) and Cavalcanti (1981, 1984) that disseminated the critiques of the new left in Brazil. I do not consider their critiques vulgar or not very rigorous. On the contrary, their ponderations are in general well elaborated, especially in the case of Bracht. The same cannot be said of several of his disseminators. A commentary on the theme can be found in Lovisolo (1995). It is also worth mentioning the works of Proni (2002), Torri and Vaz (2006) and Bracht (2013), which also present and discuss aspects of the analyses of the new left on sport.

It is about football and its position in Brazilian society, in view of this contrast caused by a theory constructed from the point of view of the ghetto (the sport is universal), that I will deal with in the following pages.

Social Drama

To study the Brazilian dilemma, DaMatta occupies himself, as stated, with elements that were once uncommon in the social sciences. Instead of focusing on political and economic structures in their socio-historical contexts, on how parties and power relations are organized in the "official" world, on military power or on the sciences, DaMatta privileges events and occurrences that in principle were considered "unserious", "disposable" or "secondary" by Brazilian elites, including intellectuals and those of progressive tradition. If the thematic panorama in the humanities is today much more open and wide, with approaches and objects of all kinds and registers, it was not so when the author developed the most significant part of his work.

DaMatta is interested in carnival, religious festivals, military parades, gambling, queues, traffic, football, through which he develops categories of analysis not only to understand such events with strong popular tradition, and practices that determine everyday life, but also to develop a theory of Brazilian society as a whole. It is through marginal themes—with the exception of certain literature, Jorge Amado, for example, whose importance for him is beyond doubt, but which is still popular—that it was possible for him to develop his ideas about Brazilian society. To understand Brazil "inside out" does not mean, however, to ignore the relations of the universes of politics and economics, of art and university, but to understand them also in their paradoxes, through these other manifestations that seem, at first sight, to be their antithesis.

Brazilian modernity would be a sui generis combination of paradoxes that would escape a coherence model that would make opt for certain social characteristics in detriment of others. It is a matter of incorporating them in a common axis, even acknowledging their specificity. For DaMatta (1979, 1997), Brazilian society combines modern aspects with others of colonial tradition, characteristics that are valid for public life (the street), but that are contradictory with the private sphere (the home). In this sense, writes the anthropologist:

> The fact is, however, that Brazilian society is prodigious in presenting combinations and connections that, at first sight, are entirely out of place or even impossible. Thus, it is easier to be catholic and umbandist, millionaire and socialist, aristocrat and populist, at the same time, than to be each one of these things in a given moment of existence. Just as occurs at the level of society, where we combine, in a theoretically complex way, state authoritarianism, familistic patronage and a modern capitalism that operates efficiently in many areas. We are usually ideological and impersonal in the street and adopt traditionalist common sense at home, when we function governed by an ethic of personal and family relations. (DaMatta, 1986, p. 103, our translation)

If, for the critic Roberto Schwartz, the key ideas of European liberalism are incorporated in the slavery context of Brazil at the end of the nineteenth century, constituting a paradigmatic case of "ideas out of place" (Schwarz, 1977), for DaMatta, the problem is not that we have too much capitalism, but not enough of it, since:

> We live in a society where there is systematically an intense and functional relationship between a market system coupled with a legal apparatus founded on universal laws and on the individual as subject; and imperative networks of personal relations that operate hierarchically, maintaining the old elitist privileges. "[...] a system where the market and universal laws only operate downwards, in the sense of those who do not have a representation by name, relations or family property. The root of our authoritarianism, thus, would be in this simultaneity or in this capacity to relate family ties, friendship and cronyism (with their ethics of patronage and considerations) and a system of universal laws constantly put in check by the logic of personal ties. (DaMatta, 1986, pp. 103–104, our translation)

To understand such contradictions that make up the Brazilian specificity and that are manifested in football, DaMatta uses, supported by the structuralist tradition represented, in this case, by Max Gluckman, Victor Turner, Clifford Geertz and Claude Lévi-Strauss—the category of "social drama". Associated to the concepts of "myth" and "rite of passage"—and to the idea that the "structure remains"— drama allows, according to DaMatta (1986, pp. 103–104), to articulate the day-to-day observations with the values present in society, because it synthesizes and puts in suspension, problematizes the norms, relations and institutions. It is an expression of the society that, for the good structuralism, relocates itself in each of the spheres it institutes. Drama, as we will see in the specific case of football analysis, represents a structure that simultaneously reveals and hides (DaMatta, 1982).

The analysis undertaken by DaMatta (1986, pp. 103–104) attacks the "utilitarianism" of social phenomena, particularly football. It would not be the case of identifying which social or political project football is serving, but of verifying its specificity as a social manifestation. He disagrees that sports must necessarily be a practical consequence of other labor and utilitarian activities; on the contrary, he sees in sports an activity whose aesthetic expression may be considered in the foreground.

> The world did not begin with men seeking food and waging war. The spirit gave the primordial impulse, if we can really speak of it, as much by the body as. If I may paraphrase Lévi-Strauss, I would say that the first dart was not only good for killing, but also for amusing, decorating, and thinking. (DaMatta, 1982, p. 24, our translation)

He disagrees, therefore, with the necessary link between these two spheres of social life—sport and work—an important idea for the European New Left, made famous by the well-known book by Rigauer (1969), but whose centrality had already been pointed out, among others, by Adorno (1997a, 1997b) and Habermas (1958). Football would not be, therefore, a space of political utilitarianism either.

For DaMatta, in the last analysis, it is a sphere that, if not distant, remains somehow independent of the immediate political relations, by characterizing itself as a space of national identity and unification, raising self-esteem configured as good memories, of individuals and groups. In this regard, taking into consideration the 1998 World Cup in France and the upcoming elections—especially the presidential ones, which opposed a left-wing candidate to a liberal one running for reelection—DaMatta is asked if the performance in the World Cup could benefit candidates, and which ones, taking into consideration a possible success of the national football team. In the opposite direction to utilitarianism, he answers

> Only a wizard could say that. I assume so. That there is a connection between winning the Cup and being proud of Brazil. That makes it possible for efficient administrations to take advantage. However, I must remember that the oppositions can also benefit from the victory by drawing attention to points that have not been seen or things that have not been accomplished. In addition, that victory would give courage to change. In defeat, which is a general disaster, everyone is scorched. (DaMatta, 1998b, June 14, p. 10, our translation)

Then he states, perhaps exaggeratedly, that he is struck by the absence of a link between football and politics in Brazil, which is present in other countries such as Argentina, Russia and Germany. For DaMatta, politicians know that football is a serious matter in Brazil to risk using it as a vector of promotion: "maybe because they are Brazilians and respect the people in their passions and traditions, they [the politicians] know that taking a ride on football provokes a negative reaction; because people know who loves football and who has no interest in the sport and has never stepped foot in a stadium" (DaMatta, 1998b, June 14, p. 10, our translation).

It has not been negligible, on the other hand, the approximation of politicians in general with football, in which, as public figures, they are not prevented from cheering. General Emílio Garrastazu Médici, dictator in the post of president of the republic between 1969 and 1974, got very close to the three-time world champion team in 1970, even being mentioned as a fan of the sport in a Jorge Ben's song. Besides, DaMatta (1996, p. 173 and p. 200) was not able to resist the temptation to put in the same scheme the 1994 World Cup conquer by the national football team and the victory of Fernando Henrique Cardoso, with the respective implementation of the economic plan that leveraged his candidacy, facts that would mark, he says, a "new time" for the country. The temptation to which even the German Thomas Fatheuer (1995) could not resist to adhere.

In the next sections, we will look at two categories of analysis: identity and destiny.

The "Specificity" of Brazilian Football and National Identity

This chapter is interested in the characterization of football as a "genuinely Brazilian" cultural element, capable of generating a national identity closely linked to the way it is practiced in Brazil, commonly called "futebol-arte" (football-art). It is not a matter, then, of discussing whether this characterization, which takes the form of mythology about Brazil in various parts of the world, is correct. The myth is not open to discussion. More important is to debate, within the framework proposed by DaMatta, the strength of this "positive image" about the Brazilian way of being.

DaMatta (1998b, June 14) considers fundamental the path of a sport that "came from outside", from the "foreigner", where everything is "chic", and develops among

Brazilians a series of new meanings, in a process he determinates "positive acculturation". His works share the imaginary of football-art and use it as a tool for a peculiar reflection on the identity of Brazilians in relation to the football played in Brazil. In Brazil, football would be first a game or even a sport experienced as a game, because it is related to other spheres of action than those that take place on the field. Firstly because the word game in Portuguese, unlike play in English, is related to luck and mischance, and it is not by venture that football is associated with a popular betting game, the sports lottery. Moreover, there is in football, as elsewhere in the whole Brazilian society, a marked presence of religious elements and superstition, in which the idea of destiny plays an important role (DaMatta, 1982, 1986).

There is a game that takes place on the field, performed by the players as a professional and sportive activity. There is another game that takes place in real life, performed by the Brazilian population, in its constant search for change to its destiny. Moreover, a third game performed in the "other world", in which entities are called to influence and, by doing this, promote transformations in the different social positions involved in the sportive event. All this reveals how a given institution—in this case, the Football Association, invented by the English—may be differentially appropriated. (DaMatta, 1986, p. 107). There would be, therefore, a unique configuration, with specific values and norms, determined by the way, in which a modern and universal cultural element is singularly appropriated.

In football, according to DaMatta (1979), it is possible for the "individual" to become a "person", since it is in the team that he can show his uniqueness, express himself in a peculiar way. The anthropologist opposes, therefore, to the thesis of "fungibility" in sport, which claims that athletes would be fungible because, once reified, they would be performing technical functions aiming at performance, which would occupy, with enormous centrality, the sportive scene. In other words, the action is worth, but not the actor, because the means are of interest, turned into ends (Vaz, 1999).

DaMatta (1982, 1986) can only go against the thesis of fungibility because, for him, Brazilian football differs strongly from European football, characterized by ball control, improvisation and individuality. This particular style of playing football, in which the "ways of being Brazilian" are recognized, would be characterized by the ambiguity of the "malandro", a symbolic figure in our social imaginary, who circulates between the spheres of legality and illegality; of the clear and the hidden; of the implicit and the explicit, and whose strength would also be related to the fact that in Brazil the version football is the one which is performed.

For the anthropologist (DaMatta, 1982) Brazilian football, in comparison—again—with European football, is characterized by having a "jogo de cintura" (being quite flexible), by "bending without breaking", dissimulating, improvising and elegantly getting out of adverse situations, usually by moving the body and creating an aesthetically valued game. As a metaphor of everyday life, football would then express a "way of being Brazilian", since it takes a lot of rascality to be able to deal with a highly modernized society on one hand, but on the other, with patriarchal characteristics and clientelistic relationships.

Rascality can be a highly positive and necessary characteristic, which expresses our subjectivity to deal with social objectivity.[4] Both the football player and the politician need the rascality and "jogo de cintura", they need to know how to move the body in the right direction, causing confusion and fascination in their opponents, creating unsuspected harmonies (DaMatta, 1982, 1994).

In fact, the foot-played version of football (football) has prevailed to a greater degree than the hand-played versions typical of Anglo-Saxon environments, such as rugby. It is worth highlighting, however, the unquestionable presence of footy football in England, whose national league is now the most attractive in the world. The English still hold the world title, and football (football for them, not football) has taken root in Great Britain as one of the key elements of working-class culture. At the same time, the United States has also found in football a popular spectacle, albeit with different emphases throughout history, as is the case in the 1930s (Clausen, 2014), the period with Pelé in the league (1975–1977), and the more recent experience, which includes the strength of the women's version of the sport.

DaMatta's (1996) interpretation is curious. According to him, sports played with the feet suppose a higher dose of imponderability, if compared to those played with the hands, in which the demands of control, precision and, mainly, forethought are much higher. This would be the case of the United States of America, not only in sports, but also in the type of parliamentary representative democracy that is exercised there. In his words (DaMatta, 1994, p. 16, our translation):

> When played with the feet, football becomes less predictable, which insinuates the ideas of luck, destiny, predestination, and victory. With this, we can immediately link football with religion and transcendence in the Brazilian case, something much rarer to occur when it comes to sports such as volleyball, swimming, and athletics. [...] moreover, the use of the foot, differently from the use of the hands, forces the inclusion of the whole body, emphasizing above all the legs, the hips and the waist, those parts of the human anatomy that, in the case of the Brazilian society, are target of an elaborated symbolism.[5]

Football-Art and Modernization: Against the Idea of the "Opium of the People"

For a long time, Brazilian elites, also left-wing, understood football as the "opium of the people", expression taken as a fundamental concept by Janet Lever (1969). For DaMatta, on the contrary, it is a "drama of social justice". Simply saying that football is the opium of the people, according to DaMatta (1982, 1986), nothing more than to corroborate class inequalities and the prejudice that says that the masses are always ignorant, that it is necessary that the elites say what is right or wrong, without acknowledging their turn and voice. After all, "if we continue to insist that football

---

[4] Soares (1994) made a beautiful study about rascality in football, with emphasis on the testimonials of Brazilian football players and former players, in which appear the intricacies and difficulties in conceptualizing the necessary rascality of the game and the reprehensible rascality in daily life.

[5] See also DaMatta (1996, pp. 43–44).

is an instrument of mystification of the ignorant masses who should be going to the theater, reading novels or discussing politics, we will only be repeating an elitist formula and leaving aside the possibility of studying the implications of football in Brazilian society" (DaMatta, 1986, p. 90, our translation).

In this sense, football would not be a phenomenon of alienation, even if we can recognize the existence of an often excessive interest in relation to it, and that evidently it is not possible to be all the time with perfect awareness of everything (Idem, ibidem). On the contrary, "consciousness is focus [and] football defocuses some things [...] and focuses others, usually their just opposite." (DaMatta, 1998b, June 14, p. 10). Football would be a space of recognition of our virtues (but also of our failures, said Nelson Rodrigues), and an expression that, as said, not only "makes us forget", but also subverts the order of things, resists the abuses linked to patriarchy, cronyism and friendship.

Modern sports, and specifically football, subverts, according to DaMatta (1996), a logic that may be condensed into a lapidary phrase, still present in the daily life of Brazilians. It is a question with which one of the interlocutors seeks to intimidate the other, usually located lower in the strong Brazilian social hierarchy. It is the slogan: "Do you know who you are talking to?"

Football would also be one of the rare opportunities for Brazilian society to organize itself collectively around a common goal, acting in a coordinated way, which would contrast, again, with traditional representations of politics and economics. DaMatta (1982) recognizes, however, that this could mean not only the suspension, but also the concealment of class conflict. After all, the church, the state, the literature, the social sciences, the university, the financial system, the armed forces, the bourgeoisie, none of these would have been able to promote the necessary confidence for the positive construction of national identity. On the other hand, football would still be a field of experiences of success, victory and achievement, and, as such, it would have an undeniable integrative force. Especially the marginalized would have the opportunity to win with their teams.

They feel, then, that their performance in the stadium as fans[6]—as a suffering audience that gives itself unreservedly to its club and heroes—produces tangible results and complete victories. This victory that the masses, perpetually deluded by dishonest rulers, are effectively unaware of in the fields of education, health and, above all, politics (DaMatta, 1994, p. 170).

Along with its character as an integrating force, football would be, as already mentioned, an excellent representation of democracy, an example of a cultural event in which the rules are universal and known by all. In it, the rules cannot be changed by who is winning or losing, and there is no place for coups, but for the "alternation between winners and losers that, projected into social life, is the basis of the most authentic democratic experience" (DaMatta, 1994, p. 170).

---

[6] There is a relevant weight in the word "*torcida*" or "*torcedor*", in Portuguese language, different from what is found, for example, in German (*fan* or *anhänger*) or English (*fan*) or even in the Spanish spoken in Spain (*afición* and *aficionado*). Similar to what happens in the Argentine Castilian, *hinchada* and *hincha* denote, like *torcida* and *torcedor*, a capacity to interfere in the course of the game. On aspects of this theme, see works by DaMatta himself (1994) and Fatheuer (1995).

This experience should be expanded to other spheres of social life, where popular weight is often not felt with the necessary vigor. After all:

> How good it would be if the people would do with the governors what they do with the national team coaches. Would not it be wonderful to see that governor take a civic beating from a popular indignant? I bet if it happened to politicians that they would really turn into administrators of public affairs. In addition, Brazil would win again in football. (DaMatta, 1996, p. 23, our translation)

The comparison between the team's coach and the President of the Republic makes sense, since both are figures with great symbolic strength in Brazil, to whom the national imaginary allocates immeasurable forces. In this context, DaMatta establishes an interesting relationship between the imaginary roles of the coach and the tribal priests, since the former, like the latter, may have glory and power, but be killed in the next moment, falling into disgrace after an unbearable defeat.

> Therefore, he [the coach] is not only the person rationally responsible for the team. He is, above all, the guy who has the tremendous responsibility of making everything work out, articulating, like a "pai de santo", technique with good fortune, physical preparation and intuition, inferiority with superiority. In our football, a great team is not enough, because you need luck and race to win. "Race" to which we Brazilians give a positive sign, because, in this context, we make it signal love, pride, will to win and, above all, competence and performance, these basic elements that until today are not criteria for the political game. (DaMatta, 1996, p. 44, our translation)

For DaMatta, it is fundamental the extremely modernizing role that competition plays with equal chances, an element based on merit, essential to sport, which opposes the relationships that presuppose and support personal favoritism.[7]

> Finally, football provides Brazilian society with the experience of equality and social justice. By producing a complex spectacle, but governed by rules that everyone knows, football symbolically reaffirms that the best, the most capable and the most meritorious can win. That the alliance between talent and performance can lead to uncontested victory. Thus, if everyday life presents us with the powerful and the powerless people who never change places, football presents us with a spectacle in which winners and losers systematically alternate, therefore, that alternation in glory is the glory in alternation - the basis of modern equality and justice. (DaMatta, 1994, p. 17, our translation)

It is established again, the idea that it is not a problem that we have capitalism, but that it is insufficient, mixed with backward and colonial values, is posed again. It is curious, again, that DaMatta considers, paradoxically, that what we have as the best are, in opposition to North American society, our traditional values. It is in this mosaic in which sources prevail, perhaps too freely chosen, that DaMatta constructs, at all risks, his interpretation of Brazil.

---

[7] Other anthropologists who have directly or indirectly studied sports and football, such as Alba Zaluar (1991, 1994) and Lovisolo (1995), agree with DaMattasconsist, mutatis mutandis.

Drama and Setting

> Interestingly, there is a parallel between my ideas and those of
> Norbert Elias regarding the relationship between sport and society.
> However, Elias, after all, is German, and I am Brazilian,
> so they always talk about Elias.
> If you have to quote someone, quote Elias.
> (DaMatta, 1998a, p. 205).

Norbert Elias showed how sport corresponds to the civilizing process and is an important part of it, by appeasing emotions and internalizing disciplinary marks. Unfolding his central argument, he verified, with Eric Dunning and others, how football and other sports were generated in the English social and political structure (Elias & Dunning, 1986).

It is possible to recognize the theoretical effort on DaMatta's part that led him to similar results, although without the same pretension of universality, a fundamental topic of Elias's theory on the civilizing process. DaMatta is interested in the specificities of Brazil, the dilemmas and paradoxes that constitute our identity.

Anyway, also for the Brazilian anthropologist, sports, and specifically football, play a preponderant role, we could say, in the process of "civilization" of our society (Lucena, 2004). Football, he says, teaches that there are rules to be followed, that it is possible to lose without dishonor, disciplining for a complex order, different from that of ancient societies, in which inequality would not only be permanent, but desirable. Sport would dramatize the conflicts that no longer need to be avenged with blood and death, but resolved in an appeasing way. According to DaMatta (1994, p. 14, our translation): "[…] such dissensions are now not only institutionalized, but programmed, planned, and transformed into a good spectacle to think and dramatize, as Claude Lévi-Strauss and Nelson Rodrigues would say."

Unlike Elias, however, DaMatta almost equates modernity with capitalism, which forces him to admit the idea that equality of chances is part of the game of imaginary construction, and therefore, however he avoids saying it, there is ideology and, in this way, alienation. With some care, perhaps it can be said that drama, as a permanent structure and that renews itself, is a way of understanding, of thematizing complex social configurations. DaMatta and Elias are close in what refers to the weight they attribute to structure. For DaMatta (1979), what matters is what remains, the similarities among social phenomena, which authorizes him, for example, to speak of carnival as a single festival, even if with significant differences in its regional manifestations.

In Elias, structure is also fundamental, but in a somewhat different sense than in DaMatta, for whom the "social drama" represents a moment, a synthesis of everyday life, problematizing it, presenting new paths, revealing and hiding. Elias (1988, 1991) undertakes his methodology of analysis starting from the more or less stable configurations, structures or patterns, formed by chains of increasingly complex interdependencies that refer to rational, but not foreseen interlacements, involving the social dynamics and the modeling of the psychological apparatus. We should highlight the character of these changes involved in the interdependence of individuals (or people,

DaMatta would say), which obey an unplanned dynamic, but which have observable direction, according to Elias, since the most remote times of civilization (Elias & Dunning, 1986).

Perhaps the fundamental difference is that the types of civilization and modernity predicated by DaMatta have a different component, thought from the Brazilian specificity. It is a playful component, of game, which resembles, but is not equal to, the notion of balance—a component of the game—defended by Elias. For him, sport helps to maintain a balance between tensions—generally prohibited in daily life, by the growing internalization of rules and external pressures—and the ordered protection against bodily violence. In other words, a combination between expression of emotions and their regulation. What is fundamental is the simulation or dramatization of the clash, with the corresponding tensions under control, so that there may be catharsis (Elias & Dunning, 1986).

In DaMatta, sport also appears as a vector of this balance, in which the civilizing force of the rules plays a key role. Differently from Elias, however, it is not only a matter of maintaining the aspects of pulsional gratification, mediated by sport rules and structures. It is a matter of verifying, in the ways in which sport, and specifically football in Brazil, is interpreted and organized, the spaces of affirmation of identity and social cohesion, which, incidentally, do not correspond—but could or should correspond—to social organization as a whole.

If we can summarize what has been said, football is a universalized sport, but it constitutes a universe of its own in Brazil. Its framework is offered by characteristics that find their special affirmation among us, such as the ways of practicing this sport. It is a peculiar form of modernization that combines technique and tactics with rascality, competitiveness and respect for rules, all as symbolic expressions that integrate our identity and cohesion. We need to be aware, therefore, of the decisive role played by football in our model of modernization, which, as we have seen, is related above all to a positive metaphor, a drama that synthesizes desires for a more just and harmonious society, which should dispense with inequality and establish its values based on merit and competence.

In this sense, while in England, there is a correspondence between the parliamentary regime and the institution of sports, both with pacifying effect (Elias & Dunning, 1986) in Brazil this connection is disjunctive, according to DaMatta, since football is, in our context, precisely the counterpoint of the political organization.

Football and Its *Miracles*, Like What We Want It to Be

> I read the classification for the World Cup as a presage that Brazil is going to be right. Right in our own way, by the internal elaboration of what we are and not by the dumb and colonial acceptance of what comes from the outside.
> (DaMatta, 1996, p. 42, our translation).

There seems to be a certain fantasy in DaMatta's assertions regarding the relationship between the constitution of contemporary Brazil and football. It sounds exaggerated, for example, to say that football is a barometer for Brazilian society, that when football is bad, something is wrong. Well, DaMatta states, as seen above, that football resists the social logic demarcated by politics, by the national economy, in short, by the "serious" world. More logical, within its own framework, would be to say that if football is doing badly, something in itself is not doing well. On the other hand, on the other hand, it would be the case of saying that politics and economics matter little, an idea that DaMatta evidently does not defend.

There is even the impression that DaMatta, in studying the myth and drama of football, incorporates and substantiates mythological elements in his own analysis, reinforced in many cases by the usually polemical tone of the essayist, and by the eventually circumstantial—but, paradoxically, coherent—character of his chronicles. In a way, this is recognized by himself, when he says that he has terrible relations with "this crap called *reality*" (DaMatta, 1998a). Or, then, when criticizing the dazzle with post-modernism, with what it would bring of new: "But, at its core, what is good in post-modernism is not new. I have always known that anthropology is not science. You see what you look for, you find what you want. Another aspect that post-modernists highlight is the text; Writing well has always been fundamental." (DaMatta, 1998a, p. 199, our translation).

DaMatta seems to incorporate, alongside the shrewd observation of everyday life, allegorical elements that help to compose a kind of sphere of desires and emotions about Brazil. This is an almost religious belief, which is expressed in phrases like: "And when someone reads of Brazil's victory, it is not news, but a presage." (DaMatta, 1996, p. 37, our translation). Not by chance, the anthropologist also often speaks of "miracles" in football, the first of them "is to be what we want it to be" (DaMatta, 1996, p. 56). Wishful thinking is, by the way, also not far from DaMatta's Oeuvre itself.

In Favor of Brazil and Its Modernity

In contrast to "pessimistic" views of Brazilian society and its historical formation, DaMatta has an undeniably positive and optimistic view of Brazil, but one that is often critical, especially of the national elites. It is better to be a country characterized by football and carnival than by wars, which reaps lives and spread violence, he says. (DaMatta, 1982, 1996). It is better to play sports, dramatizing conflicts in which one can lose with honor and win again—something that can also be read, without difficulty, in Elias.

In a country where "democracy has always been a misunderstanding", as Sérgio Buarque de Holanda had already stated, the idea seems to be to seek a balance, a balance that is configured in its own modernity, also finding new faces in football. Thus, DaMatta recognizes contemporary elements in Brazilian football that relativize the idea (or ideology?) of "football-art". If this sport ceases to be "malandro" and "cheerful", to become "caxias" (stiff) and "very serious" (DaMatta, 1996, p. 49), it is because it transforms itself along with modernized society in structures and styles. The expression of this was, according to DaMatta, Fernando Henrique Cardoso's way of governing.[8]

Still with regard to the relationship between traditional politics and football, the claim that there is no link between football and politics in Brazil is somewhat strange. With so many professional politicians embedded in the world of football, and even in the face of the eventual parliamentary effort to debate (or not debate) it, it seems wrong not to consider this relationship.

I would also like to recapture a point, mentioned in the introduction of this text. One of the fiercest criticisms made by the "new left" to sport refers to the fact that it is strongly linked to the "principle of performance" (Leistungsprinzip), in which competition evidently plays a decisive role. The critique of sport developed mainly in Western Europe understood that it reproduced and reinforced capitalist relations, instrumentalizing bodies and alienating consciences.

Roberto DaMatta, as we may notice, stands against this. For him, the thesis of alienation through sports must be, although not completely disregarded, certainly criticized for being elitist, full of prejudice against popular practices (DaMatta, 1998a). Besides, according to his works, sport does not depersonalize, making the individual get lost in a universal fungibility, but, on the contrary, it gives him the possibility of becoming a "person". It is difficult, however, to speak against depersonalization, but not to criticize, and even to defend, the presence in the Brazilian imaginary of the ideas of "destiny", or of a "game played in the 'other world'."

It is in the sense of "becoming a person" that DaMatta evokes competition as a democratic practice, in the opposite direction to the hierarchies based on kinship, cronyism and patrimonialism. Competition would be, therefore, a modernizing vector in a society in which the values of colonial life, of a weakened public sphere, are still strongly determinative.

> The fact is, however, that the old Breton sport conflicted with traditional values. Accustomed to playing and not competing, Brazilian society, built on favors, hierarchies, clients, and still full of the rancor of slavery, reacted ambiguously to football. The strange game that, with its emphasis on performance, democratically produced winners and losers without depriving any of the players of their names, honors or shame. It was necessary for this society marked by traditional values to learn to separate the rules of the men and of the game, itself before football could be openly appreciated among us. Thus, it was certainly this humble activity, this game invented to amuse and discipline that, in Brazil, became the first defender of democracy and equality. (DaMatta, 1994, p. 12, our traslation)

Perhaps there is a lack on DaMatta's considerations regarding football, a more solid foundation for a comparative sociology that takes football and other sports beyond the United States into account. We remain curious to know to what extent the

---

[8] Rocha (1996) and Fatheuer (1995), both based on Da Matta, develop the argument that, in general terms, football as an art form does not disappear, but it gives way to new forms of games that correspond, in a certain way, to the sociopolitical moment being experienced (fatheuer) and to an expansion in the repertoire of games and consequently in the national identity (Rocha). In both cases, the figure of the Brazilian three-time Formula 1 champion Ayrton Senna appears as a paradigm.

Brazilian singularity is placed, especially in the importance given to the uncertainty of the game, to "supernatural influences", to luck and mischance. Note that in other countries results are also attributed to the influence of divinities or to the "divine" character of the players.[9]

Another important issue is the designation of football as a model of cohesive and harmonious participation. We cannot disregard that this organization often results in orchestrated violence, in the irrational and unmediated relationship within and between fans. Also, in this context, the spectacle-sport is overvalued. The minimization of its character as a product in the schemes of the cultural industry seems to be exaggerated, just as the price paid by athletes to reach high performance is not even mentioned. Expressive sports results are generally achieved at the cost of a lot of organization and hard work, as Da Matta would point out, but also through a lot of violence against the body.

Finally, it should be noted that DaMatta's works are an interesting reference for understanding our social dynamics. They are not only instigating interpretations, but also research material in which we can read the meanings we attribute to the country and what we expect from it.

References

Adorno, T. W. (1997a). Freizeit. In *Gesammelte schriften* (10–2, pp. 645–656). Suhrkamp.

Adorno, T. W. (1997b). Ästhetische theorie. In *Gesammelte Schriften*, 7. Suhrkamp.

Archetti, E. P. (1998). El potremo y el pibe. Territorio y pertenencia en el imaginario del fútbol argentino. *Nueva Sociedad, 154*, 101–119. https://nuso.org/articulo/el-potrero-y-el-pibe-territorio-y-pertenencia-en-el-imaginario-del-futbol-argentino/.

Archetti, E. P. (2001). *El potremo, la pista y el ring. Las patrias del deporte argentino*. Fondo de Cultura Económica.

Bracht, V. (1986). A criança que pratica esporte respeita as regras do jogo... capitalista. *Revista Brasileira de Ciências do Esporte, 7*(2), 62–68. http://revista.cbce.org.br/index.php/RBCE/issue/viewIssue/45/34.

Bracht, V. (1989). Esporte—estado—sociedade. *Revista Brasileira de Ciências do Esporte, 10*(2), 69–73. http://revista.cbce.org.br/index.php/RBCE/issue/viewIssue/53/25.

Bracht, V. (2013). *Sociologia crítica do esporte: Uma introdução* (4th ed.). Unijuí.

Cavalcanti, K. B. (1981). A função cultural do esporte e suas ambiguidades sociais. In L. P. Costa (Ed.), *Teoria e prática do esporte comunitário e de massa* (Vol. I, pp. 301–316). Palestra.

Cavalcanti, K. B. (1984). *Esporte para todos: Um discurso ideológico*. Ibrasa.

Clausen, D. (2014). *Béla Guttmann: Uma lenda do futebol do século XX*. Estação liberdade.

DaMatta, R. (1979). *Carnaval, malandros e heróis: Para uma sociologia do dilema brasileiro*. Zahar.

DaMatta, R. (1982). Esporte na sociedade: um ensaio sobre o futebol brasileiro. In R. DaMatta et al. (Eds.), *Universo do futebol*. Pinakotheke.

DaMatta, R. (1986). *Explorações: Ensaios de sociologia interpretativa*. Rocco.

---

[9] A striking example is the case of Diego Maradona and the mythology that was created in Argentina around him. It is worth reading his autobiography (Maradona, 2000) and Eduardo Archetti's works (1998, 2001) about Argentinean football.

DaMatta, R. (1994). Antropologia do óbvio. *Revista USP, 22*, 10–17. https://doi.org/10.11606/issn. 2316-9036.v0i22p10-17.

DaMatta, R. (1996). *Torre de babel*. Rocco.

DaMatta, R. (1997). *A casa e a rua: Espaço, cidadania, mulher*. Rocco.

DaMatta, R. (1998a). Uma antropologia da sociedade brasileira: Entrevista com Roberto DaMatta (interview granted to Marcos Lanna e Pedro Rodolfo Bodê de Moraes). *Revista de Sociologia e Política,* (10–11), 195–211. https://revistas.ufpr.br/rsp/article/view/39284.

DaMatta, R. (1998b, June 14). Vitória na Copa não terá dono. *Jornal do Brasil*, p. 10.

Elias, N. (1988). *Über den prozess der zivilisation* (2nd ed.). Suhrkamp.

Elias, N. (1991). *Die gesellschaft der individuen*. Suhrkamp.

Elias, N., & Dunning, E. (1986). *Quest for excitement: Sport and leisure in the civilizing process*. Blackwell.

Fatheuer, T. (1995). Das vaterland der fussballschuhe: Eine kleine sozialgeschichte des Brasilianischen fussballs. *Lateinamerika, 19*, 21–37. http://www.jahrbuch-lateinamerika.de/jb-19. html.

Habermas, J. (1958). Soziologische notizen zum Verhältnis von arbeit und freizeit. In H. Plessner, H. E. Bock, & O. Gruppe (Eds.), *Sport und Leibeserziehung* (pp. 28–46). Piper & Co.

Lever, J. (1969). Soccer: Opium of the Brazilian people. *Transaction, 2*, 34–43.

Lovisolo, H. (1995). *Educação física: A arte da mediação*. Sprint.

Lucena, R. (2004). *Sport und sportkritik im zivilisations- und kulturprozess. Analysen nach Adorno & Horkheimer, Elias und DaMatta*. Afra.

Maradona, D. (2000). *Yo soy el Diego de la gente*. Planeta.

Proni, M. W. (2002). Brohm e a organização capitalista do esporte. In M. W. Proni, & R. Lucena, (Orgs.), *Esporte: História e sociedade* (pp. 31–61). Autores Associados.

Rigauer, B. (1969). *Sport und arbeit*. Suhrkamp.

Rocha, E. (1996). As invenções do cotidiano: O descobrimento do Brasil e a conquista do tetra. *Pesquisa de Campo,* (3–4), 9–20. https://ludopedio.com.br/biblioteca/as-invencoes-do-cotidiano-o-descobrimento-do-brasil-e-a-consquista-do-tetra/.

Schwarz, R. (1977). *Ao vencedor as batatas*. Duas cidades.

Soares, A. J. (1994). *A malandragem no gramado*. UFES.

Torri, D., & Vaz, A. F. (2006). Do centro à periferia. *Revista Brasileira de Ciências do Esporte, 28*(1), 185–200. http://revista.cbce.org.br/index.php/RBCE/article/view/46.

Vaz, A. F. (1999). Treinar o corpo, dominar a natureza: notas para uma análise do esporte com base no treinamento corporal. *Cadernos Cedes, 19*(48), 89–108. https://www.cedes.unicamp.br/pub licacoes/edicao/282.

Vaz, A. F. (2002). DaMatta: Futebol como drama e mitologia. In M. W. Proni, & R. Lucena (Orgs.), *Esporte: História e sociedade* (pp. 139–164). Autores Associados.

Zaluar, A. (1991). O esporte na educação e na política pública. *Educação & Sociedade,* (38), 19–44. https://repositorio.ufsc.br/handle/123456789/115599.

Zaluar, A. (1994). *Cidadãos não vão ao paraíso*. Escuta; Editora da Unicamp.

Chapter 10
Neymar, Football and the Formation of a Neoliberal Culture

Michel Nicolau Netto and Sávio Cavalcante

Neymar da Silva Santos posted a vent on his Instagram account in January 2019. Father of that who is considered the best and most expensive Brazilian player in activity, he argued that he was tired of the "socialist system" that would prevails in football, which allegedly considers all players equally. His son, Neymar Jr., had been injured in a match (PSG vs. Strasbourg) and was being criticized by the French and the Brazilian press. In the father's opinion, the criticism was unfair because it curtailed his son's talent, since they recommended his son to stop dribbling in order not to provoke the opponents ("Pai lembra lesões para rebater críticas a Neymar: 'Ter talento não pode?'" ESPN, 2019, January 25).

Neymar "the father" is one of the partners—along with his ex-wife and Neymar Jr.'s mother, Nadine Santos—in the company NR Sports, which manages the personal brand, image and contracts of his son. This post is the starting point for the analysis we propose in this chapter: Which structural conditions present in contemporary capitalism make it possible to mobilize a notion of socialism to complain about an injury suffered by an athlete in highly commodified football competitions?

In this chapter, we offer an answer built through the lenses of sociology. It is not the only one possible. As this book demonstrates, football involves a set of complex relationships that can be observed by different fields of knowledge. Sociology is one of them, and a necessary one, whether it be for those who are only interested in the game, or the sport itself, or for those who have society as their main focus of attention. The sociological endeavour in any field is fraught with difficulties of various kinds. The usual feeling is that taking on this task, that is, naming the forces that affect the fields—and, when necessary, seeing in the subjects the expressions of broader social processes—, nullifies what makes them particular. Worse, it takes

M. N. Netto (✉) · S. Cavalcante
University of Campinas, Campinas, Brazil
e-mail: mnicolau@unicamp.br

S. Cavalcante
e-mail: saviomc@unicamp.br

© The Author(s), under exclusive license to Springer Nature Switzerland AG 2021
S. S. Giglio and M. W. Proni (eds.), *Football and Social Sciences in Brazil*,
https://doi.org/10.1007/978-3-030-84686-2_10

away their beauty, their irreducible character. We would like to warn the reader, then, that it is precisely this enchantment, which encourages us to sketch an answer.

The core of the argument that will be developed here can be formulated as follows: at the same time that it reproduces the most specific and enchanting features of the sports practice, football carries in itself its own mechanism of production of behaviours and values that is deeply anchored in a social context that crosses its borders. We can safely say that this context is far from representing a socialist system. Rather, it is capitalism we are talking about. More specifically, about global economic processes that require a particular type of conduct and subjectivity.

More than a hundred years ago, when Max Weber set himself the challenge of understanding the cultural conditions that had made possible the emergence of the capitalist system, he identified in real people a "spirit" that transcended them— they were bearers of something greater than themselves. He highlighted Benjamin Franklin's lines, such as "remember that time is money", and "[money] is procreative by nature and fertile". And so, Weber (1958, p. 78) observed: "[…] it is the spirit of capitalism which here speaks in characteristic fashion, no one will doubt, however little we may wish to claim that everything which could be understood as pertaining to that spirit is contained in it."

We will signal as the main material base of this spirit the process of commodification, which here can be understood as the tendency to transform elements of a certain phenomenon into something that acquires a price in a certain market, entering, thus, into a determined production and circulation system. By using this concept to analyse football, we are not claiming that the sport can be reduced to it: not everything in football has become or has been becoming merchandise. At the same time, however, we affirm that this process is becoming increasingly extensive and intense in football. More extensive, because it encompasses more and more elements of this practice. More intense, because the commodification process intensifies in each element. Let us see an example to get out of the abstract: the supporter's passion. This will never be reduced to a commodity; the supporter will never be a mere consumer, like a shoe buyer who can enjoy several brands simultaneously. However, it is a fact that such passion is currently undergoing a commodification process, which occurs as with the supporter-membership system, in the sale of team products, etc. A recent example: the 2019 sponsorship agreement between the Brazilian football team Sport Club Corinthians Paulista, which has one of the two largest fan base in the country, and the BMG bank. Under the agreement, Corinthians receives a sum of money from the bank (reportedly R$ 12 million per year) for exposure of the sponsor's brand on the shirt and other materials. In addition, the bank will create a financial product aimed directly at Corinthians fans.

Half of the bank's profit from this product will be allocated to Corinthians: R$ 18 million per year, according to the Corinthians Board of Directors. The bank and the team's Board of Directors obviously hope that Corinthians fans' passion can be quantified and standardized to the point of *functioning* as a commodity. Once again, this does not mean that passion will be reduced to this—the supporter will continue to love his team in different ways—, but rather, that this has become a fundamental dimension of the relationship between team and supporter.

There is still another dimension of the commodification process. We understand that its intensification and extension have implications in people's personal practices or, returning to Weber, in life conducts. The fan, the manager and the athlete start to conduct their practices determined (i.e., their actions are coerced in different ways) by the commodification process. In this text we will try to understand this phenomenon through the analysis of the player—and the *brand*—Neymar. We believe it is plausible to consider that, through the words of Neymar "the father", it is the spirit of contemporary global capitalism that speaks to us. This happens because, besides being a son and a player with rare skills, Neymar Jr. is a brand and, as such, a commodity to be "valued". We take the player as an object of study in this sense because, from him, a significant part of the current cultural production can be described and analysed in its concrete form.[1]

Certainly, Neymar Jr.'s dribbles and goals are not determined only by "the naked self-interest, [by] than callous of cash payment", as Marx and Engels underline when describing the bourgeois order in the *Communist Manifesto*. The charm—or the "magic" of football—may still always be found in a throw or a match. But as the authors of the *Manifesto* have warned, this enchantment can also "melts into air" (Marx & Engels, 2008). Let us tell a bit of that story here.

The Commodification of Football-Spectacle

We start from the theoretical assumption that the individual has their life conduct predisposed by the structures that surround them. This way, to understand a football player's attitudes (specifically Neymar, our character here) and his relation with the neoliberal subject, it is necessary that we start with the history of the process of football spectacle commodification.

Let us remember that when Adi Dassler, in 1954, convinced the German coach Sepp Herberger that his players would have a better chance in the World Cup Finals if they wore Adidas boots, neither Herberger nor the players imagined the possibility of asking for money in exchange for wearing them. The practice had been common since the 1936 Olympics, when the German shoe manufacturer Gebrüder Dassler had obtained permission from the Nazi government to offer their products to German athletes. The relationship between sports champions and their shoes seemed as a guaranteed way to expand the market, and the Dassler brothers (Adi and Rudolf) did not shy away from going beyond government authorization and also offered their shoes to the enemy: Jesse Owens, the black man who defied the racism of the Nazi

---

[1] This text was concluded in February 2019. Therefore, two landmark cases in the athlete's career remain absent from it. The first, the accusation of rape made by Nájila Trindade against Neymar Jr. He denied the allegations and accused her of extortion. Police closed the case. The second, the racist insult he claimed to have suffered from an opponent in a match in September 2020. Both cases require a more accurate treatment, which was not possible here. We consider, however, that the arguments developed in this text—the imbrication of the player as a person and as a brand—contribute to the analysis of important dimensions of these cases.

government, also wore Dassler shoes. In fact, the brothers' adherence to Nazism had been no greater than their adherence to the capital (Smit, 2007).

Soon after, however, competition between shoe companies would become more aggressive, and the mere supply of sporting goods, insufficient. In 1960, at the Rome Olympics, the sports apparel company Puma made a ground-breaking deal with the German runner Armin Hary. The company not only gave him the shoes for the 100-m finals, but also guaranteed him a cash payment to wear them. That act was forbidden at the time because it hurt the Olympic rules of amateurism, officially in force up until the Olympic charter (a type of constitution that rules the Olympic movement) of 1978. Even the commercial exploitation of the use of sportive materials of a certain company by an athlete used to be controlled, and the sports apparel companies could not tie the name or the image of an athlete directly to a product. Thus, "when advertising they were forced to disguise the identity of any athletes pictured by blurring their faces or placing a black band across their eyes" (Smit, 2007).

However, already at that moment, the interest of companies in using major sporting events to promote their sports shoes, and that of athletes in being paid for this bond began to impose a new economic order on sports. Still behind the curtains, in 1968, at the Mexico Olympics, some athletes received up to US$ 10,000 from Adidas or Puma to compete in their shoes. Overtly, since the World Cup was not regulated by the rules of amateurism, English players received £1,000.00 for their feet in the 1966 World Cup Finals.

These amounts are insignificant when we think about the contracts of the big stars of football today. However, this is the origin of a history marked by the process of commodification of the sport that we are interested in reviewing, and the presence of Adidas and Puma is no coincidence. Their founders, Adolf (Adi) and Rudolf (Rudi) Dassler, inherited a shoe business from their father (Christoph Dassler) and trans-formed it into the company Gebrüder Dassler Sportsschuhfabrik, Herzogenaurach (Dassler brothers, sports shoe factory, Herzogenaurach), which operated until 1948, when the brothers split up and founded their respective companies: Adi founded Adidas and Rudi, Puma. The history of competition and enmity between the two is well known, subject of books, documentaries and TV series, so we will not go over it again here. We shall only highlight that, in their engagement in this competition, sports companies became involved in sports politics and became influential agents in the production field of the sports spectacle (Oliveira, 2015).

Adi's son, Horst Dassler, made good use of the social capital acquired during the years working with his father. As Barbara Smit reports, in 1956, at the Melbourne Olympics, while Horst was trying to convince athletes to wear Adidas shoes, he knew the world's sporting elite and established a strong reputation as a sports busi-nessman. After the games, Horst took over the company's operations in France, and the distance from his family allowed him to undertake his own vision for the business. João Havelange's victory for president of the *Fédération Internationale de Football Association* (FIFA) in 1974 became a turning point in Dassler's path and for the commodification of sports. Havelange defeated the Englishman Stanley Rous, president between 1961 and 1974, who had been notable for his criticism of the commercialisation of football, but who was seen by non-European countries as elitist and not concerned with the expansion of the sport outside of Europe (Jennings, 2006). In the campaign, Havelange focused precisely on non-European countries' votes, promising to increase the number of national teams participating in the World Cup and the funds allocated for the development of football in those countries. Havelange even used his Brazilian ancestry as a way to oppose the British Rous. After being elected, he also expanded the myth of racial democracy by stating that being Brazilian:

> It was an advantage for me when I became president of FIFA, that since a small child I have lived together with all the different races and understood their mentalities. It is nothing new for me to be in FIFA's multi-racial environment […] In São Paulo and Rio there are streets with Arabs living on one side and Jews on the other side and they live in the same street in perfect harmony. (Tomlinson, 2014, pp. 1580–1584)

With the victory, Havelange needed money to fulfil his promises. Today FIFA has 390 employees, but in the late 1960s it was still a small institution with only four employees and no resources to fulfil campaign promises (Tomlinson, 2014). The commercial exploitation of sport attracted Havelange and Horst Dassler. The German had approached, in the early 1970s, Patrick Nally, advertising manager and partner, with Peter West, from the company Westnally. Although the term "sports marketing" was only coined at the end of the 1970s (Proni, 1998), West and Nally's company had already developed their beginnings in the USA, establishing connections with important executives from companies such as Coca-Cola. It was precisely with Coca-Cola, through Nally and Norst, that FIFA, now presided by João Havelange, signed its first sponsorship contract, in 1976. Coca-Cola is the first company to sign an advertising contract with FIFA directly, and not through the host countries committees, to sponsor the World Cup for 12 million Swiss francs (Smit, 2007). In 1983, Nally and Dassler founded the sports marketing company ISL—International Sport and Leisure—which, until their closing in 2001, had in their history several scandals and businesses with numerous sports entities, including FIFA and the International Olympic Committee (IOC) (Brewer, 2017; Chade, 2014; Jennings, 2006; Tomlinson, 2014).

It is from Dassler and Nally's team that, after the 1984 Olympics, the marketing programme "The Olympic Partner"—TOP arises, named by a former ISL employee, today's IOC consultant and former Rio 2016 consultant, Michael Payne, as the "Olympic turnaround" (Payne, 2006). In fact, TOP signified a new relationship between events, sport and capital, having been subsequently adopted by FIFA (also by the hands of Dassler and Nally) and served as the basis for all agreements in professional sport today. The programme is based on the sale of the exclusive rights, by product category, to associate a given brand with the Olympic brand (Oliveira, 2015) and points to serious transformations.

In FIFA and IOC versions, the marketing plan of mega events (World Cup and the Olympics) came to be controlled by these organization, and no longer by national committees, that is, a process that we may call denationalization of the production of these events. We borrow the concept of denationalization from Saskia Sassen (2006), who defines it as the process in which a series of functions created on a national basis are transferred to transnational entities. In the case at hand, this has developed in two ways. Firstly, FIFA and the IOC took over the exclusive use of symbols and terms, something that was previously the right of local committees, or was not protected at all. For example, the Olympic symbols had been the property of National Olympic Committees since 1950, when the US Olympic committee (USOA) won a lawsuit against the bread brand Helms, which had registered the Olympic rings as their property soon after supplying their products at the 1936 Olympics (Barney et al., 2004). Similarly, FIFA has increasingly undertaken efforts to protect certain symbols as their own. For example, up until 1994, the name of the World Cup varied from country to country. In 1966, the official poster referred to the event as World Cup, but in 1970, it was called World Championship, as it was in Brazil in 1950, with the subtitle: Jules Rimet Cup. Since 1994, all editions have been called World Cup, and from 2002 on, the registered term is FIFA World Cup, followed by the name of the country. The effort to maintain control over the name and symbols of the World Cup is immense: in Brazil, FIFA has registered 1116 trademarks with the National Institute of Industrial Property (INPI); in 2006, they registered the German World Cup logo in 153 countries and sued 3300 companies in 84 countries that allegedly used the registered symbols without authorization (Chade, 2014).

With control over their symbols—or rather, with the appropriation of symbols that refer to collective knowledge and experiences and that were then transformed into brands—FIFA and the IOC can offer companies the exclusivity of attaching their names to the Olympics and World Cup brands. The deliberate scarcity produced by these relationships is precisely the basis of their business. Thus, the rarer the possibility of linking a brand to the sports brands, the more profitable the relationship becomes. To that end, the organizations have restricted the number of sponsors, focusing more and more on global brands with great capacity to spend *marketing* resources. The change is radical. In 1972, the German Olympic Committee signed 628 advertising contracts with companies for the Munich Olympics, mostly local firms that received from the committee the right to use the Olympic brands and exhibit their brands at the event. For this, each paid US$ 50,000 (Barney et al., 2004, p. 155). In 2016, between the Worldwide Olympic Partners and Official Sponsors categories, there were 16 sponsors that, together, paid around US$ 2.25 billion. In the case of the World Cup, between FIFA Partners and FIFA World Cup Sponsors, there were 14 sponsors who jointly disbursed around US$ 2 billion (FIFA, 2015, May 28–29). It is interesting to note that these sponsors do target a global market, which is evidenced by the fact that most of them were present at both the South Africa and Brazil Cups (Table 10.1).

We have seen so far, therefore, that mega events have become global platforms for brands due to the increasing insertion of the mercantile logic in these events, and the denationalization of their production, increasingly controlled by FIFA and the IOC. However, this can only occur because the events in fact have become of global interest. It does not even matter if a country is competing, or if it has chances of winning, the event interferes in the daily lives of people anywhere. This process is achieved largely through television and, today, the Internet. The first television broadcasting of a mega event took place in 1936, with the Garmisch-Partenkirchen

Table 10.1 FIFA partners and FIFA World Cup sponsors

2010 South Africa	2014 Brazil
Adidas	Adidas
Coca-Cola	Coca-Cola
Emirates	Emirates
Hyunday (Kia)	Hyunday (Kia)
Sony	Sony
Visa	Visa
Budweiser	Budweiser
Continental	Continental
Castrol	Castrol
McDonald's	McDonald's
Mahindra Satyam	Johnson & Johnson
MTN	Hello
Seara	Moy Park
Yingli Solar	Yingli Solar

Source FIFA

Winter Games, which was repeated with the Summer Olympics of the same year, also held in Germany. In these two sporting events, as well as in the London (1948), Helsinki (1952) and Melbourne (1956) Olympics, and in the first World Cup (1954) broadcasts, they were limited to a few countries, to a few stretches of the competitions, and with a few days delays. However, in the 1950s, the Soviets launched the *Sputnik* satellite and 18 European countries—and, with a few hours' delay, the USA, Canada and Japan—watched the 1960 Olympics on television (Oliveira, 2015; Zimbalist, 2016). Television broadcasting has relevant impacts in what matters to us here. First, because it becomes the main source of revenue for events. In 1956, in Melbourne, for the first time the concept of television rights, and the governance policies of their sales emerged (Barney et al., 2004) copying the American model, where already in the 1950s the Baseball League charged US\$ 6 million for the broadcasting rights of their games for a five-year contract (1951–1956) (idem, ibidem). Television rights have been rising edition by edition: in 2014, they generated US\$ 2.47 billion for FIFA, and US\$ 2.35 billion for the IOC in 2016.

Secondly, television ensures that sponsor brands are broadcast worldwide. Thus, the brands present in the World Cup stadiums were captured in 2014 by 34 cameras (five more than in 2010) and broadcasted to 239 countries and territories. Furthermore, through contract with the broadcasters, FIFA has guaranteed, since 2002, that all matches are broadcast in full, which includes both the entrance of players (with the camera capturing the Adidas ball) and the post-match interviews that the players give with a sign of the event sponsors behind them.

FIFA also ensures that all rebroadcast footage is identical, regardless of territory, as it is produced solely by HBS under FIFA's licence. This means that local broadcasters cannot choose which images to transmit, nor can they interrupt the broadcast, giving

FIFA complete control over the images. It is through this control that FIFA—and the same is true for the IOC—tries to assure to the sponsoring brands that they will be the only ones seen during the matches, and in the way they wish to. In fact, in the 2014 World Cup General Law (Lei No. 12,663/2012 June 5), one of the main guarantees given to FIFA by the State was that there would be no room for the so-called ambush marketing, i.e. the disclosure of brands, products or services, with the purpose of achieving economic or advertising advantage, through direct or indirect association with the Games, without FIFA's authorization (Lei No. 12,663/2012, June 5, art. 32).

Thus, sports present in the field of spectacle production are definitely tied to commercial interests; every gesture of the athletes, every image they produce, all of it is immediately transformed into merchandise. Major sporting events today operate following FIFA's and the IOC's model described here. This is the case of the Champions League, completely reformulated in the 1990s, especially after the company TEAM—Television, Event and Media Marketing—, responsible for developing ways "to produce the league brand", was hired by the Union of European Football Associations (UEFA). That was when the league created an anthem (Handel's version of "Zadok, the priest," with the chant "Champions" at the end), a logo and a colour pattern. All stadiums that hold matches for the championship are standardized and, as TEAM (apud King, 2004, p. 56) states, "irrespective of whether you are a spectator in Moscow or in Milan, you will always see the same stadium dressing materials, the same opening ceremony featuring the 'starball' centre circle ceremony and hear the same UEFA Champions League Anthem." With this, in the same way as FIFA, UEFA guarantees their sponsors that no matter where they are, the spectator will see the same images: those of the brands.

The history of mega events merchandising reveals the logic of the commodification process that spreads across the various elements of sporting practices, which conditions the conduct of agents involved in them. In the case of football clubs, since the early 1980s they have lost their shame with their shirts—sacred for some—and have made them available for companies interested in displaying their brands, with much more prominence than that of the club's crest. This adds to the competition among teams a second and fiercer dispute: for money, by the clubs.

What we can do is point out a general process that, although unequal, operates as a system from the richest to the poorest of agents. Thus, both in Brazilian and European clubs, the logic of the commodification process is equally observed. A symptom of this is the transformation of fans into consumers (Dubal, 2010; Webber, 2017). The metamorphosis occurs through the creation of programmes (in Brazil called "stakeholders-supporters") in which the supporter becomes a permanent, instead of casual, consumer (such as the one who buys the ticket on the day of the game). Furthermore, their place to cheer live is being transformed, with stadiums being renovated and increasingly resembling consumption temples, not only in its architecture and the intensive presence of consumer goods, but also through the behaviour expected from fans, who have become as well disciplined as consumers, bearing similar rights and duties. Thus, in England (and in several stadiums in Brazil), "all-seated stadiums" have been adopted (Hollanda, 2017), and it has become common for a person to ask (or shout) for another to sit down, arguing that he has paid for the ticket and has the right to watch the game sitting down. The consequence of this is that the fan with little money matters less and less. In Brazil, they still connect with their team through the TV—some of the games continue to be broadcast on open TV—because going to the stadium has become increasingly difficult for them.[2]

But here we are concerned with another agent: the football player. It is clear that we are thinking, at this point, only of the athlete at the top of this process, who plays in high-profit teams and in leagues of global dimensions. What interests us is to know how the becoming of the successful player in this scenario is determined by the broader process of football commodification.

The Commodity "Football Player" and the Neymar Case

When we refer to commodification—of sport, of clubs, of their relationships with supporters and of the very making of players—it is important to recognize both differences and similarities in relation to other activities that are subject to the same process. The analysis we make here requires some considerations, albeit limited, regarding a very extensive debate in the field of human sciences.

Let us take the example of factory production. The owners of a given company have a sufficient amount of monetary resources to buy land, facilities, machinery, supplies and the lifetime of workers who, because they do not have their own means of production, sell their labour force in exchange for wages. The company's money then functions as capital: it is invested in the production of a given commodity aiming at obtaining a profit at the end of the cycle. In this sense, a car factory, for example, may spend years designing a new product, but it knows that the investment will pay off after the serial production of thousands or millions of copies of the original prototype. The value of goods, according to Marx (2001), has an objective determination: it is measured by the labour time socially necessary for the reproduction of these copies, which also needs to reach stores and, finally, consumers.

In the middle of the nineteenth century, when Marx began the research that gave rise to *Capital,* production in these typically capitalist moulds was found in a very small part of the world. Realizing that this logic was necessarily self-expanding, Marx predicted that the greater part of material production (in the sense of tangible goods, which can be dissociated from those who produced them) would be subordinated to

---

[2] According to Alexandre Kalil, former president of Atlético Mineiro, one of the most popular clubs in Brazil, and current mayor of the capital of Minas Gerais, Belo Horizonte, Brazilian football needs to "copy [the models of other countries in which] the poor watch on TV and the rich go to the stadium. Is that discrimination? No. Then they tell me: Are you inventing this? No, I am copying the world. […] This is not my opinion, no, this is copying the model that has worked in the world. It is like the city hall forbidding someone to sell *pastel* [fried pastry] for 30 reals and saying that it has to be 1 real for poor people. Hold on, it's my pastel; it's not yours, no! Whoever thinks that football is a cultural asset [to be widely accessible to the population] should go to the government with a proposal and the government should subsidise the clubs. I have nothing against it, but I think we have to take care of the readjustment of [Public Health System], education, the structure of the country before" (Interview to L. Oliveira & T. Fernandes, 2019, February 18, our translation).

this pattern. One reason is its technical efficiency. In a first moment, capitalists hire wageworkers to produce under "traditional" technical conditions. Later, they create their own technical means to increase productivity. Marx further stated that labour and commodity production are swallowed up by two complementary processes: *formal subsumption and real subsumption to capital.* In the first (formal), the relations of production are altered by means of the waging of the "free" worker. In the second (real), the technical means themselves and the subjectivity of the workers are moulded according to the objectives of production.

The last decades of the twentieth century witnessed the expansion of the capitalist logic in a wide variety of sectors, not necessarily only in manufacturing. Capitalist companies began to compete for activities beyond the world of production of physical and tangible goods. The capitalist industrial logic expanded, reaching the field of "services" such as health, education, leisure, social reproduction of families, etc.

Here is the point that interests us: when a social activity becomes determined by this economic logic, it tends to "import" the demands present in the production of goods in traditional sectors. The capital invested in sports requires a rationalization of the activity that makes it possible to compare this investment and the possibility of return to so many others that the markets may offer. It is true that investments can be made "at no cost" due to someone's personal passion, something very common in football, which shows how the economy is always overdetermined by social forces.[3] However, non-rational business strategies—in the sense of maximizing return—are increasingly challenged by large investment funds that operate impersonally. This is the force that drives the commodification of football's inherent relationships: rational calculation—and, through it, greater control over the predictability of earnings—needs to be extended to all the pieces that make up this sphere to the point of knowing how much one profits from the investment of each dollar or real through each of these pieces: the sales of shirts, tickets, the image rights to broadcast matches and, of course, the players that are bought and sold in a specific market.

As pointed out in the previous item, a key piece in the gears of this industry is the dispute around the construction, consolidation and dissemination of brands. The relationship between merchandise and brands is old, but it gains an unprecedented role in capitalism between the 1970s and 1980s. As Paulani (2016) observes, the purpose of brands becomes broader than potentiating the sale of goods. They intend to "generate value"[4] by themselves by creating an intangible heritage independent even from the products themselves, a particular and unique relationship with consumers who identify themselves in some way with what the brands claim to represent.

When we say, then, that contemporary capitalism seeks to subsume football as much as possible, the consequence, from the point of view of the human factor essential to the sport—the player—, is that his training needs, increasingly, to deal

---

[3] Not to mention the strategy, also rational, so common to football, to "launder" illicitly obtained resources.

[4] The process of brand creation, according to Paulani (2016), does not generate value, but allows companies to extract profit by creating a mechanism analogous to the "monopoly rents" discussed by Marx.

with two problems simultaneously: how to obtain the maximum efficiency in terms of the skills needed for practice and, at the same time, how to make them seem to integrate the image of an athlete to the point of singularizing him, i.e. to the point that he can live up to what his brand promises. The formation of the athlete and brand Neymar is, in this sense, especially significant. Through it, we will also see how the "neo-liberal subject", as named by Dardot and Laval (2014), is engendered and justified.

To that end, it is worth to follow the journey of Neymar's career as narrated by the well-known Brazilian sports journalist, Paulo Vinícius Coelho (2014). In *O planeta Neymar: Um perfil*, PVC—as he is known—presents the story of a Brazilian teenager "predestined to become an idol". In the context of intense competition among young people, from a very early age, and dispute for a successful professional career, the qualifier "predestined" attributed by the journalist to the protagonist of his book could not go unnoticed.

If the expression had come from Neymar or his family, Christians who attend the Peniel Baptist Church in the city of São Vicente, it would be understandable to consider the extent to which the notion of Calvinist predestination discussed in the classic study by Weber (1958) resonates with it. However, the term came from the pen of the journalist and author of the book, which allows it to be interpreted in a more secular register. It is a narrative, therefore, more attuned to the secular liberal discourse that begins with the identification of scarce skills in a young man who is a "rough diamond" and, through much effort and dedication, achieves an exceptional technical performance and financial success.

Amidst so many other talented youngsters, Neymar stood out for, from an early age, controlling a different set of skills: Neymar kicks with both his feet, he heads, he shoots on his chest, he makes throws, he disarms opponents, he sets up attacking moves… in short, he brings together a wide repertoire of footballing qualities— whereas most players cannot even be as proficient in just one of these skills (Coelho, 2014). His ability to use his left foot, even though he is right-footed, is testament to his hard work in training, which has helped him hone a talent that would have come "straight from the factory". A skill that coaches and especially the player's father—who is also, let's not forget, his career manager—have contributed to.

When Neymar was only ten years old, Zito—one of the greatest legends in Santos Football Club's history and, at the time, an employee of the club responsible for the youth categories—was delighted to see him play for Portuguesa Santista. His enthusiasm convinced Marcelo Teixeira, then president of the team, to find a way to put him in the youth categories of Santos. However, in Santos they were only for boys over 12 years old. So the solution was to create a new category, especially to incorporate Neymar.

It is important to highlight that the building of Neymar, the player, was simultaneous to the building of Neymar, the brand. What is interesting from the sociological point of view is that such overlapping processes cannot be explained only by intentions or individual desires, but by a set of relationships that pave the way of individual choices. That is to say that the existence of a global market and the expectation of participating in the world of high figures had the promise from Santos FC probed, as early as 13 years old, by Real Madrid. The path had been opened by the proximity of the athlete manager and agent Wagner Ribeiro with the Spanish club, since Ribeiro had recently sold another Santos player to Real Madrid, Robinho.

Neymar, accompanied by his father and Ribeiro, went to Madrid to meet the team, do some tests and stayed there for about two weeks. He was offered a millionaire contract, an apartment for the family and school for his sister Rafaella (Pinheiro, 2007, October).[5] Unlike another future global star, the Argentine Lionel Messi—who already at that age migrated definitively to Barcelona—Neymar decided to return to Brazil.

The complex confluence of interests and desires that clashed in this decision helps to understand the dual formation of the player-company. According to Daniela Pinheiro (2007), Ribeiro stated that he was in favour of that excellent business. From Neymar father's point of view, it was necessary to accept the decision of his son who, sad, would not get used to life in Madrid, would miss his friends and Brazilian food. But PVC's report touches on another, quite plausible, dimension for the father to be afraid:

> Would there be room in the near future for him in a squad bloated with superstars whose transfer fees had cost Real [Madrid] a fortune? Or would he, like many other young talents, be forced to accept a plan B and be loaned out to minor Spanish teams such as Granada, from the city of the same name, or Rayo Vallecano, from the Vallecas district of Madrid, and *risk not fulfilling the destiny of the great footballstar that everything indicated was reserved for him*? (Coelho, 2014, p. 66, our emphasis, our translation)

In the sociological analysis we propose here, it is not a matter of assessing the moral correctness of the decisions made by each agent in this process. It is important to identify the factors that objectively weigh in a decision that requires a very different ability from that of a right-handed person to kick well with his left foot. It is necessary to have a commercial vision, a feeling for business capable of discerning the best opportunities to obtain and expand revenue.

The equation used to refuse the contract also included the fact that the harassment by the Spanish people would necessarily generate a counterpart from Santos FC. In the football market, the expectation for the future price of the diamond already polished would justify an audacious plan in the present. Santos board then offered a contract that guaranteed the player R$ 2 million signing bonus, to be paid in instalments until the athlete turned 19. Therefore, while the other players of Santos sub-15 category received an allowance of R$ 180 reals, Neymar went on to earn a

---

[5] The article by Daniela Pinheiro (2007, October) in *Piauí* magazine about Ribeiro states that "they offered $3 million to have him immediately. Because of his young age he could not sign a work contract. The club even got Neymar's father a job as a mechanic at an Audi factory, the team's sponsor, to justify the family's moving".

salary of R\$ 16 thousand.[6] Marcelo Teixeira did not believe that this disparity would create a bad environment among the other athletes:

> I swear I didn't think about any of that. The only risk I pondered was that of him suffering an injury and becoming unfit for football. It was a risk, no doubt, but the only one I could see. I trusted in luck. I also believed in what I saw in front of me. Neymar had a family base. He wasn't going to get lost. To this day, his family accompanies and supports him (Coelho, 2014, p. 75, our translation).

Another attempt to sign the player occurred in 2010, this time by the English club Chelsea. When the proposal reached 35 million euros, Neymar's father and Ribeiro considered it impossible to refuse. A new offer from Santos's board of directors was successful by raising his salary to R\$ 600 thousand and, a key point, transferring 70% of the image rights—advertising contracts and television licence made by the club using the player's image—to the star. In 2011, Real Madrid came forward again and raised the proposal to 60 million euros.[7] Once more Santos used the image rights and gave the player 90% of what they were entitled to. The Brazilian club thus achieved something very rare in the current global market, that is, to hold a high level player in the country for long. With this, it also gained a lot, in titles and expansion of the fan base. The values, for Neymar's family, were impressive: not counting salaries, just for image rights, Neymar may have received around 12 million euros annually, a higher amount, at that moment, than the "galactic" Cristiano Ronaldo (Coelho, 2014). The departure from Brazil occurred only in 2013, in a controversial negotiation with Barcelona that, according to estimates, earned Neymar's family company 60 million euros and caused, in addition to the resignation of the president of the Catalan club, an intense legal dispute.[8]

In fact, as signalled by Teixeira, Neymar is the object, until today, of a family business of high income. And it is not only about the amounts obtained in salary negotiations with clubs, but, increasingly, about the marketing of the brand. Neymar

---

[6] According to an article published in the newspaper *Folha de São Paulo* (Mattoso & Garcia, 2018, June 12), Luis Alvaro de Oliveira Ribeiro, president of Santos since 2009, used to say, "jokingly, that Neymar, the father, deserved the Nobel Prize in economics. That's because he went from being an ex-employee of CET (traffic engineering company) to a ruthless negotiator, with a millionaire asset in his hands". The article also brings the statement of Fernando Silva, who participated in negotiations with the player: "Neymar [the father] is a guy who understoond what was around his son and prepared himself for it."

[7] At the same time, the doors seemed to be open at the rival Barcelona. Neymar-father met with the then president of the Catalan club, Sandro Rosell, at a dinner, and reportedly told friends something like: "I took a shower, put on my best clothes, put on a little perfume, went to the restaurant and practically said: 'eat me, Sandro!'" According to PVC, "the metaphor was about the way he offered his son to Barcelona's teeth" (Coelho, 2014, p. 73).

[8] While Santos claimed to have received 17 million euros, Barcelona claimed to have paid 57 million. The case has generated several disputes in the courts due to payments not officially accounted for. Neymar's father admitted that he received 10 million euros as a way to ensure the sale of his son to Barcelona, even before the legal signing of the contract, which could be considered a pre-sale. It is important to note that this amount had already been transferred to Neymar when he was still a Santos player, and even before the match for the FIFA Club World Cup in 2011, played precisely against the Catalan club, his future employer.

was the player with the most sponsorship contracts in the world in 2018, with 35 arrangements (Sheen, 2018, December 10). In 2016, shortly before moving to Paris Saint-Germain, he was better paid by these contracts than by the salary he received from Barcelona. The advertising contracts are made between the sponsors and the company that manages the career and image of Neymar, the NR. The player, by contract, receives 15% of all agreements, just like a highly paid employee of a company. The other 85% goes to the company's partners, and the player's father and mother (Garcia, 2018, August 21).

It is important to take a step back in this story to get a sense of the magnitude of the changes. As we saw above, until the 1960s, players were not paid for using certain sporting materials. Even after that, when they started getting paid for it, the remunerations were specific, referring to one game, as it happened with Pelé, who got money for wearing Puma boots in the 1970 final. Cruyff may have been the first soccer player to have a permanent contract (an endorsement) with a sponsoring company, precisely Puma. This change is decisive to the extent that, once permanently linked to a brand, the player must observe his own behaviours having this brand in his mind and body.

What is most important for us to note is that, just like big events and clubs, stars are becoming brands themselves. Recently, some players have started to be described by acronyms—CR7, NRJ—, and this is not a mere simplified way of referring to them. In fact, these acronyms are trademarks, registered by companies that aim to commercially exploit the image of players. The stars they refer to earn huge salaries, but it should be noted that this income is only part of their revenues. As the table below shows, with data from 2018, on average 20% of the revenues of the 20 best-paid players in the world come from advertising contracts (Table 10.2).

Note that there is a huge salary concentration (38.78%), and even more of sponsorship (61.03%), in the three best-paid players. In fact, these players have brands—assessed by the possibility of attracting sponsors who, in turn, are anchored in the ability to reach consumers—that compete with many clubs. The US$ 47 million received by Cristiano Ronaldo alone represents almost half of what his new club, Juventus Turin, managed to collect in 2018: US$ 102 million. Neymar's US$ 17 million correspond to 15% of what his team, Paris Saint-Germain, raised in advertising contracts (Sujith, 2018, October 13). Neymar's contracts represent the same amount that the Brazilian club Grêmio collected in 2018, lower, in Brazil, only to the contracts of the clubs Palmeiras, Corinthians, Flamengo and São Paulo (Iasnogrodski, 2018, December 2).

On NR Sports' own website (under the "Neymar Jr. and the market" tab), Neymar is presented as one of the biggest influencers and trendsetters, since in 2018 he had more than 60 million likes on Facebook, more than 104 million followers on Instagram, and more than 40 million on Twitter, and had almost 800,000 subscribers on his official YouTube channel (Netto & Cavalcante, 2020, p. 248). The unquestionable marketing potential of Neymar Jr. is strongly emphasized, and his name and image are presented as effective brand promoters, which can be linked to different types

Table 10.2 Income of the world's top players in 2018

	Name	Team	Position	Salary + Bonus (millions US$)	Endorsements (million US$)	Total (millions US$)	Endorsements/Total (%)
1	Lionel Messi	Barcelona	Forward	84	27	111	24.32
2	Cristiano Ronaldo	Real Madrid	Forward	61	47	108	43.52
3	Neymar Jr	PSG	Forward	73	17	90	18.89
4	Gareth Bale	Real Madrid	Forward	28.6	6	34.6	17.34
5	Paul Pogba	Manchester United	Midfielder	25	4.5	29.5	15.25
6	Oscar	Shanghai	Forward	25.9	1.5	27.4	5.47
7	Luis Suarez	Barcelona	Forward	19.9	7	26.9	26.02
8	Wayne Rooney	Everton	Forward	22	5	27	18.52
9	Sergio Aguero	Manchester City	Forward	17	6.5	23.5	27.66
10	Angel di Maria	PSG	Forward	20.6	2	22.6	8.85
11	Kylian Mbappe	PSG	Forward	20	1.5	21.5	6.98
12	Thiago Silva	PSG	Defender	21.4	1	22.4	4.46
13	James Rodrigues	Bayern Munich	Forward	16.8	5.3	22.1	23.98
14	Graziano Pelle	Shandong Luneng	Forward	21.1	1	22.1	4.52
15	Hulk	Shanghai	Forward	21	1	22	4.55
16	Zlatan Ibrahimovic	Los Angeles Galaxy	Forward	15.5	5.5	21	26.19
17	Gerard Piquet	Barcelona	Defender	17.5	3.3	20.8	15.87
18	Antoine Griezmann	Atlético de Madrid	Forward	16.7	3	19.7	15.23

(continued)

Table 10.2 (continued)

	Name	Team	Position	Salary + Bonus (millions US$)	Endorsements (million US$)	Total (millions US$)	Endorsements/Total (%)
19	Yaya Toure	Manchester City	Midfielder	17.1	2.5	19.6	12.76
20	Cavani	PSG	Forward	18	1.5	19.5	7.69
	Total			562.1	149.1	711.2	20.96

Source Forbes (https://www.forbes.com/athletes/). Own elaboration

of products, aimed at various audiences. NR Sports even states that it has worked from the beginning to reinforce the prestige of this unique player and build a brand of worldwide impact, that is, to transform Neymar into one of the most desired icons of the advertising market.

The Formation of the Neoliberal Culture

An interesting dimension of the processes described here coming from football is that they can be narrated within the register already naturalized by the culture corresponding to the "spirit" of contemporary capitalism. Merchandising is a process that is expressed in almost all spheres of social life, and it is not difficult to find a myriad of other cases—such as artists, for example—in which subordination to the logic of the capitalist market also requires the building of an entrepreneurial being in each individual. The recurrence and intensity of these situations provide a natural aspect to socially and historically determined processes. If amateurism is left behind, why should we be surprised at the radicalization of professionalism and the power of investments that lead to the improvement of stadiums, championships, etc.?

For the same reason, the personal trajectory of Neymar and his companies is possibly and understandably celebrated as a case of resounding success: the perfect conjunction of a boy's rare skills for football and a family's for business. The million-dollar market that is now at his disposal is only fitting retribution for the union of natural talent, effort and business savvy. How many of the young boys, especially from working-class families, would not wish to be Neymar?

The fascination that this story provokes is unquestionable, as well as the charm that Neymar's moves can generate in football aficionados. From a certain angle, the narrative of personal stories of overcoming and success is as old as capitalism. The critical consideration in this regard is already known: it is stories like this that keep thousands of young people striving and betting on success, despite the slim chances of obtaining a prominent place in the market. It is cases like this that drive proposals from entrepreneurs to "diamonds" that, for the most part, will remain rough and will join the ranks of hard work in other activities throughout life.

When they continue to bet on their projects, the rule is a standard of living very close to the standard condition (unequal and low) of the Brazilian labour market as a whole. In a survey conducted by the Brazilian Football Confederation (CBF) with figures from 2015, of the 28,803 contracts then registered in the country, 82.4% were for up to R$ 1000. Another survey, with different numbers obtained from the Ministry of Labour in 2016, accounts 12,880 athletes with an average monthly salary of R$ 3653—an average amount similar to that of professional categories such as margarine manufacturing technician or documentary dispatcher, as the article notes. In salary brackets, 39% receive up to R$ 1000, and 73% up to R$ 3000. It means, the 1% top-earners players receive more than the 78% poorest ones (Sabino & Garcia, 2018, May 4).

The same article reports as typical the story of Kauê Ceccacci, coincidentally a player for Portuguesa Santista, the first club in the amateur phase of Neymar's career. Typical, because it is about a 23-year-old player hired by teams of lower divisions and with a minimum wage contract. It is worth reading the article (Sabino & Garcia, 2018, May 4, our translation):

> He [Kauê Ceccacci] admits to wanting what ten out of ten footballers in the country crave: fame, fortune and moving to European football. "The kids who start in football nowadays think precisely that. That's what's on TV," he says. It is a responsibility he carries with him from an early age. His talent on the futsal court earned him a full scholarship to study at one of the most expensive private schools in the area around the city of Santos. "I see Neymar's success ... That's what we're aiming for. Football is a life project, also for helping people, like he did by opening an institute to care for children in the region [Instituto Neymar Jr. in Praia Grande]," says the player who, without a manager, searches alone among his network for an opportunity for the next season, which only begins in seven months.

As we have said, the projection of success stories as a form of incentive to thousands of postulants is not new and is part of the foundation of the liberal worldview. Yet there are significant qualitative and quantitative differences.

The first refers to the huge disparity of "return on talent" that is perceived between the situation of Neymar and that of thousands of other Kauês. To some extent, the widening of inequality that necessarily accompanies commodification processes is justified internally to the neoliberal reasoning, because it is seen in terms of increasing efficiency to the extent that the system of "winner takes all" stimulates even more the struggle for success. Moreover, if commodification is the mechanism par excellence of the rational calculation of income, there is no inequality that can be morally evaluated as unjust. This kind of income disparity, moreover, has already been naturalized in the wider corporate world, especially in the financial sector, the hegemonic fraction of neoliberalism. In the case of global football, the issue is not without perversity. Neymar is not a million times more skilled than Kauê. Even if the technical issue is always present in the game itself, it is the "positioning" of his brand in a global market that gives him such a distance of financial income.

However, the reference to a social project with children as a justifying element at the moment a successful trajectory is crowned is not secondary. In more mundane and concrete terms, people continue to need mechanisms of broader moral justification for their existence, despite the extreme corporate individualism of the neoliberal culture.

As Boltanski and Chiapello (2009) observe, contemporary capitalism has found a path of reinvigoration not only because of new techniques and productive strategies, but also because of the ability it has demonstrated to seize the yearnings of social critique that addressed the loss of meaning of the activities under its domain. Young people in various parts of the Western world who, especially in the late 1960s, questioned its bureaucratic, alienating and predictable pattern, were urged to rediscover a sense of existence by converting their personal projects into something greater than a fattened bank account. If they could fulfil their dreams through the efficiency of the capitalist technique, they could also satisfy human "needs" of the most varied kinds.

The ultimate goal, as Neymar, the father, announced several times, was for his son to be "happy".

It is precisely this role that brand building can also fulfil. Earlier, in the description of Neymar's company, principles and values that transcend the sports practice are mixed: an influencer that evokes authenticity, relevance, charisma and ability—as NR Sports states. The return for the talent, even for its unreasonable distribution, could be more legitimate if it touched and benefited a larger group of people.

One question remains: to what extent can a human-entrepreneurial type, which concentrates so many unequal pressures and forces within oneself, express oneself coherently and live in an "authentic" way?

The Neoliberal Subject in Sport

Football players, as we have seen so far, insert themselves in an increasingly commodified universe, present in the championship they play, in the team they play in and in themselves, as their own company. The merchandising imposes itself so strongly on the players' lives that they no longer have control over countless ordinary and daily situations, to the extent that they too become part of the life of a brand. It does not mean that they cease to have "agency" and become passive entities of external forces, but that, when acting, conditions imposed on their being-company will always be present.

In practice, Neymar's "personal" life is simultaneously Neymar-company's life. Let us look at some recent facts. His romantic relationship with the famous Brazilian actress Bruna Marquezine could not escape repercussions and market relations. At the 2016 Olympics, when Neymar was football champion and climbed the Maracanã tribunes, apparently to resume his relationship with Bruna, he met her with open arms, and on his girlfriend's T-shirt there was a huge Adidas logo printed, in one of the most interesting cases of "ambush marketing" of those games (Netto, 2019). An underwear brand exploited the couple's intimacy and made them their poster boy and girl. When they were surrounded by cameras, together or apart, Bruna and Neymar had to use products from their sponsors.

The commodification of the player's life became more evident in two episodes. The first occurred when he turned 27. With a broken metatarsal, he thought of cancelling the planned party. However, "Neymar's birthday is now an important commercial date for partners, sponsors, and for the player himself," and the party is provided for in the contract (Marques et al., 2019, February 6). Cancelling a party for him is not only a voluntary will, it is a breach of contract. The second case occurred shortly after the 2018 World Cup. With the defeat in the championship, the criticism over Neymar for allegedly simulating fouls took a large dimension, echoing in the press around the world and jamming social media. Neymar kept quiet and, when he did speak, he did so in a corporate way, recording a commercial for one of his sponsors in which he narrates his fall with phrases like "you don't know what I went through in life", and ends up turning his request for help, which presupposes a justification of his actions, into a sale of razor blades.

Like other cases of international football stars, he guides his strategic career decisions, above all, by the need to reach individual achievements at the expense of collective victories. The transfer to Paris Saint-Germain is the most representative and controversial case, not least because of the questions raised about the possibility of accomplishing these goals.[9]

Perhaps the most glaring symptom of the precariousness of the principle of authenticity, which he shared with other PSG players, was the discovery by Football Leaks—reported by broadcaster *France 2*—of the "ethics bonus" offered by the French club to its squad. Among the requirements was the obligation to greet and applaud the fans of his own team at the end of each game. Like any merchandised process, the bonus varies from player to player: Neymar receives the highest amount, with an estimated 375,000 euros per month for the contractual clause. Kylian Mbappé pockets 117 thousand euros monthly, while Daniel Alves and Edinson Cavani earn 70 thousand euros and Thiago Silva takes 33 thousand euros.[10] Each applause, as on a supermarket shelf, has its price.

Dardot and Laval (2014) offer a thought-provoking framework of analysis of "manufacturing the neo-liberal subject" and identify continuities and changes in relation to the constructions of the original liberalism. In the view of traditional liberalism, the Benthamian man was the calculating man of the market and the productive man of industrial organizations. The neoliberal man—they explain—is a competitive man, entirely immersed in global competition. The sphere of sport, as the authors argue, plays a key role in the production of this new subjectivity, i.e. a man of competition and performance, a being made to win, to be successful. The competitive sport, even more than the idealized characters of the company leaders, continues to be the great social theatre that reveals the gods, demigods and modern heroes. Thus, they are perfect incarnations of the self-made entrepreneur, who does not hesitate for an instant to sell to the highest bidder, without much regard for loyalty and fidelity (Dardot & Laval, 2014).

Let us go back to the beginning, to Neymar-father's outraged comment. The party that Neymar, even if he wanted to, could not cancel due to commercial contracts, was threatened by a fracture in his foot caused in a game in which his marker tried, three times, to take the ball away from him. Something, in fact, very difficult to do, given the technique, speed and the player's ability to control the ball and escape his opponents.

---

[9] A British commentator accurately summarized the feeling: "It's easy to forget that buried somewhere in the middle of all this is a staggeringly talented footballer; one who attracts medals like a jam sandwich attracts ants and who could conceivably end his career on some sort of par with Pelé, Romário and Ronaldo. Equally, he is hardly the first footballer to choose to leave a successful team, and nor is he the first to be motivated by fame, money and personal accolades. But he is perhaps the first to do it all so nakedly, and to such obscenely lucrative ends." (Hess, 2019, July 10).

[10] See "Por bônus PSG, obriga atletas a aplaudirem torcida; Neymar recebe R$ 1,6 mi". *UOL*, November 9, 2018.

Where did Neymar-father's anger come from? On social media and on TV shows that discuss football, many identified, at the start of the move, a very questionable characteristic of Neymar. The player was running in the middle of the field, essentially towards his own team's goal. He seemed to be holding the ball, thus, unnecessarily. Not to say that he is to blame for his own injury, but that his style of game unnecessarily increases the risk of contact.

Criticism of the excess, the "flamboyance" and the individualism have always accompanied Neymar's career, despite the goals, the beautiful moves and the championships won. What usually escapes these discussions is that the line on which Neymar needs to walk is unstable precisely because he needs to find, as the liberal fiction of the *homo economicus*, an optimal point—most of the time, as unreal as the liberal fiction—between being victorious in an essentially team sport and, at the same time, stand out individually, singling out not only his performance—which has always existed in football and in the athletes' search for glory—but, above all, in a way that enhances his image, his brand (something bigger and with more people involved than just him).

Dardot and Laval (2014) note that, when the entrepreneurial subject links his narcissism to his own success combined with that of the company, in a climate of competitive war, the slightest setback of fate can have extremely violent effects. Although controlled in his Instagram account, Neymar-father's reaction can be read in this record.

The exposition elaborated here aimed to show that, although disconnected from a credible diagnosis of reality—like so many other complaints of "socialism" that we see in the current political scenario in Brazil or in other countries—it becomes minimally comprehensible when we recognize that, through its mouth, the new spirit of capitalism speaks. This new spirit needs to justify the return on its investments. As Boltanski and Chiapello (2009) remind us, capitalism does not justify itself and needs to resort to other areas of social life. In this sense, it finds its justification in what is most essential in football: its collective strength, the engagement of fans, the identification among fans and between them and their teams, the union of players in the locker room, the need for a collective game, no matter how much one tries to boast an individual. However, the more this spirit tries to justify itself on these bases, the more tensions and disenchantments can arise with the intensification of commodification. Neymar is just one point in this process. It is still to be seen whether there will be another way and, if so, what role personalities like him will play.

References

Barney, R., Wenn, S., & Martyn, S. (2004). *Selling the five rings*. The University of Utah Press.

Boltanski, L., & Chiapello, È. (2009). *O novo espírito do capitalismo*. São Paulo: Martins Fontes.

Brewer, B. D. (2017). The commercial transformation of world football and north-south divide: a global value chain analysis. *International Review for the Sociology of Sport, 54*(4). https://doi.org/10.1177/1012690217721176

Chade, J. (2014). *A Copa como ela é—A história de dez anos de preparação para a Copa de 2014.* São Paulo: Breve Companhia.

Coelho, P. V. (2014). *O planeta Neymar: Um perfil.* São Paulo: Paralela.

Dardot, P., & Laval, C. (2014). *The new way of the world: On neoliberal society.* Verso.

Dubal, S. (2010). The neoliberalizatioin of football: rethinking neoliberalism through the commercialization of the beautiful game. *International Review for the Sociology of Sport, 45*(2). https://doi.org/10.1177/1012690210362426

FIFA. (2015, May 28–29). *FIFA financial report 2014.* 65th FIFA Congress, Zurich. https://img.fifa.com/image/upload/e4e5lkxrbqvgscxgjnhx.pdf

Garcia, D. (2018, August 21). Por contrato, Neymar destina 85% dos lucros com publicidade aos pais. *Folha de São Paulo.* https://www1.folha.uol.com.br/esporte/2018/08/por-contrato-neymar-destina-85-do-lucro-com-publicidade-aos-pais.shtml

Hess, A. (2019, July 10). The fall of Neymar: where PSG's ill-tempered talisman has been going wrong. *FourFourTwo.* www.fourfourtwo.com/features/fall-neymar-where-one-worlds-greatest-players-has-been-going-wrong#4azrlVcQ5sob1Yk7.99

Hollanda, B. B. B. (2017). 8 questões para pensar as torcidas organizadas de futebol. *Ludopédio, 92*(6). https://ludopedio.org.br/arquibancada/8-questoes-para-pensar-as-torcidas-organizadas-de-futebol/

Iasnogrodski, F. U. (2018, December 2). Os maiores patrocínios dos 12 grandes clubes brasileiros. *90min.* https://www.90min.com/pt-BR/posts/6236928-os-maiores-patrocinios-dos-12-grandes-clubes-brasileiros

Jennings, A. (2006). *Foul! The secret world of FIFA: Bribes, vote rigging and ticket scandals.* Harper Sport.

King, A. (2004). The new symbols of European football. *International Review for the Sociology of Sport, 39*(3). https://doi.org/10.1177/1012690204045599

Lei No. 12.663 (2012, June 5). Dispõe sobre as medidas relativas à Copa das Confederações FIFA 2013, à Copa do Mundo FIFA 2014 e à Jornada Mundial da Juventude—2013, que serão realizadas no Brasil. http://www.planalto.gov.br/ccivil_03/_ato2011-2014/2012/lei/l12663.htm

Marques, J. H., Almeida, P. I., & Lopes, P. (2019, February 6). Por que Neymar deu festão de aniversário mesmo de muleta e com pé lesionado. *UOL.* https://www.uol.com.br/esporte/futebol/ultimas-noticias/2019/02/06/por-que-neymar-deu-festao-de-aniversario-mesmo-de-muleta-e-com-pe-lesionado.htm

Marx, K. (2001). *O capital: Crítica da economia política. Livro I.* Boitempo.

Marx, K., & Engels, F. (2008). *The Communist manifesto.* Pluto Press.

Mattoso, C., & Garcia, D. (2018, June 12). Empresário, Neymar pai cobra de todo mundo, inclusive do filho. *Folha de São Paulo.* https://www1.folha.uol.com.br/esporte/2018/06/empresario-neymar-pai-cobra-de-todo-mundo-inclusive-do-filho.shtml

Nicolau Netto, M. (2019). *Do Brasil e outras marcas: nação e economia simbólica nos megaeventos esportivos.* São Paulo: Editora Intermeios.

Nicolau Netto, M., & Cavalcante, S. (2020). Futebol e capitalismo global: Mercadorização do esporte e a formação de uma cultura neoliberal. In S. S. Giglio, & M. W. Proni (Orgs.), *O futebol nas ciências humanas no Brasil* (pp. 232–254). Campinas, SP: Editora da Unicamp.

Oliveira, N. G. (2015). *O poder dos jogos e os jogos de poder: Interesses em campo na produção da cidade para o espetáculo esportivo.* Editora UFRJ.

Oliveira, L., & Fernandes, T. (2019, February 18). "Estádio é para rico". *UOL.* https://www.uol.com.br/esporte/reportagens-especiais/entrevista---alexandre-kalil/

Pai lembra lesões para rebater críticas a Neymar: "Ter talento não pode?" (2019, January 25), *ESPN Brasil.* https://www.espn.com.br/futebol/artigo/_/id/5209833/pai-lembra-lesoes-para-rebater-criticas-a-neymar-ter-talento-nao-pode

Paulani, L. (2016). Acumulação e rentismo: Resgatando a teoria da renda de Marx para pensar o capitalismo contemporâneo. *Revista De Economia Política, 36*(3), 514–535. https://doi.org/10.1590/0101-31572016v36n03a04

Payne, M. (2006). *Olympic turnaround: How the olympic games stepped back from the brink of extinction to become the world's best known brand*. Praeger.

Pinheiro, D. (2007, October). O agente globalizado. *Piauí*, (13). https://piaui.folha.uol.com.br/mat eria/o-agente-globalizado/

Por bônus, PSG obriga atletas a aplaudirem torcida; Neymar recebe R$ 1,6 mi. (2018, November 9). *UOL*. https://www.uol.com.br/esporte/futebol/ultimas-noticias/2018/11/09/por-bonus-psg-obriga-atletas-a-aplaudirem-torcida-neymar-recebe-r-16-mi.htm

Proni, M. W. (1998). Marketing e organização esportiva: elementos para uma história recente do esporte-espetáculo. *Conexões, 1*(1), 82–94. https://doi.org/10.20396/conex.v1i1.8638015

Sabino, A., & Garcia, G. (2018, May 4). Jogador brasileiro ganha quarto salários mínimos por mês em média. *Folha de S. Paulo*. https://www1.folha.uol.com.br/esporte/2018/05/jogador-bra sileiro-ganha-quatro-salarios-minimos-por-mes-em-media.shtml

Sassen, S. (2006). *Territory, authority, rights: From medieval to global assemblages*. Princeton University Press.

Sheen, T. (2018, December 10). Neymar is world's most branded footballer with 35 endorsement deals for Nike, Beats, Qatar National Bank and Red Bull. *The Sun*. www.thesun.co.uk/sport/foo tball/7941752/neymar-brands-nike-jordan-beats-qatar-bank/

Smit, B. (2007). *Pitch invasion: Adidas, Puma and the making of modern sport*. Penguim.

Sujith, M. (2018, October 13). Ranking the top 10 clubs with the highest sponsorship revenues. *Sportskeeda*. https://www.sportskeeda.com/football/top-10-clubs-with-the-highest-sponsorship-revenues-ss

Tomlinson, A. (2014). *FIFA: The men, the myth, the money*. Routledge.

Webber, D. M. (2017). "Playing on the break": Karl Polanyi and the double movement "against modern football". *International Review for the Sociology of Sport, 52*(7). https://doi.org/10.1177/1012690215621025

Weber, M. (1958). *The Protestant ethic and the spirit of capitalism*. Scribner's Press.

Zimbalist, A. (2016). *Circus maximus: The economic gamble behind hosting the Olympics and the World Cup*. Brookings Institution Press.

Chapter 11
A Modernity that is not Complete? Ideas and Interpretations About Brazilian Football

Juliano de Souza and Wanderley Marchi Júnior

Introduction

In the well-known and referenced text *"The liberal adventure in a patrimonialist order,"* the Brazilian sociologist Raymundo Faoro tried to discuss, based on some Weberian categories of social understanding—categories, it is always important to remember that these categories had already emerged as central in the Brazilian author's work since the time he wrote his classic book *Os donos do poder* and published it for the first time in 1958. The author's argument developed in the text in question, in line with the theoretical analysis that permeates his entire work, is that civil society was not constituted in Brazil as the basis of society, and, on the contrary, what would characterize this type of social formation would be the predominance of a political order in which individuals basically exercised the role of rulers or ruled (Faoro, 1993, p. 16).

In painting this interpretative panel about Brazilian social formation, Faoro makes use of a dualist theoretical approach, in which the coexistence of the two aforementioned orders—patrimonialism and liberalism—, from a certain historical period on, culminated with the establishment of a society marked, in particular, by the predominance of a type of "politically oriented capitalism" (Faoro, 1993, p. 16). This suggested diagnosis is translated in an unmistakable way in Faoro's terms, when he argues that Brazilian society—even in the context in which he wrote his essay— possessed the characteristics of these two modalities: "inheritor of Portuguese patrimonialism, it received, with independence, the impact of the English world, already modern, adopting the capitalist and liberal mask, without denying, or, as we would say with more property, without overcoming patrimonialism" (Faoro, 1993, p. 17).

J. de Souza (✉)
State University of Maringá, Maringá, Brazil

W. M. Júnior
Federal University of Paraná, Paraná, Brazil
e-mail: marchijr@ufpr.br

The expressions "liberal adventure" or "capitalism as mask," in this sense, can be read as categories employed by Faoro in order to mark the difficulties with which the liberalist project was asserted in Brazilian society and, more than that, with the purpose of pointing out the relative shortcomings of this society before world capitalism.

These ideas, as we will suggest in the course of the article, in a way go back to Sérgio Buarque de Holanda's own notion of "man cordial," acting as an objective and structural referent of what the author of *Roots of Brazil* envisioned, at the level of individual subjectivities, as a typical ideal standard of Brazilian conduct. Whether, however, in terms of individual ways of acting, or, consequently, in terms of the functioning of social structures and institutions, the fact is that these ideas denote the existence of a historical articulation, to some extent problematic, between a core of pre-modern action and a core of modern action, leading to a reading whose greatest effect is the interpretation of the modernization process of Brazilian society through the optics of backwardness and deviation in relation to the centers of world capitalism.

In the following pages, we seek to demonstrate how these ideas ended up being appropriated and replicated in the Brazilian football context. Here, this context is understood as a space of multiple social meanings that—among other logics and processes—was also constituted by virtue of the interweaving of the analyses of different cultural specialists or, more precisely, from a kind of "invisible cordon" interconnecting academic discourses and journalistic and literary common sense discourses (Juliano de Souza, 2014), so that this articulation of ideas would happen in order to assert an interpretation of Brazilian football in which both the critical analyses about the phenomenon itself and the possible solutions for the dilemmas inherent to the circulation of this sport practice in the country were presented having as idealistic comparative reference the logic of modernization of European football and the process of modernization of European society.

If our line of reasoning is correct, these dated efforts, often without direct relation to each other, are in the core of the constitution of an enduring "intellectual family"— in the sense attributed by Brandão (2005)—within the sociocultural studies of football in Brazil. It is also because we believe in this diagnosis that we resort to Brandão's propositions for the sociology of intellectuals, in order to (I) consider those most representative texts that were produced within this lineage and (II) demonstrate the elective affinities between the works of authors from different historical contexts, but that, by using a set of similar analytical categories, strengthened a particular theoretical conception. Parallel to this approach, we also mobilize Jessé Souza's (2006, 2009) "theory of selective modernization," due to its critical-reflexive potential that allows us to restore the feedback logic between theory and common sense in the construction of an interpretation of the modernization process of Brazilian football through the optics of backwardness and deviation.

The Thesis of Backwardness and Deviation in the Brazilian Football Context

As an initial analysis, it is important to highlight that, in terms of understanding the structural and institutional dynamics that take place in the Brazilian football context, the "intellectual family" mentioned here will turn its attention, above all, to those aspects of social action that manifest themselves in a more reflected and rational way in this *locus*. This obviously does not mean that the authors who integrate this first lineage have availed themselves in an orthodox way of the Weberian perspective of understanding society, in which rationalization assumes a central and paradigma passe tic role to qualify the meaning of social action and, more than that, to explain that what is called modernization is the result of the complex process of expansion of instrumental rationality to various regulatory spheres of life. What occurs in these studies can be read as an introspective and not very nuanced affiliation to Weber's argument, because of the social, political, and intellectual effects of the circulation of Weber's ideas in Brazil.

It is worth noting that perhaps no other sociologist among the canons has influenced the production of Brazilian social thought as much as Max Weber. There is, in this sense, a need to make a Weberian "theory of theory effect" in Brazil, and, in part, this project has already been carried out in the collection *O malandro e o protestante:* A tese weberiana e a singularidade cultural brasileira, organized by Jessé Souza (1999). What, however, we are interested in emphasizing with this argument is, first, that Weber (2004) conceives protestant ethics as "midwife of modern rationalism" and, second, that here in Brazil, there was a concern on the part of our main interpreters to find substitutes or equivalents for the protestant ethics in order to explain both the logic of backwardness and the cultural singularities of our modernizing process (Jessé Souza, 2006, p. 25).

But let us reserve our attention, at least for now, to the image of deviation, in order to locate how it took shape and was materialized in studies about football. Before that, however, we should point out that, if in terms of the great interpretative works on Brazil, the comparative referent mobilized by the authors was the USA, as Jessé Souza (2006, p. 33) argues, in the sociology of football, in what it received influence from theoretical analyses that oppose liberalism to patrimonialism and vice-versa, the ideal pursued was, and still is, European football, even because in the USA the variant of football played with the feet was definitely not the one that prospered the most. Let us see how this trend of thought ends up being implicitly translated in Proni's (1998, p. 205, our translation) words:

> Towards the end of the 1970s, despite the aforementioned efforts, a certain consensus emerged that the professional structure of Brazilian football was lagging far behind that of European football. It was not uncommon for proposals for the modernization of Brazilian football to appear, with reference to the new organizational model being developed in Europe: the so-called "corporate football". In fact, while Brazilian clubs continued to be passionately managed and to depend on fluctuating revenues, while disorganization prevailed in the federations, with frequent changes of dates and match schedules, in some European countries football was already better planned and better managed, with several teams testing

new marketing strategies and implementing modern methods of sports management, such
as more permanent sources of revenue and more profitable championships [...].

This reading perspective denotes, between the lines, a theoretical belief that understands that the major social changes and ruptures start from institutional modifications legally assessed. The correlative of such changes in football would reside
in demands, such as, for example, the professionalization of managers, the recon-
duction of relations between club and athlete, and above all the transformation of
clubs into companies (Rodrigues, 2007, p. 172). Such claims, in turn, would not
be articulated ideas without concrete social referents, and, among other occasions,
they would be supported by the approval of Law No. 8,672/93 (Zico Law), in 1993,
and Law No. 9,615/98 (Pelé Law), in 1998, constituting dynamics indicative of the
modernizing spirit that then aroused in our football, at least from the point of view
of institutionalized political processes.

It is understandable that in the scope of jurisprudence, specialized sports media,
politics, and the national public debate itself, emotional traits are bound to denote
a desire to equate the current administrative structure in Brazilian football with
the management structure of European football. In the applied context of sports
marketing itself, of which the book *Futebol-empresa—A nova dimensão para o
futebol brasileiro* signed by Roberto Mack (1980)—is an emblematic example of the
circulation of ideas legitimized by the spokespersons of this "intellectual family,"
it is accepted, with less reticence, this type of idealism leading the analysis. Less
justifiable, however, is this type of initiative being conveyed, even if implicitly, in
the academic-scientific production.

To have a slightly more precise dimension of how strong and penetrating these
ideas are in the context of supply and demand of the football debate in Brazil, we
could refer to the final of the Fédération Internationale de Football Association (FIFA)
Club World Cup played between Santos and Barcelona at the end of 2011. On that
occasion, numerous explanations were mobilized in the different media outlets to
justify the defeat suffered by the São Paulo team. Reinaldo Azevedo, on the Web site
of *Veja* magazine, commented: "Look at the degree of professionalism that Spanish
football has reached and compare it with the pterodactyls, starting with the CBF,
who look after Brazilian football. What was seen yesterday in Japan was the triumph
of method over poetry out of place" (Azevedo, 2011, December 19, our translation).

In turn, this "poetry out of place" referred to by the journalist constitutes a nostalgic
appeal to the supposed Brazilian "futebol-arte" long forgotten (according to his text),
and, then, an allusion to the fact that, for a greater excellence of results in football, it
would not be enough only the individual "gingado" of some athletes. Because of the
structural arrangement evidenced in that context, the comparison between Brazilian
football, associated on the occasion to the figure of Santos FC, and European football,
represented by the Barcelona SC, was imposed and was revived in a naturalized way
by the agents. On one side, we would have the strength, the rational management, and
the method. On the other hand, we would have the scarcity of resources, emotional
management, corruption, and to once again refer to the metaphor suggested in the
excerpt quoted, "poetry out of place."

Curiously, and also in reference to the decision of the FIFA Club World Cup held at the end of 2012—by the way, involving a European club and a South American club—, again these ideas that Brazilian football—and, more broadly, South American football—is overlooked in relation to European football circulated in the scope of journalistic incursions. What is interesting to observe in this plot is that the potential administrative merits of Corinthians, reflected in a competitive team that overcame Chelsea in 2012, were not used to do justice to the club's planning, but to consecrate the idea of Brazilian football deviating from European football and overvaluing the latter. An example of this can be seen in *Lance!* newspaper, in an article signed by journalist Vitor Birner and later published in his blog, with the suggestive title "Corinthians has been more European than Chelsea." In it, statements such as: "Corinthians has been much more European than the English teams"; "In the Blues, the mess is big"; "I think Parque São Jorge is in Europe and Stamford Bridge here in Brazil" (Birner, 2012, December 10).

Another suggestive example in as much as this idealistic and Eurocentric reading of Brazilian football is concerned that has been widely circulating in the print and broadcast media in the country may be contemplated in a text written by journalist Mauro Cezar Pereira, published in the Web site of newspaper *O Estado de S. Paulo*. When referring to the aforementioned final of the FIFA Club World Cup involving Corinthians and Chelsea, the journalist argues—by the way, in very passionate terms and as if it were more than an obligation of the European sports media to know, strictly speaking, Brazilian football and national clubs:

> Corinthians has fans, tradition, titles, a sponsor, a stadium being built, a lot of media, and a good football team. How was it possible for a Club of such caliber to be practically ignored by many European fans and journalists until the victory in the final? And let's be clear: had someone else been the Brazilian representative in Japan, it wouldn't have been any different. The football played here is virtually unseen abroad. And that needs to be faced by us, so that we can find problems and think of solutions. [...] Yes, the Brasilerao is to a European fan or journalist what the Costa Rican league or the Colombian Postobon league are to us. Bad luck for the English reporter who doesn't know Corinthians or bad luck for those who have so much tradition in football and can't attract the world's attention? Stop, think. The enemy of progress in our football lives at home. (Pereira, 2012, December 17, our translation)

Idealistic and ethnocentric comparisons such as this one are common and routine in the Brazilian sports press, especially on the occasion of matches between local and European clubs. It would be a mistake, however, to think that such comparative discourses between Brazilian football and football practiced in Europe are something recent and restricted to the scope of professionals who compete within the journalistic field. On the contrary, this kind of diagnosis was and has been present also in other fields of production of material and symbolic goods offered and consumed in the core of this society, as well as in the understanding of those very agents who made history in the Brazilian football context. An example of this can be seen in the figure of João Saldanha, who, in his acknowledged text *Subterrâneos do futebol* (Football underground), published in 1963 and re-released in 1980, had already demonstrated his amazement with the structure of European football, or, better said, with the way football was managed in Europe. Let us note how this idea shines through in a unique way in some passages of his book (Saldanha, 1980, our translation):

> The European countries compensate, to a certain extent, for their disadvantages with a training truly worthy of the name, with a human material bearing better hereditary health and with a strategic and tactical application of play at a higher level. (p. 120)

> In Europe, the boy of this age, in the most developed countries, still wears pants and is in school. The Brazilian is already an adult. The life he leads forces him to face problems as such. (p. 120)

> The Brazilian player is one of the least durable in activity, among all those from other countries. Nílton Santos and Jair da Rosa Pinto are mentioned all the time because they played for a long time. One played twenty-four years, which is exceptional, and the other has been playing for sixteen years. In Europe there are hundreds of players who have played for twenty years. And that's no big deal. (p. 162)

> Any first division team, where there is professionalism in Europe, has top class coaching. Someone could argue that "we are right and they are wrong". That it is our spontaneity and anarchy that are good. The proof is that "we won two World Cups over them". This is absolutely false. Anarchy is not a form of development in any sector of human activity. (p. 166)

João Saldanha, it is important to remember, shared a worldview dear to both the footballing context of action, in which he was able to establish himself as coach of Botafogo do Rio de Janeiro and of the Brazilian national team, and the media field, where he worked as a journalist and sports chronicler. His idealism, in this sense, is due to this double socialization. The fact that he saw and experienced in loco some of the problems that have historically permeated Brazilian football and Brazilian society, coupled with the social force of the theoretical interpretations that were sweeping the country, may be understood as a condition that led Saldanha to perceive in European football—and, by extension, in European society—an exemplary source for the modernization of Brazilian football. However, this interpretative proposal of his, although attentive to a series of fundamental issues such as the dynamics that gave rise to the exploitation of child labor in the country, is easy prey to comments that may be read as eugenic, Eurocentric, and, above all, permeated by a belief in the "futebol-arte" that is supposedly practiced here.

If, within the specialized sports chronicle, this idealistic proposal of comparison between Brazilian and European football is to a certain extent justifiable due to the passion and lack of distance of these agents from what was played and built within the limits of this context of sports action, much less understandable is the penetration of these idealistic comparisons in those studies of academic-scientific value and renown. Our argument is built, and therefore, in order to demonstrate that ideas such as these stand as an obstacle to a more realistic reading of social processes carried out in Brazilian society, whether sporting or not, from an analytical emphasis on the structural specificities of the formation of a country, in which, according to Jessé Souza (2003), slavery reigned for almost 400 years, in a contrary movement to what occurred, for example, in the process of modernization of European societies, in which slavery was presented as an institution merely marginal when not absent.

It is worth noting that it was even to account for this dilemma of the Brazilian social formation that an intellectual of the size of Florestan Fernandes based a considerable part of his analyses on a kind of idea of "conservative modernization,"[1] with the main purpose of problematizing the ambiguity with which the bourgeois revolution took place in Brazil, that is, based on a dynamic of technical modernization leveraged by a growing process of urbanization and industrialization that ensured the maintenance intact of the structures of power and inequality inherited from the colonial period and the slave system. Situated under another conceptual apparatus, it was a conservative modernization embedded in a bourgeois revolution imposed from "top to bottom" and, therefore, partially (Fernandes, 2006).

This analysis undertaken by Florestan would decisively influence the production of several Brazilian intellectuals in the most varied instances and areas of academic investigation. Moreover, in this work, so to speak, the proper foundations were laid for what would come to be called dependency theory—whose assumptions would animate much of the reflection developed in the so-called Paulista sociological school (Arruda, 2001; Bastos, 2002)—and that, beyond the field of Brazilian social thought, would spread, in due course, to other branches of social investigation, such as art, culture and, especially, to the field of study we are discussing here, football.

We have, however, the impression that some of the studies of Brazilian football that were based on this concept of conservative modernization, as evoked in Florestan's writings, unilaterally demonstrated, from an ontological point of view, what would be the equivalents of this historical process of modernization imposed from "top to bottom" in the context of football action or even in sport more broadly. In other terms, these authors could only or only aimed at perceiving the normative and legal character of this modernizing impetus in football, i.e., they did not pay attention to those less reflected aspects of social action and, above all, to the dynamics of the actors involved in this process. On the other hand, the studies that focused on recovering the dimension of the agents' *habitus*—in the sense attributed by Bourdieu—possibly only reinforced those ideas already legitimized in the local football belief system. In order to investigate and problematize some of the ways in which these readings act and were legitimated in the Brazilian football action context, it is necessary to dwell on some analytical positions presented by Proni (1998) and Rodrigues (2007). To this end, it is worth reproducing in full some fragments and impressions that were extracted, respectively, from their works:

> In concluding this section, it is important to highlight that some of the most striking structural transformations in Brazilian football took place during undemocratic political regimes. State intervention in this field has always been based on corporativist principles, resulting in what we may qualify as a process of "conservative modernization". This is because, while it promotes the introduction of modern norms and institutions, it does so without radically breaking with the archaic power structure, seeking whenever possible to reconcile the interests of the different segments involved. Besides, it is a modernization "from top to bottom", that is, imposed by the will of the state and that was not discussed by organized society. In

---

[1] As far as we know, this concept was originally employed by the sociologist Barrington Moore Junior (1975) to point out the differences between the English, North American, and French modernization processes that culminated with the development of capitalist and democratic societies and the German and Japanese modernization processes that led to the ascendancy of fascist regimes (Pires & Ramos, 2009, p. 413).

short, the Brazilian state played a decisive role in the main moments of restructuring of professional football. Both the induction to professionalism and the creation of the CND, during the first Vargas era, and the implementation of the national championship, the regulation of the football player's profession and the creation of CBF, during the military dictatorship, may be interpreted as important steps towards updating Brazilian football in relation to European football, on the one hand, and the search for a disciplined civil life and national integration through sport, on the other. Regardless of the reasons for such intervention, what matters is that during the first fifty years of its existence, professional football required state tutelage in order to structure and grow. (Proni, 1998, pp. 203–204, our translation)

Regarding the modernization of Brazilian football by the Pelé Law, the predominant perception of the athletes is that the new sports legislation modernized only some elements of our football (69%). This is very relevant data in the present analysis, since we defend the thesis that the Pelé Law represents one more face of the conservative modernization in Brazil, in which most of the changes are imposed from above, in an attempt to preserve the interests of dominant groups, as Florestan Fernandes (1976) understands it. In the case of football, there was a restructuring of football to accommodate the interests of managers and businessmen, often to the detriment of the players' interests. For 17% of the players, Pelé Law fully modernized our football (Rodrigues, 2007, p. 308).

The concept of *habitus* helps us in the analysis and in the understanding of the emergence of new professional behaviors and attitudes of the football player, endowed with a typical *habitus of* professional, business, and bureaucratic football. The athletes' perceptions are evidence of this *habitus*, especially those related to the importance of the unions and the players' awareness of their rights. The changes in the regulation system of labor relations in European football have created conditions for the advent of a more politicized football player, aware of his rights and participative. The modern player is endowed with a new ethic, a professional *habitus* distinct from the behaviors prevailing at the time of associationism as a standard of organization of clubs. It is expected that, with the end of the pass, the same happens in Brazil (Rodrigues, 2007, p. 312).

As we can notice in these excerpts, both authors refer to the conservative modernization of Brazilian football, letting transpire between the lines the desire for a complete modernization that, it seems, should have European football as a structural reference. There is, in this sense, an idealism implicitly surrounding these arguments, as if the modernizing process of European society and its football would constitute an adequate and efficient salvationist model to be "copied," with the major purpose of solving some of Brazilian football's dilemmas and even of the society surrounding it.

Moreover, within this, lineage seems to stand out the idea that the state would be an evil of origin in Brazil, while the market would emerge, par excellence, as the "kingdom of virtue." According to Jessé Souza (2009), this valuation scheme mutually attributed to the Brazilian state, and the market is typical of the interpretations that are based on the theoretical paradigm of personalism/patrimonialism. According to Jessé Souza (2009, p. 106), the personalism/patrimonialism schema—imposed as one of the dominant interpretative paradigms of Brazilian society—refers decisively to the effort engendered by Sérgio Buarque de Holanda in his classic text *Roots of Brazil*, published in 1936.

It is worthwhile to follow how this interpretation, dominant until today within the social sciences in the country, takes shape in Sérgio Buarque's own terms:

> In Brazil, it can be said that only exceptionally have we had an administrative system and a body of officials purely dedicated to and based on objective interests. On the contrary, it is possible to observe, throughout our history, the constant predominance of particular wills that find their own environment in closed circles little accessible to an impersonal order. Among these circles, the family has undoubtedly been the one which has been most strongly and freely expressed in our society. And one of the most decisive effects of the undisputed, absorbing supremacy of the family nucleus—the sphere par excellence of the so-called "primary contacts," of the ties of blood and heart—is that the relationships created in domestic life have always provided the obligatory model for any social composition among us. This occurs even where democratic institutions, founded on neutral and abstract principles, pretend to base society on anti-particularist norms. (Holanda, 1995, p. 146, our translation)

This is a well-known passage from *Roots of Brazil*, which also reveals some influences that were exerted on him by Gilberto Freyre's ideas gathered in *Casa-grande & Senzala*, 1933, especially regarding the reading of the Brazilian personalism constituted in the patriarchal family nucleus, as proposed by the Pernambuco intellectual (Freyre, 2006). The thesis of personalism rests on the reasoning that the way of living in the tropics, as we can see in the previous quote, is guided by personal ties of protection and favors rather than the impersonal ties typical of a so-called complete modernization process. This is the pre-modern core that would supposedly affect this society, at least from the point of view of a tradition of thinkers including Sérgio Buarque, Faoro, and DaMatta.

It happens that for Sérgio Buarque, patrimonialism is an extension of personalism, so that the author, inspired by a more Weberian reading of society, points out that in Brazil there was not a fully bureaucratic state, but a patrimonialist state whose administrative body would guide its interventions through criteria based on personal relations and favors. It was also with the purpose of theoretically articulating this analysis that Sérgio Buarque built the ideal figure of the "cordial man," that is, of a man who, being molded by the family, ended up being also guided in the sphere of politics or economy by primary feelings such as love or hate. Holland, in this sense, performed a mirror inversion of the "positive" version with which Freyre conceived the "unique society" that was formed here and gave it "negative" contours, so that his interpretation of Brazil clearly gained a kind of "critical charm" (Jessé Souza, 2009, p. 55). It should also be noted that this intellectual tradition, according to Jessé Souza (2009, p. 60), faces a curious internal theoretical tension, since individuals of the personalist society behave as "cordial men" only when they act in the state. In turn, when they act in the market, these same "cordial men" are virtuous beings. Thus, the dominant Brazilian interpretation anchored in the patrimonialist scheme tends to demonize the corrupt state as the "evil of origin" of the nation, so that it is only necessary to correct the defects of state policy to leverage Brazilian development. On the other hand, it tends, by self-exclusion, to consecrate the market as the "realm of virtue," that is, as an institution that has the agents that produce, create jobs, and promote the true development of the country (Jessé Souza, 2009, p. 79).

Notwithstanding, however, this theoretical overview presented, it is important to note that this first lineage of sociocultural studies of football in the country, even if supported by analytical assumptions embedded in the binomial personalism/patrimonialism, retains the relative peculiarity of not associating, for example, the so-called corruption schemes of national football only to the sphere of the state, but also to that of the market.[2] In this sense, the "cordial man," at least in the scope of investigations about football in the country, would also inhabit this second institution. Let us observe the words of Proni (2007, p. 20, our translation):

> In short, currently assessing the changes introduced by modernization, the market logic seems to have increased exclusion and widened inequalities in this field. The management of clubs and federations is still marked, in general, by accusations of corruption and illicit enrichment. The class of professional players remains disunited. The teams complain that they are victims of the action of unscrupulous businessmen. The "Fan Statute" has been frequently breached. Therefore, the moral principles that should underpin the construction of a sports culture consistent with that moralizing discourse have not yet been consolidated, and nothing indicates that this will occur in the coming years.

It is important to mention this fragment extracted from another work by Proni, because it demonstrates that Brazilian football, then ruled by the logic of the market, would still be guided, according to the author's analysis, by a kind of doubtful ethics that tends to corruption. However, a decisive point of inflexion is verified, for this argument, as it seems, was not woven by Proni from only the capital of personal relations of the personalist theories that, perhaps without realizing it, he incorporates to his interpretation, but from the capitals of impersonal relations such as those preconized in the theory of fields of Bourdieu.

Notwithstanding these analytical potentialities present in the works of Proni (and also of Rodrigues) with support in the Bourdieusian theoretical tradition, this author may be idealizing, perhaps inadvertently, the free action of the market as an alternative for the modernization of football in the country. It should also be noted that the inspiring matrix of this project should be European football, which, after World War II, according to Proni himself (1998), "modernized" drastically from a strong wave of influence of North American liberal capitalism. This modernization, however, should not be configured only as a copy of a model. As Rodrigues warns: "even having the European football model as a [successful] model, we should not simply imitate it, without a careful adaptation to our reality" (Rodrigues, 2007, p. 239).

---

[2] This argumentative proposal, among other possibilities, can be found in the doctoral thesys of Aldo Antônio de Azevedo entitled "From the old to the new cartolas: An interpretation of power and its resistances in the clubs, facing the impact of the football-corporate relations" (our translation). In that thesis, in which the author proposes to address the issue of power and its resistances in Brazilian football, it is developed the hypothesis that the "old structure" of power embodied in the figure of the so-called "cartolas" of football, even if under another guise, remains in the so-called management of corporate football that, since the 1980s, began to be pursued more incisively in Brazil, concomitantly with the emergence of the modernizing discourse of this sporting practice. It is argued that the entrance of the market in this "game" of interests reflects only a partial modernization in the power structure in Brazilian football, since the empirical data accumulated in the thesis indicate, in the author's own terms, not only a reproduction or permanence of the "old cartolas" in power, but the production of a "new cartola" of football, i.e., the capitalist company (Azevedo, 1999).

In synthesis, the institutional lag of the modernization process of football in Brazil, in light of a greater opening of the market tangentiated by the new legislative proposals put into effect (especially the Zico Law and the Pelé Law), coupled with the remnants of an emotional, conservative, protectionist, familialist management, prone to corruption, in other words, disposed to appeal, whenever it is convenient, to the famous "Brazilian way of doing things"—as we can glimpse in some moments of the arguments of Proni (1998) and Rodrigues (2007) —, would constitute an unmistakable evidence of what, based on Florestan Fernandes (2006), these authors called conservative modernization of Brazilian football.

Having made these analyses and theoretical correlations, it is worth advancing the argument and discussing in more detail a second aspect that predominates in this lineage and that, in fact, maintains close connections with the interpretations located thus far, namely the widespread idea, particularly in the media field, and by extension, in the realm of common sense, that Brazilian football is, par excellence, a *locus* for the exercise of the most varied forms of corruption.

In this particular, when we confront this idea with the discussions that were developed in the previous pages, it is possible to deduce an implicit logic through which the "cordial man"—based on his affective and favoritism policy—emerges as an agent that prevents a complete modernization of football in the country. In other words, the "nature" of the so-called "cordial man," as it is expressed in the conduct of some emblematic figures that structure, for a long time, the Brazilian football context of action—namely managers, coaches, athletes, referees, etc.—, is what would explain all sorts of corruption carried out in national football, corruption rarely thought of from the angle of impersonality in Brazil and often explained from the standpoint of personalism.

It is worth emphasizing that, with these analyses, we do not wish to deny or repress the processes of corruption that can be empirically verified in the structure of Brazilian football during various historical moments, with respect to a dynamic that has been present and recurrent in any other society or even in world football as a whole. Our argument, therefore, is that corruption in itself is not an obstacle to the modernization of Brazilian football, as patrimonialist readings would have it, but, above all, it constitutes one of the faces of the very process of modernization of football in Brazil, according to a common logic that mobilizes both the center and the periphery of capitalism. Furthermore, we cannot agree with a reading implicitly rooted in the belief in a kind of innate predisposition of Brazilians to corruption, be they of the elite or of the "rabble," as if their reasons for acting were the result of a deviant modernization experience and, more seriously, as if only in Brazil was there a "jeitinho" (an improvised fix) for everything.

Therefore, the major theoretical drawback of these readings when they are applied to the field of sociocultural studies of football is that, through them, besides idealizing and exalting the supposed complete modernization carried out in the European context of football action, they disregard part of the structural and symbolic dynamics that were central to the emergence of the Brazilian context of football action. In other words, a questionable interpretation is built that these relations are nothing more than pre-modern, archaic, and outdated ways in which football circulates among different social groups in Brazil. More than that, it lists, at first hand, a series of national figures as protagonists of a corruption that has delayed and would delay the development of this sporting practice in the country, and, as a result, it puts in the background the existence of a network of corruption that organizes the distribution of football, in its feature of spectacle, around the world.

This intellectual tradition, which sees corruption as the mechanism responsible for delaying the development of this sport in Brazil, and for preventing it from being built in an ideal way, along the lines of European football, both in terms of the objective organization of the spectacle and the subjective forms of cheering, tends to take on a conservative and pseudo-critical character, since it envisions, on the one hand, a structure of modernization of Brazilian football that more directly suits the interests of the groups that hold the greatest amount of economic capital, and, on the other hand, by underestimating the fact that football, in its condition of spectacularized product, is the monopoly of a non-transparent institution that operates alongside other affiliated institutions, which help regulate the logic of football distribution within the different countries, whether South American or European, based on questionable precepts and marked by controversial cases of corruption, as suggested by Juliano de Souza et al. (2014).

In the wake of what is being said, it is necessary to warn that these ideas that emerge from attempts to understand Brazilian football from a personalist perspective often disguise themselves as mere "conspiracy theory" which, when appropriated by the mechanism of "sports talk," has helped to consolidate—from the symbolic-emotional codes proper to the sport—a logic of expansion of the capitalist market through the supply and demand of cultural goods. If this mechanism were not enough, these ideas launched by intellectuals have the "scientific" prestige necessary to be perpetuated in time and space. The notion of "man cordial" is a categorical example of this, since, by decisively influencing the production of Roberto DaMatta—who "made the head of modern Brazil" (Jessé Souza, 2006) by proposing a particular sociability dynamic to Brazilians based on his sociology of the "jeitinho" (improvisation)—, it remained preserved and, in other ways, contributed to legitimize one of the dominant perceptions of Brazilian football in common sense, in the spheres of cultural production and in the academic field itself.[3]

Long before DaMatta articulated these precepts in his emotional theory of action, however, we can see these ideas of corruption based on the Brazilian personalist schema being conveyed in some well-known texts in the field of football history and sociology, namely *O negro no futebol brasileiro* (*The black man in Brazilian soccer*), authored by journalist and writer Mário Rodrigues Filho (original version dated 1947 and updated version 1964), and *Subterrâneos do futebol* (Football underground), by

---

[3] It is important to note, according to the sociologist Jessé Souza (2009, p. 37), that the ideas of Gilberto Freyre, Sérgio Buarque de Holanda, Roberto Damatta, or any other intellectual win the hearts and minds of people not because these subjects started reading the main productions of these authors and became convinced of their arguments. What happens is that these ideas, when finding institutional support and being appropriated by dominant social groups, gain legitimacy and become concrete practices and modes of action that are spread throughout the social fabric through the radius of action of the fields of symbolic production.

João Saldanha, 1963. For his part, historian Joel Rufino dos Santos, in his 1981 *História política do futebol brasileiro,* also corroborated this scenario, especially when seeking to establish homologies between those events played out in the political world and the events then unfolding in the context of Brazilian football action (Santos, 1981).

What is similar in these readings is that they all resorted to the mythical figure of the "malandro"—equivalent to Mário de Andrade's Macunaíma—perhaps replacing the figure of the North American "protesting pioneer." Note well that many situations described in the texts by Rodrigues Filho (2003), Saldanha (1980), and Rufino dos Santos (1981)—the "jogo do bicho" (a betting game based on drawing numbers), the famous "bicho pela vitória" (a bonus for victory), the athletes' escapes from the concentration camp, the attempts at bribery, doping, the suspicious actions of referees and officials, etc.—were explained in the light of the "malandragem" (rascality) and "jogo de cintura" (malleability) that supposedly distinguished Brazilian society from others. In our view, therefore, this type of analytical stance tends, on the one hand, to folklorize corruption and, on the other, to elevate Brazilian football to the dimension of the unexpected (a "box of surprises") in the collective imagination. Such condition, therefore, guarantees commercial notoriety to football for being something potentially controversial and that is close to the sensationalist everyday life in which many people are socialized in Brazil.

But it is not all mere speculation, conspiracy, and ideology. In fact, there is a series of empirically verifiable corruption processes in the Brazilian football structure. We could refer to several emblematic examples. However, two facts deserve greater attention. In the first place, we should mention the scandal that involved refereeing in the 2005 Brazilian Football Championship. Reportedly, there was manipulation of results with a view to favoring Internet bettors. Referee Edílson Pereira de Carvalho, then a FIFA member, ended up being arrested by the federal police (Rizek & Oyama, 2005, September 24). One of the interesting effects of this occurrence is that it affected the national sports imaginary in the sense of contesting the reliability of the Brazilian title won by Corinthians on that occasion.

Secondly, it is necessary to mention the Parliamentary Investigation Commission (CPI) of football requested on March 11, 1999, installed on October 17, 2000, and finalized in mid-2001 (Azevedo & Rebelo, 2002; Schmidt Filho, 2005). The main reason for convening this CPI was to investigate whether there were irregularities in the contract signed for ten years (1996–2006) between the multinational Nike and the Brazilian Football Confederation (CBF). However, improbities were also discovered in the management of the clubs.

In a summary text published in *Motrivivência* magazine containing parts of the final report presented by the parliamentary commission of inquiry on August 27, 2001, journalist and CPI advisor Carlos Azevedo, together with Federal Deputy Aldo Rebelo—petitioner and president of the CPI—stated that the contract signed between CBF and Nike conferred an absurdly abusive power to the multinational on decisions concerning the Brazilian football team (and even the youth and women's national teams). The main conclusions of the authors were expressed in the following terms.

CBF was converted into a millionaire business agency that exploits the image of the Brazilian team. Money flows: in 2001, CBF receives US$ 25 million only in sponsorship from Nike and Ambev. The money disappears: CBF's current liabilities reach R$55 million and accumulated losses reach R$25 million. How has the CBF spent so much money? The function of CBF is to promote football in the country, from the main national team to the youth football. But Brazilian football is going from bad to worse: the national team is a shadow of its past glories; the best players are sold abroad; grassroots football, which develops new stars, is abandoned. Young players, exported en masse, with adulterated documents, false passports. Underage athletes are trafficked and subjected to exploitation, hunger, disease, and even prostitution in foreign countries. The CBF "system" disorganizes football, submits the calendar to pressures from sponsors such as TV stations, and from political interests; for this, it corrupts club and federation officials. And it culminates with the bankruptcy of football (Azevedo & Rebelo, 2002, p. 18).

It is important to note that the authors articulated a series of facts in sequence to explain the crisis in Brazilian football. There are mutual factual references to processes alluding, on the one hand, to the scope of action and intervention of the public initiative sedimented in the figure of the state, in reference to a range of relations established between politics and football in Brazil through a dialogic perspective that, over the years, has been proving to be a constant (Guterman, 2009), and, on the other hand, to the scope of action of private initiative expressed in market logics. Furthermore, the main explanations for the disorganization of football in the country are centered on CBF's interventionist power, which denotes an implicit interest in exempting the state's participation in this process. According to the authors' report, CBF uses power at its pleasure, so much so that, in its contract signed with Nike, it agreed to clauses that, in favor of the multinational's marketing interests, went against its autonomy and, more seriously, hurt the character of sport as Brazilian cultural heritage and the Code of Consumer Protection (Azevedo & Rebelo, 2002, p. 8).

In addition to these criticisms, the authors record, albeit without due theoretical support, an important movement in world sport (and society) that significantly affected the bases of supply and consumption of modern football. Let us follow along in their own words:

> The commercialization of sports, and particularly of football, has created, over the last few years, a new situation in which a large flow of capital has come to involve sports activities. The sale of image use rights of teams, clubs and players to companies of sports and other products, the sale of the broadcasting rights of matches on TV, radio, internet, etc.; the transfers of players between clubs and from one country to another, all of this, added, has greatly surpassed the former source of resources that was the income resulting from the sale of stadium tickets. In a more recent phase, large investor groups, including multinational investment funds, attracted by football's economic potential, have been entering the sector, sponsoring and becoming co-managers of clubs and players. This type of interference, aimed at seeking profits and results that enhance the image of the sponsoring brand, has exerted an influence that is subjecting football to rapid changes and distortions. In Brazil, as the activity is still managed in an amateurish way and business is largely done informally, the result has been an increase in corruption. And a picture of contrasts is created. On one hand,

TV stations, investment and marketing companies, businessmen and players' agents make high profits; a good number of managers get personally rich; a minority of players receive high salaries. On the other hand, entities and clubs plunge into a deep crisis, in many cases reaching insolvency. Most athletes receive low salaries and have no retirement system. The quality of football is declining, and the stadiums are becoming empty. And also abandoned, without reforms and maintenance, offering little comfort and even becoming a threat to the fans' safety. (Azevedo & Rebelo, 2002, p. 1, our translation)

In this excerpt, Azevedo and Rebelo (2002) argue, in a normative tone, that global changes in football, brought about by the market, coincide with unilateral interests, and that here in Brazil, due to informal and amateur management, these interests reach an extreme level and result in corruption that impedes the development of football and the return to a "past of glories," as they seem to idealize in their text. The limit of this type of reading, even if it perceptively perceives corruption as something that relates both to the sphere of the market and the state, is not being attentive to the fact that corruption specializes and refines as the social system becomes more differentiated, and this in any society or in any social sphere.

This theoretical reconstruction of reality escapes Azevedo and Rebelo, which is perfectly understandable even because of the *habitus* they share and the interests that permeate their worldviews. Moreover, even if they observe some important ruptures in the sports field, these agents—sufficiently socialized in the universe of hegemonic representations about football in Brazil—move according to the "invisible cordon" that interlinks intellectuals, politicians, journalists, chroniclers, and civil society around a personalist belief that not only projects the "malandro" and his famous "jeitinho" as structuring elements of national politics, but also echos the idea that a process of conservative modernization was imposed on Brazilian football.

It is essential to emphasize that the media field in Brazil, as in any other modern society, although it is not the locus that originally produces these ideas, has an important role in the generalization of these same ideas to civil society. Gurgel (2004, p. 33) points out that, in the context of the CPI, the predominant discourse in the media ceased to be guided by the modernizing ideal resulting from the greater flexibility of Brazilian football to market logics and, as a response, began to advocate a moralization of football in the country due to the crisis arising from allegations of corruption and, above all, of the CPI.

Despite, however, the displacement visualized in the media discourse, this field as a conductor of ideas produced in other cultural spheres only returns to the agents, with an appearance of knowledge of cause, what they, ultimately, already expect to hear by virtue of the process of cultural socialization to which they are subjected since the first links they build with this sporting practice, i.e., that football in Brazil is a fruitful space for the exercise of corruption; that conflict resolution in the context of football action takes place primarily in a personalistic manner; that football in the country is not being modernized; that football is a business that effectively interests the few, etc. Note that these common-sense readings, despite the influences exerted by those who form public opinion in the country, reinforce the idea of deviation of Brazilian football in relation to European football, constituting ontological correspondents of the patrimonialist theory.

Notwithstanding, however, this logic of mutual feedback that seems to be established between the interpretative pictures painted about modern Brazil and the sphere of common sense from which emanates a quantity of empirical material that will later corroborate these theoretical analyses, it is necessary to emphasize that, by adopting this critical line of reasoning as outlined here, we are not denying that there are ruptures in Brazilian football and that these have correlations with what happens in the political, economic, or media sphere. Our reservation, on the contrary, resides in the way these ruptures are explained in the sphere of science, due to the insidious penetration of beliefs routinized in common sense based on the analytical categories idealized by the main interpreters of Brazilian society, who, as we have seen, helped to build, many times without considering this dimension, a project of nation and society based on the personalist/patrimonialist scheme.

Final Considerations

Notwithstanding the ideological character that guides the core of intergenerational relations analyzed in this text, it is worth noting that one of the main merits presented by this "intellectual family" problematized here, as one of the most enduring lineages of thought in the field of sociocultural studies of football in Brazil, is to analyze the social and cultural processes played in the context of football action as structured in the country, in the light of the two main institutions that guide and support modern life, namely the centralized state and the competitive market. This type of methodological orientation, however, is not enough to respond to the fact that the representatives of this lineage in the academic sphere are still linked to those political-theoretical analyses that tend to think Brazil and its modernization experience emphasizing precisely the images of backwardness and deviation in relation to the center of world capitalism and, what is disturbing, explaining such process based on a series of pre-modern categories such as the notions of "homem cordial" and "jeitinho brasileiro."

It is not too much to emphasize that this introspective affiliation is supposedly not perceived by the authors, which ultimately ends up demonstrating the strength with which these categories of thought spread to the various constituent spheres of Brazilian society. In fact, it is difficult to break with this set of ideas, especially because the agents are socialized, from an early age, in this structure of thought that, as we seek to argue, prescribes readings and interpretations replicated in countless ways in the most different cultural fields.

The partial construction, therefore, of the Brazilian social reality based on the ideas of a series of dominant intellectuals has the potential to explain why authors, such as Proni and Rodrigues, even if supported by Bourdieu's theoretical framework—for whom modern life is built and sedimented unavoidably from relations of dispute for "impersonal" capitals (namely cultural capital and economic capital)—are led, at various moments in their arguments, to weave analyses based on the complex nucleus of tensions and relations that, throughout history, have been placed in the area of social thought, cultural capital and economic capital—, are taken, at various moments of their arguments, to weave analyses based on the complex core of tensions and relations that, throughout history, were placed in the area of Brazilian social thought between, on the one hand, patrimonialism/personalism and, on the other, liberalism of political and economic type.

As a final observation, it should be noted that this theoretical lineage, by focusing on the analytical program that we have tried to highlight throughout the text, ended up establishing a kind of neutrality relationship with broader social conflicts. In other words, by emphasizing the tensions between a nucleus of pre-modern societal formation marked, as is believed, by corruption—and another nucleus of modern societal formation—in which the transparency of acts and institutions is supposed to prevail—, social conflicts and, in particular, class conflicts are sidelined in these explanations, at least in the domain of the studies we revisited. Therefore, by ideal-izing a greater spectrum of market action in the Brazilian football context, regarding a dynamic that took place in European football, without imputing, perhaps, greater damage to social groups that enjoy this sporting practice there, such interpretations, in the case of a peripheral society such as Brazil, in which the dynamics of social conflicts has its relative particularities, end up matching the wishes of certain social groups that envision a football spectacle not only more modern but also restricted to certain interests.

In short, by not taking into account these political effects that a structural modern-ization of Brazilian football in the exact European mold would represent in the context of the relations between different social groups, accentuating even more the inequal-ities of opportunity between those who make and those who consume the spectacle of football in the country, it is that the adepts of this lineage allowed themselves to idealize the imperative need for a process of modernization of Brazilian foot-ball through European logic, as if this were not already underway, but according to a dynamic that is not exclusively European, but of late globalized capitalism. By focusing its analytical scope on these processes, this "intellectual family" could not stick to the way in which certain symbolic-emotional aspects, beyond the myth of the "cordial man" and the "culture of improvisation," were being activated in the relationships that the different social groups built throughout the process of emer-gence and consolidation of the Brazilian football context of action. These theoretical developments, however, are reasons for other reflections and future contributions.

References

Arruda, M. A. N. (2001). *Metrópole e cultura em São Paulo no século XX*. Bauru: Edusc.

Azevedo, A. A. (1999). *Dos velhos aos novos cartolas: Uma interpretação do poder e das suas resistências nos clubes, face ao impacto das relações futebol-empresa*. (Doctoral Thesis in Sociology), Universidade Nacional de Brasília, Brazil. https://repositorio.unb.br/handle/10482/35366

Azevedo, C., & Rebelo, A. (2002). A corrupção no futebol brasileiro. *Motrivivência*, (17), 1–18. https://periodicos.ufsc.br/index.php/motrivivencia/article/view/5923

Azevedo, R. (2011, December 19). Santos x Barcelona: no futebol, cabe o inesperado, mas não o milagre. *Veja*. https://veja.abril.com.br/blog/reinaldo/santos-x-barcelona-no-futebol-cabe-o-inesperado-mas-nao-o-milagre-ou-o-que-faz-messi-ser-messi-ou-ainda-neymar-sera-um-dia-neymar/

Bastos, E. R. (2002). O pensamento social da escola sociológica paulista. In S. Miceli (Ed.), *O que ler na ciência social brasileira (1970–2002)*. São Paulo: Sumaré; Brasília: ANPOCS.

Birner, V. (2012, December 10). Corinthians tem sido mais europeu que o Chelsea. *Lance*. https://blogdobirner.virgula.uol.com.br/2012/12/10/corinthianstemsidomaiseuropeuqueo-chelsea/

Brandão, G. M. B. (2005). Linhagens do pensamento político brasileiro. *Dados, 48*(2), 231–269. https://doi.org/10.1590/S0011-52582005000200001

Faoro, R. (1993). A aventura liberal numa ordem patrimonialista. *Revista da USP*, (17), 14–29. https://doi.org/10.11606/issn.2316-9036.v0i17p14-29

Fernandes, F. (2006). *A revolução burguesa no Brasil: Ensaio de interpretação sociológica* (5th ed.). São Paulo: Globo. (Original work published in 1975)

Freyre, G. (2006). *Casa-grande & Senzala* (51th ed.). São Paulo: Global. (Original work published in 1933)

Gurgel, A. (2004). O futebol no campo econômico: Construção jornalística da Copa do Mundo de 2002 como negócio. (Master's Dissertation in Communication and Semiotics), PUC, São Paulo. https://sapientia.pucsp.br/handle/handle/4358?mode=full

Guterman, M. (2009). *O futebol explica o Brasil: Uma história da maior expressão popular do país*. São Paulo: Contexto.

Holanda, S. B. (1995). *Raízes do Brasil*. São Paulo: Companhia das Letras. (Original work published in 1936)

Mack, R. C. V. (1980). *Futebol-empresa—A nova dimensão para o futebol brasileiro*. Palestra.

Moore Júnior, B. (1975). *As origens sociais da ditadura e da democracia*: Senhores e camponeses na construção do mundo moderno. São Paulo: Martins fontes.

Pereira, M. C. (2012, December 17). Futebol jogado no Brasil não atrai interesse lá fora. Culpa dos brasileiros ou dos estrangeiros? *ESPN Brasil*. http://www.espn.com.br/blogs/maurocezarpereira/298586_futebol-jogado-no-brasil-nao-atrai-interesse-la-fora-culpa-dos-brasileiros-ou-dos-estrangeiros

Pires, M. J. S., & Ramos, P. (2009). O termo modernização conservadora: sua origem e utilização no Brasil. *Revista Econômica do Nordeste, 40*(3), 411–424. https://www.bnb.gov.br/revista/index.php/ren/article/view/367/315

Proni, M. W. (1998). *Esporte-espetáculo e futebol-empresa*. (Doctoral Dissertation in Physical Education), FEF-Unicamp, Brasil. http://repositorio.unicamp.br/jspui/handle/REPOSIP/275330

Proni, M. W. (2007). Ética e futebol no Brasil: argumentos para reflexão. *Esporte e Sociedade, 2*(5), 1–28. https://periodicos.uff.br/esportesociedade/article/view/48016/27933

Rizek, A, & Oyama T. (2005, September 24). Jogo sujo: A máfia do apito do futebol brasileiro. *Veja*. (1924), 72–80. http://arquivoetc.blogspot.com/2005/09/mfia-do-apito-no-futebol-brasileiro.html

Rodrigues Filho, M. (2003). *O negro no futebol brasileiro* (4th ed.). Rio de Janeiro: Mauad. (Original work published in 1947)

Rodrigues, F. X. F. (2007). *O fim do passe e a modernização conservadora no futebol brasileiro (2001–2006)*. (Doctoral Dissertation in Sociology), UFRGS, Porto Alegre, Brazil. https://lume.ufrgs.br/handle/10183/11434

Saldanha, J. (1980). *Os subterrâneos do futebol*. José Olympio.

Santos, J. R. (1981). *História política do futebol brasileiro*. São Paulo: Brasiliense.

Schmitz Filho, A. G. (2005). A CPI do futebol: Agendamento e processualidades sistêmicas. (Doctoral Dissertation in Communication Sciences), Unisinos, São Leopoldo, Brazil. https://www.yumpu.com/pt/document/view/6498306/universidade-do-vale-do-rio-dos-sinos-unisinos

Souza, J. (1999). *O malandro e o protestante: A tese weberiana e a singularidade cultural brasileira*. Brasília: Editora da UNB.

Souza, J. (2003). *A construção social da subcidadania: Para uma sociologia política da modernidade periférica*. Belo Horizonte: Editora UFMG; Rio de Janeiro: IUPERJ.

Souza, J. (Org.) (2006). *A invisibilidade da desigualdade brasileira*. Belo Horizonte: Editora UFMG.

Souza, J. (2009). *A ralé brasileira: Quem é e como vive*. Belo Horizonte: Editora UFMG.

Souza, J. (2014). O "esporte das multidões" no Brasil: entre o contexto de ação futebolístico e a negociação mimética dos conflitos sociais. (Doctoral Dissertation in Physical Education), Universidade Federal do Paraná, Curitiba, Brazil. https://acervodigital.ufpr.br/handle/1884/37212

Souza, J., Almeida, B. S., & Marchi Júnior, W. (2014). Por uma reconstrução teórica do futebol a partir do referencial sociológico de Pierre Bourdieu. *Revista Brasileira de Educação Física e Esporte, 28*(2), 221–232. https://doi.org/10.1590/1807-55092014000200221

Weber, M. (2004). *A ética protestante e o espírito do capitalismo*. São Paulo: Martin Claret. (Original work published in 1905).

Chapter 12
FIFA, BRICS, and the Soft Power Discourse: Analysis of the World Cup in South Africa, Brazil, and Russia

Marco Bettine

Introduction

South Africa, Brazil, and Russia hosted the FIFA (Fédération Internationale de Football Association) Men's Football World Cup this century. This chapter works with the dialectic relationship between these countries—as an international political–economic group—and FIFA, to the extent that both the federation and the BRICS had strategic interests in such mega-event, whether at domestic, regional, or global levels.[1]

I intend to analyze how these countries use the men's football World Cup as a discourse to expand their "soft power" or their public diplomacy, or simply their propaganda,[2] a discourse that FIFA markets (Schausteck et al., 2016; Brannagan et al., 2014, 2016; Almeida et al., 2015; Ziakas, 2015; Brathen et al., 2014; Damo et al., 2013; Cornelissen, 2011a; Manzenreiter, 2010).

I am not taking the category of soft power in a naive way; I know that it is often used as a justification for hosting mega-events, being considered as one of their intangible legacies. The legacy issue itself is controversial, as much is said about it during the candidacy period, probably to garner political, social, and economic support, but the concrete fact is that the "legacy" theme is little studied after the event in the Global South axis (Horne, 2017).

---

[1] Research Grant: Fundação de Amparo à Pesquisa do Estado de São Paulo, Funding Group. Process: 2018/11558–6.

[2] The papers suggested below go into more detail on host country promotion, soft power, gentrification, and the state of exception: Almeida et al. (2015), Braathen et al. (2014), Brannagan & Rookwood (2016), Brannagan & Giullianotti (2014), Cornelissen (2011b), Damo & Oliven (2013), Manzenreiter (2010), Schausteck & Graeff (2016), Ziakas (2015), Grix & Lee (2013), Grix et. al. (2015).

M. Bettine (✉)
University of São Paulo, São Paulo, Brazil
e-mail: marcobettine@usp.br

I intend to develop in this study three theoretical topics and a more generalist consideration. The theoretical topics will be: (1) discuss the concept of soft power in the context of the Global South and its limits; (2) present the evaluations of the men's football World Cup through some international media; and (3) the BRICS as FIFA's new market. At the end, I shall seek to make some considerations on the possible reasons that led these countries to host this mega-event and what are FIFA's interests in such countries.

Some problems were raised by researchers who are concerned with FIFA's performance in the contemporary world; among them, I highlight the lack of clarity in the choice of host countries; the choice of hosts with potential for legislative changes in favor of FIFA's financial partners; and countries with endemic corruption, which would facilitate FIFA's agreements with global partners and the local political elite.

Based on these concerns, which are not only mine, but those of a large number of football enthusiasts, I propose three sub-areas of analysis: (i) soft power in the context of the globalized world; (ii) use of mega sporting events by peripheral nations to increase their soft power; and (iii) international media as an impact factor on the evaluation of countries abroad and possible influence on their soft power.

But, before starting the theoretical discussion, I would like to explain to the reader what the BRICS stands for and why I state in this chapter that these countries invested heavily in major sporting events.

A Panorama of the BRICS in Mega Sporting Events

BRICS is a geopolitical acronym that identifies new global actors (Brazil, Russia, India, China, and South Africa). Its use is part of a political–diplomatic mechanism that is constituted at a moment of redesign of global governance, in which the perception of the deficit of representativeness and, therefore, of legitimacy of the structures created after the fall of the Berlin Wall, becomes more and more acute.

The BRICS, despite the geographical and cultural distance, has in common the understanding of the unequal distribution of power in international relations. Their main objective is to reform the international order, whether in the UN, IMF, or WTO.

Brazilian researchers, particularly from the Alexandre de Gusmão Foundation (Funag), a public entity linked to the Brazilian Ministry of Foreign Affairs, in a 2012 meeting discussing Brazil, the BRICS and the international agenda, stated that there is a common interest among these countries for a geopolitical positioning that redistributes power in the international sphere, adding to this the interests of each nation. The BRICS are (a) for China, a convenient way to position itself as a world leader, exert global influence, and reduce that of the USA without exposing itself or taking risks alone; (b) for Russia, a channel for dialogue with the USA and a space to regain its strength in global demands; (c) for India, a space for its multilateral demands and to protect itself against Pakistan; (d) for Brazil, a means to expand its political strength beyond South America and improve its image in the world; (e) for

Table 12.1 Four Mega Sport Events

Summer O. G	Winter O. G	FIFA World Cup	Commonwealth games
2000-Sydney	2002-Salt Lake City	2000-Japan and South Korea	2002-Manchester
2004-Athens	2006-Torino	2004-Germany	2006-Melbourne
2008-Beijing	2010-Vancouver	*2010-South Africa*	*2010-Delí*
2012-London	*2014-Sochi*	*2014-Brazil*	2014-Glasgow
2016-Rio de Janeiro	2018-Pyeongchang	*2018-Russia*	2018-Gold Coast
2020-Tokyo	*2022-Beijing*	2022-Qatar	2022-Birmingham

Four mega sporting events (FIFA Men's World Cup, Summer Olympic Games, Winter Olympic Games, and the Commonwealth Games) will be used

South Africa, a way to gain the trust of global actors (especially in relation to human rights) and to be the spokesperson of Pan-Africanism.

The biggest sports enterprises use the typical strategies of international relations for foreign trade demands, like customs tariffs, contracts international relations and horizontal relations with other economic blocs. Another point, what has become evident in the twenty-first century is the strategic use of sport for international political and economic promotion, as well as the intention to reinforce domestic agendas, political legitimacy and national cohesion (Table 12.1).

Just to alert the reader about the importance of the Commonwealth Games in this table, remember that this competition between countries linked to the British Empire began in 1930, occurs every four years, and in 2022 will be in its 22nd edition. In 2010, it was the first time that the games were held in India, even this country figuring in 4th place in the overall medal table, in a total of 70 confederations (countries) recognized by the Commonwealth Games federation.

By 2022, the BRICS will be at the forefront as the host of Mega Sport Events, and there will be two Summer Olympic Games, two Winter Olympic Games, three World Cups, and one Commonwealth Game.

In this chapter, the theoretical effort will be to analyze the FIFA Men's Football World Cup and to focus on just one mega sporting event. However, nothing prevents us from making use of China and India's experiences, if required, to clarify any obscure point or interesting example.

Is *Soft Power* a Concept of Public Diplomacy or Just Propaganda?

Since this is a chapter, I will not delve into the "theory of soft power," its critiques, its followers, or its limits. I can affirm, however, that the use of soft power in a mechanistic way in peripheral nations is a very serious problem to the extent that the first objective of its creation was to use it as a theoretical tool destined to analyze

Western economic powers in a specific conjuncture—post-perestroika, glasnost, fall of the Berlin wall, and the failure of real socialism in Eastern Europe and USSR. The concern of political scientists was to understand the role of the United States of North America in this new world scenario and how this country could exercise other forms of power, besides those already used by the Pentagon.

A year after the fall of the Berlin Wall, Joseph Nye[3] presents a book about the changing forms of American power in the world, gaining several supporters and making him a reference/celebrity in the debate about international relations. His theory seemed very simple to understand: Power is fluid, there is intangibility, and there are other ways for a country to exert its world influence without using economic embargoes or *Agent Orange*,[4] such as movies, technologies, or bilateral alliances of cooperation agreements in strategic areas such as energy.

Nye's great theoretical bet, which did not come true in concrete reality, was that with the end of the Cold War, military and economic coercion would be less effective in the search for prestige and international influence, allowing nations to pursue their objectives through other paths and to ascend within the established order without necessarily destroying its institutions and agreements (Nye, 2004). I claim that it has not been realized in concrete reality due to the post-September 11 "war on terrorism." Since this period we live in a permanent state of exception, with personal data being watched whit governments, even secret prisons. Even the German Chancellor Angela Merkel, theoretically an ally of the USA, suffered the invasion in personal data in 2015 (Reuters Staff, 2015, July 8).

Answering the question posed in this item—soft power, public diplomacy, or propaganda?—it seems to me that the soft power category is closer to propaganda, which uses strategies of global scope, such as movies and series in the area of entertainment; broadcast and online newspapers for news; and Mega Sport Events for sports. Public diplomacy is associated with the promotion of a country's image abroad, through diplomats and consuls concerned with the relationship between foreign policy and civil society, in an effort to democratize and make transnational public policies more transparent.

Researchers such as John Horne, Wolfram Mazentereiter, Richard Giulianotti, and Andrew Zimbalist are some of the authors who criticize the idea of applying soft power to sporting events; particularly elsewhere (Almeida, et al. 2018), I have stated that the category soft power attempts to minimize imperialism or coloniality in forms of power. And that power in international relations, in its various forms of expression, remains bureaucratic power in the Weberian sense of the term, applied to the politics

---

[3] Joseph Samuel Nye Jr. is an American political scientist and co-founder of the theory of interdependence in international relations and the theory of neoliberalism. He pioneered the theory of soft power. His category became popular with the use by members of the American government, which ends with the beginning of the Trump administration.

[4] Agent Orange is a mixture of two herbicides. It was used in the Vietnam War. In the period 1961–1971, American troops sprayed 80 million liters of herbicides containing 400 kg of dioxin over Vietnamese territory. These defoliants destroyed the natural habitat, left 4.8 million people exposed to Agent Orange and caused irreversible diseases, especially birth defects, cancer, and neurological syndromes in children, women, and men in the country.

between countries developed by Hans Morgenthau (2003), who defines power as a struggle between forces that are not necessarily antagonistic, since to want power is to have and hold on to power, regardless of ideology. I advanced in Morgenthau's studies to extend the idea of power not as a means, but as an end in itself. In this case, the (imperialist) nation uses elements of cultural and social co-optation to impose its strength in the international political game.

> Therefore, the nation that manages to make its culture prevail over others would have more "heterodox soft power". Because the dominant nation is in the hearts and minds of the dominated nations, it could yield its power through the principles of traditional soft power. Ultimately, soft power can only be used if its primary foundations include a dominant nation's violence, imposition and strength over a dominated one. It would be neocolonization of culture itself in a globalized society (Almeida et al., 2018, p. 1356).

Authors who advocate critical thinking as to what we call intangible legacies, as would be soft power, harshly criticize the causal relationship that is established between hosting a FIFA World Cup and having one's agendas met in terms of international demands—see Brazil's intentions to have a seat as a permanent member of the UN Security Council—showing that hosting this event involves changes in the most diverse aspects of the country, from political and legal, to urban mobility and housing. The spending of billions of dollars, the supposed profit, and a massive audience do not represent, by themselves, the success of the event and may result in huge failures, as analyses made in Beijing, Sochi, South Africa, Brazil, and Rio de Janeiro (Almeida & Gutierrez, 2018; Ziakas, 2015; Cornelissen, 2011a, b; Ahlert, 2007; Preuss, 2007).

The imposition of FIFA agenda to host countries reveals a huge gap, as an example, the legal–institutional changes in Brazil to meet the demands of international sports organizations (Toledo et al., 2015); one can consider this loss of state autonomy as a true state of exception, evidencing how fragile democracies such as those of BRICS end up using public money in the promotion of mega-events (Damo, 2012; Damo & Oliven, 2013).

FIFA has become a global actor in international relations that has an aggressive, authoritarian, and fraudulent strategy, as a *modus operandi*, in the choices and agendas to hold its event. I believe that the arrest in 2014 of FIFA's leaders in the middle of the World Cup in Brazil was an important step to unveil the pose of "good lady" that this entity propagated. FIFA is a transnational company, which seeks profit for its partners and leaders, makes agreements without *accountability,* and does not take responsibility for human rights in its interventions. I like to call FIFA a hurricane, *FIFA's Hurricane,* which leaves traces of destruction wherever it goes—homeless populations, public neglect, workers' deaths, and gentrification. When questioned, the federation places the blame on the local government and states that everything was in contract and we move on to the next "victim," that is, host city.

These statements may seem, at first, ideological, without theoretical basis. To those who think so, I suggest reading internationally recognized texts for the reader to realize how much FIFA and its partners are doing a disfavor to football, such as Horne (2017) on political contestation and abuses in the area of human rights; Hill et al. (2016), which criticize the way football presents itself in the contemporary world; Tomlinson (2014), who discusses the lack of governance and transparency at FIFA; Chappetel (2018), who addresses the need for regulation of international sports agents such as the IOC and FIFA; Bayle and Rayner (2018), who draw a parallel with the Nixon scandal by using the term "FIFAgate," a reference to recent corruption scandals at the federation. These are only examples in the academic field. Other initiatives of civil society groups also act with the intention of curbing FIFA's corruption and protecting football as a world cultural heritage; such groups have built international articulations, such as (a) Play the Game; (b) Against Modern Football; (c) Sport for the Peace; and (d) Articulação Nacional dos Comitês Populares da Copa.

The FIFA Men's Football Cup in BRICS

South Africa in 2010, Brazil in 2014, and Russia in 2018 have hosted the last FIFA Men's World Cups. Each nation wanted to use the event's visibility to promote their agendas in the three spheres: domestic, regional, and global. There is a time stamp, a collective memory built by the World Cups have a mnemonic sphere in terms of culture, leisure, and tourism and have an aura of memories, especially for those who have as a time marker the World Cups, I do not know South Africa and Russia, but Brazilians build part of their memory from the experiences of the World Cup. Simoni Guedes synthesizes with mastery in her text "O Brasil nas Copas do Mundo: tempo 'suspenso' e história" (Brazil in the World Cups: "suspended" time and history):

> The World Cups constitute, for Brazilians, true national rituals, occasions in which Brazil-ianness is celebrated, a symbolic construction of national unity, "suspending", in a way, the differences and inequalities that permeate the social structure. In order for this process to take place, it is necessary that these periods constitute their own time and their own history. This process supposes the "suspension" of daily time, establishing extended holidays and activating the memory of the participation of Brazilian teams in World Cups (Guedes, 2002, p. 1, our translation).

This way of thinking about the relationship between football, Brazil, and the World Cup was transformed in 2013, when we had the June Days in Brazil, just before the Confederations Cup began. Bastos (2017), Avritzer (2016), Dantas et al. (2016), and Szwako (2016), discussing the impasses of democracy in Brazil, show us a very consistent reading of the 2013 protests up to the 2016 parliamentary coup. Another important study to understand the population's rejection to the Confederations Cup and the FIFA World Cup in Brazil is the study by Ângela Alonso (2017), called "A política das ruas: protestos em São Paulo de Dilma a Temer" (Politics of the streets: protests in São Paulo from Dilma to Temer).

Another interesting point to be analyzed in relation to the 2014 World Cup held in Brazil concerns the existence of a symbolic football narrative; an example of this phenomenon was the defeat of the Brazilian team to Germany, the "Mineiratzen," a reference to the "Maracanazo" in 1950. These fictional names, over time, become constructed stories, creating a universe of tales and chronicles, filmic, and journalistic, which are more in the world of fantasy than of reality. Discussing the myth issue,

Anthony Pereira's article (2014, June 13) published in *CNN* addresses these issues, as well as the fears that hovered over the 2014 World Cup.

The fear was shared with foreign vehicles such as *CNN, BBC, Daily Mail, New York Times, The Guardian, Le Monde,* which demonstrated a distrust regarding the holding of the World Cup in Brazil, evidenced in their editorials. For example, Jenny Barchifield (2013, June 30), in an article for the *Daily Mail*, explained that anti-government protestors marched near the Maracanã stadium before the Confederations Cup final, demonstrating their outrage at the billions of dollars the Brazilian government spent on the Mega Sport Events instead of investing in public services.

In June 18, 2013, the *BBC* mentions the protests in Brazil and the spread of *hashtags*, like "#nãovaitercopa". According to the report, about 200,000 people marched through the streets of Brazil's largest cities against the rising costs of public transportation and the expense of hosting the World Cup (Mirchandani, 2013, June 18).

It is true that during the World Cup, through legislative changes imposed by FIFA, particularly Law No. 12,663/2012—known as the General Law of the Cup (Toledo et al., 2015)—there was greater control over protests; through violence, organized groups and social movements were dispersed and put into illegality, thanks to a series of measures, including the use of anti-terrorism legislation (Freixo, 2014, April 17). This caused foreign newspapers to change their opinions regarding the unfeasibility of the World Cup. *The New York Times,* for example, said that the 2013 predictions of doom (the arenas would not be ready in time, violent street protests would threaten the supporters, and strikes at the airports and in the subway would hinder thousands of visitors) had not been confirmed. These predictions of chaos were constant worries in the days leading up to the World Cup. But after the tournament started, the situation was quite different. The quality of the spectacle and the comfort of the fans ensured the success of public opinion, and the thrilling games provided the perfect drama for television (Border, 2014, June 17).

In the Brazilian case, the 2014 World Cup, as Brazil's propaganda abroad (soft power), showed a weakened democracy, with politicians who violated the democratic pact, and an advance of a conservative agenda.

In South Africa, the issue of overcoming *apartheid* and the representation of pan-Africanism set the tone for the speeches of South African leaders in international media reports—these were the country's demands. For example, *The Guardian*, in a report by David Smith (2010, June 13), points out Africa's problems and the little media attention given to the various civil wars taking place in the continent. The fascination caused by Africa's first World Cup concealed frequent terror and famine.

Like Brazil, South Africa has had to reform its laws to adapt to the burdens of FIFA, with courts that have been specially established to deal with situations involving FIFA's interests. Marina Hyde (2010, June 20) did an excellent report (published also in *The Guardian*) on the draconian actions of the South African government to calm FIFA's nerves in the face of urban violence in the host cities. Concerned with undoing its image damaged by crime before the tournament, the South African government agreed to the creation of 56 World Cup tribunals across the country—an initiative that was praised by FIFA.

In South Africa, FIFA's statute forbids informal commerce near official areas such as stadiums and venues of events involving FIFA (fan parks, accreditation centers, official training areas, hotels). The documentary *Trade Mark 2010*[5] by journalist Rudi Boon presents this scenario. Newton (2009) presents the removal process for the construction of structures related to the World Cup, project *N2 in Cape Town,* with 20 thousand displaced people.

In 2018, when Russia hosted the World Cup, differently from previous events, a journalism more concerned with FIFA's actions, which started to appear in 2013, with the coverage of the protests in Brazil, had already been consolidated. Another point to be highlighted again was the arrest of high-ranking officials of the International Football federation in 2014 and 2015, making a sweep in the entity. The World Cup in Russia begins with much discussion about the corruption of the entity, accusing Russia of lack of transparency in the process of choosing the country to host the Cup and distrust about Putin's relationship with FIFA.

Western journalists began a massive coverage of "FIFAgate." *The New York Times* described in detail in its editorial the accusations based on the FBI investigation that began in 2011, pointing to widespread corruption in FIFA over the previous two decades, mainly linked to the dispute for the right to host the World Cups in Russia (2018) and Qatar (2022), as well as marketing and television contracts. In 2015, with the arrest of FIFA's top management in Zurich, the biggest scandal in the world of football became public.[6]

Russia, which has always had difficulty imposing its agenda in the West, had to deal with the international civil society demanding transparency and governance from FIFA and its partners—something that Russia itself does not have. Another important point to note was the exponential increase in spending by the host countries for the event. Three BRICS countries—South Africa, Brazil, and Russia—that hosted the last World Cups had huge expenses in the realization of this sporting event.

---

[5] Watch the documentary through this link: http://apublica.org/2012/02/FIFA-manda/.

[6] Involved in the case are: Chuck Blazer—Former Secretary General of CONCACAF; Alejandro Burzaco—CEO of the channel Torneos y Competencias; Aaron Davidson—Chairman of the Board of Governors of the North American Soccer League; Rafael Esquivel—President of the Venezuelan Football federation and member of the CONMEBOL executive committee; Eugenio Figueiredo—Former President of the Uruguayan Football Association and former President of CONMEBOL; José Hawilla—Owner and founder of Traffic Group; Hugo Jinkis—President of Full Play Group; Mariano Jinkis—Vice-president of Full Play Group; Nicolás Leoz—Former president of CONMEBOL; Eduardo Li—President of the Costa Rican Football federation, member of FIFA's executive committee, and member of CONCACAF's executive committee; José Marguiles—Secretary of Traffic Sports Brasil; José Maria Marin—Former president of the Brazilian Football Confederation and former governor of São Paulo; Julio Rocha Lopez—President of the Nicaraguan Football federation, FIFA development director, and former president of UNCAF; Costas Takkas—Former secretary general of the Cayman Islands Football Association; Daryll Warner—Jack Warner's son and former FIFA development director; Jack Warner—Former FIFA vice president, former CONCACAF president, and former Minister of National Security of Trinidad and Tobago; Jeffrey Webb—President of CONCACAF, president of the Cayman Islands Football Association, and FIFA vice president; Carlos Chavez Landivar—Former president of the Federación Boliviana de Fútbol and former treasurer of the South American Football Confederation.

How can one understand that nations with greater HDI (Human Development Index) problems were the ones that most "invested" (spent) on the FIFA World Cup? How were the BRICS nations used to inflate the mega-event?

The *New York Times* called the Russian Cup the Putin's Cup (Smith, 2018, June 13). After the event's opening speech, the same *NYT* denounced some actions of the Russian government that demonstrated the opposite of the sense of brotherhood extolled during the ceremony: annexation of Crimea, support for separatists in eastern Ukraine, indifference to the suffering of the Syrian people, murder of Kremlin critics abroad, imprisonment of activists, and banning the defense of homosexuality on social media (Macfarquhar, 2018, June 13).

Foreign newspapers played a very limited role during the World Cup in Russia, either because of Putin's strength on the world stage or because of the internal control of domestic issues; there is no doubt that there was a shielding by the government of the news broadcasted during the staging of the World Cup in Russia.

Unlike what happened in Brazil and South Africa, countries in which the international media were able to discuss problems such as income distribution, urban violence, public spending, transparency, police violence, corruption, gentrification, in the Russian World Cup, these same media channels were limited to discussing the country's war and expansionist policies.

In my opinion, there is a perverse relationship between FIFA and the BRICS. There is, however, a greater affinity with South Africa and Brazil than with Russia, which once "owned" half the world at the time of the USSR, and which brings with it a whole ideological and military burden, as a counterpoint to countries that are only regional emerging economies, which have little attention in the asymmetrical international power relations. This reinforces the thesis that soft power only exists if a nation knows how to historically use its military and economic strength to conquer its agendas. Russia—and Putin, particularly—knew how to shield the event, showing only what it wanted to show, recalling the German effort in the Berlin Olympics.

Final Considerations

In these considerations, I would like to try to answer some questions pointed out in the introduction, systematizing a coherent explanation from the consulted literature and the selected materials.

FIFA markets its product, the men's football World Cup. To sell it, it relies on the attractive resource of soft power, which translated into the Global South means propaganda. For a long time, the host country of FIFA's Hurricane will remain in the world media's sights and will be able to conclude its commercial agreements in a neoliberal environment.

Table 12.2 World Cup costs

Country	General costs (in billions)
Russia (2018)	US$ 17.6
Brazil (2014)	US$ 15
South Africa (2010)	US$ 8.6
Germany (2006)	US$ 4.6

Source Exame and *The Guardian* (figures updated to 2018)

FIFA used all its political strength, added to the will of rising leaders from the Global South, to give new directions to its organization. It sought agreements with countries that had great interest in using its brand to expand its global network, and this generated astronomical numbers, as seen in Table 12.2.

The BRICS, given their representativeness deficit and their interest in expanding strength and power in the global geopolitical game, has fed the Hydra's FIFA. In Greek mythology, the Hydra is a dragon with serpent heads, with two main characteristics: The first is its venom—lethal when simply exhaled (in the BRICS, the World Cups have left a trail of corruption, displaced people, violence to human rights, and obscurity); the second is that for each head of the serpent cut off two others are reborn (Even with the investigations, FIFA and its partners built, through a "game of corruption and power", spurious ways of managing football and, consequently, the World Cup).

The emphasis on consumption is diametrically opposed to a social redistribution for the host countries of the event. The recovery of the city for the production of tourist attractions produces yet another gentrification of the urban space in the name of regeneration, with a consequent negative impact on the poor communities affected. The use of public funds to finance a private event produces gaps in public accounts that lead in sequence (South Africa and Brazil) to an action of fiscal austerity and legislative changes in social security and labor guarantees.

Recent mega-events in the BRICS (including in China and India) have demonstrated: (a) evictions of poor populations without a compensation process; (b) abuse of mainly immigrant workers; (c) changes in civil rights and curtailment of social movements; (d) threats, intimidation, and imprisonment of engaged free media journalists.

This is the picture of the BRICS as host of the Summer Olympic Games, the Winter Olympic Games, the FIFA Men's World Cup, and the Commonwealth Games.

To finish, it is worth remembering that, in 2013, then-FIFA Secretary General Jérôme Valcke stated that less democracy is sometimes better for organizing a World Cup (Reuters Staff, 2013, April 24). On January 2016, after allegations of corruption, Valcke was banned by the FIFA Ethics Committee until 2028 and fined 100,000 Swiss francs.

References

Ahlert, G. (2007). *Assessing the impact of the FIFA world cup Germany 2006*. Gesellschaft Für Wirtschaftliche.

Almeida, B. S., Bolsmann, C., Marchi, W., Jr., & Souza, J. (2015). Rationales, rhetoric and realities: FIFA's world cup in South Africa 2010 and Brazil 2014. *International Review for the Sociology of Sport, 50*(3), 265–282. https://doi.org/10.1177/1012690213481970

Almeida, M. B., & Gutierrez, D. (2018). O soft power do Brasil e a cobertura da mídia internacional da Copa do Mundo da FIFA 2014. *Licere, 21*(2), 226–257.

Almeida, M. B., Gutierrez, D., & Graeff, B. (2018). Foreign media reports about Brazil's mega sporting events: Soft power, periphery and dependence. *Movimento, 24*(4), 1353–1368.

Alonso, A. (2017). A política das ruas: protestos em São Paulo de Dilma a Temer. *Novos Estudos CEBRAP*, (special issue), 49–58.

Avritzer, L. (2016). *Impasses da democracia no Brasil*. Civilização Brasileira.

Barchfield, J. (2013, June 30). More missiles and tear gas in Brazil as 5,000 anti-government protestors march near Maracana. *Daily Mail*, Confederation Cup 2013.

Bastos, P. Z. (2017). Ascensão e crise do governo Dilma Rousseff e o golpe de 2016: Poder estrutural, contradição e ideologia. *Revista De Economia Contemporânea, 21*(2), 1–63. https://doi.org/10.1590/198055272129

Bayle, E., & Rayner, H. (2018). Sociology of a scandal: The emergence of 'FIFAgate.' *Soccer & Society, 19*(4), 593–611. https://doi.org/10.1080/14660970.2016.1228591

Border, S. (2014, June 17). At the world cup, Doomsday predictions give way to smaller hiccups in Brazil. *New York Times*.

Braathen, E., Sørbøe, C. M., & Mascarenhas, G. (2014). BRICS, megaeventos esportivos e o Rio de Janeiro como uma "cidade de exceção". *Tensões Mundiais, 10*(18–19), 327–362.

Brannagan, P., & Rookwood, J. (2016). Sports mega-events, soft power and soft disempowerment: International supporters' perspectives on Qatar's acquisition of the 2022 FIFA world cup finals. *International Journal of Sport Policy and Politics, 8*(2), 173–188. https://doi.org/10.1080/19406940.2016.1150868

Brannagan, P. M., & Giullianotti, R. (2014). Soft power and soft disempowerment: Qatar, global sport and football's 2022 Word Cup finals. *Leisure Studies, 34*(6), 703–719. https://doi.org/10.1080/02614367.2014.964291

Chappelet, J. L. (2018). Beyond governance: The need to improve the regulation of international sport. *Sport in Society, 21*(5), 724–734. https://doi.org/10.1080/17430437.2018.1401355

Cornelissen, S. (2011a). More than a sporting chance? Appraising the sport for development legacy of the 2010 FIFA world cup. *Third World Quarterly, 32*(3), 503–529.

Cornelissen, S. (2011b). The geopolitics of global aspiration: Sport mega events and emerging powers. *The International Journal of the History of Sport, 27*(16–18), 3008–3025.

Damo, A. S. (2011). Produção e consumo de megaeventos esportivos: apontamentos em perspectiva antropológica. *Comunicação, Mídia e Consumo, 8*(21), 67–92.

Damo, A. S. (2012). O desejo, o direito e o dever: A trama que trouxe a Copa ao Brasil. *Movimento, 18*(2), 41–81.

Damo, A. S., & Oliven, R. G. (2013). O Brasil no horizonte dos megaeventos esportivos de 2014 e 2016: Sua cara, seus sócios e seus negócios. *Horizontes Antropológicos, 19*(40), 19–63. https://doi.org/10.1590/S0104-71832013000200002

Dantas, A. T., Jabbour, E. K., & Sobral, B. (2016). A recriação conservadora do Estado: Impasses no reformismo progressista e popular e o golpe de 2016. *Revista Da Associação Nacional De Pós-Graduação e Pesquisa Em Geografia, 12*(19), 5–38. https://doi.org/10.5418/RA2016.1219.0001

Freixo, M. (2014, April 17). Lei para coibir protestos na Copa trata manifestante como terrorista. *Especial UOL*.

Grix, J., Brannagan, P. M., & Houlihan, B. (2015). Interrogating states soft power strategies: A case study of sports mega-events in Brazil and the UK. *Global Society, 29*(3), 463–479. https://doi.org/10.1080/13600826.2015.1047743

Grix, J., & Lee, D. (2013). Soft power, sports mega-events and emerging states: The lure of the politics of attraction. *Global Society, 27*(4), 521–536. https://doi.org/10.1080/13600826.2013.827632

Guedes, S. L. (2002). O Brasil nas Copas do Mundo: Tempo "suspenso" e história. *Reunião Brasileira de Antropologia* (XXIII RBA), Associação Brasileira de Antropologia.

Hill, T., Canniford, R., & Millward, P. (2016). Against modern football: Mobilising protest movements in social media. *Sociology, 52*(4), 688–708. https://doi.org/10.1177/0038038516660040

Horne, J. (2017). Sports mega-events—Three sites of contemporary political contestation. *Sport in Society, 20*(3), 328–340. https://doi.org/10.1080/17430437.2015.1088721

Hyde, M. (2010, June 20). World Cup 2010: Fans, robbers and a marketing stunt face justice. *The Guardian.*

Lafer, C. (1982). *Paradoxos e possibilidades: Estudos sobre a ordem mundial e sobre a política exterior do Brasil num sistema internacional em transformação.* Nova Fronteira.

Macfarquhar, N. M. (2018, June 13). Thank soccer, and Trump: Putin has a chance to woo the world. *New York Times.*

Manzenreiter, W. (2010). The Beijing games in the western imagination of China: The weak power of soft power. *Journal of Sport & Social, 34*(1), 29–48. https://doi.org/10.1177/0193723503509358968

Mirchandani, R. (2013, June 18). Brazil protests spread in Sao Paulo, Brasilia and Rio. *BBC,* World Latin America.

Morgentau, H. (2003). *A Política entre nações: A luta pelo poder e pela paz.* Imprensa Oficial do Estado de São Paulo; Editora Universidade de Brasília.

Newton, C. (2009). The reverse side of the medal: About the 2010 FIFA world cup and the beautification of the N2 in Cape Town. *Urban Forum, 20*(1), 93–108. https://doi.org/10.1007/s12132-009-9048-y

Nye, J. S. (2004). *Soft power: The means to success in world politics.* New York: Public.

Pereira, A. (2014, June 13). Brazil 2014: Exploding the myths of sun, samba, soccer. *CNN.*

Preuss, H. (2007). The conceptualisation and measurement of mega sport event legacies. *Journal of Sport & Tourism, 12*(3–4), 207–228. https://doi.org/10.1080/14775080701736957

Reuters Staff. (2013, April 24). Soccer: Less democracy makes for an easier world cup—Valcke. *Reuters.*

Reuters Staff. (2015, July 8). U.S. spy agency tapped German chancellery for decades: WikiLeaks. *Reuters.*

Schausteck, B. A., & Graeff, B. (2016). Displacement and gentrication in the "city of exception": Rio de Janeiro Towards the 2016 Olympic Games. *Bulletin International Council of Sport Science and Physical Education* (70), 54–61.

Smith, D. (2010, June 13). As football fever grips the nation, terror and famine in Africa go unreported. *The Guardian.*

Smith, R. (2018, June 13). Russia welcomes the world, for better or worse. *New York Times.*

Szwako, J. (2016). O fascismo contemporâneo brasileiro ou o mundo segundo o conservadorismo. *Escuta,* (special issue).

Toledo, R. M., Grix, J., & Bega, M. T. (2015). Megaeventos esportivos e seus legados: Uma análise dos efeitos institucionais da eleição do Brasil como país-sede. *Revista De Sociologia e Política, 23*(56), 21–44. https://doi.org/10.1590/1678-987315235602

Tomlinson, A. (2014). The supreme leader sails on: Leadership, ethics and governance in FIFA. *Sport in Society, 17*(9), 1155–1169. https://doi.org/10.1080/17430437.2013.856590

Ziakas, V. (2015). For the benefit of all? Developing a critical perspective in mega-event leverage. *Leisure Studies, 34*(6), 689–702. https://doi.org/10.1080/02614367.2014.986507

Chapter 13
Football and Anthropology in Brazil

Arlei Sander Damo

Not so long ago, it was usual to start a text about football denouncing the prejudice of the academic world against the sport or claiming the scarcity of publications, even in Brazil. Within this multidisciplinary field, anthropology has an outstanding role, especially in Brazilian case, and this may be evidenced by seminal contributions, by the volume and quality of thesis and dissertations, by the institutional insertion in academic events and awards in related competitions, and by the continuous renewal of the themes.

However, there is no unanimity nor anyone authorized to state, on behalf of a collective, what anthropology of sport or football is or should be. This observation echoes a broader phenomenon of thematic dispersion, noted in the broader spectrum of the anthropological discipline, impacted, since long and irreversibly, by the need to reinvent itself from epistemological clashes concomitant to the collapse of colonialism. In this sense, proliferation of themes, theories, and networks of influences that have accompanied Brazilian anthropology over the last three decades is remarkable, with the exponential growth of graduate courses and, by extension, of research production. In this scenario, even the canonical and perhaps simplest formulation of what anthropology is, based on the etymology of the word, is uncertain. One can no longer even affirm that anthropology is the study of humanity as a species, since classic distinction between nature and culture has been questioned in detriment of bolder proposals about the status of humans and non-humans—including, here, animals, objects, and other beings such as algae, viruses, and bacteria.

For each version of anthropology practiced in contemporary times, there is or there could be a way of approaching sports, and this could make a succinct presentation unfeasible. An alternative is to present football itself from the perspective of these investigations carried out on or about it, highlighting the most recurrent and consensual aspects among us. In other words, even though we have very diverse theoretical

A. S. Damo (✉)
Federal University of Rio Grande do Sul, Porto Alegre, Brazil

backgrounds and methodological influences, as a result of the disciplinary dispersion already mentioned, it is feasible to identify the accumulation of productions
around some objects. It is also possible to note important thematic shifts over the
four decades that separate us from the first thesis in anthropology and in Brazilian
social sciences (Guedes, 1977).

In order to address this proposal, the chapter is subdivided into three parts. Firstly,
I present a synthesis of the reductionist interpretations of football, which have obliterated or contributed little to its consideration as a relevant theme for social sciences.
In the second part, I try to show how anthropology has contributed to broaden the
understanding of football as a social and cultural fact. Consistently with the principle
of diversity, one of the pillars of our discipline, I try to explain how it is possible to
address different issues from the broadening of the understanding of what football
itself is, a plural and multifaceted fact; therefore, we have been using more and more
frequently the term "footballs." In the third part, I emphasize identities and otherness, because, around this issue, there is a remarkable concentration and convergence
of studies. Finally, I provide a brief narrative, in diachronic way, presenting some
thematic transitions that occurred in the spectrum of Brazilian anthropology. I believe
this will help the reader to understand the variation in scientific production at the
intersection between sensitive dynamics in relation to social changes and internal
dynamics concerning theoretical and methodological debates.

From Football to Footballs

It is difficult to think about the development of sport anthropology apart from other
contributions, notably from related areas, such as sociology and historiography.
Urban anthropology, which has developed since the second half of the twentieth
century and, particularly in Brazil, from the 1970s onward, has a notable multidisciplinary influence, differently from the anthropology of indigenous societies, also
called ethnology. Hence, it is frequent that anthropologists work in collaboration
with historians, although anthropology is characterized more by researching present
time and, therefore, privileges synchrony. I make this caveat because the subsequent
paragraphs could suggest to an unaware reader the intrusion in the field of historians,
by approaching football in a diachronic way.

British court edicts indicate that folk football games have been played since the
Middle Ages, commonly during periods of religious festivals and not infrequently
declining into generalized violence. There is also information about *calcio*, played
in Florence region, in Italy, and it is possible that other forms close to football were
practiced in Europe before the nineteenth century. It is notable, however, that such
games were only legally admitted, and even recommended by moralists and peda-
gogues, after undergoing a process of regulation. In this effort of containing violence,
male boarding schools, especially English public schools, played an important role,
and their graduates were equally responsible for the creation of clubs and leagues,
important for the institutionalization and stabilization of the rules of the games.

Rules, by the way, besides modulating violence, instituted differences among sporting disciplines and enabled them to be practiced within a wider radius. This is the case of football, whose codes, initially formulated by students at Cambridge University around 1848, were later reformulated and institutionalized by a group of young Londoners who, in 1863, founded the Football Association. These youngsters changed football rules played in the city of rugby, still today known as rugby, allowing the use of hands and the tackle, as well as modifying the shape of the ball, changing the arrangement of the goals, and abolishing the scrum, among other less relevant details. In parallel with the codification, associations were set up to monitor the rules, such as the International Board, that became FIFA, the international agency which owns the legal monopoly on spectacle football.

The sporting diaspora started in England took place under the auspices of British imperialism. Football association was identified with the working classes and ostensibly practiced in the more industrialized regions of Northern England, whereas rugby and cricket were more aristocratic. One of the remarkable developments in the diaspora, an example of early globalization, was the spread of the football association to almost every continent, wherever there was the presence of Englishmen—usually working in the establishment of railways, electricity companies, textile industries, and banks. The exceptions were the former colonies, where there had been a long English presence, which chose rugby or cricket because they seemed more exclusive. The exception was the USA, whose independence was earlier and more disputed. As North Americans needed to establish certain differences from the metropolis, they changed the rules of rugby football to such an extent that emerged what is called in Brazil "American football"—from cricket, they made baseball, and football association became just "soccer."

Although football association became known around the world as soccer, it would never cease to be seen as an English sport—in Brazil, it was called the "noble Breton sport"—and part of the "English way of life." The game arrived little by little in our country, being played initially by English sailors on the beaches of Rio de Janeiro and by boarders in some elite schools. Charles Miller and Oscar Cox were two names that stood out, in São Paulo and Rio de Janeiro, respectively, in the spread of football among the local elites. Generally speaking, football spread in Brazil from the urban centers to the outskirts, but there are exceptions, such as in Rio Grande do Sul (Mascarenhas, 2001). In this state, Brazil's southernmost, football first developed in the urban agglomerations along the borders with Uruguay and Argentina, and in the cities of Rio Grande, due to its seaport, and Pelotas, the province's economic and cultural dynamo at the end of the nineteenth century.

Parallel to the diaspora, popularization occurred. This process, still little investigated by historiography, is characterized by the appropriation, by popular groups, of the rules of the game, of certain body techniques, and of some values of amateur sports. In Brazil, popularization was characterized by a successful encounter between English codes and the wide repertoire of body techniques of popular groups. Popularization also implied the appropriation of sport management technologies, with the proliferation of clubs and associations in districts, workers' villages, factories, and so on (Antunes, 1996). Certain clubs, which originally consisted of a modest group of friends, managed to mobilize their communities, organizing excursions to neighboring cities, providing amorous flirtations and distraction on weekends. In Bangu's case, where athletes and managers were recruited from the workers of a textile industry located in the city of the same name, on the outskirts of Rio de Janeiro, the club's organization and community support reached such a point that the team began to face the Rio elite on equal terms. Cases like this became frequent, with teams from the periphery challenging and, not infrequently, defeating the teams of white, wealthy good guys.

Popularization forced a modality of functional democratization (Lopes, 1994), from which many elite clubs banned football from their interior, claiming that the game attracted unwanted fans. Those who chose to continue with football started hiring proletarian players, often black and mulattos, to cope with the increasing performance demands. Upper classes, then, took over management of the clubs, where they remain until today, leaving the mundane and, from the 1930s onward, remunerated practice to the egresses of the popular groups. The rivalry involving some associations was heightened by media support, which occurred simultaneously with the professionalization of athletes. The disputes once confined to the cities became regionalized and, around 1970, nationalized.

Although it is the spectacularized matrix that comes to mind when one talks about football, one cannot forget the diversity of footballs. The multiplicity of names— *futsal*, footvolley, beach soccer, *racha*, *pelada*, football seven, table soccer (button football), *pebolim* (foosball), *futebois*,[1] etc.—is a strong indication of diversity, which nuances are not limited to the rules or to the body techniques employed, but include different materials, spaces, times, purposes, and meanings. This is the case of women's football, for example. Its rules do not differ from the football in which men predominate, but its historical, cultural, and political conformation suggests a specific approach.

Too much emphasis on the spectacularized version of football is one of the problems that anthropology, which has always been committed to diversity, seeks to correct. I have suggested that the diversity of football could be grouped into five distinct circuits (Damo, 2019),[2] each marked by certain specificities that need to be considered when one intends to take football as an object of investigation. Although these circuits may vary from one context to another, the distinctions were thought from a broader set of variations, for example, the presence of public, money, media, legislation, or even—and above all—the discrepancy in terms of function and meaning. Besides the spectacularized circuit, organized by FIFA, I have suggested thinking about the specificity of the community circuit—in Brazil, better known as *futebol de várzea* (lea football)—in which spectacle-like characteristics are present,

---

[1] This is a performance practice, carried out in some regions of Brazil, in which football matches are played with the presence of wild bulls on the field.

[2] Originally (Damo, 2007), I had suggested the term matrix and four main distinctions. Later (Damo, 2019), I evaluated the possibility of using the notion of circuits, inspired by Zelizer (2005), and added a modality, women's football.

but in a less pronounced way. This means less public, amplitude, resources, control of violence, media visibility, demand in relation to athletes' performance, etc.

School circuit, on its turn, would be associated with school and physical education classes. The practice follows pedagogical guidelines and purposes, being football confined, in this case, to a modality among others for body practice. The bricolage circuit would be the one in which games are played in the most diverse spaces and times, with the adaptation of rules and equipment according to contingencies and away from state or official sport agencies' controls.

Finally, there is women's football. Its rules and body techniques are the same as those belonging to other circuits, but presents a very singular trajectory in Brazil, having been banned for several decades (Kessler, 2015). The circuit of women's football is not the same as women's football—this is the conventional way in which sports institutions point what they call "naipe," a distinction marked by biological sex and that has evolved to hormonal descriptors. It is also not an exclusive circuit for women because, although they are the practitioners, a large part of the teams/clubs and competitions are run by men. There are many clashes linked to the body and gender politics associated with this circuit, and the way they are faced helps to rethink the social history of men's football, something somewhat naturalized by the fact that it is usually men who write this narrative. Despite the fact that the partitions—in matrices, circuits, or any other name—may be revised, the tendency is to assimilate the plurality and diversity of football.

Identities and Otherness

Football rules are based on the agonistic structure of the game. As Lévi-Strauss (1965) would argue, the game is a disjunctive rite, insofar as the teams compete in a situation of supposed equity hoping that one of them will be the winner in the end—and the other, the loser. On a deeper level, perhaps we could think of a dispute in which one kills or dies, even if in a simulated way. This is true for all games, including those that pertain to the social circuit, although, in this case, to kill or to be killed is reduced, with some exceptions, to ephemeral fluctuations of mood in virtue of circumstantial success or failure. In the spectrum of spectacle football, the competitors are professionals, and, for them, the matches are far from being a pleasant pastime. This is because bold and exuberant performances are required of them, sometimes strenuous and even sacrificial. After all, they are paid to represent a community that may reach millions of fans who project themselves onto them.

To understand the dynamics of cheering, it is necessary to go beyond an aesthetic analysis—at least an aesthetic conception of the Kantian type, in the manner of Gumbrecht (2006)—because the supporters do not go to the stadium to watch a sublime spectacle, plenty of virtuous or unusual moves. This may occur sometimes, but what mobilizes them, above all, is a type of bond established beforehand and nurtured over time. Being committed to one of the parties is a condition to fully experience the football excitement; a "supporter passion," as Bromberger well wrote:

"c'est la passion partissane qui donne sens, sel et intérêt à la confrontation. [...] La partisanerie est la condition nécessaire pour assurer un maximum d'intensité pathétique à la confrontation" (Bromberger, 1998, pp. 272–273).

"Club belonging" was a neologism coined to account for the identity bond that is specific to the spectacle football, but which could well be extended to other sporting spheres—rugby in Australia, New Zealand, and South Africa; baseball, basketball, and football in the USA, among others (Damo, 2002). The notion of club belonging specifies, in the spectrum of cheering, a militant public segment, not necessarily by attending stadiums, not even by the bond to organized groups, but by affective engagement. Unlike sympathizers, who choose their teams according to circumstances, and sometimes conveniences, fans follow the same team during their lives and extend the emotions lived in the space-time of the game beyond it, and, sometimes, their actions may be considered irrational.

Thus, taking the issue of engagement as central to understand the spectacle football, it can be stated that there are, strictly speaking, two main strategies of audience formation, with a competition circuit and a history of confrontations and rivalries corresponding to each one of them. One of these circuits, currently economically and politically controlled by FIFA and its partners, basically focuses on events in which teams representing nation-states compete. Another circuit, broader and less subject to FIFA's interference, but still under its tutelage, is composed by multiple disputes of club competitions—it includes from a continental competition, such as the Champions League or Copa Libertadores, to amateur football leagues, restricted to cities or neighborhoods.

One of the essential differences between these two circuits for anthropology corresponds to the symbolic order, as it concerns the modality of engagement of respective publics.[3] In other words, the fuel that moves the circuit of nationalism comes from the identification of supporters with the teams that represent the nation. It is, therefore, an identification that slips from the scope of nationalism to football. The task of identification between a small collective—a team of 11 athletes—and another, very extensive—integrated by those who recognize themselves as members of a nation—is much easier in this case. However, it is not enough to dress the football team with the colors of the national flag for the magic of identification to appear; the metonymic relation is not produced naturally (Gastaldo, 2002). Converting a team of players into a living symbol of the nation requires a certain investment, but it is not something that demands miraculous strategies. Just observe how, on the eve of important competitions, such as World Cups or Continental Cups, there is an intense mobilization in order to promote this displacement of meaning, from the nation to the national team and vice versa.

This task, in general, falls to the sports media without, however, being a planned deliberation. As a matter of fact, the media has its own reasons to promote such

---

[3] When suggesting that club commitment is essential to the spectacle football, I am not assuming that all supporters are equally implicated by this modality of identity appeal, nor the consumers of the spectacle, whether in stadiums or elsewhere, are an indistinct mass of fanatics. I admit, therefore, Giulianotti's (2005) suggestions as a sociologically adequate and even essential cutout for the understanding of disputes around cheering, regarding moral, aesthetic, and economic modulations.

events and to do its press converges in relation to the interests of the promoting entities—cases of FIFA, UEFA, CONMEBOL, and so forth. Intellectuals are mobilized
quite often, and the preference leans, obviously, on specialists in themes related to
the formation of national identity. In recent years, these mega-events have received a
strong marketing boost, so that commercial advertising has produced pieces aiming
to link their products to nationalist feelings with the expectation of boosting sales
and, in doing so, end up raising and strengthening such feelings. In countries like
Brazil, where it lacks events and heroes capable of unifying and condensing national
belonging, the football team organized for the World Cup and other similar competitions ends up fulfilling this function. Games of the CBF team in cups—which we
simply call Brazil, at best the Brazil national team—are treated as sacred events,
surrounded by a series of taboos, such as the suspension of labor activities, whereas
Independence Day is considered a mere holiday, except for the military.

On certain occasions, the state may be involved in these mega-events and, in these
cases, the celebration that should be secular ends up generating controversies. A
striking example occurred in the 1978 World Cup, organized and won by Argentina,
at the time ruled by a bloody military dictatorship, which took advantage of the
occasion to promote itself. The strategy may have yielded immediate results, but
these did not prevent the crumbling of the regime a few years later. After three
decades, approximately, Argentines are promoting the trial of the military accused
of torture and murder in that period, at the same time that they give new meaning
to the achievement of 1978. As Archetti (2006) exposed, at the present, a clouded
coloring is attributed to that achievement, to the point that some of the players who
were in the field feel ashamed.

The 2014 World Cup is also an example of how problematic state, nation, and football bonds can be. Between 2007 and 2014, Lula and Dilma's left-wing governments
provided approximately 13 billion dollars to finance the renovation of stadiums and
meet other structural requirements made by FIFA (Damo & Oliven, 2014). On the eve
of the inauguration of new arenas, in 2013, there were intense street demonstrations
contesting the public spending, with President Dilma being grossly booed whenever
she dared to attend the stadiums. What was usually a ritual of celebration of Brazilianness became the stage for political disputes that ended up with the appropriation
of national symbols—and even the symbols of the CBF team—by certain sectors of
society, contrary to the administrations led by the Workers' Party. The demonstrations that began with collectives and parties to the left of the Workers' Party—urged
to make agreements with patronage parties to ensure governability—ended up being
appropriated by right-wing and far-right groups that would later be decisive in the
parliamentary coup that deposed Dilma Rousseff in 2016, in Lula's imprisonment in
2018, and in the election of Bolsonaro in 2018 (Damo, 2020).

In parallel to the circuit driven by nationalism, there is the one integrated by
football clubs. In fact, there are multiple circuits, in general consolidated from continental, national, regional, and even local borders, although the latter remain at the
margins of the spectacularization. Unlike the circuit of nationalism, which benefits
from an already established identification, the production of identities in the spectrum
of clubism is a more complex process, since football clubs are, in general, secular

entities. Using the same process of nationalism, it is easy to identify a team with a company, a school, a political party, a cause, or a city. However, the so-called big football clubs, which integrate the elite of the national circuits, have managed to extrapolate such boundaries, draining to their surroundings heteroclite belongings until arranging them in order to produce an identity of their own. If we observe identities and differences that constitute rivalries in clubism, we will notice how they are impregnated with elements drawn from the broader spectrum of society—in the Brazilian case: region/state, class, and race/ethnicity, basically.

An important part of the emotions experienced on the occasion of the games is given by the fact that the individual recognizes himself as a member of a collectivity that transcends him, as it is proper to the religious sphere. The strength perceived in the crowd is subjectively experienced, from the superimposition of the "I" to the "we." This sort of experience, a kind of *communitas*, is widely studied by anthropology since the work of Turner (2013), and it is no surprise to find it in the spectrum of football. It is important, in any case, to highlight that the public that goes to stadiums, where *communitas* is easier to be noticed—but not in all spectacles, of course—does it based on an engagement given beforehand which is dramatized on the way to these sacred places, in their surroundings or inside them, so that feelings of collective belonging are then touched and an effervescence of the same kind observed in religious events is produced (Bromberger, 1995).

Clubism could then be considered a modality of modern totemism (Damo, 2002). The choice of totems, which certain societies chose animal species, is a cultural arbitrariness (Lévi-Strauss, 1962). That is why Durkheim (1996 [1912]) described the use of the flag in the context of the French Revolution as a modality of totemic representation, in the same way that the appreciation and devotion to football clubs— gremismo, coloradismo, flamenguismo, and any other of these "ismos"[4]—would be. It is important to note, however, that, although individuals are free to choose their totems—they do so, as a rule, by affective influence, from friends or family—they are constrained by the logic of the system that defines affinities and rivalries. If you love Palmeiras, the system will say you not only have it above all different clubs, but you also hate Santos, São Paulo, and, above all, Corinthians—Brazilian clubs from the state of São Paulo; if you love Internacional, from the state of Rio Grande do Sul, you will necessarily hate Grêmio. In a certain way, and this is perhaps the most important consideration in this regard, the relationship among clubs or, as one might prefer, the rivalries and loyalties has a symbolic nature partly detached from the empirical world, insofar as, both here and within the nation, traditions are invented.

To understand the history of clubism, it is essential to take into account the process of symbolic thickening of disputes, considering factual events—games, goals, scorers, etc.—and personal experiences. As important as or even more important than the moves of a game, the experience of having lived them is what effectively matters to the fans. After all, winning and losing are part of every fan's biography, which is why the biggest rivalries are between clubs whose performances constantly

---

[4] Translator's note: "Ismo," in Portuguese, corresponds to the suffix "ism" in English.

alternate over time. It makes no sense for Manchester United to have Colchester United as its biggest rival.

The space of football, particularly the one focused on the spectacle, reveals a generous source of questions to be investigated, to the extent that it offers extensive and multifaceted arrangements in terms of identities and otherness. The agonistic structure of the game, which presupposes a well-demarcated dispute between an I (or we) and an other (or others), greatly favors the establishment of identification and differentiation. Since the game is a disjunctive rite, and the parties in dispute are inseparable from the dynamics of the event, it is enough if one of them refuses to fulfill the role structurally assigned to it—it stops attacking or, what gets worse, stops defending—for the game to lose its meaning. Adversaries in a game are, from this point of view, essential partners, because the dispute raises the presence of another against whom and also with whom one plays. And the same goes for the case of rival fans; after all, they are like two sides of the same coin and could not exist without the other.

In the universe of spectacle football, the question of representation is openly posed as a drama to the fans. The idea of representation implies mediation and, therefore, negotiation. Although victory is an important component in the assertion of a team or a player before the fans of a football club or national team, the idea of what is a good or bad representation exceeds, considerably, the question of results. Dedication, courage, bravery, and commitment are also valued, even in defeat. Just as there is a history of books and another one for reading practices, there is a history of games and there should be another one reporting how fans are involved in them. In order for us to reconstitute the practices of cheering—which implies asking for whom, how, where, with whom, and for whom—it is necessary to broaden our understanding horizon about the meanings of belonging, be it to a team that represents a club or a nation-state.

In the spectrum of football club belonging, there is a type of engaged participation that practically operates in a parallel logic, because it is mediated by another totemic system, constituted by organized groups. In Brazil, such groups are known as Torcidas Organizadas[5] (TOs); in other countries, they receive different designations, without a precise translation: In Argentina, they are called *barrabravas;* in England, hooligans; and in Italy and France, *ultras.*

Since the early days of spectacle football, there have been groupings of fans inclined to participate more effusively in events. We have few records of how this process occurred, although assumptions indicate that these fans may have remained isolated or grouped slowly, in a spontaneous way. *Torcida*[6] was the name given to a kind of turban made with a scarf, a creation of the French fashion designer Paul Poiret in the 1920s, which became fashionable among the elite women of Rio de Janeiro, who, at the time, were frequent visitors to the stadiums. It seems that women were the most effusive part of the audience, and the term "*torcida,*" which identified them,

---

[5] Translator's note: The expression "*torcida organizada*" (TO) could be adapted, in English, into "football organized supporters" or "organized groups of football/soccer fans."

[6] Translator's note: Literally, "torcida" is also translated into English as "twisted."

started to be used in a generic way, as a synonym of engaged audience and later as football audience. Then, the verb—"*torcer*"—was declined, probably during the 1930s, when the Portuguese speaking of English terms occurred, concomitantly with the popularization of football (Leite Lopes, 1994).

Around the 1930s and 1940s, when stadiums with capacity to hold 30 thousand people or more were built, these more enthusiastic supporters started to be seen as a problem for the clubs, to the extent that their willingness to encourage the team was the same as that to create conflicts. One of the football clubs' strategies, with the recommendation of the public authorities, was to discipline these individuals. That is how the uniformed supporters' groups emerged, a block that at the same time added new elements to the spectacles, with influences taken from carnival—confetti and serpentine, brass band, war cries, etc.—and enabled the institutions to exercise some surveillance (Hollanda, 2010).

By the 1970s, some of these groups became more autonomous, and the clubs lost some of their ability to rule them. With the consolidation of a national competition circuit, from 1971 onward, with the performance of longer displacements, these groups began to experience more radical experiences—it would be one thing to go from home or work to a stadium; another thing would be to move between cities and states in trips that could last a day or more. This type of adventurous mobility has favored the increase of male participation in TOs, particularly of young men willing to face physical challenges, starting with the strenuous trips in precarious vehicles. This was not the only reason why confrontations became frequent, but it certainly contributed to it until, in the 1990s, fights became routine, and TOs started to be labeled as marginal groups (Toledo, 1996). The confrontation strategy of the state apparatus, basically reduced to violent repression, only contributed to increase the belligerence of the TOs, which began to recruit and value cadres with a Spartan disposition for increasingly brutal clashes (Hollanda, 2010; Teixeira, 2004).

Brazil is not alone regarding the resurgence of violence among organized supporters, which is why some of the explanations for this phenomenon must be sought outside the football field. The profile of this audience, mostly young and male, helps to understand the willingness for corporal confrontation. The absence of any other strategy than the use of repression by the state apparatus, observable with small variations in almost all countries, had effects contrary to those expected. The disdain of the clubs, or even the acquiescence of their leaders, allowed the prolif-eration of bellicose and self-interested leaderships, who often lend their services to political disputes inside and outside the club in exchange for various privileges. Finally, the strained relationship between players and fans, which occurred with the glamorization of the profession and the purchasing power of athletes employed by the big clubs, contributed to the increase of tensions.

Many of the reasons that explain the resurgence of violence in other spheres of society and, particularly, its modus operandi also help to understand what is happening in football. This is the case of state violence directed at stigmatized groups, such as the poor and blacks, one of the reasons why confrontation with TOs has reached unacceptable levels. It is also the case of the worsening of conflicts among

TOs, parallel to the dissemination of firearms, which has multiplied fights with serious injuries and deaths, in the vicinity and on the way to the stadiums.

Two additions to this intriguing question must be mentioned. The first one is that football is a sport, and, as such, it is a way of waging war by other means, but there are always those who forget it is "another way" and do it by conventional means. It gets worse when this somebody is an institution or a manager who knows—or should know—that the type of entertainment that pays huge dividends is a form of "playing with fire," because the motto for the increase of interest in the spectacle is inseparable from the promotion of tensions and rivalries involved in it. The second addition has to do with the condition that TOs cannot be reduced to the production of violence, as is sometimes heard and read in the media. TOs are responsible for the co-production of spectacles, and without them stadiums lose much of what makes them fascinating. This happened recently in Brazil, when an attempt was made to remove TOs from the new arenas, under the pretext that they were supposed to become spaces of entertainment for well-to-do families—in other words, white middle and upper-class families. Quickly, however, the lack of animation, choreographies, and shouts of support was noticed, so TOs were reintegrated.

Football as an Object of Brazilian Anthropology

As previously mentioned, the field of sports studies in which football is remarkably prominent is multidisciplinary, but it is not so by force of prior planning or influence of any theoretical strand. This is particularly correct for the case of Brazilian produc-tion, marked by collaboration among researchers from different areas. To date, there has been no attempt at a theoretical synthesis of this production—there are only bibli-ographical surveys—and I would venture to affirm that it is quite uneven in terms of the interest of the disciplines in the theme. Anthropology and historiography, for example, have systematic productions, while political science and economics have shown little interest. The unplanned regime of collaboration makes the task of isolating the contribution of a specific discipline difficult, even more so if the person responsible for this task is directly involved, in this case an anthropologist dealing with the influence of anthropology. To minimize this risk, I will try to avoid, from now on, dealing with football studies in a broad perspective, limiting myself to punctuate the main themes investigated over these four decades in the spectrum of Brazilian anthropology and the reasons why they emerged or evanesced.

If it were the case of establishing a milestone of studies on football in Brazil, it would be the master's thesis defended by Simoni Lahud Guedes in 1977, at the Graduate Program in Social Anthropology of UFRJ, the Museu Nacional. Until then, we had sporadic contributions on the subject, with an essayistic bias, some from social scientists such as João Lyra Filho, Anatol Rosenfeld, and Gilberto Freyre, others from intellectuals of the most varied hues, including chroniclers such as Nelson Rodrigues, José Lins do Rêgo, Lima Barreto, and Carlos Drummond de Andrade, among others. The reasons that justify the scant academic production on football in Brazilian social sciences coincide with those prevailing in different contexts (Elias & Dunning, 1992, pp. 39–99; Bromberger, 1998), and two should be added.

First justification concerns the late development of social sciences in Brazil, which was institutionalized only after 1950 (Miceli, 1989). In the case of anthropology, the pioneering role in research in this university spectrum belongs to the Museu Nacional, an institution that housed the first postgraduate program with master and doctoral degrees in the 1970s. The fact that the first anthropological incursions were made in this institution was no accident. Although Guedes' thesis is ground zero, the publication taken as reference is the collection *Universo do Futebol*[7] (UF), organized by Roberto DaMatta (1982) with a text he originally published outside Brazil and with the collaboration of young anthropologists linked to the Museu Nacional, including Simoni Guedes herself.

The second justification has to do with the appropriation of sports, especially football, by both Civilian Dictatorship (1937–1945) and Military Dictatorship (1964–1985). It prevailed among the emerging social sciences—especially those who followed a Marxist bias, very strong in the 1960s and 1970s—the idea that sports were, in fact, a sort of "opium of the people." Writing something that was not a denunciation against football alienation was a kind of taboo, even in alternative newspapers. It is interesting to note there is a significant gap between the text published in a Recife newspaper by Gilberto Freyre in the 1930s, republished with minor changes in the 1950s as a preface to Mário Filho's book *O negro no futebol brasileiro* (Rodrigues Filho, 2003 [1947]), and a book of essays written by the German art critic Rosenfeld (1993 [1974]) in the 1970s. Rosenfeld, perhaps because he was a foreigner, could afford to look at institutions considered as peripheral when interpreting Brazil, whereas the native intellectuality was focused on economics and politics—and not unreasonably. The publication of UF, in 1982, coincided with the end of the military dictatorship and the intense political mobilization for direct elections. No one would think that the effects of UF were immediate, triggering a wave of researches, although it is recognized as a milestone in Brazilian and Latin American production (Alabarces, 2011; Giglio & Spaggiari, 2010).

UF's texts and, above all, DaMatta's writings are clearly influenced by Gilberto Freyre, who gave prominence to aspects of private life and daily life, highlighting the contribution of Afro-Brazilian culture—cuisine, religiosity, sexuality, and so forth—until then neglected. The article "Football mulatto," published in 1938, is an exaltation of Leonidas da Silva's performance in World Cup, held in France that year, which Freyre tracked on the radio, like all Brazilians (Velho, 2004). In this apology to Leonidas—the sensation of that World Cup—Freyre reaffirmed the thesis of his masterpiece, *Casa-Grande & Senzala* (Freyre, 2006 [1933]), suggesting that miscegenation qualified Brazilians with virtues such as creativity, expressiveness, and daring, very different from what evolutionists, for whom miscegenation was synonymous with degeneration, had claimed until then.

DaMatta's writings on football are in line with Freyre's perspective (Damo, 2014) and continue the arguments expressed in *Carnavais, malandros e heróis* (DaMatta,

---

[7] Translator's note: Could be translated into "Football Universe."

1980), his most successful book and one of the classics of Brazilian anthropology. Brazil, DaMatta claimed, is more complex, creative, and instigating when analyzed from its popular institutions, those that remained on the margins of the militarized state and the Catholic Church, for example. Football, DaMatta suggested, was not "opium of the people," as the dictatorship tried to make it be. Just like in carnival, it was a space of popular expression, where black and mulatto people—in the case of carnival, this included women, gays, and other social renegades—acquired visibility and recognition. Although flawed on the issue of gender (1996), DaMatta's text focuses on the contribution of black and mulatto players, as well as on the effusive participation of the public in stadiums, in which popular aesthetics stand out. The fact that the control of football institutions—clubs, federations, media—was a white men matter was not relevant.

DaMatta even argued that football was more transcendent than a sport, being appreciated by Brazilians as a game, and that its cosmology implied the intervention of extramundane elements and the possibility of the weak beating the strong. In this aspect, DaMatta's text is aligned with the rising trends in Brazilian urban anthropology at the time, of appreciation of popular culture, and in tune with the "point of view of the natives," as in the famous interpretation of the Balinese cockfight by Clifford Geertz a few years earlier. As enunciated by Geertz in "Deep play: notes on the Balinese cockfight" (1973), anthropology should not be concerned with wide-ranging universal formulations or the explanation of social phenomena, but it should try to understand native interpretations. This meant, ultimately, that the important thing was not whether or not football alienated fans from political issues, nor how it did so, but to know what people imagined, thought, and experienced when involved with the games and the whole discursive production around these events. Stadiums could be like circuses, although this would no longer be the core of the debate, because what would matter, from then on, was to know why and how one laughed at the clown.

If the cockfight, after "Deep play ...", ceased to be a frivolous event, no one would have any reason to dispute the relevance of football as a social fact. For Geertz, cockfighting was a metaphor of real life; it was men who actually fought, and the social drama experienced around the fights would reveal the true Balinese ethos. DaMatta did not plagiarize Geertz; he had already been discussing Brazilian popular rituals and heroes from anthropological literature using the concept "social drama" (DaMatta, 1982). However, the translation of Geertz's book in Brazil, the first version in 1979 and the second in 1989, and its resounding success between the mid-1980s and 1990s, when all his work was then translated, gave even more support to those who were thinking of approaching football. Intermittently, other publications appeared throughout the 1980s, some of them important for subsequent generations, as in the case of Leite Lopes' texts (), but rarely constituted by long-term ethnographic fieldwork, one of the characteristics of anthropological production.

From thematic point of view, one can notice in the production of the period marks of a kind of social division of intellectual labor on the nation-state, this institution so dear to the West. In the spectrum of social sciences, there is a tendency to impute to anthropology—and we could include historiography under this register—the authority on the thematic of the nation (collective identification, rituals, myths, and heroes), while sociologists and political scientists deal mainly with issues involving the state—political parties, public policies, police violence, protest movements, etc. Based on this inclination, one can understand the reasons why anthropological production of this period, but not only, emphasizes topics involving the relationship between football and nation.

This articulation proved to be very fruitful after dictatorship ended, as it allowed emphasizing the associationist mobilization of supporters, in their clubs or in smaller segments such as uniformed fans (and then organized fans), but especially the occupation of the public space, to the point of stadiums being considered as such. Football showed a vibrant and hopeful nation, even if authoritarianism had assaulted conventional political institutions during dictatorship, especially in the period when AI-5 (1968–1978) was in force. Fans' participatory enthusiasm could be interpreted as an indication that the nation was escaping the control of the militarized state, rather than corroborating the alienation thesis. The Brazil revealed in the surroundings of football fields was more polyphonic, heterodox, and poetic than the one glimpsed in other public spaces.

Simoni Guedes and Leite Lopes were important researchers in the transition from the first to the second generation of anthropologists, and Luiz Henrique de Toledo's thesis, awarded by the National Association of Social Science Researchers (ANPOCS) in 1995, may be taken as a milestone in this process. The award helped consolidate football as a serious topic, and the ethnography soon converted into a book (Toledo, 1996) served as a reference for other investigations that would follow, marked by extended fieldwork, dialogue with international productions—Bourdieu, Elias, Archetti, Bromberger—and progressive, though not radical, distancing from media and memorialist narratives (Damo, 2016).

Toledo's thesis was finished when the "Pacaembu battle" took place, a generalized fight inside the field between supporters of Palmeiras and São Paulo after the final of a juniors' championship. The unfortunate episode that came to an end with over one hundred injured and one dead due to beating, all duly recorded by television, brought to the light the discussion on the escalation of violence among TOs, a theme already widely discussed internationally. The debate was then instigated in the national media and in the field of public security, which seemed to have suddenly discovered what was going on behind the scenes of the games and immediately started to blame organized supporters, labeling them as marginal, infiltrated criminals and anti-sports agents. Instead of stigmatizing the TOs, Toledo sought to understand the meaning of engagement and the multiple faces of its dynamics according to the point of view of the fans themselves, paying attention to their aesthetic and political performances.

This perspective opened space for an extensive series of ethnographies on supporters, organized or not, favored by the fact that many of those interested in the sports theme were young people, then engaged in clubism and TOs, to the point of attending the panels duly uniformed. In the wake of this discussion, several papers emerged expanding the scope of the relationship of supporters with their clubs, the constitution of bonds and rivalries. Ethnographies were replicated in contexts outside the Rio de Janeiro–São Paulo axis, where they initially predominated due to the concentration of research institutions and also of clubs with expanded media visibility.

At the broader level of Brazilian economy and politics, the 1990s were strongly impacted by neoliberal policies, characterized by privatization of state-owned companies, concession and delegation of public services to private agents, and adoption of corporate governance models. Two neoliberal amendments to sports legislation directly impacted football, the so-called Zico Law, enacted during Fernando Collor de Mello's government (1990–1992), and Pelé Law, during Fernando Henrique Cardoso's first administration (1995–1999). These laws followed, in general terms, the codes practiced in Europe, which were also impacted by the strategy of expanding the labor and commercial markets.

During the Military Dictatorship, Brazilian state intervened in the organization of professional football from a more political perspective—football at the service of national integration, one of the axes of the dictatorship—than from a market perspective. With the end of dictatorship, spectacle football entered a crisis due to management problems at clubs and federations, which were unable to organize a proper calendar and cope with the harassment of European clubs that recruited the stars of the national team. Spectacles lost quality, and audience was scarce, especially as television started showing games from European championships, where Brazilian stars now played.

Zico Law relaxed the status of clubs, allowing them to act as companies, and Zico himself, a star player of Flamengo and of the Brazil national football team in the 1980s, created a "prototype," the CFZ Rio, which ultimately proved to be unfeasible. Pelé Law relaxed the statute that regulated the athletes' bond with the clubs under the pretext that, until then, they were "slaves" of the managers. Competitions started privileging big clubs, articulated around an elitist entity called Clube dos 13, with the expansion of the national calendar in detriment of the regional ones, which would lead to the precariousness of the work of players not linked to clubs belonging to first and second national divisions. The chaotic organization of the competitions persisted, with things changing directions, until 2003, when TV Globo gave an ultimatum to the clubs and practically took over the management of national competitions.

Although they have contributed little to the professionalization of the calendar management, both legislations, as a whole, have created a favorable scenario for the increase of transactions involving players, and this has had repercussions both in the emergence of a new professional—the player's agent—and in dissemination of a business model for managing the training, commercialization, and career of athletes. With the increase of globalization, Brazil went from being a "star producer" to a "commodity producer," given the proliferation of training centers and the intensification of workforce transfers to international market—especially the European one—as a strategy of local clubs to increase their revenues (Damo, 2007).

Transformations with a market bias reverberated in Brazilian production from the late 1990s, with several investigations on training and circulation of players (Damo, 2007; Pimenta, 2001). In a sense, a displacement of object is noted, with the problematization of issues involving the movement of people, borders, careers, and the spectacularization, although questions about identity—national, as formulated in the 1980s, and club, in the following decade—remained high. Questions, however, would be different: What is Brazil's place in a globalized economy? What are the links between mobility of players and other Brazilian emigrants? Which agencies and agents are responsible for the intensification of player flows? What is the relation between the players' departure and the entrance of merchandises such as T-shirts and images of European games in Brazil? What leaves Brazil along with Brazilians? The work of Rial (2008), known in the field for contributions on globalization, focused on the lifestyle of Brazilian players who are in the international market—including Europe, the USA, Japan, among others—and of their families. Still in the spectrum of studies on training/production and circulation of players carried out in the field of anthropology, the works of Pisani (2012), Spaggiari (2014), and Palmiéri (2015), among others, stand out.

Spaggiari (2014) focuses on training activities at a community club in the western outskirts of São Paulo. With strong influences from Brazilian urban ethnography, the dissertation, now turned into a book, straddles the boundary between community football and spectacle football, as Spaggiari follows the families and agents of boys who begin their training in a club in the outskirts of São Paulo and then continue on a pilgrimage through the circuit of the big clubs, aiming at professionalization. It is interesting to notice, in this dissertation, the transit through different disciplinary fields, in particular the gift, kinship, family, childhood, and youth, among others. It is an exemplary work of research conducted in and with football—in its circuits, with its agents—and not about football, one of the hallmarks, perhaps, of anthropology. It is not the game itself that one wants to apprehend, or not only. It is the social fact in its complexity; if we have boys in any training center, we have a family project. As football is not isolated, we notice that, in Brazil, this project modality that is observed in football has certain class marks, in this case, the popular class, as Rial (2008) had already shown, when unveiling the taste and lifestyle of players and their expatriate entourage.

The announcement of Brazil's candidacy to host mega sporting events—World Cup 2014, in 2007, and the Olympic Games 2016, in 2010—impacted the production ambivalently. Mega-events are not the prototype of enterprise accessible to ethnography, a sort of research that values face-to-face interactions and performs better in small-scale events, where it is possible for the researcher to move with ease among members of the group with which he conducts his incursions, establishing a relationship of trust and complicity. Both the World Cup and the Olympic Games are events whose decisions are centralized by private companies—including FIFA and the IOC—in partnership with state agencies. Accessing the backstage of this plot is almost impossible, and participant observation is hindered. On the other hand, public speeches—including figures on spending and presumed benefits—are almost always suspect, and the access to them are mediated by other agencies. Paradoxically, mega-events presented themselves as an opportunity, as there was a social demand for publications that were more consistent than those conveyed by the media, and, at the same time, an ordeal, given the difficulties of facing the challenges that an original research would require with the disciplinary resources at our disposal. Still, we tried to do something, working on the periphery of the works, paying attention to the social impacts, and, above all, to the implications of arenization for the dynamics of cheering (Curi, 2012).

Money has been present in football since its modern origins, although it was denied in amateur times, only to be later admitted and legalized with the advent of professionalization of players, something around the 1930s. It was after popularization of television broadcasting, in the 1970s and 1980s, and the increase in advertising that came with it, that football reached another marketing stage. Stadiums until then used to collect money through ticketing became advertising targets, and then marketing invested against the supporters' spaces themselves. The stadium as a whole—from its location to its name—and each of its interior spaces started being thought of based on a monetary logic. "Terraces areas,"[8] where the audience with lower purchasing power was concentrated, became labeled as threatening. Those people so close to the field, waiting for an opportunity to invade it, would have to be civilized or removed, as in fact happened.

The organized supporters are a by-product of the terraces for good and for bad—it is not the case to separate the wheat from the chaff. They were able to organize, in the sense of purifying and improving, the dispersed aesthetic and political expressions that constituted, for long decades, the terraces. Soon the leaders showed up, and they captured that ecstatic anarchy and ended up, in a sense, preying on the creativity and imagination of the collectives formed ad hoc. Among other things, they began to use, strategically, such repertoires in political fights for their own benefit, as those fought behind the scenes in the clubs. The organized fan clubs managed to reinsert themselves in the arenas because they are politically articulated groups and have an aesthetic capital considered indispensable to the spectacle. What was banned, in the end, was the anarchic passion of anonymous fans.

It is still too early to assess the impact of arenization, a form of elitization, on anthropological production, but it is admittedly that it significantly changes the way stadiums have been interpreted. DaMatta's paper published in UF seems obsolete if we look at the audience that comes to new arenas. Football seems to have become a spectacle to the taste of elites, as if returning to its origins, when it arrived in Brazil as a symbol of a modernity consumed by those who imagined themselves, thereby Europeanized. Maybe it is not the case of abandoning the stadiums, because social processes follow their courses and we may have other changes from now on. If it is true that the less wealthy strata were excluded, it is also true that stadiums became less hostile to the presence of women. The TOs, initially excluded, have been recovering their spaces, and new political movements are emerging, contesting both elitization of clubs and their management models and the political legacy of TOs, which, it seems, have always been more concerned with ensuring privileges for themselves than politically representing other fans, ensuring popular participation in football.

There is certain exhaustion of some themes and the need to rethink them. In this sense, renewed works have been emerging that are, in part, of dispersion in relation to spectacle football, with the emergence, for some time now, of research carried out on

---

[8] Translator's note: In Portuguese, this area is called "geral."

other football teams or even on other sports, which means removing from spectacle football its hegemonic position. Since dialogue in the spectrum of anthropology is not only among those who work with football, but also with those who investigate sports in general or even body practices that are not defined as such, it is more likely that new questions will be formulated by those who carry out research in spaces dominated by football than this sport being abandoned. Works about women's football are certainly a novelty, not only because they complement what we had done so far, basically among men, but because they question a series of theoretical assumptions, including the way we have been dealing with gender issues. This bibliography coming from those who work with women's football brings an updated literature on gender, and the same goes for the case of the notion of "dissonant sports" (Camargo, 2016), as the concept shuffles sporting practices and the values with which they have been identified. Although it is not a work carried out in the field of anthropology, but quite influenced by it, I believe that Aguiar's (2018) dissertation about an openly gay-organized fan club, still in the 1970s, helps us to rethink the theoretical paths traced so far.

I wish I could have said more about studies on football held among indigenous communities. Despite the extraordinary potential, given the passionate way in which these people dedicate themselves to the practice of football in Brazil and to the cultivation of symbols related to clubs or to the Brazil national football team, we have had few bolder investigations. One of them, which deserves to be highlighted for its in-depth fieldwork and the theoretical support of ethnology, is the ethnography of Vianna (2008) carried out among the Xavantes. We have, however, other researches on competitive body practices, the most prominent conducted in Alto Xingu region and centered on the Kalapalos (Avelar, 2010; Costa, 2013).

Conclusion

"Anthropology of football and image" was the name of the first panel to appear in an anthropology event in Brazil and, probably, in Latin America. According to Carmen Rial, who coordinated this panel with Leite Lopes, the objective was indeed to discuss papers related to football, but the term "image" was added because there was a certain fear that only with "football" would not succeed through the scrutiny of the scientific committee of Reunião Brasileira de Antropologia (RBA)[9] held in Brasilia, in 2000. The following year, the Curitiba edition of Reunião de Antropologia do Mercosul (RAM)[10] took place, where I had the privilege to coordinate a panel along with Simoni Guedes. This one was called "Anthropology of Sport," at my insistence and against the wishes of Guedes, who always thought football was more

---

[9] Translator's note: Brazilian Meeting of Anthropology, RBA, is the largest and most relevant anthropology congress in Brazil. It is held every two years in a different city within the country.

[10] Translator's note: Mercosul Meeting of Anthropology, RAM, is another important congress in South America. It takes place every two years in a different country, alternating with RBA.

important than sport for Brazilian anthropology, lined up with DaMatta's thought, and not without reason. After these occasions, there was always a panel on this theme in anthropology events, but the term sport always prevailed, although the works were mostly about football. These details help us to understand how important football is to anthropology, because, more than any other sport, it is fully woven into Brazilian society and culture, particularly male values and lifestyles. We often study football—national representations, gifting, conflicts, etc.—and not the sport itself.

By the way, the angle of gender, poorly formulated by DaMatta, took a long time to be perceived and only recently has been corrected. It decisively influenced the conduct of work in the spectrum of anthropology—and perhaps related areas—as if naturalizing male prominence. Although we have made progress in relation to questions of race/ethnicity and even in relation to the multiplicity of footballs and their localisms, we still owe a lot in relation to gender, something that may be in the process of being rethought after the androcentric dispersion noted in recent years in events and publications in our field.

We have been greatly favored by the expansion of graduate programs in Brazil and in a particularly accentuated way throughout the first decade of 2000, in which research received more generous public contributions than in other times. Perhaps, we have lacked bolder international insertion and dialogue, although the problem is not the quality of our work.

Despite the diversity, with some convergences that I tried to explore here, what unites us is, undoubtedly, ethnography, and it will be through it—ethnography is not only fieldwork, obviously—that we will overcome a certain strangulation observed after the mega sporting events, in particular the 2014 World Cup, and everything that happened in its surroundings. Not even the fact that spectacle football has been captured by the elites, at least the on-site spectacles, will keep us away from this circuit, but the focus will certainly be different from when the studies started four decades ago.

References

Aguiar, L. A. (2018). *De "são bichas, mas são nossas" à "diversidade da alegria": Uma história da torcida Coligay*. (Doctoral Dissertation in Human Movement Sciences), UFRGS, Porto Alegre, Brazil. https://www.lume.ufrgs.br/bitstream/handle/10183/184514/001080189.pdf?sequence=1

Alabarces, P. (2011). Veinte años de ciencias sociales y deportes, diez años después. *Revista Da Alesde, 1*(1), 11–22. https://doi.org/10.5380/alesde.v1i1.22598

Antunes, F. (1996). O futebol na Light & Power de São Paulo. *Pesquisa de Campo*, (3–4), 51–64. https://ludopedio.org.br/biblioteca/o-futebol-na-light-power-de-sao-paulo/

Archetti, E. (2006). Argentina 1978 and after: Military nationalism, football essentialism, and moral ambivalence. In A. Tomlinson & C. Young (Eds.), *National identity and global sports events* (pp. 133–148). Sunny Press.

Avelar, G. (2010). *Valores brutos: Lutadores do Alto Xingu*. (Master's thesis in Social Anthropology), Museu Nacional, UFRJ, Rio de Janeiro, Brazil. http://www.dominiopublico.gov.br/pesquisa/DetalheObraForm.do?select_action=&co_obra=200636

Bromberger, C. (1995). *Le match de football: Ethnologie d'une passion partisane à Marseille, Naples et Turim*. Éditions de la Maison des Sciences de L'Home.

Bromberger, C. (1998). *Football, la bagatelle la plus sérieuse du monde*. Bayard.

Camargo, W. X. (2016). Dilemas insurgentes no esporte: As práticas esportivas dissonantes. *Movimento, 22*(4), 1337–1350. https://doi.org/10.22456/1982-8918.66188

Costa, C. E. (2013). *Ikindene hekugu: Uma etnografia da luta e dos lutadores no Alto Xingu*. (Doctoral Thesis in Social Anthropology), UFSCar, São Carlos, Brazil. https://repositorio.ufscar.br/handle/ufscar/233?show=full

Curi, M. (2012). *Espaço da emoção – Arquitetura futebolística, torcida e segurança pública*. (Doctoral Thesis in Anthropology), UFF, Niterói, Brazil. http://ppgantropologia.sites.uff.br/wp-content/uploads/sites/16/2016/07/MARTIN-CHRISTOPH-CURI-SP%C3%96RL.pdf

DaMatta, R. (1980). *Carnavais, malandros e heróis* (2nd ed.). Zahar.

DaMatta, R. (Ed.). (1982). *Universo do futebol: Esporte e sociedade brasileira*. Pinakotheke.

Damo, A. S. (2002). *Futebol e identidade social: Uma leitura antropológica das rivalidades entre torcedores e clubes*. Porto Alegre: Ed. UFRGS.

Damo, A. S. (2007). *Do dom à profissão*. São Paulo: Hucitec.

Damo, A. S. (2014). Del opio de los pueblos a la antropología de lo obvio: Lectura crítica de los escritos de Roberto DaMatta sobre futbol. *Lúdicamente, 3*(6), 1–12. https://publicaciones.soc iales.uba.ar/index.php/ludicamente/article/view/4261

Damo, A. S. (2016). Posfácio – Novas abordagens sobre o esporte em ciências humanas no Brasil. In E. Spaggiari, G. Machado, & S. S. Giglio (Eds.), *Entre jogos e copas – Reflexões sobre uma década esportiva*. São Paulo: Intermeios; Fapesp.

Damo, A. S. (2019). Futebóis: da horizontalidade epistemológica à diversidade política. *Fulia, 3*(3), 37–66. https://doi.org/10.17851/2526-4494.3.3.37-66

Damo, A. S. (2020). A tragédia que a Copa legou ao Brasil: as Jornadas de Junho e a efervescente anticorrupção. *Interseções: Revista de Estudos Interdisciplinares, 22*(2), 167–200. https://doi.org/10.12957/irei.2020.54488

Damo, A. S., & Oliven, R. G. (2014). *Megaeventos esportivos no Brasil: Um olhar antropológico*. Campinas: Armazém do Ipê.

Durkheim, E. (1996). *As formas elementares da vida religiosa*. São Paulo: Martins Fontes. (Original work published 1912)

Elias, N., & Dunning, E. (1992). *A busca da excitação*. Lisboa: Difel.

Freyre, G. (2006). *Casa-grande & senzala: Formação da família brasileira sob o regime da economia patriarcal* (51th ed.). São Paulo: Global. (Original work published 1933).

Gastaldo, É. (2002). *Pátria, chuteiras e propaganda: O brasileiro na publicidade da Copa do Mundo*. São Paulo: Annablume.

Giglio, S. S., & Spaggiari, E. (2010). A produção das ciências humanas sobre futebol no Brasil: Um panorama (1990–2009). *Revista de História*, (163), 293–350. https://doi.org/10.11606/issn.2316-9141.v0i163p293-350

Giulianotti, R. (2005). Sport spectators and the social consequences of commodification: Critical perspectives from Scottish football. *Journal of Sport and Social Issues, 29*(4), 386–410. https://doi.org/10.1177/0193723505280530

Guedes, S. L. (1977). *O futebol brasileiro: Instituição zero*. (Master's thesis in Social Anthropology), Museu Nacional, UFRJ, Rio de Janeiro, Brazil.

Gumbrecht, H. U. (2006). *Eloge du Sport*. Maren Seull Éditteurs.

Hollanda, B. B. B. (2010). *O clube como vontade e representação: o jornalismo e a formação das torcidas organizadas de futebol no Rio de Janeiro*. Rio de Janeiro: 7Letras.

Kessler, C. S. (2015). *Mais que Barbies e ogras: Uma etnografia do futebol de mulheres no Brasil e nos Estados Unidos*. (Doctoral Thesis in Social Anthropology), UFRGS, Porto Alegre, Brazil. https://lume.ufrgs.br/handle/10183/131770

Lévi-Strauss, C. (1962). *La pensée sauvage*. Plon.

Lévi-Strauss, C. (1965). *Le totémisme aujourd'hui*. PUF.

Leite Lopes, J. S. (1992). A morte da alegria do povo. *Revista Brasileira de Ciências Sociais*, *7*(20), 113–134. http://www.anpocs.com/images/stories/RBCS/20/rbcs20_09.pdf

Lopes, J. S. L. (1994). A vitória do futebol que incorporou a pelada. *Revista USP*, (22), 64–83. https://doi.org/10.11606/issn.2316-9036.v0i22p64-83

Mascarenhas, G. (2001). A *"bola nas redes" e o enredo do lugar: Uma geografia do futebol e seu advento no Rio Grande do Sul*. (Doctoral Thesis in Geography), USP. São Paulo. http://pos.ffich. usp.br/node/45227

Miceli, S. (1989). *História das ciências sociais* (Vol. 1). São Paulo: Vértice; Idesp.

Palmiéri, J. C. (2015). *Um mundo em vários movimentos* – Uma etnografia sobre futebolistas de base. (Doctoral Thesis in Social Anthropology), UFSCar, São Carlos, Brazil. https://repositorio. ufscar.br/handle/ufscar/7291

Pimenta, C. A. M. (2001). Novos processos de formação de jogadores de futebol e o fenômeno das "escolinhas": Uma análise crítica do possível. In P. Alabarces (Comp.), *Peligro de gol: Estudios sobre deporte y sociedad en América Latina* (pp. 75–97). Buenos Aires: CLACSO.

Pisani, M. (2012). *Poderosas do Foz: Trajetórias, migrações e profissionalização de mulheres que praticam futebol*. (Master's thesis in Social Anthropology), UFSC, Florianópolis, Brazil. https:// repositorio.ufsc.br/handle/123456789/100982

Rial, C. (2008). Rodar: A circulação dos jogadores de futebol brasileiros no exterior. *Horizontes Antropológicos*, *14*(30), 21–65. https://doi.org/10.1590/S0104-71832008000200002

Rodrigues Filho, M. (2003). *O negro no futebol brasileiro* (4th ed.). Rio de Janeiro: Mauad. (Original work published 1947).

Rosenfeld, A. (1993). *Negro, macumba e futebol*. São Paulo: EDUSP.

Spaggiari, E. (2014). *Família joga bola: Constituição de jovens futebolistas na várzea paulistana*. (Doctoral Thesis in Social Anthropology), USP, São Paulo, Brazil. https://www.teses.usp.br/teses/ disponiveis/8/8134/tde-01062015-180120/pt-br.php

Teixeira, R. C. (2004). *Os perigos da paixão: visitando jovens torcidas cariocas*. São Paulo: Annablume.

Toledo, L. H. (1996). *Torcidas organizadas*. Campinas: Autores Associados.

Turner, V. (2013). *O processo ritual*. Petrópolis: Vozes. (Original work published 1974)

Velho, T. B. (2004). Gilberto Freyre e o futebol-arte. *Revista USP*, (62), 233–238. https://doi.org/ 10.11606/issn.2316-9036.v0i62p233-238

Vianna, F. L. B. (2008). *Boleiros do Cerrado*. São Paulo: Annablume.

Zelizer, V. (2005). Circuits within capitalism. In V. Nee & R. Swedberg (Eds.), *The economic sociology of capitalism* (pp. 289–321). Princeton University Press.

Chapter 14
An Ethnographic Game of Fluid Categories of Analysis

Enrico Spaggiari

The decisive conversation for the development of my master's research (Spaggiari, 2009)—and for its success regarding more its completion and less the subsequent appreciation of the textual product—started like this:

> Boy: - You're not a scout, then?
>
> *I: - No, I am a researcher, anthropologist, I study at USP.*
>
> Boy: - Not even a businessman?
>
> *I: - No, I come to observe the classes and trainings, it's part of my study.*
>
> Boy: - The guys tripped... they were even fooling around in front of you, giving elastic band, pen, thinking they could make to a team there...

During the first three months of fieldwork in Cidade Líder, an area in the eastern part of Sao Paulo city, I got in contact with different actors: teachers, schoolkids, parents, local shopkeepers, among others. But I did not use to get close to the children and youngsters, keeping just brief dialogues, mostly for practical purposes: "What time is it?", "hold my cap while I play," "throw the ball here." This dynamics went on and on until the day I talked to this boy, then 12 years old, who decided to sit next to me on a wall near the football field where the neighborhood football school players were training.

The conversation went on for a while, when the boy asked me again: "And why are you here? Is it to help the teacher?" More than 20 min of conversation followed, in which I tried to explain what the research was about, what anthropology was, what it was for, etc. The boy did not let the conversation end, asking about my presence there, but mainly about the usefulness of watching children play football, since I was not a teacher, nor a coach, nor a scout, nor a manager. I could not satisfy the boy's curiosity and suspicion, mostly due to the fact that I honestly used, in the wrong way, terms such as *theory, classification, concept,* and *category* to answer his questions.

E. Spaggiari (✉)
University of São Paulo, São Paulo, Brazil

© The Author(s), under exclusive license to Springer Nature Switzerland AG 2021   227
S. S. Giglio and M. W. Proni (eds.), *Football and Social Sciences in Brazil,*
https://doi.org/10.1007/978-3-030-84686-2_14

As in a philosophical competition, I found myself caught in a sophist trap (Huizinga, 2005), about to be defeated after my last card: "That is why we use categories, to be able to analyze what was observed." Again, another minute of silence. When the conversation seemed over, the boy stammered: "I think I understand." And he added: "It's not a big deal. It's just like football." Surprised, I asked him why he compared it to football. He answered: "It must have category." Defeated in the sophist duel, now it was my turn to be speechless for a minute.

As a key moment in the fieldwork, the boy's approach proved to be very intriguing. "It must have category" brings together football and anthropology, two apparently distinct kinds of knowledge, two initially disparate interests, but whose articulation has fed the production of knowledge that sometimes goes beyond the academic scope.

Body, Game, and Sports

The relationship between football and anthropology dates back to reflections on games and body practices in traditional societies proposed by classical anthropology, as pointed out in the article "Games in culture," by Roberts et al. (1959), which drew attention for its goal of systematizing the point of view of anthropology on sports and game.

> The beginning of Anthropology concern about sports must be searched in the XIX century [...] in this aspect, the works devoted to the compilation of games, both in Europe and America, stand out. Most of these early works are ethnographic and ethnological, concerned about pointing out the similarities and differences between the physical-sportive practices and the games of different communities. (Medina & Sánchez, 2003, p. 12, our translation)

Among those first anthropological analyses, which still did not turn to experiences associated with the so-called modern sports, the famous text by Marcel Mauss on body techniques stands out, defined as "the ways men, from society to society, in a traditional way, know how to use their bodies" (Mauss, 2003, p. 401). For the French author, body techniques are also socially constructed because they are culturally transmitted from generation to generation, varying according to the cultural context, but they can be interpreted in different ways and present themselves in different ways. Thus, they become traditional because they are relevant and meet the interests of the society in which they are developed. Those interests cannot just be understood by the functional-utilitarian key, but also by the presence of elements of a symbolic efficacy in daily gestures and acts, such as eating, swimming, and walking. This way, as Mauss had already emphasized, corporality should be understood in a relational way, since a plural set of elements permeate the construction of corporal techniques in the long term.

Since then, the body has been a central theme in anthropological research on sporting practices, which requires problematizing certain notions of corporality as methodological appropriations, avoiding reifying them as a prompt research descriptor, which may be covered by ethnographic data (Toledo, 2007, pp. 256–257), or even as illustrative forms. As Toledo emphasized, it is about considering the body as "a methodological way to achieve a new access to the object, because it is potentially content and form, object and method of observation" (2007, pp. 258–259, our translation).

The contributions of classical anthropology also reach the debate involving the uses of the concepts of sports and game—entertaining and agonizing, fun and serious—which mobilized studies of several authors from other areas, such as Johan Huizinga and Roger Caillois, about the meanings of sports in modern societies. For Lévi-Strauss (2005, pp. 46–49),[7] games and rituals are symmetrical and opposite forms of social organization. The game would create events from structures, with an equal space for two teams submitted to the same rules, which leads to disjunction throughout the dispute, producing the difference, with some disadvantage on one side. The rite, on the other hand, would create structures from events, starting from asymmetry to create a conjunction, bringing closer, and equalizing the two sides of the dispute.

Despite the relevance of those classic works, Brazilian anthropological production on football has designed a very particular academic trajectory, focused on the sociocultural and academic dynamics of a country undergoing a process of national integration and urban and industrial transformation. Although it is not the purpose of this chapter to make a detailed survey of the expressive bibliography of anthropology on football, which is a challenge faced by several recent bibliographic reviews from the point of view of the social sciences (Alabarces, 2004; Damo, 2016; Giglio & Spaggiari, 2010; Guedes, 2010; Toledo, 2001), the text presents a linear, but not systematic, balance of anthropological production, guided mainly by certain analytical units and methodological orientations that have remained for three generations—suggested by Damo (2016)—as well as by the emergence of new themes and questionings.

Football, Drama, and National Identity

In Brazil, the first contributions of the human sciences to the study of football date back to the 1940s: the essay "O papel da magia no futebol" (The role of magic in football), by Mário Miranda Rosa, and sociologist Luiz Aguiar Costa Pinto's review of the recently released book *O negro no futebol brasileiro* (The black man in Brazilian soccer), by Mário Filho.[1] However, the presence of such theme in the academic scene was sporadic until the end of the 1970s,[2] with emphasis, over this long period of time, on the essayistic works of some Brazilian intellectuals—such as Gilberto Freyre and João Lyra Filho—on the theme of the nation and the formation of a national identity. Those works were problematized mainly based on issues related

---

[1] Both were published in *Sociologia*, the first scientific journal of Social Sciences in Brazil, published by Escola Livre de Sociologia e Política de São Paulo at the time (now FESPSP).

[2] Among the productions, one can highlight Anatol Rosenfeld's essay "O futebol no Brasil" (Football in Brazil), published in 1973 (Rosenfeld, 1973).

to race, ethnicity, and popular classes that surrounded the deterministic explanations for the victories and failures of the Brazilian national team in World Cups between the 1930s and 1980s—a long period that cannot be dissociated from the turbulent Brazilian political context.

Reflections on national identity play a key role in consolidating a more porous academic scenario for studies on the sporting phenomenon in Brazil. Given its ability to disassociate itself from a vast spectrum that includes many other sports, football holds a certain hegemony in various instances, including in the Brazilian academic environment, which can be explained by the various connections of this sport with the nation. The first researches produced in the field of anthropology are symptomatic of this observation.

It is common ground to state the pioneering nature of the collection *Universo do futebol: Esporte e sociedade brasileira* (Football universe: Sports and Brazilian society), organized by anthropologist DaMatta et al. (1982), regarded as the first theoretical attempt to view football as an object of cultural analysis. Before that, however, the master's dissertations of Guedes (1977) and Araújo (1980), both in the Postgraduate Program in Social Anthropology of Museu Nacional (UFRJ), had already announced the emergence, in the late 1970s, of more methodical investigations dedicated to understand football as an object of study. It is worth emphasizing the relevance of the work of Simoni Guedes for the consolidation of the sportive phenomenon in the academic field of social sciences; her continuous performance in congresses and guidance for new researches in the following decades were fundamental for that. However, due to restrictions on the circulation of dissertations and theses, Roberto DaMatta's propositions, summarized in *Universo do futebol*, drove the investigations conducted by different generations of researchers in the following decades.

Universo do futebol (1982) has as its main attribute the anthropological view of four researchers: along with DaMatta, Luiz Felipe Baeta Neves, Simoni Guedes, and Arno Vogel, all associated, at that time, with Museu Nacional, in Rio de Janeiro. Each author wrote a text—DaMatta also wrote the introduction—on different aspects, but somehow united by the same initial objective: to analyze football as a national institution, expressed in the idea of Brazil as the *country of football*. This refuted the consolidated perspectives of the time, which dissociated sports and society, linking football to certain social roles: ideological instrument, factor of popular alienation, and opium for people.

As in his analysis of carnival, another contemporary phenomenon of popular and mass culture,[3] DaMatta points out that his interest comes from the fact that these phenomena are privileged means to understand significant issues of Brazilian society, since they highlight and problematize aspects of everyday life, which justifies, for the author, the popularity of football and carnival in the country. The dichotomy

---

[3] Roberto DaMatta aimed, in most of his work, to understand numerous aspects of Brazilian society, such as carnival, trickery, public and private, democracy, and also football. Although this last aspect is perhaps the least read and cited in his work, such analyses undertaken by the author as of the late 1970s were decisive to make the first investigations in the sports field legitimate (and possible).

between sports and society has thus overcome, seeking to understand this activity as part of society and not opposed to it. In order to build his argumentative line, the author starts mainly from Victor Turner's concept of *drama*. DaMatta sees football as a *social drama*—a vehicle for dramatizations of crucial problems—in order to understand Brazilian society in a more general way. The dramatization in football would express and reveal values, relations, or ideologies; that is, drama would be the way society would let itself be read or perceived, or, as Geertz (1989) states, the way society tells its own story to itself.

The unfolding of football as a manifestation of popular culture endowed with "a remarkable multivocality—a complex vocation that allows one to understand and experience it simultaneously from many points of view" (DaMatta, 1994, p. 12, our translation)—reveals the reason why the *anthropology of sports* has been treated, in many moments, as the *anthropology of football*, as noted by Guedes (2010). This also raises some criticism due to the fact that the author, in a way, essentializes the fact that football is a national institution that allows Brazilian society to talk about it to itself. Geertz (1997), for example, criticizes the use of the concept of *drama* elaborated by Victor Turner, which can be a "formula for all seasons" turning obviously different subjects into insipidly homogeneous ones. Such perspective will have to be studied by a second generation more concerned to investigate and problematize the processes and relations—harmonic and conflicting—that operate in the construction of football as a national symbol.

The propositional qualities of the works of DaMatta, Simoni Guedes, and their peers fostered a unique theoretical configuration to understand the complexity of football as an articulating phenomenon of various symbolic elements. Inspired by readings of classic anthropological monographs, the analytical framework designed by this first set of anthropological researches proved to be original and bold, especially for being supported by interpretations and ethnographies related to the Brazilian context.

This does not imply that the foreign literature devoted to such sportive phenomenon was disregarded upon the Brazilian production, even though its appropriation has occurred, at times, in a quick, limited, and not very deep way. Among the established foreign authors who were—and are—important references for those who have dedicated themselves to studies on football in Brazil, even beyond the borders of social sciences, it is worth highlighting the influence of sociologist Norbert Elias's analyses (together with Eric Dunning) on the importance of modern sports for the domestication of violence in Western societies from the nineteenth century and on the acting of groups of supporters in England; on Frankfurt School sociologists who conducted a critical analysis of sports as an alienating element of the cultural industry; and on Pierre Bourdieu's sociology of practice, widely used through concepts such as field, action, and *habitus*. It is, therefore, a diversified set of authors, not restricted to those mentioned above, whose work would also become compulsory reading for a second generation of researchers who attempted, through constant dialogues with what was produced inside and outside Brazil, to theoretically advance in the 1990s and 2000s.

The production of this period aroused some important debates and themes for sport anthropology, but instead of regarding football as one of the national symbols, this second generation set out to investigate the dynamics and practices of the incubation process of a football *ethos*. To this end, they focused on football as a multi-faceted phenomenon that reaches numerous social and cultural dimensions, not only in its spatial–temporal locus of spectacularized ritualization, but also at the level of everyday practices. Thus, instead of focusing on *dramatizations* as conceptual instruments of mediation between society and football, priority was given to a procedural, relational, and situational analysis of the plurality of practices and representations of the football phenomenon.

Anthropology of Sporting Practices

In a sports scenario that experienced profound transformations related to the marketing vocation of a continuous project of football spectacularization, the Brazilian production of the 1990s and 2000s started to be dedicated to the various agents who get in on the football field—shared by Toledo (2002) in *professionals, specialists, supporters,* and *officers,* the latter group added by Damo (2007). In this fruitful period, when a gradual increasing process of dissertations and theses could already be observed, the researches, formerly contingent, became more systematic[4]—although erratically regarding the quality of production—and contemplated several themes: the insertion and participation of blacks in football; the relationship between football and national identity; discussions about styles and football schools, especially about a "Brazilian-style game," better known as "art football"; the circulation of players in international football; the training of young players, among others. Among the main themes, researches on organized fans, greatly influenced by the proliferation of conflicts and violence cases in stadiums in the early 1990s, had a decisive impact on the process of expanding the scenario of studies on sports in Brazil.

Thus, in general, the second generation managed to sediment and refine the theoretical and methodological frameworks based on an anthropological production focused mainly on ethnographies that sought to identify the point of view of the players that make up the sports field, as well as to avoid certain generalizations still observed in other areas of knowledge. Those researches, some of which were even awarded by the National Association of Social Sciences Researchers

---

[4] Some names, among others that could be mentioned, emerge as representative of this second generation: Luiz Henrique de Toledo's research on organized fans, representation forms and the formation process of a football field; Carmen Rial's on family projects and the circulation of Brazilian football players abroad; José Paulo Florenzano's on the agency and management of people in football around the rebellion and politicization of players; and Arlei Damo's on club belonging, football matrixes, and the formation of football players.

(Anpocs),[5] expanded the scope beyond the sports universe, creating dialogues with other subfields within the disciplinary tradition itself, such as urban anthropology and visual anthropology. In addition, the rapid circulation of research results and easy digital access to a growing amount of bibliography has led to the strengthening of ties with South American peers. In institutional terms, the outstanding production has given visibility to the theme in the main journals of social science area,[6] in addition to expanding and consolidating spaces for discussion inside and outside Brazil, which encouraged the movement of expansion of works in the last decade.

The second generation has left a significant production that advanced not only in quantity, but also in quality, but it was still seeking to establish itself in the face of other traditional fields of anthropology. In this sense, the successive working groups held in national and Latin American academic forums and the organization of academic events specifically focused on the theme of sports were essential. Such collective spaces for contact and debate among researchers with different institutional links were decisive in the long process of strengthening the field of studies and research on sports in Brazil.[7] Although the quantity and quality of researches presented at those forums might vary, their permanence over the last two decades is also symptomatic of the academic consolidation of the theme. It is also worth highlighting the performance of numerous research centers and study groups in several public and private universities,[8] as well as the consolidation of specific disciplines on football and sports in graduate programs of institutions. Against the solidified discourse that the production on the sportive phenomenon was small, Toledo warned:

> For some time now, dissertations and theses that deal with the sport dimension no longer make the remark that the subject lacks a consistent bibliography. This remark, often converted into lack of care or unpreparedness in the bibliographical review, was taken by surprise in the last decade with the *boom* of works on sports in Brazil and the consolidation in the academic environment of areas that gave a less sporadic treatment to the theme. (Toledo, 2001, p. 135, our translation)

---

[5] Anpocs awarded the master's research of Toledo (1996) as the best Social Sciences Dissertation of 1994 and the doctoral research of Arlei Damo (2007) as the best Social Sciences Thesis of 2006.

[6] It is also worth mentioning the creation of magazines specialized in publishing research on football, such as *Pesquisa de Campo* (Field Research), published by Núcleo de Sociologia do Futebol (Center of Sociology of Football)—linked to the Department of Social Sciences of Instituto de Filosofia e Ciências Humanas of Universidade do Estado do Rio de Janeiro (UERJ) and coordinated by sociologist Maurício Murad. Initially intended to be published every six months, the journal was discontinued after its fifth issue due to lack of funding, but its pioneering spirit was decisive for the strengthening of football studies in social science courses in Brazil.

[7] I highlight the working groups at Anpocs, the Brazilian Meeting of Anthropology (RBA) and the Mercosur Meeting of Anthropology (RAM), as well as the three editions of Symposium on Football, organized by Núcleo de Antropologia Audiovisual e Estudos (NAVI) of the Department of Anthropology of UFSC, and the three editions of the International Symposium of Studies on Football, organized by the Football Museum (Pacaembu/SP) in partnership with LUDENS—Interdisciplinary Center for Studies on Football and Recreational Modalities (University of São Paulo).

[8] For a more detailed survey of research groups focused on the study of sports in human sciences, mostly formed in the last two decades, see Ferreira (2009).

In the anthropological field, especially, it was no longer appropriate to say that academic literature on football was scarce and insufficient; after all, as Damo (2016, p. 338) points out, "we jumped from a production on a handmade scale in the 1980s (or without scale, to be precise), to a production in an almost industrial regime in the following decades" (our translation). But, in fact, the production was still far from the deserved relevance, considering the importance of the theme in Brazil, as Toledo (2001, p. 135, our translation) rightly pointed out: "In some academic journals of recognized visibility in the scientific field, we can observe a derisory number of works that have sports as theme. This, somehow, reflects a field still in formation and in institutional statement."

Supported by the contributions and advances of research conducted in previous decades, a third generation—of anthropologists, categories, approaches—has emerged, dedicated to expand and diversify interpretative keys, theoretical discussions, and methodological approaches, to problematize new themes, reflections, and issues related to football expressions and practices, as well as to scrutinize other sport modalities. Thus, anthropological production, until then marked by the prominence of football, has gradually diversified in recent years.

This change is not associated with a possible retraction in its research framework, but rather, as noticed by Guedes (2010), to the expansion of the empirical field of produced analyses. Indeed, other kinds of practices—volleyball, basketball, rugby, sailing, horseback riding, swimming, skateboarding, surfing, martial arts, etc.—began to be viewed by approaches that go beyond, to some extent, traditionally studied dimensions. As Guedes attests, this insurgence has been impacting the football hegemony in the scope, now, of an *anthropology of sporting practices,* which seeks to account for a greater thematic mobility and the coverage of other dimensions beyond those centered on practices considered competitive and high level, such as the spectacularized matrix of football. For Toledo and Costa (2009), the *anthropology of sporting practices* allows the confluence of practices that conjugate certain hybrid symbolic principles and that are not necessarily circumscribed to the sportive domain. This condition updates, therefore, what is conventionally called *sport* by broadening and deepening new theoretical and methodological possibilities. Thus, a production is revealed with a multiform profile and already partially synthesized in recent collections (Spaggiari et al., 2016).

In addition to the plurality of sportive practices, it would be impossible not to give due emphasis on the impacts that the organization of major world sportive events in Brazil has caused in studies on football and on the sportive phenomenon in general. This *sporting decade* may be understood as a period marked by the emergence of expectations, euphoria, speculations, indignations, and rebellions in relation to certain processes and agencies around their controversial organizations.[9]

---

[9] Although it is possible to map some episodic events that preceded this period—such as the "Peace Game" of 2004—it can be considered that the debut of this decade took place in 2007, when the Pan American Games and the Para-Pan Games were held in Rio de Janeiro, and continued until 2016, with the Olympic Games and Paralympic Games, also in Rio de Janeiro, which were unprecedented in our country. In addition to events held under the seal of the International Olympic Committee (IOC), other important competitions took place in several Brazilian cities in between the period

The World Cup and the Olympic Games were the main mega-events of the *sporting decade*. The fact that Brazil hosted both of them was strategic in many ways, especially regarding its political and economic projection in an international scenario. However, the mobilization for achieving such condition generated burdens to the public coffers, reverberating, in fact, too many impacts of all sorts. Negotiations between state agents, multinational private corporations, and the world's leading sporting entities—FIFA and the IOC—were judged by many contrasting positions: some considered the use of public resources in mega-events a worthy investment, others argued that such an initiative would entail only exacerbated and unnecessary expenses that could be better applied in public policies for the benefit of the entire population.

Thus, between use and abuse of public funds, the distrust to the over-promoted "legacies" provided by mega-events was significant during this decade. Such suspicion was expressed, above all, through the actions of popular movements and effusive political and social clashes, such as the June 2013 Days, which gave visibility to numerous issues that went beyond the sporting arena (urban appropriations, real estate speculation, violence, public transport, national sovereignty, etc.). After all, as argued by anthropologists Damo and Oliven (2013), not only issues of monetary economy were at stake, but also of moral economy.

The mega-events provided, to a certain extent, new perspectives for studies on the football theme in Brazilian anthropology, which problematize from issues of the spectacularized level, related to events of extensive and global proportions, to investigations on local and circumscribed social practices and networks, but no less complex, which also make football a phenomenon of contemplation, *sportstalk* (Eco, 1984) and *discussability* (Bromberger, 1998). Although incipient in the bibliographical set, the flourishing of a recent thematic diversification of the works produced in the period in question allows us to rethink the centrality of football in the Brazilian academic and sports scene, however, not in the sense of questioning its prominence, but rather to update the constitutive dynamics of such scenarios, which are increasingly multifaceted. One of the challenges for future investigations is to try to understand how the social, economic, and political impacts are articulated to the different processes of esportivization, which go through the ambivalences of the relations between amateurism and professionalism, and how they contribute to the understanding of the representativeness of sports in political, recreational, and aesthetic daily life.

The projection of a critical reading of the political issue in the sports universe was undoubtedly one of the main "legacies" of this troubled *sporting decade*. Reflections on impacts of mega-events in Brazil go through tangible and intangible aspects, some

---

mentioned above; however, none of them had the same repercussion as the football spectacles promoted by FIFA, namely the 2013 Confederations Cup and, most importantly, the 2014 World Cup.

considered more relevant than others: infrastructure, urban interventions, transportation system, professional training, telecommunications, security, tourism, projection of the country's image, economic opportunities for host cities, use of new stadiums, increased physical activity, investment in school sports, etc.

Ethnographic Displacements

The inquiry into the relations between football and politics has gone beyond the mega-events in the country and has gained visibility in several areas. It is not only about a decade of mega-events, but about the manifestations of the sporting phenomenon in an expanded and plural perspective, which goes beyond the temporal cutout of this definition, covering dynamics of remarkable resonance in the political, economic, media, and educational fields among others. The expansion of the political issue throughout this period, yet in an apparently diffuse manner, proved to be expressive and catalyzed the search for new meanings for the relations between sports and politics, which, until recently, had been little explored in studies on football.

This last statement also reveals what is perhaps the critical point of a vast anthropological production that, in fact, has overlooked the relationship between football and politics—which can also be observed in the notable absence of this theme in political science, as Guedes points out (2003). There was, from the 1980s on, a hasty appropriation of criticism of an ideological reading of the sporting phenomenon—and more specifically football—fomented by the expression "football is the opium of the people" (or "the opium of the masses"). The consequences of this refusal expanded to such an extent that there began to be a rejection of approaches that linked political aspects to sporting aspects. By disassociating culture and politics, similar mistakes of those who only defended the alienating role of sports were being repeated. Football and sports practices, in general, may have political and ideological uses, which are even recurrent cases in the sports universe.[10]

Thus, if politics, on the one hand, has always been related to football, on the other hand, the restlessness of the last decade has made it a recurrent theme of research, instigating reflections on the flows of power that cross both institutional and more informal and everyday dynamics, in a broad scenario that articulates nation-state, transnational economy, new social movements, club entities, redemocratization, debates on gender and ethnicity, etc.

Two themes, among the many that could be mentioned, have gained relevance in anthropological production, receiving due and overdue in-depth studies. The first,

---

[10] It is worth pointing out that some anthropological studies have invested in the reading of the relationship between football and the state, focused on criticizing the capitalization of professional football by authoritarian regimes in different contexts, places, and periods. Other researches, especially the one by Florenzano (1998, 2009), focused on spaces of resistance, such as the *Democracia Corinthians* (Corinthians' Democracy) movement, and the protest manifestations of sportsmen and other personalities linked to the sport, such as Reinaldo, Paulo César Caju, Afonsinho, among others.

on women's football,[11] amateur or professional, concentrates a significant part of the discussions on gender, corporality, and empowerment. As a space of homosociability and of a certain model of masculinity (Damo), football—and the world of sports in general—is a phenomenon that has been dominated by men, guided by masculine values and structured on the basis of power relations that promote inequalities of gender and sexuality and, consequently, asymmetric conditions of action and movement in the sporting universe. Like other sporting practices, football is marked by institutions and spaces of power where gender and sexuality are constituted and reproduced in a system in which heteronormativity is imposed (Butler, 2003).

Hegemonic and normative representations can be observed in several levels that cross the football system, both in the spectacularized and media dimension of the phenomenon and in its everyday forms. However, it is possible to observe the construction of specific forms of femininity in spaces related to a practice considered as hegemonically masculine; also, an approach to the representations of femininity in the football system raises questions related to the constitution of masculinity. It is, therefore, an exercise of denaturalizing a phenomenon marked by an asymmetric relationship between the genders and thus destabilizes representations that associate attributes, behaviors, styles, and corporalities to the masculine and feminine. After all, masculinity and femininity are not fixed, rigid, and stable identities, but multiple, flexible, and transitory ones.

If the issue of masculinity in football has already been addressed from an anthropological point of view (Archetti, 1999; Guedes, 1998), more recently the gender category has been incorporated by research on women's football. Later, but not far from the long period of restriction to the practice of sports by part of the Brazilian population, such studies have contributed to the strengthening of the gender theme by focusing on an heterogeneous universe of practices experienced in different contexts, seeking to understand the local, particular, and creative agency beyond the institutional, marketing, and media structure associated with the spectacularized matrix (Almeida, 2018; Kessler, 2015; Pisani, 2018).

By questioning the naturalization of a social marker of difference in a universe also crossed by other markers—such as sexuality, race, generation, and class—such studies have stimulated the interest for new themes and research approaches in the area, broadening the questions to several forms of participation other than football practice, as well as for an understanding of variations in other sport modalities. Thus, the expansion and deepening of research and efforts to understand the practices and social agents that make up the universe of women's football may contribute not only to problematize the football hegemony associated with a gender model guided by a binarism favoring what is adjectivized as masculine, but also to enrich

---

[11] According to Kessler (2015), the denomination "*feminine football*," which meant the sport in institutional terms, has been overlooked before the expression "*women's football*" or "*football played by women.*" Several studies have pointed out that the category "feminine" is a generified description of sporting practices that refers to the construction of a single, normative, and hegemonic model of femininity associated with the feminine–masculine dyad.

the various contemporary debates that have addressed issues related to gender intolerance, hegemonic heteronormativity, invisibilization of practices, heteronormative values, homoerotic affective experiences, and new arrangements of empowerment.

The second theme, which is not new in the academic production on football, on the contrary, has a remarkable centrality in the process of consolidation of the theme in anthropology and involves the transformations of supporters' practices, the ways of cheering, in face of the process of updating sports equipment. A discussion questions the controversial construction of arenas and renovations of football stadiums for mega-events in the country, but that extends to negotiations and disputes related to other sports venues that were not directly associated with the 2014 World Cup. It is worth emphasizing, once again, that many of those effervescent discussions that have fed recent research are not exactly new. The process of modernizing and transforming football stadiums into arenas, undertaken in recent years, for instance, had already been observed when stadiums were built or renovated in other periods, with the due differences and singularities of each movement (Damo & Oliven, 2014).

Fragmentation, control, and hierarchization that mark new architectures, globally propagated by mega-events and ruled by a "FIFA standard," generate impacts and transformations in the form of supporters' sociability, including the exclusion of lower-class people with less purchasing power (Curi, 2012). Thus, the process of transformation of sports venues, guided by values such as multifunctionality, comfort, safety, and technology, ends up conflicting with a playful sociability (Toledo, 2010), whose ways of cheering change continuously, triggering a diverse performative repertoire that accumulates gestures, musicality, and corporality.

This management of spectacularized football, however, is not limited to changing and reconfiguring the ways of cheering and sociabilities that make up the internal scenario of stadiums. The transformations in sports venues reach other levels of supporting experience, whose effects spread around the urban spaces of metropolises, by supporters, and imply updates of the dynamics of appropriation and circulation by terminals and transport flows, shops, streets, meeting spots, etc. Thus, the changes and permanences demand from supporters a continuous "making up the city" (Agier, 2011), in face of new uses of spaces, urban equipment, different logics of spatialization, unknown routes, and other types of unforeseen events. Whether by changes in the place of the city to be occupied, or by changes in the form of appropriations of spaces in the same region, such updates of cheering, as revealed in the dissertations by Bocchi (2016) and Mandelli (2018), pose challenges, from the anthropological point of view, for thinking about belonging, mobility, and cityhood.

Similar challenges are faced by other researches that seek to articulate studies about football with other lines of thought within anthropology, both when taking the city as a fundamental dimension to scrutinize the daily and political plots that permeate amateur football and the production of young footballers (Spaggiari, 2016) and when dialoguing with ethnology to investigate body and sport practices in Amerindian contexts (Costa, 2013; Vianna, 2008), or even to reflect, as already mentioned, on dissonant practices and gender issues (Camargo, 2012). Interfaces announce new paths and theoretical and methodological arrangements that would enrich the anthropological production on football, as Toledo rightly pointed out:

An "Anthropology of sporting practices" should be attentive to these dynamisms and not confine its investigation to sporting events, in the same way that an urban anthropology should not be restricted to explaining the urban phenomenon, the city itself as an independent variable. (Toledo, 2001, p. 137, our translation)

Final Remarks

The two thematic axes indicated above are representative of the recent body of research related to an anthropology of football, but they do not exhaust it. It is a field of studies that has grown gradually and whose various angles are directed toward central issues in anthropology—from research on events of extensive and global proportions, to analyses of local and circumscribed, but no less complex, social networks and practices. This perennial and expressive production, briefly outlined here, ensures a vast field that can still be explored by new bold and daring contributions, regardless of the constraints that may be imposed by the institutional and political environment that surrounds them. The *sporting decade*, in fact, offered a new and polyphonic research agenda guided by political dynamics, but composed of more empirical than theoretical efforts, which requires a continuous theoretical and methodological review, with a critical and rigorous stance, in order to update certain paradigms and analytical keys (race, national identity, ways of cheering, etc.) that were and still are decisive for the constitution of the anthropological field of studies on football in Brazil.

The complex current scenario, presented only in a panoramic way in this chapter, requires a constant process of renewal that can draw much from an inventive and symmetrical transdisciplinary debate, as well as from the comparative and dialogical effort to what has been produced about other sports and sporting experiences. However, this renewal will depend, above all, on the theoretical and methodological investments that will feed future anthropological reflections on different football expressions and practices. In this sense, the centrality of ethnography in anthropological thought must be given due prominence.

The ethnographic perspective, a methodological and analytical unit that interconnects classical and contemporary issues worked over three generations, has an essential role in the constitution of an anthropological field marked by creativity and the unprecedentedness of its theoretical propositions. Ethnography shows itself open to the imponderables of the field, to what is unpredictable, detached from predefinitions and certainties, so that it can refine the theoretical models. As a specific form of construction of theoretical knowledge that occurs in conjunction with data collection, ethnography cannot be summarized as the empirical application of theories, nor as a way to fit information and data into preconceived models and categories. The dialogue of researchers with their interlocutors and the continuous confrontation with data and field experiences make ethnography a constitutive part of the theoretical effort of anthropological knowledge. Thus, theory and empirical research do not occur at different times, since ethnography is, at the same time, method and theory. As Strathern (1987) states, it is from the relationship between two techniques of theorizing—anthropologists and interlocutors—that anthropological knowledge emerges, the result of the "ethnographic encounter" (Oliveira, 2000, p. 24) between the various experiences and interpretive constructions.

In this movement of seeking to understand the plurality of native points of view in their own terms, ethnography allows anthropologists to question the homogenizing reproduction of diffuse and heterogeneous realities reduced to inoperative and simplifying dualities. In the field of football studies, certain dichotomous assumptions obscure the multiplicity of relationships established among various social actors, which leads to the profusion of essentializations that contribute little to advances in the theme. It is up to ethnography to emphasize the relational nature of some dualized schematizations, highlighting the congruences, permeabilities, and intersections of conceptual polarizations that persist in anthropological studies on football—such as game and sport, seriousness and playfulness, amateurism and professionalism, daily life and ritual.

Finally, but back to the beginning of this chapter, that boy was right when he said that in anthropology, as in football, "It must have category," after all, the prominence of anthropological reflections and studies on football cannot be dissociated from the concepts and analytical schemes forged over the last four decades. But the same can be said of the new questionings and theoretical advances catalyzed by numerous ethnographies, because only a close look at the processes, relationships, and situations will allow us to understand the complexity of the multifaceted game of practices, conflicts, and tensions that constitute the football phenomenon.

References

Agier, M. (2011). *Antropologia da cidade*: Lugares, situações, movimentos. São Paulo: Terceiro Nome.

Alabarces, P. (2004). Veinte años de ciencias sociales y deporte en América Latina – un balance, una agenda. *Revista Brasileira de Informação Bibliográfica em Ciências Sociais*, (58), 159–180. http://anpocs.com/index.php/bib-pt/bib-58

Almeida, C. S. (2018). *Do sonho ao possível*: Projeto e campo de possibilidades nas carreiras profissionais de futebolistas brasileiras. (Doctoral Thesis in Social Anthropology), UFSC, Florianópolis, Brazil. https://repositorio.ufsc.br/handle/123456789/191267

Araújo, R. B. (1980). *Os gênios da pelota*: Um estudo do futebol como profissão. (Master's Thesis in Social Anthropology), Museu Nacional, UFRJ, Rio de Janeiro, Brazil. https://www.scribd.com/document/385563368/ARAUJO-Ricardo-B-Os-Genios-Da-Pelota-Futebol-Como-Profissao

Archetti, E. (1999). *Masculinities: Football, polo and the tango in Argentina*. Berg.

Bocchi, G. M. M. (2016). *Do estádio do Pacaembu para a arena Corinthians: Etnografia de um processo de "atualização"*. (Master's Thesis in Social Anthropology), USP, São Paulo, Brazil. https://teses.usp.br/teses/disponiveis/8/8134/tde-10032017-152856/pt-br.php

Bromberger, C. (1998). *Football, la bagtelle la plus sérieuse du monde*. Bayard.

Butler, J. (2003). *Problemas de gênero*. Civilização Brasileira.

Camargo, W. X. (2012). *Circulando entre práticas esportivas e sexuais: Etnografia em competições esportivas mundiais LGBTs*. (Doctoral Dissertation, Interdisciplinary Doctorate in Human Sciences), UFSC, Florianópolis, Brazil. https://repositorio.ufsc.br/xmlui/handle/123456789/96147

Cardoso de Oliveira, R. (2000). *O trabalho do antropólogo*. São Paulo: UNESP.
Costa, C. E. (2013). *Ikindene hekugu: Uma etnografia da luta e dos lutadores no Alto Xingu*. (Doctoral thesis in Social Anthropology), UFSCar, São Carlos, Brazil. https://repositorio.ufscar.br/handle/ufscar/233?show=full
Curi, M. (2012). *Espaços da emoção: Arquitetura futebolística, torcida e segurança pública*. (PhD Thesis in Anthropology), UFF, Niterói, Brazil. http://ppgantropologia.sites.uff.br/wp-content/upl oads/sites/16/2016/07/MARTIN-CHRISTOPH-CURI-SP%C3%96RL.pdf
DaMatta, R., et al. (1982). *Universo do futebol: Esporte e sociedade brasileira*. Pinakotheke.
DaMatta, R. (1994). Antropologia do óbvio. *Revista USP*, (22), 10–17. https://doi.org/10.11606/issn.2316-9036.v0i22p10-17
Damo, A., & Oliven, R. G. (2014). *Megaeventos esportivos no Brasil: Um olhar antropológico*. Campinas: Autores Associados.
Damo, A., & Oliven, R. G. (2013). O Brasil no horizonte dos megaeventos esportivos de 2014 e 2016: Sua cara, seus sócios e seus negócios. *Horizontes Antropológicos, 19*(40), 19–63. https://doi.org/10.1590/S0104-71832013000200002
Damo, A. S. (2007). *Do dom à profissão: A formação de futebolistas no Brasil e na França*. São Paulo: Hucitec.
Damo, A. S. (2016). Novas abordagens sobre o esporte em ciências humanas no Brasil. In E. Spaggiari, J. Machado, & S. S. Giglio (Orgs.), *Entre jogos e copas: reflexões sobre uma década esportiva* (pp. 330–350). São Paulo: Intermeios.
Eco, U. (1984). A falação esportiva. *Viagem na irrealidade cotidiana* (pp. 220–226). Nova Fronteira.
Ferreira, A. L. P. (2009). *O estado da arte da sociologia do esporte no Brasil: Um mapeamento da produção bibliográfica de 1997 a 2007*. (Master's thesis in Sociology), UFPR, Curitiba, Brazil. https://acervodigital.ufpr.br/handle/1884/18362
Florenzano, J. P. (1998). *Afonsinho & Edmundo: A rebeldia no futebol brasileiro*. São Paulo: Musa.
Florenzano, J. P. (2009). *A Democracia Corinthiana: Práticas de libertação no futebol brasileiro*. São Paulo: FAPESP; EDUC.
Geertz, C. (1989). *A interpretação das culturas*. Rio de Janeiro: Guanabara. (Original work published 1973).
Geertz, C. (1997). *O saber local: Novos ensaios em antropologia interpretativa*. Petrópolis: Vozes. (Original work published 1983).
Giglio, S. S., & Spaggiari, E. (2010). A produção das ciências humanas sobre futebol no Brasil: um panorama (1990–2009). *Revista de História*, (163), 293–350. https://doi.org/10.11606/issn.2316-9141.v0i163p293-350
Guedes, S. L. (2003). Lógicas da emoção. *Revista Brasileira De Ciências Sociais, 18*(51), 179–183. https://doi.org/10.1590/S0102-69092003000100015
Guedes, S. L. (1977). *O futebol brasileiro: Instituição zero*. (Master's thesis in Anthropology), Museu Nacional, UFRJ, Rio de Janeiro, Brazil.
Guedes, S. L. (1998). *O Brasil no campo de futebol: Estudos antropológicos sobre os significados do futebol brasileiro*. Niterói: Eduff.
Guedes, S. L. (2010). Esporte, lazer e sociabilidade. In L. F. D. Duarte, & C. B. Martins (Eds.), *Horizontes das ciências sociais no Brasil: Antropologia* (pp. 431–456). São Paulo: Anpocs.
Huizinga, J. (2005). *Homo Ludens: O jogo como elemento da cultura*. São Paulo: Perspectiva. (Original work published 1938).
Kessler, C. S. (2015). *Mais que Barbies e ogras: Uma etnografia do futebol de mulheres no Brasil e nos Estados Unidos*. Doctoral Thesis in Social Anthropology. Porto Alegre, Graduate Program in Social Anthropology-UFRGS.
Lévi-Strauss, C. (2005). *O pensamento selvagem*. Campinas, Papirus. (Original work published 1962).
Mandelli, M. C. (2018). *Allianz Parque e rua Palestra Itália: Práticas torcedoras em uma arena multiuso*. (Master's Dissertation in Social Anthropology), USP, São Paulo, Brazil. https://www.teses.usp.br/teses/disponiveis/8/8134/tde-08032019-152307/pt-br.php

Mauss, M. (2003). As técnicas do corpo. In *Sociologia e Antropologia*. (pp. 399–422). São Paulo: Cosac Naify. (Posthumous book published 1950).

Medina, X., & Sánchez, X. (2003). *Culturas en juego. Ensayos de antropología del deporte en España*. Icaria.

Pisani, M. S. (2018). *"Sou feita de chuva, sol e barro": O futebol de mulheres praticado na cidade de São Paulo*. (Doctoral Thesis in Social Anthropology), USP, São Paulo, Brazil. https://www.teses.usp.br/teses/disponiveis/8/8134/tde-11102018-110139/pt-br.php

Roberts, J. M., Arth, M. J., & Bush, R. R. (1959). Games in culture. *American Anthropologist, 61*(4), 597–605. https://doi.org/10.1525/aa.1959.61.4.02a00050

Rosenfeld, A. (1973). O Futebol No Brasil. *Revista Argumento, 1*(4), 61–85.

Rosenfeld, A. (1993). *Negro, macumba e futebol*. São Paulo: Perspectiva.

Spaggiari, E., Machado, J., & Giglio, S. S. (Orgs.) (2016). *Entre jogos e copas: reflexões sobre uma década esportiva*. São Paulo: Intermeios.

Spaggiari, E. (2009). *Tem que ter categoria: Construção do saber futebolístico*. (Master's Dissertation in Social Anthropology), USP, São Paulo, Brazil. https://www.teses.usp.br/teses/disponiveis/8/8134/tde-02022010-133343/pt-br.php

Spaggiari, E. (2016). *Família joga bola: Jovens futebolistas na várzea paulistana*. São Paulo: Intermeios; FAPESP.

Strathern, M. (1987). The limits of auto-anthropology. In A. Jackson (Ed.), *Anthropology at home* (pp. 16–37). Tavistock.

Toledo, L. H. (1996). *Torcidas organizadas de futebol*. Campinas: Autores Associados; Anpocs.

Toledo, L. H. (2001). Futebol e teoria social: aspectos da produção acadêmica brasileira (1982–2002). *Revista Brasileira de Informação Bibliográfica em Ciências Sociais*, (52), 133–165. https://ludopedio.org.br/biblioteca/futebol-e-teoria-social-aspectos-da-producao-cientifica-brasileira-1982-2002/

Toledo, L. H. (2002). *Lógicas no futebol*. São Paulo: Hucitec; Fapesp.

Toledo, L. H. (2007). Posfácio—corporalidade e festa na metrópole. In J. G. Magnani, & B. Mantese (Eds.), *Jovens na metrópole: Etnografia de circuitos de lazer, encontro e sociabilidade* (pp. 265–266). São Paulo: Terceiro Nome.

Toledo, L. H., & Costa, C. E. (Eds.). (2009). *Visão de jogo: Antropologia das práticas esportivas*. São Paulo: Terceiro Nome.

Toledo, L. H. (2010). Torcer: metafísica do homem comum. *Revista de História*, (163), 175–189. https://doi.org/10.11606/issn.2316-9141.v0i163p175-189

Vianna, F. (2008). *Boleiros do Cerrado*. São Paulo: Annablume.

Chapter 15
Garrincha, Pelé and Maradona: The *Sporting Sacred* in Times of Football Icon Veneration

Luiz Henrique de Toledo

The South American Trinity

Pelé, the saint,[1] and *Maradona, Mano de Dios* are the names popularly given to two widely known images that are now easily accessible through digital search engines. For decades, they have served to stroke the imagination of fans, stoke controversies, begged the comparison of their backgrounds and careers and highlighted in an expressive fashion how fragments of elusive narratives and concepts of the sacred have generated novel representations in the field of sports. Today, these images continue to give rise to an endless source of new internet images of these two players. Therein, they witness not only past playing styles and the sensory perceptions of a football that historically, particularly in Latin America, has been embedded within syncretic popular knowledge about these objects undergoing the process of sacralization.

Historically and across the world, sports have birthed numerous lay idols. These "living gods" are adored, feared or hated by noisy moral and political groups always willing to engage in the widest possible range of forms of contemplation and/or destruction of images. This classifies the sports domain as an endeavor far from fleeting, disinterested or merely playful. The fans can become true iconophiles, gathering into their subjectivities a pantheon of idols and images that inflame their "selves" and give rise to mediations between subjectivity and the game. Hundreds of thousands of players never achieve or maintain idol status. Thus those exceptional players and become masters of techniques and creativity. They mirror fans' behaviors, serve as a link for socialization, become signs of contemplative rituals and mediators of a sports culture that ripples throughout popular culture.

---

[1] In his technical records, this image receives only the singular name *Pelé 1960–1969*, as can be verified in <https://colecaopirellimasp.art.br/autores/119/obra/429>.

L. H. de Toledo (✉)
Federal University of São Carlos, São Carlos, Brazil

At a time when commercialism has pervaded fandom and destitute sports idols of their moral ballast, they have been transformed ubiquitous and innocuous businessmen who capture and deconstruct forms of the game in the movement sciences. In this process, they have forged an athlete persona based on individualistic motivational therapies (see, for example, see the numerous self-help theories that have invaded sports). This process absorbs a great part of these idols' free that becomes increasingly dedicated to growing their market share. This, in turn, generates controversy between forms of idolatry and iconoclasm in the public arena. The powerful forces of sports institutions like FIFA keep on demanding mega-events designed to spur further consumption. Meanwhile, policies are being drawn up to manage forms of fan support and football idol worship.

Building on the ideas of academics such as Bruno Latour about the most phantasmagorical interventions of rationality, we live in a time when the critical mind uncovers shows the hands of humans acting everywhere in order to trounce the sanctity of religion, the belief in fetishes, the cult of the transcendent, the icons sent from heaven and the strength of ideologies. For him, the more the human hand can be seen to have worked on an image, the weaker the image's claim to truth will be (Latour, 2008, p. 117).

Contemporary football is becoming more and more oriented toward financial gain and statistical productivism resulting in another type of "sportive truth" in which professional ethics has been divorced from the fans' values and the ambiguous meanings attributed to the role of great players. These players are, in turn, defined exactly by their ability to improvise, to play tricks and by their unique styles of play. The fans, who have been turned into consumers, have been obligated to behave in an aseptic manor within new sports arenas that have been turned into stages for a distant, impersonal performance.

A football without mediators is not exactly what is preached. However, the relationship between the making of plays or goals and the fans' lived experience (how to dress, how to watch, how to behave) has been increasingly taken over by the filter of the inscribers[2] and freed from any background noise or ambiguity that they had once shared with the fundamentals of the sport. For at least three decades, in Brazil and worldwide, it has been decreed within this ethical and aesthetic space that is subject to numerous political, economic, religious and ideological influences, and it has been decreed that "unnecessary" dribbling should be restrained, any "unruly" intimate behavior of players should be denounced, that the "maladjusted" fan behavior should be condemned, and that the "uncontrollable" cities surrounding the new arenas should be tamed. These arenas appear as silent physical figurations of mega-events in landscapes, as was seen in some of those inert monuments scattered throughout Brazil on the occasion of the 2014 World Cup.

---

[2] Latour, in the book *Laboratory Life*, speaks of the numerous devices used in scientific experiments (e.g., a spectrometer) that manipulate the raw data when writing scientific statements and ends up masking the process itself, making the literary inscriptions (the reports and their graphs, points, etc.) appear as rational and exact procedures. Inscribers came to invent what scientists have come to conceive as being objective reality, the external nature and not something that, in truth, was invented by these inscribing procedures and machines.

In this sense, managing the football of spectacle pivots around a certain limitation or containment of the neighboring experiences by players and fans alike of the creative, magical, and "unproductive" activities outside the instrumental motives; one such unproductive activity is the intangible exercise of the "fan faith." Today, the supposedly mega-professionalized football tries to quickly redefine notions historically constitutive of sports, such as competitiveness, sporting meritocracy, technical performance, so as to triumph without the presence of what might be called the more irrational or magical elements. The greater control and the assumption of marketing directors, personal stylists, managers, performance analysts, professionals of body and soul aim at the search for the most tangible properties within a corporate dynamic that supports contemporary football. It implies the production of new images, a less baroque aesthetic in line with these other periods of former idols, but also, and for that very reason, cleansed by the commercialized globalism that the football spectacle has become.

The "FIFA standard," in imposing itself as a multi-situated sporting order, brought the dictates of a new era, aiming to manage, in addition to all urban, political and economic reordering, documents such as the General Law of the Cup, which stipulates the types of images produced, the choice and management of signs and symbols (mascots, posters, images), and even the food allowed at its events. See, by way of example, the tremendous controversy that ensued at the 2014 World Cup Brazil about controlling the sacred street food, the famous *acarajés*, that are traditionally served to fans on match days at the Salvador, Bahia headquarters.

But such a movement, obviously, can never be taken as a linear and continuous process of mechanic cleansing, since insurgent movements, spurred by either by players or fans, have arisen occasionally, in opposition to the so-called modern world football. These pushes have taken a critical position relative to the aesthetic control of FIFA, and, even if they have not achieved significant effects, they have at least contradicted and widened the qualitative understanding of the phenomenon.

Returning to the old images of Garrincha (Mané), Pelé or Maradona, that for many years encouraged and animated a fan aesthetic. Yet, they cannot evoke a nostalgic, idyllic time, as, in fact, nothing of the sort ever existed. Rather, they serve to enable the search for fresh, less-fetishized images of contemporary football idols that may result in a more complex aesthetic reading of this football that is controlled by consumerist instrumentality.

Images and Production of Sports Emotion

Latour proposes a concept the "iconoclash" which refers to ambiguous phenomena that perform mediating and displacing functions in the war between religious, artistic, ideological and scientific convictions. Football is a form of sports that intensely dialogues with all these other domains, as it also occasionally produces iconoclashes who stir up controversies in opposition to or that destabilize the more controlled iconoclastic attempt by the organizers of contemporary professional football to cleanse the phenomenon.

It is worth pointing out the more general idea that football images can extrapolate the instrumental meanings they were intended to convey and can continuously yield ambiguous meanings. I am guided by Latour's notion of image: any sign, work of art, inscription or figure that acts as a mediator to access something else (Latour, 2008, p. 114). However, I choose to use less the conceptual instrumental of some aesthetics[3] or visual anthropology or image, because what matters is less he mimetic and representational potential of images in the apprehension of the other or "something else," but the enunciation of the images as other, or rather, as artifacts whose physical form performs an action, i.e., they are possessed by actions, in short, they are images that play (Barbosa & Cunha, 2006; Hikiji, 2012; Ingold, 2007; Novaes, 1988; Silla, 2012).

Thus, images of Pelé, Maradona and finally Garrincha that have long enjoyed the scrutiny of millions of fans. The particular players have been chosen, precisely due to the fact that they have been continuously reappropriated as idols, built up, destroyed and rebuilt.[4] They are, themselves, iconoclasts within the symbolic sports order. Some ambiguity insinuates itself in this continuous process in which narrative forms extrapolate the strict football universe, making their biographies establish interesting counterpoints, independently of their owners, both in the sports world or within the artistic, religious or political establishment.

For a long time off the pitch, these idols continue dialoguing very closely and connecting experiences in temporal folds that explode into comparative images whenever they are triggered in the fans' memory or in media narratives. In a quieter fashion, these images still today may reclaim their voice in the continuous comparative exercise to each new striker that arises to claim the status of idol.

Chosen as icons by the collective bodies of fans in their respective periods, these players have witnessed the hyperbolization of the bodily, moral, technical and ethical features of their images. The images, in turn, keep stoking the tension between the condition of sacralized idols exposed to relentless fan contemplation, on the one hand, and successive biographical[5] desecration, on the other, that aims to limit them

---

[3] Some works establish the relationship between aesthetics and sports, such as the classic text by Michel Leiris (2001) on bullfighting, and Gumbrecht (2007).

[4] In commemoration of the 150th anniversary of football, the newspaper *O Estado de São Paulo* of 26/10/2013 published an insert in which presented "the dream team of 150 years of football," whose selection criterion was the participation of players who made a difference in World Cups. Once again, sports trinity was portrayed.

[5] In 2013, there was an intense debate throughout the Brazilian press about biographies. On the one hand, there are artists and some public figures opposed to the publication of unauthorized biographies. On the other, biographers and part of the public felt that such bans evoked the time of the dictatorship when free expression was curtailed. In any case, biographies can serve as examples of iconoclashes, as they destroy and rebuild their characters. They inhabit, I argue, the terrain of ambiguities. They produce and are in themselves interesting mediations through which the paradoxical relationships between fans and idols can be scrutinized. That same year, Pelé returned to the media scene with the headline: "New book about Pelé has copies that can cost up to R$

to the realm of purified technique of the scientific imperatives that try to explain their talents. Objectivity is continuously subjected to the iconoclastic pressure of the multiple facets of football modernization, as advocated by the "FIFA standard."

The building up, destruction and reconstruction of the images of these idols serve as paradigmatic examples that are multiplied infinitely in regional contexts. They take the form of figures, cartoons, street posters, collages, graffiti of more artistic or popular natures, photographs either amateur or professional, and they set themselves against the idea that enjoyment of the game can be increasingly afforded by the direct search for some purified and objective "sports truth."

The attempt to destroy sacralized images in conjunction with biographical revisionism go on to generate new images and signs that feed many other forms of sacralization and desacralization. Until even technique itself is challenged as being all too human (*did Garrincha really play all that much?*). I would say that, in these times of fan sociability in arenas, there is almost a competitive sacralization between means and ends. What seems to matter is less the players and their plays than the monumentality of the facilities, the spread of the fans rather than the gathering of souls. Essential are the perfect sights for selfies, the safe and comfortable parking lots, the big screens displaying images of beautiful fans, both men and women, a retractable roof sheltering everyone from bad weather which is nothing other than the domestication of both nature that is outside and the intimate and rebellious nature of the protagonists of the spectacle.

This chapter addresses those idols of the past amidst the controversies surrounding the forms assumed by modern day iconoclasm which occasionally attempt to simply extirpate, purify or remove them from the ubiquitous condition of idols and mediators of the passion for the game. Maradona, who has been banned from the stepping on US[6] soil, is frequently ridiculed in the media in images that capture him hanging around stadiums in images that showcase his moral and physical and decadence. Another example comes from advertising spots that turn Pelé into a supporting actor of the Ronaldo phenomenon during the 2014 World Cup. In the same year, equally oversized images were seen of Neymar billboards served the less than subtle function of this aesthetic process of purifying and updating the former idol. The already distant memories of Garrincha inscribe him as a player with a naive personality and asymmetric body who was the product of historical chance. This essay aims to reinsert them using available factual images in other spirals of meaning, therefore working in counterpoint to the corrosion of a volatile historical memory and broadening the potential sacredness that made and makes them extra-serial players. Pelé, Maradona

---

5.5 thousand." Available at <www.correiodeuberlandia.com.br/author/agenciaestado/>. Accessed on 2013, October 25.

[6] "Armando Diego Maradona has not set foot in the USA since he was suspended from the 1994 World Cup for doping and had his visa suspended. The former Argentine star had intended to return to the country this year [2018], to attend the trial of the case he opened against his ex-wife, Claudia Villafañe, in Miami. However, according to his lawyer, Maradona has again had his request denied. Matiás Morla attributes the denial to the fact that the former player insulted US President Donald Trump. Available at <https://veja.abril.com.br/placar/maradona-e-proibido-de-entrar-nos-eua-apos-insulto-a-trump/>. Accessed on 2019, January 7.

and Garrincha, out of the world or out of the fields, meet again and again with the fan's imagination in a luxurious profusion of mediations that still confer a transcendent quality on the game from the fan's point of view. This takes place because the sacral, sensual and handcrafted images search for the most varied and unpredictable forms of beauty.

However, even in the name of fair play, of refined field technique, of the selective beauty of the spectacle, of the theatrical security of the fans, a series of ambiguous signs are imposed that simultaneously create and put at risk this football order. This uncertain play between the meanings of images and their continual reappropriations can be understood in Latour's conceptualization. According to him, "iconoclasm" is when we know what is happening in the act of breaking statues or idols—in a gesture of intolerance and fundamentalism—and what the motivations are for what presents itself as a clear project of destruction. On the other hand, "iconoclash" is when one does not know, when one hesitates when disturbed by an action for which there is no way of knowing, without further investigation, whether it is destructive or constructive (Latour, 2008, p. 113).

The Game and the Sacred

A seminal author in the conceptual struggle between play and sport, Caillois, establishes the sacred as being pure expressive content, an "indivisible force" in contrast to the pure form assumed by the notion of a game (applied, in this case, to football), whose interest, in short, would be confined within itself. We are dealing with the sacred as an instance of transcendence and the game as an instance of immanence. Two "purities" are separated by a logical void which, when approached from reality, has produced two new ways of understanding it: escaping from serious life issues, hence the function of the game is seen to be a disinterested activity, while seeking (emotional) rebalancing in the face of danger and life's mysteries refers to the relationship with the sacred.

Such arguments, quite recurrent and transfigured in many ways by literature, try to establish a clearer border between what authors like Huizinga blurred when they disseminated the concept of a game as the epicenter of any form of sociability and implying that even the sacred is a game. Caillois, following Durkheim and Mauss's classification system of genus and species, warns that there is a "sacred-profane-playful" hierarchy. Although "sacred" and "playful" resemble each other, in that they are both opposed to practical life, they occupy symmetrical situations vis-à-vis it. Play must fear it, since it breaks it or dissipates it at the first shock. On the other hand, the sacred has the power, it is believed, to elevate it (Caillois, 1988, p. 159).

Power can be seen to decrease as you pass from the sacred to life and, finally to play, as if proposing the experience of a *homo* triplex and not only duplex, as suggested by the dualism manifested by the coexistence of opposites in the same being (reason and sensibility) Durkheim's sociology. The problem is that Caillois ends up separating the sacred from the game, interposing between them a supposedly more legitimate and properly morphological instance which he calls the domain of (profane) life. This, in principle, following the line of French sociology, gives rise to a typology of game symbolism that he went on to explore further, separating facts (life) from values (the sacred and the game).

Sociologist Elias (1992) sees the game as a human phenomenon that coincides with the production of all social life, locating individuals one by one, two by two, three by three, *n* by *n*, in endless networks of relations. His concept of chains of interdependence,[7] so to speak, tends to desacralize the foundations of dualism in the entire Durkheimian tradition that advocates a stabilizing apriorism of the social (sacred) as a background instance of associated life. In Elias, the game appears to cease being properly a potential expression, standing neither beyond nor below the social taken as an example of the sacred.

Thus, the Elisean desacralized game, product as it is of unplanned movements in the history of associated individuals, retakes a more central methodological position, to the extent that the universality of interactive relationships can assume various hierarchical, egalitarian, competitive or cooperative powers. Said powers, in turn, established the causal nexus of social dynamics in which the concept of the game becomes the very contents of these social interactions. Thus, the notion of game returns to the condition of form, historical form it is true, but a space to be filled by interdependent ludic or non-ludic experiences.

Images, on the other hand, as instances possessed by actions would appear to have some advantage over concepts insofar as, once taken as agentive cultural artifacts, they merge with play, sacredness and other instances within the repertoire of cultural objects and things, softening the potency of a priori conceptualisms that would separate and hierarchize play and sacredness relative to life.

Pelé, The Saint

The iconographic field of football constitutes a space of symbolic experimentation and proximity of different spheres, discursive rearrangements, semantic shifts of all kinds, serving as a kind of reactor of symbolizations that continuously feeds the practice and the taste for the practice. Creation and reiteration, invention and reification move in a gear of continuous discursive and image production about the game that allows the free mobilization of many spheres of sociability, among them the domain of the sacred and of the enjoyment of sportive beauty.

Forms of sacralization in popular culture, in football in particular, are induced irrespective of the intent of institutions, churches or their priests, and of specialists in the rhetoric of the authorized word. They carry the feelings of millions of vicarious spectators who expose their convictions on the great stages of the stadiums. It is

---

[7] Chains of interdependence is an expression coined by Norbert Elias to designate how social life connects (the economic connects to the political, which connects to the sacred, which connects to entertainment and so on).

very common to take as a motto this approximation between football and the sacred to state that fans give their "lives" for and in the game, in a commitment and an immersion that far transcends mere commercial enjoyment.

There is nothing new about the association between football and the sacred, either in the social sciences or in the activities that portray this relationship and direct it to produce some identity, whether by academic, journalistic or aesthetic means.[8] It is worth speculating once again, however, about this relationship, and I will do so based on the notion of "the sporting sacred."

In the image of "Pelé, the saint,"[9] by chance, the photographer managed to capture the confluence and superimposition of two planes that, in turn, skillfully yield a third, unexpected and impactful representation. The viewer's eye is redirected even paralyzed and the led to scrutinize and then absorb the enigmatic image that leaps to the eye. A mirage or a kind of miraculous image captures us suddenly, but it can deceive as well, because it sets up a relationship that, once fixed, transpires and is revealed in its unequivocal message. The image acts on certain powers and mobilizes two fields of knowledge. First, we have the corporeality and physicality of football, in tandem with representations of the sacred that is mobilized by memory to reorient viewers' perceptions and reaffirm common sense in the face of an extraordinary player. What we have here is, firstly, a visual and emotional experience that appears to lead to the notion of displacement. It is an iconoclash of the sporting sacred. We leave behind the football match to arrive at something beyond it that also imposes a discontinuity and almost devoid of causality. This scarcely perceptible image will lead to neither victory nor defeat, because it is suspended in time, autonomous in relation to technique and lacking commitment even to the game itself. These are the effects manipulation of an image of the idol that would be above, beyond or below the historicity that imposes tangible limits to football as a worldly practice.

In the background of the photographic composition, a band can be seen playing the protocol national anthem before a game. In front, stands Pelé, neither petrified nor scenically framed, but portrayed in a pre-Mannerist style, in which it feels as if his body is about to give a pendular leap to catch the ball. The other teammates are deliberately cut out of the composition which, by focusing on Pelé, showcases the intense notion of presence and individual hyper-determinism of his exceptional calling for football.

The image also evokes an iconic gaze à la Monalisa that projects itself from the face of the star complete with a *sfumato* and perspective. It matters little whether we

---

[8] References to a sporting sacred are present in the prose of playwright Nelson Rodrigues. See, for example, Rodrigues (1994).

[9] In the collection of the estado agency, "Pelé 70 years," available on the web since October 22, 2010, some of the most popular images of Pelé taken by Domício Pinheiro can be found. Available on <https://internacional.estadao.com.br/blogs/olhar-sobre-o-mundo/pele-70-anos/>. Accessed on August 1, 2019. Domício Pinheiro was the photographer who became known for recording the most iconic images of Pelé. He had a solo exhibition called *Pelé* at Galeria Fotóptica in São Paulo in 1972 and participated in a group exhibition in 2002, entitled "Pelé: a arte do rei", at Museu de Arte de São Paulo Assis Chateaubriand (Masp). Available at <https://colecaopirellimasp.art.br/autores/119/obra/429>. Accessed on August 1, 2019.

are looking at a photograph (using an optical illusion) or a painting (which would raise doubts about the intent of the representation and the represented). It is as if the whole Western tradition of the personal portrait were taking the lead, but with the addition of sacredness that is conveyed by the juxtaposition of the two planes. Pelé's elusive and somewhat oblique gaze only intensifies the mystery and the proximity to the various traditions through which the notion of the portrait has flowed, making the sacralization of the human and of the self a powerful symbolic mechanism of the individualizing ideologies that have triumphed in our societies, which, by the way, invented sports (Elias, 1992).

Pelé is awaiting the whistle, restlessly giving an unfocused gaze. We have no idea whether he is paying attention to the anthem or is worried about the match. What is more, through a coincidental juxtaposition, the frame captures Pelé in an optical illusion. A trick of light reflects off a tuba immediately behind his head adorning him with a magical halo looking as if it were taken directly from some sacred painting. In another reference to Monalisa, Pelé appears to be addressing us directly with his oblique gaze, or directly questioning each of us, each fan or rival, bringing us to his level by a staring game, which we maintain and immediately return to him in an endless match, an endless synergy. It is as if we could swap places with Edson, the common man, who is deconstructed in the next instant by Pelé with halo who overcomes any existential doubts about his sports career.[10] Consequently, the halo above his head and his scrutinizing gave that leaps out of the photo to capture us fight among themselves to seize the meanings. One, that is the halo, guides our gaze upwards, toward a bit of the sky, while his eyes already bring us back to an awareness of the mundaneness of the game, just before the match. They invite everyone to dive into the clash that is about to begin, to the earthly, yet elusive world of football, thus positioning us as spectators. This disjunction manifests the sporting sacred, which does not eschew ambiguity but weakens it, producing disparate planes, that are inconclusive and abundant in meanings and copresences. In the beginning, it was just one more commitment of the national team, but from the game, it became an icon in pure unshaken image, synthesizing the unexpected union between the game and sacredness, supported immediately by the photographer's cunning, sensitivity or chance that expanded the fans' imagination when faced with the magical football displayed by Pelé.

Another expression of the sacralization of the mundane football world dealt with Pelé as well. Journalist Edgar de Oliveira Barros of the *Diário da Noite* published a plea: "Pelé, play for us!" This was a supreme call for the game in which a distrustful Brazil would end up suffering a surprising defeat by the Portugal team led on the field by Eusébio in the 1966 England World Cup.

During the 2014 World Cup, a popular movement arose in opposition to the huge event and to the political context that surrounded it. On the streets of São Paulo, handmade images in unusual scenarios showed Pelé all suited up for the match who

---

[10] Pelé is well known in the public sphere for separating his heroic character from the common person of Edson Arantes do Nascimento, his birth name. He usually self-names both in the third person (Silva, 2008; Toledo, 2004).

Fig. 15.1 Excerpt from *Pelébeijoqueiro*, by Luís Bueno, art instructor at Istituto Europeo di Design (IED).[11] Photo: Luiz Henrique de Toledo

---

[11] In an interview with the website Super FC, from Belo Horizonte, on August 1, 2019, the street artist maintains an equidistance between Pelé the citizen and Pelé the athlete: "Some people get mad at me because of Pelé's stories with his daughter or the proximity of involvement in FIFA scandals. I also think he could have been more Maradona. He is very powerful in himself. He did not need to align himself with power […]" (as cited in Toledo, 2020, p. 365, our translation). Other works from this artist's collection can be seen in Palhas (2016, November 8). For more on other political features of Pelé's career as an athlete and citizen, see Toledo (2004, 2019), Silva(2008), and Souza (2018).

in the day-to-day life of the metropolis comes across an affectionate Monalisa. His back is turned, and his expression is hidden, but he is the object of a rare, warm and physical embrace by DaVinci's character (see Fig. 15.1). More desecrated than *Pelé, the saint*, we now see a more mundane, perhaps needy Pelé, presented by the collage by Bueno. The figure establishes a dialogue with another poster immediately beside it reading "Vai ter culpa? (Will you be to blame?)" in a play on words referring to the motto of the opposition movement "Não vai ter Copa! (There's not going to be a World Cup!)."[12] Countless intertextual readings and other spirals of meanings are prompted.

The position of the *Não vai ter Copa* Movement is undoubtedly, contrary to the proclaimed positions of the flesh and blood Pelé, a player who largely built his reputation by bringing football prowess together with the proximity or political promiscuity vis-à-vis the sports' centers of powers of the sport. He promoted a

---

[12] The phrase "Vai ter Culpa?" (Will you be to blame?) appears next to the image, ironically referring to the "Não vai ter Copa" protest movements which that across the country in 2013 and 2014.

vigorous marketing career that carefully controlled his image as an entrepreneur.[13] Besides the warm embrace, Pelé also kisses the face of Monalisa whose cheeks are graced with the Brazilian national colors, green and yellow. He appears to stroke her hair in an obvious moment of tenderness by two teammates or fans celebrating a goal in the stands. The rustic street poster, ephemeral like all street art, but captured by many anonymous cell phones, brought the idol back into a transversal narrative in an improbable alliance in which, once again in his condition of idol, promoted the ambiguous atmosphere that surrounded this championship making it a milestone of the ongoing crises of political representation going on in Brazil at that time. By taking refuge in the arms of Monalisa, *Pelé, the saint* was once again able to serve as an omniscient witness to such unpredictable changes. Until that moment, countless anonymous people had walked by that image on Avenida Paulista, the busiest avenue in the country's most populous city and enjoyed that unusual encounter that repositioned the idol in the historical spiral.

The Hand of God

Maradona faced the world (on and off the pitch) mobilizing the sacred in sports, claiming for himself the sacralization of technique in that photo shot in a 1986 World Cup match that swept up the mass of fans.[14] It was the *Pibe* (Maradona's Spanish nickname) recreating the precise number of centimeters he lacked at the instant of the fatal header to the opposing goal—the opportunistic and supplementary contribution of the left hand that reached up to the ball as if it were an extension of his head to ensure the path of immortality in the victory over the English. Moreover, it was the left hand rather than the right hand which, in long-lasting Western symbolism, expresses polarity between the sacred and the profane; the left hand represents ineffable danger, all that is suspect, cursed, and forbidden (Hertz, 1980).

Maradona was later questioned about the fraud, an irregular goal in the view of the International Football Board that was caught and broadcast on worldwide television. There he placed between himself and the universalism of the rules of men the concurrence and fatalism of the divine, of the supreme forces that draw from

---

[13] See Souza, 2018 for a critique of the exaggerated media image of Pelé's performance as a successful businessman.

[14] Available at <https://www.techtudo.com.br/noticias/noticia/2013/01/britanico-mike-stimpson-recria-fotografias-classicas-usando-lego.html>. access on 2019, December 13. For more details, see "the story behind the photo of the 'mano de Dios'," text of June 22, 2016, by Leo Lepri, in honor of the 30 years of this goal. Available at <http://globoesporte.globo.com/blogs/especial-blog/latinoamerica-futbol-club/post/historia-por-tras-da-foto-da-mano-de-dios.html>. Accesed on 2019, October 1. "Mano de Dios" also received mentions in musical records in biographical lyrics, such as that of popular artist Rodrigo, who, in a fragment of his song "Mano de Dios," sings: "carga una cruz en los hombros por ser el mejor, por no venderse jamás al poder enfrentó. Curiosa debilidad, si Jesús tropezó, por qué él no habría de hacerlo …." Audio and lyrics available at <www.letras.mus.br/rodrigo/196494/traducao.html>. On Youtube at <https://youtu.be/8J6zWO9X7Gu>. Accessed on October 1, 2019.

each one of us a supplementary, sacrificial, superhuman will, the last drop of blood in the service of destiny. Cheating was necessary, therein the retroactive designs of a nation in historical dispute with the English were fulfilled. It was God, some god or another, who had helped him score that goal against the English and the trick would win over the world and be recognized as The Hand of God. The recreation of the play in Legos[15] brings the dimensions of the drama even closer to the level of playfulness in which this Lego *Pibe* ends up cheating the pragmatism and the instrumentality of the rules.

Was his jocular, irresponsible and cheeky explanation set against the positive law of rules or respect for the popular cultural mass from which he was raised as a poor boy, leftist, son of God and football player? Who defines and delimits the acts and sentences of a good or bad, condescending or severe, particular or universal god? Here, the notion of mediation serves to capture these decisions and cultural choices made in a fast fraction of a move that creates the space of doubt, then of indignation for many. In any case, within the political and ethical football debate, and despite FIFA's central role in homogenizing the forms of the spectacle. Like a trickster mediator (Queiroz), Maradona called the world's attention to take part in this great sports controversy.

To gain eternity in the pantheon of football, to defeat an archrival at any cost, to rejoice in such a stratagem and to be misinterpreted as an atavistic manifestation of the anti-game may compose the bundle of motivations through which the interpretations of the *Mano de Dios* have walked and still are walking. However, the collateral and possibly more interesting effects of such a gesture may be anchored, albeit belatedly, in a Dadaist maxim that advocates the disorientation of the spectators as a way of apprehending aesthetic judgments, which are imposed on that which is ambiguously perceived as appreciable or not, ugly or beautiful. The most paradigmatic example are Duchamp's well-known ready-mades, especially the piece called "The Fountain" which is, in truth, nothing more than a mere urinal present in numerous public bathrooms. These works elide frontiers and dislocate a work of art from its canons by resemanticizing a common object, imposing that "the only personal intervention [of the artist] possible in a work would be the choice" (Ades, 1991, p. 86, our translation) as a strategy or tactic of disorientation.

A disconcerting, misleading gesture, a mixture of refined football technique and a crude, unsportsmanlike attitude, the choice of "bad technique" in *Mano de Dios* lends itself to recalling the most ironic attitudes of the wasteland and its anonymous cohabitants, places where cheating is rife as constitutive of the game, where seriousness is imposed by the limits of common play, among common people. *Mano de Dios*, therefore, bothers us precisely because it falls short of the expectations of those who, accustomed to domesticating their heroes, expect from them only correctness,

---

[15] See Youtube as "La mano de dios' al estilo lego" <https://youtu.be/5_c_m5eDe-i>. Or at <www. google.com/search?q=la+mano+de+dios+ao+estilo+lego&rlz=1c1nhXl_en-brbr702br702& sxsrf=acYbGntXrQWsYcreDveldzsK7fceaDenZQ:1,573,298,388,610&source=lnms&tbm= isch&sa=X&ved=0ahuKewicsnccgd3lahWbhrkGhX0YameQ_auieygc&biw=1350&bih=608>.

wisdom, fairness, to channel the technical potential in the quantitative production of the football spectacle.

Maradona, in a gesture of fractions of a second, frustrates the sports establishment by revealing his irony, just as did Picabia, another Dadaist, who wrote the following thought a hundred years ago:

> You are always in search of an emotion that has been felt before, just as you like to get back from the dyer an old pair of trousers, which look new as long as they are not looked at too closely. Artists are like dyers. They don't let themselves be ensnared by them. The real modern works of art are not made by artists, but, quite simply, by men (Picabia, 1920, p. 44, our translation).

Another image of Maradona on the internet is closer to that of *Pelé, the saint* brings to the theme of the sacred the sacrificial dimension, very different from the contemplative figure of the Brazilian player. It also includes the presence of a halo as a sign of the sacred, but it is less definite and is attached to the player's head, clearly imposed there by some graphic technique. This image also hyperbolizes the *Pibe*'s corporality, containing as it does the iconic representation of the crucified Christ's body,[16] highlighted against a dark background, evoking a not so well realized idea of infinitude, emptiness and temporal suspension on the occasion of Christ's torment. From the back, however, Maradona's ordeal can neither be witnessed nor participated in. Hence, the fraud surreptitiously reappears in an image that was intended to be serious, but which seems more to find the star in a deep sleep rather than to externalize any form of suffering.

The references in this case are obvious. Hence, the lesser impact of this image, given the somewhat *kitschy* staging that precludes any notion of chance and displacement that so mobilizes the image of *Pelé, the saint*.[17] It is only an approximate representation, intended to be dramatic, but that does not capture the potentiality of surprise because it is made using the calculating coldness of computer graphics. *Pelé, the saint*, without any conscious scenic ostentation or obvious representation of the sacred, becomes more effective and mysterious. Therefore, the mystery can be seen more as resulting from the displacement rather than an immediate or intentional reference to any particular religious tradition.

The sporting sacred revealed an even more productive contrast between Pelé and Maradona, beyond their sports and political careers. Starting from these images

---

[16] Available at <https://mundod.lavoz.com.ar/futbol/maradona-y-la-historia-de-la-pelota-de-pla stico-el-dia-del-doping-en-el-mundial-1994>. Accessed on February 20, 2020.

[17] Other "conscious" and too evident attempts to use images to link the sacred to football can be seen in the article entitled "Swiss painter transforms Pelé, Zico, Sócrates, Maradona and other players into saints" (December 19, 2004)., in which portrays aureole players: "Artist David Diehl has created 12 paintings in which he places the faces of famous athletes and former athletes like Pele, Zico, Socrates, Maradona, Totti on top of sacred images such as those of Christ, the Virgin Mary and other saints, Icons of football' aims to show the religious aura of the players. The canvases were painted on wood and metal plates, many of them decorated with gold." Available at <https://extra.globo.com/esporte/pintor-suico-transforma-decoratedwithgold>. Available at <https://extra.globo.com/esporte/pintor-suico-transforma-pele-zico-socrates-maradona-out ros-jogadores-em-santos-14877770.html>. Accessed on January 7, 2019.

described, it introduces the comparative notion of unpredictability as a symbolic substance that brings together facts, objects, words and circumstances that are not under the objectifying lens of the relations of cause and effect. Hence its enormous efficacy as an iconclash. Unpredictability, it is worth recalling and was central for a long time to the football techniques of both Pelé and Maradona, who were seen across the globe as the principal representatives of the South American corporal "magic."

The Bowlegged Angel

We hardly find representations of a sanctified (or diabolized) Mané Garrincha. As an angel, he would be hierarchically inferior to the saints, therefore more complicit with men. This is revealed in the abundance of images that stop at his bowlegs, images that suggest the effects of an improbable physicality, a special phenomenon of nature to express in abundance his excessively human nature. He is, however, a human who should, due to his physical condition, have been banned from playing sports.

As an angel Mané is above the ball, not next to it on the ground, nor even below it, a routine situation found in a game where the ball is permanently thrown from one side to the other, over the top, as they say, either through the disastrous kicks and the clumsy dodges of the defenders, either by throws or plays, more plastic and valued situations, provided they are well executed.

To approach the representation of an angel Mané is to impose the notion of infinitude, that is, continuous, multidirectional displacement, which then produces another form of symbolic displacement: from the categories time and space so appeased by the laws of the game to the effects of a singular sportive surrealism that arose from the feet of Garrincha, a master in making the improbable into something so simple.

But even the most canonical representations of surrealism at their most dreamlike—some of which are nothing more than a regression to pre-Cubist forms, according to Duarte (1995)—Magritte's beautiful, winged images did not fully represent this overly diluted current in painters like Salvador Dalí. Their images would not serve to totalize or convincingly capture the restlessness of Garrincha's playing style that, far from being excessive, was hyper-representational and literary. It seemed to suggest something more pre-logical, antiverbal and sublime that evaded the beautiful while being compared to other surreal experiences.

Garrincha's game was not inebriated by the excess of rehearsed moves and symmetrical and precise juggling. Nor did he hide the ball like a magician. It was almost a mediunic automatism that imposed itself on the body, which was the seat of all the creative potential of his football. The obviousness of the almost unattainable dribbles was given to the "space that was his own." That is why he did not waste "time with the slowness of reasoning, he did not [suffer] the temptation of deviations in the path of intelligence" (Campos, 2000, p. 28). The dribbling seemed to be born before the nature of his irrepressible physical complexion, which beforehand already intimidated the opponent by displacing in him not only his ambiguous body, but above all, in the hierarchy that imposed itself on the ways of thinking about playing. It is as if we could affirm that, when thinking in front of Mané, any adversary ended up at the mercy of his fatal feints. Pure energy detached from his body to be accountable more to sensibility than to reason.

For some, he intimidated the very elitist and deterministic notion of the athletic body present in football. Galeano (1996, p. 28) tells that when Garrincha started to play football, the doctors disappointed him. They diagnosed that those crooked legs would allow him to become a sportsman. He was a poor young man, with childish behavior, who as a child had had polio and gone hungry. An ignorant and lame young man, with an S-shaped spine and both legs crooked to the same side.

Insisting on the idea of seeing in Mané the corporal performance of some "sporting surrealism," through the automatism of the creative luxury of his dribbling, perhaps his style would be closer to the apparently "simple" forms and economy of lines of a Miró, the one among other painters who knew best how to understand or practice a surrealism dictated by the games of the most radical alterities. He elevated the surreal perspective not as a hallucinatory dimension of some omnipresent self (a cheesy sacred), nor explorations of intimate landscapes or obvious superimpositions of contrary elements and elusive sexual symbolism, but rather by the continuous, experimental play with the otherness he encountered along the way: "Strictly visual and antiliterary Miró's poetics places him alongside the free trace of the child and the supposedly illogical gesture of the insane" (Venâncio Filho, 1995, September 4, our translation).

That could also help explain Mané's inexplicable calmness in the face of the most fearsome of adversaries. His was an attitude that could never be interpreted as innocence, ignorance (in the intellectual sense of the word) or disdain, but rather pity before the difference cannibalized by his football. Preying on adversaries, and not necessarily participating in the political ethics of *parliamentarization* that Western civilizational life imposed (Elias, 1992) on modern consciences, left him below or beyond the ethical and political limits of what is defined as sport itself.

Here, the approximations with the universes transfigured in the ideation of the other present in the surrealist oneiric domain cease. Radicalizing his corporeal relationship with the other, with the unconscious or illusionist mediations, Mané gave way to presentification, to corporality, to the domain of form, to the body as the seat of codes that access the interaction with the other.

For Mané, it was not enough to defeat his adversaries by his dribbling. No, his aim was to produce in the body of the other a physical and psychological dislocation of meaning. That is why Garrincha called all of his opponents by the name of João, which in Brazil is a reference to *João Bobo*, the traditional child's punching toy that swings from side to side without ever escaping the punches. Garrincha made all his adversaries topple over when faced with his dribbles on the field. They became like nobody subjugated by the Garrincha effect. Nevertheless, the goal was aimed, the goal is (was) necessary,[18] but not at the expense of the productivist compulsion of the game as entertainment.

---

[18] As Paulo Mendes Campos claims in a book with the same title.

We can freely associate between Garrincha's feet (see Fig. 15.2) with images from *Abaporu*, a painting in which the dimensions of the character's feet invade and stand out throughout the canvas. A man who eats people, the *Abaporu,* by painter and modernist Tarsila do Amaral, a well-known artist cultivated in the intellectual avant-garde of the early twentieth century, represents the unconscious monsters recounted told by black women in their childhood. *Abaporu* would be an exercise in Brazilian surrealism, anchored in a sociology of miscegenation celebrated by Gilberto Freyre, presented to Oswald de Andrade and that went on to inspire the anthropophagic literary movement, followed by musical tropicalism (Caetano Veloso, Gilberto Gil among others), and some aesthetic movements, such as the Oficina Theatre by playwright José Celso Martinez Corrêa.

He who eats people, playing at being a football player, Abapuru is perhaps the best painting to define Garrincha, being the one who placed his body and his corporality at the disposal of the sporting sacred. His surrealism in sports differs from the colorful reminiscences of Tarsila that set up an immanent cannibalism. Most of the time he was portrayed in black and white, like the colors of his favorite team, Botafogo de Futebol e Regatas. When passing over opponents lying on the ground, Garrincha also devoured them in his path toward the goal.

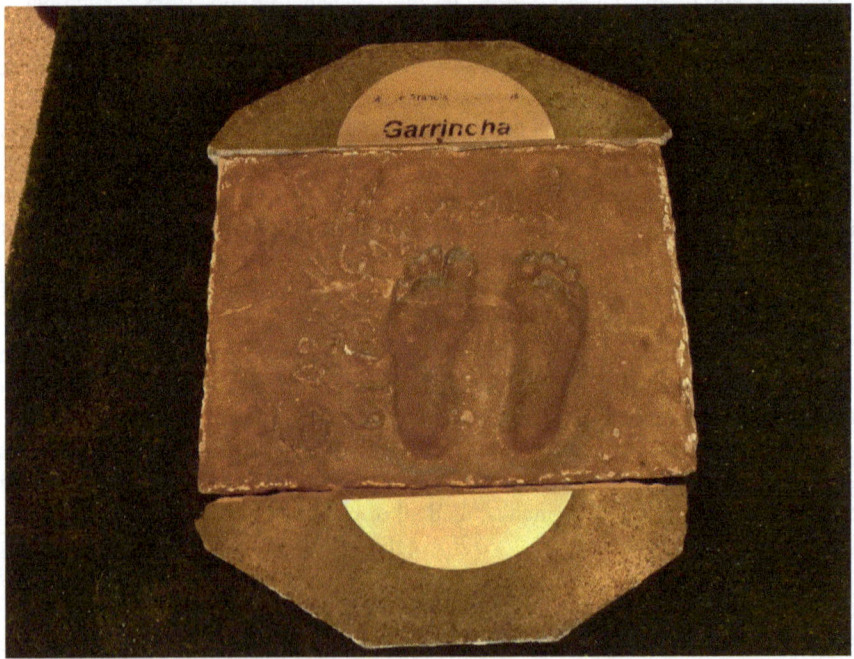

Fig. 15.2 Cast of Garrincha's feet on the Maracanã Stadium's Walk of Fame. Photo: Sérgio Settani Giglio

Final Considerations: The Sporting Sacred

In the sporting sacred, what we see in abundance is the continuous interplay of the objects of faith put at the service of the intrinsically corporal gestures of football. They are prostrations, reverences, ablutions of bodies, products and producers of individualized spaces of belief. They are marked, scarred, tattooed, covered, exhausted bodies, which give flow and establish the subtle relationship between the materiality of the game and the ineffable perception of the extraordinary.

In the popular domain, the presence of the religious multiverse in football is abundant and exceeds the most institutionalized forms, achieving the sphere of the sacred, but not any sacred but straining the secular universe of the game. The search for this sacred in the players' gestures, in the cries and chants from the stands, in the fans' corporality, in the manipulated objects and ready-mades, or in the images, expresses decisive moments of ecstasy and affliction. In short, they are captured by the media and ubiquitously experienced by the fans throughout the vast reaches of the country wherever there is a field, a ball and people willing to feel the strong and contradictory, overwhelmingly human, emotions of football.

The elevated concept here, therefore, would be that of the sacred rather than that of religiosity itself, which, if mobilized, could lead us back to some more institutional notion of a sacred image collected in churches, temples, *terreiros*, or imposed by the acute religious controversies that animate stern proselytizing conflicts and often intolerant (Giumbelli, 2002), which achieved the order of iconoclastic reason rather than objects.

The images of the sporting sacred mobilize and spread through other symbolic repertoires, hybrid and elusive, corporal, image above all, since they simultaneously express seriousness and jocularity. This sacred certainly feeds on religiosity but also on other forms of sacredness inherent in the mismatches that only the notion of power as concentration and unequal management of exceptional qualities can capture so well.

The sacred, made secular, is able to almost irresponsibly elevate a player to the condition of saint or king, an instant or event to the condition of saga (Sahlins, 2005), a mistake to redemption or suffering, a swear word or war cry fired from the stands to forms of prayer.

Moreover, such hybridity works both ways and what has been made sacred can quickly be converted into the profane, or what is worse, can be demonized. What is cheered one moment is booed the next. This instability and doubt are what feeds the sportive becoming of each fan in front of his idols. Are we going to win or lose? Are we going to stay or are we going to fall? Is he injured or faking it? A genius or a beast? And it is from this inconclusive and dissimulating game that the powers of this *sporting sacred* spares no effort to manipulate heterocycle elements in the production of amalgams. Bundles of meanings thrive. Sacralizing in football, in short, is independent of the forms of adherence to specific religious denominations, although they appear and should not be obliterated precisely because they release the most reifying acts of faith, which then spread transfigured in the condition of gestures, plays, techniques, fans, objects (halos, crowns, wings, mantles, etc.), images (cartoons, comic strips, photographs) and performances on and off the field. It is the very nature of the symbolic role in creating the ineffable and the transcendent that is inherent to the mysteries of football.

References

Ades, D. (1991). Dadá e surrealismo. In N. Stangos (Ed.), *Conceitos da arte moderna* (pp. 81–89). Jorge Zahar.
Barbosa, A., & Cunha, E. T. (2006). *Antropologia e imagem.* Jorge Zahar.
Caillois, R. (1988). *O homem e o sagrado.* Lisboa: Edições 70. (Original work published 1939–1950).
Campos, P. M. (2000). Mané Garrincha. In *O gol é necessário. Crônicas esportivas* (pp. 23–29). Rio de Janeiro: Civilização Brasileira.
Duarte, P. S. (1995). Gravuras e obras gráficas. *Catálogo da Mostra Miró* (p. 6).
Elias, N. (1992). *Em busca da excitação.* Lisboa: Difel.
Galeano, E. (1996). *El fútbol a sol y sombra* (2nd ed.). Ediciones del Chanchito.
Giumbelli, E. (2002). *O fim da religião. Dilemas da liberdade religiosa no Brasil e na França.* Attar.
Gumbrecht, H. U. (2007). *Elogio da beleza atlética.* São Paulo: Companhia das Letras.
Hertz, R. (1980). A preeminência da mão direita. *Religião e Sociedade*, (6), 99–128. https://edisci plinas.usp.br/pluginfile.php/3131843/mod_resource/content/1/Hertz_Preemin%C3%AAncia%20da%20m%C3%A3o%20direita.pdf
Hikiji, R. S. G. (2012). *Imagem violência. Etnografia de um cinema provocador.* Terceiro Nome.
Ingold, T. (2007). *Lines: A brief history.* Routledge.
Latour, B. (2008). O que é *iconoclash*? Ou, há um mundo além das guerras de imagem? *Horizontes Antropológicos, 14*(29), 111–150. https://doi.org/10.1590/S0104-71832008000100006
Leiris, M. (2001). *O espelho da tauromaquia.* São Paulo: Cosac Naify.
Novaes, S. C. (1988). O uso da imagem na antropologia. In E. Semain (Org.), *O fotográfico.* São Paulo: Hucitec.
Palhas. (2016, November 8). Quem é o artista que espalha o Pelé beijoqueiro pelo mundo? *Sonhe.cc.* https://sonhe.cc/quem-e-o-artista-que-espalha-o-pele-beijoqueiro-pelo-mundo/
Picabia, F. (1920). *Jesus-Christ Rastaquouère.* Paris Booksellers Publishers.
Queiroz, R. S. (1987). *Um mito bem brasileiro. Estudo antropológico sobre o saci.* Polis.
Rodrigues, N. (1994). *A pátria em chuteiras. Novas crônicas de futebol.* Companhia das Letras.
Sahlins, M. (2005). Cultura e ação na história. *História e cultura: Apologias a Tucídides* (pp. 121–178). Jorge Zahar.
Silla, R. (2012). Percepção, religião, tempo e nação, ou um parlamento de linhas. In C. A. Steil, & I. C. M. Carvalho (Orgs.), *Cultura, percepção e ambiente: Diálogos com Tim Ingold.* São Paulo: Terceiro Nome.
Silva, A. P. (2008). *Pelé e o complexo de vira-latas: Discurso sobre raça e modernidade no Brasil.* (Doctoral Dissertation in Cultural Anthropology), Universidade Federal do Rio de Janeiro, Rio de Janeiro, Brasil. https://www.historia.uff.br/nepess/arquivos/teseanapaula.pdf
Souza, D. A. de. (2018). *Pra frente, Brasil! Do Maracanazo aos mitos de Pelé e Garrincha, a dialética da ordem e da desordem (1950-1983).* São Paulo: Intermeios.
Toledo, L. H. (2019). *Remexer anotações. O trabalho de um antropólogo arguidor.* Editora da UFSCar.
Toledo, L. H. (2004). Pelé: Os mil corpos do rei. In J. Garganta, J. Oliveira, & M. Murad (Orgs.), *Futebol de muitas cores e sabores. Reflexões em torno do desporto mais popular do mundo.* Porto: Campo das Letras; Universidade do Porto.

Toledo, L. H. (2020). Garrincha, Pelé e Maradona: O sagrado esportivizado em tempos de icono-clastia futebolística. In S. S. Giglio, & M. W. Proni (Orgs.), *O futebol nas ciências humanas no Brasil* (pp. 354–380). Campinas: Editora da Unicamp.

Venâncio Filho, P. (1995, September 4). Surrealistas nos trópicos. *Folha de São Paulo.* https://www1.folha.uol.com.br/fsp/1995/9/04/caderno_especial/18.html

Chapter 16
When Does the World Cup 2014 Event Start and End?

Martin Curi

When we hear the term "event," we often think of some outstanding event, perhaps unique, that shall remain in the memory of those involved, including for the historical consequences that shall suddenly alter daily life in some manner. In the case of mega sport events, this imagination is present through the notion of "legacy," which is promised by individuals interested in organizing them.

In the Brazilian case, this legacy is expressed via the country's desire to become modern, developed and, thus, part of the so-called First World. One of the most renowned statements in this sense is that of former President Lula: "We are no longer second class, we are first class."[1] Former Sports Minister Orlando Silva,[2] in a book summarizing the proceedings of the seminar "Management of legacies of sports mega-events," wrote (Silva, 2008, p. 19): "The book also illustrates the growth and progress of the host country through texts that focus on economy, culture, social inclusion, environment, urban regeneration, marketing management, and research projects." Statements indicate a belief in the immediate and automatically beneficial effect of mega sport events for the host country despite the fact that studies presented at the mentioned seminar do not necessarily indicate the advancement and strengthening mentioned by the former minister.

Due to the little evidence of the promised improvements, opposition to mega-events has increased, and warning of the possible negative consequences derived their realization in Brazil (Mascarenhas et al., 2011; Sánchez et al., 2014). As an example, it is possible to quote the following excerpt from the *Dossier of the Popular Committee of the World Cup and Olympics in Rio de Janeiro*:

---

[1] Former President Lula on the day of the choice of Rio de Janeiro as host city for the 2016 Olympic Games (*O Globo*, October 3, 2009, as cited in Curi, 2020, p. 381, our translation).

[2] Orlando Silva, Minister of Sport from 2006 to 2011.

M. Curi (✉)
Fürth, Deutschland

© The Author(s), under exclusive license to Springer Nature Switzerland AG 2021
S. S. Giglio and M. W. Proni (eds.), *Football and Social Sciences in Brazil*,
https://doi.org/10.1007/978-3-030-84686-2_16

The first version, released in March 2012, drew a comprehensive picture of the situations of human rights violations related to the interventions of the World Cup and the Olympics, involving issues of housing, mobility, work, sports, public safety, information, participation, and economy. Unfortunately, about two year after that report, we can see the worsening of the situations reported.

(Comitê Popular Rio da Copa e das Olimpíadas do Rio de Janeiro, 2014, p. 7, our translation)

This means that a legacy cannot be so easily interpreted as positive or negative. In fact, it can be said that it is in dispute, as argued elsewhere (Curi, 2013). In other words, the consequences of a so-called legacy event do not occur from one day to the next, but rather depend on discursive disputes and historical evaluation, which begins before and continues after events. Previous quotes from defenders and opponents of mega-events date back to 2008, 2009, 2012 and 2013, i.e., long before the very period in which these were held. Therefore, one might ask whether the World Cup event lasted from June 12, 2014, to July 13, 2014—its official period—or whether it had already begun well before and continued after.

Events do not exist objectively but depend on cultural evaluation. Sahlins (1985) argues that history is culturally ordered in different ways in different societies, according to the schemes of signification of things. The opposite is also true: Cultural schemes are historically ordered because, to a greater or lesser extent, meanings are re-evaluated when realized in practice.

Let us discuss here the relationship between static cultural structure and social change. We are embedded in the cultural structure of our society, and hardly anything happens that, in fact and immediately, sensitively alters our daily routine. We live with our families, go to work, go shopping and get together again with our family for dinner. On the other hand, we have the distinct sensation that we live today in a different society than 10, 50 or 100 years ago. That is, in a direct comparison between different historical periods, we observe some kind of social change. But normally, such transformation occurs so slowly that we do not notice it in our daily lives.

That is, not every action is a historical event (Sahlins, 1985). Between August 24, 2002—the date of Rio de Janeiro's selection to host the 2007 Pan American Games— and July 13, 2014—the date of the World Cup final—there were many actions and incidents, but very few can be classified as events.

It seems to be an exercise of personal reflection, which can be questioned by the reader, that both the announcement of Rio de Janeiro as the host of the Pan American Games 2007 and the Games themselves were not events with lasting impacts for that city and Brazil. In this case, it is necessary to remember that the cultural importance of this multi-sports competition is reduced in Brazil, largely because it is considered only a continental version of the Olympic Games, which also explains its limited significance in other continents. One might affirm that this limited cultural significance also applies to the 2013 confederations cup.

Other moments that could be interpreted as major events—for example, the announcement that Brazil would host the 2014 World Cup or the games of this tournament itself—were not as significant in their entirety. Since Brazil is perceived as the "country of football," it was only a matter of time, in the popular imagination, that a World Cup would take place here again. At the time of the choice of the host country for 2014, there was only one candidate—Brazil—so there was neither competition nor surprise in the decision.

Brazilians are used to watching the national team's matches in World Cups every four years; the 2014 World Cup matches should not be considered, therefore, extraordinary events, with one exception: the 7 × 1 defeat against the German team in the semifinal. This match may be seen as an event for several reasons: its outstanding importance as a semifinal, the home defeat of the "country of football" and the score of this match, which surpassed all existing records in this sport up to that moment—largest defeat of the Brazilian team in number of goals, largest defeat of a cup host, largest defeat in a semifinal.

A second event with outstanding cultural significance was the announcement of Rio de Janeiro as the host city for the 2016 Olympic Games, on October 2, 2009. Unlike the Pan American Games, the Olympic Games have an outstanding cultural significance worldwide. As Brazilians are much less interested in this multi-sport competition than in football tournaments, such a choice meant something new, that is, something that does not easily fit into existing cultural structures.

Finally, the third significant event was the so-called Jornadas de Junho de 2013, in reference to the demonstrations that took place in several Brazilian cities during the Confederations Cup this year, mainly between the 17 and 20 of June. These protests represented a novelty in that the media attention of the sporting event was used by protesters to give visibility to their demand for social and political changes. Thousands of Brazilians participated in the demonstrations, and the importance of these acts was highlighted by the media.

The examples cited provide evidence of Sahlins' (1985, 2000) argument that an event, in order to be defined as such, needs to somehow go beyond ordinary action and interfere with cultural and social structures. In anthropology, we know several models of structure. Perhaps, the first reflection on the structure of a society was presented by Marx (1981), who was interested in material structures.

In this author's view, the structure of society is defined based on the position occupied by its members in relation to the means of production. In his analysis, the bourgeois would be the owners of the means of production, while workers would only have the labor power of their own bodies. Thus, the structure of society would be characterized by economic inequality. Social changes would occur through the redistribution of material goods.

Another model of structure was called structural functionalism by Radcliffe-Brown (1952). In this case, society is understood as a body in which there would be several entities with functions aimed at ensuring its maintenance. Thus, a social change would be an interference in this functional structure, for example, the exclusion or addition of an entity or the redefinition of functions.

The structuralism of Lévi-Strauss (1963) defends the existence of structural models in the thought and communication of peoples. These structures would not necessarily have a material base, nor functions other than that of structuring thought and making communication possible. They would not be determined, but strongly related to each other, by empirical reality. These structures would have the form of a model with symbols and their relations. Therefore, social change would occur in the case of reevaluation of these relations or exclusion or addition of symbols.

Finally, Geertz (1973) radicalizes this reflection on culture and says that man is an animal tied to the web of meanings that he himself has woven. It would be possible that this web has no relation with empirical reality and exists only discursively in the exchange of symbols whose meanings would be understood. In this sense, social change would imply a change of meanings.

Sahlins himself also thought about cultural structures and their definition. For him, culture would be a socially constructed arrangement of categories and would be in a continuous structural transformation. It would be a symbolic process. That arrangement would be the "culture-as-constituted"; but Sahlins calls attention to the existence of a "culture-as-lived," which would be the interpretation and the realization that each individual would make of the "culture-as-constituted." This individual project would be dominated by the individual's pragmatism and rationality that would influence and could even change the "culture-as-constituted," depending on some conditions. Sahlins (2000) points out (i) the improvisations that can be logically motivated by analogy, metaphor or similar things, (ii) the institutional freedom to do it and (iii) the author's position in a social hierarchy that gives structural weight to his action, makes it have more or less consequence for others.

Despite considering the empirical reality of institutional freedom and actor power based on social hierarchy necessary for social change, Sahlins (2000) interprets the social change as a symbolic process of the functional displacement of the relations between signs in personal action and the practical reassessment of signs in the famous "context of the situation." On the other hand, there are the considerations of Bourdieu (1987), who interprets social structure as a set of fields in which there would be disputes for the available capitals. Thus, the author emphasizes more the social hierarchy than the symbolic structure. The symbolism is present in his concept of symbolic capital as the power of a person to define a situation, i.e., to define the meaning and symbolic value of a sign. Social change, for Bourdieu, would be changes in the social hierarchy, and these could also occur through the re-signification of symbols.

We can see, from what has been said so far, that there are various ways of defining structure. In anthropological thinking, there is the hierarchical, functional and symbolic structure. Continuity will be given to the considerations of Sahlins, who agrees with the functionalist conception of institutions in our societies. But, in his view, these are not automatically beneficial for the majority of members of a society, so he questions their functionality, although they are necessary to organize concrete actions such as the Olympic Games, demonstrations or football matches.

Therefore, it is valid to propose an analysis of hierarchical, institutional and symbolic changes as of the mega sporting events. For one to be able to speak of an event, these changes must take place suddenly, to a considerable extent, thus being perceived by the members of a given culture. Sahlins (2000) also analyzes three moments of an event: concretization, unleashing of forces and totalization. Concretization refers to the representation of the central categories of a given culture by persons, objects or acts. The second element is the incidents themselves that the author calls unleashing of forces. Finally, the totalization concerns the consequences of what happened in the sense of the attribution of meanings to the event by those involved.

We can analyze the three situations mentioned above—the announcement of Rio de Janeiro as host city for the Olympic Games, the 2013 demonstrations and the 2014 World Cup semifinal—making use of Sahlins' theoretical considerations. The materialization happens, in the case of the announcement, through President Lula, who, in his speech, symbolizes and formulates a social ascension. In the situation of the June 2013 Days, the protesters on the street represent the people and their definition of Brazilian democracy. Finally, in the 2014 semifinal, the Brazilian team represents the Brazilian nation that mirrors itself in a European nation, represented by the German team.

The second element, which Sahlins calls triggering, refers to the events themselves: the procedure of the election of the Olympic City, in the first case; the progress of the demonstrations with their demands and the reactions of the police, media and politics, in the second; and the semifinal match between the teams of Brazil and Germany, with the defeat of the hosts by 7×1, in the last case.

Finally, totalization occurs in the attribution of meanings that can be quite diverse. It is questionable whether the choice of Rio de Janeiro as Olympic City in fact led the Brazilian population to evaluate Brazil as a developed country. In the case of the 2013 demonstrations, it seems that in fact they had the meaning of an active people who know how to demand their rights. But one must also consider that the definition of the meanings of the 2013 Days is still under dispute. Finally, it seems that the 2014 semifinal is being interpreted as evidence of Brazilian inferiority before the developed countries of Europe—therefore, a contradictory meaning compared to the moment of Rio's election as Olympic City.

The examples show how difficult it is to evaluate the meanings of these events and how the perception of a radical change is quite relative. In fact, the possibilities of interpretation offered here are subject to discussion and certainly many people will disagree with them. There are other possible interpretations. It is also questionable to what extent there was actually social change in relation to the hierarchical, institutional or symbolic structure of Brazil. It is not noticeable, for example, that the hierarchical structure of the country has changed. The symbolic discourses on Brazilian inferiority in relation to Europe and the ways to overcome this situation are not new. Regarding institutional changes, one can perhaps perceive a slight change in the sense of a gain in power of the Brazilian Olympic Committee and a more prominent presence of some social media.

Methodology

We observe how difficult it is to analyze changes in the social structure brought about by events. As a German living in Brazil and working with mega sport events, I had the opportunity to follow a specific part of the preparations for the World Cup, mainly involving institutions from Germany and Brazil. It is interesting to reflect on the strategies of these institutions, to what extent they were agents of the sport events and to what extent they caused or felt the consequences of the ruptures in the social structure.

A work was developed during the 2014 World Cup as part of a project called "embassy of the German fans."[3] This is a mobile service point, usually in a van, for German fans at World Cups and European championships. At the embassies, basic information about the country can be found.

In Germany, in every city with a first division team, there are so-called fan projects,[4] social welfare institutions for adolescent fans of these clubs. These projects were founded in the decade of 1980 as a preventive measure against violence around football matches. The national coordination (KOS)[5] of these projects decided to organize, as of the 1992 Euro Cup, in Sweden, the "fans embassy" in response to the violent incidents with German fans at the 1990 World Cup, in Italy, and with inspiration in a similar project that already existed in England.

I have a degree in social work from the University of Nuremberg, and I did my obligatory internship at the project for fans of the city of Karlsruhe. Thus, I had the opportunity to make contact with the employees of the national coordination, who knew about my migration to Brazil in 2002. They hired me to be part of the project of the embassies of fans at the Euro Cup 2004 in Portugal, given my knowledge of the native language.

At that moment, the supporters' embassies were no longer an isolated initiative of German institutions, but a project derived from the initiative of seven countries: England, Italy, The Netherlands, Czech Republic, France, Switzerland and Germany, which came together under the name Football Supporters International.[6] Thus, fan embassies were offered to several countries, with funding from UEFA[7] and the European Union, as a collaboration and exchange project.[8]

In the context of the present chapter, it is important to highlight the political interest in making the European Union appear to be a cohesive and peaceful federation. Certain international political intentions enabled the funding and, therefore, the project itself. In practice, the work was based on a lot of improvisation, given the lack of local structure; for example, Lisbon city hall lent us a room, to be used as a secretariat, which had no electricity or water.

I was invited again to work at the 2006 World Cup in Germany. This time, I was responsible for the Brazilian fans. The organizing committee of this World Cup, with strong influence from the German government, decided to create a marketing plan through which the world soccer tournament should be used to improve Germany's

---

[3] In German: *Deutsche Fanbotschaft*.

[4] In German: *Fanprojekte*.

[5] KOS—Koordinationsstelle der Fanprojekte: <www.kos-fanprojekte.de> .

[6] International Football Fans: <www.fanseurope.org>.

[7] The European football confederation: Union of European Football Associations.

[8] See the report entitled *Fans' embassies at international tournaments*, published by Football Supporters International (2005).

image. It was analyzed that the country had a bad image due to the historical events of National Socialism and World War II. According to this analysis, Germany would be perceived as unfriendly and hostile to foreigners. Therefore, it was imperative to present the host country as cheerful and hospitable.

This stance of the German government became visible because there were events in preparation for the World Cup that were funded by the Friedrich Ebert Foundation (FES),[9] of the Social Democratic Party, which was in the German government at the time. FES organized, together with the KOS, a preparation seminar in December 2005, with events in Hamburg and Frankfurt.

Before that, an event for Brazilian fans was organized in São Paulo, for which I was hired. The FES was interested in knowing what the expectations of fans from other countries were regarding the World Cup that would take place in Germany. In April 2006, an international meeting of fans was held at the FES headquarters, in Bonn. In other words, a German government party used its foundation to give a profile to the World Cup and thus make its political proposals explicit in this mega sport event.

This is the political reason why a comprehensive fan and visitor program with various elements was financed: *Fan Fests*, *Fan Camps* (cheap accommodation), *Helpline*, *Fanguide* printed and *-online* in German and English. In addition, fixed fan embassies were set up in all cities. The physical structure consisted of a container with counter, computers, telephone and information materials where fans were attended to.[10]

Thus, the posture adopted to receive foreign fans was quite different when compared to that assumed in previous championships. The *Fan Fests* were organized in city centers, with FIFA's endorsement, who perceived that this was yet another space to place advertisements. The World Cup Organizing Committee wanted to give a good reception to all fans, even to those without tickets and with little money, and, therefore, created accommodation options and train tickets at affordable prices. The fan was no longer seen as a threat, but as a welcome visitor.

The program aimed at the welfare of fans and visitors was only possible because it met, on the one hand, the political and economic interests of the institutions involved—as FIFA, German government, German football federation, coordination of fan projects, World Cup Organizing Committee—and, on the other hand, the interests of German traders. In addition, there was an infrastructure and know-how to organize it. The funding was guaranteed by the German government and the German Football Association.

For the 2008 tournaments in Austria and Switzerland, 2010 in South Africa and 2012 in Poland and Ukraine, I was not invited, but I know that there were fan embassies and other offers such as *Fan Fests*. It was already the beginning of the preparation for the 2014 World Cup.

---

[9] For more information: <www.fes.org.br>.

[10] See the report entitled *Welcome Fans—The World Cup 2006 fan and visitor programme*, published by the coordination of fan projects (KOS, 2006).

The 2014 World Cup

In 2012, the German consulate in Rio de Janeiro invited me to some events. The first ones I remember were the broadcasts of the German national team's Euro Cup matches on big screens in the Germania society. Later, I received invitations to the celebration of the National Day of Germany, at the consul's residence,[11] where I was introduced to several employees of the consulate, the Goethe Institute, German journalists and other members of the German community in Rio de Janeiro.

In 2013 and 2014, the year of "Germany in Brazil" was organized by the federal association of German industry (BDI), the Goethe Institute and the German government, with the support of several German and Brazilian companies and institutions. The project promoted events of several natures in the cultural, scientific, political and other areas, presenting Germany to Brazilians. The most prominent ones were the lighting of the Christ the Redeemer monument with the colors of the German flag and the parade of the samba school Unidos da Tijuca with the theme "Germany," in Carnival 2013.

Still in 2012, the Goethe Institute Rio got together to prepare a cultural program that, among other events, included a series of lectures with soccer as a theme, an art exhibition about this sport with the title "the game only finishes when it ends," and the *KulturTour*, a truck that traveled all over Brazil promoting cultural presentations. In May 2014, I published, with two colleagues, the *Pequeno dicionário do futebol alemão e brasileiro* (Little dictionary of German and Brazilian football), funded by the German consulate in Rio de Janeiro, the Goethe Institute Rio, the alliance of Ruhr universities and DAAD (German research funding). The launches took place at the football seminar in São Paulo and at the Goethe Institute in Rio de Janeiro.

The choice of Brazil as a guest country for the Frankfurt book fair, in 2013, and the invitation to Germany to participate in the book biennale, in Rio de Janeiro, that same year, were also important elements. At the Frankfurt book fair, the German football federation organized a stand called "culture stadium," with several roundtables, two of which I participated in, talking about Brazilian football. As part of the event, a football match was held between two teams of writers, one Brazilian and one German. These players/writers presented texts and poems at the culture stadium.

These events of the year of "Germany in Brazil" can be interpreted as a *marketing* plan to expand relations between the two countries and improve Germany's image in the perception of Brazilians, taking advantage of the World Cup. This small sample, based on my own experiences, shows the complexity of this strategy, which involved the participation of a wide range of institutions.

At the end of 2013, my conversations with the KOS began to organizing the fans' embassy for the following year's World Cup. Once again, the national coordination team found partners to make the project feasible. In this case, the fact that the Society for International Cooperation (GIZ),[12] a German state-owned company that carries out international projects for the government of its country, mainly the Ministry of

---

[11] German Unity Day, October 3.

[12] Available at <https://www.giz.de/en/html/index.html>. Accessed on March 19, 2020.

Foreign Affairs, made it much easier, for international cooperation, to support sports projects, one of the investment countries was Brazil.[13]

In 2014, GIZ organized an exchange between fans from Germany and Brazil. In January of that year, young fans from Berlin, Düsseldorf, Dortmund and Augsburg visited the cities of São Paulo, Rio de Janeiro, Fortaleza and Brasilia to meet local fans. The group also included employees from the aforementioned Fan projects, from the KOS and from the association of German municipalities and social scientists. The group met, in addition to Brazilian fans, representatives from the states and city halls, and Brazilian scientists.

At the end of March, the second part of this project was developed, with the visit of a Brazilian delegation to Germany, which I did not take part in.

Between February 9 and 19, 2014, the preparation trip, the most important part of the organization of the fans embassy, took place. A few days before, an employee of the German consulate contacted me to schedule a visit to the World Cup Organizing Committee (CO), in Riocentro, Barra da Tijuca. She, another consulate employee and me visited the committee, being welcomed (after passing through X-ray control) by the general manager of competition and team services—Frederico Nantes—and by the manager of spectator services—Marco Sansoni, an Italian who had already worked at the Winter Olympics in Turin. We presented the idea of the embassy of fans and asked for the support of the OC. We took the reports of the 2006 World Cup, documents unknown to them. There was no surprise with the project presented because, according to them, they had already received delegations from England, the USA, Netherlands and South Korea with similar intentions. In principle, they liked the idea, but said that the OC was responsible for what happened inside the stadiums, and since the embassy of fans would operate on the street, the responsibility was usually the responsibility of the municipalities.

Next, they called the heads of media and protocol, with whom the consulate staff was very interested in talking. The main interest was related to the protocol for visits of high-level politicians from the German government to World Cup matches. The organization of these visits, which are very common, is the responsibility of the diplomatic corps. The biggest concern was the fact that Germany has a president (head of state) and a prime minister (head of government), and the stadiums at World Cups are not prepared to receive two representatives from the same country.

The start of the preparatory trip for the fans' embassy was in Fortaleza; we then went on to Recife, Salvador, Belo Horizonte, Rio de Janeiro, Porto Alegre and São Paulo. The group was formed by a representative of the KOS, one from the German Football Association (DFB), two employees of the German diplomatic corps (one from Rio de Janeiro and the other from Brasilia), a German police officer, a member of the International Police Exchange Program and myself.

---

[13] <www.giz.de/expertise/html/9911.html>.

In general, we followed the same routine in all cities. We were welcomed by local employees of the German diplomatic corps[14] and, together with them, visited representatives of the city and state governments responsible for the local organization of the World Cup, the control centers with police officers, the stadiums and possible locations for the fans' embassy in the city centers and print shops for the printing of our information material. In Fortaleza and São Paulo, I met with city and/or state employees that I had already met on the previous trip with GIZ.

Thus, favorable conditions were created for the joining of forces and the sharing of costs between the German Football Association (DFB) and the German government to pursue different interests. The DFB wanted to prepare the World Cup to serve its customers—the fans—and to create conditions for the team to win the title; the KOS sought to ensure the organization of the fan embassy; the diplomatic corps aimed to improve its knowledge and its way of operating in the country; the police were interested in security technologies.

At the end of the trip, we knew, in general terms, the cities and had some idea of where to locate the fans' embassy. We knew who was responsible for the necessary permissions, and it was agreed that the German embassy, in Brasilia, would send official requests for the reservation and use of the place. The trip, which was marked by the meeting and exchange of many business cards—an intense networking—ended in São Paulo, where the colleagues from DFB and KOS took the plane back to Germany and the others went back to Brasilia or Rio de Janeiro.

In the following months, the organization of the embassy of fans was completed, with arrangements such as the purchase of tickets, hotel reservations and the space for the embassy. There was also another meeting worthy of mention. The interior committee of the German parliament came to Brazil to check the conditions of the host country of the World Cup. I was invited to have breakfast with the deputies, whose main concern was the security situation for German fans, especially after the demonstrations that took place in Brazil during the Confederations Cup in 2013.

I was impressed by the fact that the German parliament sent a group of deputies to gather information about security—these clarifications, in fact, were accessible through the work of German police officers who were in Brazil through an international exchange program and who accompanied the embassy of fans. They worked at the German embassy in Brazil and had the task of producing reports about the public security situation in the country. On the other hand, there were also Brazilian police officers in Germany and other countries.[15]

The World Cup opened on June 12, 2014, with the match between Brazil and Croatia (3–1). The first match of the German team was scheduled for 16 June in Salvador, so the work of the team from the fans' embassy began on 13 June in that city.

The team consisted of 12 people: one KOS employee, one DFB employee—both had participated in the preparation trip—another KOS employee, four local fan

---

[14] Consulates General in Recife, Rio de Janeiro, Porto Alegre and São Paulo; Honorary Consulates in Fortaleza, Salvador and Belo Horizonte.

[15] <www.interpol.int/en>.

project employees (from the cities of Magdeburg, Osnabrück, Gelsenkirchen and Hoffenheim), a fan manager from a German Club (VfB Stuttgart), three journalists (one had already participated in the GIZ trip) and myself.

For the execution of our work, we received from the DFB sponsors a van and two cars painted in the colors of Germany, the sponsors' symbols and the "supporters' embassy" identification. Our task was to place these vehicles at a central location in the city where the German team would be playing a few days before the match, keep them there on the day of the match and leave them there until the next day. The employees of the fan embassy were uniformed in blue clothing, provided by a DFB sponsor, to serve German fans on their way to the stadium.

A key instrument was a fanzine, a small magazine called *Helmut* containing information about the host city, the stadium and the opponent. It was distributed free of charge and could establish contact between the embassy and the fans. The content of the fanzine was also made available online. The three journalists on the team were responsible for producing *Helmut* and the Web site. Finally, we had a mobile phone number that functioned as a helpline. German fans could call if there was any problem, knowing that they would speak to someone in German.

With slight variations, this routine was repeated in all cities. Right after one of the games, the team of journalists produced, in about 24 h, the content of the fanzine, which was sent via email to the printer in the city of the next game. Then, we traveled to the place of that game in order to reconnoiter it. The day before the game, we received *Helmut* from the printer and set up the fans embassy in the city center. In addition, we were present inside the stadiums during the seven games of the German team.

Initially that was our job, but in fact there was much more than just the dialogue between my colleagues and the fans. To begin with, we always had four employees of the German diplomatic corps, of which two participated in the preparation trip, at the fan embassy, to attend to consular cases, and one was a press officer to document the project.

DFB sold tickets to the German national team matches through the "fan club national team,"[16] which also offered a "Fancamp," a cheaper accommodation near the city of Recife. The Seleção fan club used the fan embassy as a support point to serve its customers, placing a tent next to our van. We received, during the World Cup, several visits from high officials of the DFB and from different German governmental levels, such as consuls, ministers and managers from several areas of the DFB. In addition, police officers who had participated in the preparation trip also attended the fan embassy.

It is worth remembering that the fan embassy is organized by KOS, the Fan Projects Coordination, and that most of its employees come from these projects. They are social workers who do social work with teenage fans at a local level in Germany.

At one point, during the World Cup, one of my colleagues said the following: "This is strange. It has little to do with social assistance." This observation is quite

---

[16] Fan Club nationalmannschaft: <http://fanclub.dfb.de/start>.

significant, as it highlights the fact that the audience of a World Cup is different from that of club matches at local or national level. The World Cup is mainly for adults who have enough money to pay for travel and tickets to the tournament. This type of audience probably does not understand the work done by the embassies as being typical of the one they usually associate with welfare; on the contrary, the work of the fan embassy is far removed from their original idea of this activity. Why, then, does it continue to exist?

This aspect can be explained through the gains that each institution involved obtains with the project. The fan embassy is much more than a service to support fans; it is an ephemeral platform institution, which articulates the most diverse interests. For the KOS, it is a showcase of its work expertise and a tool to maintain good relations with the DFB and governmental institutions, which are the funders of this national coordination and of the fan projects in Germany.

For the DFB, it is a service to serve and maintain relations with its customers— a relatively inexpensive service, because the costs can be shared with the German government and the sponsors. The employees of the fans' embassy do not need a work permit and are dismissed after the tournament. DFB sponsors have, with the supporters' embassy, an opportunity to insert their brand in the center of the World Cup space, a place of media interest. It is not easy to place a brand in this area, because FIFA restricts the visibility of all brands that are not its sponsors. Nicolau Netto (2014a) calls this phenomenon "image control."

This media visibility is the reason why governmental institutions and high politicians seek the fan embassy. Moreover, it explains why both the diplomatic corps and the KOS hired journalists who documented the work and produced images, preferably with some famous character visiting the fan embassy. Thus, the German government can present Germany as a country concerned with dialogue with the host country.

The same strategy could be seen at the "TOR" kiosk, on Leme Beach, organized by the German consulate during the World Cup. Diplomatic representations from other countries had the same idea and also created their own spaces in several host cities. In addition, GIZ continued the work started at the beginning of the year with the exchange of fans and organized several events in several Brazilian cities, including creating an agenda with social projects for the German chancellor and interior minister (GIZ, December 2014).

The media in different countries responded well to the fan embassy because it provided it with great press material, such as good photographs and recordings, and because there were always a good number of fans around. Many articles were published in the German and other countries' media about the project.

It can be seen from these descriptions that there was a strong investment in a marketing project aimed at presenting Germany to the world in a positive way. Not that it is "only" about marketing, but this project is the result of a conjunction of existing institutions whose interests converged to carry out the work. The result was well evaluated by those involved.

Here, we described the strategies and actions of German institutions. But other countries behaved in a similar way. For example, the visit of heads of state and ministers to the host country of a World Cup is quite common. Other countries also organize fan embassies. The great example is England, where a supporters' association carries out a project with a profile very similar to that of Germany. In the Netherlands, the private company Orange Supporters Club[17] is the partner of the Football Association and organizes parties and the "orange march" on days of the national team matches. Brazil itself invests in a *nation branding* strategy using events, biennials and fairs, as Nicolau Netto (2014b) describes.

The World Cup as an Event

After describing the experiences of the mega-events, the Euro Cup (2004) and the World Cup (2006 and 2014), it is important to return to theoretical considerations about structure and event. Once again, it is difficult to see any significant changes in the social or cultural structure of either Germany or Brazil and it is therefore difficult to talk about an event. The various institutions described, such as the diplomatic corps, the DFB, the KOS, the fan projects, the FES, the GIZ, the police, the sponsoring companies or the various governmental institutions, have existed for quite some time and were not created because of the World Cup. The youngest of these is the KOS, which was founded in 1993. Considering that, in little more than a decade, it managed to develop to the point of playing an important role in the organization of the 2006 World Cup in Germany, we must admit that the KOS has made significant progress, a slow and gradual movement without ruptures.

Remembering the notions of hierarchical, institutional and symbolic structure, we can also state that none of the institutions significantly changed their social status for better or worse at the 2014 World Cup. No institutions were extinguished or created. Both the supporters' embassy and the World Cup Organizing Committee are short-lived institutions, but neither represent novelties that suddenly change the hierarchical or symbolic structure of a country. In fact, many Germans and Brazilians are unaware of the idea and existence of a supporters' embassy.

The analysis of changes in the symbolic structure remains. A common thread, especially between the World Cup of 2006 and 2014, is that German governmental institutions pursued the strategy of improving Germany's image in Brazil and other countries. To evaluate if this strategy was successful is, of course, highly speculative. I personally have the impression, without any empirical data, that Germany's image in Brazil has improved, but this change has already been happening for some years and therefore cannot be attributed to the World Cup.

What can be observed is, on the one hand, a continuous and slow development that changes structures gradually and not abruptly, which would lead to the rejection of the event concept to describe a World Cup. On the other hand, we can note that there are initiatives that consciously target the host country and the time of the World Cup, indicating its highlighted importance, which would be an indication of the possibility of using this concept. This description recalls Braudel's (1984) concepts of

---

[17] Available at <https://www.supportersclub-oranje.nl/>. Accessed on March 19, 2020.

time level, of short duration time and its events as opposed to long duration time and its structures. It is possible to propose that events also have structures. The three cited at the beginning of this text—the choice of Rio as Olympic City, the 2013 demonstrations and the 2014 World Cup—were announced and planned, most importantly, with a typical ritual structure. There were official openings with parties and speeches by top representatives of the institutions involved, as well as official closings with award presentations and status changes provided by these achievements. All these elements need to be, and have been, planned for the long term.

To this effect, there must be institutions that, throughout history, have structured themselves administratively and accumulated the symbolic significance required to lend weight to events, which is, in the events analyzed, precisely the case of the CO, FIFA, governments and sports associations involved. In the words of Bourdieu (1987), these institutions managed to accumulate economic, cultural, social and symbolic capital.

But part of this ritual structure of events is composed of a certain unpredictability, which implies the opportunity to expand the capitals at stake, but also the risk of losing them. This is what Sahlins (2000) means by "institutional freedom." At the moment of the event, the people and institutions involved assume the risk of losing. This freedom allows the reallocation of resources in a sudden way and with unplanned directions, allowing the entry and performance in a country of foreign institutions such as FIFA, but also of the supporters' embassy.[18]

But let us return to the 2014 World Cup and the report on German institutions that invested in building a positive image of their country. It is worth considering that all these efforts would not have had the same effect without the German team's 7–1 victory over Brazil in the semifinal and the victory in the final, which represents the greatest cultural capital. And despite all the planning, including by the team itself, these events were not predictable or controllable. The "7–1" has an immense symbolic value for Brazil, for Germany and, probably, also for other countries. It is the event that will be remembered and discussed for a long time.

Thus, we realize the weight of symbolic value that is culturally constructed, but in an uncontrollable way, and that in fact defines an event. The moment of the choice of Rio as Olympic City has already begun to be forgotten, and the 2013 Days still have a certain symbolic weight in Brazil, but the big event, including internationally, was the semifinal of the 2014 World Cup. That is, once again we see that there is a planned part and an unpredictable part in events. It is exactly this hybridity and liminality that in anthropology are considered typical of rituals (Archetti, 2003; Turner, 1967).

---

[18] In fact, the host state must legally allow the entry of a foreign institution such as FIFA. In every World Cup, there is a contract between FIFA, the host state and the local football federation (in the Brazilian case, CBF). Formally, it was the CBF that organized the cup and not FIFA. But, obviously, FIFA will not choose a country to host the cup if this contract is not signed.

Conclusion

This text intends to have shown that there are many people and institutions involved in mega sporting events that act in a planned manner over the long term. Many of these actions take place unnoticed by most people. Institutions defend their interests, but usually fail to significantly alter the structures of societies. When this kind of change is achieved, we are talking about an event.

Therefore, the concept of *event* refers to a short space of time with ritual characteristics, in which the values of a culture are being altered. The event becomes a mega-event when it provokes international attention from the media, populations and institutions. The term "values" is consciously chosen because we are talking not only about economic capital but much more about the symbolic power that is predominant in events. It also means that the beginning and the end of an event are defined by the ritual beginning and end of liminality.

It is important to highlight that *alteration* means that even the supposedly powerful participate in an event in a risky way. There is the possibility of losing their capital, and there are examples of this, such as the former governor of Rio de Janeiro Sérgio Cabral, the PT government, the coach of the Brazilian national team Luiz Felipe Scolari or some players of this team, especially Fred and Dante.

One way to protect oneself against the unpredictable nature of the ritual structure of events is to create long-term institutional alliances and thereby strengthen the social capital of those involved. This is what the German institutions I have worked for have done at various mega sport events. Despite the unpredictable and uncertain nature of events, it is possible to influence developments with strategic measures in small steps that barely alter the structure.

Whether or not this strategy has been successful depends crucially on the assessment of those involved. The power of definition is only partially in the hands of the institutions that represent the event's core cultural categories and that usually use some ceremonial, such as an opening or closing ceremony, a speech or the presentation of an award. Each individual that participates in events defines what an event is and how it should be evaluated. Thus, they define the legacy for themselves. This explains the very different evaluations of the World Cup.

References

Archetti, E. (2003). *Masculinidades*. Antropofagia.
Bourdieu, P. (1987). What makes a social class? On the theoretical and practical existence of groups. *Berkley Journal of Sociology*, (32), 1–49. https://edisciplinas.usp.br/pluginfile.php/2290040/mod_resource/content/1/Bourdieu%20-%20What%20makes%20a%20social%20class.pdf
Braudel, F. (1984). *O Mediterrâneo e o mundo mediterrânico na época de Filipe II*. Martins Fontes. (Original work published 1949)
Comitê Popular Rio da Copa e das Olimpíadas do Rio de Janeiro. (2014). *Megaeventos e violações dos direitos humanos no Rio de Janeiro* (Dossiê). CPRCO. https://comitepopulario.files.wordpress.com/2014/06/dossiecomiterio2014_web.pdf

Curi, M. (2005). Embaixada da torcida brasileira. Projeto de serviço social durante a Copa do Mundo de 2006 na Alemanha para acompanhar os torcedores brasileiros. *Esporte e Sociedade, 1*(1). https://periodicos.uff.br/esportesociedade/article/view/47957

Curi, M. (2020). Quando começa e termina o evento Copa do Mundo 2014? In S. S. Giglio, & M. W. Proni (Orgs.), *O futebol nas ciências humanas no Brasil* (pp. 381–398). Editora da Unicamp.

Curi, M. (2013). A disputa pelo legado em megaeventos esportivos no Brasil. *Horizontes Antropológicos, 19*(40), 65–88. https://doi.org/10.1590/S0104-71832013000200003

Football Supporters International. (2005). *Fans' embassies at international tournaments.* FSI.

Geertz, C. (1973). *The interpretation of cultures: Selected essays.* Basic Books.

GIZ (Deutsche Gesellschaft für Internationale Zusammenarbeit) (2014, December). Using the world cup to harness the potential of sport for development. Bonn: GIZ GmbH. https://www.sport-for-development.com/imglib/downloads/bmz-giz2014-en-german-development-cooperation-sfd-activities-during-world-cup.pdf

KOS. (2006). *Welcome fans*—The world cup 2006 fan and visitor programme. Frankfurt am Main. https://www.yumpu.com/en/document/read/5062639/welcome-fans-koordinationsstelle-fanprojekte/52

KOS. (2014). Die Copa aller Copas—Fanbetreuung bei der Weltmeisterschaft 2014 in Brasilien. Frankfurt am Main. *Kosmos 8.* Frankfurt am Main. https://www.kos-fanprojekte.de/fileadmin/user_upload/materialien/KOSMOS/KOS-kosmos8-2014-screen.pdf

Lévi-Strauss, C. (1963). *Structural anthropology.* Basic Books.

Marx, K. (1981). *O capital.* Civilização Brasileira. (Original work published 1867)

Mascarenhas, G., Bienenstein, G., & Sanchez, F. (2011). *O jogo continua: Megaeventos esportivos e cidades.* Eduerj.

Nicolau Netto, M. (2014a). Copa do Mundo e o controle das imagens. *Anais do 38º Encontro Anual da Anpocs.* Caxambu.

Nicolau Netto, M. (2014b). Os sentidos da diversidade e da modernidade nas campanhas promocionais contemporâneas da Embratur. In G. Pontes, M. B. Castro, & M. S. Santos (Eds.), *Diálogos interdisciplinares: Literatura e políticas culturais* (pp. 1–26). Eduerj.

Radcliffe-Brown, A. (1952). *Structure and function in primitive society: Essays and addresses.* The Free Press.

Sahlins, M. (1985). *Islands of history.* The University of Chicago Press.

Sahlins, M. (2000). *Culture in practice: Selected essays.* Zone Book.

Sánchez, F., Bienenstein, G., Oliveira, F. L., & Novais, P. (2014). *A Copa do Mundo e as cidades.* EDUFF.

Silva, O. (2008). A importância dos legados de megaeventos esportivos para a Política Nacional de Esporte no Brasil. In L. DaCosta et al. (Eds.), *Legados de megaeventos esportivos* (pp. 19–20). Ministério do Esporte. http://www.sportsinbrazil.com.br/livros/livro_legados_esportivos.pdf

Turner, V. (1967). *The forests of symbols: Aspects of Ndembu Ritual.* Cornell University Press.

Part III
Other Areas

Chapter 17
Football and Communication Studies in Brazil: Fences and Crossroads of an Indisciplinary Field

Édison Gastaldo

In the historical genesis of the contemporary world, and particularly in Brazil, it is interesting to note the almost concomitant emergence of modern sport and of the mass media by the end of the XIX Century. Created in England and exported worldwide by the British naval and commercial power, the sporting *ethos* became, during this period, an ideal of conduct for the illustrated elites all over the world. In the same period, the graphic arts and audiovisual communication technologies experienced extraordinary advances: photography, telephone, phonograph, cinema and offset printing, still in the XIX Century, provided technological conditions for the emergence of these two important foundations of mass culture of the XX Century: mass media and sports.

More than parallel phenomena, sports and mass media have built each other reflexively. The "spectacular" (that is, "to be seen") characteristic inherent to sports competitions and their power of collective mobilization (by the metonym that places nations or neighborhoods within pitches, tracks or rings) articulate perfectly with the emergence of offset printed newspapers, aimed at a large number of readers, within the urban expansion process by the turn of the Century.

In Brazil, games and competitions have been part of the national culture since colonial times. Although in the colonial and monarchic periods, the most popular games were linked to Iberian colonization and the rural economy, such as cockfights and horse racing on a straight track, modern sporting events emerged mainly in the urban environments, such as turf and rowing.

In the pages of the first mass newspapers published in Brazil, the last page was traditionally dedicated to sporting results, initially of races and regattas (Melo, 2016). In a few years, the supremacy of sports practices in Brazil was definitively conquered by football. Without needing the highly specific geographical conditions demanded by rowing, and involving communities, neighborhoods and associations in their collective game logic, football clubs quickly spread throughout Brazil at the

---

É. Gastaldo (✉)
Personnel Study Center and Fort Duque de Caxias, Rio de Janeiro, Brazil

beginning of the XX Century. The modern press, with its large circulation daily news-papers, contributed decisively to the separation of roles between two very distinct groups: the players and the fans, creating the basis for the phenomenon we now call "spectacle football".

Thus, this reflective construction of both phenomena throughout the twentieth century shows that communication and sport not only have much in common. In fact, the very form that both contemporarily assumed is largely the result of this interaction.

Nevertheless, in the Brazilian academic field of communication, the theme of sports is still somewhat marginal. Some indicators of this situation: For example, no working group has ever been dedicated to it at the National Association of Graduate Programs in Communication (Compós). At the Brazilian Society of Interdisciplinary Studies of Communication (Intercom), the working group "sports media" had a somewhat erratic existence, having disappeared and reappeared many times over the past few years. I would like to highlight here the strenuous efforts of José Carlos Marques (UNESP/Bauru) and Ary Rocco (USP/São Paulo) in keeping it running throughout this time.

In this chapter, I will seek to explore some elements of the intersection between communication and football, highlighting some of the disciplinary "fences" that structure this academic field in Brazil and some paths explored in theoretical and methodological terms, in communication and other related areas, such as anthro-pology, sociology and physical education. My intention is to present angles of research with good development potential on a set of phenomena to which commu-nication studies (particularly in Brazil), throughout history, have dedicated relatively little attention, considering their relevance in Brazilian culture.

Reflections on the Fields of Sport and Mass Media in Brazil: An Indisciplinary Approach

Sporting phenomena, as we have seen, constitute journalistic facts since the early days of the modern press, in the mid-nineteenth Century. In Brazil, sports practices arrived along with the winds of modernity, by the end of the XIX Century. In less than 20 years, slavery was abolished (1888), the Empire was toppled (1889), yellow fever was eradicated (1904–1908), and downtown Rio de Janeiro was rebuilt (1902–1906). During this effervescent period, known in Rio de Janeiro as the "*Belle Époque* carioca*", in addition to the slavery abolishing and the Proclamation of the Republic, rowing clubs (such as Clube de Regatas Botafogo, from 1894, and Clube de Regatas do Flamengo, from 1895) and, a little later, football clubs (Fluminense Football Club, from 1902) were also founded. On the history of the creation of football clubs in Rio de Janeiro, see Mattos (1997).

Since the practice of sports began to become an index of modernity and alignment with international elites, the coverage of sports facts and events became part of the daily life of modern press in Brazil. From the Sunday results of horse races and rowing competitions to the popularization and the gradual consecration of football as a national sport, there was growing space for media coverage of sporting events. In 1908, for instance, Jean Claude Bernardet (1979) reports that the first public movie sessions in São Paulo already presented local soccer matches. The entry of new communication technologies in this scenario expanded the already strong bonds between sports and the media. The beginning of broadcasting (particularly Rádio Nacional, in the 1930s) not only gave rise to a Brazilian "school" of live sports broadcasting but also raised the audience of soccer matches to millions, given its transmission capacity, which covered the entire national territory (Soares 2002). A not neglectable consequence of this historical moment of maximum media centralization in Rio de Janeiro—the capital by then—was the dispersion of supporters of Carioca clubs throughout the Brazilian hinterland, even today. The consolidation of international sports competitions, such as the Olympics and World Cups, also acted as a powerful stimulus to the development of communication technologies worldwide. During the 1938 FIFA World Cup, the first intercontinental radio transmission was made; the Tokyo Olympics (1964) was the first TV transmission to cross the Pacific via satellite; the 1998 World Cup saw the first international high-definition television (HDTV) broadcast; at the South Africa World Cup (2010), the first international TV broadcast in 3D was made; in 2014, in Brazil, the first broadcast in 4 K; and in Russia, in 2018, the first broadcast in UHD, besides, on the field, the VAR system, the so-called video referee (FIFA/COI), was adopted.

Thus, the convergence between football and media is historical and of fundamental importance for the understanding of contemporary processes of social mediatization of football. However, the academic field of communication still devotes relatively little attention to the theme, at least if we take into account the diversity of approaches in the area, manifested in indicators such as the small number of research groups registered at National Council for Scientific and Technological Development (CNPq), working groups in congresses of the area and number of specialized journals. As I have argued some time ago (Gastaldo, 2010a), the subject of football and sports—in all its multiple unfoldings—"belongs" much more to the area of physical education than to any other, by ample majority in all criteria above.

For example, in the Directory of Research Groups CNPq, there are only nine groups registered in the field of communication with the term "sport" in their menus, in a universe of more than 660 groups, of which more than 250 in the area of physical education. Among registered groups that include the term "football", from a total of 67, only five relate to communication.

I want to make it clear that there is excellent research and relevant bibliographic production on communication and football in Brazil, but that, in the academic area of communication, research on football and other sports lacks greater institutional affirmation, at the level of the relevance of the phenomenon and the quality of the existing production.

Despite the numerical superiority of physical education, areas such as anthropology and sociology have presented, for over 30 years, consistent and relevant theoretical and methodological production on sporting phenomena, a bibliography that exerts great influence on the field of physical education. The "social studies of sport", an expression I use to describe this broad spectrum of research, are essentially transdisciplinary (or "indisciplinary", as suggested by Luiz Carlos Rigo) and may also be found in the fields of psychology, literature, history, geography, education, etc. Thus, communication students who intend to review the literature on sports phenomena may need to "jump over some fences" to find more interlocution.

Some Theoretical and Methodological Paths in Research on Soccer and Communication in Brazil

In order to collaborate with students and scholars of communication who are interested in researching phenomena related to the football universe, I will comment in this topic some theoretical strands and possible methodological paths for the development of research on this universe in a communicational perspective. Obviously, this is not an exhaustive categorization, nor a catalogue of any kind. They are just examples of possible approaches and indications of relevant literature that I hope can be of value to students and researchers.

Practices and Experiences in the Football Universe: The Ethnographic Perspective

The ethnographic perspective is characteristic of anthropology and was originally employed for the study of societies without writing. For a good introduction to this method, see Winkin (1998). Briefly, it is a research method which consists of a combination of two techniques: "participant observation", the direct, intense and prolonged coexistence of the researcher in the fieldwork situation, and "ethnographic fieldwork diary", the detailed and systematic reporting of field experiences. Other research techniques are usually involved, such as interviews and the production of maps, photographs or videos. The production of an ethnography demands patience, methodological discipline and a rare research input: time. One cannot force the people in whose company an ethnography is constructed to trust a researcher just because s/he wants to, and building trust takes time. In anthropology, the conduct of ethnographies is grounded in a broad theoretical and methodological base; it is, so to say, the methodological heart of the discipline. For researchers in other fields, such as communication students, it is important to beware of frivolous apprehensions of the method. It is slow, laborious and full of pitfalls (on the "traps of ethnography", see Cardoso, 1986). There is no "prohibition" against doing ethnographies outside the field of anthropology, but it requires a lot of willingness and extensive complementary bibliographic and methodological training.

To investigate sports phenomena, the ethnographic perspective can be very useful in media reception studies with groups of supporters. Usually, the first idea about an ethnographic study on soccer fans consists of making participant observation in stadiums. There are interesting communication phenomena there, both face-to-face and mediatized. Several anthropological studies have been dedicated to examine the organized fandom, such as the work of Pimenta (1994), who analyzed the logics of the discourses of masculinity and violence of these associations, and that of Toledo (1996), who investigated organized fandom in São Paulo in terms of their political concert and relationship with the football clubs and with other institutions—especially the police. Another ethnographic work on organized fandom was published by Damo (2002), in this case in Rio Grande do Sul, in which he analyzes the lyrics of supporters' chants and other aspects of everyday life in stadiums. An ethnography that emphasizes the social use and the supporters' definitions of the stadiums architectural space—by comparing, from the users' point of view, the traditional model with the "arena" model—is the Doctoral Thesis of Curi (2012), carried out at the João Havelange Olympic Stadium, the "Engenhão", in Rio de Janeiro.

Another ethnographic approach between football and communication includes the reception of mediated football in public places, such as bars and restaurants where football matches are shown on television. I have conducted several ethnographic works in these environments, both regarding the daily life of club football in Rio Grande do Sul (Gastaldo, 2005) and in Rio de Janeiro (Gastaldo, 2010b), and during the ritualized period of the World Cup (Gastaldo, 2009, 2013). In any of the cases, the reception of mediated soccer adapts well to the particularities of the ethnographic method. As it occurs in smaller spaces than a stadium, one can easily carry out maps, countings of participants and interviews with regulars. The "entry into the field" (a quite difficult situation depending on the researched context) is relatively simple: Since these are public places, it is enough to go to the bar or restaurant, sit down and observe.

In addition, specific groups such as organized fans, managers, players, aspiring athletes and businessmen (Damo, 2007), among other actors of the sports media scene, can be researched by this perspective, as well as the productive routine and professional practices of radios, TV stations and newspaper (Martins, 2007), in the discursive construction of sport as a media phenomenon (Rial, 2003).

Talking About Football: Analysis of the Media Discourse

The pages of daily newspapers provide plenty of research material in discourse analytical perspective that is dedicated to football phenomena. There are several research techniques referred to under the general term "discourse analysis". Usually, the discourse in question consists of written texts, and for the analysis of journalistic texts, there is already ample and well-known current bibliography in the field of communication (e.g., Maingueneau, 2001; Charaudeau & Maingueneau, 2006). In terms of printed media, the chronicles and even the daily news about major sporting events offer a wide field of investigation on social representations, value systems, identity, memory and sociability related to the soccer universe. The sports editorial, for supposedly dealing with less "serious" topics than politics or economics, is usually less restrictive to journalists' personal expression, resulting in a journalistic style that is much lighter, ironic, passionate and metaphorical than those found in other editorials. In Brazil, the master of the genre was undoubtedly Nelson Rodrigues, who, with his unmistakable style, helped to build and/or consolidate many mythologies surrounding the memory of Brazilian football. In this sense, it is worth mentioning the book by José Carlos Marques (2000) that analyzes Nelson Rodrigues' work on football. Based on the reading of 350 chronicles, many of them unpublished in book form, this is a reference work for students and researchers.

Another important book is *A invenção do país do futebol*, a collection organized by Helal et al. (2002). In this book, I highlight the debate about another important name of social theory on football in Brazil: Mário Rodrigues Filho, Nelson's older brother and author of the classic *O negro no futebol brasileiro [The Black Man in Brazilian Football]*, published in 1947 (Rodrigues Filho, 2007). The book by Helal, Lovisolo and Soares criticizes the naïve adherence to Mário Filho's version of black participation in football by social scientists over many decades. Even today, themes such as Fluminense's "rice powder" (supposedly used by black players to look "whiter" to the audience) and the narrative of the possibility of social ascension of black players through football are taken for granted, when there are several historical and sociological inconsistencies to be discussed. I also highlight in this collection the debate about "sports idolatry", a phenomenon of interaction between media discourse and social imaginaries that, in newspapers, radios and television stations, mythify the image of extraordinary players like Pelé, Zico, Ronaldo or Neymar. This is an important point of convergence between media communication and soccer culture.

Despite the strong methodological emphasis of discourse analysis on reading written texts, other research techniques, such as semiotics or narrative analysis, can be employed in the research of discourses in other media, such as radio, photography, cinema or television. In 2000, I published an article analyzing the Brazilian narrators' voice-overs of the 1998 World Cup final, in France (Gastaldo, 2000). Five Brazilian television channels broadcasted this competition. Since the images were generated by French television, it was relatively simple (although laborious) to transcribe and compare the way announcers and commentators described what was being seen on the field. In this case, the humiliating Brazilian defeat. The unexpected result led to a series of discursive mechanisms of "consolation" of the audience by sports press professionals, synthesized in the title of the article, "The Champions of the Century", taken from a commentator's line: "We lost a game, but we are the champions of the XX Century" (Gastaldo, 2000).

In my doctoral thesis, done in 1998 and published in book a few years later (Gastaldo, 2002), I used another communicational approach about sports, apart from journalism. I analyzed the representation of Brazil, of Brazilians and of football in advertisements aired before, during and after the World Cup. The advertisements are a very interesting media object for analysis, due to their magical logic and relatively free of commitments with "the facts", being a vehicle of very significant mythifications, metaphors and hyperboles (on this theme, see also Rial, 1999).

Finally, in terms of narrative or discourse analysis, I would highlight the analysis of fiction productions, such as films, books and novels, in which football plays a prominent role. It is an object relatively seldom explored in Brazilian fictional production, but with great possibilities for an academic reading. As an example, I highlight the article by Melo and Knijnik (2009), in which they analyze the representation of soccer in two Brazilian films of the 1980s.

Voices from the Past: Historical Analysis of Media Texts

The nodal point of the articulation between communication and sports seems to reside in the journalistic speech about the sporting facts. The permanence of the printed page (unlike the volatility of the radio and TV waves) means that the use of old newspapers is often the main source of data on past sporting events. Considering the weight that, in the football universe, the past has over the present, the research of historical basis on the discourse of the sports press represents an important methodological contribution to the study of "myths" which represent and shape actions in the present, but whose "mythical past" is documented in the press and occurred less than one hundred years ago.

In the pages of old newspapers, we can find out details about Friedenreich's performance in the 1919 South American championship or comments on the Brazilian defeat in the 1950 World Cup final. Besides the already mentioned debate around *O negro no futebol brasileiro*, another important research to have historical press data as methodological foundation was Simoni Guedes' (1998) study on João Lyra Filho's writings in the 1950s and the debate on race and national identity in Brazil. Lyra Filho, besides being the head of the Brazilian delegation in the 1954 World Cup, was also a politician and journalist. The analysis of his texts allowed us to take a more sophisticated look at the terms of the debate between eugenics and miscigenation in the Brazilian intelligentsia in the 1950s, a period in which the ideology of the "football country" was being consolidated.

It should be noted that, as in any historical research, it is always necessary to critique the sources: The fact that a given version was published in a newspaper does not imply that the fact occurred exactly as it was reported, or even that it effectively occurred. The "fact" to be taken into account is that "that" version was published on that day. Factors such as the editorial orientation of the newspaper, the political moment lived in the period and even the idiosyncrasies of the journalist (that in the sports press often assumes the support for a certain club) can decisively influence the terms in which a given version is published in a newspaper. I highlight in this sense the Master's Dissertation in Communication by João Paulo Teixeira about the historic Carioca Championship of 1923, won by Vasco da Gama with a team that included black and mixed race players. Analyzing the sports pages of newspapers of that year, Teixeira (2010) questions several of the interpretations and narratives of

Mário Filho about the "racism" of which the Vasco da Gama team would have been victim, contesting even factual data, such as the alleged narrative of a generalized fight, with invasion of the pitch, to which the newspapers of 1923 make absolutely no reference.

Another interesting approach to deal with the football past is the so-called oral history or "life history". Research technique created by historians, but widely used by anthropologists and social scientists, consists in recording and systematically analyzing testimonies of people who experienced the events narrated firsthand. For a classic approach on oral history, see Queiroz (1991). As in any other research of historical analysis, it is always necessary to critique the sources. Even more so in a domain as nuanced by affections such as the remembrances of the football universe. Many good researches have been carried out based on oral history interviews. This technique is particularly important to bring to light aspects of the football universe that are not published in newspapers, for not being part of the dominant narrative. I highlight here, among others, the work of Reis and Souza Jr. (2018) on the vicissitudes of women's football in São Paulo and of Luiz Carlos Rigo and his group (Rigo, 2005) on what he calls "infamous football" (without fame, forgotten) played in the floodplains and in amateur tournaments in the far reaches of the country, in his case, in the extreme south of Brazil. This is a meticulous work to recover fragmented memories, which articulates photographs, notes, clippings and posters to the recorded narratives of the interviewees. A symbolic archeology of "soccer universes that only left fragments behind". But that existed, nonetheless.

In Conclusion

This chapter sought to present elements to think about the productive confluence between communication and football as a research agenda. After presenting the relevance of studies on the crossing of these themes, the three methodological paths outlined here are just a stimulus to reflection. Other possibilities are also productive, such as the research on the political economy of sports communication, analyzing the complex web of power relations between clubs, federations and media corporations; on gender relations in the sports media; or on social interactions in communities and supporters' blogs and Web sites on the Internet, just to name a few examples.

I would like to make clear the potential for theoretical development of the convergence between communication and football and its indisciplinary character: Without jumping over some "fences", one cannot advance in this field. My final caveat would be that, although there is no problem in being influenced by theories and methods from other disciplinary fields, caution and seriousness are needed in their use. To avoid the risk of "barroom psychology" in anthropological, sociological, pedagogical or historical versions, it takes more than a quick walk through other people's fields: It takes time, reading, hard work and qualified interlocution. The communicational perspective on football can allow developments that illuminate both what we know about football and what we know about communication.

References

Bernardet, J. C. (1979). *Filmografia do cinema brasileiro: 1900–1935*. Secretaria da Cultura do Governo do Estado de São Paulo.

Cardoso, R. C. L. (1986). Aventuras de antropólogos em campo ou como escapar das armadilhas do método. In R. C. L. Cardoso (Org.), *A aventura antropológica: Teoria e pesquisa* (pp. 95–105). Paz e Terra.

Charaudeau, P., & Maingueneau, D. (2006). *Dicionário de análise do discurso* (Dictionnaire d'Analyse du Discours) (F. Komesu, Trans.). Contexto.

Curi, M. (2012). *Espaços da emoção*: Arquitetura futebolística, torcida e segurança pública (Doctoral Thesis in Anthropology). Niterói: PPGAS/UFF, Brazil. http://ppgantropologia.sites.uff. br/wp-content/uploads/sites/16/2016/07/MARTIN-CHRISTOPH-CURI-SP%C3%96RL.pdf

Damo, A. S. (2002). *Futebol e identidade social: Uma leitura antropológica das rivalidades entre torcedores e clubes*. Editora da UFRGS.

Damo, A. S. (2007). *Do dom à profissão: A formação de futebolistas no Brasil e na França*. Hucitec.

Gastaldo, É (2000). Os campeões do século: notas sobre a definição da realidade no futebol-espetáculo. *Revista Brasileira de Ciências do Esporte, 22*(1), 105–124. http://revista.cbce.org.br/index.php/RBCE/article/view/757

Gastaldo, É. (2002). *Pátria, chuteiras e propaganda: O brasileiro na publicidade da Copa do Mundo*. Annablume; São Leopoldo: Unisinos.

Gastaldo, É. (2005). O complô da torcida: Futebol e performance masculina em bares. *Horizontes Antropológicos, 11*(24), 107–123. https://doi.org/10.1590/S0104-71832005000200006

Gastaldo, É. (2009). Ritos da nação: uma videoetnografia da recepção coletiva da Copa do Mundo no Brasil. *Revista Brasileira de Ciências do Esporte, 31*(1), 209–222. http://revista.cbce.org.br/index.php/RBCE/article/view/644

Gastaldo, É. (2010a). Estudos sociais do esporte: Vicissitudes e possibilidades de um campo em formação. *Logos: Comunicação e Esporte, 17*(2), 6–15. http://www.logos.uerj.br/PDFS/33/01_logos33_gastaldo_estudossociais.pdf

Gastaldo, É. (2010b). As relações jocosas futebolísticas: futebol, sociabilidade e conflito no Brasil. *Mana, 16*(2), 311–325. https://www.scielo.br/j/mana/a/zMLqFHnSgJtGfmXWmtCvyTR/?lang= pt&format=pdf

Gastaldo, É. (2013). O fato social total brasileiro: Uma perspectiva etnográfica sobre a recepção pública da Copa do Mundo no Brasil. *Horizontes Antropológicos, 19*(40), 185–200. https://doi. org/10.1590/S0104-71832013000200007

Guedes, S. L. (1998). O povo brasileiro no campo de futebol. In *O Brasil no campo de futebol: Estudos antropológicos sobre os significados do futebol brasileiro* (pp. 19–38). EDUFF.

Helal, R., Lovisolo, H., & Soares, A. J. (2002). *A invenção do país do futebol*. Mauad.

Maingueneau, D. (2001). *Análise de textos de comunicação* (Analyser les textes de communication) (C. P. Souza e Silva, D. Rocha, Trans.). Cortez.

Marques, J. C. (2000). *O futebol em Nelson Rodrigues*. Educ; Fapesp.

Martins, M. N. (2007). *Sala de Redação: Um estudo etnográfico das dinâmicas e estratégias de enunciação dos apresentadores* (Monograph for undergraduate degree in Communication), UNIFRA, Santa Maria, Brazil. https://lapecjor.files.wordpress.com/2011/04/marcel-neves-martins.pdf

Mattos, C. (1997). *100 anos de paixão: Uma mitologia carioca no futebol*. Rocco.

Melo, V. A. (2016). O esporte: uma diversão no Rio de Janeiro do século XIX. *Revista Brasileira de Estudos do Lazer, 2*(3), 49–66. https://periodicos.ufmg.br/index.php/rbel/article/view/494

Melo, V. A., & Knijnik, J. D. (2009). Futebol, cinema e masculinidade: Uma análise de "Asa branca, um sonho brasileiro" (1981) e "Onda nova" (1983). *Revista Portuguesa de Ciências do Desporto, 9*(2–3), 183–191. https://rpcd.fade.up.pt/_arquivo/artigos_soltos/vol.9_nr.2-3/1.5.pdf

Pimenta, C. A. (1994). *Torcidas organizadas de futebol: Violência e autoafirmação*. Vogal.

Queiroz, M. I. P. (1991). *Variações sobre a técnica de gravador no registro da informação viva*. T. A. Queiroz.

Rial, C. S. (1999). Japonês está para TV como mulato para cerveja: Imagens da publicidade no Brasil. In C. Eckert, & P. Monte-Mór, (Eds.), *Imagem em foco: Novas perspectivas em Antropologia.* Editora UFRGS.

Rial, C. S. (2003). Futebol e mídia: a retórica televisiva e suas inmplicações na identidade nacional, de gênero e religiosa. *Antropolítica, 14,* 61–80. https://drive.google.com/file/d/0B9HwgBRe_UoI cXd4LVI4Q2h6Mnc/view?resourcekey=0-jnW-cyhAxPxE2XkGIoLu5w

Rigo, L. C. et al. (2005). Memórias de corpos esportivizados: A natação feminina e o futebol infame. *Movimento, 11*(2), 131–146. https://doi.org/10.22456/1982-8918.2872

Rodrigues Filho, M. (2007). *O negro no futebol brasileiro.* Rio de Janeiro: Mauad (Original work published 1947)

Souza, Jr., O., & Reis, H. H. (2018). *Futebol de mulheres: A batalha de todos os campos.* Autor Esporte.

Toledo, L. H. (1996). *Torcidas organizadas de futebol.* Autores Associados; Anpocs.

Teixeira, J. P. (2010). 1923: Investigação sobre a existência de racismo no noticiário esportivo carioca. *Contemporânea, 8*(2), 28–42. https://doi.org/10.12957/contemporanea.2010.790

Winkin, Y. (1998). *A nova comunicação: Da teoria ao trabalho de campo.* Papirus.

Chapter 18
Sport and the Media in Brazil: Vices and Virtues of a Secular Marriage

José Carlos Marques

Introduction

As it is widely known, Brazil was chosen to host, in the second decade of the twenty-first century, the two major sports mega-events of today: the Football World Cup (in 2014) and the Olympic Games in Rio de Janeiro (in 2016). These facts, by themselves, would already justify the need to discuss the sport and its social implications in our country, given the imbrications that such events establish with the local culture, economy and politics. In the case of the communications field, the relevance is amplified if we bear in mind that the World Cup and the Olympics are currently two of the most significant events in terms of the advertisers' market and press agencies' investment in terms of media coverage (print, radio, television and Internet). Furthermore, these two mega-events only conquered the dimension they have today due to the media apparatus that was dedicated to them by media companies all over the planet throughout the twentieth and twenty-first centuries.

If it seems to be so easy to justify the presence of sport in our contemporary life scenario, why is it—sportstill today the target of discrimination by the Brazilian academia and even of a significant part of the communication market? Why is it that in the Brazilian scientific entities, with rare exceptions, sport is still considered a "minor subject"? Why is sport, in the TV medium, increasingly associated to the "non-serious" sphere of life, due to its approach to the entertainment area?

What we still see today is the result of the little prestige of research on sport in the field of communication and human sciences. Perhaps because the tradition of studies on the subject that predominated in Brazil in the 1960s, 1970s and 1980s, based on a neo-Marxist view of the sportive phenomenon, has preferred to highlight the aspects in which sport is associated to discipline and alienation, as a result of society after the Industrial Revolution of the nineteenth century. From this standpoint, sport would be relegated to a leisure activity, free time or non-working time, and thus, it would

J. C. Marques (✉)
São Paulo State University, São Paulo, Brazil

291

be kept away from the important issues that regulate social life, serving only the interests of the ruling classes. Although this critical tradition of Marxist analysis on sport has gained new contours in the last decades, it still seems to influence several sectors of Brazilian academia.

An example of this is the observation of Freitas Filho (1985) when he explains that the popular participation in texts about sports published in newspapers maintains a structural and harmful ambiguity: if, on one hand, the reader performs the exercise of discussing his micro-reality (but linked almost exclusively to the fate of his club or of a particular player), on the other hand, he does not realize that, in this exercise, he is being increasingly removed from his real world. Therefore, the alleged specialization of the sports discourse serves only to hide the discourse that would really matter—the economic or political contestation of the "public thing":

> Today, when we read a chronicle or a commentary in the newspapers the day after the games, we have the clear impression that the analysis is being made by a theorist, a deep scholar of the subject, when they are simply journalists who make them without, for that, having had the need to attend specific courses. The language and the level of complexity of the sport allow this kind of easy access to its universe, not closing its doors neither to the informants (journalists) nor to the informed. (...) Unlike other sectors, such as economy and politics, where the masses are not allowed access to its 'backstage', in sport, this is used almost in a compensatory way. (Freitas Filho, 1985, p. 55, our translation)

In the case of social communication courses, namely in Brazilian public universities, it is rare that there are subjects that establish the relation between sports and communication itself in their curricula. This only happens, in some cases, in private educational institutions, which usually changes their curricular grids with more agility, focusing on more immediate professional applications.

If the view sport receives from academia is still highly influenced by the so-called critical school, an equally discouraging scenario is dedicated to it by the communication market. The Brazilian journalism field has also grown and solidified viewing sports as a subject pertaining to an equally "minor" editorial when compared to the "important editorials" (Politics, Economy, International, etc.).

This entire scenario, however, underwent major changes in Brazil from the end of the twentieth century. The experience of a democratic regime, with direct elections for all executive positions in the country, ensured by the Federal Constitution of 1988, seems to have buried part of the commonplace perpetuated during the Military Regime in our country that football, for example, would be the "opium of the people"; i.e., it would be a sport at the service of dictatorships, as an element of numbing the masses. Furthermore, the achievements of Brazilian football after the re-democratization of the country and the new studies on sport conducted by researchers in Brazil as of the 1980s were responsible for resizing part of the view of the sport phenomenon in Brazilian academia. All this took place at a time when football was no longer viewed with such prejudice in universities, and at a happy coincidence with Brazil's victory in the 1994 World Cup in the USA. After this achievement, Brazil would participate in two more finals in the following World Cups: second place in France 1998 and the title in 2002 in South Korea and Japan.

Thus, since the 1990s, we have witnessed an effervescence with football due to the Brazilian National Team having reached three consecutive World Cup finals. It is only natural, therefore, that football would once again become the focus of advertising, the advertisers' market, the visual arts, literature, communication, the human sciences, and cinema in our country. Likewise, the sport intensified its presence in academia, especially in communication and humanities courses, as had never occurred before, especially in the universities of São Paulo, Rio de Janeiro, Rio Grande do Sul and Minas Gerais. Today, this is a trend that seems to point to the increase and solidification of research on the subject, something extremely healthy and necessary for us to move forward in search of greater quality and reflection around the possible relationships between communication and sport in our country.

It is not about any favor around the sport or football. Paulo Perdigão's (2000) account of the defeat of Brazil's national team in 1950, in the first football World Cup organized in the country, shows us the importance of this modality in the country's social bosom. This sport manages to be, in the country, the only sport that leaves such deep marks in the popular imagination—both in the spectacular victory (see 1970, in Mexico) and in the drama of defeat, the biggest example of which is the final with Uruguay, at Maracanã, in 1950:

> The uncontrolled and irrational eagerness gave way to its reverse, and the impulse of creativity succumbed to the impulse of destructiveness: there remained the anguish of feeling that the nation had died on the lawn of Maracanã, and also a hopelessness about the effectiveness of any collective project. It seemed a facticity, against which nothing can be done - the tropical version of Nordic nihilism, according to which life is a succession of obstacles until death, the final defeat. (Perdigão, 2000, p. 29, our translation)

And, under this aspect, we have that the mobilization of Brazilian fans around the World Cup matches attests well the approximation between football and popular culture in our country. In 1962, the newspaper *Diário de Notícias,* in Rio de Janeiro, referred thus to the days of the Brazilian team games:

> What is said... That truly Brazil is the country of football and carnival. That whoever doubts this can be very sure now with the transmissions of the World Cup that Rio, at least, stopped entirely to listen to the game. That even in the banks there were loud radios listening to the game and one could very well enter, go inside the safe, and leave calmly. (*Diário de Notícias*, 1962, June 2, p. 7, Second Section, our translation)

For the Brazilian press, Brazilian victories in football have always been elevated to the condition of important theme and deserving of highlighting, especially in newspapers with more popular appeal. When the Brazilian team won the 1962 World Cup in Chile, the newspaper *Última Hora* on Monday (1962, June 18), one day after the decision against Czechoslovakia, ran the following front-page headlines: "World Cup is ours for another 4 years"; "People sing the final victory in the four corners of the country: 'Even without rice and beans, Brazil is two-time champion!'".

In view of all this, it is observed that the printed media, in face of the fierce competition of large business conglomerates, could no longer ignore the power of sports, especially the economic mobilization arising from the advertising market in times of World Cup, something that intensified more sharply in 1994, the year of the World Cup in the USA. At that time, the newspaper *Folha de S. Paulo*, in an analysis by its ombudsman, reflected well this new posture of newspapers in face of the new reality imposed by football: "Sport itself has changed, and never influenced so much the behavior, nor created so many idols, nor launched so many fashions, nor moved so much money as in the last years." (Nogueira de Sá, 1994, July 20, p. 6, our translation).

Based on these initial considerations, this article aims to analyze the particularities of the coverage conducted by print, radio and TV media in Brazil regarding the sports scene, in a historical retrospective that dates back to the twentieth century and that focuses on the second decade of the twenty-first century. We start from the assumption that, nowadays, sports represent a phenomenon with several consequences, since different sports modalities—and, in the case of Brazil, football in particular—launch fashions and behaviors, stimulate the advertising world and the global economy, promote the emergence of technological innovations and create identity relations between different social groups.

The Print Medium and the Primacy of Sports Coverage

In the early twentieth century, sports started to occupy timidly the pages of the main Brazilian newspapers—at first without specialization of journalists, who worked in an amateur way. But it would not be long before the sports sections would gain more and more space, to the point of becoming, by the end of the twentieth century, the target of major sponsorships within the newspaper. After Brazil won the 1970 World Cup for the third time, the main newspapers of the Rio-São Paulo axis began to dedicate more and more space to the coverage of this sport during the following World Cups, even more so due to the massive investments that began to involve the televised broadcasting of the games. And, with the omnipresence of television in the mediation of this event, the print media needed to reinvent its work before the power of the image on TV monitors. One of the main resources used was the summoning of writers, journalists, singers, sportsmen and other celebrities, who started to sign chronicles and columns in the main Brazilian newspapers, as a way to compensate coverage that was intended to be increasingly objective and close to the referent. And the path taken by football between amateurism and professionalism in our country has its similarity in the trajectory of the sports press. Until the early 1940s, the sports columnist occupied the lowest position in the hierarchy of newspapers, and football kept a discrete prominence in the written press: "Like police journalism, sports journalism was a kind of bastard child" (Fonseca, 1997, p. 126, our translation).

When football matches and championships started to become more frequent in Brazil, around the 1910s, it was common for reports on the games to occupy a full page of the most important newspapers in Rio and São Paulo. And the report that was read was, in fact, a chronicle of the whole event: the weather conditions in the city were described, the spectators' state of mind, the flow of people around the stadium and, finally, all the moves of the match, minute by minute. The texts contained short sentences, the result of the game was never disclosed at the beginning of the text (there was no headline at the time), and there was a predominant concern with the detailed description of all the throws that arose during a football match, with the refinement of not forgetting any detail. The reports also showed a detailed description of the episodes surrounding the game—hence, perhaps, lies the fact that the term "chronicler" has been adopted to represent the work of this press professional who began to occupy himself with football reports in newspapers. In this sense, the chronicle is based on the sport in the sense of "historical report," through the use that the term had acquired in the Middle Ages. The texts about sports and football, in the Brazilian press, take on the character of chronicles in the sense that they represent, at the beginning of the invention of the sports press in Brazilian newspapers (when neither radio nor TV existed), a narration of historical facts according to a chronological order.

On the other hand, if Umberto Eco sees the sports press as the "denial of all discourse" (1984), it is equally visible that on sports journalists has been settled, with relative ease, the mantle of lack of expertise, unpreparedness and alienation. This image certainly comes from the circumstances that were the basis for football coverage in Brazil in the early twentieth century:

> The functions were not fixed or, even less, compensated. Most of the 'chroniclers' worked for free, just to have the opportunity to write in a newspaper, since this was their inclination, and to be able to, especially, defend their club, because, at that time, like today, the 'chronicler' had his favorite club, with the difference that, before, at that time, nobody made a secret of it. On the contrary: the shields on the lapel of the 'chroniclers' were common and their presence in the celebrations of triumphs was indispensable. The professional writer, but who made the press a simple "free job", could be both "chronicler" of sports on Sunday, as police writer on Monday, theater critic on Tuesday, street reporter on Wednesday, political observer on Thursday or - which was not rare - all this at the same time ... There was no specialization. (Neiva, 1954 as cited in Pedrosa, 1968, p. 9, our translation).

Although the quote demonstrates, in general, the conditions of amateurism that are the basis of the craft of Brazilian journalism, it is worth emphasizing that it is precisely in the figure of the sportsman that the stigma of political alienation is intensified. One of the possible explanations lies in the fact that the action of the sports journalist, a priori, does not have the power to cause significant changes in political systems or in more complex economic structures. The very matter that serves as fuel was seen at first only as contemplation or entertainment and did not require the professional of the area to correlate facts or to exercise greater considerations with political or economic circumstances:

> The sports reporter's greater freedom of action - more granted than properly conquered, if taken into account the Brazilian social system - led him to be considered as an alienated person, who would not know how to make the connection between his area of action and the general context of society. (Fonseca, 1997, p. 128, our translation).

As there was not the profession of sports journalist and neither specialization among journalists appointed to report sports events, the sportsman appears marginalized in the press. Any "focus," upon arriving at a newsroom, was assigned to cover sports or police news, as the possible consequences of his unpreparedness would not interfere in the "serious side" of the reader's life. Stigmatized, discriminated and having to fight for a better quality in their work, the sports professionals got organized and got together to found an association that would represent the new category. That is how the Sports Writers' Association appeared in Rio de Janeiro (on 1917, May 3).

Pierre Bourdieu (1983) also offers relevant analyses that explain why the concept of alienation has been so strongly applied to sports, as advocated by Umberto Eco. The French sociologist shows how school institutions saw in sports a way to occupy, at a lower cost, the adolescents and children who were under their full time responsibility:

> When the pupils are on the sports field, it is easy to watch them, they devote themselves to a 'healthy' activity and direct their violence against their colleagues instead of directing it against the installations themselves or tormenting their teachers. Undoubtedly, this is one of the keys for the dissemination of sport and for the multiplication of sport associations which, originally organized on a beneficent basis, progressively received the recognition and the help of public authorities. (Bourdieu, 1983, p. 146, our translation).

Anyway, as of the moment sport started its professionalization process, the same happened to sports journalism: the enrichment of football and its professionalization are directly related to the strengthening of the sports press in Brazil. As soon as sportive events started to acquire social importance, it became inevitable that the press focused on such spectacles. In São Paulo, for instance, the newspaper *A Gazeta* launched, as early as the late 1920s, a weekly publication dedicated to sports coverage. Later, the importance of football allowed the newspaper to launch, in December 1928, the 'Gazeta Esportiva' as a weekly until 1930. Tomáz Mazzoni, an outstanding personality in the São Paulo sports scene, ran this newspaper from 1930 to 1940, which became a daily publication as of 1948. *Gazeta Esportiva* ceased publication in December 2001, when its staff began to devote itself to maintaining a Website (www.gazetaesportiva.net) specialized in sports news.

In Rio de Janeiro, the most important sports daily in the last century was *Jornal dos Sports*, which became the property of Mario Filho (brother of Nelson Rodrigues) as of August 1936. *Jornal dos Sports*, surprisingly, did not circulate for a long time on Mondays—the day on which readers are normally most interested in news of the weekend's events. In any case, for several years in the 1950s, the newspaper's front page bore the inscription (our translation): "The sports morning paper with the largest circulation in South America".

The improvement of the sports press does not hide, however, some marks pointed out by Tomáz Mazzoni (1939, 1950). These characteristics remained for a long time tied to the figure of sports journalists and can still be widely observed today, especially in vehicles of lesser expression. Among these particularities, we highlight the fact that the sports coverage still maintains a club mentality, regionalist, partisan and passionate:

> Impartiality was completely left aside in the chronicles and commentaries on interstate games. In local games, extreme clubism prevailed. The chroniclers were not professionals, with rare exceptions. (...) They thus created a very partisan chronicle and there is no doubt that they are largely responsible for the formation of sports education in Brazil. (Mazzoni, 1939, p. 116, our translation).

After half a century, it is observed that the lack of professionalization and commitment of sports men still continue to surround the aura of the sports journalist. Even today, one notices that many professionals prefer to maintain a good neighborhood policy with athletes and managers so that "sources" are maintained and so that the paths at the clubs do not close to their performance—"journalists have to maintain friendly relations with players and managers of the major clubs, which often make them hostages of their profession". (Murray, 2000, p. 212, our translation). Even in journalistic writing manuals, the theme recurs: "The independence of the newspaper and the reporter must be maintained at all costs, especially when there are sports tours. No favors (lodging, payment of tickets, and others) should be accepted". (Erbolato, 1981, p. 15, our translation). And one of the biggest critics of this unethical practice within sports journalism, journalist Juca Kfouri, never tires of explaining the contradictions of the Brazilian press:

> In the Brazilian sports press, today, we don't know if the guy is a poster boy, event promoter, athlete's manager, press officer, if he works for a club or for a media outlet. You don't know if the journalist receives from CBF or from the newspaper. Without a doubt, there is a promiscuity between journalists and the media, which makes them get mixed up. (Kfouri as cited in Gomes & Carrano, 2000, pp. 49–50, our translation).

Criticism of the poor training of Brazilian sports journalists—a condition that accompanies them since the early days of football development in the country—does not stop there. The American journalist and Brazilianist Matthew Shirts has already referred in the following terms to the partiality of our sports press:

> The low cultural level of some sports chroniclers, the mediocrity of others, or the simplism of the pretension of the Brazilian general chronicle, establishes and maintains a rather high degree of alienation. One sees, in their discourse, a bourgeois vision of power, without the analysts themselves, nor the readers. It is a matter of reproducing in the football discourse the classist, bourgeois pattern. (...) It is maintained, therefore, within this vision, the intact system: the bourgeois values are strengthened. Any questioning, null. It is also necessary to emphasize that the narrative proposes models, patterns of life. (Shirts, 1982, p. 94, our translation).

Janet Lever, another American university student who was dazzled by Brazilian football after participating in an exchange program in the country in the 1970s, attests in the book *A loucura do futebol* (Football madness) the importance given to sports coverage in São Paulo and Rio de Janeiro newspapers. According to her, the Brazilian fan would have at his disposal more daily sports news than the European and American readers, considering here not only the specialized sports newspapers, but also those of general interest. Another particularity of the national press would once more prove the passionate nature of our coverage:

> Brazilian sports journalists are willing to sacrifice the privacy of stars to sell newspapers and fill all available space. American journalists write less about their private lives and more about what the players do on the field. (Lever, 1983, p. 114, our translation)

One cannot deny, however, that the sporting fact gained new dimensions after radio, at first, and television, later, emerged in the mediation of competitions, matches and events. With the increase of these two new media, print media had to set aside the mere recording of matches, as if they were minutes of results, to specialize their coverage teams. Moreover, the newspapers' sports language, with explicitly literary pretensions in the beginning, also needed to be modified. Thus, from the 1960s, we witnessed the development of sports editorials in major newspapers, which inhibited the specialized newspapers.

> When newspapers realized that, in terms of reaching the public first, they had lost out to radio and television, they chose a path that guaranteed their survival. They became, with great entrepreneurial and editorial effort, true daily magazines. It was then that research departments flourished in the major Brazilian newspapers. (Mello & Souza, 1986, p. 153, our translation)

This process in search of greater "qualification" of the Brazilian sports journalist would be intensified in 1970 with the launch, by Editora Abril, of *Placar* magazine, which sought to revolutionize sports coverage in the country. Using a more modern language, seeking new approaches in the treatment of athletes, abusing the use of images and escaping from commonplaces typical of the football environment, the magazine quickly established itself as one of the most important vehicles in the world of sports and started to influence the coverage of the main Brazilian newspapers. In this sense, sport, as a product of industrial and urban society, also acquires a structure equivalent to that seen in the manufacturing production processes.

Print Media Coverage and Competition with TV

After the direct broadcasting of World Cup matches inaugurated by radio in 1938 and by television in 1970, another significant change would only occur in 1998, when the Internet was present in the mediation of the event held in France: *O Globo, Jornal do Brasil, O Estado de S. Paulo* and *Folha de S. Paulo* created specific portals so that Internet users could follow live match results and also have access to the texts published in the respective pages of these newspapers. It is undeniable that the Internet, with the flow of information in real time, causes particular fascination in the sports enthusiast, who can seek, in national and foreign sites, the results and news on sporting events that are not covered by newspapers or by open network television (in this article, however, we will not dwell in detail on the influence of social networks and the Internet on sports coverage, since our proposal in this space is to analyze, for now, only the traditional media).

From the end of the 1960s and beginning of the 1970s, however, Brazil began to witness the predominance of television in the mediation of news and daily events. If before newspapers and radio (the latter on a larger scale) were responsible for keeping the population informed, now it would be the turn of a new electronic medium, combining image and audio, to become the great concentrator of modern man's attention at the end of the twentieth century. Bourdieu (1997) demonstrates how this change of axis happened and what are the implications for the printed media:

In the 1950s, television was little present in the journalistic field; when one talked about journalism, one hardly thought about television. (...) With the years, the relationship was completely inverted, and television tends to become economically and symbolically dominant in the journalistic field. This is signaled above all by the crisis of newspapers: there are newspapers that disappear, others that are forced to ask themselves at every moment the question of their survival, the conquest or the reconquest of their audience. (Bourdieu, 1997, p. 59, our translation)

There is thus a progressive retreat of journalism in the written press before the influence of television: The TV supplements do not stop growing in the printed media and even newspaper professionals give more and more value to the fact that they can also work on TV. In Brazilian sports journalism, this trend dates back to the 1960s, when the sports debate program *Resenha Facit* already congregated, in its time, the country's main football chroniclers: Nelson Rodrigues, João Saldanha and Armando Nogueira. This phenomenon gives rise to the analysis of the theorist and historian of literature Mikhail Bakhtin (2010), according to whom the media do not act in isolation, using only their own codification. For him, the media are not enclosed in their codifications, but contaminate each other, through the "plenivalence" of several voices: text systems cross and intersect, enabling the convergence of distinct discursive genres that cohabit the same space—hence the concept of dialogue proposed by the Russian scholar.

The newspaper, needing to reinvent its work in the face of competition from TV, begins to suffer from structural problems in this new panorama, and few manage to achieve commercial success without damaging its image. Bourdieu (1990, p. 75) takes as a contrary example the newspaper *Le Monde*, which would be at the same time large enough by circulation to maintain power with advertisers and, at the same time, "sufficiently endowed with symbolic capital to be an authority." This is the case of the newspapers analyzed here, which managed to gather and crystallize these two conditions throughout the 1970s and 1980s—although *Jornal do Brasil* went into sharp decline in the late 1990s. The written press today is faced with a choice: should it move toward the dominant model, that is, make newspapers that are almost television newspapers, or should it accentuate the difference, employ a strategy of product differentiation? This phenomenon, however, can also be framed in what Bourdieu describes from the logic of the "Trojan Horse": one introduces into the autonomous universes heteronomous producers who, with the support of external forces, will receive a consecration that they cannot receive from their peers (Bourdieu, 1990, p. 85).

In times of the World Cup, the investment remitted to football reflects well not only the importance of this sport among fans and common readers, linked to the popular sphere in our country, but also serves as fuel for those who see in this "elephantiasis" a major factor of public alienation:

The media fetishize football. They attribute self-sufficiency to it, a value in itself, intrinsic. They absolutize it. They justify its popularity as motivated by its magical power to engage people. With that, they try to explain the exhaustive football coverage. (Ramos, 1984, p. 34, our translation)

One must also recognize the position that football occupies in the context of other sports in order to better understand its importance as a cultural component in Brazil. TV stations are partners of the entities that organize the sport from the moment they acquire the rights to broadcast a competition. In our particular case, one cannot study football consumption independently from the consumption of leisure in general that it provokes in Brazil. Because of the capillarity that football has in Brazil (it passes through all social classes and age groups, and in recent decades has become an object of interest not only to men), this sport has gained a media hegemony that makes it the cause of what is conventionally called the sports monoculture of the Brazilian press. Despite the fact that this reading deserves further analysis and reflection, it should be accepted for now that football, in fact, has dictated the way in which the vast majority of television formats have focused and are still focusing on the sports fact. And given the passion with which football is treated in our society, this peculiarity has come to be accepted—and even well regarded by some segments of the public—as something positive. This is what justifies announcers, presenters and reporters shedding tears before the misfortunes of Brazilian teams or players in major competitions.

Likewise, it is accepted that TV agents can assume their partiality as enunciators of the sportive fact, assuming without problems their preferences in favor of the Brazilian national team or the national team competing in an international tournament. There is no "implicitness" in these manifestations: everything is declared, the game is frank and open, in a dimension that folklorizes these actors by the construction of images and hyperbole. The explicit display of a subjectivity that one does not want to mask makes the objective bow before the subjective, and the emotiveness manifests itself in a language that is almost always colloquial.

Given that, secularly, sports have been treated lightly and with a certain air of non-commitment by the Brazilian press (until recently, any apprentice journalist, upon arriving at a newsroom, was assigned to cover sports or police news, since the possible consequences of his inexperience would not interfere in the serious side of life), we currently have a fraying of this aspect of relaxation: television programs about sports have been "contaminated" by the sphere of entertainment through what we define here as "*standupization*" of presenters: it is necessary to divest the journalist of the formal air he maintains when dealing with other subjects; thus, the more similar to a middle-class viewer, the better. Designer clothes, sold in malls all over the country, become the standard, as well as the free movement around the studio (this also happens in some news programs, but they keep more rigidity and formality in the clothing options). The host of the sports program also tries to assume the role of a friend of all of us and therefore establishes an unusual degree of intimacy and informality. Even though there is a defined script, the teleprompter is no longer imperative—hence the opening for improvisation. And the recurrence to humor and laughter, which are neither new nor recent in the Brazilian press, is now configured as a seemingly irreversible wave.

We see, this way, how most journalists do not hide their partiality as enunciators of printed journalism and assume without problems their preferences in favor of the Brazilian team. There is no "implicitness" in their manifestations: everything is declared, the game is frank and open, in a dimension that folklorizes them by the construction of images and hyperbole. The explicit exhibition of a subjectivity that one does not want to mask makes the objective bend before the emotional, present in a colloquial language, although richly worked. This posture indicates the refusal of neutrality that journalistic analysis intends to impose on readers. Professionals who boast of being exempt or impartial are only assuming a mask that distorts their own craft.

What are the risks for the quality of information in face of this hybridization of the treatment that sports have been receiving on Brazilian television? In our view, entertaining and informing are not necessarily antagonistic actions. The problem lies in the nature and configuration of information and entertainment. When the main purpose of a television product is to seek audience through humor and laughter, there is the risk of the final result not being funny at all. The risk of going beyond the limits of common sense and good education is huge, and not infrequently Brazilian TV has been touching the bad taste and the grotesque in the caricaturization of the treatment granted to sports.

In his seminal work on the subject, José Carlos Aronchi de Souza (2004, p. 183) extends the discussion not only to the definition of genres, but also to that of formats and categories (our translation): "Format is the fundamental element for the classification of genre. Format is the language developed by television to shape a genre of television program and transmit it." It then establishes 37 genres and 31 television formats, divided into five categories: (1) *entertainment*; (2) *information;* (3) *education;* (4) *advertising;* and (5) *other.*

For Aronchi de Souza (2004, p. 106), sports programs could be classified in the information, entertainment or education category. Fundamentally, sports events (among which, broadcasts of games and competitions) would be classified in the entertainment category. Right away, the Web according to which sports broadcasts would be or should be based on strictly journalistic concepts, related only to information and interpretation of facts, begins to collapse. In the case of Brazilian TV, sports broadcasts, especially football, have historically been greatly influenced by the tradition of radio broadcasts. Narrators or announcers use, most of the time, an exacerbated sensationalism, fantasizing the plays that take place on the field. In addition, improvisation is also an important component: it means that the accuracy and precision of the report is partly lost—the announcers are thus on a plane that is also full of turbulence.

This radio influence on TV, regarding football transmissions, receives harsh and ironic words in Décio Pignatari's (1984, p. 40, our translation) provocative analysis: "Football transmissions are made on that basis, brought in, without any major concern for competence and correction." That is why sports broadcasting on TV in Brazil would reproduce the repetitive litany of the "inefficient and incompetent *Brazilian style*": "The basic characteristic of this style may be succinctly defined: it is radio on video. Like the radio sportscaster, the television camera follows the ball and not the game" (Pignatari, 1984, p. 41). Moreover, the different language of the sportscaster would pretend to escape from the ordinary linguistic register, in order to print in the verbal expression a connotative meaning, in the search for a bigger audience. Décio de Almeida Prado's statement is a testimony of that:

> The radio, in the exalted voice of the announcers, gave the games of that time a vibration that they never had, before or after, with such intensity. It is as if we were at the edge of the field, following the ball from foot to foot, but free from the limitations that reality imposes on the imagination and, above all, without the relentless witness of television. There was no match that did not have epic contours. (Prado, 1997, p. 204, our translation)

In the search for external recognition, i.e., the audience, as defined by Bourdieu, laughter and humor have been an ally of television in its mediation of sportswe would say, in fact, that it has been an ally of the press in general. TV announcers, many times coming from radio, have been known, along with commentators and sports reporters, for creating slogans, catchphrases, slogans, etc—almost all of them fun and humorous. Sports newspapers, not rarely, got used to resort to provocative headlines or catchphrases to portray competition results (such phenomenon has also started to be observed in the generalist newspapers, when the sports section started to appear in a separate section), even creating stereotyped characters to sign columns about the club they represent. Brazilian radio, in the same way, often used laughter as a tool for listener's adhesion, both in sports broadcasts and in the programs that followed the football days, the biggest example of which in São Paulo was "Show de Rádio," a set of humoristic sketches created by Estevam Sangirardi, in 1969, to play with profiles of Paulista fans. Such tradition persists in São Paulo radio, considering the permanence of sports shows that dialogue continuously with humor, such as "Estúdio 97," from *Energia 97 FM,* and "Na Geral," from *Radio Bandeirantes.*

We can say that there is a *standupization of* sports programs also refers, as the name implies, to the mobility of presenters, who started to move continuously through the scenario, free from the mechanical reading of the teleprompter. Within this new logic, one cannot sit behind a bench, simply staring at the camera. If morning and afternoon programs aimed at women try to reproduce, in the studio, the kitchen or living room of our homes, the new face of sports programs on broadcast TV tries to mimic the bedroom of the young or the schoolyard: we can sit in front of an interviewee as if we were at the foot of the bed talking to someone close, as well as we can move from side to side through screens, monitors and graphics, as if we were playing in the playground of the condominium. In a way, it is recovered, thus, a strategy of approaching the young audience established to a large extent in Brazil by the arrival of *MTV,* in the late 1990s: informality in gestures and features, use of a colloquial speech (sometimes with slang and fads), use of casual and colorful clothes, as well as great personalism in the way of addressing the viewer (by the way, some changes made by the *ESPN Brasil* pay channel in 2014, incorporated part of these trends set in motion by broadcast TV).

In the face of these attempts to expand the audience, relaxation and informality have been the rules. It is necessary to establish with the audience the same empathy that unites colleagues at recess or break time at school. And one of the artifices that connects these gears is precisely the use of laughter—to complete, thus, the aesthetics of *standup* comedy. Some of these programs—including on cable channels—often resort to performances that could figure in any theatrical humor show: journalists and presenters make imitations (vocal and corporal) of sports personalities or politicians; abuse the use of puns and catchphrases; insist on telling jokes full of commonplaces; perpetuate jokes sometimes sexist and discriminatory; provoke fans of certain clubs, etc.

Some Final Considerations

The relationship between sports and the media has long proved to be part of a mutual exchange of interests: sporting events fill spaces in the coverage of newspapers, radios, and televisions, while these, by expanding the demand and allowing the diffusion for the production of these same events, end up equally making the disclosure of the competitions and of all sponsors and organizing entities involved. This communion takes on stratospheric dimensions when we come across major sporting events or so-called mega-events.

Furthermore, the coverage that the Brazilian press destines to sports obeys general criteria of noticiability when it comes to national competitions. Thus, the TV scene is dominated by football and the country's major clubs. When we face international competitions, such as a football World Cup, coverage becomes directly subordinated to the campaign of the Brazilian team represented there. The broadcasters' attention to national athletes and teams thus depends on their competitive possibilities. Thus, the victorious participation of Brazilians ends up contaminating the media work, causing the appearance of numerous stories and reports that try to seduce the viewer to get involved in the support for a particular athlete (as we saw in December 2014, with the appearance of surfing on the screens of our channels, due to the world title in the sport obtained by Gabriel Medina).

If we accept the premise that TV networks are committed to the financial success of the sporting events they themselves broadcast—and for which they have paid for the respective rights, how can we imagine that such conflictive aspects have predominance in the coverage engendered by the TV networks themselves? One way of tacitly renouncing this more dysphoric commitment before the mega sporting events has to do with the monumental character that the media companies like to announce about their work teams—hence the wide dissemination of figures involving people involved, resources invested, hours transmitted, among other accounts.

We cannot ignore the fact that the recurrence of former sportsmen to act as television commentators only demonstrates the weaknesses of communication professionals working in Brazilian broadcasters. Almost always hostages of the sports monoculture around football, the channels resent the absence of greater sports skills among journalists and communicators, which makes a more pedagogical performance often lacking in the case of infrequent sports on TV screens—or that gain prominence only in times of Olympic Games. Hence, the overwhelming presence of former athletes, coaches, and referees with the task of commenting on the sporting event and filling gaps in the journalistic field. On the other hand, such sports professionals are not always sensitive to socio-cultural issues that involve the practice of sports or to the intricacies of football geopolitics. And, in most cases, they coat their speeches with almost always impressionistic discourses, sometimes assuming the role of the fan in front of the cameras.

Press coverage, however, remains hostage and subordinates itself to the campaign of Brazilian athletes or teams when it comes to international competitions. The victorious participation of "team Brazil" ends up contaminating the work of the press, which in turn invites readers, listeners and viewers to become increasingly integrated around the "canarinho team" or national athletes' supporters. It is a procedure of collective anesthesia, in which the Brazilian teams are usually sung and decanted in verse and prose by media agents whenever the start of a competition approaches and as soon as it begins.

In the specific case of football, regardless of the circumstances and the opponents, we always arrive at a World Cup as favorites. Every four years, it is this party and this magic that the Brazilian National Team accomplishes throughout the Cups. This phenomenon is replicated by all other sports that deserve some kind of press coverage and which have Brazilian representation in the competition. Far from being a peculiarity exclusive to the Brazilian media, such characteristic only reflects and updates ancestral practices of our communicators throughout the twentieth and twenty-first centuries.

References

Aronchi de Souza, J. C. (2004). *Gêneros e formatos na televisão brasileira*. Summus.
Bakhtin, M. M. (2010). *Estética da criação verbal*. Martins Fontes.
Bourdieu, P. (1983). Como é possível ser esportivo? *Questões de sociologia* (pp. 136–153). Marco Zero.
Bourdieu, P. (1990). Programa para uma sociologia do esporte. In *Coisas ditas* (pp. 207–220). Brasiliense.
Bourdieu, P. (1997). *Sobre a televisão*. Jorge Zahar.
Eco, U. (1984). *Viagem na irrealidade cotidiana*. Nova Fronteira.
Erbolato, M. L. (1981). *Jornalismo especializado: Emissão de textos no jornalismo impresso*. Atlas.
Fonseca, O. (1997). Esporte e crônica esportiva. In P. Tambucci, J. G. M. Oliveira, & J. Coelho Sobrinho (Eds.), *Esporte e jornalismo*. Cepeusp/USP.
Freitas Filho, L. (1985). A cobertura esportiva no rádio e no jornal. In G. K. Dieguez (Org.), *Esporte e poder*. Vozes.
Gomes, M., & Carrano, P. C. (2000). O futebol entre palcos e bastidores. Entrevista com o jornalista esportivo Juca Kfouri. In: P. C. Carrano (Ed.) *Futebol: Paixão e política*. DP&a.
Lever, J. (1983). *A loucura do futebol*. Record.
Mazzoni, T. (1939). *Problemas e aspectos do nosso futebol*. A Gazeta.
Mazzoni, T. (1950). *História do futebol no Brasil*. Edições Leia.
Mello e Souza, C. (1986). Impressões do Brasil: a imprensa brasileira através dos tempos. Grupo Machline.
Murray, B. (2000). *Uma história do futebol*. Hedra.
Neiva, A. (1954). *60 anos de futebol no Brasil*. Federação Paulista de Futebol.
Nogueira de Sá, J. (1994, July 20). A hora da virada. *Folha de S. Paulo*, (p. 6).
Pedrosa, M. (Ed.). (1968). *O olho na bola*. Gol.
Perdigão, P. (2000). *Anatomia de uma derrota* (2nd ed.). L&PM.

Pignatari, D. (1984). *Signagem da televisão*. Brasiliense.

Prado, D. A. (1997). *Seres, coisas, lugares*. Companhia das Letras.

Ramos, R. (1984). *Futebol: Ideologia do poder*. Vozes.

Shirts, M. (1982). Futebol no Brasil ou football in Brazil? In J. C. S. B. Meihy & J. S. Witter (Eds.), *Futebol e cultura: Coletânea de estudos*. Imprensa Oficial, Arquivo do Estado.

Chapter 19
World Cups' Geography: Urban Brazil in 1950

Gilmar Mascarenhas

Introduction

How can geography contribute to football studies?

Without ever getting a definitive answer, I have been asking myself this question for 25 years, but I have accumulated some interesting clues, and a lot of work since then. It all started when I attended, in 1994, at the university where I was already teaching (Uerj), the event "Futebol: Cem anos de uma paixão brasileira" (Football: One hundred years of a Brazilian passion), brilliantly conceived and organized by my colleague Maurício Murad. A surprising event, as football was still an essentially foreign subject to the academic universe. Envying historians, anthropologists and sociologists who were already able to work on the subject with some referential support, I started imagining what a possible football geography would be like. In my searches, in the "pre-Google" era, I discovered the British John Bale and the French Jean-Pierre Augustin, geographers who were practically solitary in their attempts on the subject.

With some initial reflections, I entered, in 1996, the doctorate in Human Geography at USP. In 2001, I defended my thesis on the diffusion of football in Brazil, a study in the field of historical geography, investigating how the various agents who introduced football (bachelors, railroad technicians, English factory workers, missionaries, etc.) participated in an extensive web associated with imperialist mercantile networks, which I called "the ball in the net(works)," and how this network dealt/dialogued with the internal dynamics of the Brazilian territory, that is, "the plot of the place." In short, the ways in which we Brazilians got to know and welcome that strange innovation.

One of the contributions of this study lies in weaving new explanations about how our slow and precarious national integration, triggered above all from 1930 onwards, conditioned the diffusion of this sport, generating the strength of local and regional

G. Mascarenhas (✉)
Rio de Janeiro State University, Rio de Janeiro, Brazil

rivalries that still survive. The other contribution was to highlight how a slave society based in cities inherited from the colonial past had great difficulty in breaking bodily taboos and assimilating football, contrary to much of the literature then available (Mascarenhas, 1999).

I conducted several other studies, some of them pioneering, such as the *Liga da Canela Preta* (Black Shin's League) in Porto Alegre, demonstrating how the existence of this league, a model of institutional racial segregation explicit and rare in Brazil, was related to the urban dynamics of the capital city. If in my doctoral thesis, my scale of analysis was the national territory and its imbrications with the world economy, now I was dedicating myself more properly to urban space, to the geography of the city.

In short, I believe that geography may basically collaborate in two ways within this scope. The first would be by providing elements of spatial dynamics and configuration with potential to explain phenomena of the sports field, such as for instance, the concentration of power in the main clubs located in the two national metropolises, with capacity to encompass the entire national territory as a zone of influence. The second form of geographical study would be to act in the opposite direction of the first: to verify how football helps us understand certain geographical phenomena. In this case, stadiums acquire special relevance: they produce centrality, agglutinate flows, impact their surroundings and correspond precisely to the strength that football acquired in a particular time and place. I have been working in both ways.

Brazil has recently experienced a cycle of sports mega-events, which began with the Pan American Games of 2007 and culminated with the 2016 Olympic Games, both hosted in the city of Rio de Janeiro. Throughout this period, I focused efforts on this theme, founding in 2009 the Research Group Cities and Sports Mega-events, registered in CNPq. The football World Cups are an essential part of this theme, and from this study, I accumulated data and reflections that led to the construction of the present chapter of this book.

From an essentially geographical point of view, I understand that a World Cup can serve to help unveil various aspects of a given territorial formation and its urban network, as well as the nature and contents of urbanization, in addition to feeding the reflection on regionalisms, and many other issues. The very universe of cities chosen to host the matches serves as a "portrait" of the urban hierarchy in a given historical context and can also tell us about the pattern of demographic occupation of the national territory, and thus reveal, in our case, huge "voids" in 1950: The entire Midwest and the North were excluded from the event, besides the vast semi-arid region. We thus had an almost "coastal" World Cup, consistent with a spatial structure that preceded the era of the great interiorization policies, with Brasília as a landmark, and which became more pronounced with the adoption of the military regime.

Still in a specific approach to football geography, now taking the planetary scale as a reference, a mega-event such as this can elucidate elements of the world economic and geopolitical panorama: the World Cup as a showcase of the most powerful nations, with few and impoverished African representatives, for instance. For Ignacio

Ramonet (1998, p. 55), the World Cup is an authentic "ritualized war," which reaffirms football as the best revealer of a nation's virtues. It may also show a geopolitical desire for international projection, as did Fascist Italy with the 1934 World Cup, and Nazi Germany, which held in 1936 the largest Olympic Games ever seen up to that time. Along the same line, Vargas' government intended to hold a World Cup in 1942 as a genuine Estado Novo's propaganda, but would be restrained by the outbreak of World War II, which suspended the holding of the competition (Drumond, 2009).

The study of the World Cup focused on intra-urban space, in turn, deals with the extensive (and sometimes dramatic, for the affected communities) package of reforms in the city's infrastructure, with emphasis on mobility projects, in the Brazilian case, in 2014. We can also investigate more specifically the existing football spatiality and the impact of the tournament on the stadiums. This will be the central focus of this work, given that in 1950 the size of this event did not trigger large budgets in order to intervene in the urban infrastructure. We shall not fail, however, to make slight observations and comments on the Brazilian urban network and how it was triggered to support this mega-event. In our exercise, we will attempt to place the 1950 World Cup in the context of our urbanization, framing the material interventions (creation and renovation of stadiums) and the very choice of location of the host cities in the context of urban Brazil at the time. We can establish the following question as the question of our study: What was the general state of our stadiums in 1950 and how the World Cup of that year affected it, against the backdrop of the Brazilian urban landscape of that time?

To assess the insertion of the 1950 World Cup in the production of urban space, we shall begin by presenting the pre-existing picture in our football spatiality, i.e., how our stadiums looked like when Brazil decided to organize the tournament. This retrospective will allow a clearer dimensioning of the World Cup's impact on the Brazilian stadiums. It will be presented in two moments: the conformation of our first generation of stadiums and, then, the popularization process of football in Brazil, which, as of the 1930s, required the creation of what we understand as a second generation of stadiums (Mascarenhas, 2014). Finally, in the third part, we will identify the interventions that the 1950 World Cup promoted in our stadiums to argue that this event did little to effectively change the ongoing process of renovation of our stadiums. The tournament's low impact is mainly due to Fifa's low requirements at that time, when compared to those of today.

A Supposedly Aristocratic Ritual: The First Generation of Stadiums in Brazil

Football was introduced in Brazil between the end of the nineteenth century and the beginning of the following century, as a European fad with hygienic, moralistic, cosmopolitan and rigorous social distinction traits, therefore, much more appropriate to the elite youth. In those early years, the sport was a seductive vehicle of civilizing and liberating promises. Promises of modernity and progress. In this sense, English workers, foreign missionaries and young bachelors brought from Europe not only the practice of a new sport, but especially its symbolic dimension: Football as an activity carrying unquestionable benefits, since it originated from the "good" European civilization, taking it as a healthy activity and capable of improving intelligence, character and other moral attributes. According to Hobsbawm (1998, p. 53), the world was divided between a smaller part, where "progress" was born, and other, much larger parts, where it arrived as a foreign conqueror, helped by minorities of local collaborators groups of paladins of the new habits.

Young men from wealthy families, founders of many of the first football clubs in Brazil, can be placed in this group. In short, sanctioned by supposedly modern and "cosmopolitan" groups, football arrives in Brazil precisely at the moment when Brazilian elites want to invest in breaking with the colonial past. Consequently, they practice football in a highly segregated manner, speaking English on the field of play, as an authentic ritual of class distinction.

In this sense, our first stadiums were almost exclusively aimed at the elite. Their geography is unmistakable: located in the noblest neighborhoods, and with small-sized equipment (usually a single built structure that did not even cover the entire length of one of the four sides of the field), they presented an architecture more similar to a comfortable theater. As the athletes also came from the privileged social strata, it was their family and friends who came to watch the exhibitions of the new English sport that was becoming successful in Europe. The stadium was then an ornament of the civilizing wave of Eurocentric stamp and of very restricted access, true space of elite fruition (Mascarenhas, 2009).

Several examples attest this initial moment in the history of Brazilian stadiums. In Porto Alegre, Grêmio Football Porto-Alegrense erects, in 1904, its first stadium, the first in the entire Southern region, a majestic social pavilion with only 500 seats and located in a prime area (Moinhos de Vento district), with the city's elegant hippodrome as its immediate neighbor.[1] In São Paulo, the first matches took place at the end of the nineteenth century, at the Velodrome, on land belonging to the powerful Prado family, in the Consolação district, when this area was being occupied by mansions in the context of urban expansion of a bourgeois-hygienist nature, away from the old center and away from the city that was becoming industrialized beyond Várzea do Carmo, to the East. Already in 1902, the Antarctica Company, which hosted football matches in its park intended for the leisure of employees, will be the scene of the games of the first Paulista Football Championship, resulting, then, in the construction of the Parque Antarctica stadium, one of the first football stadiums in the history of Brazil.

---

[1] Since Baron Haussmann built, in the *Bois de Bologne,* the majestic *Hipodromme de Auteuil,* conferring *glamour to* the turf (traditional popular spectacle), it was established the correlation between such object and the *Belle Époque,* spreading internationally this model, so that the physical presence of an imposing hippodrome became an instrument of urban land valuation, tending to be located in elite neighborhoods. On this subject, see Mascarenhas (1999).

Building a stadium presumes high investment, which could eventually come from a rich patron such as the Guinle family in Rio de Janeiro, which sponsored the construction of the elegant Fluminense Football Club stadium in 1906.

In this context, which was prone to improvisations due to the incipient nature of the activity, in São Paulo, there was a sports facility, the Velódromo, which served to house the first movements of the local football scene. In Recife, football matches were played in the "Campina do Derby," a space adapted from one of the city's old hippodromes. The use of such venues was mainly due to the existence of large, flat surfaces that were sufficiently large for football practice, in addition to the prior availability of a seating area for the select audience. But beyond practicality, there was also the symbolic significance of the new sport: as a sport accepted in the privileged circle of the elite, football was included in the list of sports already consolidated in the local social and sporting life.

In most cities, due to the absence of sports facilities, the first football practitioners resorted to free spaces. In Paraíba, the first games took place in 1908, at the Praça Independência, in the capital, borrowing some chairs from the Santa Rosa theater (Marques, 1975, p. 15). The same occurred in Salvador, where the Campo da Pólvora served as the stage for the first exhibitions of football, later to be held at the Rio Vermelho hippodrome. In Porto Alegre, the Farroupilha Park also hosted matches, even when the Baixada stadium already existed, due to the multiplication of clubs in the city around 1909. In Curitiba, the first match would have occurred in 1905, at the Bosque on Marechal Deodoro Street, but later the Jóquei Clube Paranaense was established as the preferred venue for matches, which also featured the field of the public force barracks.

According to a Brazilian football almanac (Klein & Audinino, 1998), in the city of Manaus, the first football games took place in the meadow of the Masonic Dispensary, but there were also venues in the Praça da Saudade and in the municipal woods. In Fortaleza, the space used by the first footballers, in 1904, was in front of the Gasometer. Later, with the activity consolidated, the clubs moved to the "Stadium do Prado." In Florianópolis, football was played on an improvised basis at the General Osório square. In 1907, in the capital of Goiás, the sport was introduced to a group of young men who took part in an exhibition at the Chafariz square. In this case, it is worth mentioning a note that reveals the degree of incipiency and improvisation: there were only six players in each team.

In short, there were many ways for those interested in practicing football to find a flat, large space compatible with the rules that came from England. We note the use of squares and parks, but hippodromes were undoubtedly privileged venues for the new sport. However, this equipment was restricted to cities where the turf was consolidated, such as Recife, Fortaleza and Curitiba. São Paulo had a velodrome and Rio de Janeiro relied on patronage to build a stadium for its first football club.

Of this first generation of stadiums, which were still wooden structures, few have survived, such as that of Fluminense FC, in Rio de Janeiro. Located in prime areas, usually those with higher real estate values, which would later undergo verticalization processes, such stadiums, once replaced by larger, "popular" equipment and located in less valued places, tended toward demolition to shelter lucrative real estate projects.

In Porto Alegre's case, Moinhos de Vento stadium, which survived until 1954, gave place to the refined park with the same name, thus ensuring the neighborhood's valorization, which remained as the most noble of the capital city until approximately the 1990s, when new neighborhoods were consolidated in the same East vector, endowed with the new amenities required by the market.

Football's popularization process would inevitably make these stadiums anachronistic. On the one hand, their reduced audience capacity could no longer cope with the growing influx of people interested in watching the matches. On the other hand, the expansion of such facilities would face physical obstacles, as they were inserted in areas of dense occupation, traditional neighborhoods, usually taking part of a block. At the same time, the fact that the stadiums are located in prime areas made any expansion project that required land acquisition more difficult. Finally, the larger and noisier influx of fans itself was of no interest to the inhabitants of such prime areas as it compromised their valuable amenities. Moreover, as football ceased to be the sport of aristocratic youngsters, it was no longer interesting to accommodate stadiums in these neighborhoods, unlike hippodromes and, later, golf courses, which remained as sports equipment to add value to the surroundings (Bale, 1994; Mascarenhas, 2018). In sum, football social evolution and its spectacularization demanded a new spatiality, addressed below.

The Party Transits to the Popular: The Advent of Concrete Stadiums

The sports movement of a given city, when it reaches a certain success and popularity, results in the creation of large geographic objects destined to exhibit and "sell" the show, with emphasis on hippodromes, velodromes, indoor gyms and football stadiums. But such objects do not always have a lasting existence in the urban landscape, since they depend on the permanence of the historical conditions that generated them. In the case of turf, there was great success in several Brazilian capitals in the late nineteenth century, but it seems that football won many of its admirers, transferring to stadiums a significant part of the public that frequented horse racing.

Football, unlike turf, cycling and rowing, followed its evolutionary course in a steady ascent, acquiring levels of popularity that challenged the existing geographical base. In the process of popularization of football, which in Brazil was consolidated in the 1920s and 1930s, we can see in Rio de Janeiro the following renovations to expand the Laranjeiras stadium and the inauguration of São Januário in 1927, then the largest stadium in South America (until the inauguration, in the following year, of the stadium of the Argentine club Independiente, in Greater Buenos Aires), materializing this process of progressive incorporation of the masses. It is precisely in this context that nighttime lighting was implemented in these two venues in 1928. The advent of lighting in football stadiums is associated not only with the growing influx of spectators, making it economically feasible to install expensive electrical systems. It can also be explained by the political project of incorporation of working classes into another sphere of social life, demanding night events, outside working hours, a different situation from the old aristocratic stadium. The presence of masses at stadiums seems to integrate, somehow, the new social pact in the formation of metropolitan urban Brazil as of 1930.

An important milestone in this transition toward a second generation of stadiums was the inauguration of São Januário stadium by C. R. Vasco da Gama in 1927. Large sized for the time and endowed with imposing architectural lines, the equipment was located in an industrial and middle-low income area, thus establishing a marked rupture with the locational pattern that, up to that time, had been in force for Brazilian stadiums. According to Fernando Ferreira (2004, pp. 73–74, our translation), some basic factors were involved in the site selection:

> The neighborhood of São Cristóvão had definitely lost any remnants of the once imperial, aristocratic neighborhood [...] had assumed the role of industrial and proletarian neighborhood, being occupied by a population predominantly of worker origin, with the old properties previously belonging to the nobles and wealthier citizens, being gradually replaced by industries and by the population with fewer resources. The combination between the availability of large plots of land at affordable prices, in the "back" of the neighborhood, with the ease of access provided by tramway transportation, added to its great infrastructure, in our view, seem to have been determining factors for the choice of São Cristóvão as headquarters for the club's imposing stadium. [...] the relative proximity to the old field on Morais e Silva street and to the port area, part of the city where the club was founded; the existence of a large Portuguese colony in São Cristóvão, comprising residents, merchants and industrialists alike; the neighborhood's identification with Portugal, built since the arrival of the Royal Family at Quinta da Boa Vista in the first decade of the 19th century.

With an estimated capacity of 40 thousand people, the stadium immediately became a kind of stage and showcase for populism. Several politicians, especially Getúlio Vargas, used the venue for major civic demonstrations. In the football field, it represented the unprecedented rise and power of a suburban club, Vasco da Gama. This club, like the other suburban clubs of the 1920s, recruited athletes from the lower classes, unlike the traditional clubs of Rio's South Zone (Fluminense, Botafogo, Flamengo, and even América, from the upper-middle-class North Zone neighborhood of Tijuca). Since the middle of the previous decade, these "brunette"[2] suburban associations had been playing in the main division of the League, but without the success achieved by Vasco, carioca champion of 1923, a conquest that shook the foundations of the football system of the time.

Another important milestone of this period was the construction of the Pacaembu stadium in São Paulo, inaugurated in 1940. In line with the spirit of the 1932 Revolution and with all the flagrant, ufanistic discourse of the "Brazilian locomotive," the São Paulo municipality erected the country's first state-owned football stadium. However, unlike Vasco, it did so in a noble area of the city, repeating the locational trend of the first generation of stadiums. It was a civic monument that, as such, required a location "consistent" with its importance and centrality in the city's social and cultural life. And there was not only the football field, but facilities for other

---

[2] Teams with black, white, and mixed-race players.

sports such as athletics and swimming (Olympic swimming pool), in addition to a multi-sport gymnasium, since the widely publicized goal was to promote a healthier, more vibrant and, therefore, presumably patriotic youth. In Vargas' words, imbued with fascist moods, on the occasion of the stadium's inauguration speech, a youth with a "high eugenic index" was projected (Negreiros, 1998, p. 87).

A year later, in 1941, Amaral Peixoto, governor of Rio de Janeiro state and Getúlio Vargas' son-in-law and appointed by him as federal intervenor, inaugurated the Caio Martins stadium in the capital city of Niterói. With due regard for proportions, it followed the same principles that had shaped the Pacaembu project: the noble location (in Icaraí neighborhood), sober lines, the existence of a true sports complex, state control and the stadium's use for pro-government civic demonstrations. In general terms, within the spatiality of the football spectacle, this was Brazil on the eve of the 1950 World Cup. Henceforth, let us see how this event impacted the football spatiality that was already in full expansion.

The 1950 World Cup and Its Peculiar Geography: Context and Impacts

The main material legacy of 1950, the Maracanã sports complex, is a geographical object that can be read as the synthesis of a peculiar combination of factors. One of them, the intense rivalry with São Paulo, which produced in the cariocas a feeling of dissatisfaction for not having a bigger stadium, despite being the most important national city. And, it is important to emphasize, it had not yet built a public stadium (state-owned), a symbol of the sport's value to the society as a whole, that is, to the project of a civilized nation. Private stadiums, owned by clubs, were considered at the time a paradox in relation to the high sporting principles of equal conditions among opponents. Another essential factor is the growth in the influx of fans, evidencing the need for bigger stadiums in Rio de Janeiro.[3]

Not coincidentally, in 1941, very shortly after Pacaembu's opening, the federal government, through the Ministry of Education and Health Gustavo Capanema, launched a tender to select the best project for the future national stadium in Rio de Janeiro. The initiative, however, foundered given political disputes between governmental spheres since the municipality immediately declared its interest and determination in building the capital's major stadium (Moura, 1998, p. 24). At the same time, the city's major clubs had been considering the expansion of their stadiums, planning to build facilities that could seat up to 100 thousand people but they stalled their

---

[3] In 1948, faced with uncertainties regarding the construction of Maracanã, a private group led by Fausto Matarazzo announced its intention to build the Estádio Nacional Sociedade Anônima (Ensa), in the suburb of Irajá, with capacity for one hundred thousand people, a project harshly criticized by *Jornal dos Sports*, which accused it of being in disagreement with the fundamental principles of the national sports policy.

projects before the announcement of the state's interest in building a large common use arena.

Another factor to be highlighted in the production of what would be the world's largest stadium is the country's historical moment, driven by developmentalism and by the perspective of aligning itself with the great "industrious" and civilized nations. Industrialization driven by import substitution, the speed of rural exodus and the formation of an increasingly active state machine, all these movements outlined an optimistic picture. And this optimism included the acceptance of monumental projects that would show the world our greatness and our technical capacity. Thus, building the world's largest stadium would be fully in line with the immediate future of the "sleeping giant".

The stadium project was criticized under allegations of priority for public investments in basic sectors such as health and education (Moura, 1998, p. 28). But arguments to the contrary reveal another conjunctural factor that favors the construction of the stadium: the validity of the discourse that emphasizes sport's presumed regenerating effect (which dates back to the nineteenth century but was revived by Nazi-fascism) and its paradoxical attribution to the modality "football" which, given its intrinsic characteristics (of unpredictable shocks, constant heartbeat variations and exaggerated efforts), is not welcomed by medicine as a health promoter, nor is it recommended as a character building ingredient. Another contradiction in this discourse that associates stadium construction with public health is the fact that such equipment encourages passivity rather than sports practice. The victory of this fragile argument reveals the strength of the ideology of sports as a trainer of a *New Man* in the context of the Estado Novo; and Maracanã as a symbol of a new era of civility and nation aggrandizement.

In addition to Rio de Janeiro, the 1950 World Cup was hosted by the cities of São Paulo (with the Pacaembu stadium, built in 1940), Curitiba (with the Durival Britto e Silva stadium, built in 1947), Porto Alegre (with the Eucaliptos stadium, built in 1931), Recife (with the Ilha do Retiro stadium, built in 1937) and Belo Horizonte (with the Independência stadium, built in 1950), the latter being the only one built specifically for the event. The exceptionality of Minas Gerais can be explained: On one hand, Belo Horizonte, an entirely planned city, was the ostensible symbol of national urban modernity (before Brasília was built) and the capital of one of the most important states in the federation, politically, historically and economically speaking. This city in vertiginous growth, symbol of progress, which walked swiftly toward the polarization of the various urban basins of Minas Gerais, gradually forming a single urban system to consolidate its centrality (Singer, 1977), did not yet have a compatible stadium.

Football was still at a relatively late stage of development in the capital city of Minas Gerais. This is exemplified by the fact that in 1929 a stadium with capacity for only five thousand people was inaugurated, belonging to the state's most popular club, Atlético-MG (Souza Neto, 2017). Belo Horizonte's desired affirmation in the context of nascent national metropolises implied in following São Paulo's then recent example (and already underway in Rio de Janeiro) and thus erect a "great" municipal stadium, an equipment that would be aligned with other monumental works, worthy of a modern and civilized urban center. The World Cup was undoubtedly a major pretext and driving factor behind the Independência stadium construction project.

Before addressing the other venues, it is worth mentioning Fonte Nova stadium in Salvador. Delays in construction prevented it from participating in the 1950 World Cup and it was inaugurated only six months after the competition, in January 1951. Bahia would follow in the aforementioned Pacaembu, Caio Martins and Maracanã footsteps by inaugurating the monumental state stadium Otavio Mangabeira, endowed not only with a sports complex, but also with a public school establishment. With modernist lines, its location is central and emblematic, next to the Dique do Tororó.

The other World Cup stadiums only underwent adaptations, such as the placement of fences and the eventual creation of tunnels and appropriate spaces for journalists, basic equipment required by Fifa who, as it transpired, made a single previous inspection visit to each of the six stadiums. Exceptionally, the stadium of Eucaliptos underwent significant expansion, increasing its capacity from 10 to 30 thousand spectators and changing sectors of stands still made of wood for concrete structures. However, such renovation is not exactly explained by the World Cup, but by the fast growth of the owner club, SC Internacional, a phenomenon that will deserve attention in the next paragraphs, as it is representative of the context of popularization of football and the formation of large fan clubs.

Porto Alegre's Internacional emerged in 1909, as an initiative of middle-class individuals to challenge Grêmio FBPA, then the main force of the nascent gaúcho football and representative of the German elites who then controlled important sectors of the economy. Since the beginning, therefore, Internacional sought to impose itself as the "native club," representative of the Luso-Brazilian segments, against the dominant, "foreign" club. In the 1930s, this club invested in the process of popularizing its image, with peculiar success.

In 1931, upon opening its new stadium (the "Eucaliptos stadium"), Internacional took an important step toward establishing its popularity for two basic reasons: it was located in the Menino Deus suburb, whereas its rival remained in the prime zone, as we have just shown. As early as 1935, a decisive Gre-Nal[4] held at the packed Baixada stadium recorded that 2/3 of those present, even though in "enemy territory," were Internacional supporters. It was evident in the "native club" the full potential of becoming a "people's club" (Noronha & Coimbra, 1994).

With new prospects, Internacional decided to absorb the "popular winds of the Campanha Gaúcha." In that 1930s, clubs from Pelotas, Rio Grande, Livramento and Bagé won seven of the ten state championships contested annually.[5] The main reason for this uncomfortable "landowner-pastoral" superiority over football in the capital was the strong influence of the plains, besides, of course, the economic power of the

---

[4] Popular name for the match of greatest rivalry in southern Brazil, with opponents Grêmio and Internacional, the two largest teams in the city of Porto Alegre.

[5] The first time that a city in the northern half of the state (with the obvious exception of the capital) placed a club in the Gaucho Championship final was in 1942, through E.C. Floriano, from Novo Hamburgo. A well-documented account of the history of the Gaucho Football Championship can be found in Dienstmann (1987).

landowners of Campanha. Adhering to the "professional" model already consolidated in Prata since the end of the previous decade, such clubs openly invested in hiring talented players, without any restrictions related to race or social origin of the athlete. Counting on funding from large cattle ranchers, football in Campanha extended its recruitment base beyond the border, inserting Uruguayan (and eventually Argentine) players of excellent technical level in their teams. In Porto Alegre, football was structured in different leagues that operated as independent circuits, reproducing the city's rigid socioeconomic hierarchy. The main league operated according to "amateurish" principles, but the growing pressure of new fans eager for victories was already leading to the incorporation of other values. As Arlei Damo (1998, p. 109) has well perceived, the prestige of a club started to be measured by quantitative criteria (wins and number of supporters), and no longer by the distinction of its participants. Progressively, the urban masses of the developing metropolis became interested in football and redefined it.

Far less tied to elitist values than their rivals, it was Internacional's turn, more precisely from 1937 onwards, to massively recruit black and poor players to reinforce their team. The obvious result was an unquestionable superiority over its opponents, winning nine of the ten city championships contested over the following decade. By adopting black and poor players, the club quickly became in the 1940s the "people's club" of Porto Alegre. Other symbols came to endorse this new image: the famous Rei Momo Vicente Rao became the leader of the crowd, animating the stands in a carnivalesque tone; an animal devoid of any nobility as the goat became the team's "mascot," accompanying it in all games, entering the field and becoming popularly known with the name of "Chica" (Noronha & Coimbra, 1994, p. 51). The "little black man" (*negrinho* in Portuguese), expressive figure of the regional folklore, expression of humility, was adopted in the 1950s as the maximum symbol of the club, and later (in 1968) the *saci,* meaning the malice and the dark powers of an excluded "blackness," became the club's representative character.

And so, football in Porto Alegre entered a new period, radically distancing itself from the obsolete aristocratic and elegant tone, an expression of the (excluding) European modernity, to "carnivalize" the stadiums and definitively insert the noisy anonymity of the crowds. In this sense, we may state that the World Cup only provided a context that enabled the making of a material investment that would not be long in coming: the inexorable expansion of the Eucaliptos stadium as well as the urgent need, in Rio de Janeiro and Belo Horizonte, to build a stadium that would be compatible with the size and functions of these two capital cities.

Concluding Remarks

Milton Santos (1996) bequeathed us a theory of places according to which they are produced from two intersecting axes: verticalities and horizontalities. In our study, Fifa and, more broadly, football's economic logic are presented as vertical vectors, i.e., those that affect places from "outside in" and "top down". Our stadiums, in turn, and our urban network in the historical period studied make up the axis of horizontalities: the Brazil that Fifa found when it elected this country to host the 1950 World Cup.

We saw that the Fifa we found was quite different from today's Fifa in as much as the level of requirements to host the great event is concerned, so that interventions in our stadiums were small in scope. In sum, the 1950 World Cup did not significantly shape new directions for Brazilian football and its spatiality. We tried to demonstrate here that a process of renovation of our stadium facilities was already underway, at least two decades before the mega-event. Such renovation, basically dictated by the physical expansion of equipment and by providing more space for popular sectors, responded to the gradual process of redefinition of football in the Brazilian society: from a sport played by and for the enjoyment of elites, football has been progressively attracting interest from popular sectors. Gradually, athletes from the "várzea" and the suburbs joined the main clubs, making the teams "mestizos." At the same time, the popular segments became interested in participating as active elements in the spectacle, while the elites discovered other sports of clear social distinction, such as swimming, tennis and golf.

As the stadiums were filled by people who worked in factories, in construction and in the informal market of the metropolis under construction, the latter effectively incorporated football into its new and complex mechanisms of social reproduction. Thus, it seemed that football was following the new structural trends that pointed to a transition toward an urban mass culture. From the 1940s on, processes of relative social integration developed and generated new spaces for sociability. We believe that the new stadiums, due to their size and ability to bring together the various social segments, actively participate in the transition from a culturally segregated city (see the urban reforms of the *Belle Époque*) to a new urban context, with Fordist nuances and endowed with elements of a "mass" culture. But we intend to invest more fully in this line of analysis in the next steps of the research.[6]

The spatiality of the World Cup portrays, to some extent, the panorama of the Brazilian urban network in the mid-twentieth century, a theme that may be further explored in subsequent studies. The significant concentration of investments and even of matches played in Rio de Janeiro expresses not only the capital city's condition, but the very strength of the city of Rio de Janeiro in the economic, social and cultural scenario at the time. The two national metropolises concentrated two thirds of the entire competition. The impoverished Northeast attended "symbolically" with only one city (Recife), with a makeshift stadium (Ilha do Retiro) and hosted only one match out of the total of 22 contested. The South region, the second most developed, had two cities (Porto Alegre and Curitiba), but hosted only four matches, that is, it had a reduced participation in the competition, whose "center" was the Southeast. To the precariousness of the communications network we must add the low budgetary capacity of the sporting event.

---

[6] Project of our authorship: "The global and the local in the spectacle city: Territory, culture and citizenship in the context of the 2014 World Cup." Approved by CNPq, Research Productivity Scholarship, 2014–2017.

We also believe that this Cup represented, on the international scene, Brazil's affirmation as an emerging power in football, civil engineering and the economy. The developmentalism that characterized the 1950s cannot be dissociated from this event, and especially from the construction of a stadium that for many decades remained as the world's largest. Also, in the national context, this Cup represents the consolidation of football as an institution omnipresent in the territory and as an undisputed national passion. It can be understood as the authentic outcome of the Estado Novo's "sports" policy, which conceived it in the spirit of Italian fascism: football as a crucial element to foster patriotism and mobilize the masses.

In 1950, Brazil experienced the beginnings of what would later become, during the years of the military regime, the formation of the state machine that planned the national territory and cities. The state presence in football would take its first steps, as we have seen, by building stadiums such as Pacaembu, in São Paulo, in 1940. In addition to the construction of Maracanã, it had a timid participation in the 1950 World Cup, but became more important as of 1968, with the dissemination of large popular stadiums in virtually all state capitals, in an evident policy of "bread and circuses." The 2014 edition reveals massive governmental participation, especially in the volume of resources, but not to offer entertainment to the urban masses. The new stadiums are aimed at segments with higher consumption capacity and tend to be managed by private initiative. In short, in 1950, we had the outline of an urban Brazil marked, at least in some sectors, by public policies aimed at including the popular strata, such as, for example, in the provision of social housing endowed with essential public services such as health and education. The new scenario points to a clearly neoliberal context in which public policies and investments favor private initiative and promote socio-spatial segregation, elitist stadiums and using the World Cup to implement urban projects that accentuate social inequalities in the city.

References

Bale, J. (1994). *Landscapes of modern sports*. Leicester University Press.
Damo, A. S. (1998). *Para o que der e vier: O pertencimento clubístico no futebol brasileiro a partir do Grêmio de foot ball porto alegrense e seus torcedores*. (Doctoral Dissertation in Anthropology), UFRGS, Porto Alegre, Brazil. https://ludopedio.com.br/biblioteca/para-o-que-der-e-vier/
Dienstmann, C. (1987). *Campeonato Gaúcho: 68 anos de história*. Sulina.
Drumond, M. (2009). Pátrias em jogo: Esporte e propaganda política nos governos de Vargas e Peron. In V. A. Melo (Ed.), *História comparada do esporte* (pp. 61–75). Shape.
Ferreira, F. C. (2004). *O bairro Vasco da Gama: Um novo bairro, uma nova identidade?* (Doctoral Dissertation in Geography), UFF.
Hobsbawm, E. (1988). *A era dos impérios: 1875–1914*. Paz e Terra.
Hobsbawm, E. (1991). *Nações e nacionalismos desde 1870*. Paz e Terra.
Klein, M., & Audinino, S. (1998). *O almanaque do futebol brasileiro: 1997/1998*. Escala.
Marques, V. (1975). *A história do futebol paraibano*. União.
Mascarenhas, G. (1999). Construindo a cidade moderna: A introdução dos esportes na vida urbana do Rio de Janeiro. *Estudos Históricos*, *13*(23), 17–39. https://bibliotecadigital.fgv.br/ojs/index.php/reh/article/view/2086

Mascarenhas, G. (2009). Globalização e espetáculo: O Brasil dos megaeventos esportivos. In V. A. Melo, & M. D. Priore (Eds.), *História do esporte no Brasil: Do Império aos dias atuais* (pp. 505–513). Editora da Unesp.

Mascarenhas, G. (2014). *Entradas e bandeiras: A conquista do Brasil pelo futebol*. Eduerj.

Mascarenhas, G. (2018). Justiça ambiental e produção do espaço nos jogos rio 2016: O paradoxo do golfe olímpico. *Geo UERJ*, (32), e32541, 1–18. https://doi.org/10.12957/geouerj.2018.32541

Moura, G. A. (1998). *O Rio corre para o Maracanã*. Editora FGV.

Negreiros, P. J. L. C. (1998). *A nação entra em campo: Futebol nos anos 30 e 40*. (Master's thesis in History), PUC-SP, São Paulo, Brazil. https://sapientia.pucsp.br/handle/handle/13003

Noronha, N., & Coimbra, D. (1994). *História dos grenais*. Artes e Ofícios.

Pesavento, S. J. (1995). Muito além do espaço: Por uma história cultural do urbano. *Estudos Históricos, 8*(16), 279–290. http://bibliotecadigital.fgv.br/ojs/index.php/reh/article/view/2008

Ramonet, I. (1998). Football et passions nationales. In P. Boniface (Ed.), *Géopolitique du football* (pp. 55–62). Éditions Complexe.

Santos, M. (1996). *A natureza do espaço: Técnica e tempo, razão e emoção*. Hucitec.

Singer, P. (1977). *Desenvolvimento econômico e evolução urbana* (2nd ed.). Nacional.

Souza Neto, G. (2017). *Do Prado ao Mineirão: A história dos estádios na capital inventada*. (Doctoral Dissertation in Leisure), UFMG, Belo Horizonte, Brazil. https://repositorio.ufmg.br/handle/1843/BUOS-B2CGRB

Ziller, A. (1974). *Enciclopédia do Atlético*. Lemi.

Chapter 20
Stadiums and Arenas as Privileged Lenses to Capture Changes in Urban Space

Fernando da Costa Ferreira

Introduction

In recent decades, we have witnessed a major transformation related to the shape and uses of spaces intended for football practice. The "stadium of the masses" endowed with a strong popular centrality (Mascarenhas, 2014), gives way to facilities with smaller audience capacity, capable (in theory) of generating continuous income and attended by an audience of greater purchasing power. The space designed by the new structures, renamed as arenas, seeks to attract a "differentiated" audience. Therein, the traditional supporter shall leave the scene, being replaced by the fan-consumer as of a mistaken association between supporter behavior and the social class to which they belong. Similar discourse is adopted to justify the expulsion of the poor population from certain portions of the urban space, "chosen" by hegemonic agents to be "renewed" or "ennobled". As a consequence, we witness the deterritorialization of economically less privileged citizens. The loss of the right to the stadium goes hand in hand with the loss of the right to the city.

Like Bromberger (1995a), we understand the equipment used for football practice as microrepresentations of society and urban space. In this sense, we intend to show the importance of the studies developed in the field of sports geography, and of the authors associated with it, for the construction of a critical view about the attempts of imposition of a mercantilist logic, which intends to reduce the stadiums, arenas, and the city to spaces of consumption, frequented by a limited portion of the population.

Although we invite to the debate authors from different fields, as this text is directly focused on the sports geography, geographers shall play a leading role in the analysis related to stadiums and arenas and their relation with the urban space. We highlight contributions developed by the triad formed by the Welsh John Bale, the Brazilian Gilmar Mascarenhas (pioneer of sports geography in Brazil and in its study under a

F. da Costa Ferreira (✉)
Instituto Benjamin Constant, Rio de Janeiro, Brazil

© The Author(s), under exclusive license to Springer Nature Switzerland AG 2021　　　　321
S. S. Giglio and M. W. Proni (eds.), *Football and Social Sciences in Brazil*,
https://doi.org/10.1007/978-3-030-84686-2_20

critical perspective, opening a new and promising field of investigations) and the US Christopher Gaffney.

This chapter is structured in three parts. The first deals with stadiums from the geographers' perspective and the difficulty in defining the meaning of the term "arena". The second part presents a history on the evolution of the shape and functions of football stadiums and how they became icons of the urban landscape, first in British cities and then in much of the world, since the mid-nineteenth century, until the Heysel and Hillsborough disasters in the late twentieth century. The final third will analyze the post-Taylor Report stadiums; the adoption of the *tradium* conception developed by John Bale; the emergence of the modern FIFA standard arenas, designed to house the fan-consumer; and the perceived differences between the space designed for arenas and the space experienced by the attending public.

Stadiums and Arenas: A Geographical Overview

Gaffney (2008) uses as main criteria to define a stadium the architectural shape, its primary use and internal spatial arrangement, delimiting as object of study, those equipment that shelter sports practiced on a natural or artificial grass fields. Disregarding indoor arenas, it comprises the stadium as a large, open-air structure, usually permanent, built and maintained with the main purpose of hosting sports events.

Following a similar path, Gilmar Mascarenhas' view on football stadiums seeks to define them both according to the physical presence and the relationship with the urban space (external configuration) and from the relationships built between the supporter and these facilities (internal appropriation). From an urban geography perspective, the author subdivides his analysis and classifies them as follows:

> Geographically, a building or equipment of collective access that behaves as a physical and symbolic centrality in the urban-metropolitan space. In the urban operational plan, it performs the function of periodic centrality, capable of attracting a large influx of visitors on match days, forcing a rearrangement in the public management of its surroundings (to ensure safety and accessibility) and generating fleeting commercial and service opportunities to the informal sector. (Mascarenhas, 2014, p. 161, our translation)

In this sense, he understands it as a space of specific sociability, accumulated memory, collectively lived, which takes place in an objective manner, in the concreteness of the place. Joining both lines, he cites the stadium as a constant, permanent centrality in the physical and cultural landscape (Mascarenhas, 2002, 2014). Gaffney (2008) states that due to its shape, size and location, coupled with the function it performs as a public space, the stadium helps shape the memories, textures and experiences we build of cities around the globe. Christian Bromberger (1995b, p. 300) goes further and extols its dual character, which turns it into "one of the few spaces where a modern urban society can give itself a material image of its unity ands its differentiations."

Gomes (2002, p. 242), in an analogy made in the opposite sense to common sense, highlights urban space as a metaphor of football, based on the observation that, when going beyond the limits of the playing field, the fundamental idea of territorial dispute, contained in football, gains the profane world and the city metaphorizes itself in football—and the stadium is one of its spheres of overflow. Furthermore, the organized fans use the term "territory" to designate an area under their domination or in dispute with rival groups (inside or outside the spaces destined for football practice).

Ferreira (2017) observes that, long before the term became popular, several stadiums were characterized by multifunctionality, serving for countless events: musical performances, civic parades, holding public competitions and college entrance exams, religious celebrations and even hosting other sports. During such appropriations, the stadium used to be frequented (also) by individuals who were averse to football and by groups excluded from the environment related to the traditional stadium. Thus, it understands the football stadium as a football territory, both in the concrete and symbolic dimensions, whose different uses produce multiple territorialities of transitory character.

In Brazil, the year 2007 can be considered a milestone in relation to the implementation of a reconfiguration regarding the form-function of our stadiums. The choice of the country to host the XX Football World Cup, in 2014, came with the realization that no sports venue was fully suitable to meet the requirements and recommendations of the *Fédération Internationale de Football Association* (FIFA), necessary for the holding of such a huge competition. Since then, new or renovated stadiums have been designated as arenas.

The term "arena", however, lacks a clear definition. Despite appearing as a counterpoint to the traditional stadium, perceived as old-fashioned, its origin dates back to very ancient structures. In Ancient Rome, the arena would correspond to the central part of Roman amphitheaters, covered with sand, where combat spectacles between gladiators or between beasts took place. According to the same source, on the occasion of certain dates or civic festivals, it served as a stage to deliver common or Christian convicts to the beasts.

The report "Multipurpose arenas" prepared by the National Bank for Economic and Social Development (BNDES) understands such structures as "facilities of different sizes such as gyms and stadiums, where events of various natures are held" (BNDES, 1997, p. 3, our translation). Even among architects involved in plans to build or renovate the 12 stadiums used in the 2014 World Cup, there is no consensus as to what they would actually be.

The duo responsible for preparing the reconstruction project of the Mané Garrincha stadium (also called Nacional stadium), in Brasília, has distinct visions. In a simple but didactic analogy, Eduardo de Castro Mello compares stadiums to saucers, with low bleachers and far from the playing field. Arenas, on the other hand, would look like cups, with a greater inclination of the bleachers and the approximation of the audience to the pitch. His son, Vicente de Castro Mello, takes a pragmatic view, understanding this new denomination as a marketing strategy to more easily sell the new, or remodeled, sporting equipment, increasing the collection with sponsors (Ferreira, 2020). Thus, the arena would arise as a way of getting rid of the image associated with the ancient stadium, understood as a territory focused on the practice of sports, once in a while appropriated by temporary territorialities that escape from its primary function. Its main purpose would be to offer paid entertainment services, associated with the use of its facilities which, in the traditional stadium, remained idle most of the time.

Daniel Hopf Fernandes (2013, p. 65), CEO of the office responsible for the Arena Pernambuco's construction project and Maracanã's retrofit, understands stadiums as places for the almost exclusive practice of football, while arenas are designed to host a large number of different events. Although matches remain as the prime use, they are not necessarily the activity that shall generate the highest volume of revenues. For that to happen, football would need to stop being seen as a sport and start being understood as entertainment, something that, according to Fernandes, is a concept not yet assimilated by most agents involved in these plans. In his understanding, while stadiums would tend to suffer, over the years, with the process of degradation and devaluation, arenas would be consolidated as reference points and attract investments.

Geraint et al. (2007) perceive *stadia* as buildings designed to house sports that require greater space for the unfolding of the action, whether outdoors or with structures designed using roofing. However, they admit that *stadia* may refer to large arenas as long as, in addition to their multiple uses, they are designed to house musical concerts, being fundamental the existence of a roof (fixed or retractable) that covers the entire playing field. The authors' understanding for these post-modern structures is related, as we will see in the third part, to the *tradium* conception.

In Brazil's case, the imposition of the architectural standard associated with arenas arises as a way of trying to mark the opposition between the ancient stadium—comfortless, dirty, unsafe, with unpleasant odors, homophobic, misogynistic—and new structures designed to host events other than football (Mascarenhas, 2013). It would symbolize an expression of rupture with the traditional stadium's idea of backwardness, which would aim at attracting a new audience, of higher purchasing power and lower socioeconomic diversity and, due to the national historical context, lower ethno-racial diversity.

Arenas work as a factor of distinction in multiple scales: architectural (as icons of urban space within the context of promoting the image of cities), social (status symbol), cultural (imposition of a new standard of behavior and ways of using these spaces) and technical (incorporation of cutting edge materials and technological devices).

As part of this process, traditional stadiums and gyms lose their toponymity identity (replaced by coveted naming rights) and their ties to their original sporting families (football stadium, athletics stadium, multisport gymnasium) and are now categorized as multipurpose or multifunctional arenas. Traditionally, the stadium has a baptism name and a popular denomination that identifies it before the population. In the stadium that becomes an arena, the adoption of a commercial name is naturalized which at the end of the contract, disappears and may be succeeded by another. In these new facilities, due to increasingly more expensive entrance fees and the prohibition of traditional ways of supporting, perceived as being inadequate to resigned environments, sociocultural exclusion gives way to socioeconomic exclusion. Using the term established by Haesbaert (1997), there is an ongoing process of concrete and symbolic deterritorialization of the traditional supporter which, it is worth emphasizing, is prior to the arenization process of part of our stadiums.

Football Stadiums in the Nineteenth and Twentieth Centuries

The Welsh John Bale, the first geographer to study in detail the football stadiums, their importance in the landscape and their centrality in the urban space, tries to explain the evolution of this sport and the spaces intended for its practice. The author follows two paths: The first one is related to the change in the arena's shape that, in a little over a century, went from an open space to a commercialized closed space, and, finally, to a technological space; the second one concerns the degree of spatial confinement of the participants and, mainly, of the spectators. We can notice in the internal architecture of the remodeled arenas and stadiums an increasing atomization of the cheering act and the imposition of rigid behavioral rules. Taking as reference the contribution of Gaffney and Mascarenhas (2005–2006), we witness, at the current stage, the attempt to transform these places, from spaces of celebration into disciplinary spaces.

Bale (1993) is based on Lefèbvre's idea that the transformation of space into commodity is one of the main characteristics of capitalism. Thus, sports, especially football, emerges as another element to be turned into commodity, a product to be sold in spaces intended for its use, reflecting the processes of economic, social and spatial specialization that occurred in society as a whole.[1]

Football stadiums appeared in the urban landscape of the UK in the second half of the nineteenth century, providing better accommodation to a growing audience, willing to pay a certain amount of money to watch the matches. The use of earthen banks, inclined and built around the field, marked the first attempts to create better conditions for the audience to watch the matches. The possibility of increasing revenue from the charging of tickets with different values strongly influenced the internal configuration of football stadiums from the sectorization of these spaces.

Some geographical aspects were also taken into account in the configuration of the modern stadium. The more affluent spectators were able to watch matches seated at stands, mostly built on the western side of the stadium, i.e., facing the sun (matches were played in the afternoon), thus enabling a better view of the unfolding action. The installation of a roof for this sector (often only in the central part) eased the spectators' suffering with the rigors of the British Isles' climate, especially wind and rain. The less fortunate were left with the open sectors to the east (facing the sunset), north and south (behind the goals)—thus, with a less favored view of the field of play,

---

[1] According to the author, there are records that in 1874, Aston Villa charged tickets for their matches with the pitch being enclosed by ropes (the boundaries of the pitch would be formally demarcated by white lines eight years later).

with the audience generally seated standing—known as terraces, bringing football closer to popular theater.

As to the location of the built equipment, the traditional British stadiums followed two main patterns, with strong influence on the spatial distribution of its fan base: the proximity to transport terminals (especially railway stations), enabling access from different points of the city and even from neighboring locations; the proximity to factories, responsible for strengthening the team's ties with the surrounding population, restricting the spatial reach of its sphere of influence.

In the early twentieth century, the Scottish architect Archibald Leitch led the first great revolution related to the shape of football stadiums. If, at first, they used to follow an elliptical shape, with an uncovered stand that sloped behind one of the goals, inspired by the majestic Roman amphitheaters (Giulianotti, 2002), the difficulty clubs had in expanding or acquiring new land plots given the accelerated growth of cities forced him to adopt the rectangular shape for the stadium, coupled with the construction of imposing covered bleachers, overlapping in two rows (doubledeck), which made it possible for clubs to expand the capacity of their sports venues and generate higher revenues, thus creating the classic stadium standard in the UK which consequently been copied in much of the world.

One notices, however, an important difference between *football* stadiums in the British Isles and those also built *for football* in continental Europe. While in England such facilities were owned by the clubs, erected in the heart of urban centers as specific territories only for football practice (except Wembley), on the continent it was common to find publicly funded buildings located in more distant areas, with the possibility of other sports uses inside them (by building an athletics track around the playing field or by sharing it among teams of different sports) or as part of sports complexes comprising gyms, courts, aquatic centers, etc. (model adopted, for instance, at the Maracanã multisports complex). Bale establishes a comparison between football stadiums, located in densely populated working-class areas in English cities, and tennis clubs, located in elegant and distant suburbs. For the author, the social heterogeneity of the British sport, therefore, was reflected in its geographical arrangement in the city (Bale, 1993, p. 20).

Football's continuous growth in popularity brought with it fanaticism and consequently, an increase in the number of conflicts recorded inside the stadiums between groups of the same fan base and notably between rival supporters, leading to greater segregation and crowd control not only by social class but also by club affiliation. In the UK, rowdy supporters were given the name of *hooligans*, a term that, just as the sport they codified, spread across the planet. To combat such acts, solutions were adopted for stadiums that brought them closer (in a much less subtle way) to the Italian stage model (separation of the stage from the audience made by the pit and the curtain), present in theaters since the sixteenth century. The first measure was to prevent the public's free movement around the stadium with the confinement of visiting fans in *pens*, located at points of worst visibility, separated from the field and from the opposing fans by bars, fences and barbed wire fences. Even for the local fans, the conditions of the facilities were not satisfactory. Cases of overcrowding and clashes involving fans often took place inside and around the football fields, reaching a significant contingent of supporters each season.

Giulianotti (2002), when analyzing the main tragedies that have victimized fans in football matches around the globe, cites, in addition to the inefficiency of *anti-hooliganism* measures, which often turned against the safety of the spectators themselves, turning the fields into veritable traps, the following causes: natural disasters; precarious and overcrowded facilities; panic in the crowd. Among so many events with fatal victims, we can cite as the most emblematic the massacres of Heysel, in Brussels (1985),[2] Hillsborough, in Sheffield (1989),[3] with the tragic toll of 39 and 96 deaths, respectively. Such events, although preceded (and succeeded) by many others, represented saturation points, milestones for radical changes in the configuration (physical structure and frequency) of stadiums in continental Europe and the UK in the first instance and, subsequently, in other regions of the planet.

In the UK, a commission was established to investigate the causes of the Hillsborough disaster, with the release of a document produced by the appointed authorities. Presented in its definitive version in January 1990, the Taylor Report, prepared by a team led by Lord Taylor of Gosforth, contained a series of recommendations aimed at increasing the comfort, safety and control of crowds attending football stadiums. This was not the first document presented with this intention, but it had as a differential the fact that, instead of blaming the fans, it pointed out as the main responsible for this and other disasters the clubs, the authorities, the police and the way the press approached the subject. In the name of security, stadiums, many of them built before World War I and endowed with precarious facilities, were transformed into veritable prisons, whose hostile architecture to the public contributed to situations of collective panic, such as the one that occurred in the city of Sheffield, assuming such proportions.[4]

---

[2] Before the start of the final of the European Cup at *Heysel Park in* Brussels, Liverpool fans broke through a barrier formed by only six police officers and invaded sector Z, occupied mostly by Juventus fans who had bought tickets with moneychangers. As well as taking over the opposition stand, the *hooligans'* intention was to attack anyone in front of them. Trapped, the Italian fans concentrated next to a side wall, which could not withstand the excessive weight and gave way, the same happened to the pitch's separation fences. In total, 39 people died (many from suffocation, crushing and/or trampling) and 454 were injured.

[3] The Hillsborough stadium (considered one of the best in the UK), owned by Sheffield Wednesday, was chosen to host the FA Cup semi-final match against Nottingham Forest. The insufficient number of turnstiles for the entrance of Liverpool fans, in the section reserved for them, behind one of the goals (called *terrace*), led to a major uproar, due to the damming of the crowd. In accordance with the security requirements of the Popplewell Report, the newly refurbished terrace had been divided into four sub-sectors known as *pens*. When the police finally decided to open the gates as a way to more quickly drain the public towards the inside, the lack of indicative signs caused the human mass to follow to the closest subsectors, causing their overcrowding (something that did not happen in the other two *pens* located at the ends). The pressure of the crowd, which kept on entering, made that, in order not to be crushed against the "protection" fences, many fans tried, as an extreme attitude, to jump over the bars towards the lawn. The police, not understanding the gravity of the situation and trained to treat movements of supporters as acts of disorder, instead of allowing the access to the pitch, even beat some of them to make them return to their *pens*. As a consequence of this succession of errors, 96 people died and almost 800 spectators were injured in an enclosure free from the presence of *hooligans*.

[4] Among the main proposals prepared by the commission, we can highlight: greater standardization and rigidity as to stadium construction and renovation standards; adoption of the *all-seater stadium*

Stadiums and Arenas Post-Taylor Report

Hollanda and Reis (2014, p. 14) understand Heysel and Hillsborough as temporal milestones responsible for the union of efforts of authorities (at different scales) with the police forces aimed at preventing, containing and punishing violent acts in stadiums and surroundings. In parallel, the adoption of a set of policies aimed at "sanitization, gentrification and modernization of stadiums" sought to ward off and inhibit the presence of potentially aggressive groups.

The new management model of stadiums and associated events was quickly replicated to other parts of the world, resulting in a change in the profile and attitude of the audience due to the reduced capacity of the renovated equipment and the elimination of popular sectors. The grounds *of* the turn of the twentieth to the twenty-first century came to be managed by a commercial logic of American inspiration. Alvito (2014) points out the clubs' managers as responsible for changing the profile of the audience attending the stadiums. They envisioned the possibility, by offering safe and comfortable equipment, to attract an audience with higher purchasing power and lower offensive potential, the fan-consumer. Based on an approach inspired in Michel Foucault's ideas, Gaffney and Mascarenhas (2005–2006) suggest a new political anatomy of the stadium, bringing it closer to the predictability characteristic of current theater and cinema audience behavior.

Bale (2003, p. 135) employs the term *tradium* (trade + stadium) as a way of naming post-modern structures planned without the concern of being exclusively linked to a single sport, transformed into multisports, multifunctional spaces and of flexible use, with declared commercial purposes. In his understanding, the stadium returned to its pre-modern form of multifunctional use of space, returning to being "a gigantic entertainment hall".

Along similar lines, FIFA (2011, p. 45) suggests that plans prepared for stadiums built or renovated to host competitions under its seal, include the possibility of holding entertainment and other sports events as a strategy to make them financially viable. The issue of affordability has encouraged owners of new stadiums to transform them into multipurpose arenas, allowing for use unrelated to the main sports function. In several countries, there are examples of successful initiatives: shopping centers, health clinics, fitness centers, hotels and conference facilities. Thus, diversification in ongoing use increases the "self-sustainability" and "feasibility" of new arenas.

If, as we have seen, there is no clear definition of what an arena is, its vocation emerges explicitly by providing that multifunctional stadiums, despite having football matches as their primary purpose, host other modalities as a way to increase revenue generation (FIFA, 2011, p. 44). There is a reservation, however,

---

model with all fans accommodated in numbered seats (even acknowledging that the presence of standing supporters was not intrinsically unsafe); fan identification contained in the ticket; removal of barbed wire barriers or any other sharp object separating the public from the field of play and other parts of the stadium; elimination of sectors in which the first steps would receive spectators seated at points whose floor is located below the level of the field of play; prohibition for the same fan to purchase lots of tickets.

for the construction of athletics tracks, which would keep the public away from the playing field.[5] Another important source of funds is the holding of entertainment events, including concerts, festivals, plays and business and consumer fairs. The use of synthetic turf, another example of technical advances long held back by the organization, is now encouraged as a means of extending the life of the pitch.

The new spaces are designed to house different uses related to the provision of services and paid entertainment enabling ongoing income generation. These environments should be as predictable as the lobby of an international airport or the interior of a shopping center. At the operational level, the division into four separate sectors (which can be fractioned) seeks to avoid contact between rival groups. The accesses need to be wide, well signaled and have the presence of stewards (scattered around the outside and inside), prepared to answer any questions and avoid unpleasant surprises. A clean, clear and airy environment, with an abundant supply of toilets and eating facilities, contributes to the maintenance of order, discouraging vandalism and the occurrence of other inappropriate behaviors. The ambience created should favor impulse consumption, with stores and kiosks prepared to turn club passion into income, offering from a wide range of official products to supporter membership plans. Nothing should hinder the experience of the spectator of a football match. According to FIFA (2011, p. 111), the identification of sectors and rows should be clearly displayed in the circulation areas in an easily located place. When spectators arrive at an unfamiliar stadium, the path to their seat should be clearly marked and easily identifiable. It is important that spectators move fluidly so that they do not become impatient and frustrated. In other words, the process of entering the arena cannot be stressful or unnecessarily time-consuming. And the same can be said for exiting the stadium.

Seated in their covered, numbered, unbreakable and fireproof seats, the field of vision of the four lines of the pitch must be free of any obstacle, something partially guaranteed by the steeper slope of the stands and, if necessary, by a security team, responsible for (initially) politely approaching those who have difficulty assimilating the new standard of behavior in force. A powerful sound system and high-definition screens display goals from historic matches, chants and images of the fans, various statistics, (many) advertising messages, as well as images of the match and the audience. With luck, the fan/spectator/customer can be focused (the chances increase if accompanied by family or a romantic couple) and "explode" in joy, live, for the entire country. The high-speed Internet allows the experience in the stadium to be, after the photographic or video record, immediately posted, shared and liked. All this, duly monitored in an internal control room, equipped with closed circuit TV. On behalf of the preservation of heritage and public safety, all movement of fans and other players involved in the realization of a match is duly monitored.

Mascarenhas seeks to advance this discussion by admitting the income generation potential of new arenas for clubs and their administrators without forgetting, however, the impact brought about by new spaces designed by hegemonic players on traditional

---

[5] A very expensive but possible solution would be the adoption of retractable stands, such as those at the *Stade de France*.

ways of cheering. His main criticism falls on the reduction of the multifunctional character of these spaces to a purely economicist conception. For the author:

> The dominant rhetoric praises such equipment as being endowed with multi-functionality by means of the recurring adjective "multiuse". In reality, this is an architectural adequacy that enables the operation of shops and restaurants inside the stadium, as well as hosting major musical, religious and other events. Undoubtedly, the modern arena multiplies its commercial capacity by making the equipment's functions more flexible. However, as far as the engaged supporter is concerned, what one notices is the opposite movement, of accentuated restriction of his behavior, reduced to the passive condition of watching seated. Therefore, contrary to what is enthusiastically disclosed by hegemonic agents, various interdictions standardize the ways of cheering and wave to the supporter the clear reduction of the effectively "multifunctional" nature of the traditional stadium, which was the true carrier of diversity of uses: not only watching [to] spectacles, but being the protagonist, and inventing forms of collective expression, singing, dancing, eating, and drinking. (Mascarenhas, 2013, p. 157, our translation)

Gaffney and Mascarenhas (2005–2006) understand the end of Maracanã's *geral*, consummated in 2005, as part of this process in which arenas emerge as symbols of modernity in counterpoint to the "old" stadium. The permanence of the traditional popular sector represented the vestige of a past era that does not agree with the modern demands of sports production.

It is possible to draw a new parallel between the *tradium* and the FIFA standard stadium when we analyze the strong surveillance and control apparatus existing over the public, both with the escorting of groups of visiting supporters, since their arrival in the city until the match, and with the installation of modern monitoring systems inside the stadiums. Bale draws on the idea of the panopticon present in Michel Foucault's *"Discipline and punish"* to define the football stadiums of the current stage. The new fixtures are conceived as technological artifacts, being named as multipurpose arena, with its internal configuration may vary according to the spectacle it hosts. The sectorization, or hypersectorization,[6] acquires such a degree of sophistication that contact between different sectors and free movement within the same sector (through the adoption of marked seats) are practically impossible. With the introduction of the *all-seater* standard, the old places intended for standing audience (*gerais* in Brazil and *terraces* in England) were eliminated, replaced by comfortable individual seats, corporate boxes or sectors reserved for the presence of families, with the reduction of audience capacity largely offset by a significant increase in revenue. Thinking about the potential role of stadiums in the debate on the right to the city, Mascarenhas (2013) suggests that:

> In face of the concept of city-scenery, it does not seem strange to propose the notion of "stadium-scenery", considering how much its current configuration and regulation lend themselves much more to behaved and adequate staging to television broadcasting than to a space of free collective manifestation. Milton Santos (1987) had already put bluntly how the capitalist society restricts the access to citizenship rights to those able to pay: the

---

[6] Ferreira (2017) coined the term "hypersectorization" with the purpose of identifying the growing fragmentation of the spaces destined to football stadiums' frequenters in order to prevent their free movement through the resigned sporting equipment. At the same time, one notices a trend towards the reduction or even elimination of popular sectors.

"citizen-consumer". However, it seems that we are facing a new situation, which radicalizes the association of consumption with rights of access to the polis: it is the impoverishment of public life through spatial segregation (insularization) combined with the aforementioned staging, the result of the emerging normative apparatus. [...] The acclaimed modernization of football stadiums is inserted precisely in this process, since it aims to remove from their enclosures all those behaviors considered inappropriate to the new order of passive consumption of the football spectacle. The current "FIFA model" conceives the modern stadium as equipment intended to a specific audience, "extra", select, solvable, willing to pay dearly for technology, comfort and safety. a "familiar", "orderly" audience, which goes to the stadium to consume the spectacle and not to seek for traditional forms of protagonism that are of no interest to the new hegemonic model. Still at the level of modernizing rhetoric, it is intended a "civilized" stadium, as opposed to chaos and "barbarism", supposedly reigning in the previous model, considered vulnerable to uncontrollable mass movements and subject to the action of "dangerous" social groups. It is remarkable how this discourse on stadiums faithfully reproduces the neoliberal thought. (Mascarenhas, 2013, pp. 158–160, our translation)

In terms of internal appropriation, Ferreira (2017), when studying the behavior of Maracanã's frequenters after the 2014 World Cup, notices that the space conceived by hegemonic actors does not fully correspond to the space experienced by the public present. The ambience produced varies according to a number of factors, such as: sector of the stadium, schedule, latest results and the opponent. In decisive matches or in derbies of greater rivalry, it is common to find demonstrations of exacerbated behavior (considered inconvenient) in the partitions where pre-established order should reign. There is then a growing clash between different ways of cheering and watching the games. Little by little, cries of "Sit down!"—initially banned from the Brazilian arenas—were heard again. At the same time, we witness a growing movement that calls for the "repopularization" of football, which consists in regaining the atmosphere existing in traditional stadiums, without losing the advances perceived by the public present at the arenas, especially the cleanliness and comfort of the environment and the significant reduction of acts of vandalism and violence.

Around the globe, it is possible to notice, albeit timidly, small but significant victories by fans who prefer to cheer without the cramped conditions caused by the rules in force in the concourse. In Germany, 15 of the 18 stadiums/arenas used in the 2018–2019 *Bundesliga* season had areas intended to receive fans who do not need the comfort of seats. In Brazil, we can mention Itaquerão,[7] which, although designed as a FIFA standard arena, after the 2014 World Cup, had the chairs fixed in the North sector, a portion occupied by the traditional fanatical fans, removed. In Maracanã, the northern and southern upper sectors, despite the maintenance of the original configuration, are occupied by fans who maintain the traditional culture of watching the matches standing up, without the risk of being reprimanded by the stewards. This achievement was possible due to negotiations involving representatives of supporter collectives, the police and the consortium that used to manage the stadium/arena.

---

[7] Itaquerão is the popular name that identifies the Corinthians Arena, built in the district of Itaquera, East of the city of São Paulo. In 2020, the building was renamed *Neo Química Arena* due to the sale of the naming rights to a pharmaceutical group for the next 20 years.

Conclusion

The shape, location, function and forms of appropriation of stadiums reflect the urban space and the society in which they are inserted. Equipment that were built between the second half of the nineteenth century and the last quarter of the twentieth century were designed to shelter collectivities of all classes, arranged in separate sectors according to purchasing power. In the arenas of the twenty-first century, in the same way we notice in the areas desired for the expansion of real estate capital, there is a clear intention to "clean" these environments from groups understood as culturally and/or economically undesirable. The renovation project of these spaces consists in replacing the traditional frequenter by a clientele belonging to the middle, upper-middle and upper classes. It is then built a discourse that seeks to justify the deterritorialization of the less fortunate fans and low-income citizens, who reside in the desired areas for the expansion and the consequent reproduction of capital, concentrated in the hands of hegemonic agents.

In this context, the traditional stadiums, perceived as dirty, macho, and violent environments, are replaced by arenas, equipment marked by comfort, safety, "multi-functionality" and respect for diversity. In the name of a discourse that seeks to exalt the inclusion of traditionally excluded groups, we witness the imposition of a logic aimed at attracting a public with greater purchasing power, passive in behavior and active in consumption. At the same time, based on a mistaken association between social class and public behavior, we witnessed a process of exclusion of former frequenters belonging to less favored classes.

At the same time, it is possible to find, in stadiums and cities, resistance movements undertaken by hegemonized agents. Mascarenhas (2013, p. 155) points out that the rich movement of stadium appropriation makes it a unique element in the social reproduction of the city. The active posture of groups of supporters who claim the party's protagonism, refusing to limit their performance to the role of passive spectators and consumers, configures an act of resistance to the attempt of imposing a single behavioral norm in contemporary stadiums/arenas. The same thought applies for social movements that claim, for all citizens, the right to the city.

In the case of stadiums/arenas, they have not lost their organic character, constituting objects in constant transformation. Their numerous transitory micro-territorialities result from a complex game of forces in which tensions and contradictions found in the urban space are constantly produced, reproduced and represented, and which should be understood as a reflection of a broad social context. The main contribution of sports geography lies in the adoption of a critical perspective that provides the researcher, based on analyses produced in the sports field, with subsidies to think of stadiums, arenas and the city as possible spaces experienced by all, not only by privileged groups.

References

Alvito, M. (2014). *A rainha de chuteiras: Um ano de futebol na Inglaterra*. Apicuri.

Bale, J. (1993). *Sport, space and the city*. Routledge.

Bale, J. (2003). *Sports geography* (2nd ed.). Routledge Taylor & Francis e-Library.

Banco Nacional de Desenvolvimento Econômico e Social (BNDES). (1997). Arenas multi-usos. Rio de Janeiro: BNDES, Área de Operações Industriais 2, Gerência Setorial 2. www.bndes.gov.br/SiteBNDES/export/sites/default/bndes_pt/Galerias/Arquivos/conhecimento/relato/aren-mul.pdf

Bromberger, C. (1995). *Le match du football: Ethnologie d'une passion partisane à Marseille, Naples et Turin*. Éditions de la Maison des Sciences de l'Homme.

Bromberger, C. (1995). Football as world-view and as ritual. *French Cultural Studies, 6*(18), 293–311. https://doi.org/10.1177/095715589500601803

Fernandes, D. H. (2013). A nova infraestrutura de arenas e a Copa de 2014: Impulsionando a cadeia de entretenimento no Brasil. *Cadernos FGV Projetos, 22*, 62–69. https://fgvprojetos.fgv.br/pub licacao/cadernos-fgv-projetos-no-22-futebol-e-desenvolvimento-economico-social-0

Ferreira, F. C. (2017). *O estádio de futebol como arena para a produção de diferentes territorialidades torcedoras*: *Inclusões, exclusões, tensões e contradições presentes no novo Maracanã*. (Master's thesis in Geography), Universidade do Estado do Rio de Janeiro, Brazil.

Ferreira, F. C. (2020). Estádios e arenas como lentes privilegiadas para capturar as transformações do espaço urbano. In S. S. Giglio, & M. W. Proni (Orgs.), *O futebol as ciências humanas no Brasil* (pp. 508–523). Editora da Unicamp.

FIFA. (2011). *Football stadiums: Technical recommendation and requirements* (5th ed.). https://www.scribd.com/doc/100501692/FIFA-Football-Stadiums-Technical-recommendation-and-req uirements-5th-edition

Gaffney, C. T. (2008). *Temples of the earthbound gods: Stadiums in the cultural landscapes of Rio de Janeiro and Buenos Aires*. University of Texas Press.

Gaffney, C. T., & Mascarenhas, G. (2005–2006). The soccer stadium as a disciplinary space. *Esporte e Sociedade, 1*(1). https://periodicos.uff.br/esportesociedade/issue/view/2390

Geraint, J., Sheard, R., & Vickery, B. (2007). *Stadia: A design and development guide* (4th ed.). Elsevier; Architectural Press.

Giulianotti, R. (2002). *Sociologia do futebol*: *Dimensões históricas e socioculturais do esporte das multidões*. Nova Alexandria.

Gomes, P. C. C. (2002). *A condição urbana*. Bertrand Brasil.

Haesbaert, R. (1997). *Desterritorialização e identidade*: *A rede gaúcha no Nordeste*. Eduff.

Hollanda, B. B. B., & Reis, H. H. B. (2014). Introdução. In B. B. B. de Hollanda, & H. H. B. Reis (Eds.), *Hooliganismo e a Copa de 2014* (p. 13–19). 7Letras.

Mascarenhas, G. (2002). O lugar e as redes: Futebol e modernidade na cidade do Rio de Janeiro. In G. Marafon & M. Ribeiro (Eds.), *Estudos de geografia fluminense* (pp. 127–142). Infobook.

Mascarenhas, G. (2013). Um jogo decisivo, mas que não termina: A disputa pelo sentido da cidade nos estádios de futebol. *Revista Cidades, 10*(17), 142–170. https://revista.fct.unesp.br/index.php/revistacidades/article/view/3238

Mascarenhas, G. (2014). *Entradas e bandeiras: A conquista do Brasil pelo futebol*. Eduerj.

Taylor, L. J. (1990). *Hillsborough Stadium disaster: 15 April 1989* (Inquiry by the RT Hon Lord Justice Taylor, final report). London: HMSO. https://www.jesip.org.uk/uploads/media/incident_reports_and_inquiries/Hillsborough%20Stadium%20Disaster%20final%20report.pdf

Chapter 21
The Football Industry in Brazil

Marcelo Weishaupt Proni

Introduction

In the 1990s, the major football clubs in Brazil began to test professional management methods and new sports marketing tools to increase their revenues and their sports competitiveness. The success of the Palmeiras–Parmalat partnership (1992–2000) became quite emblematic and stimulated the entry of large companies not only as sponsors, but as investors and co-managers of the business. Although "Brazilian football"[1] had great market potential, the gap in the commercial exploitation of this business by the major national clubs in relation to the main football centers in Europe was growing (Aidar & Leoncini, 2000). The predominant discourse in the sporting press mistakenly claimed that the adoption of a purely economic rationality in the management of clubs and in the organization of tournaments would be enough to solve the financial instability of the major national clubs and to bring them on par with European competitors (Proni, 2000).

Another important vector to mark the development of the football industry in Brazil is the change in the legal framework and in the institutional environment. In this sense, it can be said that the regulation of the "club-company"—which began with the Zico Law (1993), advanced with the Pelé Law (1998) and subsequently underwent occasional revisions in 2000, 2003, 2011, and 2015—has not only accompanied the ongoing changes but has also marked their direction. However, despite the new

---

[1] The analysis is focused on men's professional football. The women's tournaments, which began to be played in 1989, received little media attention and did not attract sponsors. In 2013, the Brazilian Football Confederation (CBF) created the Brazilian Women's Football Championship. Starting in 2019, all clubs in the men's first division league will be obliged to maintain a women's team. However, the revenues (and expenses) of the women's league are still negligible compared to those of the men's league.

M. W. Proni (✉)
University of Campinas, Campinas, Brazil
e-mail: mwproni@unicamp.br

legislation and the adoption of marketing strategies and new management methods, the highest level of revenues of the richest leagues (especially the English, Spanish, German, Italian, and French) were not reached.

Over time, the organization of tournaments has improved and there has been a remarkable growth in the annual revenues of the "national elite football clubs." In 2003, the 20 most prestigious teams earned total revenues estimated at R$650 million (Somoggi, 2015), which was equivalent to €180 million. In 2019, the sum of the gross revenues of the 20 clubs that competed in the Série A of the Brazilian Football Championship reached R$5.6 billion (Itaú-BBA, 2020), or approximately €1.2 billion. Using a deflator to correct the effect of inflation in Reais,[2] the total revenues of the elite clubs in 2019 were 3.3 times higher than in 2003. However, the gap in relation to the main football centers in Europe remained.

As of 2003, the Brazilian Championship started to be played in a new format, with the title being won by the team with the highest number of points obtained throughout the competition. Since then, the financial power of the teams became even more determinant, as in order to be champions it became indispensable a high expenditure to hire the best players and coaching staff (previously, clubs with less economic power could eventually reach the final phase of the tournament). It should be noted that teams had to strengthen their partnership with the major sports media (especially with TV Globo) to expand their revenues. And the priority given to the teams with the largest number of fans (i.e., greater marketing return) favored the valuation of sponsorship contracts, enabling the hiring of talented players to improve the quality of the show and increase its attractiveness (Reis et al., 2014).

Over time, the disparities between clubs belonging to the national elite have increased and contributed to distinct trajectories on the sports field. During the past two decades, a few "big clubs" have performed well financially (allowing them to increase their share of total revenues), while others have achieved relatively more modest revenues, with most elite clubs facing recurrent difficulties in balancing their budgets.

In this new era, chronic financial imbalances caused a significant increase in the level of indebtedness among the elite clubs. The situation of insolvency, especially with regard to tax debts, led the federal government to take measures that sought to help clubs equate their debts and, at the same time, demanded greater responsibility in financial management. Two government initiatives stand out in this regard: the creation of "Timemania"—a lottery with 80 teams emblems—in 2006; and the Program for the Modernization of the Management and Fiscal Responsibility of Brazilian Football (Profut) in 2015. However, in most cases, the financial imbalances were not overcome and the problem continued to be discussed in the National Congress.

It can be stated that such chronic financial imbalances and the persistent mismatch in the capacity to generate revenues caused the club-company to develop in Brazil in

---

[2] The accumulated inflation in Brazil, measured by the General Market Price Index (IGP-M), for the period from December 2003 to December 2019 was 160%.

a way that lagged behind the richer European football centers.[3] In fact, most of the elite teams continued to sell their key players to cover deficits. Even the better-off Brazilian teams were unable to compete with the salaries paid in the well-structured European leagues and continued as suppliers of star players.

Similarly, financial inequality has also manifested itself internally, reproducing the hierarchical relations between "big," "medium," and "small" clubs and accentuating the asymmetries of power between teams from the traditional centers (São Paulo, Rio de Janeiro, Belo Horizonte, and Porto Alegre) and teams from the peripheral regions (other state capitals and cities in the interior of the country). Undoubtedly, this is not an exclusive characteristic. Such hierarchy, reinforced by the concentration of power, is a common element in all relevant national football leagues, a consequence of the prevalence of a mercantile logic in the organization of professional football.

The objective of this chapter is to offer an interpretation of the development of the football industry in Brazil. The analysis of the financial situation of the elite clubs allows one to argue that it is an "unequal and combined development." It starts from the observation that this unique business is fully inserted in the context of globalization. Three hypotheses are examined: (i) the main Brazilian clubs have adapted to the changing conditions of economic competition and to changes in national sports legislation; (ii) Brazilian football tends to remain economically lagging behind the main centers of Europe, occupying a place in the semi-periphery of this "global value chain"; (iii) the amplification of the asymmetry of economic power among the elite clubs is a trend inherent to the unequal development of the football industry in Brazil.

The text is composed of six more sections. The second section provides a brief overview of the expansion and characteristics of the football industry in Europe in order to establish parameters for the proposed interpretation. The third section highlights the legislation that has regulated the economic activity of football clubs in Brazil since the 1990s. The fourth section analyzes the increase in revenues of the elite national clubs between 2003–2019 and the asymmetries in economic power that currently exist. The fifth section focuses on the problem of the big clubs' high indebtedness (caused by recurrent budget deficits) and the federal government's efforts to try to solve the problem. The sixth section discusses some current challenges for the development of the Brazilian football industry. The last section adds some concluding remarks.

An Overview of the Football Industry in Europe

The term "football industry" generally refers to a singular branch of business conducted by the soccer clubs of a national league (Szymanski & Smith, 1997),

---

[3] According to Giulianotti and Robertson (2009), the economic and sporting inequalities between the top South American leagues and the top European leagues increased from the early 1980s. This mismatch in club-company development has widened since then.

but it can also be used to analyze market structures and competitive strategies at the international level.

The metamorphosis of this business completely changed professional football in the last quarter of the twentieth century (Giulianotti, 1999; Proni, 2000). Until 1974, the Fédération Internationale de Football Association (FIFA) imposed strict restrictions on the penetration of economic interests in football, but under the presidency of João Havelange sponsorship contracts and the commercialization of the show were allowed. The transition to new models of club management was gradual and initially took place in European football centers, later reaching other continents.[4] It started with the adoption of business management methods in traditional clubs (non-profit sports organizations), progressed with the partnership between clubs and investors interested in exploring a potentially very profitable business, and deepened with the transformation of the ownership structure of clubs, which assumed the legal form of a company (limited liability company or joint-stock company). In some countries, the "club-company" constituted as a corporation has been allowed to go public on the stock exchange, but this has not become the predominant trend in European clubs.

The UK was the first European country to allow clubs to adopt the legal form of limited liability company (controlled by majority shareholders). In the 1960s, they were already described as a special kind of "company" (Vinnai, 1970). But at that time, professional football was a very particular business, due to market characteristics and restrictions on economic competition among clubs, which depended on each other for financial support. In particular, the behavior of firms (clubs) was not based on a "profit-maximizing model" but on a "utility maximizing model" (in this case, sports victories), preventing the adoption of a conventional business rationality (Sloane, 1971).[5]

In the 1970s, the number of European clubs with a professional management of the professional football department (i.e., with rational methods of financial management and with budget planning and execution) was increasing. Traditional clubs had already abandoned amateur management, generally based on passionate decisions, and sought to increase their competitiveness through solid financial conditions. But this was not yet the rule. In Italy, for example, clubs had high social security

---

[4] It is important to mention that the National American Soccer League (NASL), created in the USA in 1967, pioneered the adoption of marketing strategies to promote the sport (such as the signing in the 1970s of renowned stars such as Pelé, Beckenbauer, Cruyff, among others) and increase revenues. Although it was not a league affiliated to FIFA (so it could go against the guidelines of the federative system and adopt its own rules), it probably influenced the changes that occurred later in Europe.

[5] According to Bühler (2006), this business had unique characteristics, which distinguished it from others by the following aspects: (a) the economic success of the club depended on its sporting success; (b) the financial management was conducted in an environment of high uncertainty (and low predictability of results), making long-term planning difficult; (c) it was necessary to reconcile competition and cooperation (the clubs were competitors, but needed each other to produce the product and enhance the spectacle); (d) the manager's objective was not to maximize profits (football clubs prioritized the sportive performance); (e) the high loyalty of the fans propitiated a special relationship of the club with its clients; (f) the clubs did not seek to expand their market share through competitive prices, nor did they need marketing actions.

debts, some teams were used for "money laundering," and allegations of match-fixing appeared.

The transition to a new era was boosted in the following decade. The expansion of income sources for clubs was enhanced by the release of advertising on athletes' uniforms in 1981 (FIFA maintained the ban only for national teams) and, shortly afterward, by the negotiation of the TV broadcasting rights of the championships, which stimulated the hiring of players that could raise the quality of the spectacle and attract more audiences.

Another decisive factor was the change in the legal nature of the clubs, which occurred at different moments in each country. In 1981, the Italian government approved a new legislation to discipline professional football and supervise the business, inducing the transformation of clubs into commercial companies owned by private economic groups (such as Juventus, controlled by the Agnelli family, owner of Fiat). In return, the RAI (public television station) started broadcasting Italian Championship matches and helped boost the clubs' revenues. In 1990, there was a similar legal reordering in Spain, which required the conversion of clubs into a "sports joint-stock company" with responsible financial management (Real Madrid and Barcelona were allowed to continue as civil society organizations, but subject to tax and legal rules equivalent to those applied to commercial companies).

In the 1990s, the major European leagues began to devise more sophisticated marketing plans to enhance business value. The Premier League (founded in 1992) became an example of financial success. In Germany, meanwhile, legislation allowing the conversion of the football club into a joint-stock company was passed in 1998, but with the "50 + 1 rule," ensuring that control of the club remained with a portion of its fans (two exceptions were allowed: Bayer Leverkusen, owned by the Bayer group, and Wolfsburg, controlled by Volkswagen).

The first club to trade shares on a stock exchange was Tottenham Hotspur in 1983. But in the 1980s, English football was still not a profitable activity and was not seen as an investment by shareholders. This situation changed ten years later with the Premier League, after the government intervention to combat hooligans and make stadium modernization viable (financed by a public agency), prioritizing the comfort and safety of fans. The financial restructuring of clubs, the increase in the value of sponsorship and exclusive broadcasting contracts, and the rise in ticket sales revenues made the business profitable, which allowed several clubs to make an initial public offering (IPO) on the London Stock Exchange to capitalize and increase their market power (Manchester United was the most successful in this strategy). However, the entry of football clubs in the capital markets has not had the same success in other European countries and cannot be seen as an inevitable trend (Proni & Libanio, 2016).

At the end of the twentieth century, when the economic activities of football clubs came to be governed by the commercial legislation of each country and by European law,[6] football began to be seen as a genuine business, capable of generating significant revenues and increasingly similar to other economic activities in which cartels are formed—even though the clubs' objective remained the maximization of victories rather than profits (Szymanski & Kuypers, 1999). The growing volume of money involved and the size of the potential market (due to its integration into a very profitable branch of the entertainment industry) began to attract the attention of big businessmen. The conversion of traditional football clubs into emerging companies was made possible by the exploitation of these valuable brands (with national or international reach), which changed the principles that guided the management of clubs and leagues. Understanding consumption patterns and changes in consumer behavior became a relevant factor for marketing actions in this field. The financial indicators became indispensable to assess whether the clubs were economically competitive.

But it must be stressed that, at the start of the new millennium, many economists still did not consider that football had become an important branch of business in the European economic landscape, given that the elite clubs were seen as "medium-sized" companies, considering their cash flow and number of employees, even though some aroused great public interest and received media attention from global players (Bühler, 2006).

This perception has changed as an increasing number of "super clubs" (Andrews, 2015) have moved toward the annual revenues of "large companies" and have adopted corporate governance guidelines. The European football market (summing the revenues of all leagues and federations in the 2018–2019 season) was valued at €28.9 billion, with the top five leagues earning €17 billion and accounting for 59% of total revenues (Deloitte, 2020b). Indeed, this market has grown strongly over the last 20 years and continues to expand.[7] One can even draw an analogy with "global value chains" since the international network of companies (clubs and leagues), centered in Europe, has grown in size and focus on the production and commercialization of football spectacles and the valorization of brands (Brewer, 2019).

In the "football business,"[8] different interests are at stake, taking into account the various stakeholders that interact in this scenario: clubs, federations (leagues), players, agents, sponsors, investors, media, government, organized fans, and spectators. The economic interaction between these multiple stakeholders is configured

---

[6] For example, the ruling of the Court of Justice of the European Union against UEFA (Union of European Football Associations) in the "Bosman case" in 1995 abolished the "pass law" and redefined employment relations in football.

[7] In the 2000–2001 season, the only club with annual revenues exceeding €200 million was Manchester United (€217 million). In the 2018–2019 season, according to the Football Money League 2020, there were 21 European clubs with revenues above this level. Manchester United's turnover had expanded significantly (€712 million), but was outperformed by Real Madrid (€757 million) and Barcelona (€841 million), the first club to exceed €800 million (Deloitte, 2020a).

[8] For a broad overview of the issues discussed in recent studies on the "football business," see the handbook edited by Chadwick et al. (2018).

into two "relationship chains" (Aidar & Leoncini, 2000): one concerning the organization and production of the sporting event, and the other concerning the marketing of the show (and brands).

The development of the football industry induced organizational learning, since the old ways of managing clubs and organizing tournaments became anachronistic. The strategic repositioning of clubs was necessary in view of the evolution of football as a business—which, in turn, made the aforementioned interactions between the players more complex. Like other leading corporations, European elite football clubs also had to plan long-term strategies and had to adapt to changes in the environment in order not to become obsolete. In particular, they were required to empower themselves to increase efficiency in producing the spectacle and exploiting existing markets (Leoncini & Silva, 2005).

Both domestically and internationally, new spaces of competition have been formed among clubs endowed with symbolic capital and economic power, which undertake efforts to achieve prominent positions within and outside the sports field. As the football industry consolidated, clubs were challenged to constitute a "corporate identity," but without losing their "club identity"—an ambiguity that was expressed in the term "club-company" (Albino et al., 2009).

The term "club-company" is more fluid than the definition found in the legal field, usually related to the legal form adopted by the club (although such definition may vary from one country to another, according to the national legislation).[9] From the economic point of view, the conversion of the football club into a company became more complex as time went by. The adoption of business management methods and the predominance of a mercantile mentality in the 1970s already denote the initial transition to a business model. In the 1990s, the legal form becomes one of the criteria to identify club-company types, while the symbiotic relationship with television and the partnership with investors became essential to configure a more advanced stage of development. In some countries, the football industry took on the characteristics of an oligopoly (Manoli, 2014).

Given the deep structural and institutional differences that characterize the various national spaces, it is evident that there is not a "superior model" to be copied, there being different arrangements that enable an efficient economic performance and a high sports performance. Five parameters that interfere in the club-company's performance can be mentioned: (a) ownership structure, (b) governance model, (c) company size, (d) market structure and dynamics, (e) competition strategy.

The ownership structure of football clubs varies on the international scene: in some countries, a non-profit civil association predominates (but with corporate management); in others, a corporate identity (limited liability company or joint-stock company) is the dominant legal form. Even in some countries, there are different legal

---

[9] In Brazil, the determination of the legal nature of the club-company is based on legal criteria and falls under art. 982 of the Civil Code of 2002 (Perruci, 2017).

structures.[10] The important thing is to understand who holds the control of the club-company (it can be an economic group, an owner, the majority shareholders, or the associated fans), because this affects the degree of freedom of the managers (elected or hired) and the decision-making processes within the organization.

Corporate governance criteria applied in football clubs are closely related to the ownership structure (Dimitropoulos, 2014) and are adapted to current legislation and sports regulations (and conventions). They establish relationship standards between the management (board of directors) and owners (partners or shareholders), shape the definition of strategic objectives, and interfere in the relationship with sponsors, employees, players, and supporters. Companies organized as corporations have the board of directors and the CEO elected by the shareholders' meeting. If governance is oriented toward the interests of shareholders (with regard to brand value and equity appreciation as well as dividend distribution), performance evaluation is centered on the balance sheet and financial statements. But the governance model can also be oriented to serve the interests of other influential stakeholders and impose other priorities. Hence, governance in football is at the service of the most powerful groups (Gammelsaeter, 2018).

Clubs that have reached "large company" status have greater access to funding sources, greater spending capacity (investment and current expenses), and greater competitiveness in economic terms. The ranking of the 30 European clubs with the highest annual revenues in the 2018–2019 season (Deloitte, 2020a) shows Barcelona at the top, with record revenues of €841 million, followed by Real Madrid (€757 million), Manchester United (€712 million), Bayern Munich (€660 million), Paris Saint Germain (€636 million), and Manchester City (€611 million). Note that 15 teams had revenues exceeding €300 million, while the other 15 had revenues exceeding €170 million. Together, the 30 listed football clubs generated a record business income: more than €11 billion this season. This ranking brings together the clubs with the highest market share among those playing in the UEFA Champions League or the UEFA Europa League. But one caveat is important: Although these clubs play a leading role in this "big business" and act like multinational companies, their economic power does not compare to that of the giant transnational corporations that sponsor them.[11]

The way a club-company operates depends on the structural conditions of the market in which it competes and on the dynamism of the entertainment industry of which it is a part. In this sense, teams from countries with high per capita income

---

[10] For example, in the UK, "football clubs can take one of several different legal structures, the most common of which are: (1) unincorporated association; (2) private company limited by guarantee; (3) private company limited by shares; (4) community interest company (CIC) (which can either be limited by guarantee or shares); (5) registered society (which can either be a Co-operative or a Community Benefit Society)" (The Football Association, 2015, p. 6).

[11] Giulianotti & Robertson (2009) agree with the argument, but emphasize that major European clubs have many similarities with "transnational corporations" in that (i) they have introjected corporate structures and norms, (ii) their specialized workforce is drawn from different nations, (iii) their main product (the spectacle) is aimed at markets with global reach, and (iv) their marketing strategy is centered on branding.

(where entertainment consumption is expressive) have an advantage over teams inserted in unstable economies (where the average household spending on entertainment is low). One should also consider the characteristics of the national league to which the club is affiliated, since it directly influences the negotiation of broadcasting rights (and may establish rules for sharing) and the attraction of sponsors (depending on the size of the attendance), and delimits the scope and direction of the marketing strategies adopted by clubs.

The leading clubs in Europe adopt different competition strategies (both in the economic field and in the sports field), which imply in different ways of conceiving the business and evaluate the success or failure of a management. In this sense, five strategies can be identified within the football industry (András & Havran, 2015): (a) "success-circle strategy" (victories in the sports field allows to expand revenues, while financial success promotes an improvement in sports competitiveness, producing a virtuous circle); (b) "transfer-strategy" (the revenue from the sale of players is essential to keep the competitiveness of the club, which makes it essential to invest in training young talent, seen as the basic competence of the company); (c) "commercial-strategy" (the managers' priority is placed on the budget balance and on the activity profitability, even if this represents little expressive sportive results); (d) "synergy-strategy" (the club is managed by a business group in search of mutual benefits, establishing a connection between the club's sporting performance and the group's economic performance); (e) "l'art pour l'art strategy" (if the club is owned by a large number of members and has great tradition, the management is directed to obtain or expand prestige, focusing on sportive results).

Some examples help to understand the variety of business models in European football.

Real Madrid and Barcelona are examples of clubs that have remained as civil society organization but have professionalized management and adopted basic principles of corporate governance (transparency, fairness, accountability, and corporate responsibility). PSG is an example of a club that is owned by a single owner. In 2011, it was bought by QSI, an investment fund linked to the Qatari government, and its CEO Nasser Al-Khelaïfi became the club's president. Manchester City is an example of a club with one controlling group and two investor groups. In 2008, it was bought by the Abu Dhabi royal family and became the property of Sheik Mansour bin Zayed; in 2015, the City Football Group sold 13% of the shares for US$400 million to a Chinese investment consortium, China Media Capital; in 2019, the US investment firm Silver Lake Partners bought 10% of the shares for US$500. These four clubs seek to maximize wins (not profits), but have distinct ownership structures.

Borussia Dortmund, for its part, is an example of a company that has floated on the capital market but is not subordinate to an economic group. In 2000, this sports club with more than 145,000 members created Borussia Dortmund GmbH & Co. KGaA (BVB) and listed on the Frankfurt Stock Exchange. Professional football remained under the control of the club. Minority fractions of the shares were acquired by Evonik (main sponsor), Signal Iduna (which holds the naming rights to the stadium), and Puma (sportswear manufacturer), while 60% of the shares were spread among small shareholders, mainly fans. In other words, although it is a "public company" (controlled by a board of directors), it can be described as a "publicly owned sports club."

The case of Manchester United is also unique. After was listed on the London Stock Exchange in 1991, its shares appreciated by over 500% in the first four years. In 2005, the American multimillionaire Malcolm Glazer became the owner of the club (with 98% of the shares), which was worth £800 million at the time, and withdrew the club from the stock exchange. In 2012, it returned to the stock market, but now on the New York Stock Exchange, with the initial public offering of 10% of its shares, having raised £150 million (the market value was valued at $2.3 billion). But investors were left with just 1.3% of the voting shares, meaning the Glazer family remained in full control of the club. The shares have appreciated in value as revenues and profits have risen. In 2018, the club reached an estimated market value of over $4 billion. However, the stock price depreciated in the following two years.

Generally, clubs with the size of a "large company"—according to the criterion of operational revenue—are valuable brands (they have intangible assets of great economic value), belong to a national league with international projection (potentializing their marketing actions), have a high level of competitiveness (essential to sustain their position in the market), and adopt competition strategies typical of market leaders (sales do not depend on price but on the quality and visibility of the product, customer loyalty, and the capacity of brand internationalization).

However, even in Europe's richest leagues, there are several clubs that have the revenues of a "medium-sized" company, do not have the same brand projection, cannot maintain a high level of competitiveness, operate in regional markets, and need to sell their best players. This is the case of teams like Real Valladolid (a Spanish sporting limited company controlled by the investment group led by Ronaldo Nazário—R9, former Brazilian center-forward) and Udinese Calcio (owned by Italian businessman Giampaolo Pozzo, who adopted the motto "buy low, sell high"). It was also the case of Leicester City until 2010, when it was bought by the Thai group King Power for £39 million (the club changed levels after winning the Premier League in 2016, and reaching a turnover of €179 million in the 2017–2018 season).

Clubs with marginal participation in a large market (or inserted in a smaller market) face difficulties caused by competitors and do not achieve the same effectiveness in marketing actions. Often, the difficulty in expanding revenue sources and the high cost of remaining in the first division of the national championship force medium-sized clubs to regularly seek the valuation of their main players to obtain additional revenue from the sale of the "economic and federative rights" (for registration and transfer) of these players.

Note that a corporate club can go bankrupt, causing serious damage to creditors, but can then be reborn with a different legal personality. This was the case with Napoli, which accumulated a debt of €70 million, was declared bankrupt by the courts in 2004 and relegated to Serie C (the third and last division of Italian professional football). The club was reborn on the initiative of film producer Aurelio de Laurentis, who bought the company's estate and changed the name to Napoli Soccer. In 2006, the name was changed back to Società Sportiva Calcio Napoli. The club managed to return to Serie A in the 2007–2008 season and regained its place among Italy's top teams. Parma's case was more serious. It was declared bankrupt in 2004 (following the bankruptcy of Parmalat in 2003) and was relegated to Serie D of the Italian league (amateur division), being forced to start again under another name (Parma Football Club). A second bankruptcy occurred in 2015, forcing them to once again change their name (Società Sportiva Dilettantistica Parma Calcio 1913) and start again from the fourth division. In June 2017, the acquisition of 60% of the club's shares by Chinese investor Jiang Li Zhang was announced. In 2018, the club managed to gain access to return to Serie A of the Italian Championship.

Another example is Glasgow Rangers, a traditional Scottish club acquired in 1988 by steel magnate David Murray. The club became a public limited company, then went public in 2000, but was unsuccessful and had to abandon the capital markets. In 2012, after being convicted of tax fraud, Glasgow Rangers went bankrupt, with debts totaling £134 million. A new company was founded (The Rangers Football Club Ltd) to rescue the club. After three consecutive accessions, it returned to the first division of Scotland in 2016. In the 2020–2021 season, the club became Scottish champion for the 55th time.

In short, it is worth noting that the size of the market, the economic environment and the institutional framework vary greatly from one country to another and condition the field of action of the corporate club, resulting in different stages of development of the "football industry" in Europe. As in other businesses governed by mercantile logic, this game produces winners and losers. Furthermore, the adoption of a business mentality by football clubs and the corresponding concentration of economic power cause a series of imbalances in the sports field, shaking the federative system foundation, changing the organization of tournaments, and reshaping the relationship between clubs and their supporters (Szymanski, 2007). And despite the proclaimed economic success of football in European countries, one cannot hide the excessive indebtedness of many clubs, threatened with bankruptcy and exclusion, nor the commercial exploitation to which supporters are subjected (Kennedy & Kennedy, 2012).

The Legislation Regarding the Economic Activity of Football Clubs in Brazil

Initially, it must be clarified that the transition to "football business" in Brazil was a long process that began before the changes in sports legislation. An important milestone was the formation, in 1987, of the "Clube dos 13"[12] to represent the commercial interests of the elite clubs in negotiating the rights to broadcast games. But at that time, the professional management of football was at an incipient stage and

---

[12] Clube dos 13 was an interest representation entity founded by the following teams: Atlético-MG, Bahia, Botafogo, Corinthians, Cruzeiro, Flamengo, Fluminense, Grêmio, Internacional, Palmeiras, Santos, São Paulo and Vasco da Gama. In the period 1997–1999, the group grew to 20 teams.

the financial condition of the major Brazilian clubs was very fragile. Furthermore, the detrimental economic conjuncture (stagnant GDP, hyperinflation, devalued exchange rate, and high interest rates) and the low level of the national per capita income kept the major clubs vulnerable to international competition, driving the exodus of players to Europe (Proni, 2000).

There was a significant change in the economic environment in Brazil in the mid-1990s. After the adoption of the new currency (Real) in 1994, macroeconomic stability fostered optimistic expectations as to the international competitiveness of national clubs, favored by the appreciation of the exchange rate. However, Brazilian football had structural conditions that were very different from those found in the main European centers (Proni, 2000). For instance, the smaller size of the companies that sponsored Brazilian teams and the lower purchasing power of supporters in comparison with Germany, England, Italy, France, and Spain. Furthermore, the near-monopoly of TV Globo in the broadcast of the main national tournaments, the little information on the billing of pay television and the financial fragility of most clubs weakened the negotiating power of Clube dos 13 in the signing of contracts for broadcasting rights.

Many politicians believed that the main cause of the gap in relation to Europe was the anachronistic institutional framework that governed professional football (and prevented the modernization of club management). To overcome the problem, the Zico Law (Law No. 8672/1993) sought to induce the creation of the "club-company," and the Pelé Law (Law No. 9615/1998) even required the transformation of the legal form of professional football clubs, which until then were treated as a "non-profit civil organization" and should now be legally denominated as a "business entity." However, this requirement hurt the autonomy of organization and operation of football clubs (Melo Filho, 2003).

The new sports legislation had been defended as an essential step toward the modernization of contractual relations in professional football. The aim was to reduce the financial gap in relation to countries where football industry had already consolidated in order to avoid the early loss of the best players. It was also intended to change the power structures in clubs and federations to make management transparent and eliminate managers who used football for personal interests. A third goal was to combat violence between fans and to provide more safety and comfort for fans in the arenas. In sum, liberalization within the scope of legislation was presented as a necessary condition to pave the way for market forces and forward the modernization of Brazilian football, which would provide greater efficiency in the organization of tournaments, help in the "moralization" of managers, make the entry of investors more attractive, and improve the quality of the spectacle offered to the public. This was the discourse that sought to legitimize the rupture in the current order (Proni, 2000).

However, the currency devaluation that occurred in 1999 and the problems faced by the Brazilian economy in that unfavorable context once again highlighted the financial fragility of the major national clubs. In addition, there were two other obstacles to the valorization of the spectacle and to the economic strengthening of

Brazilian clubs: the precarious organization of the main tournaments and the use of the national federation (CBF) and of the state federations to serve personal interests.

CBF and Clube dos 13 led the movement of resistance to the mandatory conversion of the sports club into "club-company." Other points of the Pelé Law were questioned, leading the National Congress to change several provisions. The Law No. 9981/2000 made the transformation of the clubs into a "business entity" optional and opened the possibility for them to constitute or hire a company to manage their professional activities. It also prevented two or more teams from competing in the same competition if they had the same owner or controller. The resistance to the conversion of the legal form was mainly due to the fact that many clubs did not have the means to solve practical and immediate problems such as tax and social security liabilities and the great uncertainty that existed about the concrete results of a change in the control of clubs.

Later, the Law No. 10672/2003—nicknamed "Football Moralization Law"—amended again provisions of Pelé Law, assuring flexibility in the definition of the legal form of the professional sports organizations (according to the regulation of the legal entity contained in the Civil Code of 2002) and keeping its conversion into "business entity" optional. But it was determined that the exploitation and management of professional sports constitute an exercise of economic activity and shall have differentiated treatment in relation to non-professional sports, in special with the requirement of financial and administrative transparency. Since then, clubs and professional football federations were required to publish the annual balance sheet and respective financial statements. The activities of professional sports entities and sports federations, regardless of the legal form in which they are constituted, are now equivalent to those of "private companies," notably for tax, social security, financial, accounting, and administrative purposes.

At the same time, Law No. 10671/2003 (known as a fan defense statute) was sanctioned, aimed at requiring transparency and credibility in the organization of tournaments, establishing proper conditions for ticket purchase and public accommodation, requiring measures to ensure greater safety in stadiums, as well as penalizing managers responsible for damages or violations of such rights and fans who incite violence or chant discriminatory, racist, or xenophobic songs.

Therefore, it can be said that the process of modernization of the legislation that regulates the economic activity of football clubs in the country was consolidated in 2003. However, some gaps generated opportunistic conduct and legal insecurity (Perruci, 2017). To make matters worse, the strong economic recession (between the end of 2008 and mid-2009) increased the number of labor conflicts. In this context, the need to improve the legislation to eliminate those gaps became evident.

In this sense, Law No. 12395/2011, called "New Pelé Law," introduced changes with the intention of protecting the "training club," limiting the action of the "intermediaries" and ensuring the balance of rights and duties of clubs and players. There was the introduction of the indemnity clause (in favor of the club) and of the compensation clause (in favor of the player), destined to prevent that contractual conflicts be solved only based on the labor legislation. Likewise, the determination of the percentage corresponding to the "image rights" and the characterization of such right as having a civil, and not labor, nature. An attempt was made to make clearer the distinction between employment relationship, sports bond, and assignment of economic rights.

Note that a specific rule for international transfers has been included. In cases where the athlete breaks the contract in advance to contract a new labor contract with a foreign club, the new law kept the unlimited fixation for the value of the sports indemnity clause, seen as a protection for the investments of national clubs in face of the economic power of foreign clubs. This protection against abusive economic power is reinforced by the rules regulating international transfers of players (FIFA, 2019).

It should also be mentioned that the new law instituted the joint liability in the payment of the indemnity clause; that is, if it is evidenced that the new employer club (third party) enticed the athlete, it will be jointly liable for the payment of the indemnity for the termination of the employment agreement with the former employer club. One may notice the attempt to avoid that players bound to small-sized clubs be enticed by large clubs.

However, after the 2014 World Cup, the financial situation of most of the elite clubs remained precarious. To solve the problem of indebtedness with the Federal Government, the Sports Fiscal Responsibility Law (Law No. 13155/2015, which established the program called "Profut") was approved, establishing principles that should guide the financial management, as well as transparent and democratic administration practices for professional football entities. Profut established special rules for the installment payment of tax debts. It also sought to curb reckless management within football clubs (and federations): Regardless of the legal form adopted by the club, managers became subject to compensation for losses caused. Note that the articles of the bill creating a special taxation regime (with simplified and reduced taxes) for clubs that convert to a corporation were vetoed.[13]

In short, the improvement of the legislation brought relevant advances: The legal equalization of clubs with companies (even without the obligation to change the legal form), the guarantee of decent and respectful treatment for the supporter (client), the balance between the protection of the economic rights of the club and the labor rights of the player, and the requirement of civil responsibility of the managers. However, the regulation of the economic activity of football clubs should not be seen as a panacea for the diagnosed ills. The financial gap in comparison with other centers (the main reason for the continuous exodus of young talents) was not reduced; the political power in the clubs and federations remained in the hands of a few "amateur" managers; the publication of the balance sheet did not ensure the desired transparency; corrupt managers continued to use their positions for personal enrichment; the saturation of games in the national calendar continued; the issue of violence among fans was not solved; and the occurrence of homophobic acts and racial abuse was not prevented.

As of 2016, other bills related to sports legislation (in particular, to professional football) were under discussion in the National Congress, but still with no outcome

---

[13] On the clash between interest groups that pressured the federal government and congressmen for the approval or veto of specific articles of that bill; see Matias and Mascarenhas (2018).

by the end of 2020. It is clear the interest of the Legislative Power in inducing a modernization of football clubs in Brazil guided by a strictly economic rationality, based on the belief that it is possible to adopt a business model similar to those adopted in large European teams. However, it should be considered that such regulation is not the only determining factor, and that football clubs cannot be forced by a legal imposition to move toward a more efficient club-company model. The main determining factor is the very dynamics of competition between clubs in this highly competitive market (Aidar & Faulin, 2014).

It should be emphasized, finally, that the discussion about the economic organization of professional football is not restricted to the elite clubs and has impacts on a much larger set of clubs, companies, and individuals. An estimate of the size of the football market in Brazil for the 2017 season, considering the revenues of all professional clubs,[14] state federations and CBF, showed a total volume of revenues of R$6.25 billion (Sports Value, 2018), which was equivalent to €1.7 billion at the time. Football clubs accounted for 88% of the total, with 20 clubs generating R$5.05 billion (81% of the market), while CBF earned R$544 million (9% of total revenues). In turn, a study funded by CBF estimated that the "football production chain"[15] induced the movement of R$52.9 billion in 2018 (approximately €12 billion), with all registered clubs and federations moving transactions estimated at R$11 billion, another R$37.8 billion were moved by the other links in the chain, R$3.3 billion refer to salaries and charges (direct and indirect), and R$761 million were paid in taxes; in addition, this production chain had the potential to generate around 156 thousand jobs in Brazil (Ernest Young & CBF, 2019).

Expansion of Elite Club Revenues and Asymmetries in Economic Power

As of 2003, the quality of the financial statements published by football clubs (mainly those that regularly participate in the Series A of the Brazilian Championship) started to improve. Thus, it is possible to measure the growth of the football clubs market in Brazil in the period 2003–2019 and analyze the market concentration ratio and the main economic asymmetries among clubs.

The early 2000s were marked by an unfavorable economic environment for football clubs. In 2001, the national economy already showed clear symptoms of chronic crisis. In 2002, the unemployment rate went up again and the exchange rate suffered

---

[14] In 2017, there were more than 700 professional football clubs registered with CBF (distributed in 27 state federations), with 128 teams competing in the four divisions of the Brazilian Championship (20 in Series A, 20 in Series B, 20 in Series C, and 68 in Series D). The elite clubs account for less than 3% of the total number of professional football teams in Brazil.

[15] The football production chain is formed by five links (Ernest Young & CBF, 2019): clubs and federations; sponsors; media groups; sporting goods companies; and supporters. Furthermore, service supply companies (transportation, lodging, food) are demanded for the holding of competitions and the government collects taxes derived from this productive chain.

a strong devaluation. In 2003, there was a severe recession in the country (with an increase in the interest rate, a drop in the purchasing power of salaries, and a growing number of unemployed), which affected the football business. But the financial situation of the elite clubs did not deteriorate much because the contract between Clube dos 13 and TV Globo was renewed.

At the time, São Paulo was the club with the best financial situation, with total revenues of R$95 million in 2003 (equivalent to € 27 million that year), far ahead of its competitors—the top-5 included Corinthians (R$55 million), Flamengo (R$53 million), Cruzeiro (R$52 million), and Palmeiras (R$51 million). Together, the five clubs with the highest revenues accounted for 38% of the "football clubs market," estimated at R$805 million (€ 222 million) in 2003 (BDO-RCS, 2011). Although some revenues fluctuate from one year to another (mainly those from transfers of players), the revenue differences between the clubs of the Series A stemmed from inequalities in the management methods adopted and, mainly, in the ability to exploit the respective market potential (Proni & Zaia, 2014).

As of 2004, the Brazilian economy resumed its growth trend, with progressive improvement of economic indicators and increased confidence of companies to invest and diversify their activities. Football revenues followed this upward trajectory, making the turnover double (in nominal values) in four years, exceeding R$1.6 billion in 2007 (equivalent to €620 million, in a context of exchange rate appreciation). The marketing strategy was beginning to go beyond the goal of expanding revenues. Now, some elite clubs sought to create a "corporate identity," redefine their organizational culture, and revalue the relationship between the club and its supporters (Albino et al., 2009).

The Brazilian economy experienced a recession between the last quarter of 2008 and the first half of 2009. But elite clubs did not present a drop in revenues, probably because the Clube dos 13 signed a contract with TV Globo for the broadcast of the Brazilian Championship (2009, 2010, and 2011 editions) for R$1.4 billion (approximately €560 million). The main problem at that time was the reduction in the sale of players to Europe (since many European clubs were greatly affected by the financial crisis that shook the economies of their countries). It should be mentioned that, in December 2008, Corinthians repatriated Ronaldo (R9), innovating with a very successful marketing campaign, which led the Club to raise its financial level.

In 2010, the Brazilian economy had a very positive performance. The high GDP growth (7.5%) was driven by the increase in public spending, the supply of credit and the rise in household consumption, leading to strong formal job creation, and higher salaries (and stimulating the expansion of the advertising market). The appreciation of the Real (against the Dollar and the Euro) contributed to keep inflation under control. In this scenario, the revenues of the elite clubs grew again, but at a slower pace than before the crisis.

The Brazilian football market, summing up the revenues related to the 2010 season, was estimated at R$2.2 billion (BDO-RCS, 2011), or €1 billion according to the exchange rate at the time. The first position in the ranking was occupied by Corinthians (R$213 million), followed closely by Internacional (R$201 million), while São Paulo fell to third position (R$196 million). Completing the top-5 were

Flamengo (R$129 million) and Palmeiras (R$122 million). These five clubs generated over R$860 million in revenues, about 39% of the total revenues in Brazilian football that year.

In early 2011, the exchange rate was still appreciated, allowing the richest Brazilian clubs to pay high salaries to their top stars, even if they were not comparable to the salaries paid by major European clubs. This allowed Flamengo to repatriate Ronaldinho (R10), another famous striker established in Europe, also with the expectation of obtaining increased revenues with a bold marketing plan (however, disputes over sponsorship contracts made the club pay the player's millionaire salary alone). It also made it possible for Santos to delay the sale of Neymar, a young talent, and to win the Copa Libertadores that year.

It is essential to highlight that, in 2011, there was a radical change in the negotiation of broadcasting rights of national tournaments with TV companies, which was centralized by Clube dos 13. In February, Corinthians disaffiliated from the entity for not agreeing with the rule of division of TV money and started negotiating directly with TV Globo. In the following weeks, other big clubs were also convinced to negotiate separately. Clube dos 13 lost its function and imploded.

So began the cycle of preparation for the 2014 World Cup. Some clubs decided to invest in the construction of a multipurpose arena or in the modernization of their stadiums, with the intention of increasing their revenues from ticket sales and event rental. The most successful example was Palmeiras' arena (named Allianz Parque), inaugurated in November 2014. The construction company paid the renovation costs on the condition that it would manage the arena for 30 years, and Palmeiras would receive an increasing percentage of the revenues obtained during this period. On the other hand, the construction of the Corinthians Arena (where the World Cup opening ceremony was held) was considered a disastrous strategy due to the debt assumed by the club, which forced it to allocate the stadium's revenues (ticket sales, store rentals, events, and naming rights) to pay the loan granted by a federal government bank. These are two very different business models, with diverging impacts. Corinthians had achieved record annual revenues of R$358 million in 2012[16] (driven by the extra money from TV and the titles won: champion of the Libertadores Cup and the Club World Cup), but in 2014 revenues dropped to R$258 million (and one of the causes was the lower box office revenues). Palmeiras, on the other hand, showed a leap in revenues between 2014 and 2015, reaching R$301 million, mainly due to the increase

---

[16] At the time, this was equivalent to €132 million, which would place the club in the world's top-20. The *Football Money League 2013* identified this outstanding financial performance of the club, even without taking into account revenues from the sale of players and other sources: "Brazilian club Corinthians are the highest placed non-European club with revenues of €94 m. This places the current FIFA Club World Champions amongst the clubs immediately below the top 20. A growing economy has contributed to increasing broadcast and commercial revenues for Brazil's top clubs. These factors combined with the substantial stadia investment committed or planned in both Brazil and Russia in order to host the next two World Cups, in 2014 and 2018, means that clubs from these countries potentially have a strong platform to challenge the dominance of clubs from Europe's "big five" Leagues, and hence enter the lower half of our top 20, in future years." (Deloitte, 2013, p. 4).

in ticket sales, the success of the supporter program (Avanti), and the increase in the value of sponsorship.

The favorable economic situation and the atmosphere of optimism kept the revenues of football clubs growing. Between 2010 and 2014, the sum of the annual revenues of the clubs considered as the protagonists (12 teams) and the other clubs that competed in the Brazilian Championship during that period (15 teams) increased from R$1.7 billion to R$3.2 billion (approximately €1 billion at the time) (Itaú-BBA, 2018). Once again, there was a change in the ranking of the elite clubs according to annual revenues. In 2014, the top-5 were occupied by Flamengo (R$325 million), Corinthians (R$258 million), São Paulo (R$253 million), Cruzeiro (R$222 million), and Grêmio (R$206 million). These five clubs accounted for 40% of the total revenue generated by the elite clubs.

The long and perverse economic recession in 2015 and 2016 (marked by a rise in bank interest rates, a significant increase in unemployment, and a drop in the average real salary) had little impact on the revenues of the elite clubs. Despite the weak economic recovery between 2017 and 2019, club revenues once again grew strongly. The aggregate revenue of the main clubs reached R$5.6 billion in 2019 (equivalent to more than €1.2 billion at the time) due to the new broadcasting rights contracts, the increase in revenues from ticket sales (including supporter loyalty program), and mainly due to the increase in player transfer revenues (Itaú-BBA, 2020). In fact, the outflow of players abroad was stimulated by the strong exchange rate devaluation during this period.

Table 21.1 shows the operating revenues of the football clubs participating in the Brazilian Championship Series A in 2019. Flamengo (€187 million) remained top of the ranking, while Palmeiras (€141 million) took second place, Internacional (€92 million) climbed to third place, Grêmio (€87 million) moved up one position, while São Paulo and Corinthians were overtaken. In fact, Santos (€86 million) only achieved fifth position because of the transfer of Rodrygo to Real Madrid (€40 million).

The main source of revenue in Brazilian football continued to be television (broadcasting rights represented 41% of the total). The share of the other sources was much smaller: transfers of players (23%); ticket sales and stadium (15%); advertising and sponsorship (11%); other revenues (10%). The differences in the composition of revenues among the protagonist clubs should be highlighted. For example, in 2019, dependence on television was greater in Corinthians (53%) and Vasco da Gama (53%); the share of sponsorship and advertising was greater in Palmeiras (21%); ticket sales (including supporter loyalty program) had greater share in Fortaleza (26%) and Internacional (23%); and the share of transfers of players was greater in Santos (53%).

It should be noted that the top-5 obtained a volume of revenues equivalent to 48% of the total computed, which indicates a high concentration of economic power in the hands of a few clubs. In 2019, Flamengo's operating revenue was more than twice that of São Paulo, more than four times that of Vasco da Gama, seven times that of Fortaleza, and more than ten times that of Chapecoense.

Table 21.1 Total operating revenue and revenue sources (R$ million)

	Club	Operating revenue	TV rights	Sponsorship, advertising	Ticket sales	Transfers of players	Ordinary revenue[a]
1	Flamengo	841	330	93	171	191	650
2	Palmeiras	635	214	135	108	104	531
3	Internacional	414	155	48	94	109	305
4	Grêmio	391	165	56	83	88	303
5	Santos	389	111	16	24	205	184
6	São Paulo	374	137	34	48	97	277
7	Corinthians	359	189	80	36	18	341
8	Athletico-PR	355	160	21	50	98	257
9	Cruzeiro	290	106	18	33	108	182
10	Atlético MG	256	121	22	27	58	198
11	Fluminense	249	108	9	22	89	160
12	Vasco da Gama	199	106	19	16	7	192
13	Botafogo	186	83	11	17	38	148
14	Bahia	182	71	16	17	41	141
15	Fortaleza	120	43	10	31	6	114
16	Ceará	98	46	8	23	15	83
17	Goiás	96	67	6	9	1	95
18	Chapecoense	80	39	14	12	5	70
19	Avaí	71	50	4	2	3	68
20	CSA[b]	...	...	...	...	...	...
	Total	5585	2301	620	823	1281	4304

Clubs in the Brazilian Championship Series A: 2019
[a]Operating revenue without the amount obtained from transfers of players
[b]Centro Sportivo Alagoano (CSA) has not yet released its 2019 financial statement
Source Itaú-BBA (2020). Own elaboration

Considering annual revenues without taking into account the value obtained from the transfers of players, the top-5 would be formed by Flamengo (€ 144 million), Palmeiras (€ 118 million), Corinthians (€ 76 million), Internacional (€ 68 million), and Grêmio (€ 67 million). These five clubs could be considered as "large companies," while other leading clubs would still be at a lower revenue level.[17] Because of the devaluation of the exchange rate in 2019, only two Brazilian clubs had ordinary revenues exceeding €100 million, but both were well below the top-30 in Europe.

Table 21.2 shows the operating expenses of the elite clubs in 2019, highlighting the employee costs (salaries, charges, benefits, image rights, and other operating

---

[17] In Brazil, the criterion for identifing a "large company" is an annual operating revenue regularly higher than R$300 million.

Table 21.2 Total operating expenses, employee costs, and investments (R$ million)

	Club	Operating expenses	Employee costs[a]	Investments[b]	Championship standings
1	Flamengo	566	358	270	1°
2	Palmeiras	456	303	177	3°
3	Corinthians	370	272	109	8°
4	São Paulo	346	234	174	6°
5	Cruzeiro	346	215	85	17°
6	Internacional	298	190	81	7°
7	Grêmio	280	139	88	4°
8	Santos	255	166	58	2°
9	Atlético MG	231	169	42	13°
10	Athletico-PR	229	124	75	5°
11	Vasco da Gama	174	121	16	12°
12	Fluminense	159	106	13	14°
13	Botafogo	136	87	31	15°
14	Bahia	135	82	47	11°
15	Chapecoense	100	75	3	19°
16	Fortaleza	99	51	10	9°
17	Ceará	86	32	12	16°
18	Goiás	72	51	21	10°
19	Avaí	57	23	4	20°
20	CSA[c]	…	…	…	18°
	Total	4395	2798	1316	

Clubs in the Brazilian Championship Series A: 2019
[a]Including expenses with transportation, lodging, and meals
[b]Sum of expenses with transfers of players, youth teams, and infrastructure
[c]Centro Sportivo Alagoano (CSA) has not yet released its 2019 financial statement
Source Itaú-BBA (2020). Own elaboration

expenses) and the expenses with investments, whose largest share refers to the expenses with transfers of players (the economic rights constitute an intangible asset of the club). The ranking is similar to that of revenues, but some clubs change positions (for example, Santos and Cruzeiro). It should also be noted that there are differences in the profile of expenses: in Corinthians and Atlético-MG employee costs represented almost three quarters of the operating expenses; in Grêmio, half of the total; and in Ceará, only 37%.

Flamengo's high investment volume (€ 60 million, i.e., 32% of its operating revenues) is noteworthy. It was the club that spent the most on the transfers of players—but it obtained an amount almost with the sale of players as high as the one spent with the arrival of new stars. In contrast, Vasco da Gama obtained a very small amount with the sale of players, which contributes to restrict its investment capacity.

In general, the clubs that spend the most on the investments and employee costs are those that occupy the top positions in the Brazilian Championship, while those that spend the least are those most at risk of falling to the Series B.[18] In 2019, Flamengo (champion) had employee costs 2.5 times higher than Grêmio (4th position), more than 4 times higher than Botafogo (15th position), and more than 15 times higher than Avaí (20th position). And in the case of the volume of investment, this disproportion was even more expressive, due to the differences in spending on improving the quality of the squad. In fact, the greater the asymmetry in economic power between the protagonist clubs and the supporting clubs, the greater the imbalance in the sports competition (the same tendency is verified in the main European leagues).

From an economic point of view, it can be assumed that the clubs with higher cash generation capacity and with the most "valuable brands"[19] are the most capable of acting as a "market leader" company. Generally, the clubs with the strongest brands in the market are the ones that can better exploit marketing actions, increase the value of sponsorship contracts, earn more from TV rights and sell tickets at high prices, thus increasing their market power. As a consequence, they are able to raise their current expenditures and investments, which provides greater chances of maintaining a level of sports competitiveness above the other competitors. This, in turn, makes them more attractive to investors, more visible in the media to attract sponsors and better financing conditions, reinforcing this virtuous circle. Other elite clubs try to enhance the brand to increase their revenues and spending, a necessary condition to remain as protagonists (facing the threat of losing competitiveness). On the other hand, clubs with marginal participation in the market have great difficulty in remaining in the Brazilian Championship Series A, that is, to remain in the national elite.

In short, there is no doubt that there was a strong quantitative growth of the football industry in Brazil between 2003 and 2019, well above the growth of the Brazilian GDP during this period. Simultaneously, the economic inequality between the clubs of the Series A increased, reinforcing market concentration (i.e., a large market share in the hands of a few clubs). This asymmetry of economic power has unbalanced the conditions of sports competition, but CBF never saw this imbalance as a problem.

The Problem of Excessive Indebtedness of the Elite Clubs

In parallel to the expansion in revenues of the elite clubs, there was an excessive increase in the level of accumulated debt. In most cases, the indebtedness was not planned; i.e., it did not result from a strategy to finance investments, increase

---

[18] Of course, surprises may occur, such as the fall of Cruzeiro (17th position) in 2019.

[19] A more sophisticated methodology to determine the economic power of football clubs refers to the "brand value," taking into account the number of fans, characteristics of the national market, and the volume of operating revenues. The physical assets of the clubs and the economic rights over players are not considered in this methodology. The four most valuable Brazilian teams in 2018 were Flamengo (R$1.95 billion), Corinthians (R$1.74 billion), Palmeiras (R$1.53 billion), and São Paulo (R$1.20 billion) (BDO-RCS, 2018).

sports competitiveness and enable greater revenue generation in the long term. In other words, it was a debt resulting from budget imbalances and incompetent or irresponsible financial management.

In fact, despite the fact that sports legislation demands responsible management from clubs, expenses grew above revenues, producing recurring deficits. Between 2003 and 2005, the 20 clubs with the highest revenues together had an accumulated budget deficit of R$106 million. As of 2006 these deficits increased. In the period 2006–2011, the accumulated losses of the elite clubs reached R$2 billion (Sports Value, 2018)—approximately €870 million according to the exchange rate in 2011.

In the vast majority of these clubs, a variety of circumstances increased the demand for "working capital" (money needed to pay salaries and other current expenses and keep the business running smoothly). Many clubs have had to take out short-term bank loans and request advances on revenues (e.g., from sponsors or TV Globo), compromising future revenues. Delays in the payment of taxes and accumulated debts with players and coaches occurred frequently, increasing tax and labor liabilities. To sign new players, some clubs borrowed from investors or intermediaries.

In 2006, the sum total of the debts of the elite clubs was in the region of R$1.3 billion (€465 million). Tax debt accounted for half (52%) of the total debts, and the other half corresponded to civil and labor debts (25%) and loans (23%). This insolvency situation, particularly with respect to tax debts, led the federal government to take measures to help the clubs to settle their debts and normalize tax payments. Law No. 11,345/2006 instituted a new lottery ("Timemania") with the intention of creating an additional source of income and enabling the payment in 240 installments of tax debts and pending debts with the Employee Severance Indemnity Fund (FGTS).

But this new lottery, effective in 2007, did not generate the expected revenues. Many clubs struggled to honor their obligations in the following years. Those that did not pay the installments saw their debt increase because of interest and fines. At the same time, budget imbalances continued to produce more debt. In 2010, the sum of the net debts (i.e., discounting cash availabilities) of the elite clubs reached R$3.6 billion (€1.6 billion), of which one third corresponded to debts that could be paid in installments through Timemania (BDO-RCS, 2011).

In 2012, the set of 20 clubs had a small budget surplus (R$36 million). After that, they had high losses again: R$418 million in 2013 and R$612 million in 2014 (Sports Value, 2018). Although the club-company model adopted in Brazil was not one oriented to generate profits and distribute dividends, the chronic problem of recurrent deficits had worsened.

Despite the progressive increase in the operating revenues of the clubs, the level of indebtedness continued to grow. In 2014, it reached an estimated amount of R$6.7 billion – approximately €2.1 billion at the time. The five most indebted teams were: Botafogo (R$845 million), Flamengo (R$698 million), Vasco da Gama (R$597 million), Atlético-MG (R$491 million), and Fluminense (R$440 million) (BDO-RCS, 2017). It should also be mentioned that the investment in construction or renovation of the arena (stimulated by the World Cup in Brazil) increased the debts of Corinthians and Athletico-PR.

The tax debt of the elite clubs exceeded R\$3.2 billion. The amount tripled between 2010 and 2014, possibly because several clubs had to acknowledge charges that were in judicial dispute, or decided to delay taxes and labor charges waiting for a new debt refinancing. Due to the serious financial crisis of several professional football teams, the State had to intervene again. The solution, still in 2014, was the inclusion of these clubs in the Tax Recovery Program (Refis). Over 30 clubs joined this program to obtain relief from part of their active debts with the Federal Government and renegotiate the installment payments. But Refis alone would not solve the problem.

In February 2015, the Attorney General of the National Treasury disclosed information on the fiscal and tax debt of the universe of Brazilian teams, estimated at R\$3.7 billion (Proni & Libanio, 2016) (at the time, €1.1 billion). In order to make Brazilian football a "financially healthy activity," Law No. 13,155/2015 was sanctioned in August to refinance tax and labor debts of professional football clubs. The Profut allowed the installment payment of tax debts in up to 240 months (with a reduction of 70% of fines, 40% of interest, and 100% of legal charges). The club that did not comply with the required counterparties[20] would be subject to lose the conditions for refinancing its debts. On the other hand, the state federations and CBF would be obliged to penalize any affiliated club without debt clearance certificates and may even be relegated from the division in the respective tournament. To ensure the effectiveness of the new legislation, in January 2016, the Public Authority for Football Governance (APFut) was created, to supervise the clubs registered in Profut (at that time there were 111 teams).

Profut forgave R\$579 million (€129 million) in interest and fines on taxes owed, increased pressure on clubs for financial fair play, and temporarily contributed to curbing the growth of debts and improving financial indicators for elite clubs. In fact, even during the economic recession that occurred in 2015–2016, the 20 elite clubs had significant surpluses: R\$173 million in 2015 and R\$443 million in 2016. This was only possible because Profut reduced spending on tax and interest payments in 2015, and because the clubs received bonuses in 2016 for having signed a new broadcasting rights assignment contract. In 2017, the surplus was only R\$28 million. Thus, in these three years, the clubs totaled a surplus of R\$644 million (Sports Value, 2018)—around €180 million. However, individually, the financial performance was quite distinct: Some clubs had positive results, while others had recurrent losses. It is worth mentioning that Flamengo's net debt, which started to have a competent financial management as of 2015, was reduced to R\$430 million in 2017, due to a strong reduction in its bank debt and tax debt.

---

[20] Main counterparties: (a) pay tax, social security, and labor obligations on time; (b) pay players' salaries on time, including "image rights"; (c) spend, at most, 80% of gross revenue on professional football; (d) maintain a minimum permanent investment in youth football and women's football; (e) adopt a progressive schedule for reducing the budget deficit (it should not exceed 5% as of 2019); (f) publish standardized and audited financial statements (which must be submitted to an autonomous fiscal council); (g) do not anticipate revenues forecast for future mandates, except in specific situations; (h) respect the maximum period of four years for the mandate of the sports manager (one reappointment allowed); (i) include in the statute the immediate removal of the manager who practices reckless management (and his ineligibility for at least five years).

Table 21.3 Total net debt, tax debt, onerous debt, and short-term debt (R$ million)

	Club	Net debt[a]	Tax debt	Onerous debt[b]	Operating debt[c]	Short-term debt
1	Atlético-MG	746	259	348	139	323
2	Botafogo	708	459	130	119	285
3	Cruzeiro	707	271	142	293	529
4	Corinthians	652	223	97	332	400
5	Vasco da Gama	567	351	123	93	273
6	Flamengo	563	231	53	280	229
7	Palmeiras	530	59	170	301	294
8	São Paulo	526	115	190	222	338
9	Athletico-PR	506	11	459	36	167
10	Santos	461	182	36	139	188
11	Internacional	443	164	92	186	274
12	Fluminense	407	199	48	156	193
13	Grêmio	235	93	60	82	95
14	Bahia	174	127	5	42	60
15	Fortaleza	37	13	6	17	20
16	Goiás	24	22	−10	12	3
17	Ceará	16	7	5	5	4
	Total[d]	7302	2786	1954	2454	3675

Clubs in the Brazilian Championship Series A: 2019
[a]Total net debt is composed of three types: operating, onerous, and tax debt
[b]Refers to debts with banks, suppliers, and other companies
[c]Refers to liabilities with clubs, players, and intermediaries
[d]Total for 17 clubs. Chapecoense, Avaí, and CSA are not included
Source Itaú-BBA (2020). Own elaboration

Table 21.3 shows that, together, the 17 clubs in the A Series of the Brazilian Championship had, in December 2019, a total net debt of R$7.3 billion (€1.6 billion, due to currency devaluation), of which R$ 2.8 billion (€606 million) resulted from tax debt, R$2 billion (€425 million) corresponded to net onerous debt and R$2.4 billion (€533 million) referred to net operational debt. It is also important to note that half of the total net debt (almost R$3.7 billion, or about €800 million) was short-term debt, which includes financial obligations whose maturity is less than one year.

The five most indebted clubs were: Atlético-MG (€166 million), Botafogo (€177 million), Cruzeiro (€157 million), Corinthians (€145 million), and Vasco da Gama (€126 million). It is important to note that there were differences in the debt profile. Looking at short-term debt, Cruzeiro was the club with the most critical situation (75% of the total debt). In opposition, Goiás had a very low short-term debt (12.5% of the total debt). Botafogo had the highest tax debt, and Athletico-PR was one of the lowest. Corinthians had the highest net operating debt (mainly liabilities with other clubs and with players), followed closely by Cruzeiro. And Athletico-PR had the highest net onerous debt (resulting from the financing of the modernization of its arena).

Table 21.4 shows an important accounting indicator: EBITDA (earnings before interest, taxes, depreciation, and amortization), which informs the volume of the company's "cash flow generation" and is used to assess its financial health. The high EBITDA recorded for the elite clubs as a whole (R\$1.1 billion, €240 million) was possible thanks to the high volume of revenues from the negotiation of players (Itaú-BBA, 2020). Once again, the highlights were Flamengo and Palmeiras, which were responsible for 40% of the cash generation. Corinthians had negative EBITDA because it spent more than it could afford and the revenue from transfers of players was relatively low. In turn, Cruzeiro's disastrous financial management caused very high losses, which made it impossible to pay short-term financial liabilities.

The ratio between the volume of short-term net debt and EBITDA is an indicator of the company's capacity to honor its most urgent financial commitments. In the

Table 21.4 EBITDA, net debt per EBITDA, and short-term debt per EBITDA

	Club	EBITDA[a]	Net debt/EBITDA[b]	Short-term debt/EBITDA[c]
1	Cruzeiro	−66	−	−
2	Corinthians	−27	−	−
3	Atlético-MG	14	52.1	22.6
4	Vasco da Gama	17	32.6	15.7
5	São Paulo	28	19.1	12.2
6	Botafogo	40	17.7	7.1
7	Internacional	90	4.9	3.0
8	Fluminense	74	5.4	2.6
9	Fortaleza	9	4.1	2.2
10	Palmeiras	161	3.3	1.8
11	Athletico-PR	114	4.4	1.5
12	Santos	124	2.9	1.5
13	Bahia	42	4.2	1.4
14	Flamengo	238	2.4	1.0
15	Grêmio	100	2.3	0.9
16	Ceará	12	1.3	0.3
17	Goiás	19	1.3	0.1
	Total[d]	989	7.4	3.7

Clubs in the Brazilian Championship Series A: 2019
[a]Earnings Before Interest, Taxes, Depreciation, and Amortization
[b]Ratio between total net debt and EBITDA
[c]Ratio between short-term net debt and EBITDA
[d]Total for 17 clubs. Chapecoense, Avaí, and CSA are not included
Source Itaú-BBA (2020). Own elaboration

case of the elite teams, it can be seen that Goiás, Ceará, Flamengo, and Grêmio were in a very comfortable situation in 2019 (index less than or equal to 1.0). When the index is above 3.0, the risk of default becomes very high, as is the case of Botafogo. In turn, Santos's situation was misleading because it would not be able to repeat such a high EBITDA in the following years. The condition of clubs with this index higher than 10.0 can be considered extremely serious, because ordinary companies that remained in this situation for a few years would have already gone bankrupt. However, in the case of São Paulo, Vasco da Gama, and Atlético-MG, the result was an explosive increase in indebtedness. Finally, it should be clarified that negative EBITDA makes it unfeasible to calculate this indicator, but there is no doubt that Cruzeiro and Corinthians presented an unsustainable situation in 2019, facing a very high short-term debt.[21]

In summary, the evolution of the financial situation of the clubs of the national elite between 2014 and 2019 showed divergent trajectories. Few clubs demonstrated a consistent and sustainable condition, while several failed to address the problem of excessive indebtedness, even after Profut.

There are indications that the economic inequalities among the elite clubs have widened in the recent period, not only because of differences regarding market power, but also because of differences in the level and quality of indebtedness (Lopes, 2018). And although CBF claimed to be concerned about the issue, it continued to connive with the excessive indebtedness of the big clubs.

It can be stated that—similarly to several European teams—the major Brazilian clubs have adopted corporate management, but have remained focused on sports performance and have not been concerned with obtaining profits. The competition strategies adopted differed over time according to circumstances, including the level of indebtedness. In general, the managers of the elite clubs maintained the discourse of "l'art pour l'art strategy" due to the way they conceived the business and evaluated the success or failure of management. Some clubs used the operating profits to reduce debts or increase investments in squad improvement (as in the case of Flamengo and Palmeiras). But the majority continued to believe that their financial problems could be solved by selling their best players and that they could sustain a high level of expenses even without a high cash flow generation.

---

[21] Cruzeiro is the main recent example of disastrous and irresponsible financial management. In 2019, the club's financial crisis was responsible for its relegation to Series B. In 2020, the club was punished by FIFA with the loss of six points in the national tournament and a ban on registering new players due to a debt default with clubs from other countries. In turn, Corinthians was forced to reduce expenses and lost competitiveness in the sports field, despite being a large company.

Current Challenges for the Development of Football Industry in Brazil

To understand the current challenges of the development of the football industry in Brazil it is necessary, first of all, to understand the more general context in which it is situated.

In the last quarter of the twentieth century, football became a product of the "cultural industry" fully inserted in the context of globalization, a process that can be identified in four dimensions: geographical, commercial, digital, and social (Beek et al., 2018). It can be said that globalization has raised competition among football clubs to another level of complexity. A highly valued business branch with very particular structural and institutional characteristics has gradually been consolidated, making it possible (for a limited number of clubs) to adopt competition strategies and financial management models similar to those of the corporate world.

This mutation, which broadened the scope of action of the "club-company," originally occurred in the most advanced European centers of football and gradually spread to other countries. Governance models had to adapt to each country's legislation and to the way the league interacts with the national federation (Boillat & Marston, 2016). Therefore, the development of this business branch has national specificities.

The discussion on the development of the football industry in globalized capitalism has been guided by a systemic perspective based on the "Global North–South political–economic divide" (Brewer, 2019). Caution is needed when applying this classification, as football leagues in some economically advanced countries—such as the USA, Canada, Sweden, Scotland, Austria, and Japan—do not have a leading role in the global value chain that has formed around football. Moreover, the major leagues in Latin America, Africa, and Asia exhibit distinct stages of development in the "global football industry" (Pifer et al., 2018). But what is relevant is that the economic development of football in the countries of the Global South occurs in an articulated manner (in many cases, a subordinated manner) to the main European centers, a result of the "international division of labor" in the global football market.

According to Giulianotti and Robertson (2009), the "underdevelopment" of football in countries like Argentina, Brazil, and Uruguay remained directly linked to the fragilities of these national economies. The vulnerability to foreign competition—amplified by economic instability in these countries—has made many South American clubs economically dependent on the export of players, mainly to Europe. Therefore, South American football has remained trapped in the dynamics of underdevelopment, in which the low rate of return on invested capital and the perpetuation of exacerbated indebtedness force clubs to sell their most valuable "assets" prematurely.

The unequal and combined development of the football industry is a phenomenon that has intensified in the twenty-first century. However, the growing inequality puts the sustainability of the system in question. It is likely that the financial success of the "super clubs" and the enormous market concentration has caused an increased risk of financial failure for most of the national leagues that sustain the international governance system, and therefore for most of the clubs that make up the bottom of the financial pyramid at the global level (Andrews & Harrington, 2016).

The functioning of the global value chain in world football is based on the sporting interdependence between clubs (provided by FIFA and the continental confederations) and on the connection between the supply of skilled youngsters and the production of spectacles. In the era of globalization, the internationalization of the workforce has intensified, in which a flow of young talents toward the richer European leagues predominates, as clubs with greater market power recruit the best players from other nationalities (Velema et al., 2020). At the same time, the shows produced in the major European leagues are exported to more than a hundred countries (consumer markets), extending the reach of sponsorships and enhancing the brands of the strongest clubs.

In the first two decades of the twenty-first century, an increasing number of football clubs in Europe have adopted two growth strategies used by large corporations to expand their revenue streams: "business diversification," which seeks to take advantage of the opportunities opened up by advancing digital technologies[22]; and "international diversification," which aims to expand participation in foreign markets[23] (Schmidt & Holzmayer, 2018). Clubs with a large corporate size have started to use digital marketing methods and communicate with their fans—whatever their nationality—through blogs and social media. At the same time, football championships began to be broadcast via streaming platforms and computer applications. In this way, the power asymmetry between the richest clubs in the five major European leagues (which operate like multinational corporations) and the major Latin American clubs (which still remain focused on traditional sources of revenue and national markets) has widened.

Another recent trend in the new order in world football is the expansion of "multi-club ownership," when an economic group owns (or takes control of) several clubs (Pastore, 2018). This new business model sees the formation of multinational conglomerates that operate in several national markets around the world. Several reasons make this investment attractive, such as making a brand gain global exposure, expanding the ability to discover young talent, and giving experience to players who need to develop their potential. Two well-known examples are the City Football Group (CFG)—majority shareholder of clubs in eight countries (England, United States, Australia, India, Belgium, France, Uruguay, and Bolivia), as well as holding

---

[22] The football business has entered the digital age in search of new revenue sources. Many clubs started to produce personalized content to change the relationship with their fans and expand their markets. The new technologies applied in the entertainment field have stimulated the adoption of new business models and the reformulation of growth strategies. In the digital media world, three "waves" of opportunities for club revenue expansion stood out: (1) digital commerce (more attractive content for customers, effective distribution, fairer pricing), (2) digital consumption (customer loyalty, sharing of data on preferences, lower operating costs), and (3) digital identities (social networks, crowdsourcing, increased engagement, brand enhancement) (Dellea et al., 2014).

[23] For an analysis of the internationalization strategies adopted by Barcelona, Paris Saint Germain, Manchester United, and Bayern Munich, with a focus on markets in Asia and the USA; see Dincer (2019).

shares in clubs in Japan, Spain, and China——and Red Bull (RB)—owner of clubs in four countries (Germany, Austria, USA, and Brazil). In both cases, there is a main club, based in one of the five major European leagues, while the other clubs are located in strategic markets.

It can be said that the elite clubs in Brazilian football occupy an intermediate position in this global value chain. Brazilian teams export players to Europe, Asia, and North America; at the same time, they import South American players to reinforce their competitiveness. The football fans in Brazil follow the main European tournaments (live broadcast of the matches, replays, and specialized news); at the same time, the Brazilian Championship is broadcasted to dozens of countries (although it is not as highly valued as the championships of the main European leagues). Furthermore, it must be emphasized that the devaluation of the Real in relation to the Dollar and the Euro stimulates the export (and makes it difficult to retain) the best players. Although the elite clubs are at a disadvantage when compared to their European competitors, they have much higher annual turnover than other South American clubs that participate in the "Copa Libertadores da América."

Secondly, to understand the current challenges of the development of the football industry in Brazil, it is necessary to identify the parameters that delimit the performance of the club-company. More specifically, it is necessary to examine the enduring connections between (i) the legal–institutional framework, (ii) the characteristics of the market structure, and (iii) the competitive strategies adopted by the elite clubs.

(i) The change in the legal–institutional framework began to be outlined in the 1990s. Subsequently, the legislation was adjusted according to the pressures exerted by different actors that operate in this field. Furthermore, as the Brazilian clubs had an anachronistic institutional culture, the modernization based on business rationality caused tensions, and contradictions within these sports institutions.

The elite clubs avoided conversion into a "business entity" and remained a "non-profit sports organization." This option was probably motivated by the attempt to keep the power structure intact. But it was also justified by the possibility of not losing tax exemptions and by the fear of the consequences that a financial failure could entail (i.e., not to risk bankruptcy and sports disaffiliation).

(ii) The market structure of football in Brazil is characterized by segmentation (clubs are ranked according to the leagues in which they participate, which have state, national, or international reach) and by the concentration of economic power (the elite clubs represent less than 3% of the total number of registered professional clubs and are responsible for more than 80% of total revenues). Therefore, the elite teams do not perceive the teams from other divisions (which occupy a marginal position in the market) as competitors. Furthermore, the concentration of income generated within the elite clubs has increased: The top-5 highest annual revenues accounted for 38% of the revenue generated by teams that participated in the Brazilian Championship Series A in 2003; and they were responsible for 48% of that total in 2019.

In the last two decades, the new competitive conditions in the national football market have induced an increase in the concentration of economic power in a few clubs, reinforcing the asymmetries in terms of sports competitiveness and further unbalancing the tournaments (the number of teams that have a real chance of winning national competitions is increasingly smaller). In other words, the inequality within the group of elite clubs has widened, with cumulative advantages for those with more media exposure and greater capacity to generate cash (therefore, they can spend more on salaries and investments).

(iii) The competition strategies adopted by the clubs of the national elite encompass four areas of action: commercial, financial, technological, and sports. A competent and efficient management should seek the convergence of the objectives stipulated in these four areas and the articulation of the actions undertaken. To do so, it is necessary to incorporate corporate governance guidelines (to ensure that the interests of all involved are contemplated), use marketing tools to expand revenues (by exploring different markets), control spending (to generate budget surplus), renegotiate debts (and improve the quality of debt), incorporate new technologies (in the areas of training and physiology), and to assemble a strong squad capable of winning tournaments (high-level players and coaching staff). However, most large Brazilian clubs are still unable to execute an integrated strategy, despite the presence of specialized professionals in the various departments of the club.

For a club-company to be successful, management guided by strategic planning is required. The board of directors needs to know the strategies of its competitors, to plan for long-term growth, to mobilize all the people involved to share the same vision of the future, and to create synergies that strengthen its potential and reduce its weaknesses. However, few clubs in Brazil have adopted effective management based on strategic planning. Therefore, few clubs are able to compete in this branch of business according to the rules imposed by global competition.

The connections between these three parameters are long-lasting. The legal–institutional framework (the national legislation, the rules defined by FIFA, and the organizational culture of CBF) and the way the football market is structured (a type of "competitive oligopoly" combining concentration and product differentiation) affect the competitive strategies adopted by the clubs. But the clubs' capacity for action also plays a relevant role in this process, provoking institutional and structural changes over time. Therefore, strategic management must be based on the understanding that the market is dynamic and that the correlation of forces is modified by the success or failure of the competitive strategies adopted by the elite clubs.

Up to this moment, the failure of the financial management of large Brazilian clubs has not resulted in exclusion from the market (because the club does not go bankrupt, nor is prevented from playing exclusive tournaments of the national elite). On the other hand, the market allows the entry of new competitors (small teams that rise in the sporting hierarchy). But while there are no "barriers to entry," remaining in competitions designed for elite clubs is made difficult by the disproportion between budgets (revenue expansion is limited by the number of fans and the space granted by the sports media).[24]

Third, to understand the current challenges of the development of the football industry in Brazil it is necessary to analyze the economic and financial performance of elite clubs –those that are the protagonists of this business—in order to measure the power asymmetries within the Brazilian Championship Series A and the mismatch in relation to the major European leagues. In this way, it is possible to assess the degree of external dependence (or current stage of subordination) and discuss the consequences of increasing asymmetries.

Although the elite clubs adopted business management and earned increasing revenues, they did not become highly profitable companies, nor did they start behaving like profit-maximizing firms. Instead, management remained focused on trying to maximize wins. And since the increase in expenses could not be contained, most of these clubs had deficit budgets most of the time. As a result, some became highly indebted entities.

The vast majority of elite clubs remained unable to pay salaries equivalent to those seen in foreign leagues and dependent on the sale of their key players. In the 2018 season, Brazilian football had a surplus of US$327 million (R$1.2 billion) with international transfers. This record turnover can be explained, in part, by the devaluation of the exchange rate: It is more advantageous for a foreign club to buy a player from a Brazilian club when the Dollar and the Euro are appreciated against the Real. In recent years, the exporting profile that characterizes Brazilian clubs has been strengthened—even though several elite clubs have started to sign foreign players from secondary markets, often with the intention of reselling them later.

In parallel, many elite clubs continued to rely on the complacency of the federal government to survive. The pressure exerted by clubs on the State to adopt paternalistic policies was recurrent. The main demand was always the forgiveness of part of the debts with the Union (and the payment of the debt in installments under special conditions). Recently, some clubs have demanded a special tax regime to enable their conversion into a corporation, either to receive investments from private groups or to enable them to resort to judicial reorganization (temporarily suspending the debt collection).

The need for greater oversight of the financial transactions of football clubs became evident in 2019, when the Public Prosecutor's Office opened an investigation to investigate irregularities committed by Cruzeiro's board of directors. Until then, the very high level of debt of some clubs was not a concern for CBF (which did not take the necessary measures to curb irresponsible financial management, as required by law). Shortly afterward, in an agreement with the elite clubs, CBF announced the

---

[24] The initial success of Red Bull Bragantino (created in 2019, champion of the Brazilian Championship Series B that year and a new member of the national elite since 2020) proves: A club-company without a large fan base can become a protagonist in Brazilian football if it has the investment capacity.

adoption of a "financial fair play" rule (to be implemented in the Brazilian Championship—Series A and Series B—between 2020 and 2023) inspired by the model developed by UEFA.[25]

In Brazil, the elite clubs depend on television for the production of spectacle and for the valorization of sponsorship contracts. As many of them are financially fragile, they have become subject to the dictates of the TV Globo, holder of the broadcasting monopoly. The absence of competitors allowed the corporation to obtain extraordinary profits, while the revenues passed on to the clubs were divided disproportionately.

The differences in the economic-financial performance of the clubs that compete in the Brazilian Championship Series A produce long-term consequences. The unequal market power of these clubs influences the differences in sports competitiveness, making it increasingly difficult for a "medium-sized" club to compete with a "big-sized" club (i.e., one with large economic size). This disproportion implies, over time, amplifying the existing imbalances in terms of capacity to spend on hiring, salary payments, and investment in infrastructure. Thus, it is likely that in the coming years, the big clubs with better results in terms of financial management will be able to further expand their spending capacity, leaving their direct competitors behind and gaining greater prominence at the international level. The asymmetries within the Series A are growing, and there is no way of knowing which clubs currently considered "big" will be able to compete with the top-5 clubs.

Finally, to understand the current challenges of the development of the football industry in Brazil it is necessary to mention the impacts of the economic crisis caused by the COVID-19 pandemic. Unlike previous periods of economic recession, this time the losses are greater (matches were suspended for three months in the first half of 2020, then played without attendance at arenas), with losses in revenue that cannot be offset by broadcast contracts (even TV Globo is going through a financial crisis).

All clubs, regardless of size, have sought to reduce expenses. Since personnel expenses represent a high fixed cost, the elite clubs have negotiated temporary salary reductions with players and coaching staff (usually 25% of salary). There have also been layoffs in some clubs. In addition, in December 2020 the House of Representatives approved a bill to suspend the payment of Profut installments for the duration of the nationwide "state of public calamity."

---

[25] In Europe, between 2008 and 2011, there was a significant increase in financial losses recorded by a group of more than 716 teams. In this context, UEFA established the "financial fair play" (spending control rules for indebted clubs), which started to be applied from the 2013–2014 season (Peeters & Szymanski, 2014). The intervention contributed to the turnaround in football club finances. Fearing the possible sporting punishments, clubs adjusted. Losses decreased by 70% between 2011 and 2014. In 2018, the European Club Association (ECA) announced a new version, "financial fair play 2.0," to curb exorbitant spending by some teams, which unbalanced the competition. Two new control parameters would be added: a maximum level of debt in relation to the club's EBITDA (net debt cannot be much higher than the cash flow generation); and a limit on spending on player transfers (during the transaction window, the value of acquisitions can exceed that of sales, but the difference cannot exceed €100 million).

The crisis is still ongoing. For this reason, it is not possible to estimate the total loss for each of the elite clubs, nor to predict which of these clubs will suffer the most. The increase in debts was an inevitable consequence, and several clubs have become more financially fragile. It is likely that some clubs will recover their financial health more quickly, while others may not be able to fully recover.

An additional observation: the pandemic is inducing clubs to adapt more rapidly to the digital era. Some clubs have begun to negotiate broadcasting rights with streaming platforms and have started to produce content for social networks with the intention of expanding the relationship with their fans and increasing marketing revenues. It is likely that few Brazilian clubs will be able to follow the trend observed in European big clubs and make the transition to a new business model. In any case, this trend also reinforces the increasing inequalities within professional football.

Concluding Remarks

This chapter has offered an interpretation of the specificities of the football industry in Brazil. Five findings can be highlighted:

(i) Over the last three decades, changing conditions of economic competition (both internationally and domestically) have forced the major Brazilian clubs to adopt increasingly complex business strategies.

(ii) The national sports legislation was modernized, but it did not change the ownership structure of clubs and allowed the maintenance of a hybrid governance model.

(iii) During the period 2003–2019, Brazilian football continued to lag economically behind the major centers in Europe. Furthermore, the very high indebtedness of most of the elite clubs indicates a very fragile financial health.

(iv) During this period, the asymmetry of economic power among the elite clubs widened. This trend—an inevitable result of the development of the football industry in Brazil—leads to a chronic imbalance in sporting competition.

(v) It can be said that the football industry has grown significantly in Brazil, but this was not enough to change the intermediate position reserved for the country in this global value chain.

To stimulate a more comprehensive reflection, six propositions can be added:

(1) Understanding the development of the football industry in Brazil as an "unfinished process," compared to what has occurred in European countries, implies assuming—wrongly—that the big national clubs can reach the same level of revenues and the same market power achieved by the super clubs, which are the leading corporations globally.

(2) From an economic point of view, the development of the football industry in Brazil can be characterized as *problematic* because it is a process: (a) structurally *uneven* in terms of business viability (which reinforces the high disparity

in market power among the elite clubs); (b) financially *deficit-ridden* for most clubs (which causes an uncontrolled level of debt); (c) genetically *dependent* on the export of the best players (which maintains a secondary position in the global soccer market); and (d) strategically *controlled* by the television corporation that holds the broadcasting monopoly (which conspired to implode the Clube dos 13).

(3) The significant growth of revenues, the lack of transparency, and the low capacity to inspect transactions have brought other problems that go beyond the economic sphere and corrupt the sports field, making state intervention necessary to ensure the suitability and credibility of the institutions involved. In 2015, the National Congress established a Parliamentary Commission of Inquiry to investigate crimes (illicit enrichment, money laundering, currency evasion, corruption, and swindling) involving the CBF and the World Cup Organizing Committee. Although many crimes were denounced, this parliamentary investigation had no effective consequences.

(4) The development of the football industry in Europe has provoked dissatisfaction among fans because of the increase in season ticket prices and reactions against the transfer of ownership of traditional clubs to foreign groups. In Brazil, the increase in ticket prices also excluded low-income fans from the new arenas, but the big clubs started to distribute tickets to the organized team supporters, which help to make the spectacle more exciting. It is difficult to predict how these fans will react if their team fails in the new economic order of football.

(5) In Europe, in recent years, the imbalance in the correlation of forces in national and continental leagues has increased because of the growing concentration of economic power. Several "super clubs" clashed with UEFA because of economic interests (and for being contrary to "financial fair play") and proposed the creation of the European Super League. Although this threat to the federative system is not perceived in Brazil, the lack of solidarity among the elite clubs is clear, as is their indifference to the other professional football clubs.

(6) The drop in revenues caused by the global pandemic deeply impacted the financial management of the national elite clubs, but does not seem to have altered the general characteristics and main trends of the football industry in Brazil. Therefore, the findings presented here remain valid.

References

Aidar, A. C. K., & Faulin, E. J. (2014). O negócio do futebol. *Cadernos FGV Projetos, 8*(22), 46–60. https://fgvprojetos.fgv.br/sites/fgvprojetos.fgv.br/files/fgvprojetos_caderno_futebol.pdf

Aidar, A. C. K., & Leoncini, M. P. (2000). As leis econômicas e o futebol: A estrutura do novo negócio. In A. C. K. Aidar, J. J. Oliveira, & M. P. Leoncini (Eds.), *A nova gestão do futebol*. Editora FGV.

Albino, J. C. A., Carrieri, A. P., Figueiredo, D., Saraiva, F. H., & Barros, F. R. S. (2009). Sport Club Internacional e a constituição da identidade corporativa de "clube-empresa." *Organizações & Sociedade, 16*(48), 81–100. https://doi.org/10.1590/S1984-92302009000100004

András, K., & Havran, Z. (2015). New business strategies of football clubs. *Applied Studies in Agribusiness and Commerce, 9*(1–2), 67–74. https://doi.org/10.19041/APSTRACT/2015/1-2/13

Andrews, M. (2015). Bein special: The rise of super clubs in European football. [CID Working Paper No. 299], Center for International Development, Harvard University. https://bsc.cid.harvard.edu/files/bsc/files/andrews_299.pdf

Andrews, M., & Harrington, P. (2016). Off pitch: Football's financial integrity weaknesses, and how to strengthen them. [CID Working Paper No. 311], Center for International Development, Harvard University. https://www.hks.harvard.edu/publications/pitch-footballs-financial-integrity-weaknesses-and-how-strengthen-them

BDO-RCS. (2011). Indústria do esporte: Finanças dos clubes de futebol do Brasil em 2010. BDO Publicações. https://docplayer.com.br/12935469-Industria-do-esporte-financas-dos-clubes-de-futebol-do-brasil-em-2010.html

BDO-RCS. (2017). 10° valor das marcas dos clubes brasileiros: Finanças dos clubes. São Paulo: BDO Publicações. https://www.bdo.com.br/pt-br/publicacoes/noticias-em-destaque/10%C2%BA-valor-das-marcas-dos-clubes-brasileiros

BDO-RCS. (2018). 11° valor das marcas dos clubes brasileiros: Finanças dos clubes. São Paulo, BDO Publicações. https://www.bdo.com.br/pt-br/publicacoes/noticias-em-destaque/11%C2%BA-valor-das-marcas-dos-clubes-brasileiros

Beek, R. M., Ernest, M., & Verschueren, J. (2018). Global football: Defining the rules of the changing game. In S. Chadwick, D. Parnel, P. Widdop, & C. Anagnostopoulos (Eds.), *Routledge handbook of football business and management* (pp. 20–32). Routledge.

Boillat, C., & Marston, K. T. (2016). *Governance models across leagues and clubs.* (Editions CIES – Collection réflexions sportives, Vol. 5). Neuchâtel: Centre International d'Etude du Sport. https://www.cies.ch/fileadmin/documents/CIES/Governance_II_-_Models_across_leagues_and_clubs.pdf

Brewer, B. D. (2019). The commercial transformation of world football and the North-South divide: A global value chain analysis. *International Review for the Sociology of Sport, 54*(4), 410–430. https://doi.org/10.1177/1012690217721176

Bühler, A. W. (2006). Football as an international business: An Anglo-German comparison. *European Journal for Sport and Society, 3*(1), 25–41. https://doi.org/10.1080/16138171.2006.11687777

Chadwick, S., Parnel, D., Widdop, P., & Anagnostopoulos, C. (Eds.). (2018). *Routledge handbook of football business and management.* Routledge.

Dellea, D., Zahn, F., et al. (2014). Football's digital transformation: Growth opportunities for football clubs in the digital age. Switzerland: PwC Sports Business Advisory; International Football Arena; Exozet. https://www.pwc.ch/en/publications/2016/Pwc_publication_sport_footbal_digital_transformation_aug2016.pdf

Deloitte. (2013). *Football money league 2013.* Edited by Dan Jones. Deloitte Sports Business Group. https://www2.deloitte.com/content/dam/Deloitte/uk/Documents/sports-business-group/deloitte-uk-deloitte-football-money-league-2013.pdf

Deloitte. (2020a). *Football money league 2020.* Edited by Dan Jones. Deloitte Sports Business Group. https://www2.deloitte.com/bg/en/pages/finance/articles/football-money-league-2020.html

Deloitte. (2020b). *Annual review of football finance 2020.* Edited by Dan Jones. Deloitte Sports Business Group. https://www2.deloitte.com/uk/en/pages/sports-business-group/articles/annual-review-of-football-finance.html

Dimitropoulos, P. (2014). Capital structure and corporate governance of soccer clubs: European evidence. *Management Research Review, 37*(7), 658–678. https://doi.org/10.1108/MRR-09-2012-0207

Dincer, A. (2019). *The internationalization of leading European football clubs in Asian and US football market.* (Master's Dissertation, Sports Business and Management), University of Liverpool, United Kingdom. https://www.academia.edu/41251815/The_Internationalization_of_Leading_European_Football_Clubs_in_Asian_and_US_Football_Market

Ernest Young, & C. B. F. (2019). *Impacto do futebol brasileiro.* Confederação Brasileira de Futebol. https://conteudo.cbf.com.br/cdn/201912/20191213172843_346.pdf

Fédération Internationale de Football Association (FIFA). (2019). *Regulations on the status and transfer of players.* 2019 edition. Zurich. https://resources.fifa.com/image/upload/regulations-on-the-status-and-transfer-of-players-2019-october-2019.pdf?cloudid=kgfplkndqjekwitobec1

Gammelsaeter, H. (2018). Points, pounds, and politics in the governance of football. In S. Chadwick, D. Parnel, P. Widdop, & C. Anagnostopoulos (Eds.), *Routledge handbook of football business and management.* Routledge.

Giulianotti, R. (1999). *Football: A sociology of the global game.* Polity Press.

Giulianotti, R., & Robertson, R. (2009). *Globalization and football.* Sage.

Itaú-BBA. (2018). Análise econômico-financeira dos clubes de futebol brasileiros – 2018: dados financeiros de 2017. (C. Grafietti, Coord.). https://www.itau.com.br/itaubba-pt/noticias/noticias-e-conteudo/analise-economico-financeira-dos-clubes-de-futebol-brasileiros-2018

Itaú-BBA. (2020). Análise econômico-financeira dos clubes brasileiros de futebol: demonstrações financeiras de 2019. (C. Grafietti, Coord.). https://static.poder360.com.br/2020/07/Analise-dos-Clubes-Brasileiros-de-Futebol-2020-ItauBBA.pdf

Kennedy, P., & Kennedy, D. (2012). Football supporters and the commercialisation of football: Comparative responses across Europe. *Soccer & Society, 13*(3), 327–340. https://doi.org/10.1080/14660970.2012.655503

Késenne, S. (2006). The win maximization model reconsidered: Flexible talent supply and efficiency wage. *Journal of Sports Economics, 7*(4), 416–427. https://doi.org/10.1177/1527002505279347

Leoncini, M. P., & Silva, M. T. (2005). Entendendo o futebol como um negócio: Um estudo exploratório. *Gestão e Produção, 12*(1), 11–23. https://doi.org/10.1590/S0104-530X2005000100003

Lopes, M. (2018). Análise da situação financeira de grandes clubes de futebol no Brasil (2009–2017). (Undergraduate Monograph in Economics), Unicamp, Campinas, Brazil. http://www.bibliotecadigital.unicamp.br/document/?code=001090515&opt=1

Manoli, A. E. (2014). The football industry through traditional management theories. *Scandinavian Sport Studies Forum, 5,* 93–109. http://sportstudies.org/wp-content/uploads/2014/11/093-109_vol_5_2014_manoli.pdf

Matias, W. B., & Mascarenhas, F. (2018). A constituição do programa de modernização da gestão e de responsabilidade fiscal do futebol brasileiro (Profut): Atuação parlamentar e grupos de pressão. *Motrivivência, 30*(56), 190–208. https://doi.org/10.5007/2175-8042.2018v30n56p190

Melo Filho, A. (2003). Autonomia de organização e funcionamento das entidades de prática e de direção do desporto brasileiro. In C. M. Aidar (Org.), *Curso de direito desportivo.* Ícone.

Pastore, L. (2018). Third party ownership and multi-club ownership: where football is heading for. *Rivista di Diritto ed Economia dello Sport, 14*(1), 23–58. https://lombardi-football.com/wp-content/uploads/sites/2/2020/10/Third-Party-ownership-and-multiclub-ownership.pdf

Peeters, T., & Szymanski, S. (2014). Financial fair play in European football. *Economic Policy, 29*(78), 343–390. https://www.jstor.org/stable/24029569

Perruci, F. F. (2017). *Clube-empresa: Modelo brasileiro para transformação dos clubes de futebol em sociedades empresárias.* D'Plácido.

Pifer, N. D., Wang, Y., Scremin, G., Pitts, B. G., & Zhang, J. J. (2018). Contemporary global football industry: An introduction. In J. J. Zhang & B. G. Pitts (Eds.), *The global football industry: Marketing perspectives* (pp. 3–35). Routledge.

Proni, M. W. (2000). *A metamorfose do futebol.* Campinas: Instituto de Economia da Unicamp. https://www.eco.unicamp.br/colecao-geral/a-metamorfose-do-futebol

Proni, M. W., & Libanio, J. P. (2016). O futebol brasileiro na bolsa de valores? *Revista de Gestão e Negócios do Esporte*, *1*(2), 178–200. http://revistagestaodoesporte.com.br/pluginfile.php/341/mod_resource/content/1/5_O%20Futebol%20brasileiro%20na%20Bolsa%20de%20Valores.pdf

Proni, M. W., & Zaia, F. H. (2007). Gestão empresarial do futebol num mundo globalizado. In: L. Ribeiro (Org.), *Futebol e globalização*. Fontoura.

Proni, M. W., & Zaia, F. H. (2014). Financial condition of Brazilian soccer clubs: An overview. *Soccer & Society, 15*(1), 108–122. https://doi.org/10.1080/14660970.2013.854572

Reis, R. M., dos Remédios, J. L., Telles, S. C. C., & DaCosta, L. P. (2014). The football business in Brazil: Connections between the economy, market and media. *Motriz, 20*(2), 120–130. https://doi.org/10.1590/S1980-65742014000200001

Schmidt, S., & Holzmayer, F. (2018). A framework for diversification decisions in professional football. In S. Chadwick, D. Parnel, P. Widdop, & C. Anagnostopoulos (Eds.), *Routledge handbook of football business and management* (pp. 3–19). Routledge.

Sloane, P. (1971). The economics of professional football: The football club as a utility maximizer. *Scottish Journal of Political Economy, 18*(2), 121–146. https://doi.org/10.1111/j.1467-9485.1971.tb00979.x

Somoggi, A. (2015, maio 5). Finanças dos clubes brasileiros em 2014. https://pt.slideshare.net/AmirSomoggi/finanas-dos-clubes-brasileirosmaio-de-2015-amir-somoggi

Sports Value. (2018, maio). Finanças dos clubes brasileiros em 2017. http://www.sportsvalue.com.br/wp-content/uploads/2018/05/Sports-Value-Financas-Clubes-Brasileiros-Maio18.pdf

Szymanski, S. (2007). The future of football in Europe. In P. Rodriguez, S. Kesenne, & J. Garcia (Orgs.), *Sports economics after fifty years: Essays in honour of Simon Rottenberg*. University of Oviedo Press.

Szymanski, S., & Kuypers, T. (1999). *Winners and losers: The business strategy of football*. Viking.

Szymanski, S., & Smith, R. (1997). The English football industry: Profit, performance and industrial structure. *International Review of Applied Economics, 11*(1), 135–153. https://doi.org/10.1080/02692179700000008

The Football Association (The FA). (2015). *Club structures: A guide to club structures for national league system and other football clubs*. Muckle LLP.

Velema, T. A., Wen, H.-Y., & Zhou, Y.-K. (2020). Global value added chains and the recruitment activities of European professional football teams. *International Review for the Sociology of Sport, 55*(2), 127–146. https://doi.org/10.1177/1012690218796771

Vinnai, G. (1970). *Fußballsport als ideologie*. Europäische Verlagsanstalt.

Chapter 22
The Controversy Over the Introduction of the VAR in Brazil

Sérgio Settani Giglio and Marcelo Weishaupt Proni

"The future is here." That is the headline of *FIFA 1904* magazine published in August 2018.[1] The main theme of this edition was the discussion on technology in football. Although this theme encompasses many aspects, the choice of a photo of the video assistant referee (VAR) staff in action for the cover of the magazine shows that FIFA is aware of the importance of this innovation not only in the production of the spectacle, but in the development of professional football itself in the coming decades. VAR is presented as an important improvement and an inevitable condition for the effectiveness of fair play in football. The impact that technology can have on the dynamics of the game, as emphasized by FIFA, is no longer restricted to players' training, but also contributes to refereeing. It was seen as marking the beginning of a new era.

The experience of using VAR in the 2018 World Cup in Russia is seen as successful. It is often evoked to justify the change in the rule, reinforcing that this is a path of no return. The data presented shows that in 64 matches, 455 consultations and 20 evaluations were carried out at the edge of the field, which resulted in 17 changed decisions and only three confirmed (i.e., only at a few times, the initial decision of the field referee was maintained). The text also states that the accuracy of refereeing decisions increased from 95.6% without VAR to 99.3% with its use (Monioudis, 2018, p. 13).

It should be noted that for a long time, the International Football Association Board (IFAB) resisted the adoption of VAR and other technological innovations that could change the dynamics of the game, diverging from the trend that prevailed in

---

[1] Available at https://issuu.com/fifa/docs/eng_2c8fb978b3932c.

S. S. Giglio (✉) · M. W. Proni
University of Campinas, Campinas, Brazil
e-mail: ssgiglio@unicamp.br

M. W. Proni
e-mail: mwproni@unicamp.br

other sports. The rule change was approved at the 132nd IFAB annual meeting in March 2018, after two years of testing in 20 official tournaments in various countries. The change was intended to be based on the motto "minimum interference, maximum benefit".

At the 2018 World Cup, FIFA President Gianni Infantino justified the decision and predicted that several serious arbitration mistakes would be avoided or corrected, at least in competitions where the new technology was used. He said that, despite initial fears, the VAR system had worked well. He also stated that this innovation means progress and has been adopted not to change football but to make refereeing fairer, cleaner, a resource to help the main referee make the right decisions (Homewood & Radnedge, 2018, July 13).

Presented as the solution to problems in football, apparently the four situations—goals, penalties, red cards, and player identification errors—in which VAR can be requested to indicate its simplicity. However, even with VAR, refereeing errors and omissions continued to occur, which caused many complaints and questions from athletes, coaches, and officials. The video resource does not remove an essential element of the application of the rules: their interpretation. In many countries, VAR has generated heated controversy. In Brazil, in particular, many personalities who produce or comment on the game have publicly positioned themselves for or against the innovation.

Our intention in this chapter is to recover the debate on the use of VAR in Brazilian football focusing on the opinions published in the national sports press until 2019, as well as to argue that in the academic environment, such debate should not be done in a dichotomous way.

We have divided the discussion into four moments. First, we present the opinions and initial impressions of journalists, players, managers, referees, and club presidents about this technological innovation. Then, we highlight the problems caused by the misuse of VAR during this introductory period. Afterward, we examine the positive effects of the imposed change and its irreversibility. We also discuss the idea of "fair play." In the last section, we suggest that VAR has become an additional element in the matrix of structural inequalities that unbalance the world of football in Brazil.

The Controversy Over VAR Portrayed in the Sports Press

VAR was officially implemented in Brazil in the second half of 2018, starting with the quarterfinals of the Brazil Cup. The final of the tournament played between Corinthians and Cruzeiro, in São Paulo, on October 17, 2018, which ended with victory of the team from Minas Gerais (2–1), was marked by two interferences of the video referee. For Leonardo Gaciba, then arbitration commentator for TV Globo, referee Wagner Magalhães was mistaken when he scored a penalty against Cruzeiro and then got it right when he canceled Corinthians's second goal (Globo Esporte, 2018, October 17).

For 2019, the Brazilian Football Federation (CBF) had the expectation that VAR would produce significant improvement in the performance of referees and reduce the controversies caused by refereeing errors. However, throughout the season, many decisions motivated by VAR interference were considered wrong. Below, we will give an idea of the debate starring well-known characters and the prevailing opinions on video refereeing, emphasizing the tournaments organized by CBF.

There was a lot of mistrust regarding the promised benefits of VAR among some leaders of big clubs. For example, before the semifinal of the 2019 State Championship, Corinthians President Andres Sanchez expressed his concern with VAR's interference in matches that should be exclusively interpreted by the referee (Ceccon, 2019, March 29):

> VAR is an irreversible thing. Now, it will take two, three years for everyone to learn. The fans, managers, players have to be a little patient. Many throws are interpretative.
>
> There will be errors and we will have to be a little patient. There is no perfection. [...] I think VAR should be "the ball went in or didn't go in, it was offside or not", and that's it. Now they put an interpretation, a foul at the start of a goal kick... It's going to get messy. It's difficult. For me, it had to be exact. But they are making interpretative throws, and this is the only country that has arbitration commentators. (free translation)

The prediction was confirmed throughout the season. In the middle of the year, Lance invited several commentators (journalists and former athletes) to give their opinions on the VAR controversy. In general, they were in favor of using the technology, but criticized the way refereeing was conducted and asked for corrections. Below are some excerpts (our translations) from the article that summarize the opinions of seven Brazilian sports commentators (Ojêda & Faustini, 2019, July 31):

Eduardo Tironi (ESPN Brasil):

> I am [in favor], but with corrections. I don't agree with reviewing fouls that occurred in previous throws that were not given by the referee. In addition, the time until the decision needs to decrease, a lot. [...] its primary use has to be in objective shots, [to check] whether the ball went in or not and to help signal offside.

Paulo Vinícius Coelho (Fox Sports):

> I'm all for it. But I think the VAR has to be used as a corrector, which was its primary function. It has to end the controversy. At the moment, it has not done this. The way it's being used is generating even more controversy in football. [...] [It was created] to correct obvious mistakes. In this case, it can increase its credibility. But VAR has been used for interpretative plays, which increases disbelief about its use. [...] That is, VAR must return to the origin of the proposal. That of minimum interference, with maximum benefit.

Tostão (Folha de S. Paulo):

> I am all for it. The purpose of correcting referees' mistakes is great. Now, the way it works has been very bad in Brazil. There is a lot of delay, and many interpretation errors, even with the image. This happens a lot because of the incompetence of the judges, which the image does not correct. I hope that these problems will be solved with time. [...] [It can be beneficial to] correct clear refereeing errors, like offside, or to indicate offside situations that the referee doesn't see, like a player punching his opponent out of play. Now, it is not up to VAR to interpret throws for the referee who is on the pitch. [...] The VAR rule leaves

no room for doubt. What is needed, in fact, is an improvement of arbitration, improve the competence of Brazilian judges. We see situations in which the referees are taking too long to reach a decision on a specific play.

Mauro Beting (Turner):

It wasn't so much before, because I understand that the rule is interpretative, and referees can see the play in different ways. But, even in offside situations, we see that VAR will minimize the "mistakes" and "hits" and, even so, end up creating others, keeping the controversy going. overall, the balance of VAR is positive. [...] Firstly, we have to put less pressure on the VAR booth. There has to be fewer silly penalties, like clear pulls. We journalists have to be careful to avoid making comments without knowing the VAR protocol and not fight VAR. You can't ask to shorten the time, for example. No matter how long it takes, the important thing is the fix. [...] in principle, we have to give a time for the entry of VAR in the match. This was what happened in other technology tests previously. Now, I'm in favor of the referees to show more personality. If they disagree with the marking of the video referee, it's their responsibility.

Juca Kfouri (UOL and Folha de São Paulo):

I am in favor. As long as it is used well and not as it is being used by CBF and Conmebol, who give the impression of wanting to demoralize it at any cost. [...] [The main benefit is] being able to do justice in refereeing. [...] VAR has to be the least interventionist and as fast as possible.

Casagrande (TV Globo):

Look, I still can't get used to VAR. But I think it's because of the way some referees behave on the pitch. the feeling is that the judges now have a loss of conviction when refereeing fouls. They use VAR as a shield all the time. It seems like they blow the whistle first and then wait for the video referee to give his verdict. [...] [It should be used] in doubtful penalties, in aggression that the referee didn't see, in difficult offside situations. but not all the time. The referee, who is on the pitch, is the one who has to run the match. [...] Some referees need to change their conduct. They need to stop listening to VAR all the time. In addition, the video referee cannot interfere all the time in what happens on the pitch, which slows down the matches.

André Kfouri (Lance!):

Although it is mandatory to remember that the video referee is in action for the first time, for example, in the Brazilian championship, it should be noted that the delay to check bids that seem simple in the first *replay* (see Gabriel's goal in Corinthians-Flamengo) is certainly bothersome, but it is a price worth paying for the correct decision and the protection of the game. For now, it is necessary to learn to wait and value getting it right.

For its part, the newspaper *Folha de São Paulo* sought to hear fans' opinions on VAR (Guedes, 2019, September 8). A survey conducted by Datafolha on August 30 and 31, 2019, interviewed 2878 people over the age of 16 in 175 municipalities. The result showed that most Brazilians approve of the implementation of the video assistant referee in Brazilian football. According to the survey, 58% of respondents said the technological assistance to referees "more helps than hinder" and 29% said the VAR "more hinders than help". For 2%, the novelty "neither helps nor hinders" and another 11% "could not answer." It should also be noted that among those interviewed who said they support a football team, 63% said VAR helps the most, 31% said it hinders the most, 2% said it neither helps nor hinders, and 5% could not answer. In other words, almost two-thirds of Brazilian fans approved of the introduction of video refereeing.

But the delay in the decision of the field referee continued to bother, and criticism of undue interventions or omissions multiplied in the second half of the year. We will mention here some of the most resounding opinions.

Arnaldo Cezar Coelho, former referee and commentator for the TV Globo, said he was still in favor of using the technological resource to correct "glaring errors," but was emphatic in stating that the way VAR was being used in Brazil was disastrous (Amaro & Fernandes, 2019, August 17):

> I'm in favor of technology to clear up some doubts, but the way it's being used VAR is a disaster for football in many ways. First, because it contradicts everything the rule states. The rule states that the game is played dynamically, without wasting time. [...] By the time it creates a business that leaves the game stopped, it's already conflicting. The worst thing is that football has lost its essence. The goal is not celebrated by players, fans and even less narrators. The fan watching the game doesn't know whether to celebrate or not. (our translation)

Renato Gaúcho, Manager of Grêmio, complained about the lack of uniformity in the interpretation of plays. After the disqualification of his club in the Brazil Cup, in the second semifinal match against Athletico Paranaense, in Curitiba, on September 4, 2019, he questioned the criteria used by the referee for the interpretation of doubtful bids and charged CBF and Leonardo Gaciba, President of the Refereeing Commission, for actions (ESPN Brasil, 2019, September 5):

> CBF, Gaciba, has to put only the referees in a classroom, talk to them and lay down a single rule: this is a penalty, this is not a penalty. Every weekend, a referee can't come up with his own rule. That's it. This is for the good of football. And I am for VAR. It's for the good of football. Now, enough of seeing a throw-in that is [awarded] a penalty, on the other side it's not a penalty. What can you do? (our translation)

Also in September, the newspaper *O Estado de S. Paulo* published a report stating that more than half of the directors of clubs of the national elite asked for changes in VAR. Of the 20 clubs in the series consulted on the video referee, eight did not want to give an opinion and 12 spoke out. The opinions were convergent: They said it is necessary to make corrections in the implementation of new procedures. For example, Maurício Galiotte, President of Palmeiras, said at the time (Campos et al., 2019, September 17):

> Palmeiras is 100% in favor of the technology, of using VAR. The technology has justice as its principle, so we understand that it is beneficial, and we have to fight for it. However, what we think is that it is a tool that deserves adjustments. The time it takes to make the decision has to be reduced. I think the images that are being analyzed at the time of VAR should be exposed to the public, and perhaps the audio could also be released. (our translation)

For his part, Guilherme Bellintani, President of Bahia, took up an old claim—the professionalization of refereeing—and stressed the need for greater transparency in the use of VAR (Idem, ibdem):

The professionalization of refereeing is the necessary step for the video referee to be better used. Professionalization brings with it more training, more analysis capacity, in short, general technical quality. And the second thing is transparency. I don't see why the dialogues are not usually shown and the images too, even if it is to acknowledge mistakes. (our translation)

The CBF Refereeing Commission agreed with the claims regarding transparency and promised to make available in real time the images captured by the VAR cameras for those watching the game on TV and release the audio of the communication of the field referee with the video referee for any club that requests it. However, this was not enough to diminish the criticism.

Another episode that fueled the controversy occurred in the 1–1 draw between Internacional and Palmeiras, on September 29, 2019, in Porto Alegre. After the match, Mano Menezes, then the manager of the latter team, complained about the adoption of different criteria in the arbitration of the Brazilian championship, which would be prejudicing Palmeiras and favoring Flamengo (referring to its games against Internacional and São Paulo). Mano was very incisive in the press interview. When comparing matches of the teams that were competing for the Brazilian Championship title, he said that VAR was producing different interpretations of doubtful situations. In other words, since there was no single line of conduct, different understandings of the use of VAR were interfering in the definition of the champion team (Band Esporte, 2019, September 29).

After that match, Mauricio Galiotte was even more explicit and said that several arbitration decisions were purposely favoring Flamengo. The president of Palmeiras was suspended for 15 days by the Superior Court of Sports Justice (STJD). Later, José Carlos Peres, President of Santos, expressed the same thought and was also suspended for 15 days by the STJD. In these accusations, the problem was not the VAR itself, but the biased performance of the arbitration.

Another case of undue interference by VAR occurred in the goalless draw between Cruzeiro and Fluminense in Belo Horizonte on October 9, 2019. Henrique, Captain of the Minas Gerais team, in an interview after the match, criticized the excessive interference of VAR, which, in that match, canceled a goal by Fred due to an alleged foul by Robinho in a move that preceded the goal. For him, the referee should judge whether the player had the intention to obstruct the opponent. In this case, the teammate was off balance and fell, and his foot accidentally hit the opponent. So, it is better to let the main referee judge whether it was a foul or not.

Vanderlei Luxemburgo, the then manager of Vasco da Gama, also spared no criticism of the refereeing. After the match against Ceará, in Fortaleza, on October 26, 2019, a 1–1 draw in the Brazilian championship, he questioned the criteria adopted by the video referee to assess whether or not there was offside (ESPN Brasil, 2019, July 20):

I want to send a message to Gaciba, once again. His [match referee] interpretations... there has to be a single criterion. I watched the Flamengo vs. Gremio match, which was refereed by an Argentinean referee. At no point was VAR called. Now we have four referees in the game. [...] against Corinthians it was the same move as today. Then he takes that business there [referring to the offside review by VAR] and thinks we're idiots. He sets the ruler wherever he sets the ruler. I want to see the field open, put the boards, which are references, for us to have a reference of the boards with the offside line. (our translation)

The accumulation of criticism led former referee and Fox Sports commentator Carlos Eugenio Simon to say that the misuse of VAR was not only damaging the quality of the show, but it was also damaging the referee on the field (Blog do Simon, 2019, October 30, apud Giglio & Proni, 2020, pp. 769–770):

VAR was initially conceived to be a luxury assistant in the football spectacle. However, in the Brazilian championship, it quickly stole the scene and became the main actor. As a result, the referee, who is responsible for commanding the actions regarding the application of the rules of the game, ended up becoming a secondary character whenever the scene refers to a crucial play of the match. At times when such throws occur, the electronic assistant influences decisively in the deliberations of the referee. This influence is not always positive for the development of the game, as we can see in several matches of the Brazilian Championship, where, with undesirable frequency, there is no shortage of complaints about wrong decisions made from the intervention of the VAR booth. The electronic eye may even be ruthless, infallible, but its images are subject to the scrutiny of the human eye, which is far from perfection. This frame is detrimental to our football. In addition to irritating players and coaching staff, outraging fans and generating blunt criticism from the sports press, it wears down and weakens the authority of the referee on the field, attracting the disgust of the fans present at the stadium. Let's face it, in such a turbulent scenario, it is rare for a professional to exercise his function with the serenity and firmness expected from someone with the responsibility of making decisions in a spectacle that involves the passion of millions of people and financial interests also in the millions. (our translation)

Given the frequent criticism of the video referee, the CBF Refereeing Commission conducted a survey with the clubs of the "Serie A" of the Brazilian championship to analyze the use of the feature in the season. According to Leonardo Gaciba, the teams approved the technology almost unanimously. He praised the result of the "Tour of VAR," which interviewed 584 people, including players, members of technical committee, and leaders of 17 teams. According to the former referee, the approval rate (adding "agree" and "strongly agree") for the continuity of the video referee was 94.1% (Matos & Almeida, 2019, November 21). In fact, the survey indicated that all relevant actors did not want the end of VAR but rather its improvement.

We should mention, in addition, that a survey by UOL Esporte included a question on VAR in its annual opinion poll, conducted with players who played in the Brazilian championship. For most of the interviewees, the introduction of the technological resource had somehow improved national football. Of the group of one hundred players in the "Serie A," 64% responded that VAR "improved football," 33% said the video referee "did not help improve," and 3% abstained on this question (UOL Esporte, 2019, December 26). That is, despite the controversies, the protagonists of the show seem to have approved the novelty.

There was a lot of controversy surrounding the way the video assistant referee interfered in the main football tournaments in the country in 2019. We can intuit that most players, coaches, managers, referees, and commentators, as well as most fans, were convinced that this technological innovation represents an inexorable modernization (since it was introduced by FIFA in the World Cup). But, in general, the refereeing continued to be much criticized and the criteria used, much questioned.

"All Unanimity is Stupid"

Undoubtedly, there has been an effort to build a consensus around the positive aspects of the use of VAR in football matches. But we must pay attention to the fact that there is no unanimity about it. If "all unanimity is stupid," as Nelson Rodrigues (1949/2003, p. 13) said, not being unanimous about VAR can be a good thing. Even at the risk of falling into the trap of duality between good and bad, right and wrong, it is necessary to expand the polarization and highlight arguments that question more strongly the introduction of VAR.

Arnaldo Ribeiro, Commentator for SporTV, stated that he is one of the main enemies of this innovation in Brazil, putting himself in opposition to the main colleagues in sports debates, and questioned the statistics that show a decrease in errors in football refereeing. In the same direction, André Rizek, Host of SporTV, said he hates VAR because he wants to shout goal, but now the shout is stuck in his throat (Giglio & Proni, 2020, p. 771).

Journalist Breiller Pires, in an opinion piece for El País, was very perceptive in relating the implementation of VAR to the Netflix series called "Black Mirror." He recalled a phrase that said that the future is not a distant spark, but a bright light burning in your eyes (Pires, 2018, March 17). Similarly, the cover of *FIFA 1904* had a similar message: "The future is [already] here." Is VAR a technology that burns our eyes?

This future—shaped by video refereeing—places refereeing at the forefront of the interests of the game of football. This has implications that go beyond the key of fairness in the game and that "my team will not be harmed." As presented so far, it should be clear that the implementation of VAR seems to be a road with no return. Therefore, it should have a greater participation of all agents that make up the world of football in order to improve it.

Technology has been present in high-performance sports for a long time and has been changing, even invisibly, the way sports are played. All materials that make up a football game are influenced by technology, from the corner flag to the care of the lawn, from the ball to the uniform, and from the cleats to the monitoring players' performance.

To deny the use of technology is, in fact, to deny the evolution of sport itself. However, there are many problems regarding the way VAR has been used, starting with its early implementation, without effective tests and debates. When VAR appeared in the 2016 FIFA Club World Cup, presented through a discourse in defense of justice, few people realized that the new technology could bring about other injustices. Arnaldo Ribeiro did not spare criticism to VAR because it amplifies the referee's interference in the soccer game, increases the number of interruptions, and cannot completely avoid interpretative errors. For him, if VAR was here to stay, there was the risk of ruining the show (Giglio & Proni, 2020, p. 772).

To support the argument, we must resort to the instigating and provocative analysis of Pierre Bourdieu in his book *On Television* (p. 19):

I'd like now to move on to slightly less obvious matters in order to show how, paradoxically, television can hide by showing. That is, it can hide things by showing something other than what would be shown if television did what it's supposed to do, provide information. Or by showing what has to be shown, but in such a way that it isn't really shown, or is turned into something insignificant; or by constructing it in such a way that it takes on a meaning that has nothing at all to do with reality.

When an image goes to VAR, the context is lost, that image is frozen. In case of offside, an imaginary line is drawn to prove the truth about the play. The speed of the shot gains another aesthetic dimension, that of slow motion (we invite you to watch the whole game in slow motion), of zoom, that is, of the detail that cannot be seen with the naked eye. Is this not a sport of human beings anymore?

What is most striking about the introduction of VAR is that the tests done before its implementation in the World Cup, and now in several countries, including Brazil, were not done in matches of youth leagues. The question that remains for FIFA, which is very conservative about changes in the dynamics of the game, is why it did not test VAR in competitions with less visibility. FIFA is interested in adding value to its product, football, by giving it a technological dimension and a sense of fairness.

After two years of testing, VAR officially arrived at its first World Cup in Russia in 2018. Seen as an innovation, VAR was used in several first round matches. Given the novelty, like a new toy, it was widely used (17 times in 48 matches). It was left aside during the final phase of the competition, as if the toy had already lost its appeal when it came to the knockout phase matches (it was used only three times in 16 matches).

A phrase said by Croatian Manager Zlatko Dalić, during an interview after the defeat to France in the World Cup final, is symptomatic that times were different. For him, "VAR is good for football." On that occasion, a penalty was scored against Croatia after consulting VAR. Although he disagreed with the penalty, he considered the presence of VAR in matches a step forward. At that moment, Dalić had all the conditions and enough space in the media to make a harsh criticism of VAR and FIFA. He did not do it.

We will show in this space, by questioning the offside rule and presenting four emblematic cases, how VAR has created injustices while announcing the exact opposite, and how difficult are the decisions of football referees, especially in balanced games. For this, we will essentially dialog with Bourdieu (1996).

It is very common to hear insults to referees for their decisions; however, the resource they have available is only what can be seen. So, in the view of many people, it would be fair the aid of cameras so that possible errors of arbitration are corrected. The question that arises is not that simple. Could the cameras capture all angles of a throw, i.e., would it be seen in 360 degrees? Couldn't the pressure to consult VAR quickly cause the referee to rush his decision?

Or, if we want to change the angle of the questions to spice up the debate, even if the cameras captured all the angles, would that solve the doubt of the throw? Wouldn't the slow-motion replay produce a look at a throw that does not exist? It is worth remembering that the game is not practiced in slow motion. Many plays are performed at high speed; watching the play in slow motion looking for the precision of the play will end up taking away the essence of the game, its speed. A strong push, when viewed in slow motion, turns into a simple long contact. Slow motion is worth only for the aesthetic dimension it produces for the viewer. Nothing more than that.

We will now detail two common offside situations. As a starting point, we will present the typical situation in which there is an offside caused only by a few centimeters, which makes it difficult for the assistant referee to see, as the players are moving. Many will defend the need for the presence of the video referee to decide on offside situations such as this one and, thus, not harming the progress of the match or even the final result. In this example, the offside is not exactly a mistake made by the assistant referee; in fact, it is impossible to notice those few centimeters when positioned on the side of the pitch, with several players moving at speed. Thus, we understand that the referee was right insofar as the decision was made based on what it was actually seen. The referee inferred that the player was not offside, and, therefore, the goal was legal. Even if the frozen image showed the offside line, the failure to mark the player's irregular position would not represent an error. The reader will question the argument; after all, if the television indicated that the footballer was offside, how could the assistant be right when validating the goal? He got it right because that was the referee's decision in a difficult game. Football is not made for perfection; on the contrary, its fascination lies precisely in the imperfection of the facts. And, how we know, to err is human.

But fans do not care about the inaccurate side of the game. They want their team to win and not be harmed. Let us go back to the scene: The player was offside, a few centimeters ahead, but the assistant referee did not notice and let the play continue. The throw ends in a goal. The referee points to the center of the pitch. Before restarting the match, however, a notification is sent that the video must be checked verifying the exact position of the players. In doing so, they realize that the attacker was ahead and disallowed the goal. The video referee will then be extolled as a great invention, as something that really brings justice to the field of play.

It is interesting to mention that VAR appeared to be a savior for difficult offside situations. But it ended up requiring rethinking rule 11—offside—which is basically about preventing attackers from having a significant advantage over defenders. Strictly speaking, the rule says that a player is offside if any part of his head, body, or feet is in the opponents' half of the field (excluding the halfway line) and if any part of his head, body, or feet is nearer the opponents' goal line than the ball and the opponent's second-last player. The hands and arms of players, including goalkeepers, are not considered.

If offside is one of the most controversial refereeing decisions, why not review the rule? Why, instead of stating that the player is offside if any part of his head, body, or feet is closer to the goal line than the opponent, there is not discussion about establishing, with the help of technology, a greater accuracy in this information?

It is likely that the offside rule will be revised due to the use of VAR, because it no longer makes sense to penalize a player who is a few inches ahead of his opponent. In other words, the technological innovation should induce a change in rule 11. A better criterion should be established to confirm that an attacker is in an advantageous position over the defender. For example, technology could draw the line and point out that at least one whole foot of the player is fully in front of the opponent. If this happens, there will be an undue advantage for the player who is ahead of the second-last defender. For critics, if there is no significant change in this way of interpreting offside, VAR will be involved in many controversies.

There has been a major change in the application of the rule 11. Under FIFA's new protocol, the assistant referee must not raise his flag to point out offside before the attack is completed (i.e., let the play proceed, assigning the video referee the task of checking whether there was offside). This solution produces a change in the dynamics of the game, to the extent that, in many cases, the goals scored are, in sequence, annulled after consultation with VAR. Perhaps this has brought a lot of frustration and less responsibility to the head referee.

For critics, the VAR protocol was born with the motto of minimal interference, but in fact it has multiplied the interference and damaged the dynamics of the game. The problem was not VAR, but the way it was being used. Furthermore, the adoption of VAR has even changed the discussion about who is to blame for the defeat.

Facing the criticism received, FIFA President Gianni Infantino acknowledged that occasional wrong decisions based on the use of VAR can occur because of the lack of experience of those who are using the new technology. Therefore, the use of VAR must be improved. And it is also necessary to review the rules of the game. He stated that the offside rule and the handball rule have evolved over time and that it may be necessary to review these rules, not because of VAR, but because FIFA wants to foster attacking football and avoid injustice (Warshaw, 2020, December 7).

Speaking on television, Bourdieu (1996) says that it is possible to turn an everyday event into something extraordinary and make the audience interpret ordinary qualities as being extraordinary. Bringing this to football, we can say that offside (which is an ordinary move of the game) is transformed with VAR and seen as something extraordinary, and its marking (or not marking) can determine the final result by itself.

VAR produces the "reality effect," concept used by Bourdieu (1996, p. 21) to analyze how television affects viewers. Obviously, the focus of Bourdieu's text is not football, but his reflections help us to think on this theme. Because television shows images and actions and makes people believe in what they show. When the VAR is consulted, the attention is focused on the referee, while the protagonists lose importance. In short, the choices that are produced on television are somehow choices without a subject. Why can't the request to consult the video referee be made by the team captain or the manager of the team that feels aggrieved? One way not to harm the dynamics of the match and not trivialize the plays would be to limit the number of consultations to VAR.

To contest FIFA's claim that VAR was not changing football but making it fairer and cleaner (Monioudis, 2018), we present four situations in which the video referee was used and did not produce the expected effect of justice. The exalted idea of cleanliness is somewhat mistaken as an argument for the presence of VAR. The four cases that illustrate the misuse of this technological resource highlight the reasons why the use of VAR has been so criticized during the implementation period.

The first example occurred in the 2016 FIFA Club World Cup. In the semifinal match between Kashima Antlers and Atlético Nacional, the first official use of VAR in FIFA competitions took place. Orlando Berrío, of Atlético Nacional, knocked down Daigo Nishi inside the penalty area. Hungarian referee Viktor Kassai did not signal the penalty but was warned by the video referee. The big problem in this opening match was not the penalty that was awarded, but that the referee did not award it. They disregarded the fact that Daigo was in an offside position at the start of the match.[2] It was a mistake that could not have happened, given the idea that VAR would prevent injustices.

The second case occurred in 2019 in a German second division championship match between Holstein Kiel and Bochum. Bochum player Ganvoula received a long throw-in inside the opponents' penalty area. He controlled the ball and crossed it from outside the box. Before the ball went out of play, Michael Eberwein, a Kiel player who was warming up behind the goal, with the clear intention of preventing it from hitting the advertising board, which was likely to delay play, touched the ball when it was on the line. His action of cushioning the ball was interpreted by the video referee as an infraction, causing the field referee to review the throw. According to the rules, if someone who is not inside the four lines of the pitch directly interferes with play, a direct free kick is awarded. As the substitute's action allegedly interfered with play inside the penalty area, a penalty kick was awarded against Kiel.

This is a clear case of improper use of VAR. Despite what the rule says, the referee's interpretation was disregarded when the maximum penalty was awarded. The rules only exist when the referee makes them work, which is done through his interpretations. In the aforementioned match, there was no intention of interfering in the game, preventing a goal from being scored or anything else that could benefit the reserve player's team. The ball was heading toward him and the athlete only placed his foot in order to cushion it. If there is no common sense in applying the rules, we will have situations as bizarre as this one.

The third event also took place in the final of the Club World Cup, but this time in the 2019 edition. Mané, from Liverpool, received a deep ball between the Flamengo defenses. The Flamengo player Rafinha, who was behind the Senegalese, tried to prevent the shot with a sliding tackle as Mané entered the penalty area. The striker was off balance, and his shot was not on target. The referee Abdulrahman Al-Jassim, Qatar, scored a penalty and showed a yellow card to the Brazilian player.

The throw-in was reviewed by VAR, and the referee changed his decision. He did not call a foul and withdrew the yellow card. The big issue was that the images shown on television, from different angles and in slow motion, did not allow a safe conclusion. Due to the speed of the play, it was difficult to find the exact moment in the slow-motion image of the Brazilian player's contact with the Liverpool player.

The complexity of the shot showed that the new technology is not yet able to avoid mistakes. Would Rafinha's subtle touch on Mané's foot have been enough to hinder the aim of his shot? Was the foul, if it occurred, outside or inside the area? If the images were inconclusive, why did the referee decide to change his initial decision?

---

[2] The offside is only visible with the use of technology as Daigo was just inches in front of Berrío.

What escapes this technological dimension in the attempt to ensure a fair decision is exactly what cannot be eliminated: the interpretation of the referee. Even with the use of video, which allows the referee on the field to review the play from different angles, doubts may still persist.

We cannot assume that some referees make mistakes intentionally. It must be understood that they are always being asked to make quick decisions; moreover, they cannot make mistakes. But what is a referee's mistake if not a decision (sometimes wrong) in the face of what he saw? "Ah, so let's bring in VAR to solve that." Not everything is solved with the video referee. On the contrary, its presence often creates more confusion.

Because of the introduction of VAR, which in some games has led to several long stoppages, football has become more boring. The players, in order to disrupt the referee's life, are constantly misleading him. Some will say that this kind of thing is inherent to football, it is part of the show. Under the discourse of justice, VAR ends up legitimizing the assumption of neutrality of the referee. According to Breiller Pires (2018, March 17), the variables that make football a land far from equality were ignored, and the illusion that video refereeing would promote isonomy was created.

The spectacle needs to be recreated, and there are many doubts whether the video referee helps or not in this process. If we already have players who put their hands over their mouths to cover what they are saying to their colleagues or even to the referee, there will also be an increase in the number of athletes making the gesture with both hands indicating a screen, suggesting that the referee asks for the assistance of VAR. And thus, football is put on the background.

The fact is that there are "flaws" and situations that VAR cannot solve, especially those related to the interpretations of the referee, which are subjective and are part of the specificities of this sport. The way VAR was initially used generated a lot of criticism and mistrust.

Bourdieu (1996, p. 19) states that "television calls for dramatization, in both senses of the term: it puts an event on stage, put it in images. In doing so, it exaggerates the importance of that event, its seriousness, and its dramatic, even tragic character." And all this dramatization is not dissociated from the interpretation of who is in the studio.

Some will say that, with the introduction of VAR, there is no longer any possibility of match-fixing, there are no more errors. However, we believe that, on the contrary, these possibilities have now increased. How is that possible? Well, we now have more than three people, far away from the "heat of the moment," who will solve many impasses that occur on the field. It will be the opinion of those who are outside the game, without access to what the television does not show, that will decide the fate of the game. With this supposed neutrality (and acting almost anonymously), it may be easier to manipulate decisions. To show or not to show the red card? Watch the throw by VAR and the decision will be the most correct. Is that the truly the case?

It is necessary to return to Bourdieu (1996, pp. 19–20) because he adds that "the world of images is dominated by words." If this was not the case, VAR would only be the video and communication with the assistants who are in the game.

The latest example of misuse of VAR happened in the 2018 Copa Libertadores match between Boca Juniors and Cruzeiro. Dedé, from Cruzeiro, jumped to dispute a ball and, without realizing the approach of Andrada, the goalkeeper of Boca, violently collided with him. When the referee saw the VAR, Dedé was sent off. Look at the gravity of the decision: It was a random throw, the collision happened exclusively because the two players were only looking at the ball. It was a "work accident," as the commentators like to classify. Therefore, the exclusion of the Cruzeiro player was unfair.

The introduction of VAR has put the referee at the center of the football spectacle when it should have made him invisible. Stopping the game and heading to the side of the pitch create disruptions in the way football is played. Brazilian football seems unable to escape this narcissistic dimension in the name of justice, and, in doing so, becomes its hostage.

It should be noted that technology enhances the transformation of football, at the same time that, through VAR, it imprisons the game; it wants to be more real than reality. Football definitely becomes a virtual product of television. Its existence is increasingly conditioned to the technological apparatus and becomes progressively more distant from those who make the spectacle of football: athletes, coaching staff, refereeing quartet on the field, journalists, and even fans.

Justice is Slow and Sometimes Fails

The final of the 1995 Brazilian Championship was played on December 17, in São Paulo. Botafogo became champion with a 1–1 draw against Santos. The match was marked by disastrous refereeing by Márcio Rezende de Freitas and his two assistants. Three clear errors durant the match decided the title of the tournament. Perhaps this is one of the main examples of how the correct use of VAR could prevent great injustices in football.

Botafogo had won the first match in Rio de Janeiro 2–1, and, according to the rules, Santos would be champion with a simple victory in the second leg. Túlio opened the scoring for Botafogo halfway through the first half. The striker was in an illegal position on the play, but the assistant referee did not signal any offside and the goal was validated. Early in the second half, Santos tied with a goal from Marcelo Passos, but before there was a hand touch of Marquinhos that the referee did not see. Later, Camanducaia scored another goal for Santos, after a free kick. Although the striker was in a legal position and the assistant did not raise the flag, the referee decided to cancel the goal. We can speculate that, if there had been VAR at that time and the three refereeing errors had been corrected, Santos would probably have been the 1995 Brazilian champion.

Despite the disastrous refereeing, Márcio Rezende de Freitas won the Charles Miller Award for best referee of the year, offered by TV Globo, and continued to be honored by CBF Refereeing Commission. After retiring, he became a refereeing commentator for the same network. In an interview granted in 2012, he admitted the mistakes made in the 1995 final and argued that referees are subject to make mistakes, just like players, but the burden is greater on referees. His statement reinforces the contribution that VAR can offer (Leitão & Rodrigues, 2012, October 10):

> Sometimes technology doesn't even see what it has to see. I don't know if it is a villain [for showing refereeing mistakes]. Sometimes you need an image, and you don't have that image. Technology doesn't see everything, because it is operated by humans. They are fallible humans too, and sometimes they make mistakes, just like the referee does. Only, if we use this analogy, the thing falls more to the referee's side than to the collection of the image [VAR] that didn't exist. (our translation)

Márcio Rezende de Freitas also became the central character of another great injustice committed by referees in Brazilian football, precisely in the match that marked his farewell as a FIFA referee, at the age of 45. In a decisive match of the 2005 Brazilian championship, Corinthians and Internacional played out a 1–1 draw in São Paulo on November 20. Tevez scored the first goal for the home team; Rafael Sobis equalized for the visitors early in the second half. In the 28th minute of the second half, the key moment came when Márcio Rezende missed a clear penalty kick in Internacional's favor. Fabio Costa, Corinthians' goalkeeper, knocked down Tinga, Internacional's midfielder, inside the area. In addition to not writing down the penalty, Marcio Rezende sent off the athlete of Internacional after applying the second yellow card for alleged simulation. The tie allowed Corinthians to remain in the lead (with two rounds remaining) and become that year's Brazilian champion. Evidently, VAR could have avoided this "blatant error" and made the title match fairer, in the perspective of Internacional.

These two examples help understand the main argument in favor of VAR: to avoid gross refereeing errors and make the outcome of the game "fair" (i.e., ensure that the score reflects the greater or lesser competence of each team in attacking and defending, without undue interference from the referee or external factors). This is the center of the controversy registered and fomented by the national sports press in 2019. But, after all, has VAR increased "justice" in Brazilian football? In this regard, let us see what the president of the CBF Refereeing Commission, Leonardo Gaciba, thinks (Storti, 2019, December 13):

> At no time did FIFA promise perfection. We are there so there is no unquestionable error, the rest remains part of it. There will be a residual of errors, despite the powerful tool. The general public will have to understand that there are plays where there is no consensus ever, because it depends on interpretation and, in those plays, the video referee should not interfere. We should be concerned with the mistakes where there is consensus. (our translation)

According to a survey conducted by the Refereeing Commission after the end of the Brazilian championship, the number of "serious errors" fell from 188 in 2018 to 36 in 2019. "Serious errors" were considered to be incorrect refereeing decisions that affected the outcome of the match, such as validating an illegal goal, canceling a legal goal, misusing a red card, giving a non-existent penalty, or not awarding a penalty. In addition, the success rate in protocol situations was estimated at 98.4%. In this sense, there is no doubt that VAR has contributed to a significant reduction in refereeing errors.

There were other important gains, according to the Commission (Storti, 2019, December 13). The "grabbing" between players in the penalty area was drastically reduced, the average number of fouls decreased compared to the previous edition, and there was a drop in the number of cards compared to the previous year. In other words, VAR has contributed to reducing violence and inhibiting malice that went unnoticed by the referees. For example, it has become unlikely that a player will assault an opponent without the referee or assistant referee noticing (as occurred in the case of Luis Suárez's bite on Italy's Chiellini at the 2014 World Cup). It has also become easier to prove that an athlete disrespected a professional colleague (e.g., by spitting in his face or poking his butt). The technology is also probably reducing attempts to cheat the referees by scoring a goal with their hands (as Corinthians forward Jô did, in a game against Vasco da Gama, also in the 2017 Brazilian Championship). In other words, by forcing athletes to respect the rules and improve their conduct on the field, VAR may contribute to increasing fair play in Brazilian football.

Another controversial issue concerns the delay in the evaluation of a throw made by the video referee, which interrupts the game and affects the dynamics of the spectacle. The average time consumed by the VAR in Brazil was very high in 2019, compared to what was seen in the games of the European leagues or even in the 2018 World Cup games. According to the Refereeing Commission's survey, there were 755 stoppages in 380 games of the Brazilian championship, an average of practically two stoppages per match. Each stoppage for evaluation by VAR spent, on average, one minute, but when it was necessary to analyze the dispute by the field referee, the average stoppage time reached almost three minutes. FIFA recommends that the time consumed by the video assistant referee does not exceed 1 min and 15 s. It is worth mentioning: The greater the number of stoppages in a match, the lower the chance of the time consumed by the VAR being reset (as an addition after 90 min).

The intention of the Refereeing Commission was to increase the efficiency of VAR in order to reduce the length of stoppage time, as recommended by FIFA. To this end, greater caution would be necessary to ensure that the number of interferences in a single match is not too high. Another measure envisaged was to ensure transparency in decision-making. It was expected that the acceptance of the use of this technology would increase, and criticism would decrease (Magatti, 2019, December 24).

Obviously, VAR is not infallible, but it has been perceived as "good" and "necessary" because it is "fairer." We should therefore rephrase the question: What kind of "fairness" is being sought in contemporary football?

The concept of "justice" has been defined in different ways by philosophers, jurists, sociologists, educators, and even economists. Each school of thought defines "justice" according to a specific purpose, so controversies exist over which definition is most appropriate for examining each particular issue.

In the sports field, the definition of "justice" may also be a matter of controversy. Pierre de Coubertin's Olympic ideology already defended that modern sport should be governed by impersonal rules that ensure isonomy among athletes (and also among teams). However, the understanding of what fair play is has changed in recent decades, and the aristocratic–bourgeois ethic has given way to new ethical commitments in the era of globalization and multicultural interactions.

According to the International Fair Play Committee, "fair play" is a complex concept, which comprises and incorporates a series of fundamental values that are not only essential to sport, but relevant in everyday life. Its constitutive elements are fair competition, respect, friendship, team spirit, equality, sport without doping, and respect for written and unwritten rules. It also includes the following virtues: integrity, solidarity, tolerance, care, excellence, and joy.

The FIFA Fair Play Code consists of ten golden rules. The original meaning is that victory loses its value if it is not played in a loyal, honest, and fair manner. An important lesson is to respect everyone: opponents, teammates, referees, and spectators (and fight for equal rights). A crucial rule is to reject bad influences: reject drugs, racism, homophobia, violence, and gambling. The sporting spirit can be summed up in the following idea: "play to win but accept defeat with dignity".

We may consider that, in theory, VAR contributes to "fairer" and more "correct" refereeing. Thus, it may encourage fair play in professional football, provided it reinforces points of the FIFA code of conduct—especially respect for the rules, referees (accepting their decisions) and opponents, and equal treatment. But this suggestion needs to be better evaluated.

Sandel (2009) teaches that the idea of "justice" can be understood through three approaches: utilitarian ethics, libertarian ethics, and virtue ethics. The first emphasizes the maximization of the utility of goods and services, the efficiency of the rules that regulate human conduct, aiming at the welfare or happiness of individuals. The second understands that justice is related to the freedom of individual choice and the equity of opportunities, and it may be necessary to correct failures in the functioning of markets and combat preexisting social disadvantages. The third involves the cultivation of virtue and concern for the common good. This third approach is more appropriate for the discussion of moral dilemmas. According to Sandel (2009), justice does not only correspond to the right way of distributing goods, as it also concerns the right way of evaluating conducts. Therefore, it cannot be defined a priori, since it is necessary to discuss the nature of moral dilemmas to determine the procedures that ensure the effectiveness of ethical principles that should guide individual actions in contemporary societies.

FIFA Fair Play Code could be framed in this third approach presented by Sandel, considering that the publicized discourse extols the promotion of peace and equality among peoples and collaboration to make the world a better place.

However, the way the term "justice" has been claimed in the debate on VAR seems to fit better in the first approach. The arguments of the advocates of the use of this revolutionary technology seem to be based on a utilitarian ethic and on the valuation of efficiency, in which arbitration is understood as an element that should value neutrality, without interfering with the laws of competition. The result of the competition is fair provided that (i) the rules are applied equally to all, (ii) the arbitrators are not subject to external pressures, and (iii) the punishments are assigned impartially.

It is also important to consider the concern to avoid a deep inequality in competition conditions (second approach). In order for competition to be fair, FIFA separates men and women, young people and adults, and maintains a hierarchy among teams, with "divisions" that express the level of competitiveness. But there is no concern about the differences in economic power between teams playing in the same tournament, which cause imbalances in the competition. Furthermore, it is important to emphasize: There is no room for moral dilemmas, nor for questioning the effectiveness of the ethical principles that should guide the players' conduct on and off the field (third approach).

In short, there is a lot of confusion in the debates about VAR, without making it clear what kind of justice can be expected in a football match. There are those who want to discuss the merit of the winning team and others who doubt the neutrality of the referee; those who question the objectivity of the rules and others who highlight the flaws in the system; those who highlight the personal dramas and ecstasies and others who emphasize the institutional structures and dynamics. It is therefore difficult to reach a consensus on the criteria to define when arbitration is fair and when justice fails.

Final Remarks

The reflection we are proposing gave voice to the opinions, the criticisms, the regrets, the reactions, in order to highlighting the controversies, make a balance of mistakes and successes, and weave a plot, paint a picture, propitiate a new consciousness. We chose a nonlinear path of argument, based on the explanation of conflicting opinions to emphasize the counterposition of interpretations about our object of study. Following Norbert Elias' (2007) advice: to study contemporary social processes (when the subject of knowledge is immersed in its object of study), we need to adopt an analysis perspective that reconciles "involvement and detachment" to generate reflections congruent with the complex reality and make pertinent questionings.

In the academic environment, such debate should not be done in a dichotomous way. To discuss the ongoing changes in Brazilian football brought about by the adoption of VAR, we show a variety of individual views and specific episodes (highlighting opinions published in the media) and seek subsidies in theoretical approaches for more far-reaching propositions. We oscillate between the particular and the general, aiming to better understand what is lasting and what is transitory, what is fact, and what is opinion.

We did not pretend to make sense of disconnected events, nor to reconcile troubling feelings. Instead, we have left room for personal doubts and impressions, so that the reader himself can interpret the polemics presented throughout the text. With this intention, we still want to add some considerations to stimulate critical thinking.

VAR is a product of the technology of our time. For its defenders, it is a poison that heals; for its critics, it is a medicine that kills. There is no doubt that the novelty has produced, as we have tried to show in several ways, ambiguous results. It is the medicine that, depending on the dose, turns into poison. The way VAR was introduced in Brazil, in the opinion of many characters, put at risk the health of the patient, or rather, the dynamics of the show. Although the intention was to eliminate errors to ensure "fair play," as many authorities claimed, VAR ended up producing other problems. It became inconvenient in Brazil. It was necessary to adjust the dosage, but how to harmonize all the interest groups that make up the football structure? Disregarding the divergent views and prioritizing only one point of view led to an increase in tensions and reduced the promised benefits.

FIFA's euphoric discourse was deconstructed, and the reasons that led it to announce that "the future is [already] here" were questioned. The future only exists if it is connected to the past and the present. If it is disconnected from these other times, we will have an empty future, an idea without adherence to reality. Sometimes, the consequences of well-intentioned actions can be unwanted.

VAR brought with it two concerns: How to prevent the interference of this technology from damaging the quality of the spectacle and the enjoyment of the fans? How to prevent the discussion about the VAR's mistakes from becoming more important than the performance of the protagonists?

The criteria for the use of VAR were presented in Brazil as an imposition of FIFA, but they were not merely technical criteria. In a short time, the risk of causing many fissures in the delicate balance of emotions that makes the football spectacle a unique experience became evident. Fortunately, the IFAB and the CBF Refereeing Commission were willing to make adjustments and corrections to the protocols, so that VAR would not continue to be seen as inconvenient and would not turn football into a boring spectacle to watch, which is certainly not interesting for television channels, nor for sponsors. In other words, they understood that it is necessary to get the dosage right so as not to break the flow of the show and not to bore people.

FIFA's initial speech disregarded the need for professionalization of referees. This reinforced the idea that technology supplies all the deficiencies that the human dimension can produce. Since CBF did not invest in the professionalization of refereeing, the production of the show was compromised. VAR was adopted in Brazil without sufficient training and capacity building to ensure a significant improvement in refereeing conditions.

VAR has become an irreversible innovation, but corrections to avoid distortions and to speed up consultation were required. Despite these criticisms, there was also the expectation that the use of technology, in connection with the demands and preferences of the protagonists, could change the game for the better. Ensuring that the referee's gross errors no longer spoil the show, nor compromise the work done by countless professionals throughout the season, could undoubtedly represent a major advance. And avoiding unsportsmanlike conduct also seemed to be a valuable benefit.

Finally, it should be noted that the introduction of VAR has reinforced the existing divide between amateur and professional football.[3] But it is important to emphasize that this innovation widened the gap between the most prestigious professional football leagues (whose revenues allow VAR to be funded) and the least prestigious professional football tournaments (the lower divisions of the Brazilian Championship

---

[3] It is too early to tell if the change in players' conduct at matches (fair play) caused by VAR will influence the behavior of amateur athletes who play football on the weekends.

and most state championships, where VAR was not adopted). Therefore, VAR has become an additional element in the matrix of structural inequalities that unbalance the football world in Brazil.

References

Amaro, G., & Fernandes, R. (2019, August 17). Arnaldo Cezar Coelho detona VAR no Brasil: "É um desastre". *O Estado de São Paulo*. https://esportes.estadao.com.br/noticias/futebol,arnaldo-cezar-coelho-detona-var-no-brasil-e-um-desastre,70002970500
Band Esporte. (2019, September 29). Mano Menezes: VAR não pode ter camisa, não pode ter estádio (video interview). https://economia.uol.com.br/videos/?id=mano-menezes-var-nao-pode-ter-camisa-nao-pode-ter-estadio-04024C9C3568C0B96326
Bourdieu, P. (1996). *On television*. The New Press.
Campos, C. et al. (2019, September 17). Mais da metade dos clubes do campeonato brasileiro pede mudanças no VAR. *O Estado de São Paulo*. https://esportes.estadao.com.br/noticias/futebol,mais-da-metade-dos-clubes-da-serie-a-pede-mudancas-no-uso-do-var-no-brasileirao,70003011497
Ceccon, B. (2019, March 29). Andrés não concorda com uso do VAR para lances interpretativos. *Gazeta Esportiva*. https://www.gazetaesportiva.com/times/Corinthians/andres-nao-concorda-com-uso-do-VAR-para-lances-interpretativos/
Elias, N. (2007). *Involvement and detachment*. (The collected works of norbert Elias, Vol. 8). University College Dublin Press.
ESPN Brasil (2019, 5 September). Renato: "O Gaciba vai dar uma palestra pra gente sobre o VAR na sexta à noite, será que eu devo estar lá?" (video interview). https://www.espn.com.br/video/clipe/_/id/6034174
ESPN Brasil (2019, July 20). Vasco: Depois de comemorar que VAR não apareceu, Luxemburgo explica: "não sou contra o VAR, mas como é usado" (video interview). https://www.espn.com.mx/video/clip/_/id/5856532
Globo Esporte. (2018, October 17). VAR rouba a cena na final entre Corinthians e Cruzeiro; Gaciba analisa lances. *GloboEsporte.com*. https://globoesporte.globo.com/sp/futebol/copa-do-brasil/noticia/var-rouba-a-cena-na-final-entre-corinthians-e-cruzeiro-gaciba-analisa-lances.ghtml
Giglio, S. S., & Proni, M. W. (2020). A polêmica sobre o VAR no Brasil. In S. S. Giglio, & M. W. Proni (Orgs.), *O futebol nas Ciências Humanas no Brasil* (pp. 761–787). Editora da Unicamp.
Guedes, M. (2019, September 8). Maioria dos brasileiros aprova árbitro de vídeo, mostra Datafolha. *Folha de São Paulo*. https://www1.folha.uol.com.br/esporte/2019/09/maioria-aprova-uso-do-var-no-futebol-mostra-datafolha.shtml
Homewood, B., & Radnedge, C. (2018, July 13). Soccer: Infantino says VAR means the end of offside goals. *Reuters*. World Football. https://www.reuters.com/article/soccer-worldcup-fifa-infantino-idUKL4N1U941U
Leitão, C., & Rodrigues, D. (2012, October 10). Apitei: Márcio Rezende admite erros na decisão de 95 entre Santos e Bota. *GloboEsporte.com*. http://globoesporte.globo.com/futebol/brasileirao-serie-a/noticia/2012/10/apitei-marcio-rezende-admite-erros-na-decisao-de-95-entre-santos-e-bota.html
Magatti, R. (2019, December 24). Leonardo Gaciba faz balanço positivo do VAR e projeta mudanças para 2020. *O Estado de São Paulo*. https://esportes.estadao.com.br/noticias/futebol,leonardo-gaciba-faz-balanco-positivo-do-var-e-projeta-mudancas-para-2020,70003135756
Matos, J. E., & Almeida, P. I. (2019, November 21). CBF faz pesquisa com jogadores e técnicos: 94% aprovam continuidade do VAR. *UOL*. https://www.uol.com.br/esporte/futebol/ultimas-noticias/2019/11/21/cbf-faz-pesquisa-com-jogadores-e-tecnicos-94-aprovam-continuidade-do-var.htm
Monioudis, P. (2018). Coaching and officiating tools for the big stage. *FIFA 1904*, August. https://issuu.com/fifa/docs/eng_2c8fb978b3932c

Ojêda, A., & Faustini, V. (2019, July 31). VAR na berlinda! Polêmica prossegue, mesmo com a tecnologia no futebol. *Lance!* https://www.lance.com.br/futebol-nacional/var-berlinda-polemica-prossegue-mesmo-com-tecnologia-futebol.html

Pires, B. (2018, March 17). Árbitro de vídeo: Isso é muito "black mirror". *El País*, Brasil. https://brasil.elpais.com/brasil/2018/03/16/deportes/1521237292_742570.html

Rodrigues, N. (1949/2003). *A mulher que amou demais*. Companhia das Letras, 2003.

Sandel, M. (2009). *Justice: What's the right thing to do?* Allen Lane.

Storti, V. (2019, December 13). Com VAR, comissão de arbitragem comemora redução de 80% nos "erros capitais" no brasileirão. *GloboEsporte.com*. https://globoesporte.globo.com/futebol/brasileirao-serie-a/noticia/comissao-de-arbitragem-comemora-reducao-de-80percent-nos-erros-capitais-no-brasileirao.ghtml

UOL Esporte. (2019, December 26). Pesquisão 2019. https://www.uol.com.br/esporte/reportagens-especiais/pesquisao---futebol-brasileiro---2019/

Warshaw, A. (2020, December 7). No return: Infantino defends VAR saying people, not tech, are the problem. *Inside World Football*. http://www.insideworldfootball.com/2020/12/07/no-return-infantino-defends-var-saying-people-not-tech-problem/

Part IV
Transversal Themes

Chapter 23
Life Projects, Women and Football

Osmar Moreira de Souza Júnior and Heloisa Helena Baldy dos Reis

The longing journalist João Saldanha (1917–1990), a man of strong opinions and a fierce opponent of the military dictatorship, was always categorically opposed to the practice of football by women. On one occasion, in a lecture to university students, when asked about women's football he said: "I'm against it." In an attempt to explain himself and counteract the astonishment and disappointment of the women in the audience, the journalist argued: "The guy has a son, who takes his girlfriend to meet him. The father asks the classic question: 'Do you work or study? I work,' she answers. What is your job? I'm a defender for Bangu'." Saldanha concluded by saying: "It looks bad, don't you think?".

The episode highlights the social discomfort caused by the simple assumption that women occupy spaces considered to be exclusively for men, as is the case of football. Although this thought was expressed by Saldanha in the 1980s, when Brazil was still going through a period of political reopening at the end of the 1964 civilian dictatorship regime, the same was true in the case of women's football, which was banned in the country between the 1940s and 1980s. One cannot ignore the historical ballast that this type of reasoning imprints on the social imaginary to this day in relation to life projects considered appropriate or not for women.

According to Velho (1987), the individual is not a passive receiver of social norms, having on them his own interpretations, fostering a field of possibilities that constitutes his decision-making and actions. Linked to the concept of field of possibilities, the author uses the idea of "project." Concepts that we consider important to understand the journey idealized and effectively traced by women's football players who played a leading role in our investigations.

Project is a rational perspective of pursuing specific ends; it links to how an individual operates with performance and options based on assessments of the reality

O. M. de Souza Júnior (✉)
Federal University of São Carlos, São Carlos, Brazil

H. H. B. dos Reis
University of Campinas, Campinas, Brazil

© The Author(s), under exclusive license to Springer Nature Switzerland AG 2021   397
S. S. Giglio and M. W. Proni (eds.), *Football and Social Sciences in Brazil*,
https://doi.org/10.1007/978-3-030-84686-2_23

in a given sociocultural context. Projects are formulated by individuals who act, combining diverse social pressures, but with a basic repertoire of alternatives and options that sets up the field of possibilities to act and plan life projects. According to Velho (1987, p. 27), this field of possibilities is "historically and culturally circum-scribed, both in terms of the very notion of individual, and of the existing themes, priorities and cultural paradigms."

In this sense, Chan-Vianna (2010, p. 38) considers that "project" and "field of possibilities" deal with alternatives built with the interpretative potential of the symbolic world of culture, and when these individual interpretations constitute common interests, it is possible to assume these groups of individuals as a "social project":

> "Project" is a conscious dimension of culture; potentially public; and directly linked to processes of social change. the action of individuals in choosing such personal or collective projects is limited by the "field of possibilities" that is socio-historical and not particular to each one. (our translation)

In this chapter, we outline an approximation with the framework adopted by Chan-Vianna, aiming to interpret how the personal and collective projects of some women who establish intense relationships with football are interwoven by fields of possibilities and by their singular choices.

This source was developed from the analysis of indirect sources, taking as "inter-locutors" the player Marta, based on the biography written by Diego Graciano; the testimonies of Aline Benevenuto and Nilda Ismael do Nascimento (Nildinha), in the documentary *Deixa que eu chuto* by the director Alves (2008); the former player (of the Brazilian national football team) Elane, in the program "Esporte Fantástico" of TV Record; as well as direct sources in two fronts, the first composed of young female candidates who participated in the "screening" of Santos Futebol Clube in 2010, and the second by athletes already inserted in the circuit of high-performance football that were playing the São Paulo Championship in 2011.

Projects of Martas, Elanes, Nildinhas, Alines, etc.

According to Diego Graciano, author of a biography of the player Marta, it was during her childhood in Dois Riachos, a small town in the countryside of Alagoas, that she began to show a great facility for practicing sports, having been invited by her physical education teacher to play in the goalkeeper position on the school's female handball team. Marta was then 9 years old. At that time, according to the testimonies of her childhood friends, the girl was already showing all her talent, including attending the boys' football matches, even against everyone's wishes. A short time later, she became a player, reinforcing the Dois Riachos boys' team in the region's championships, standing out as the team's captain and top scorer. About these experiences, Marta relates: "There was no locker room, and I changed clothes in a dark place, alone. that tournament was a little hard for me, that's why I was so happy to win a prize. I was the only woman" (Graciano, 2008, p. 41).

According to Graciano (2008), at the age of 10 Marta already had to flee from her brothers, who locked her in the house to keep her away from football and embarrassment. Some testimonials (our translation):

> They used to tell me: 'Your sister is playing football with men.' I used to take Marta home, fight with her, I even hit her hard once. But she ran away and went back to the field. (Statement by José, Marta's older brother) (Graciano, 2008, p. 48)

> I was ashamed of my sister. She didn't obey José nor me. (Statement by Valdir, Marta's brother) (Graciano, 2008, p. 51)

> One day, I stopped fighting with Marta. I saw how she ruled the field, she was the captain of those boys. Why bother a woman who is more of a man on the field? (Statement of José) (Graciano, 2008, p. 55).

Although she knew how to face any obstacle that came her way on her way to football, the fact is that Marta would not have gotten where she did if it had not been for the individual initiative of an acquaintance of her family who was moving to Rio de Janeiro; he proposed that the girl, then 14 years old, went with him and his family to Rio de Janeiro capital in order to try out for the Vasco da Gama women's football team. In her first test at Vasco, Marta seems to have reminded Garrincha's first training session at Botafogo, in 1953 (Pragmatismo, 2013, November 28): the little and unknown girl entered the field at the coach's request and soon demonstrated her daringness bending Brazilian national team players, such as Pretinha, Roseli and Formiga.

The documentary *Deixa que eu chuto* (Let me kick it)[1] presents some significant narratives for our research, of which we highlight those of Aline and Nildinha.

Aline Benevenuto was born in a family that, according to her, has always been very involved with football; besides her grandfather, who played football, her aunt also played, and this at a time when, according to her, "women's football was not very well known." Aline tells that, since she was very young, her father would take her to the Mineirão to watch Atlético's games. Her passion for playing and supporting football comes from that time. She started playing in the street with the boys, who liked the way she played, and she was even one of the first to be chosen to join the teams.

At the age of 8, Aline was already a goalkeeper on her high school's futsal team and then joined the local football school practice; the coach encouraged her and guided her to the Atlético Mineiro women's team, a club for which she had the opportunity to compete and win the Mineiro football championship in 2006. According to the player, Atlético was the best structured team in Minas Gerais, which allowed her to train on a grass field, receive occasional assistance from trainee physiotherapists and, also eventually, receive an allowance of R$ 70 (without any contractual commitment).

---

[1] Documentary that won the "Pitching GNT 2009" award, directed by Alfredo Alves, produced by Bemvinda Filmes. The documentary presents narratives of adult and young women who have an intense relationship with football.

Although the experience in Atlético was being successful from the sporting point of view, it was impossible to conciliate the performance in the club with attending a federal university; Aline, then, gave up Atlético, aware that she could not make a living with football, at that time without any recognition or financial structure for the professionalization of female football players. In her statement, she says that her dream was "one day I could make a living playing football" and, who knows, even play for the Brazilian national team (Alves, 2008, our translation).

Although she admits that playing football professionally was part of her life project, Aline explains in her account that the conditions offered for this practice imposed serious limits to this plan, which had to be reformulated and directed to her studies as a priority, making the practice of football conditional to the continuity of the higher education course. The young woman thus explains, in a rational and concrete way, aspects such as the lack of salary and work contract as barriers to the exclusive dedication to football, a situation very different from that experienced by men.

Nilda Ismael do Nascimento, known as Nildinha, played for several clubs in Brazil and abroad. At the time the documentary *Deixa que eu chuto* was produced, she was playing for SC Corinthians Paulista in the 2008 season. Nildinha said that, on television, she would always watch athletes like Roseli, Sissi and Pretinha playing for the Brazilian national team, occasions when she used to cry and tell her brother (who encouraged her) that one day she would still be on the national team (Alves, 2008, our translation).

The documentary informs that Nildinha played 39 official matches for the Brazilian national team, scoring 32 goals. She played for 11 different teams in Brazil; played in Japan, the USA and Europe; won 18 championships; and was top scorer in 13. In her accounts, the player tells about the countless difficulties she faced in this journey, for example, her mother's total disagreement and the lack of proper footwear, which often made her play in flip-flops, not rarely losing them during the game and being beaten when she returned home: "I think she thought that it was a boy thing, don't you think. it was something for boys, t not for me, you have to study and you are a girl and you are not going to play football. Just like that" (Alves, 2008, our translation).

The former player recalls that at that time she had the invaluable support of the man who, according to her, was then president of the Sports Society of Gama, a club in the Federal District where Nildinha began her career in football at the age of 18. Her speech is representative (Alves, 2008, our translation):

So, Mr. Luiz, who is the president of Gama until today, he gave us money to pay the bus fare and after that he trained us, then he gave us a snack, and the bus fare back home. That was it. I played because I really liked it, for love. And out of friendship for him. And to support myself too, because he helped me. Soon after my mother passed away, right, and then I was alone with my father and sometimes I had nothing at home. Oh my God! [Nildinha lowers her head and pauses, visibly moved]. Then there's also the part that I got pregnant, right, and he helped me in all this too, with my daughter. Practically, he helped bringing her up. That's why I played for him, out of gratitude [i emotionally again, Nildinha again lowers her head and bites her lips]. It was a bit sad, but I got through it out of love for football. [...] I saw that it was in football that I was going to get to play for a big team, starting with Gama, so I could earn my money and support my daughter. [...]

Look, I think that making dreams come true in women's football is kind of like this... you have your own house, you know, you live well. And thank God football gave me this, I have nothing to complain about.

The journey of Nildinha, as well as that of Marta, can be presented as a counter-point to that of Aline. Even having to face social pressures such as the disapproval of the mother who even beat her, then her subsequent death, pregnancy, poverty ("sometimes there was nothing at home") and raising the daughter (supposedly without the father's help), Nildinha contradicted the expectations and, probably because she trusted in her performance, took up football as a life project through which she sought to support her family (Alves, 2008).

The path taken by Nildinha reveals that the decision-making of individuals, although circumscribed to possibilities that restrict certain life projects, is not determined absolutely, admitting the performance of a free will that enabled experiences such as the empowerment by football of Nildinha and Marta. At different levels, both players conquered their goals, building successful life projects and confirming the thesis of Bourdieu (2010) of the subjective and objective experience transformation of the woman's body, through the intensive practice of sports.

A story-news on the TV Record's "Esporte Fantástico" program, in June 2011, told the story of Elane, a former football player who was a defender and captain of the Brazilian national team for more than ten years, having won three South América championships, the fourth place on Atlantic's Olympics in 1996 and the third place in the USA's World Cup. At the time of the story-news, at the age of 43, Elane was working as a bus driver in Rio de Janeiro. The story of the ex-footballer in the report "The forgotten captain" was based on her dismissal from the Brazilian team short before taking part in her second Olympic Games in Sydney, 2000. The sorrow kept regarding this event, and the consequences caused in her life were explained by Elane (Fantástico, 2011, June 4):

I was cut from the national team one month before the Sydney Olympics and never came back. Very boring, very sad, the worst moment of my life as an athlete was that moment. The day they came to my room there... "you are cut from the national team" [...] I didn't ask why, I didn't ask for an explanation, I packed my bags and the time to leave was really sad.

On the Brazilian team you are representing a million people, you are wearing the mantle of your country. You have to have everything to be comfortable, to do well what you are there to do. [reporter asks: "and what was missing, for example?" It is as I said; it was missing basic things. Like uniforms, sometimes they lacked part of the money they promised and sometimes it didn't come. Things like that.

I really resent it a lot, because it was 13 years, right? Leaving a lot of things behind, leaving family behind, everything to serve your country, your national team. And, unfortunately, you get nothing in return... I left through the back door.

It hurts, it hurts. Although today I like what I do, I am happy, I have a profession... but I never imagined this for me, right?

Elane's account reveals the frustration of the former player regarding the way the Brazilian Football Confederation (CBF) managed the Brazilian women's national team in the country. Again, we can see the situation of symbolic violence (Bourdieu, 2010) present in the relationship established by CBF with the female football players of the national team. In our analysis, as subordinates, they may feel fearful of claiming their rights, submitting themselves to conditions that could be seen as intolerable, such as not receiving the money promised by the entity for services rendered to the national team. Such subordination is probably linked to the *status* attached to serving one's country, which evokes feelings such as the one expressed by Elane when she mentioned that in the national team she would be "representing a million people."

As can be seen, the choice of the personal and collective projects of the women presented here is entangled in multiple and complex constructions of singular journey of individuals that, although they are not determined by the fields of possibilities that intersect them, are decisively influenced by them. All the manifestations of contestation, confrontation and subversion present in the life of Marta, Nildinha, Elane or Aline shape and limit the fields of possibilities of these and other women who project their lives as professional football players.

Mermaid's Chant: Projects of Girls Who Dream of Being Able to Make a Living from Football[2]

In January 2010, there were more than 1500 young women from 20 Brazilian states and the Federal District registered to participate in a screening organized by Santos FC with the objective of selecting "new talents" to join the club's prestigious women's football squad. According to one of the coordinators of the screening, 1,128 young women with ages ranging from 14 to 20 actually participated in the selection process.

The fields of possibilities that circumscribe the personal and collective projects of the candidates to become Santos players are the result of multiple and complex combination of spaces crossed by values related to different family configurations, regional, cultural, social class, sports, among others. Despite of it is possible to admit similarities between the projects idealized by the interviewees—because all share the motivation to join the career of football player in a prestigious club—both the individual path built by each of them, as their decisions and actions configure singular projects, which move according to guidelines and limitations arising from the repertoire of the fields of possibilities.

During the two days of tests at Santos FC, we followed the routine of the whole process of the screening. With the proper authorization from the coach, armed with a questionnaire script and a camera and camcorder, we approached a series of young women between 15 and 22 years old, from those who were preparing for the tests to those who had already finished (some approved for new stages, others dismissed),

---

[2] An expanded version of this research is presented in the text entitled "O canto das sereias: O futebol como atividade profissional no Estado de São Paulo," chapter of the book *Mulheres na área: Genero, diversidade e inserções no futebol,* organized by Cláudia Kessler and published by the Editora UFRGS in 2016 (Souza Júnior & Reis, 2016).

conducting interviews with 19 participants of the selection. Probably, many of these young women were not even aware that crossing gender boundaries by occupying the streets, fields and courts of the football schools, or even the schools, sharing space with the traditional "owners of the street"—the boys—is a very important and significant social achievement. By "invading" these spaces that are among the last redoubt of hegemonic masculinity in our society, these girls obviously suffer from some type of mistrust or even veiled or explicit prejudice within their own homes, as pointed out by some of the interviewees[3] (our translation):

> Ah, so, my father wasn't very supportive, he wouldn't let me play in the street. I had to start at a football academy for kids when I was about 13 years old. Then I started to play ball, but in the beginning it wasn't on the street or in a field. It was like this, my father didn't like it, but as there were girls there at the football academy for kids, I started there. [...] so, my father is now conforming, he even likes to see me play, but my mother does not like, still does not accept this thing, my grandmother also... they always criticize, my grandmother, so that I do not continue, but I do not care anymore, my father supports me now. (Teresa, 16 years old, Santos/SP)

> And there is a lot of prejudice from my mother's family, that I have to study. Of course you can't stop studying [...], but it is a man thing, these things that everyone says. (Maria, 18 years old, Juiz de Fora/MG)

> My mother supports me, so. My father does not like it much, nor my uncle... I mean, almost my whole family is against it, they say 'there is no future there, you will not gain anything with this'... It is my mother only, because if she had not brought me, I think I would not be here today. (Nayara, 17 years old, Curitiba/PR)

The concern of Teresa's parents that she should not play in the street—a public space historically considered of belonging and freedom only for men—translates a little of the expectation of many parents of girls who play football that their daughters should have a "girl's upbringing," guaranteed by means of feminizing social practices. This aspect becomes even more evident to the extent that the parents consent that the girls play football in a football academy, a place that does not have a character "as public" as the street and that has the presence of other girls, which somehow legitimizes the participation of their daughters.

In the case of Maria's and Nayara's family members, we can see a concern with the lack of future prospects in football in contrast to a career that would give them some financial security.

We found that the initial and recurring fear of these parents, mainly the mothers, would be linked to the uncertainties of a career in football, as well as to the crossing of gender boundaries that could put the daughter's sexuality under suspicion for the society and mainly in the closest circles of relationships.

Still regarding to the possibility of football becoming a professional field of action for women, the outlook of most of the interviewees (11) was not so optimistic. Luísa's speech is quite significant in this regard:

> I see that there is a lot to improve, but it has already improved a lot. It's a level at which there is no amateurism and there is no professionalism. I play on an amateur team and at the

---

[3] All names used to identify the participants—both in this study at Santos' screening and in the research with the athletes from the three São Paulo teams—are fictitious.

same time I play in the Brazil Cup against Marta. So, there is no way you can have a base, a standard level. (Luísa, 19 years old, Curitiba/PR)

When questioned about the possibility of football becoming a profession or a way of life for women in Brazil today, Luísa revealed herself to be pessimistic, stating that living off football in Brazil was still unfeasible in 2010, which led her to glimpse the possibility of playing outside the country as an alternative. The only possibility, even if remote, of pursuing a career in Brazilian football would be at Santos FC:

Here [...] maybe Santos. Many girls here in Santos, they live [off football] [...] as you saw, today there are 1,500 girls competing for a few spots here to live off football. So there's very little opportunity in Brazil, right? Outside it's something else. (Luísa, 19 years old, Curitiba/PR)

Just like Luísa, other interviewees also showed apprehension and disappointment with the situation of women's football in the country:

I think it's still too early to talk about that, right? [the possibility of making a living from football] Because I think that women's football is not as valued [...], it's not even half as valuable as men's football. But if you look at it, there has been a change, so I think that in a few years we can say that it's a profession. (Janaína, 14 years old, Goiânia/GO)

I think that to make a living from football, if you want to have a very good condition, I think it's still very... so... still restricted. But, you know, there is that salary, you can get some extra as well. To make a living from football, I think not... I mean, only if that person is outstanding. (Maria, 18 years old, Juiz de Fora/MG)

As we have seen, the interviewees acknowledge that, at the present moment, football rarely represents a concrete possibility of a professional career for women; despite this awareness, they remain hopeful that these conditions will improve in the future.

Projects of Football Players in the Course of Their Career

Our last field of investigation consists of athletes who were playing in the high-performance football circuit, competing in São Paulo's women's football league in 2011, the year in which the data was collected for the research. This research was developed in three football clubs, by means of field observations, interviews with managers and coaches and focus groups with female players (Souza Júnior, 2013).

The investigated clubs, A, B and C, present distinct administrative and structural models. The management policies adopted by them imply the delineation of different fields of possibilities, which consequently point to singular and diverse collective and personal projects. It is worth presenting some parameters that characterize the distinguish qualities of each one of the three models,[4] in order to provide a concrete

---

[4] It is important to emphasize that all data presented in relation to the three clubs refer to the conditions identified in the field research, in the year 2011, and there may be different conditions in each of the three clubs, in both previous and subsequent years.

framework to interpret the speeches of the athletes and of the other informants that point us to the objectives set by them in the football field.

- Club A: The club is the protagonist of the women's football project (the municipal government acts as an intermediary regarding the payment of the athletes only to try to disguise the employment relationship with the club); it does not have partnerships or sponsorships to maintain women's football; it pays salaries to the athletes, which vary between R$ 350 and R$ 5000 and subsidizes monthly fees for athletes in higher education.
- Club B: There is a partnership between the club and the municipal administration, and the municipal sports foundation is mainly responsible for the women's football project; a series of small partnerships is signed with sponsors that make petty expenses possible; the club, through the municipal sports foundation, pays salaries to the athletes that vary between R$ 400 and R$ 1000; it does not subsidize higher education courses, and neither does it establish a partnership with any college that grants scholarships to the athletes.
- Club C: There is a partnership between the municipal government and a local college; the club merely constitutes a way of formalizing a bond with the FPF (São Paulo Football Federation); it does not have any partnership or sponsorship due to a hindrance imposed by municipal legislation; its athletes do not receive salaries; the club's partner college offers full scholarships to the athletes in any of its higher education courses.

Due to limitations that made it impossible to carry out the focus group[5] with the athletes from club A, our parameters to discuss their projects in relation to their football careers are restricted to the speeches of the players from clubs B and C, with eventual comments about the conditions of club A, subsidized by information provided by coaches and managers, in addition to field observations.

From the perspective of the coach of club A, it had a distinction over the majority of the clubs that participated in the women's football circuit, since it offered conditions for the athletes to develop their careers with exclusive dedication, in relatively good conditions. In his words (Geovani, coach of club):

Nowadays, we've improved a little bit, right, but we still need a lot of things. We know, so, for example, here at club A, it is the club where they are able to work with football and make a living exclusively from football. [...]

We can't say that they will be able to accumulate savings by playing football, but these are girls who can have their personal consumer goods acquired from women's football. Club A has provided this for several of them, and you can already see girls buying apartments, some with cars. So, some things that we can't see at other clubs, we can see here at Club A.

As pointed out by coach Geovani, the athletes of club A enjoyed relatively privileged conditions, as they could dedicate themselves exclusively to football and make

---

[5] Group interview technique in which informants are selected who will potentially contribute to the understanding of the object of study of the research, being conducted by the mediator–researcher through teasing themes that guide the investigation of this object.

a living from it and some could even build up their assets, including the purchase of real estate.

Club B paid a salary to its athletes, in which the ceiling was five times lower than the ceiling offered by club A,[6] supposedly impacting on a relatively less stable subsistence condition, considering that this amount did not reach two minimum wages.

The fact that club C does not pay salaries to its athletes, offering them scholarships in higher education courses as the main compensation, evidences a clear delimitation in the life projects of these players if compared to the athletes of club B, as we could observe in the analysis of the profile of the participants of the focus groups in both clubs.

One aspect that draws attention in the speech of two players from club B with experiences abroad concerns the existence of contracts with athletes, even in second and third division teams. Janaína, who played in the third division of England, speculated about the possibility of the club she defended offering her a three-year contract, signaling a work regime much closer to a professional model than the bonds without contracts or with fragile contracts, such as the adoption of athletes, advocated by some Brazilian clubs.

> Researcher: And what happened for you not to continue there? The contract ended...
>
> Janaína: Oh no... I mean, I didn't want to, because it wasn't a first division team, so, maybe the money I was getting there, maybe it was... it was, let's say I changed it, it was really... it was the same as if I was in Brazil, I only wouldn't be paying my expenses, you know? So, to go there... and even more because I was not studying, so I said "ah, I'll stay here in Rio... in Brazil and try my luck to get a team and go to college...", to be able to study than... let's say I stay there, sign a contract for three years, then... three years playing, then the team is promoted and three years I will not study? So my mother used to be on my neck, you know?

In Janaína's speech, we also highlighted her mother's concern about the possibility that she would continue to play abroad and put her studies aside. In this aspect, the speech of some of the athletes, especially those who had already been playing football for a longer period of time, reveals a clear concern on the part of their families regarding the instability of a career in football and the price to be paid for a deficient school and professional education, caused by the demands of dedication to the sport.

> Gislaine: At home, it's not that I'm not supported, it's just that for my mother I wouldn't be in football, *I'd be employed, registered...*
>
> Eliane: *I don't have an employment record yet...*
>
> Isaura: *My work paper are blank...* (Focus group with club B players)
>
> My mother, she worries about this issue of, of... of a real career, right? *That football is not a career. So, she worries about me not having a job.* (Patrícia, player from Club C)
>
> In my family, my mother, because my parents are separated. My mother has always been with me and I played with her, she even played here... so, my mother was my biggest supporter, she gave me everything I wanted... my mother always supported me, and today she still talks

---

[6] Club B's payroll was R$ 15,000 per month, according to its manager. The manager of club A did not want to reveal the exact amount of their payroll, but admitted that it was between R$ 30,000 and R$ 50,000.

about age. *She is just worried about, "how long are you going to play,"* because I've already had a knee surgery and so on... and she says, *"I'm worried because of that, if you get hurt, then you won't be able to work..."* (Andreia, player from club C)

As we can see, the social costs that athletes must assume in order to embark on a career in football are high. The lack of compliance with the existing legislation for the exercise of the professional activity calls into question, for these players and their families, the legitimacy of even the existence of a career, as evidenced in the words of Patrícia, when she states that football is not a career and that her mother worries about the fact that she does not have a job. The lack of a proper work paper seems to be the most impacting burden for the athletes, as demonstrated by Eliane and Isaura, when they affirm that they do not have proper work papers or that it is "blank" (without any work record).

Therefore, although Law No. 12395/2011 regulates the performance of the professional athlete, establishing the requirement of professionalization of football athletes, thus ensuring professional performance also to women, considering that the law does not make any gender distinction—mistakenly and opportunistically—we can infer that football, when practiced by women, is equal to other sports (practiced by women as well as men), who, by the same legislation, are not obligated, but only allowed, to adopt the professional work regime, which enables the sports associations the opportunity to remain outlaw, including reducing costs with taxes and labor rights of the athletes, even though there is jurisprudence on the matter.

Finally, Gislaine sums up well the discouragement caused by this situation when she states that the athlete who dedicates herself only to football and suddenly finds herself without a club has not acquired experience in anything else, besides not having any studies; that is, the chances of reconverting the time dedicated to sport to another area of professional performance are practically nonexistent.

In addition to the difficulties resulting from the absence of professional contracts and low salaries, or even the lack of salary, the athletes reports point to other factors that make up the conjuncture that they usually classify as "the lack of structure in women's football. These adverse conditions became much more evident in the discourse of the athletes from club C, who mentioned a series of problems related to food, transportation, and especially medical and physiotherapeutic care in cases of injuries.

In this focus group, the issue of reconversion of the time dedicated to football to other areas of performance at the end of the football career was also addressed; the subject is assigned due to the discouragement caused by the early disruption in the career. As we have already highlighted in another passage related to the focus group with the players from club B, the lack of registration and proper work papers, studies and experience in another professional activity represents a ghost that surrounds the imaginary of the athletes when asked about their professional future.

It calls attention the statement of Patrícia, who conciliated her performance in football with the beginning of her career as a physical education teacher in early childhood education; she showed some anguish at the prospect of having to abandon sports to devote herself exclusively to the teaching career.

I think it is the same thing we talked about before, right? There is no way we can think ahead, not being in this environment, right? Like, *I can see myself teaching children, because I'm already working on it. But I think like this, if I am totally focused only on this, I think I don't have a satisfactory life, right*? (Patrícia, focus group with players from club C)

When the issue of the duration of a football career was addressed in the focus group with the athletes from club B, the theme that monopolized the discussion centered on the dilemma between insisting on this career, even with the precarious conditions established in the athletes' daily lives and horizons, and seeking financial stability in other areas of professional activity. We chose to cite the age of the B club athletes at the time of the research in order to facilitate the analysis of the projects of the more experienced and the younger ones.

Eliane (24 years old): *I've already thought about quitting... getting a better job...* Group: Everyone has thought about *it...*

Gislaine (29 years old): Yeah, but then you have to compare the following, let's take Roberta, 15 years old, she gets R$100 a month. If I have a snack bar and say: "Hey, girl, I'll register you and pay you 900"...

Eliane: *I think it depends a lot, because, like Roberta, 15 years old, you still have a lot to play for. Now you think about it, I am 24 years old... That is my opinion... I say "I don't have anything in life yet...", I am going to work! You know what I mean? I'm going to work to see if I can get something for myself, you know? In terms of football, you think like this, how long will football pay you this, do you understand?* Then you enter a company... like Gislaine, she's already... she's already graduated... she gets an offer today, today she's 34 years old, right... [group laughs] she gets... (Focus group with players from club B)

The athletes' speeches reveal, therefore, an age grouping in relation to the projects that each athlete can design for her life. In this sense, we note that the field of possibilities for athletes who are still at school age seems to allow for arrangements that establish football as one of the plausible alternatives for composing their plans. In the case of "college age" athletes, who are not engaged in higher education, as is the case of Eliane, or even with a completed college course, as is the case of Gislaine, but who have not yet entered the formal job market, the field of possibilities tends to presenting football as an unsustainable project from the point of view of financial stability especially.

A very emblematic question that was raised both in the interviews with managers and coaches and in the focus groups with the athletes concerns their respective perceptions in relation to the players of the researched clubs being or not being football professionals. In their perception, this status of professional athletes appeared almost unanimously, as it is possible to verify in the speeches of coaches and managers of the three researched clubs. The speech of the manager of club B is representative of this perception:

They are [professionals]. *The dedication they have, everything they do... it's an amazing thing.* I see them on the men's team... I never had any experience with the men's team to know this, but you see in the newspapers, players that run away from concentration, partying, sleeping late... and they, you don't have this concern. They, even among themselves, they charge each other, they know the right time... the dedication they have in training. They want to play even if they are injured, they try to participate, everything... *They are professionals.*

Unfortunately, our structure is not professional. It's not compatible with what they deserve. (Diego, manager of club B)

The research revealed that there is uniformity in the discourse of coaches and managers regarding the professional "work regime" of female football players of the three researched clubs. In some cases, however, there is disagreement in relation to what these individuals classify as the athletes' "professional behavior."

The athletes, on the other hand, revealed some dilemmas in relation to the professional status of their course in football. In club B, Adriana was categorical in stating that she considered herself a professional; as the discussion in the group developed, however, other aspects came up, making this initial statement diffuse.

Researcher: Do you consider yourselves football professionals? Adriana: *Yes.*

Luciana: *I think, because, the same things that men do, we also do. It's just that we don't get the same treatment as them.*

Gislaine: There *is no feedback.*

Adriana: And there's *no structure* either, right?

Isaura: People see women's football as amateur, you know? Gislaine: Because it *is amateur.*

Isaura: They can't see women's football at its peak, as professional. *They can't see us as professional,* as amateurs, as people who like it and do it because...

Researcher: Is there a difference between those inside and those outside when it comes to this professional thing? You who are inside the field, for those who are organizing... or even for those who see you playing... this view that you have here... nobody told me that don't consider professional, *all of you consider yourselves professionals,* isn't that it?

Group: *Yes.*

Eliane: But that's the difference with the Federation. The Federation already has an amateur league and women's football is amateur.

Adriana: *Because the only sport that is professional is football, right? All sports, they are amateur.* if I'm not mistaken, only football is professional.

(Focus group with athletes from club B)

Therefore, it is clear that the athletes of club B recognize themselves as professional football players, but highlight that the conditions to which they are subjected are not professional, and that they are not recognized as professionals by society in general, a fact expressed in the very speech of São Paulo Football Federation (FPF). Anyway, they bring up the legal component that they affirm, not very convicted, that establishes football as the only professional sport, while all other sports are amateur.

This statement by Adriana, which was not contested by the group, ends up projecting the conception that football recognized as professional is only that practiced by men, which reveals the identification of football practiced by women with amateur sports that suffer distinction in relation to football.

As for the athletes of club C, they initially showed resistance in identifying themselves as football professionals, referring to previous experiences in which they were in more favorable structural conditions and closer to professionalism. Patrícia's statement is noteworthy, recognizing that, due to the fact that she is working on another job or internship in the area of education, she is distant from the status of a professional athlete. Andreia's statement also demonstrates a distance from a professional model, based on the difficulties encountered by all athletes to effectively dedicate themselves to football due to the adverse conditions they face.

The argumentation of the two athletes also reports on the relevance of the legal issue for the conquest of a professional condition for football, indicating the need for registration with proper working papers as the main goal to be conquered.

Researcher: Do any of you, or do you consider yourselves football professionals? Patrícia: *I have already considered one day.*

Researcher: Yeah, when did you consider yourself? And what was different for you... that you considered yourself one day and today maybe...

Patrícia: Yeah, I think it*'s more the structure, right?* That we are... that is around us like that. For example, this time that we say that was the good time for the team here, is the time when the structure was all like, it was professional. We had everything. We had physiotherapy, we had a gym. We had everything we needed. But today, like that... *so much that I have job outside, right? I do an internship and teach children in Campinas. So I already have something else to worry about, right? And not just football.*

Researcher: Ah, you divide your time, right?

Andreia: Yeah, because it depends on the... It's like I said, right, it depends on the structure of where you are, and the value that you impose on that. There is *no point in us want to... today... we really want to dedicate ourselves, but we only have training once a week! How can we dedicate ourselves? Ah, we...*

we want to work hard, but you get hurt and there is no one to treat you. Ah, you want to eat right, but you go there and the food is all messy.

Researcher: And you, as Patrícia, have you ever felt that you were closer or had a professional structure?

Andreia: We have already had a much better structure, already... it's not that we don't want it, because what we want is the professional part. *They don't give us the professional structure.* It is not what we want, because if we had it, we would dedicate ourselves to it, right? Researcher: No, cool, Andreia. Because the idea is not to treat, as blaming you, saying 'ah, you are not professionals'. I want to see how you see yourselves, do you see yourselves as professional football players? Because sometimes I hear people say: "there are players and athletes, it's different, I don't know what it is and so on. That is not even the point. You, looking at yourselves, you say: "no, I am a professional", and even putting things together, what is a professional? Patrícia: Well, a professional player is a... if you're there, you see it as a job. If you are inside, you see it as something you need to do. And so, *within our team, we can see that half of us treat it as professional and half of us don't know how to do it. There is half that think it's a joke, it's not serious.* And so the only thing... I think *what is missing here in Brazil is this, the professionalization, right? That thing of having a signed work contract.* You know, *to have some law* that has this... that puts it into practice. (Focus group with players from club C)

Renata's argumentation was essential for the group to establish a counterpoint to the structural and legal conditions that were brought to the discussion so far in the focus group. The athlete acknowledged the limitations caused by the structural precariousness and legal restrictions, but was categorical in stating that she did recognize herself as a football professional, regardless of the adverse conditions, identifying football as her job.

Renata: [...] *we don't have this structure, but until today I still see myself as a professional athlete.* As a professional player. And, although we don't have this external structure that gives support for us to be treated like that. But inside, here, that's what we do. *We have a scholarship and we... and this is our job, after all, we have to be here during the week, we train, so it's our job, it's our profession, even if we don't have any support behind it.*

Researcher: So, Renata, don't you think that being a professional depends on the salary? Isn't it the... a condition, that without it, it doesn't exist? Do you think you can treat it as a profession, even without the salary?

Renata: *Yes, it is still a profession. That's how I see it. But logically, it can't be considered as such, because it doesn't have, as Patrícia said, the registration and proper working papers, the things, everything. But I see it as if it were a profession.* (Focus group with players from club C)

From the problematization brought up by Renata, the group began to discuss the issue through two prisms, identifying that, in general, athletes recognize themselves and dedicate themselves to football as professionals, but the people around do not share this conception, implying an unfair relationship, that Andreia regrets this and identifies it as a serious problem in order for the athletes to be able to dedicate themselves exclusively to football.

Patrícia: *I would really like to see it as a profession, sponsored and everything*, so... Andreia: *I would like it to be 100%, not only us. It is like Renata said, I also consider myself. Because I... I... for example, I will not go... I have a game on Saturday, I will* not go *out on Friday... and sleep at three* o'clock *in the morning.* We are not going to eat junk food, we know what we have to do. Physical training is physical training, you have to dedicate yourself 100%. *But the problem is that I wouldn't like it to be only us seeing it as a professional. I would like it to come from outside too, so we can do just that.* You have to dedicate yourself like a profession, right? Just do that...

Patrícia: Yes, we have the head of a professional, but, sometimes, those who we need to have this head too, don't have it.

Renata: Maybe like this. *I would say that the athletes see it as if they were professionals and... maybe the managers, some of them, don't see it as such.* They don't see women's football as ... professional. So... I guess that's it, right?

Researcher: And how about you, who did not speak, what do you think? Do you agree with them? Do you think about what they are saying?

Amanda: Yeah, I agree on both sides, because I feel professional. Because in the beginning, when I was 17, 18 years old, I joined a team, but I worked. You know what I mean? I worked with other things, I had my Money from other job, but I didn't have my money from football. And then, as things went on, I went from one team to another, so *I felt professional, even though I didn't get paid anything. Always... Always like this, college, housing and food, for me, it was great. I already felt professional, training every day.*

Researcher: Why did you only dedicate yourself to that...?

Amanda: That's right. (Focus group with players from club C)

The discouragement and revolt demonstrated by the athletes—especially the most experienced of club C—in relation to the conditions in which they develop their football careers indicate the recognition that the issue of professionalization of women's football goes beyond personal parameters, such as the desire to play and the dedication to training and to the other routines of athletes.

Challenging the Fields of Possibility and Conquering Territory

Marta, Elane, Aline, Nildinha, candidates of Santos FC, players of clubs A, B and C, all the protagonists of this study make up a universe of women who dared to challenge the social roles that have historically been delineated as appropriate for them and that would designate a standardized and normatized femininity.

By claiming for themselves the right to play football as a life project, these women break away with the fields of possibilities that are supposedly outlined as fate—such as motherhood and domestic responsibilities—and help to mark an important conquest of territory for the decolonization of female bodies, to the extent that, through football, they begin to establish a deep relationship of transformation of the subjective and objective experience of the body, ceasing to exist only for the other and beginning to exist as a body for themselves, as Bourdieu (2010) admits.

Finally, we agree with Hargreaves (1993) about the perception of change in the behavior considered appropriate for women, to the extent that sport becomes a way of life for an increasing number of female athletes; life projects led by female football players and athletes in general redimension the scope of the fields of possibilities of what is considered appropriate or not to them, sedimenting the conquest of new territories, new bodies and new narratives.

References

Alves, A. (Director) (2008). *Deixa que eu chuto* [DVD]. Film producer: BemVinda Filmes. http://alfredoalvescinetv.com.br/portfolio-type/deixa-que-eu-chuto/.

Bourdieu, P. (2010). *A dominação masculina* (9th ed.). Bertrand Brasil.

Chan-Vianna, A. J. (2010). *Meninas que jogam bola: Identidades e projetos das praticantes de esportes coletivos de confronto no lazer.* (Doctoral Dissertation in Physical Education), Universidade Gama Filho, Rio de Janeiro, Brazil.

Esporte Fantástico. (2011, June 4). Ex-capitã da seleção brasileira se tornou motorista de ônibus no rio. *Record TV.* https://recordtv.r7.com/esporte-fantastico/videos/ex-capita-da-selecao-brasileira-se-tornou-motorista-de-onibus-no-rio-15092018.

Graciano, D. (2008). *Você é mulher, Marta!.* All Print.

Hargreaves, J. (1993). Promesa y problemas en el ocio y los deportes femeninos. In J. I. Barbero González (Comp.), *Materiales de sociologia del deporte* (pp. 109–132). La Piqueta.

Pragmatismo, R. (2013, November 28). Cinco histórias marcantes de Nilton Santos. *Pragmatismo Político.* https://www.pragmatismopolitico.com.br/2013/11/cinco-historias-marcantes-de-nilton-santos.html.

Souza Júnior, O. M. (2013). *Futebol como projeto profissional de mulheres: interpretações da busca pela legitimidade.* (Doctoral Dissertation in Physical Education) Universidade Estadual de Campinas. http://repositorio.unicamp.br/jspui/handle/REPOSIP/275104.

Souza Júnior, O. M., & Reis, H. H. B. (2016). O canto das sereias: O futebol como atividade 'profissional' no estado de são Paulo. In C. S. Kessler (Org.), *Mulheres na área: Gênero, diversidades e inserções no futebol* (pp. 59–87). Editora da UFRGS.

Velho, G. (1987). *Individualismo e cultura: Notas para uma antropologia da sociedade contemporânea* (2nd ed.). Jorge Zahar.

Chapter 24
Brazil is *Hexa*: Marta's Sporting Career

Cláudia Samuel Kessler and Silvana Vilodre Goellner

Some say the sky is the limit, but for science, the universe still holds an infinity of unknown possibilities. Our world is connected to a multiverse, made up of several planets and universes connected to each other. In this multiverse, not every star has its brightness perceived. Some have their lights dimmed before they even reach our eyes. The strongest ones manage to illuminate the darkness, informing us of their presence.

In Marta's case, she managed to show the world her brightness, stronger than the shadows of invisibility to which many women are subjected. She went beyond the margins of a limiting national scenario and became a reference, an international celebrity, a football star. Her rise was rapid, like a meteor, and she remains perennial, with the eyes of the world still fixed on her and her feats.

It seems to be a consensus that football is a sport that unites several nations. Of English origin, it was appropriated by Brazilian culture and is the focus of analyses, opinions, and manifestations in several spheres, public and private, whether in events, academic articles, informal conversations, media agendas, or as a political strategy of governments and parties. We can say that football is present in the everyday life of Brazil and is considered a constituent element of its identity representation as a nation, bringing closer the existing differences between cultures valued in different regions of the country.

Despite the countless pieces of information circulating about this sport, it is important to note that the football that people usually talk about is almost exclusively football played by men. More specifically, it is a football classified as spectacular (Damo, 2008). This is the football that focuses the spotlight on the huge sums of money, international transfers with great media repercussion, and a perennial professional structure. In other words, most Brazilians are unaware of the riches of several *futebóis* that lie on the margins, which are practiced in different dimensions, in other

C. S. Kessler (✉) · S. V. Goellner
Federal University of Rio Grande do Sul, Porto Alegre, Brazil

413

microcosms, such as football for the blind, football in the countryside, indigenous football, school football, and women's football.

In Brazil, *women's football*[1] is still on the periphery of discussions and the very structuring of the sport. The rules of football played by Brazilian women are the same as those played by men, but their practice is not contemplated in the same way, fundamentally when it comes to their professionalization. One may also consider the transactions between clubs or the hiring of female players, which occur very rarely.

Brazilian sports journalism, especially the more traditional media, gives little space to women's football, and when it does, it limits itself to providing mostly information on the realization of the games and their scores. Rarely do the names of the players or other participants appear in the news, which also disregards the information on tactical and technical changes or about the lineup of the teams. At most, they announce the matches and the places where they will take place. This context allowed the former coach of the Brazilian women's national football team from 2008 to 2011, Kleiton Lima, to call the football played by women "ghost football" due to the lack of visibility of the games and players—even though the national team has built a history of achievements and international recognition. This scenario of invisibility began to change in 2015 with the emergence of alternative media that, since then, have produced content that values the sport, demonstrating knowledge about women's football, its history, structuring, and development.[2]

The aridity of this football scenario, very present in Brazilian football, did not prevent, however, women from occupying this space of masculine reserve (Maguire & Dunning, 1997) and from leaving indelible marks there, even if the official discourses often neither highlight nor consider them. It is worth noting that, since the end of the nineteenth century, Brazilian women were present in the sporting arenas: initially as spectators and later as football players.

However, their trajectories are barely visible on the national scene, despite the countless women who have dared to enter this field and record their experiences in it. One of them is representative of this participation: Marta Vieira da Silva, the athlete whose achievements have projected the football practiced by Brazilian women both nationally and internationally. Marta's trajectory is a daily testimony of the constant divisions between the sexes in Brazilian football and the need for effective actions to promote change.

---

[1] It is worth mentioning the important distinction between two terms in this text. We use the term "women's football" as opposed to the popularly used term "*futebol feminino*" (feminine football). We believe that the use of the adjective "feminine," at least in Brazil, is linked to the notion of women's fragility and sensuality, terms that also refer to the ideals of beauty and youth. Female players are constantly referred to, especially in the media, as "girls," a notion that translates the implicit need for care and supervision by someone more experienced. This notion of the feminine has invisibilized the constant imposition of male performances, which are considered as parameters of good performance in the sport and constantly hide the actions of these women as historical agents.

[2] The Brazilian team has won the following titles: South American Women's Championship (2003), Pan American Games—gold medal (2003, 2007, and 2015), Olympic Games—silver medal (2004 and 2008), South American Women's Championship—2nd place (2006), Women's World Cup—2nd place (2007).

Born in the arid northeastern backlands of Brazil, her story tells the story of an individual and collective achievement, insofar as it is very similar to that of many Brazilian women who seek in football a space for sociability, expression, and survival; women who place in the sport the dream of one day living solely from football, without needing other sources of income; and women from different regions who, just like Marta, have gone through very difficult times, either to get into the sport or to remain in it. Few of them can be considered successful if we take into account the spectacular standards. From a spectacular standpoint, the lives of these women would be analyzed from the perspective of men's football, whose practice structure is very different from the one accessible to them.

Marta achieved her dream by overcoming economic, ethnic, cultural, and sporting obstacles. She became an icon of Brazilian football, which does not mean that she has the same visibility and recognition attributed to male athletes in the sport. This observation deserves to be pointed out here in order to enhance the analysis undertaken in this chapter, highlighting the relevance of recording the sporting career of this athlete, built in a territory permeated by adversities.

Biographical Aspects

Born on February 19, 1986, in the town of Dois Riachos, in the state of Alagoas, Marta is one of the few women who has managed to rise from a region as remote and poor as the backlands of the Northeast. Living among men and women with few financial conditions, her talent took her far, earning her the chance to start her journey on international soil as a professional player.

Although Marta's trajectory is one of the most important in Brazilian football, there is still little space in the media both for women who play football and for athletes who practice sports other than men's football. About her career, Marta declared—after one of the many awards she received—that from an early age she had the goal of becoming the best football player in the world, and that she fought and worked hard for it. She then added that she did not consider herself the best in the world, but she was still ambitious, and the title motivated her to work even harder (Birrer & Wiederkehr, 2009, January 17). When asked about possible unachieved goals, Marta revealed that winning collective titles with the Brazilian team, such as the World Cup and the Olympic Games, is a dream she still intends to fight for.

From a humble family, daughter of barber Audálio and cleaning assistant Tereza, she lived with the consequences of paternal abandonment from one year and two months of age. Besides Marta, her mother had to support three other children: José, Ângela, and Waldir. Marta often mentions Dona Tereza with pride and reveres the efforts she made during her childhood and adolescence. According to the athlete, her mother's dedication was very important in her development, as Tereza was always a warrior, just like herself. Her mother would wake up early to work in the agricultural field, and when it rained, she would do cleaning work at the City Hall, without being able to see her daughter play (Sganzerla, 2009, October 13).

José, her older brother, playing the role of "man of the house," tried to keep her away from the fields where the boys played football in Dois Riachos, 189 km from Maceió. Despite his efforts of preventing Marta from playing (because of public comments), it was in this small and poor village—with a population of approximately 11,000 inhabitants, an economy based on small-scale agriculture and local commerce, as well as on resources from social programs to reduce poverty—that Marta started playing football, experiencing complicated moments not only because she was a woman, but also because she came from a very humble background.

Receiving a minimum wage for her work at the City Hall, Marta's mother depended on the help of the children and her mother-in-law to supplement the family income. Marta helped with the finances by selling popsicles and carting at the market (Sganzerla, 2009, October 13). Following the example of other fathers he knew, José demanded Marta to stay at home taking care of the household chores, fulfilling her "woman's role" as all the others did.

Instead of obeying her brother, Marta would sneak out to play. In a sandpit in the course of the dry river at the entrance to the city (which was only not used during the two months of rain, when it filled up with water), she played football under the bridge, with bamboo poles and a ball glued with hot rubber. Inspired by her older cousins, Marta had been playing with them since she was a child.

Despite adversities such as the lack of money to buy school supplies, little Marta started attending school at age 9, attending only until the 5th grade of elementary school (Monteiro, 2014, July), and then studying alone at home.

Despite recommendations not to stay among boys, as the male environment was not considered appropriate for a woman—who, according to the prevailing conservative thought, should be submissive to men, without ever pretending to be equal to them—Marta did not give up, showing, with her football and her leadership spirit, which invariably led the team to victories, that she had an assured place in that team of boys.

The Vieira da Silva family doubted that the girl could achieve anything good by playing football, especially because in the Brazilian scenario there were never any female players who had gained projection or high salaries with sports. "Stop dreaming, we can't afford that," her mother would tell her (Sganzerla, 2009, October 13, our translation). It is a fact that Brazilian football has historically benefited a small elite of men by paying them high salaries and creating opportunities for them to be hired by national and international teams. This situation is, however, beginning to show some signs of change.

The Beginning of the Career

Talent, simplicity, perseverance, leadership, and courage are part of Martha's personality. Her name, of biblical origin, means "mistress of the house," but instead of reigning in the domestic environment, she preferred to go beyond the limits of the private space, so common to women of her cultural context, and be the owner of the ball in public spaces. Audacious, Marta did not bow to adversity or reprimands. Belligerent and angry, she would kick those who irritated her. Her style of play, learned far from the football schools, and her genius moves amazed onlookers. Left-handed and 1.62 m tall, she began playing football on makeshift fields at age 7, becoming the only girl in her town to play with the boys. At the age of 9, when she watched a Corinthians match on television, she became a fan of that team, which, to some extent, saddens her, as she harbors great passion for a club for which she could never play, since until very recently the black-and-white team did not even have a women's football team[3] (Kessler & Goellner, 2016).

Determined, when she wanted to play the sport and there was no ball, Marta would make one by joining several pieces of old fabric. The first to recognize her talent was coach José Júlio de Freitas (Tota), who, in 1995, when she was 9 years old, invited her to play on a boys' team in the city of Dois Riachos, in Alagoas. In that team, Marta took turns with a player as captain and was the top scorer of the AABB Cup[4] the following year. After receiving a used football shoe that was too big for the size of her feet, Marta considered those the best football shoes there could be, even though she had to insert pieces of paper in the tip of the shoe in order to fill it up and use it.

At the age of 12, she was already playing in the youth category at Centro Sportivo Alagoano (in Dois Riachos), a club presided by her cousin Roberto, who also played for the team. At the age of 14, she started her professional career at Club de Regatas Vasco da Gama, in Rio de Janeiro, two thousand kilometers away from home. Friends and family helped the young athlete get to Rio, and Marta played for the team from 2000 to 2002.

On August 24, 2017, *The Players Tribune* published a letter written by Marta entitled "Letter to my younger self," in which, while looking back on her trajectory, she spoke to herself at the age of 14, recommending the scared and nervous teenager of yesteryear to get on the bus heading to Rio de Janeiro (Vieira da Silva, 2017). Marta had received a lot of advice to give up that three-day trip, which would lead her to become a professional football player. It was a difficult decision to make. Marta, however, since childhood had suffered with countless mean comments, judgments, and jokes; she had even been removed from local tournaments, under the allegation that that was no place for girls. All this gave her more strength and motivation to fight against the lack of support. Football had become a way out, an alternative to a new life.

As a teenager, she did not go through a specific muscle strengthening program, although she showed much more explosion and agility on the field than most athletes. The beginning of her career proved to be full of difficulties; besides being a rookie, in her team, there were several well-known and, to a certain extent, valued players of the Brazilian national team. Marta was the victim of *bullying* by many of her

---

[3] *Sport Club Corinthians Paulista* male team was created in 1910, and it has the second biggest number of fans in Brazil, around 30 million. Corinthians created a women's football team in 2016, in partnership with Grêmio Osasco Audax. In 2018, the partnership was broken and Corinthians created its own team.

[4] AABB is a social, recreational, and sports club for employees of a public Brazilian bank.

colleagues, who disqualified her thin build, her accent, and her northeastern origin. Marta reacted to this behavior of her teammates with shyness and bad humor, which led them to call her "country bumpkin" and "bush animal," making her situation even worse (Kessler & Goellner, 2016).

From 2002 onward, Marta reached higher levels and was able to play for the Brazilian national team. From 2002 to 2004, she played for Santa Cruz Futebol Clube, based in the city of Contagem, Minas Gerais. At that time, she received accommodation and a meager sum of R$ 200 per month as financial support. After being one of the highlights of the Brazilian campaign in the Pan American Games of Santo Domingo, held in 2003, in which the national team won the gold medal, Marta drew international attention and was hired in the same year by the Swedish team Umeå IK, earning a salary of R$ 3000 (Monteiro, 2014, July). Due to her excellent performances on the field, she was elevated to the position of number 10 on the Brazilian national team, which previously belonged to Sissi.[5]

Her career has grown in a meteoric way: In 2004 and 2005, she won, respectively, the third and second places of the FIFA Golden Ball; from 2006 to 2010, she was considered the best player in the world by FIFA (a feat that was repeated in 2018, becoming the first athlete, between men and women, to receive this award six times).[6] In 2007, besides the Golden Ball, she also won the Golden Boot.[7] In that same year, the Brazilian team won the gold medal in the Pan American Games in Rio de Janeiro, with Marta being the top scorer of the competition, with 12 goals. As a result, she was inscribed on the Maracanã Stadium's Walk of Fame as the first female athlete to achieve such a feat.[8] Thrilled by this reference, Marta, at 21 years of age, expressed herself thus:

> For me, it was a great emotion to return to play for Brazil after so long. Nothing could be more fitting than this medal to finish it in a memorable way. It was wonderful to be remembered alongside great players from the history of Brazilian football [on the Maracanã Walk of Fame]. I hope it will serve as an incentive for many other girls who want to play football in our country (Chahad & Paiva, 2007, July 26).

In September 2007, with the possibility of the victory of the Brazilian team in the Women's World Cup held in China, the then coach of the men's team, Dunga,

---

[5] Sisleide Lima do Amor, also known as Sissi, currently coaches the Las Positas College Women's, in Livermore, California (USA). Before Marta's arrival, she was considered one of the best players on the Brazilian national team. She was part of the first squad for the Brazilian national team in 1988. She participated in the Swedish World Cup in 1995 and in the USA in 1999, where, along with China's Sun Wen, she was the top scorer of the competition with seven goals. She was voted the second-best player in the world by FIFA, and in January 2000, she was awarded the Adidas Silver Ball. Sissi also participated in the Olympic Games in Athens in 1996 and Sydney in 2000. In 2016, she became the only Brazilian FIFA Legend, a major honor in the world of football.

[6] Winning the award was an unprecedented title in world football, which no man had won until 2019, when Messi also received his sixth award.

[7] The Golden Shoe or Golden Boot is an award given to the top scorer of the World Cup.

[8] In 2018, after receiving the Best FIFA Women's World Player of the Year for the sixth time, Marta once again left her footprint on a mold for the Walk of Fame, as the plaster plaque from the 2007 tribute had disappeared. Although over 10 years have passed, she remains the only woman to be recognized in that space.

declared to be in favor of the insertion of a pink star on the shirt of the Brazilian team, representing the expected victory of the Women's World Championship—which did not materialize in view of the defeat against Germany (Mota, 2007, September 27). According to the coach, Marta not only performed beautiful plays, but also stood out for her technique, further indicating that the player could form a "great duo" in the attack with Robinho, an athlete of the national team who at the time played for Real Madrid.

Since her first performances, Marta's technical quality has been constantly highlighted by players and sports commentators alike. She has been compared to Pelé, the "king of football," earning her the nickname "Pelé on skirts." She wears the number 10 jersey of the national team, just like Pelé, who was the top scorer in the 1950s and 1960s. Regarding the nickname given to Marta, Pelé commented that his press officer made the comparison and that he is in full agreement and added that she has an advantage: Her legs are more beautiful than his (Pelé diz que Marta é Pelé de saias, 2007, July 28).

Fast and with "great vision of the game"—as the former Brazilian national team player Sócrates pointed out—Marta's distinguishing feature is not only her refined technique, but also her creativity. About being called "Pelé on skirts," she stated: "This is a compliment that makes me very motivated, because comparing myself to the greatest football icon, the player of the century and the king of this sport, can only flatter me, but it also brings me responsibility because Pelé's legacy is practically unattainable" (Morais, 2013, February 8, our translation).

In 2008, Marta was again a silver medalist at the Beijing Olympic Games. That year was also marked by another dispute, this one in the publishing field: the controversy surrounding the publication of her biography written by Diego Graciano, an Argentine journalist who conducted extensive research, capturing almost 70 interviews and 250 photographs.[9] In the midst of a legal dispute still without result, Diego says that at the beginning of his research Marta was very receptive to the idea, having even made available her personal archive, a posture that seems to have changed when the athlete acquired greater notoriety. Such disagreement made it impossible to circulate the book he wrote about her, even though the writer claims to have authorization from the athlete written in her own handwriting.

In search of new challenges after her successful career in Sweden, Marta accepted an invitation to play in the USA in 2009, with the aim of boosting *Women's Professional Soccer* (WPS). In each of the years she played in this league, Marta played for a different team due to the American *draft* system. This uncertainty as to which team she would play for was frustrating for Marta, as she always had to start all over again. Despite the difficult situation, Marta managed to win the title of the best player in her first two seasons: the *Michelle Akers Player of the Year Award*.

With the closure of the *Los Angeles Sol* in 2010, the athlete became available for the *draft* and was the third to be chosen in this system. In 2010, Marta played for the team with the worst campaign of the previous year, *FC Gold Pride* (from

---

[9] We would like to thank Diego Graciano for his kind contribution by sending us a copy of his book "Você é mulher, *Marta!*", a biography of Marta published in 2008 by Allprint.

Santa Clara, California), a team in which the Brazilian player Sissi also played. Marta's participation helped the team win first place, and she was the top scorer of the competition. Her time in the USA ended in 2012, after the WPS activities collapsed. After that, Marta signed a two-year contract with *Tyresö FF,* a Swedish team.

Marta's determination is underscored by several professionals who have worked with her, including Alberto Montoya, her coach at *San Francisco Gold Pride,* the team with which she won the 2010 *Women's Professional Soccer* (WPS) Championship. Montoya stated that no one wants to win as much as she does and that Marta is the most "passionate" player he has seen (Pound for pound, the best football player in the world, 2011, February 20).

In 2007, Marta began to be represented by Fabiano Farah, who also represented the interests of clients such as football players Ronaldo, Roberto Carlos, and MMA fighter Vitor Belfort. About Marta's time in American football, her manager said: "She's a nomad. In the first two years, teams closed their doors, and now that she has found serious people, the league has been canceled. Marta was sad" (Pajaro, 2012, January 31, our translation).

Marta's "nomadism" and ease of adaptation are well known. In 2009, she played for the *Los Angeles Sol*; in 2010, for *FC Gold Pride*; and in 2011, for the *New York Flash*. During the year-end holidays of 2009, 2010, and 2011, Marta was in Brazil playing for Santos FC team and in the first two years helped the team win the Brazil Cup (2009)[10] and the Libertadores Cup (2009, 2010), the latter the most prestigious competition on the Latin American scene.

At that time, Marta's salary was around R$ 150,000 in the USA, while the payroll for female players of Santos FC totaled R$ 60,000. In January 2012, the club closed down the women's department and, consequently, disbanded the football team. Marta experienced this episode with great regret, not only because many of her colleagues were left unemployed, but also because it was a setback in relation to the professionalization of women's football in Brazil (Maranhão, 2012a, January 9).

Regarding her playing style, Marta is known to be explosive, fast, and skillful; she does not like to be marked and often gets irritated. During matches, she complains a lot and is energetic. At the start of her career, she was undisciplined, angry, and protested a lot in various situations. However, the experience has made her more mature, listening to others and being less impatient. She is very emotional and cries easily, especially during the tributes she receives.

Anyone who did not know Marta and saw her for the first time at one of the *FIFA Ballon d'Or Awards* might think she was an elegant athlete of any sport. Winner of the FIFA Ballon d'Or for best player[11] in 2006, 2007, 2008, 2009, 2010, and 2018, Marta performed in well-cut dresses and sported accessories considered very

---

[10] The Women's Brazilian Football Cup is a championship that has been played since 1994, but had several interruptions, such as between 2002 and 2005. Repeating this irregularity, this competition has not been held since 2016.

[11] The award for the best player of the year was created in 2001. In that year, Mia Hamm, an American player, won the award.

feminine, although she had once expressed she does not feel comfortable with dresses and high heels (Monteiro, 2014, July). On the awards stage, her countenance hardly resembled the long-suffering face of the author of so many warrior-like performances on the pitch.

Sweden: Martha's Second Home

It was winter when Marta arrived in Sweden to play for *Umea IK*, wearing just a jacket. When she got off the plane, she wrapped herself up in a jacket. In her first training session, in a gym, a woman from Alagoas welcomed her with *brigadeiros*[12] and offered to help her in the new country, which facilitated the player's adaptation (Monteiro, 2014, July). Marta played on this team from 2004 to 2008, with a starting salary of R\$ 20,000. Used to the abundant sun and high temperatures in Brazil, close to 30 °C, she was scared off by the snow, the cold that reached 15 degrees below zero, and the small daily exposure of three hours to the sun. The team's uniforms included gloves, caps, leg, and arm protection—quite different from playing barefoot, with shorts and a T-shirt, as in her homeland.

It was only two weeks before Marta turned 18. Not knowing the language, never having seen snow before and without her Brazilian friends and family, she had to adapt to an unusual and strange situation. Living in such an icy country was a drastic change, but the athlete faced it with optimism. After a long period in Sweden, she began to consider the country her "second home."

After a short season in the USA, in 2012 Marta returned to Swedish football, playing for *Tyresö FF* until 2014. After that team went bankrupt, she transferred to *FC Rosengård,* where she played until 2016. About her return to Sweden, she said: "My career started in Sweden and now I want to write a new chapter. I am happy and proud to be back here. I have a lot to thank Sweden for" (Maranhão, 2012b, February 22). She certainly did! In 2004, her first year in Sweden, she was the top scorer of the national championship with 22 goals. For the *Umea IK*, she won: Swedish Championship (2005, 2006, 2007, and 2008), UEFA Champions League (2004), Swedish Cup (2007), and Swedish Super Cup (2003–2004); for *Tyresö FF*: Swedish Super Cup (2012) and Damallsvenskan[13] (2012); And for *FC Rosengård*: Swedish Super Cup (2014, 2015, and 2016), Damallsvenskan (2014 and 2015), and Swedish Cup (2016).

Finally, on her return to the Swedish league in 2012, playing for *Tyresö FF*, she said:

> It was a very special moment in my life to be able to return to the Swedish league playing for a team that had only reached the top in 2009. Winning the championship in the last game (against Malmö) was really exciting. It had been a long time since I had experienced something so great as an athlete, and all the emotion of the people in the stands, the players...

---

[12] *Brigadeiro* is a traditional Brazilian dessert made of chocolate and condensed milk.

[13] Swedish Women's Premier League.

It was undoubtedly the most special moment for me in 2012. (Futebol feminino: Marta mira mais alto, 2013, February 28, our translation)

Kleiton Lima, former coach of the Brazilian team, talking about the importance of Marta's presence in the 2011 World Cup, said: "Thank God Marta is Brazilian. She has her feet on the ground, she is humble and yet she is brilliant. Marta is modest off the field, is very united with her teammates and has a good relationship with the younger ones" (Treinador Kleiton Lima: "Ainda bem que Marta é brasileira," 2011, July 5, our translation).

In March 2017, after playing ten seasons in Sweden, Marta had her contribution to the country recognized with the acquisition of Swedish nationality. She was then playing in the city of Malmö, for *FC Rosengård*. The club congratulated the beloved player on its official Web site, informing that she had finally obtained Swedish citizenship. Marta Vieira da Silva would now have dual citizenship (Marta obtém nacionalidade sueca e pretende morar no país ao final da carreira, 2017, March 17).

Evidently, having dual citizenship allows Marta to live and work outside of Brazil even after she retires from the pitch. Since 2017, the player has played for Orlando Pride, in the USA, and recently announced that she will marry her teammate Toni Pressley (Castro, 2021, January 7).

Political Engagement

Marta's work goes beyond the football fields. Since October 2010, she has been a Goodwill Ambassador for the United Nations Development Programme (UNDP), which develops social programs to combat poverty in the world. She occupies the same symbolic position held by personalities such as Angelina Jolie, Gisele Bündchen, Maria Sharapova, Antonio Banderas, George Clooney, Didier Drogba, Ronaldo, and Zidane.[14] Her choice was due to her personal history, marked by attitudes of overcoming and triumph in life and in sport.

Among the activities she promoted as an ambassador, in September 2011, she led the *Diamond Queens* in a match against the *Sierra Queens* in Sierra Leone (one of the poorest countries in the world). At this event, she launched the campaign "When women succeed, we all win," encouraging the empowerment of women and their greater participation in the country's legislative power.

Marta also promoted the *"Live Your Goals"* campaign, launched by FIFA in 2011. She said at the time that the campaign is very inspiring and that she would love to be more involved, as unfortunately there are many girls around the globe who have difficulties living their dream, as she herself had in her childhood. And she gave one piece of advice: "Never give up!" Because the more you love football, the more

---

[14] In July 2018, UN Women announced Marta as a Goodwill Ambassador for women and girls in sport. Marta is the only representative from Latin America to represent the UN in the fight for gender equality and empowerment. She assumes the same role as celebrities such as Nicole Kidman, Emma Watson, and Anne Hathaway (Hollywood film actresses).

enthusiastic and motivated you have to be to overcome challenges and barriers, to live your professional dream.

Energy, talent, skill, tenacity, speed, and intelligence are some of the characteristics that have led Marta to be compared to the best players in men's football, such as Lionel Messi. In December 2009, on the eve of the Ballon d'Or announcement, she thought Messi would win the award again, but if she had to choose a favorite, she would stay with Cristiano Ronaldo. Marta said that Cristiano is fantastic and she loves to watch him play, but she also has other references, such as Ronaldinho and Rivaldo (Cristiano Ronaldo é o preferido de Marta, 2009, December 21). The lack of references for the women's modality is evidenced by Marta herself, who has as idols other men, since there were few women footballers who managed to stand out worldwide.

Despite being a reference in football, Marta earns much less than an elite men's football player. The salary differences between male and female players are abysmal, and one of the reasons for this is the lack of initiative from women's football teams in securing strong sponsors and large investments. Marta, who is one of the biggest stars in women's football, earns around US$400,000 per season. According to the American magazine *Forbes*, Lionel Messi, a Barcelona player, was paid US$111 million in 2018 (Hess, 2018, June 14). Of this amount, US$84 million refers to salaries and US$27 million to advertising contracts. The highest paid Brazilian abroad is Neymar, Paris Saint Germain striker, who was receiving US$73 million in salary and US$17 million from advertising (US$90 million in total), making him the third highest paid footballer today. In 2019 FIFA Women's World Cup, Marta wore black football boots created by a movement called "Go Equal" that advocates for gender equity, asking for the same support, money, and recognition for women's sports.

On January 9, 2012, Marta took a stance on the lack of opportunities for other Brazilian players (our translation):

> I do what I can. For my part, I try to do everything I can. But it doesn't depend only on me. We are looking for space little by little, showing that we have conditions, but this has to come from all sides: from the press, the TV stations, because with them you attract sponsors, but also the government, the confederation... many people who can do something. For a long time we have been demanding, demanding, but things have not been the way they should be (Kessler & Goellner, 2020, p. 634).

The lack of governmental actions also motivated some of the athlete's statements; given her media exposure, Marta informally assumed the position of spokesperson for women who seek the professionalization of football in Brazil. In December 2012, she stated: "Brazil needs to change the way women's football is seen. You only keep a top-level athlete motivated with a salary. It's no use talking about girls being fat or out of shape if they don't get paid for it. It is difficult to demand professionalism from players who work without remuneration" (Castanho, 2012, January 9, our translation). In face of the national scenario that offers few changes to this picture, she added: "I cannot carry, nor can the other players, the weight of changing women's football in the country" (idem, ibidem). In the same sense, in another opportunity, she reaffirmed: "We have athletes who need support, need and deserve a greater prominence, structure to train, to take the name of Brazil to competitions such as the Olympics. But we lack structures, you know? Support" (Monteiro, 2014, July, p. 31, our translation).

On November 1, 2016, Brazil experienced an unprecedented moment in the history of its football: The Brazilian Football Confederation (CBF) announced Emily Lima as the new coach of the women's national team. She was the first woman to assume the position of coach of an adult national team in Brazilian football.[15] The news was widely celebrated not only because it represented an important achievement for women in football, but also because of her recognized competence to assume the position.

Emily's first challenge was the International Football Tournament, held in Manaus in December 2016, in which she led the national team to its sixth championship. After the first competition, she and the coaching staff drew up a development plan for the sport with short-, medium-, and long-term actions in mind. She called for regional squads, tried out new players, and promoted a different concept of football. In almost ten months of work, Brazil has won seven games, lost five, and drawn one. To everyone's surprise, on September 22, 2017, with less than a year of work, the CBF informed the dismissal of the coach, although she had not participated in any tournament organized by an official entity such as FIFA or CONMEBOL. This event generated a series of manifestos, culminating in the announcement by five prominent players[16] that they would no longer be serving on the national team, as well as the publication of an open letter[17] in which ten players demanded the CBF to pay more attention to women's football.

The great repercussion of the letter in the national and international press mobilized several segments of Brazilian football, which even resulted in the invitation of the then president of CBF, Marco Polo Del Nero, for a meeting with the players who signed the manifesto (Goellner, 2020, September 16). Inevitably, given her representativeness, Marta was asked about her position. In an interview with *Globo Esporte* Web site, the player said she disagreed with Emily's dismissal: "My opinion is the same as when Vadão[18] was replaced: we need time to work. Results cannot happen overnight in women's football, but we know how our culture in Brazil is based on results" (Gallindo, 2017, September 24, our translation). In the report, Marta said

---

[15] Another woman who should be given prestige for her work in football is 36-year-old Nilmara Alves, recognized for two surprising achievements: She is the first woman to obtain registration as a coach with the Brazilian Football Confederation (CBF) and has been in charge, since 2012, of Manthiqueira—a professional men's team from Guaratinguetá, which disputes the third division of São Paulo's state competitions (Pires, 2018).

[16] The five athletes who informed that they would retire from the national team were: Cristiane Rozeira, Rosana dos Santos Augusto, Francielle Alberto, Maurine Dornelles, and Andréia Rosa. Cristiane was the only one that played again in the national team.

[17] Entitled *Brazilian legends calls for reform: an open letter from female football veterans addressing the current situation in Brazil*, the letter was disseminated through social networks, with immediate repercussion in the international press. It was signed by: Márcia Tafarel, Sissi (Sisleide Lima do Amor), Juliana Cabral, Francielle Alberto, Formiga (Miraildes Mota), Rosana dos Santos Augusto, Andréia Rosa, and Cristiane Rozeira.

[18] Vadão was the coach of the Brazilian female football team from 2014 to 2016 and from 2017 to 2019.

she was part of the group of athletes who wanted the coach to remain, despite not having signed the letter addressed to the president of CBF, requesting the continuity of the work of the entire coaching staff.

> I didn't sign any letter, I didn't sign it because we have a hierarchy, and at that moment Marco Aurelio was the guy who represented the president [of CBF]. We talked to him and waited for him to reach the president. But I believe that when he got to the president, the decision had already been made. Before that I had met with some athletes and had proposed a phone call to the president, so that he could not say that he had not received the letter or any other message. But that did not happen. And only now they are putting on my back, for this simple fact. But football is like that and we are there. I will keep working as always. (Gallindo, 2017, September 24, our translation)

In expressing her sadness at her colleagues' decision to leave the national team, Marta reinforced that she would remain with the team: "I hope they'll come back so that together we can fight as we've always done all our lives. On the pitch. On a day-to-day basis. Asking for improvements, raises, whatever is necessary. but I will not stop serving the national team and fighting as I have always done" (Barlem, 2017, September 28, our translation).

Considering the strength of her statements and the representativeness of her image, women's football has gained greater exposure in the national media. It is undeniable that Marta raises the status of the teams she defends, positioning them at the top of the league tables; she is, without any doubt, a distinguished player.

Queen Marta is *Hexa*

The year 2018 reinforced the nickname "queen" that was once bestowed upon her, with the title of the best player in the world, eight years after her previous award. With the money she earns from football, Marta built two houses for family members; in one of the rooms of the house she bought for her mother—to whom Marta dedicates all her titles—in the city of Dois Riachos, she organized a small museum, in which she keeps her memories, represented by the cups, trophies, and medals she has won. In 2014, the Secretariat of Sports, Leisure, and Youth of Maceió inaugurated the "Memorial Rainha Marta" (Queen Marta Memorial) to honor the athlete. Four years later, the space was already in need of maintenance and care. According to a report published on *GloboEsporte.com* in 2018:

> After opening in 2014, the space operated for only one day and was closed for almost a year and a half. It reopened again in 2016. At the reopening, the promise made by the State Secretariat of Sports, Leisure and Youth was to modernize the place. But since then, what really changed was the state of conservation of the memorial. (Roma, 2018, July 17, our translation)

Marta's unprecedented award made it inevitable that she would be recognized by the CBF, whose museum has very little space for the trajectory of women in sport. On October 22, 2018, the so-called home of Brazilian football paid tribute to her with a huge panel on its facade displaying her image and the phrase: "Thank you, Queen—the only athlete to be elected the best in the world six times." Marta was welcomed by the institution's president, Antônio Carlos Nunes, and visited the temporary exhibition to which she lent her six trophies.

> Voted best player in the world six times, Marta was eternalized in the Maracanã Walk of Fame on Tuesday. Again. Although the concessionaire that manages the stadium since 2013 said that this was the first tribute to the Queen, the number 10 shirt had already gone through the same ritual 11 years ago: in 2007, shortly after winning the gold medal at the Pan American Games, Marta left the mark of her feet on plasterboard to be displayed in the stadium. The problem is that the plaque disappeared. And Maraca's administrators do not know where it ended up. (Caldas & Espogeiro, 2018, December 10, our translation)

In 2020, Marta was part of the plot of the samba school "Inocentes de Belford Roxo," on the second day of parades of Series A (Access Group) of Rio Carnival. The plot was: "Marta do Brasil—Chorar no começo para sorrir no fim" (Marta from Brazil —Crying at the beginning to smile at the end), which relates to her speech after Brazil's last game in the 2019 World Cup, asking for more support for women's football.

Marta's story has forged a broadening of views, perspectives, and possibilities for the football universe. The girl from the confines of Brazil brought the long-awaited *hexa* to the country:

> Throughout this year, we have spent a lot of time talking about a hexa that did not come. Now we can talk about one that has already become a reality. Brazil is already the hexa in 2018, because Marta is hexa. It is high time to fill our chests and say: The best player of all time is ours. Six times best in the world, six times Marta. (Mendonça, 2018, October 24, our translation)

In 2019, Marta became the World Cup's top scorer with 17 goals. Marta has become an idol and a source of inspiration for many young women, who see her boldness and determination as material proof that football can be possible for a woman.

Finally, it is worth noting that those who think it is quixotic dreams that prevent women's football from becoming a masterpiece are mistaken. Masterpieces are not just those that sit on dusty bookshelves and are part of the past. The current masterpieces are those that circulate, that is, in transformation, being reread, echoed, recreated. We can therefore say that utopia is the expansion of possible horizons.

While Marta is the "queen," there are thousands of other Brazilian players who hope to one day leave the post of subjects. To do so, talent alone is not enough; it is also a matter of personality, attitude, charisma, empathy, and several other factors that some insist on defining as "luck." Even if it were simply luck, these women wish to be *lucky enough* to have a suitable place to play; *lucky enough* to have a national championship to compete in; *lucky enough* to find businessmen to sponsor the teams; *lucky enough* to receive sufficient wages to support themselves; *lucky* to get significant support from FIFA and CBF; *luck* that will exist when the Brazilian government decides to restructure the sport; *luck* to have their matches televised; *luck* to step on the grass of the best stadiums and arenas in Brazil, under the lights of dozens of spotlights, surrounded by fans and camera flashes that give them visibility; and the *luck*, finally, to make their star shine, approaching the place where Marta arrived.

References

Barlem, C. (2017, September 28). Empresário diz que Marta segue na seleção; camisa 10 espera que colegas voltem atrás. *Dona Do Campinho*. http://globoesporte.globo.com/blogs/especial-blog/dona-do-campinho/post/marta-empresario.html.

Birrer, P. M., & Wiederkehr, D. (2009, January 17). Marta: "Muitas vezes choro depois de um gol", *Tages-Anzeiger*. (G. Hoffmann, Trans.) Published by *Swissinfo.ch*. https://www.swissinfo.ch/por/marta---muitas-vezes-choro-depois-de-um-gol-/7156474.

Caldas, A., & Espogeiro, L. (2018, December 10). Onze anos depois, Maracanã refaz homenagem a Marta após perder item da Calçada da Fama. *GloboEsporte.com*. https://globoesporte.globo.com/futebol/futebol-feminino/noticia/onze-anos-depois-maracana-refaz-homenagem-a-marta-apos-perder-item-da-calcada-da-fama.ghtml.

Castanho, F. M. (2012, January 9). Marta desabafa: "não posso ter o peso de mudar o futebol feminino." *Portal Terra*. http://esportes.terra.com.br/futebol/marta-desabafa-quotnao-posso-ter-o-peso-de-mudar-o-futebol-femininoquot,e07a1d81c499a310VgnCLD200000bbcceb0aRCRD.html.

Castro, L. F. (2021, January 7). Marta e Toni Pressley: casamento real do futebol à vista. *Veja*. https://veja.abril.com.br/esporte/marta-e-toni-pressley-casamento-real-do-futebol-a-vista/.

Chahad, A., & Paiva, C. (2007, July 26). Após ouro, Marta deixa os pés na Calçada da Fama. *Portal Terra*. http://esportes.terra.com.br/panamericano2007/interna/0,,OI1788332-EI8332,00.html.

Cristiano Ronaldo é o preferido de Marta. (2009, December 21). *Journal Record*. https://www.record.pt/internacional/detalhe/cristiano-ronaldo-e-o-preferido-de-marta.

Damo, A. S. (2008). *Do dom à profissão: a formação de futebolistas no Brasil e na França*. Hucitec.

Futebol feminino: Marta mira mais alto. (2013, February 28). *Batom e Futebol*. https://batomefutebol.wordpress.com/2013/02/28/futebol-feminino-marta-mira-mais-alto/.

Gallindo, A. (2017, September 24). Marta acredita que demissão de Emily foi precipitada: "A gente precisa de tempo". *GloboEsporte.com*. https://globoesporte.globo.com/futebol/futebol-feminino/noticia/marta-acredita-que-demissao-de-emily-foi-precipitada-a-gente-precisa-de-tempo.ghtml.

Goellner, S. V. (2020, September 16). Nós convidamos a CBF a trazer reformas de igualdade de gênero para o Brasil. *Ludopédio*. https://www.ludopedio.com.br/arquibancada/nos-convidamos-a-cbf-a-trazer-reformas-de-igualdade-de-genero-para-o-brasil/.

Hess, A. J. (2018, June 14). The 8 highest-paid soccer players in the world. *CNBC*. https://www.cnbc.com/2018/06/13/the-8-highest-paid-soccer-players-in-the-world.html.

Kessler, C. S., & Goellner, S. V. (2016). From out of the shadows of invisibility: Brazilian women's football and the pioneering figure of Marta. In J. N. Rosen, & M. M. Smith (Orgs.), *More than cricket and football: International sport and the challenge of celebrity* (pp. 145–162). University Press of Mississipi.

Kessler, C. S., & Goellner, S. V. (2020). O Brasil é hexa: A trajetória esportiva de Marta. In S. S. Giglio, & M. W. Proni (Orgs.), *O futebol nas ciências humanas no Brasil* (pp. 623–392). Editora da Unicamp.

Maguire, J., & Dunning, E. (1997). As relações entre os sexos no esporte. *Estudos Feministas, 5*(2), 321–348. https://periodicos.ufsc.br/index.php/ref/article/view/12151.

Maranhão, R. (2012a, January 9). Segurando o choro, Marta lamenta fim do time feminino do Santos. *GloboEsporte.com*. http://globoesporte.globo.com/futebol/futebol-internacional/noticia/2012/01/segurando-o-choro-marta-lamenta-fim-do-time-feminino-do-santos.html.

Maranhão, R. (2012b, February 22). Marta recebe camisa 100, chora e diz estar feliz por voltar à "segunda casa". *GloboEsporte.com.* http://ge.globo.com/futebol/futebol-internacional/noticia/2012/02/marta-recebe-camisa-100-chora-e-diz-estar-feliz-por-voltar-segunda-casa.html.

Marta obtém nacionalidade sueca e pretende morar no país ao final da carreira. (2017, March 17). *UOL.* https://esporte.uol.com.br/ultimas-noticias/afp/2017/03/15/marta-obtem-a-nacionalidade-sueca.htm.

Mendonça, R. (2018, October 24). Queriam o hexa? Marta trouxe, e o Brasil deve muito a ela. *Dibradoras.* https://dibradoras.blogosfera.uol.com.br/2018/09/24/queriam-o-hexa-marta-trouxe-e-o-brasil-deve-muito-a-ela/.

Monteiro, K. (2014, July). Fenômeno. *Revista TPM, 13*(144), 22–31. https://revistatrip.uol.com.br/revista/tpm/144.

Morais, C. (2013, February 8). Marta admira Ronaldo porque "batalha muito e trabalha imenso". *Zerozero.pt.* http://www.zerozero.pt/noticia.php?id=98916.

Mota, C. (2007, September 27). Dunga é a favor de estrela rosa no uniforme. *GloboEsporte.com.* http://globoesporte.globo.com/ESP/Noticia/Futebol/Selecao_Brasileira/0,,MUL112761-4482,00.html.

Pajaro, V. (2012, January 31). "Nômade nos EUA", Marta deve voltar ao futebol sueco após cancelamento da liga americana. *UOL.* https://www.uol.com.br/esporte/futebol/ultimas-noticias/2012/01/31/nomade-nos-eua-marta-deve-voltar-ao-futebol-sueco-apos-cancelamento-da-liga.htm.

Pelé diz que Marta é Pelé de saias. (2007, July 28). *GloboEsporte.com.* http://globoesporte.globo.com/PAN/Noticias/0,,MUL78950-3873,00-PELE+DIZ+QUE+MARTA+E+PELE+DE+SAIAS.html.

Pires, B. (2018, March 8). Nilmara, a técnica que desafia o monopólio dos homens. *El País.* https://brasil.elpais.com/brasil/2018/03/08/deportes/1520482900_971448.html.

Pound for pound, the best football player in the world. (2011, February 20). *The daily beast.* http://www.thedailybeast.com/newsweek/2011/02/20/pound-for-pound-the-best-football-player-in-the-world.html.

Roma, D. (2018, July 17). Mato, falta de tinta e promessa: Memorial Rainha Marta está esquecido em Maceió. *GloboEsporte.com.* https://globoesporte.globo.com/al/noticia/mato-falta-de-tinta-e-promessas-memorial-rainha-marta-esta-esquecido-em-maceio.ghtml.

Sganzerla, C. (2009, October 13). Um drible no destino. *TPM,* (92). https://revistatrip.uol.com.br/tpm/um-drible-no-destino.

Treinador Kleiton Lima: "Ainda bem que Marta é brasileira.". (2011, July 5). *Cada Minuto.* https://www.cadaminuto.com.br/noticia/127462/2011/07/05/treinador-kleiton-lima-ainda-bem-que-marta-e-brasileira.

Vieira da Silva, M. (2017, August 24). Letter to my younger self. *The Players Tribune.* https://www.theplayerstribune.com/articles/marta-brazil-letter-to-my-younger-self.

Chapter 25
Gender Expressions and the Multiple Practices of Football in Brazil

Wagner Xavier de Camargo

Introduction

This chapter invites us to rethink facts and convictions about Brazilian football that are generally taken for granted. Not only is it the dominant sport in the country, but it can be seen as hegemonic and naturalized in Brazilian culture. However, I am not dealing here with *that* football, that familiar old acquaintance that we either love or hate, we either follow or forget, the unavoidable topic of conversation in every bank line and public place during the World Cup. Nor am I referring to the sport that is supposedly representative of all Brazilian women and men, no.

I intend to play with football and think about how it has been impacted by apparently external circumstances, about how the sport has been falling apart, without people noticing or the media recognizing it. I will adopt aesthetic, corporal, and discursive expressions that have used football to create other forms of play, other ways to (re)claim identities or even to practice empowerment. I will cite examples of groups few people are likely to have even heard of, much less to have heard that they play football. I will reveal the multiple dimensions of gender that inhabit this sport and show that it is not nearly as homogeneous or uniform as supposed in its adherence to values such as "aggressiveness," "masculinity," "virility," and "machismo." All these words I place in quotes to point out their ephemeral nature and to argue that they should be stripped of the strength they have acquired when associated with sports in general and, particularly, the practice of football.

I also will avoid recounting the sport's founding myth of Charles Miller and his consequent "historical achievement." Bloch (2002) speaks about an "origin obsession," which is problematic in two ways: firstly because the very notion of a starting point is always nebulous and imprecise; and secondly because origin myths inevitably lead to glorifying people, facts, and events. This is how History (in capital letters) conforms to the narrative of the powerful, of the "great men" and erases any other

W. X. de Camargo (✉)
Federal University of São Carlos, São Carlos, Brazil

© The Author(s), under exclusive license to Springer Nature Switzerland AG 2021   429
S. S. Giglio and M. W. Proni (eds.), *Football and Social Sciences in Brazil*,
https://doi.org/10.1007/978-3-030-84686-2_25

participants, especially women and minorities. What is more, Bertolt Brecht suggests in "Questions from a literate worker" that looking into those excluded from history can offer us new and distinct clues about historical facts that were once narrated with grandiosity. More recent sources have brought to our attention the existence of games played with feet and balls in Jesuit parochial schools throughout Brazil in the mid-nineteenth century (Santos Neto, 2002) which may suggest that Miller's role be reinterpreted, merely, as the one responsible for institutionalizing the sport (Gambeta, 2015).

Even so, institutionalized football has changed considerably since the beginning of the twentieth century. Women, until then excluded from the sport, began to take up playing it here and there, in many secluded corners of the country. A series of stratagems and maneuvers hindered the spread of "official football" among women, including Decree-Law No. 3199 of April 1941, that famously prohibited them from playing simply because football was believed to be "incompatible" with the female body.[1] Historians and researchers have already pointed out how symptomatic this was of an era when bodies were prepared for work (men) and for motherhood (women). It was socially determined that women's biological bodies were better fit for the practice of lighter sports, such as gymnastics and dance, which were "composed of delicate, flexible, and graceful movements" (Pacheco, 1998, p. 47, our translation).

Gymnastics, in particular, had gained significant importance in nineteenth-century Europe and upon arriving in Brazil became a "technique of body education" (Soares, 1994) that served to promote notions of hygiene, health, and discipline.

> Building a strong, female organism was based on the three pillars of "health, strength, and beauty," because this trinomial would give rise to the strength of a generation of new beings, and consequently, of a new country. (Goellner, 2008, p. 16, our translation)

Girls' and women's bodies were co-opted by nationalist objectives, and gymnastics, in turn, acquired "the crucial role in schools of educating girls by preparing them to be future mothers" (idem, ibidem, p. 17, our translation).

From the 1940s on, "women's football"[2]—as it became known—was restricted to very rare occasions, and its erasure intensified during the military dictatorship. Until 1979, an official ban was in place on women engaging in contact sports or those considered "aggressive," yet the women persisted, and presentations and sports events (including charitable ones) are known to have taken place during this period. On the occasion of the Women's 2011 World Cup in Germany, Lucas Reis (2011,

---

[1] The title of article 54, reads: "Women shall not be allowed to practice sports incompatible with the conditions of their nature, and for this purpose, the National Sports Council shall issue the necessary instructions to the sports entities of the country" (Decreto-Lei No. 3,199 de 14 de abril de 1941, our translation).

[2] I will follow the argument of important Brazilian researchers on the subject and address this expression as "women's football" instead of "female football." Kessler (2015) and Pisani (2016), in different ways, but with similar explanations, understand that the nomenclature "female football" covers up diversity by imposing a standardization of body and gender linked to the matrix of hegemonic, male, macho and heteronormative football. Camargo and Kessler (2017) also emphasize that the adoption of this expression is because there are multiple expressions of femininities (and masculinities) in the bodies of women who practice the sport.

June 12) wrote a piece about a group of women from the small town of Araguari, Minas Gerais, who had apparently tried out and formed the first female football club in the country, Araguari Atlético Clube.[3]

Despite the precarious socioeconomic situation of women's football and its lack of recognition that is regularly decried by sports researchers, unusual events can currently be found taking place involving women's bodies, one of which is transgender football. Physiologically born female, these individuals refuse the sexual and gender identities assigned to them at birth and engage in the performativity of the football of trans men. The most visible example is the *Meninos Bons de Bola/ The Boys Good at Ball* (MBB) team, based in the city of São Paulo, which is composed of mostly brown and black individuals from less affluent social classes who have been carrying out their acts of defiance for almost three years.

Being a female football player in Brazil is far from the image conveyed by the media of beautiful, sensual, and delicate bodies (Almeida, 2016; Goellner, 2003; Kessler, 2015). Moreover, it suffers from a forced adaptation to the standards of a heteronormative "femininity" (which are markedly sexist and discriminatory). The bodies of trans men struggle against all these obstacles as well as the delegitimization and questioning of their technical football playing skills. They are buried, thus, within multiple layers of prejudice (namely transphobia), which are deposited socially and sportively upon them.

Thus, as much as "bio-women," trans men and women resist both inside and outside of football.[4] Such football players do not subject themselves completely to institutionalized determinations. They transgress barriers, whether by publicizing their activities within the all-powerful national sport, or by fighting for respect and claiming that their fight is that for the right to and recognition of their existence— including on the field.

Even seeking to "disidentify" from the gendered markings that have inhabited them since before they were born, these bodies dramatically bring gender issues to the sports arenas and are, in turn, marked by them.[5] This is worth calling attention to, because these bodies occupy the political arena as they reclaim and question the normatization of pleasure and sexuality itself (Stolke, 2000). They are, therefore, plural bodies, which showcase the inefficacy of standardization and the lack of applicability of the categorization of sex on the sports field.

---

[3] Historian Franzini (2005) uncovers occasional events prior to this historical period but points out that they were occasional and ephemeral.

[4] The nomenclature bio and trans (or techno) appear as technically produced gender artifices for Preciado (2008). On the one hand, "bio-men" and "bio-women" are those who identify with the sex they were assigned at birth, while "trans-men" and "trans-women" (or techno-men/techno-women) are those who contest this designation and have tried to change it with the help of external procedures (technical, prosthetic, performative, and/or legal). Instead of "bio," some theorists use the term "cis" (cisgender).

[5] Muñoz (1999) worked on the concept of gender disidentification of racialized *queer* bodies (*queers of color*). In his reading, disidentifications is a new perspective of the performance of activism and the survival of (sexual) minorities, which operates within, together, outside, and against dominant ideologies.

Notably, when using sex categories in sport, contemporary society relies on genitalia alone to categorize bodies. These genitalia are then manipulated like marionets in a theater ruled by heteronormativity, in which heterosexuality operates as a compulsory device and normativities are institutionalized, from sex to gender, from biology to culture (Rich, 1999). These bodies of knowledge determine whether the bodies that perform in sports arenas are allowed to be there, or if they should be banned. Camargo and Kessler (2017, p. 194, our translation) speak of these bodies of knowledge which are "imparted through discourses of authority (of the coach, the doctor, or the club), which gather together the power of discourse and predict a long life (for normative/intelligible athletic bodies) in the legitimated spaces of the sport and ostracize from society and sports, from society and sport errant, unintelligible and distinct bodies."

This chapter aims to explain that nowadays other individuals who express themselves through their knowledge of football deserve to be respected. These practitioners have politicized the sports field through practices that, at the limit, inaugurate multiple forms of football, expressions that intersect class, generation, ethnicity, ability, and gender in the performance of the game. These new actors, through their evoked identities, claim the practice as an index of their empowerment of football and within it.

The different footballs stand, simultaneously, at the margins and at the center of the spectacle of hegemonic football on a global scale, played by bio-men who are the main references of sociability, identity, and recognition in the sport. Such "footballs" are rarely made visible, and their political agents are, perversely, hidden. However, as Kessler (2016, p. 37, our translation) points out, "football is a political field, with political agents that, even when hidden, remain responsible for discursive processes and constitutive actions of the sports field of which they are part."

Thus, the "multiple footballs" are represented as polyphonic expressions of amateur groups or those called "trans people's football," "five-a-side football" (played by the blind and visually impaired), "seven-a-side football" (played by the cerebral palsied people), "women's football," "indigenous football," "gay football" have, in the end, politicized the practice of sport and offered an important critique of that football which is spectacular, merchandized, meritocratic, heteronormative, corponormative, and misogynistic.

Finally, I would like to point out that I will deal next with groups of athletes, self-identified as homo and transgender people, who play a version of the sport they call "society football" (on synthetic fields) as part of a rapidly spreading movement throughout the country. This is important for two interrelated reasons: firstly, because considering them within the multiple expressions of gender (participants of the LGBTIQ grouping) causes football to lose its canonical character that is so often constructed as masculine, virile, white, and heterosexual, while it also questions football's power to exclude these bodies. Secondly, by playing football (or conducting a ball with their feet, under the same rules and in the same spaces) such bodies propose a new aesthetic, another understanding of the sport and even a symbolic re-dimensioning of their meaning as players. I dare to say that these bodies promote dissonance from the football phenomenon (and, equally, from sport in general), which vibrates at different frequencies from within, while incorporating particular practices that are as legitimate and mesmerizing as the spectacular ones we are so familiar with. Acknowledging and building on a previous proposal (Toledo & Camargo, 2018, p. 4, our translation), I intend to point out that "[…] such gender dissonances, so visible from various ontological turns that have reached very politicized expressions, can be explored from inside this global phenomenon (so naturalized in its values) that is football." In a few words, and taking advantage of the anthropological perspective, it is as if the "multiple footballs," which spread through social and sport mechanisms, are sneakily working their way into the larger phenomenon.

LGBTIQ Football on the Court and Raising Questions About Football

To begin with, I would like to raise two issues which underlie this chapter. First, and despite the fundamental theoretical and conceptual gender productions about the "women's football" in physical education, the field of gender studies is not restricted merely to women. I do not deny the importance of numerous works at differing academic levels but talking about gender is to bring to the table something beyond binarism and the contrast between men and women. Gender is a system of norms, social conventions, and institutional practices that performatively produce and name the subject. Gender is not an immutable essence, an "identity," that is restricted to naming "bio-males" and "bio-women," nor is it a label that classifies those whose reproductive organs consist of penises or vaginas. It is a performative discursive and bodily practice through which the subject is understood and recognized politically (Butler, 2003, 2008).[6]

Second, it is important to highlight that I will deal below with groups of "men who relate affectively-sexually with other men" or "trans men who play society football," an urban practice in Brazilian cities. References to "gay football" or "gay men playing football," or "trans football" or "trans men playing ball" will be taken from the data, because they are emic terms rising from the ethnographic research and will not be used from an analytical point of view.[7]

---

[6] I have summarized Judith Butler's arguments herein and offered just two references. However, her vast body of gender theory and nuances are beyond the scope of this chapter. Complementary views can also be found in a collection about the athletic body (Butler, 1998) and the works of Preciado (2008; 2014).

[7] I do not use "gay" as an adjective of men or football because I want to escape the marketing identification that such a category carries. "Men relate affectively-sexually with other men" does not exclude any other designation they can assign to themselves. However, I avoid using "homosexuals" as an identity category, because I think that the contextual and situational dynamics of the processes that involve such identifications of these subjects is what matters. This is not new in the Social Sciences and has already been worked on previously. Among other works, see those of Braz (2007; 2012), Facchini (2008) and França (2012).

Having made these reservations, let us go on to the phenomenon. Nowadays, with regularity and frenetic excitement, festive sports events have been taking place among non-heteronormative men, who play football on synthetic "society" fields rented for the purpose. I will be looking at the phenomenon as a whole, rather than bring up the specificities of each group.

It is often said that "it all started" in 2015. However, this is not the opinion of a spectator who watched a game between the Real Gothic and MBB teams, sitting next to me at *Ocupa Pacaembu*, one event held in front of the Football Museum in the city of São Paulo in 2017. On that day, in addition to art workshops and street samba, the Museum organized games between amateur teams engaging in identity discourse work in the realm of sexuality. For that fan (our translation),

> *Gay football* started a long time ago. In the small field[s], in the square[s] of some neighbor-hoods, among the people from the cities' peripheries. Playing together is a common practice in these places. Now, this football is new, the way they did it.[8]

He was referring to "*várzea*" or floodplain football, an identity football that takes place in streets, grassy fields, in the peripheral neighborhoods, where young people stage local, urban social practices, as they get together to play ball. "That way down there," he said, was the institutionalized way, out in the open for everyone to see, just like the Museum event that took place in a prime urban area. He claimed that despite this happening at that moment, many groups would still prefer the anonymity of their neighborhoods.

From my point of view, yes, groups will exist that do not want to be linked to any form of disclosure or exposure, since what moves them is the practice of a neighborhood football, played among friends and acquaintances, which enables players to seek corporal expression. Perhaps some of these groups are not composed of cisgender men with homoerotic desires, nor by trans men. They may be genderless, non-binary, or even asexual.

Anyway, these events were happening in São Paulo and other cities, some more than others, but the so-called *gay football* was gaining fans. It started as some-thing isolated and occasional in the city of São Paulo and spread throughout the country. Some groups, such as Unicorns Brazil in São Paulo, offered opportunities for "practicing sports within the LGBTIQ community," with options including foot-ball, functional training, and running.[9] It was from the contests between teams with media attention at multiple events that prompted other teams to emerge and soon Rio de Janeiro, Florianopolis, Brasilia, Belo Horizonte, among other cities, also had one or more of these football teams.

The groups then decided to create the National League of Gay Football—LiGay or LGNF and set up a formal game schedule. The first Brazilian championship took place in November 2017, in the society arena of Rio Sport, in Tijuca/RJ, with

---

[8] Conversation recorded in a field diary: "Occupy Pacaembu," August 26, 2017.

[9] As one of the best organized, the group maintains a Web site <https://www.unicornsbrazil.com> with a range of options for Internet users to get to know them, including merchandising on sale in a virtual store.

eight male teams participating. It was called Champions LiGay, apparently in reference to the massive Champions League—UEFA, a continent-wide European football competition.

The "gay football league," as it has been called, had been undergoing cultivation since the middle of the first half of that year. I have followed some teams that played in this tournament and that were organizing during the LGBTIQ Parade of São Paulo. I reported on the so-called Diversity Games, held the day before the big parade (Camargo, 2017, June 25). Several groups participated in this São Paulo event, such as the Beescats (from Rio), who were still coming together at that time.[10]

In turn, "men who relate affectively and sexually with other men" practicing sports is not exactly a novelty. At the international level, the systematic practice of sports by LGBTIQ subjects has been recorded since 1982, when the US decathlete Tom Waddell led a process that culminated in the creation of the *Gay Games*, an Olympic competition that aims to exchange sports experiences among people excluded from other normative sport environments (Camargo, 2016; Davidson, 2006; Symons, 2010; Waddell & Schaap, 1996).

I have been studying the phenomenon of the so-called LGBTIQ sports (or, as I prefer, "sports practiced by LGBTIQ people") for over a decade in various parts of the world. What is surprising to me is the organized playing of football by groups of Brazilian men who maintain sexual and homoaffective relationships with other men and who call themselves fans of the British sport, while it was probably this very sport that had excluded them from physical exercise their entire lives. If they are subjects who had painful stories of discrimination, rejection, and prejudice in the conventional and spectacular football and even if they are people who went through bullying and humiliation in physical education classes during their student lives, why declare "love" to the tormenting sport and insist on playing it? Was their only agenda to "occupy the denied place" and "show the heterosexual world" that they can also play ball? It is an unprecedented phenomenon, incidentally, that is (still) difficult to interpret. The fact is that the number of teams is increasing and media coverage has taken off.[11]

LiGay sports events have been taking place with a certain regularity, mainly due to the positive reception that the games have received at least until the coronavirus pandemic of 2020. Many teams emerged between late 2017, when only eight of them participated in the Rio de Janeiro tournament, and late 2019, when 28 teams (25 bio-male and 3 of cis/trans women) played in the championship in Belo Horizonte, Minas Gerais (see Fig. 25.1). After the success of the late 2018 São Paulo competition, the following was published on the LiGay Facebook page (Camargo, 2020, p. 596, our translation):

> Yes, the parade has gone by, the elections have passed, and we will continue here, united, strong and showing that, in the 'country of football', gay people also play ball and that sports

---

[10] This is my recent anthropologic and ethnographic research, as a participant observer (Durham 2004), that is part of my second PhD in progress at the Federal University of São Carlos (UFSCar).

[11] This opens up many avenues for speculation of less than a scientific nature. This lies beyond the scope of this chapter, however. For an initial look at the issue, I suggest Pronger (1990).

Fig. 25.1 Empty stands at the 5th champions LiGay. (Personal archive)

are "a thing" for faggots, yes, a thing for lesbian, bi, trans, transvestite, and queer people. It belongs to whoever wants to participate!

The text makes mention of one of the most feared moments in the political history of the country, when a far right, conservative, openly evangelical candidate had just been elected President of Brazil. This candidate not only considers all the scientific and theoretical-epistemological debate in the field of gender studies as "gender ideology," but he also spread fake news during the campaign about a supposed gay kit intended to subvert "family values and good manners" in schools.

Just as The Queer Nation Manifesto (1990, June 24)—"We are here, we are queer, get used to it!"—the Facebook text called for equal representation on the sports fields as well. After all, Brazil is football country and all non-binary people who do not identify with the aesthetics of heteronormativity also want (and have the right to) play it.

In the third edition of the São Paulo tournament, the excitement in the air, in the conversations, and in the movement of people around the fields was immediately noticeable. There was an atmosphere of comradery, mingled with the festiveness that marked all the groups who felt a part of what was going on. Many had come from out of state, traveling hours by bus.

I talked to organizers, staff, players, people who attended all the editions, and newcomers who were there in São Paulo. In one conversation, for example, a player told me how important it was for him to "come out of the closet" to his family and start playing football "as a gay man" (his words, our translation):

> I didn't know that existed. I was always raised thinking that men play ball, not gays. It took me a while to understand that I, even if I was gay, could play ball. Being here has helped me, including, to reveal myself to my family, the personal side, but also the masculine side that I have.[12]

This player had just started to play on a team from Rio de Janeiro, and he was participating in his first event for LGBTIQ people. He also told me that being there "was something he had never thought of," either because of his conservative family upbringing or because he had never imagined that "gay people played football" (sic).[13]

André Machado, member of the Beescats/RJ and president of LiGay at the time, commented that interest in playing gay society football has been growing all over Brazil. The São Paulo event had brought together the full number teams, 16, that the tournament's organization could hold and the demand for participation was increasing significantly.[14]

Some of these football tournaments are connected to other events for sexual and gender minorities, such as the Gay Games, a sports mega-event, similar to the mainstream Olympic Games and which is held every four years.[15] In other words, in terms of the participants and organization, Champions LiGay resembles what takes place in that mega-event. However, my ethnographic data gathered at the championships revealed a peculiarity in the Brazilian case arising from the football monoculture that reigns in the country. And so there predominate other, localized references linked to issues that dialogue more with the hard Brazilian reality of "being gay in a country of male football players" than an activity carried out for mere leisure, entertainment, or relaxation.

Most of the participants in the first Champions LiGay were white, cisgender men, apparently educated and with a certain purchasing power that had enabled them to pay the expenses arising from the practice of sports, including materials, training, and travel to the competition venue. Today the style is different and brown and black people predominate as do teams that have to overcome financial barriers to participating in the competitions.

---

[12] Conversation recorded in a field diary: 3rd LiGay Champions, November 1, 2019.

[13] About the coming out process, see Sedgwick (2008). About this process among men who have sexual and erotic relations with other men and who also play sports, see Camargo (2018).

[14] Just as an example, in the 3rd. Champions LiGay the following clubs were present: from São Paulo, "Futeboys Futebol Clube" and "Unicorns Brazil" (host teams), "Afronte F.C.", "Bulls Football SP" and "Diversus F.C."; from Rio de Janeiro "Beescats", "Alligaytors" and "Karyocas"; from Belo Horizonte (MG) the "Bharbixas F.C." and "ManoTauros F.C."; from Brasília (DF), the "Bravus"; from Goiânia (GO), the "Barbies F.C."; from Curitiba (PR), the "Capivaras Esporte Clube"; from Porto Alegre (RS), the "Magia Sport Club" and "Pampacats"; and from Florianópolis (SC), the "Sereyos Sport Club".

[15] For more about this specific event, see Symons (2010), Bosch and Braun (2005), Waddell and Schaap (1996).

Something peculiar has been happening in the Brazilian context which is the growing participation of women in leadership positions, such as referees, coaches, physical trainers, and even team managers. Pinto (2019, January 15, our translation) reports on women's performances with football teams including Fabíola Araújo, coach of Bharbixas F.C. (MG):

> It was wonderful to be invited to train Bharbixas, because besides also being LGBT, because I'm a lesbian, I found it an incredible opportunity to contribute to the cause. Besides, they are wonderful people. Our time together was wonderful; they welcomed me in a very good way, so, it was a sum of good things.

Some of Pinto's examples raise questions: Does attributing coaching positions to such women reflect an attempt to acknowledge the role of women, unlike what happens in hegemonic football where they almost never have a voice or a say? Or do these teams lack the resources to hire male coaches for the same functions? On what basis are they invited or hired to be part of the team: voluntarily, with a signed contract or paid on an hourly basis as a freelancer?

A clear fact is that the practices are all amateur, from the subjects' participation to their training processes. Exceptions include refereeing, which must be paid, and the venues that are usually rented. It remains to be seen whether women will continue to participate in these roles over time.

As for the games themselves, of the many games I have watched, most have lacked the festive performance of sexual and gender diversity on the field at the 2017 São Paulo Diversity Games. I have witnessed the participation of a few trans men and some cisgender lesbian players (mainly in the 5th Champions, in 2019), yet most players have reproduced a standard masculine body aesthetic, with hair, unshaven beards, and muscles on display.

A milestone in the 2017 Diversity Games in São Paulo was the presence of the group of trans men, the MBB, playing futsal with a team from Rio de Janeiro. The MBB appeared to intentionally challenge the body aesthetics and the binarism that seems to reign even in environments of homo- and transsexualities. That event was characterized by the visible coexistence of less normative, less binary, and less conventional body aesthetics: masculinized bodies with vaginas; bodies with breasts, long hair, and goatees. They performed aesthetics intended to rethink the body (and by extension, gender and sex) in the middle of the twenty-first century. My field notes read,

> If the personal is political, what I saw in the competition between these trans-male football players was the explicitness of a strong political presence in a public space, in the presence of countless, frenzied television cameras, and in the eyes of inadvertent spectators. These players showed me and everyone else that they could exist in sporting spaces like that field on a pleasant autumn afternoon, offering a tense and interesting game of futsal, and that this could be the rule and not the exception!. (Camargo, 2017, June 25, our translation)

Therefore, it seems that the criticism publicly raised by the MBB social network page upon the first meeting with those gay athletes is still valid: the space of football has been appropriated by "cisgender, gay, white and defined men" (sic), who rejoiced to encounter their peers there. There would be little chance of coming across the existence of those who were different, who were abject, or of those who failed to identify with the dominant aesthetics of the athletic body under construction in these environments, a body reproducing values similar to those found in conventional society.

Bernardo Gonzalez, a trans male MBB founder and former player, explained in an interview that "most groups and players need to rethink the issues of class, gender identity, biotype, diverse aptitudes and all sorts of bizarre things that the mainstream, be it sports or otherwise, imposes on us."[16] Only then, in his opinion, will the phenomenon become productive.

From a feminist point of view, it can be argued that this space has been co-opted by the teams and has reproduced hegemonic, "toxic masculinity" regarding what they hope to attract and reject, yet these choices may jeopardize their subordinated existence (due to the issue of the players' non-normative sexuality).

On the other hand, since I have been following the football expressed by these teams, I have noticed that their athletic performance has improved considerably, both at the technical and tactical levels, which may contribute to the spread and growing visibility of the phenomenon. There are more matched plays, with better tactics. At the most recent games, the players appeared to be more homogeneous in skill level, both in terms of their game plans and ball handling. Moreover, there is an apparent concern with the homogenization of the physical/body appearance of the players, a common process if we take into account that these groups are moving toward intensifying their competition. For example, at the events I have attended several teams expressed concern with physical preparation, nutrition, and even the tactical training of athletes. As early as 2018, The Alligaytors had told me that they had hired a coach with a degree in physical education who had been developing systematic and differentiated training sessions to improve group performance. Many players reported that this strategy has become common among several teams in recent times.

Spectator numbers have risen, even if timidly, since the first Champions. Most of the visibility is the fruit of alternative media, even though the first event did receive some attention from the hegemonic media. However, it is worth mentioning that visibility remains erratic and does not quickly and automatically lead to representativeness—something that will represent the next great challenge for the sport on a national level.

Bringing homosexuality or transsexuality into sports and football is, first of all, to question the hegemony of the heterosexuality that reigns in the world of sports, legitimizing bodies, attitudes, and behaviors. In addition, placing oneself as a desiring subject outside the heteronorm (aligned with any other sexual aesthetics) highlights that not only bodies, but also the practices of pleasure, need to be rethought and reconsidered for other references than those socially accepted.

---

[16] Interview with Bernardo Gonzales, Free Skype Recorder (2019, February 16, our translation).

I would argue that football as a cultural phenomenon has already been inadvertently colonized by "multiple footballs," particularly those of the LGBTIQ community. The extent of occupation and proliferation of such expressions within mainstream football remains to be seen.

Notes for a New Understanding of Football

Their presence is political and occupying the rigid, doctrinaire, prejudiced, and binary spaces of sports has an important social function. The subjects, about whom I have previously written, elaborate, out of their own existence and their sportive manifestations, deeper political issues, which certainly impact sport and football in some way.

It is interesting to realize that, as much as we live in moments of conservatism that affect society (Brazilian and global) and that leave us pessimistic and discredited, facts such as those brought in this text demonstrate that the number of exceptions exceeds the rule, that dissonance sprouts from the system, that other sexual and bodily aesthetics may subvert the normatization of bodies that inhabit the sports world. I think that the presence of such non-heteronormative players in football is enough to show the spectacular and mediatized football, or even Brazilian sports as a whole, that there are cracks in the established certainties and that changes are underway, and that neither the "country of football boots" nor the unruliest organized fan clubs will be able to prevent.

Therefore, we can think that such fierce competition for a space for dialogue with the sport represents not only a pulverization of distinct dimensions and expressions (the multiple "footballs"), but also a transformation of the phenomenon itself, on a scale as yet unknown. As I mentioned, football is colonized from within by the "multiple footballs," among which football expressed by LGBTIQ bodies is just another one.

And to such protagonists, I issue a series of calls: that their bodily performances on the field during these matches challenge the established norms about "being male" in football; that they manage to rid themselves of "toxic masculinities" as a model of being and living; that they inhabit, perhaps and only, creative imaginations in frenetic moments of jouissance and that the challenges of playing football may lead to the understanding and construction of new ways of being-in-the-world; that these players can respect the diversity of ways, affections, and expressions in other bodies that play, understanding that gender disidentification is not an anomaly, but a critical shift of self; and, finally, that we all understand that these aesthetics of gender and sexuality, as well as body practices, may facilitate others to advance within sports, be they football, volleyball, athletics, or any other type.

LGBTIQ society football is still a recent phenomenon in Brazil, and it appears likely to grow considerably, especially because of the proliferation of groups in all states. There is a lot of space and sport to be conquered in Brazilian society. I believe that other sports will also be organized by these (or other) collectives, until leagues or tournaments of their own come to pass—as the football of trans men has done. This text has only revealed the tip of the iceberg, whose base is very wide and (still) little explored.

References

Almeida, C. S. (2016). Belas e feras, nós e as masculinizadas: Discursos, corporalidades e significações. In C. S. Kessler (Ed.), *Mulheres na área: gênero, diversidade e inserções no futebol* (pp. 107–133). Editora da UFRGS.
Bloch, M. (2002). *Apologia da história ou o ofício do historiador*. Zahar.
Bosch, H., & Braun, P. (2005). *Let the games beGay!* Gatzanis.
Braz, C. A. (2007). Corpo a corpo: Reflexões sobre uma etnografia imprópria. *Revista Ártemis, 7*, 128–144. https://periodicos.ufpb.br/ojs2/index.php/artemis/article/view/2157.
Braz, C. A. (2012). *À meia-luz... uma etnografia em clubes de sexo masculinos*. UFG.
Butler, J. (1998). Athletic genders: Hyperbolic instance and/or the overcoming of sexual binarism. *Stanford Humanities Review, 6*(2), 103–111.
Butler, J. (2003). *Problemas de gênero: Feminismo e subversão da identidade*. Civilização Brasileira.
Butler, J. (2008). *Cuerpos que importan: Sobre los límites materiales y discursivos del "sexo"* (2nd ed.). Paidós.
Camargo, W. X., & Kessler, C. S. (2017). Além do masculino/feminino: Gênero, sexualidade, tecnologia e performance no esporte sob perspectiva crítica. *Horizontes Antropológicos, 23*(47), 191–225. https://doi.org/10.1590/S0104-71832017000100007
Camargo, W. X. (2016). Esporte, cultura e política: A trajetória dos Gay Games nas práticas esportivas contemporâneas. *Revista USP*, (108), 97–114. https://doi.org/10.11606/issn.2316-9036.v0i108p97-114.
Camargo, W. X. (2017, June 25). Jogos da diversidade de São Paulo. *Ludopédio*. https://ludopedio.com.br/arquibancada/jogos-da-diversidade-de-sao-paulo/.
Camargo, W. X. (2018). O armário da sexualidade no mundo esportivo. *Revista Estudos Feministas, 26*(1), e42816. https://doi.org/10.1590/1806-9584.2018v26n142816.
Camargo, W. X. (2020). Dimensões de gênero e os múltiplos futebóis no Brasil. In S. S. Giglio, & M. W. Proni (Orgs.), *O futebol nas ciências humanas no Brasil* (pp. 589–604). Editora da Unicamp.
Davidson, J. (2006). The necessity of queer shame for gay pride: The gay games and cultural events. In J. Caudwell (Ed.), *Sport, sexualities and queer/theory* (pp. 90–105). Routledge.
Decreto-Lei No. 3,199 de 14 de abril de 1941. Estabelece as bases de organização dos desportos em todo o país. (Legislação Informatizada, publicação original). https://www2.camara.leg.br/legin/fed/declei/1940-1949/decreto-lei-3199-14-abril-1941-413238-publicacaooriginal-1-pe.html.
Durham, E. R. (2004). *A dinâmica da cultura: Ensaios de Antropologia*. Cosac Naify.
Facchini, R. (2008). *Entre umas e outras: mulheres, (homo)sexualidades e diferenças na cidade de São Paulo*. (Doctoral Thesis in Social Sciences), Universidade Estadual de Campinas (Unicamp). http://www.repositorio.unicamp.br/handle/REPOSIP/280657.
França, I. L. (2012). *Consumindo lugares, consumindo nos lugares: Homossexualidade, consumo e subjetividades na cidade de São Paulo*. EDUERJ.
Franzini, F. (2005). Futebol é "coisa para macho"? Pequeno esboço para uma história das mulheres no país do futebol. *Revista Brasileira De História, 25*(50), 315–328. https://doi.org/10.1590/S0102-01882005000200012
Gambeta, W. (2015). *A bola rolou: O velódromo paulista e os espetáculos de futebol, 1895–1916*. SESI-SP Editora.

Goellner, S. V. (2003). *Bela, feminina e maternal: Imagens da mulher na revista de Educação Physica*. Ed. Unijuí.

Goellner, S. V. (2008). "As mulheres fortes são aquelas que fazem uma raça forte": esporte, eugenia e nacionalismo no Brasil no início do século XX. *Recorde—Revista de História do Esporte, 1*(1), 1–28. https://revistas.ufrj.br/index.php/Recorde/article/viewFile/790/731.

Kessler, C. S. (2015). *Mais que barbies e ogras: uma etnografia do futebol de mulheres no Brasil e nos Estados Unidos*. (Doctoral Thesis in Social Anthropology), Universidade Federal do Rio Grande do Sul (UFRGS). https://lume.ufrgs.br/handle/10183/131770.

Kessler, C. S. (2016). Futebol ou futebóis: é plural ou singular? In C. S. Kessler (Ed.), *Mulheres na área: Gênero, diversidade e inserções no futebol* (pp. 21–41). Editora da UFRGS.

Muñoz, J. E. (1999). *Disidentifications: queers of color and the performance of politics*. University of Minnesota.

Pacheco, A. J. P. (1998). Educação física feminina: Uma abordagem de gênero sobre as décadas de 1930 e 1940. *Revista de Educação Física, 9*(1), 45–52. https://periodicos.uem.br/ojs/index.php/RevEducFis/article/view/3827/2638/.

Pinto, M. R. (2019, January 15). As mulheres que fazem a Champions LiGay. *Ludopédio.* https://ludopedio.com.br/arquibancada/as-mulheres-que-fazem-a-champions-ligay/.

Pisani, M. (2016). Uma análise inicial sobre a profissão de jogadora de futebol: Trajetórias, dificuldades, histórias de vida e migração de algumas jogadoras do Foz Cataratas Futebol Clube. In C. S. Kessler (Ed.), *Mulheres na área: Gênero, diversidade e inserções no futebol* (pp. 43–58). Editora da UFRGS.

Preciado, P. B. (2008). *Testo Yonqui*. Espasa.

Pronger, B. (1990). *The arena of masculinity: Sports, homosexuality, and the meaning of sex*. St Martin's.

Reis, L. (2011, June 12). Primeiro time feminino brasileiro é reativado em Minas. *Folha de S. Paulo.* https://www1.folha.uol.com.br/esporte/2011/06/928856-primeiro-time-feminino-brasileiro-e-reativado-em-minas.shtml.

Rich, A. (1999). La heterosexualidad obligatoria y la existencia lesbiana. In M. Navarro, & C. R. Stimpson (Eds.), *Sexualidad, género y roles sexuales* (pp. 159–211). Fondo de Cultura Económica.

Santos Neto, J. M. (2002). *Visão de jogo: Primórdios do futebol no Brasil*. Cosac & Naify.

Sedgwick, E. K. (2008). Epistemology of the closet. *Epistemology of the closet* (pp. 67–90). University of California Press.

Soares, C. L. (1994). *Educação Física: Raízes europeias e Brasil*. Autores Associados.

Stolke, V. (2000). ¿Es el sexo para el género lo que la raza para la etnicidad… y la naturaleza para la sociedad? *Política y Cultura*, (14), 25–60. https://www.redalyc.org/pdf/267/26701403.pdf.

Symons, C. (2010). *The gay games: A history*. Routledge.

The Queer Nation Manifesto (1990, June 24). *History is a weapon!* https://www.historyisaweapon.com/defcon1/queernation.html.

Toledo, L. H., & Camargo, W. X. (2018). Futebol dos futebóis: dissolvendo valências simbólicas de gênero e sexualidade por dentro do futebol. *FuLiA/UFMG, 3*(3), 93–107. https://doi.org/10.17851/2526-4494.3.3.93-107.

Waddell, T., & Schaap, D. (1996). *Gay olympian: The life and death of Dr. Tom Waddell*. Alfred A. Knopf.

Chapter 26
Football, Violence, and Democratic Politics in Brazil

Heloisa Helena Baldy dos Reis and Mariana Zuaneti Martins

There are those who argue that football and politics do not or should not mix. Neither should it relate to our institutional democracy. This purist narrative argues that football, by allowing us to experience equal opportunities and destabilize other social hierarchies, would dramatize relationships very different from those traditionally involved with politics and with the democracy that actually exists, especially in our country. In this way, football would be a sphere separated from everyday social relations, which seduce us so much, insofar as it would allow us not to ritualize the unequal and ossified democracy that confronts us on a routine basis, but rather to provide an opportunity for a true sense of meritocracy and justice, which are blocked for us by some institutions, including politics. This way of looking at football, which attributed to this sport an aura such as that of a work of art, sought to counter other discourses that mechanized its presence in society, making it merely an annex of the heap of inequalities and estrangements that afflict us daily. Briefly, we will summarize the bipolarity that traditionally involves two classical views of football, opposing the vision of "opium of the people" to the one of "drama of social justice." These are opposing pairs that compete regarding whether football is separated from social and political relations or not. However, football, it is not a sphere separated from social or political institutions, and not a mere reflection of something more important. What we will argue is that football and society are fields that feed on each other and, in this sense, are not separated from politics and, in the case of democratic societies, from the rituals of participation and democracy, as well as from their contradictions. This analytical key, which interprets football and society as complementary elements, is fundamental for us to look at the problem of violence related to football spectacles. Without observing these possible relations, we may fall into stigmatized, essentialist, or even apologetic interpretations.

H. H. B. dos Reis (✉)
University of Campinas, Campinas, Brazil

M. Z. Martins
Federal University of Espírito Santo, Vitória, Brazil

In order to develop this line of interpretation, we will present a theoretical framework, pointing out the foundations that led us to this relationship, in a dialogue that provided the first indications for the development of research on football and violence. Next, we will contextualize analyses that point to the problem of violence and its relationship with democracy in Brazil. Finally, we will outline the relationships between football, political participation, and democracy in Brazil today.

Theoretical Framework of the Relation Between Football, Society, and Violence

Research into the relationship between football and violence has enabled us to contribute to understanding the social significance of this phenomenon in society (Reis, 1998; Reis & Escher, 2006). Thus, it is not possible to talk about violence related to football spectacles without understanding the social and cultural role of football in contemporary societies and the meaning that this sport has for young people and adults (Elias & Dunning, 1992). Moreover, in our research trajectory, it became evident that prejudice and violence find fertile ground in Brazilian society, in a field of secular cultural and identity manifestations—football played *by* and *for* men. Transforming or displacing these relations may seem like a utopian dream today, when there is a clear regression in Brazilian civilization and in the civilizing advances of several western countries. However, some experiences demonstrate that these relations are always changing, making it possible to have islands of resistance. Issues involving the relationship between football, violence, society, and democracy will be the theme of this chapter.

This look at the relationship between football and society was based on a theoretical framework according to which the understanding of sport should be centered on the idea that it is part of the civilizing process experienced in Europe in the fifteenth century. The "civilizing shift" of medieval sports summarizes the process in which its rules became written and standardized, "directed towards the *ethos* of *fair play* and providing equal opportunities for all participants and with reduced opportunities for violent physical contact" (Dunning et al., 2004, p. 9). It should be noted that the relationship between the transformations in entertainment and the civilizing process occurred in a complementary way, not by unidirectional determination. Therefore, it is necessary to describe what is meant by civilizing process and how sport is inserted in it.

For the sociologist Norbert Elias, the civilizing process is a blind movement, unplanned, and without a specific direction. Therefore, to describe it, the author studied in detail the behavior and social norms from the twentieth to the thirteenth century, in order to demonstrate how changes in *habitus* and personality structures are concomitant to the formation of the modern state, constituting the features of the civilizing process that developed in the West. The development of refinements and self-control, operated at the levels of behaviors and personality, caused the control over violence and aggression within societies to be extended, which brought about a reduced capacity for subjects to feel pleasure with the suffering of others and with witnessing violence, a behavior that is also the result of an increasing mutual identification related to solidarity and mutual understanding (Dunning, 2014). Thus, talking about the civilizing process implies referring to a decreased tolerance for violence, political centralization and pacification under state control, growing social differentiation, increased chains of interdependence, and, finally, functional democratization.

In *Quest of excitement*, Elias and Dunning described the process of sociogenesis and psychogenesis of sport, i.e., the correlation between the development of social structures, state formation, pacification, interdependence chains and functional democratization and the normative and behavioral development at the level of manners and *habitus* (Dunning, 2014), understanding that both processes created the conditions under which sport was socially produced. The question that guided the authors referred to understand the reasons that made sport necessary to human beings from the XVII centuries onward (Dunning, 2003).

For Elias and Dunning (1992), in societies oriented by the need of a constant self-control of emotions and violence, in which this moderation becomes part of the personality structure, sport would be the opportunity to arise emotions, in a controlled and socially approved way. They also argue that, in an extremely self-regulated society, there was a need for an activity in which it was possible to develop some kind of socially approved and therefore also regulated lack of control.

Another factor that specifically propitiated the emergence of sports as a leisure activity in these societies was the relationship of this practice with the civilizing process that was developing in England, in the fifteenth century. For Elias and Dunning (1992), the "sportization" of leisure activities occurred in parallel with the process of political "parliamentarization" that was developing in English society, as the civilizing process allowed conflicts to be solved respecting rules defined by parliamentary conduct, thus providing the necessary conditions for the development of *fair play*. "Parliamentarization" was based on free associationism, a form of organization that housed clubs of the English nobility and, among other activities, developed the practice of sport (Murphy et al., 2000). Thus, "sportization" and "parliamentarization" are two interdependent facets of a civilizing process.

According to Dunning, at the end of the twentieth century, industrial societies had in sport an element increasingly shaping the identity, not only in individual level, but also for the affirmation of intergroup affinity actions and hierarchical structures of countries (Dunning, 2003, p. 15). Sport provided a space in which people could meet and strengthen ties. Even loyalty to a club could be a useful and unique link in an increasingly uncertain and fragmented world.

The "professionalization" of sports, in the twentieth century, brought it to a new level, with increased competitiveness, and consequently, the seriousness involved in the practice of sports (Dunning & Sheard, 1979). Along these lines, there was an increase in social identification with sport and with clubs, which also developed violence related to sporting spectacles. According to Elias and Dunning (1992), this violence, called *hooliganism*, developed within football as it became more serious, so that the excitement originating in the mimetic framework of the sporting activity itself could be extrapolated to real life. *Hooliganism* occurs among people, generally young men, and is associated with aggressive masculinity, who considered that the fight related to football is the source of a pleasant emotional excitement. Being a hooligan provides ascension for these young men (the *hooligans*), a *status* that only sport can bring them (Dunning, 2014). Evidently, Dunning (2014) was dealing with the European case, something that needs to be mediated for the understanding of the phenomenon of violence related to Brazilian football.

Fan Organizations and Violence: Traces of Democracy?

When one talks about football-related violence in Brazil, the "Torcidas Organizadas" (TOs), which constitutes groups of organized fans, are commonly mentioned. TOs[1] are autonomous youth associations, which bring together groups of supporters with affective ties with a specific football club. Their members, initially linked by club identity bonds, primarily seek sociability relationships.[2] TOs emerged in the late 1960s, on December 6, 1967, when the Flamengo Youth TO was created in Rio de Janeiro (Teixeira, 2004). In the countryside of São Paulo, in the city of Campinas, on March 23, 1969, the Ponte Preta's TO was formed, renamed as "Torcida Jovem Amor Maior" (Eleoterio, 2014). In the same year, on July 1, it was founded, in the city of São Paulo, the "Gaviões da Fiel," one of the largest TOs in Brazil (Pimenta, 1997).

According to Teixeira (2004), in the 1990s, TOs grew stronger as a group; their specificity as to the way of supporting became explicit through their own identity and the belief in the power to choose, fire and project players, coaches, and managers—relations that are ambiguous and contradictory. Toledo (1996) called such groups "militant supporters" and concluded that they would reproduce, "in the way they organize themselves, in practice and in the discourse, the most recurrent relations of society, such as hierarchies, status, prestige, authority." Hierarchies and ambiguities, in a culture of hegemonic masculinity, reproduce the prejudices and discriminations against women and LGBTQIs. Reis (2017) called them "faithful fans" due to the frequency with which they attend matches in stadiums, in the most diverse weather conditions and in terms of the team's performance.

---

[1] We also have the Federation of Organized Fans (TOs) of Rio de Janeiro (FTORJ) officially created in March 2008 with the objective of promoting dialogue between the institutions based in the state of Rio de Janeiro and the authorities, having been inspired by the association of Organized Fans (TOs) of Rio de Janeiro (Astorj), created in June 1981 and dissolved before the beginning of the 1990s, and the national association of organized fans (TOs) (Anatorg), created on 12/12/2014.

[2] For Simmel (Gastaldo, 2005, pp. 108–109, our translation), "sociability is a form of interaction in which participants show themselves at once interested and uncommitted, autonomizing their actions in the sense of avoiding any demonstration of an objective interest in the matters dealt with".

Who Are the Fanatic Football Fans in the Twenty-First Century? Why Are the Majority of Supporters in These Associations Composed of Men?

The pioneering research on fanatic fandom was conducted in the late 1980s, but especially in the 1990s, aiming to describe the identity and behavior of these youngsters and, especially, their inclination to join fights (Cesar, 1981; Pimenta, 1997; Reis, 1998; Toledo, 1996). In a first investigation, conducted in the state of São Paulo, in 2005, covering the records of some TOs, it was detected that these fans were mostly male—about 90% male fans and 10% female fans, most of them in the age range between 20 and 30 years (Reis & Lopes, 2016), although the ages ranged between 2 and 86 years. On the same track, Hollanda and Medeiros (2016) found 9.5% of women in the supporters of Rio de Janeiro and 13.9% of women in the supporters of São Paulo, indicating a small increase in female participation in these associations.

In order to better understand the supporters' profile, Reis (2016) sought to identify their age distribution, ethnicity, education, attendance to the games, the use or not of alcohol they did, important elements to understand, demographically and socially, who they were, and to draw a first picture about the way they were involved with the football spectacle.

The majority (59.8%) of the sample was young men; between 15 and 20 years old (26.9%, 15 to 17 years; 31.9%, 18 to 20 years; 21.9% between 21 and 23 years, and 19.3% between 24 and 25 years); 19.2% were black, which is quite distant from the general representation of the black population in the metropolitan region of São Paulo, where the research was carried out, which was 36.1% already in 2004. The level of education of the interviewees was compatible with their age group, and 10.2% had some educational delay (Reis & Lopes, 2016).

Regarding the involvement with the sporting spectacle, the sample can be considered loyal fans (Reis, 2017), to the extent that they were very assiduous to their teams' matches: 85.9% of them attended at least one match per week; 40.8% attended all matches, that is, two per week; and 45.1% attended one match per week.

Furthermore, among the interviewees, an expressive portion of alcohol drinkers at risk was found: 32.8% scored positively (above 8) on the research instrument "The Alcohol Use Disorders Identification Test" (AUDIT), while 67.2% scored negatively for alcohol abuse, a percentage almost double that found by Martins et al. (2008). Among young people from the interior of São Paulo, 17.9% of fans scored positively in relation to alcohol abuse.

About their leadership, in a 2015 research conducted by Lopes, Reis, Paschoa, Teixeira, Medeiros, and Hollanda (unpublished), among the 64 leaders of TO's from all over the country, 98.4% were men and 1.6% women (corresponding to one woman). All of them were older than 18 years. Among them, 54.7% self-reported as white and 42.2% as black, a rate much higher than the ones collected by Reis in 2007 and 2008, by biophenotyping, among TOs in general. Regarding the education of the TO's leaders, 82.5% had completed high school or college education, a rate much higher than the Brazilian population in general, whose percentage that reached this education is 46.1% (IBGE, 2018).

Research on profiles helps researchers to empirically support arguments that go against what has been claimed by the media, that these supporters are vandals, poorly educated, people "without family," which would justify morally reprehensible behaviors (Reis, 2017; Reis & Lopes, 2016). However, they also reaffirm previously detected patterns, especially regarding the small presence of women. This scarcity, especially in a select group of leaders, led us to inquire what would be the space of women in the football spectacle, particularly among TOs, a question that was incorporated into the questionnaire of the investigation conducted with female supporters of two clubs in the capital city of Bahia. The data from that research confirms a restricted and subordinate participation of women in the leadership of TOs. There are even reports of women being prevented from participating in spaces such as the drums or in some specific activities of cheering. There was no possibility of women supporters holding leadership positions. The claiming of female fans for equality and for rights within TOs occurs daily in the form of resistance and through negotiations. As part of this struggle, they joined the "I National Meeting of Women from the stands," held in São Paulo on June 10, 2017. Nearley, 300 female fans this meeting, from 40 different TOs (Moraes, 2018).

Prejudice, sexism, and discrimination against LGBTIQs and women, as well as against poor and black people, are normalized in our society. Not even the 1988 Constitution and other laws and conventions previously mentioned were enough to ensure an equality of gender or of ethnicity/race, among others. Within TOs, it can be noticed, through qualitative research, the presence of all possible prejudices, besides, obviously, the male domination, based on a hegemonic, aggressive and exacerbated masculinity, founded on values such as overpowering, leadership, and oppression to the less "strong" (Monteiro, 2003; Teixeira, 2004; Toledo, 1996). In Dunning's (2003, p. 33) explanation, "modern sport started out as a male preserve and that many sports continue to act as vehicles for the expression and reproduction of male aggressiveness."

Fan Culture and Brazilian Politics

One of the great problems of Brazilian culture is the lack of class identity of the subaltern and exploited strata of society, making up what Demo (1998) called "political poverty." Agreeing with the author, we understand that this type of poverty contributes to the perpetuation of the condition of exploitation of social groups that do not perceive themselves as subaltern. According to Demo, these people, by not seeing themselves as members of a group of the Brazilian social stratification—poor and black man/woman or of the most exploited working class, or even as a member of a social group that suffers prejudice, discrimination, stigmatization, physical and symbolic violence, such as the TOs—contribute to perpetuate all the inequality and violence addressed to them.

The lack of class identity makes it difficult for those fans to even realize that they are being violated by a state that should constitutionally guarantee them the democratic rule of law, which includes free speech, access to leisure, housing, work, transportation, health, and quality education—conditions sine qua non for their emancipation as human beings. Political poverty contributes to the perpetuation and reproduction of an unjust and unequal society such as Brazil's, and here it is worth bringing up a recent event in which supporters, despite being threatened by one of the candidates for President of the Republic, voted for him.

We have not even reached what Elias (1993) points out as central to the advancement of the civilizing process of any nation-state, that is, the centralized control of violence by the state. In Brazil, under the pretext of combat the daily violence in which we are immersed, the state actually ends up exercising various types of violence against the population. The residents of the peripheries of large urban centers, who live in conditions of greater vulnerability, are the most affected by this revealing posture of a state that promotes injustice and discrimination against those it should protect. Incontrovertible proof of what we are talking about is the fact that Brazil is one of the countries where there are more deaths caused by public security agents, with an average of nine victims per day.[3]

The violent and arbitrary control by public security agents is a form of state violence that, according to official data, victimizes preferentially poor and black men from large cities. The official data also admit that only a small number of these crimes are cleared up, thus configuring, according to experts, a sense of impunity and perpetuating a violent, arbitrary, and lethal police force. The police force has been authorized and defended by the politicians elected in the last election (2018), particularly by the current president of the country and the former governor of Rio de Janeiro. For these leaders, the control and reduction of violence are directly linked to the increase in the number of police officers and the freedom to "slaughter," according to the expression used by the former elected governor of Rio de Janeiro.

In addition to this deviation/excess of the Brazilian state, we could mention another entity in the power structure in Brazil that would have to repair the damage committed, the Judiciary. This, however, has historically shown itself to be selective. Unlike the other powers, such as the executive and legislative branches, which are controlled by popular vote every four years, the judiciary is only accessible through meritocracy, with no social control mechanisms. This absence of vertical accountability allows public security forces to commit their abuses/deviations/excesses without anyone being able to authorize or punish them.

The relationship between what happens in national politics and the situation of TOs has already been discussed in some studies. Toledo (1996) mentioned the fact that, in order to win the fans' votes, many club leaders and managers run for elective offices, approaching the supporters in election seasons—a clientelistic, opportunistic approach. In the October 2018 elections, however, something different happened,

---

[3] According to the 10th Brazilian Public Security Yearbook, produced by the Brazilian Public Security Forum. Available at http://memoriasdaditadura.org.br/desmilitarizacao-e-reforma-das-pol icias/index.html>. Accessed on 2018, November 6.

when the leader of a TO ran for state deputy in São Paulo. To everyone's surprise—since, at least theoretically, he defended the supporters' demands—this candidate did not receive votes from the fans he represented. This context is even more serious and amazing if we consider that, after decades facing attempts to ban TOs from the Brazilian football scene and from São Paulo, most of these fans voted other candidates, even belonging to political parties directly responsible for these attacks against them.

TOs comprise an expressively numerous group of the Brazilian population: an estimated universe of three million individuals. Therefore, for decades this space has served as an electoral springboard or of public visibility for candidates or political leaders (Toledo, 1996). Within this same debate, it is important to report herein that a good portion of those supporters, by not perceiving themselves as a violated, stigmatized, criminalized, despised, and manipulated group, have not taken up the fight against the removal from office of the President of the Republic elected by popular vote, for instance; by not being aware of the consequences of political changes for their own existence, they contribute to the onslaughts against the guaranteeing of their right to the football spectacle as leisure, to the respect of the state, to the consideration of the organizers of the spectacle. These are attacks that go against the existence of TOs as spaces of youth sociability as we know it and toward the appropriation of football by the Brazilian elite and its complete commercialization.

One of the fundamental forms of engagement is precisely the participation in the electoral process; however, such participation cannot be used by opportunistic politicians, in exchange for a few bucks on the eve of elections. It may result in the very weakening of TOs, as many of these politicians are the same ones who always spoke in favor of the extinction of the fan associations culture.

Football, Political Participation, and Democracy

Although we do not agree with the statement that football is the opium of the people, we argue here the contradictions and ambiguities of individuals whose identity is formatted by their bond with the club within fan culture. Consequences are that they relate to politics in a very conservative way, as we have shown. What about the other actors from football spectacle? Would they also be joining the conservative wave that has reached fans?

The practices of club managers have not served as an example of democracy and transparency, to the extent that they act to exclude the other actors, such as players and fans, from the decision-making process concerning football (Martins & Reis, 2017a). Even if any generalization produces injustices, we cannot fail to say that the vast majority of club managers, when they manage to get elected as city councilors, deputies or to executive positions—often anchored in the vote of football fans, as mentioned above, they do so through parties of conservative ideological spectrum, not voting in favor or proposing laws that guarantee constitutional freedoms and human rights.

These examples suggest that, if the social justice narrative does not seem to express the current moment of fan culture and participation in football, this sport would indeed be very close to the idea of being configured as the opium of the people. However, we still do not tune in with this idea, which defends a deterministic view and does not recognize the capacity and possibilities of people to negotiate, transgress, resist, transform the established social and structural conditions. In this sense, when looking at these phenomena, even if precisely based on the pessimism of reason, it is also important to pay attention to the optimism of contradiction, to play a little with the famous Gramscian quote.

When we observe football players' taking a political position, as a rule, apathy is dominant, which in other moments has already been identified as paternalism (Florenzano, 2009). Since their image is part of the product they offer to the club, besides the fear of taking a political position and losing job opportunities, players rarely seek information about national politics or football (Martins, 2017). However, there are football athletes who somehow got involved with political issues in their country, as suggested by the short series presented by former player Eric Cantona on Rebel Footballers. In this show, there are stars such as Predrag Pašić, from Bosnia, who did not want to leave Saravejo during the Yugoslavian war in the early 1990s; the Chilean Carlos Caszely, whose family was persecuted during the Pinochet dictatorship; the Algerian participant in the conflicts for independence, Rachid Mekhloufi; the Ivorian Didier Drogba, whose presence greatly contributed to his country's qualification for the 2006 World Cup, an important achievement for the unity of several ethnic groups in Ivory Coast; and Socrates, with his participation in the Corinthians Democracy and his political positions in favor of the return of direct elections for president in 1984 in Brazil. These are players who understood themselves as citizens, political actors, and chose to actively participate in the construction of the directions of their respective countries.

Corinthians's Democracy can be understood as a moment when there was, in fact, the participation of Brazilian football players in some instances and decisions of a club. The movement took place in the first half of the 1980s, a time when the country was thriving in the struggle for the return of democracy and the end of the military dictatorship established since 1964. Issues concerning the football department were brought to the Corinthians squad for discussion and deliberation, enabling some achievements, such as not having to stay away from home the night before matches. From the point of view of the board of directors, it was a period of two managements in which a more entrepreneurial vision of administration was undertaken in the club. Engaged in this movement of democratic participation, claim, collective organization, and achievement of rights (Martins & Reis, 2017b), the Corinthian players pluralized the meanings of democracy within football, encompassing the practice on the field, but also the discussions, the decisions, the political participation in their own lives, in a clear demonstration of contestation to the prevailing paternalism in social labor relations in football (Martins & Reis, 2014). They highlighted the importance of collective action, articulating themselves in political parties and in the player's union in an attempt to expand that *modus operandi* so rare in football beyond the walls of the club (Martins & Reis, 2017b).

During the period of Corinthians's Democracy, the athletes' union gained a lot of publicity in the media. In this same period, trade unionism, in general, was on the rise, marked by many general strikes (Sader, 2002), a context that, combined with a moment of politicization of football, enhanced the actions of the football players' union itself, giving it greater visibility. At the time, the players' union even threatened to initiate a strike that would paralyze the São Paulo championship, something still unheard of to this day (Martins & Reis, 2014).

Another important example of situations in which football players have taken the stage to fight for their rights in the country occurred recently, through the Bom Senso F.C. movement, which had its genesis related to the protest cycle of June 2013, protesters—conservative or progressive—gathered the streets in Brazil.

Influenced by this cycle of protest, Bom Senso F.C. brought together players willing to fight for their right to 30 days of vacation after the end of the season, something that was threatened in 2014 due to the World Cup being held in the country. Their claim for less exploitative working conditions, however, was acquiring broader contours. From then on, the movement committed itself to a broader agenda of demands for changes in Brazilian football, which included democracy in the football decision-making bodies, such as the Brazilian Football Confederation (CBF), as well as influence on federal legislation that regulates the sport. Bom senso F.C. fought for changes in the law of the Brazilian football management modernization and fiscal responsibility program (PROFUT).

The very condition of the players, who, on the one hand, are a labor force of the football spectacle and, on the other, an image of branding, sustained the political existence of Bom Senso F.C. Through the image of famous football players, it sought to reverse the negativity related to political participation. That is, the movement tried to transform political action into something that could converge to a positive image for the meaning of their claims, as well as for the political strategy adopted. In this way, collective action and bargaining would become feasible for some players, since the damage to their public image would not be prominent, especially those who were at the end of their careers, whose political participation could mean engagement with football by other means, such as management and the sports media. This moment of rise of a collective action in football aimed at transforming the status quo, however, fizzled out. Its actors suffered, somehow, retaliations, and CBF reorganized itself, so that things changed exactly to continue the way they were, as stated in the classic sentence from the novel *Il Gattopardo*, by Giuseppe Tomasi Di Lampedusa.

Just as the context of political and union effervescence in the 1980s infected football, with the emergence of Corinthians' Democracy and the strengthening of athletes' unions, the current scenario of conservatism also has repercussions among football athletes. The support of several players for the radical right-wing candidate for President of the Republic Jair Bolsonaro—such as Felipe Melo (Palmeiras); Lucão (Goiás); Gilberto (Bahia), Lucas Moura (Tottenham, England); Carlos Alberto; Ederson (former Flamengo player); Jadson and Roger (Corinthians); and former players Dagoberto, Edmundo, Cafu and Ronaldinho Gaucho—drew the attention of the media during the election campaign. The justifications employed by these athletes and former athletes for such support were that Bolsonaro would represent "the family"—that is, defending traditional and conservative values—was an outsider in politics—even though he had been a member of parliament for almost three decades—and sought solutions considered by them more appropriate to the problem of violence—such as advocating arming the population. As a rule, such justifications were supported by a discourse that conveyed hegemonic, virile, and aggressive masculinity, representative of the world of football, considered one of the last spaces in which this type of masculinity can be fully expressed (Elias & Dunning, 1992).

Such statements were also related to a religious perspective, since many of these athletes profess religions that are close to Bolsonaro's. In the case of football players, particularly, religious identity is important for the creation of bonds and adherence to a regulated routine. This is because, once these athletes circulate globally, religion becomes the spaces in which they and their families meet other Brazilians or people with whom to create bonds of friendship and trust, far from their homeland (Rial, 2008). In addition, as they become famous, these players are exposed to behaviors that would affect their discipline for trainings (such as parties, alcohol, and late nights), and for which religion, especially those of neopentecostal tendencies, would be an antidote, since their conservative perspective is supported by inner-worldly asceticism.

The fact that several players have declared a vote for Bolsonaro is something unconventional in Brazilian electoral disputes. More than a possible politicization of football players, this presents itself as a counterpoint to the Bom Senso F.C. engaged in transform football players lives by actively influencing the country's politics and advocating in a democratic agenda. In this sense, taking position in favor of Bolsonaro is a major setback in football players' political participation. Setback because it is a government that does not advocate democratic practices.

Since it is not possible to understand football without society, configurations of power, ambiguities, and contradictions get mixed up and merge. It is not football that imitates society, or society that dramatizes itself in football; what exists is a feedback between spheres that cannot be seen separately. People who fight for social change also like football, just as more collective, horizontal and democratic ways of life are also experienced and nurtured through sport. However, conservative waves also gravitate around football. Perhaps today, more than ever, Eduardo Galeano's interpretation of contemporary football is not only present, but even more necessary as a social metaphor. For him, the game has become spectacle, with few protagonists and many spectators (football for watching). The technocracy of professional sports has been imposing a football of great speed and physical strength, which renounces joy, atrophies fantasy, and forbids daring. He comments, ironically: it is rare for a daredevil player to have the courage to go off script and commit the absurdity of dribbling the entire opposing team. In other words, the joy of the body that dribbles for pure pleasure is lost, because the adventure of freedom is forbidden (Galeano, 2014, pp. 14–15).

May we all embrace and play the unfortunately ever more forbidden adventure of freedom. And may we play it not only in football matches, but may freedom and democracy be the keynote of our daily tactic and strategy to face life.

References

Cesar, B. T. (1981). *Os gaviões da fiel e a águia do capitalismo: Ou, o duelo.* (Master's Dissertation in Social Anthropology) Universidade Estadual de Campinas. http://www.repositorio.unicamp. br/handle/REPOSIP/279355.

Demo, P. (1998). *Pobreza política.* Autores Associados.

Dunning, E., & Sheard, K. (1979). *Barbarians, gentlemen and players: A sociological study of the development of rugby football.* Routledge.

Dunning, E., Malcolm, D., & Waddington, I. (2004). Conclusion: Figurational sociology and the development of modern sport. In E. Dunning, D. Malcolm, & I. Waddington (Eds.), *Sport histories: Figurational studies in the development of modern sports* (Chapter 12). Routledge.

Dunning, E. (2003). *El fenómeno deportivo: Estudios sociológicos em torno al deporte, la violencia y la civilización.* Editorial Paidotribo.

Dunning, E. (2014). *Sociologia do esporte e os processos civilizatórios.* Annablume.

Eleoterio, R. H. (2014). *As relações de sociabilidade da torcida jovem amor maior.* (Undergraduate Monograph in Pedagogy), Unicamp. http://www.bibliotecadigital.unicamp.br/document/?code= 000962489&opt=1.

Elias, N., & Dunning, E. (1992). *A busca da excitação.* Difel.

Elias, N. (1993). *O processo civilizador: Formação do Estado e civilização.* Editora Schwarcz; Companhia das Letras.

Florenzano, J. P. (2009). *A democracia corinthiana: Práticas de liberdade no futebol brasileiro.* EDUC.

Galeano, E. (2014). *O futebol.* L&Pm Pocket.

Gastaldo, É. (2005). "O complô da torcida": Futebol e performance masculina em bares. *Horizontes Antropológicos, 11*(24), 107–123. https://doi.org/10.1590/S0104-71832005000200006.

Hollanda, B. B. B. de, & Medeiros, J. (2016). Violência, juventude e idolatria clubística: Uma pesquisa quantitativa com torcidas organizadas de futebol no Rio de Janeiro e em São Paulo. *Revista Hydra, 1*(2), 97–125. https://doi.org/10.34024/hydra.2016.v1.9135.

IBGE. (2018). *Pesquisa nacional por amostra de domicílios contínua (PNADC): Educação, 2017.* Instituto Brasileiro de Geografia e Estatística.

Martins, M. Z., & Reis, H. H. (2017a). Poder, transparência e democracia nas gestões esportivas. In *Movimento é vida. (Background Paper for the "Movimento é vida: Atividades físicas e esportivas no Brasil" report), Relatório Nacional de Desenvolvimento Humano do Brasil*, Programa das Nações Unidas para o Desenvolvimento—PNUD. https://ludopedio.com.br/wp-content/uploads/ Atividades-Fi%CC%81sicas-e-Esportivas-e-Corrupc%CC%A7a%CC%83o.pdf.

Martins, M. Z., & Reis, H. H. B. (2017b). *Democracia corinthiana: Futebol e política.* Autoresporte.

Martins, M. Z., & dos Reis, H. H. B. (2014). Cidadania e direitos dos jogadores de futebol na Democracia Corinthiana. *Revista Brasileira De Educação Física e Esporte, 28*(3), 429–440. https://doi.org/10.1590/1807-55092014000300429.

Martins, R. A., Manzatto, A. J., Da Cruz, L. N., Poiate, S. M. G., & Scarin, A. C. C. F. (2008). Utilização do *Alcohol Use Disorders Identification Test* (AUDIT) para identificação do consumo de álcool entre estudantes do ensino médio. *Interamerican Journal of Psychology, 42*(2), 307–316. http://pepsic.bvsalud.org/scielo.php?script=sci_arttext&pid=S0034-96902008000200012.

Martins, M. Z. (2017). *A mercadoria do futebol.* Autoresporte.

Monteiro, R. de A. (2003). *Torcer, lutar, o inimigo massacrar: Raça Rubro-Negra! Uma etnografia sobre futebol, violência e masculinidade.* Editora FGV.

Moraes, C. F. (2018). *As torcedoras querem torcer.* (Master's Dissertation), Programa Multidisciplinar de Pós-Graduação em Cultura e Sociedade, Universidade Federal da Bahia. https://reposi torio.ufba.br/ri/handle/ri/30758.

Murphy, P., Sheard, K., & Waddington, I. (2000). Figurational sociology and its application to sport. In E. Dunning & J. Coackley (Eds.), *Handbook of sports studies* (pp. 92–105). Sage London.

Pimenta, C. A. M. (1997). *Torcidas organizadas de futebol: Violência e auto-afirmação—aspectos da construção das novas relações sociais.* Vogal.

Reis, H. H. B., & Escher, T. A. (2006). *Futebol e sociedade*. Líber.

Reis, H. H. B., & Lopes, F. T. P. (2016). O torcedor por detrás do rótulo: Caracterização e percepção da violência de jovens torcedores organizados. *Movimento, 22*(3), 693–705. https://doi.org/10.22456/1982-8918.57150.

Reis, H. H. B. dos. (1998). *Futebol e sociedade: As manifestações da torcida*. (Doctoral Thesis in Physical Education), Universidade Estadual de Campinas. http://repositorio.unicamp.br/jspui/handle/REPOSIP/275326.

Reis, H. H. B. (2016). O perfil do torcedor organizado e a política brasileira para o futebol espetáculo. *Tríade, 4*(7), 172–189. http://periodicos.uniso.br/ojs/index.php/triade/article/view/2526.

Reis, H. H. B. dos. (2017). Atividades físicas e violências: O futebol como referência. (Background Paper for the "Movimento é vida: Atividades físicas e esportivas no Brasil" report), *Relatório Nacional de Desenvolvimento Humano do Brasil*, Programa das Nações Unidas para o Desenvolvimento—PNUD. https://ludopedio.com.br/wp-content/uploads/Atividades-Fi%CC%81sicas-e-Esportivas-e-Viole%CC%82ncia.pdf.

Rial, C. (2008). Rodar: A circulação dos jogadores de futebol brasileiros no exterior. *Horizontes Antropológicos, 14*(30), 21–65. https://doi.org/10.1590/S0104-71832008000200002.

Sader, E. (2002). *Quando novos personagens entraram em cena: Experiências, falas e lutas dos trabalhadores da Grande São Paulo (1970–80)*. Paz e Terra.

Teixeira, R. C. (2004). *Os perigos da paixão: Visitando jovens torcidas cariocas*. Annablume.

Toledo, L. H. (1996). *Torcidas organizadas de futebol*. Autores Associados.

Chapter 27
Narratives About Football Hooliganism in Brazil: (De)constructing the Label "Violent Supporter"

Felipe Tavares Paes Lopes

Introduction

Explosions of rage. Tacit codes of ethics. Caravans. Preventive arrests. Courts. Popular jury. Batons that tear the skin. Iron bars that sink skulls. Corrupt cops. Honest cops. Searching to be heard. Searching for recognition. Searching for favor. Excitement-seeking. Provocations between rival groups. Stonewalling. Labels that stigmatize. Official statistics. Scientific explanations. Journalistic narratives. Sensationalism. Humiliations that remain in the shadows. Lack of preparation of security forces. The carelessness of authorities. Complicity with violence. Security cameras everywhere. Remodeled stadiums. Seats that become weapons. Pepper gas that blinds momentarily. Rubber bullets that blind forever. Advocacy for stricter punishment. Criticism of the stringency of the law. Seminars on organized fans. Inadequate public policies. Public policies yet to be implemented. Meetings before derbies. Incidental meetings. Scheduled meetings. Hospitals. Surgeries. Candles burning next to the last thread of hope. Tears flowing at the son's wake. Congratulations to the policeman who killed a "bum". Theft of the flag. Theft of life. Last-minute alliances. Long-time enemies. Racist practices. Homophobic chants. International models for violence prevention. Ideals of masculinity. Ways of life execrated. Ways of life celebrated.

This tangle of actors (human and non-human) and situations are sometimes connected, sometimes disconnected, sometimes reconnected, producing what we usually call "football violence." This violence, therefore, does not correspond to a clearly delimited, fixed, and stable object. It corresponds to several objects that, in the public debate on the subject, are excluded, reinforced, and overlap in various narratives, which designate motivations, circumstances, victims, etc. In this chapter, I discuss some of these narratives, focusing on how they construct a specific character: the violent fan. To this end, I describe and interpret some of the main research results I have been carrying out since 2008, which analyzed laws, public policies, academic

F. T. P. Lopes (✉)
University of Sorocaba, Sorocaba, Brazil

productions, news reports, and interviews with members of *torcidas organizadas* (organized groups of supporters).

This interpretation, it should be noted, will be guided by the constructionist perspective. However, I will also use concepts from other theoretical and epistemological traditions. I will use these additional concepts as if they were useful tools to solve specific problems posed by that perspective. This is certainly an unorthodox procedure, subject to potentially problematic theoretical accommodations. After all, there is always the possibility of using a sledgehammer when, in fact, the nature of the problem requires a screwdriver. I consider, however, that the potential analytical advantages provided by the articulation of the concepts discussed here are worth the risks.

Having made this clarification, I present the structure of the chapter. The chapter is organized in three sections. In the first section, I discuss the role of language in the construction of football violence. I show, firstly, that this violence is the result of conventions and ensuing this, how the texts, figures, and images that form the narratives about it often contribute to turn it into a thing, into something objective, regardless of the observer. In the second one, I deal with a myth that is widespread in these narratives: that of non-violence, which makes one believe that the relationships established in the football universe are essentially peaceful. I also discuss how this idea gives rise to the stigmatization of fans (seen as) violent, legitimating, among other things, the expansion of penal punishment. In the third and last one, I focus on the construction of these fans. In it, I show that the label of violence falls mainly on a specific group: the organized fans. I also discuss some logical and social consequences of this stigmatization, such as the legitimation of the control of these fans and their exclusion from the decision-making bodies of the football spectacle organization.

From Convention to Reification: The Role of Language in the Construction of Violence in Football

A narrative is, roughly speaking, a discourse that describes a sequence of events (Thompson, 2000). A discourse that tells a story, like the one about football violence. As I will resume subsequently, there is no narrative that captures a single truth. Narratives can, of course, be fanciful or not. They may be well founded or not. They can be more or less reasonable. But they will always be constructions that necessarily depend on the eye of the narrator, on his or her categories of perception and evaluation of the social world. Constructions have effects on reality, contributing to perform it. After all, language is, as John Austin (1998) would say, an "instrument to do things," and not just to present our ideas to the outside. In this sense, it can be said that a narrative not only tells us how an event was, but also institutes it. It participates in its constitution, therefore.

But how exactly does this participation happen? To answer this question, we need to know what the main signature systems are and understand the consequences of each of them in the process of sense making. Depending on where they are conveyed, narratives about football violence include images as primary forms of communication. Images are very present in the media, especially in television programs, and tend to have a strong appeal on public opinion. For example, the images of the so-called Pacaembu Battleground[1] were shown hundreds of times, mobilizing a series of measures to improve security in stadiums. From then on, the repression against the organized groups of supporters was intensified. In turn, academic texts, official documents, journalistic articles, etc., tend to privilege written language, which operates mainly through argumentation (Spink, 2005). Language that sometimes is accompanied by numbers, which are used, for example, to show the growth of conflicts involving football fans.

Following the reflections of Íñiguez (2002) and Ibáñez (2005), we can say that written language has changed the ways of thinking and has had numerous effects on knowledge. This is not to say that, from it, we necessarily started to think better. But instead of that, we started to think differently. In the fifteenth century, writing (and reading, consequently) suffered a real revolution with the invention of a new technology of intelligence: the press. This developed thanks to printing techniques, originally elaborated by Johannes Gutenberg. Techniques that soon spread through the urban centers of Europe, having been explored by printing workshops, mostly set up as commercial companies (Thompson, 1998).

The development of the first printing presses and the subsequent advent of the printing industry not only produced new centers of symbolic power networks but impacted on the very nature of knowledge. In other words, it was not only an important vector for the diffusion of knowledge, but also modified the way of producing and presenting it. Modification that, in turn, allowed the establishment of science as we conceive it today. After all, the author is blurred on the printed page. A book, for example, makes authorial traces diffuse and almost invisible, helping to fix the knowledge—which, in turn, feeds the ideas of objectivity, reliability, and neutrality (Íñiguez, 2002; Ibáñez, 2005).

These ideas serve as the basis for the so-called ideology of representation, fundamental to the constitution of modern scientific rationality since it advocates the belief that valid knowledge can correctly reproduce reality. That it is a faithful translation of reality and, therefore, valid for all human beings, at all times.[2] In effect, through the lens of the "ideology of representation," we are led to perceive reality as observable facts or things that can be known through an appropriate method (Ibáñez, 2005). On

---

[1] Happened in the finals of the 1995 São Paulo Juniors Super Cup, after organized supporters of Palmeiras and São Paulo teams invaded the playing field and clashed with sticks, stones, and other artifacts, resulting in the death of a fan (Lopes, 2019).

[2] The discourse of science also constantly reinforces this ideology by using the impersonal ("it is observed," "it is concluded," "it is affirmed," etc.) and realistic ("to reveal," "to uncover," "to evince," etc.) language, which makes one believe in the existence of a reality independent of an observer.

the one hand, there would be, therefore, violence-in-itself and, on the other, violence-for-us, that is, its idea or representation. And science would have the mission to bring the latter closer to the former insofar as possible.

However, following the reflections of Ibáñez (2005), we may say that we are the ones who create violence based on concrete social relations, by agreeing that certain practices should be classified as such. Notwithstanding this, would violence be reduced to the idea that we make of it? To its representation? No, because, in this case, we would fall into radical idealism. And, between Plato's certainties and Protagoras' relativizations, I prefer, as does the above-mentioned author, the latter. Allow me to explain: Constructionism starts from the basic idea that we are the ones who construct the world, that is, that everything we consider real was socially constructed. This means that violence itself is a social construction and that, therefore, it would be nothing if we did not agree on what it is (Gergen & Gergen, 2011). Therefore, from this perspective, there is no such thing as the essence of violence, which we could access through reason. This does not mean, however, that the punch, the club, the shot, and the pain do not concretely exist. Evidently, all these things exist! But they exist because we construct them as such, collectively and through "a long historical process intimately related to our characteristics as human beings" (Ibáñez, 2001, p. 258, our translation).

By refuting an essentialist conception of violence, constructionism leads us to question, consequently, any kind of reading that reifies football confrontations. That converts them into things, regardless of the operations that we articulate in the process of construction of their knowledge (Lopes & Cordeiro, 2018). To (de)reify these confrontations, constructionism invites us, therefore, to ask ourselves how they were effectively constructed. To historicize them, in short. Not in the sense of checking how, over the years, they have been interpreted and treated—as if what changed were only the looks on them and the proposed solutions; never their "essence" or "nature." But in the sense of verifying the conditions that made it possible to think them (and, consequently, to produce them). What were the practices, relations, and institutions that enabled the constitution of a field of knowledge around them?

As I have already suggested, in addition to science, the media has been a central actor in the constitution of this field and in the process of reification of violence, with the difference that it has progressively included images as primary sources of communication (Spink, 2005). This information is particularly relevant for the analysis of this process because, petrified in an image (moving or not), football conflicts appear dissociated from the processes and contradictions (social, cultural, historica,l and/or economic) that gave rise to them. They appear, therefore, as an autonomous, independent reality, that is, as a fact: ordered and finished (Chauí, 2006). This form of appearance, however, is not necessarily an illusion, a false reality, so to speak, but an abstract, immediate reality, since the way in which the referred conflicts are produced remains in the twilight.

The photo or video of a crowd of fans advancing against a group of police officers, for example, gives rise to the idea that the first are "barbarians," who oppose law and order. But its meaning may change radically if we find out that this advance was a response to the brutal beating and murder by the police forces of a black fan, mistaken for a thug. In this second case, the image formed of the conflict, as the outcome of the indignation with the institutionalized racism in the repressive state apparatus, is more clearly articulated to its conditions of production.

Like images, numbers—widely disseminated not only by the press, but also by scientific literature and public authorities—tend to be reified, that is, to be deemed as things. This perception distorts what they really are: the product of human action. An action that involves two choices, which are often related to each other: the sample (what to count) and the method (how to count) (Best, 2003). Let us begin with the sample. To measure football violence, we must first define and delimit this phenomenon. For example: Does it include only physical aggression or also chants and shouts in support of violence? What about the various forms of discrimination in the stands, should they be included? What about social injustices and inequalities? Suppose we agree that the phenomenon of violence refers only to bodily and armed clashes. Then the subsequent question is: How to count them? Faced with this methodological difficulty, we might have to redefine the sample and opt to count only the most visible and tragic results of these conflicts: homicides. But, again, we would fall into a problem of definition: What is a football-related homicide? Only that which occurs inside the stadium? But what about those that happen outside? What about those that happen inside and are the result of structural problems? Suppose we agree to count only those involving clashes between fans: What if they have other motivations, such as disputes related to drug trafficking? Again, wouldn´t we would fall into a problem of definition? And, to make matters worse, of method: how to count these homicides? Through the media? But how many of them may simply not have been reported, especially those that occurred far from the major football centers? By official data? But data in relation to what? For those cases that were tried and solved? But the investigative and judicial work is slow, and wouldn't many events be left out? Should we then include those that are under investigation? But what if it later turns out that some of them had nothing to do with football?

As we can see, the numbers regarding football violence, as any numbers, are the product of a series of conventions. It happens that, as I already anticipated, they tend to be reified and to be deemed as a reliable translation of reality. Far from being just an epistemological issue, this reification has serious social and political implications for the public debate around such violence. After all, transformed into things, into a being with its own independence, the numbers tend to become fetishes as well, determining our own actions.

By this, I do not mean that statistical productions are useless. On the contrary, they are valuable instruments for the elaboration of diagnoses of violence and, consequently, for the establishment of more adequate public security policies. However, they need to be read critically, which means problematizing–questioning their production conditions. And it is precisely from the problematizing that we can dismantle the texts, numbers, and images responsible for creating the figure of the violent supporter. To problematize, it should be stressed, does not mean simply to make problematic that which is taken for granted, natural, but also to understand how and why something has acquired the status of unquestionable evidence (Ibáñez, 2001), such as some myths related to violence in football, discussed in the next section.

From the Myth of Non-Violence to the Stigma of Violence: Narratives About Football Confrontations

A myth is usually understood as a narrative about the origin of the world and of the human being, about the origin of things: a narrative that denies reality, while explaining and justifying it. The discussion about confrontations in the universe of football very often conveys arguments, points of views and beliefs that contribute to crystallize a myth in the social imaginary: that the relations established in this universe are peaceful. Based on the analysis of Chauí (2006) on violence, I understand that this myth is fundamentally elaborated by two procedures: The first is exclusion. A procedure that makes believe that those supporters who get involved in bodily and armed confrontations are non-supporters. Bandits disguised as supporters. Thus, violence would be practiced by external agents, persons who do not participate in the supporter collectivity.

This argument is refuted by some football scholars, such as Alabarces (2012). When discussing the reasons for violence in football, the Argentine sociologist argues, among other things, that violence is an everyday thing, that is, it can be observed in the broader set of social relations. Similarly, Chauí (2006) states that Brazilian society is structurally authoritarian, that is, authoritarianism constitutes its way of being and organizing, and is not, therefore, only a feature of the dictatorships that marked our history, such as the Estado Novo (1937–1945) and the civil–military dictatorship (1964–1985). According to the philosopher, we often think that authoritarianism emerges only from time to time, with the rise of a dictatorial government, marked, among other things, by the limitation of party pluralism, media censorship and violence against insurgents. However, as we know, from the colonial period until just before the end of the Empire, Brazil lived a production regime based on slavery. This regime, according to the philosopher, has reflexes until today. In other words, current Brazilian society retains the traces of slavery, and, for this reason, its spaces are strongly hierarchical or verticalized. In these spaces, the relations are, basically, of command and obedience, between a superior and an inferior, and people are not equal in rights and feelings.

In this authoritarian context, some social groups systematically have more chances and opportunities of intervening in the course of events than others (Thompson, 2000). These various forms of domination (of class, gender, race, etc.) that permeate Brazilian society sustain economic exploitation and result in social inequalities that are not seen as violent because we are so used to them. They are very naturalized in our daily practices. According to Spink and Spink (2005), naturalizing means "treating something as normal, as given, as part of everyday life; as obvious as the morning sun and the afternoon rain" (p. 8, own translation). Our inequalities, social psychologists follow, remain as such precisely because they have become normal and unproblematic. That is why we do not recognize them as a form of violence. In fact, violence, from the point of view of hegemonic forces, is mainly present in the practices that aim precisely to transform these inequalities, such as protests, strikes, and picket lines.

Corroborating this line of thought, Galtung (1985) notes that discussions of security tend to ignore what he has termed structural violence, which "is built into the structure, and manifests itself as unequal power, and consequently as distinct life chances" (p. 36, own translation). Not surprisingly, for the author, this violence is silent and invisible. It seems as natural as the air we breathe. In the universe of football, it would express itself in several ways, such as, for example, in the exclusion of the working class from stadiums, due to the (prohibitive) ticket prices, or in the exclusion of fans in general from the public policy-making process geared at them. Thus, as these exclusions tend not to be recognized (or agreed upon) by the media as forms of violence, the ruling group (public and sports authorities) tends not to be perceived as a direct promoter of violence in football—at most, it would be an indirect promoter, to the extent that it would not be able to stop the advance of confrontations between supporters.

Alabarces (2012) also argues that violence is legitimate within the football universe. This is an information that almost never appears in the public debate on the topic. Saying that it is legitimate does not mean, however, that it is legal, but that it has consensus. As the author notes, no poll would show that fans who engage in confrontations have the support of others. However, through ethnographic research, it is possible to verify that these groups are considered as being those that defend the honor of their community and clubs. Thus, while they are feared, they are also admired and respected. It should be noted as well that the fan who claims to repudiate violence is the one who also often extols it in war cries and applauds the police when they violently repress rival fans. He is the same one who chants homophobic and sexist songs. However, as I have just suggested, since the various forms of discrimination are not seen (or agreed upon) as violent, this supporter is cleared.

Sexist and homophobic violence are denied in the football universe through the praise of virility. Football is a privileged space for the dissemination and affirmation of an "aggressive masculinity," which states that, to be a real man, one must endure adversity (Alabarces, 2012). In this context, the domination of men over women is disguised under the image of protection. Seen as fragile, the latter have their field of action limited, not being able to perform a series of activities that men do. For example, in games considered to be the most dangerous, women cannot travel in the caravans. Homosexuals, in turn, cannot even manifest affection for each other. A kiss between two men in the middle of the bleachers, for example, can provoke hostile reactions to them. Simultaneously, homophobic shouts coming from all sections of the stadiums tend to be seen as part of the fan culture—as a harmless joke with no major consequences.

The second procedure for the elaboration of the non-violence myth is the one of distinction between the essential and the accidental. If the football universe is, by nature, non-violent, then violence can only be an unnatural action. An epidemic would invade this universe to destroy its "good nature." Not by chance, the fan (considered) violent is often constructed, by the media and governmental documents, through the metaphor of nature. In this metaphor, the social world is presented from a biological point of view, as if it suffered from a disease, in this case, the (purported) violence practiced by this fan who, in turn, is represented as a "foreign body" that must be extracted from the "social body." He would be a "virus," an "excrescence," and a "disease" (Lopes, 2013, 2019; Lopes & Reis, 2017).

A "disease" of current football—both the narratives conveyed in the media and in government documents express a kind of collective amnesia of conflicts existing in the past (Lopes, 2013, 2019; Lopes & Reis, 2017). It is forgotten (or omitted) that Brazilian football was born marked by racism, by sexism, and by classism. It is also forgotten (or omitted) that there are records of confusions and fights between fans already in the early days of this football, as indicated by studies in historical perspective, such as the one developed by de Hollanda (2009). The past of Brazilian football is usually constructed as a period of peace, as a kind of paradise lost. Nonetheless, the current situation tends to be dramatized, which contributes to draw attention to the extreme and heinous character of conflicts involving fans, suggesting that they are unacceptable and morally intolerable.

In this scenario, the supporter (considered) violent would be that element that would disturb the (purported) rational and non-violent social order of football. The idea that the fan is irrational blurs or, at least, obscures the logic of conflicts inside and outside the stadiums. It erases the ideas, for example, that these conflicts are related, as we have just seen, to a specific ideal of masculinity and that they are legitimate within the football universe, or even, according to Alabarces (2012), that they produce adrenaline. They are exciting and pure desire. And that, as with the most powerful drugs, they can be addictive. It also blurs the idea that, according to the Argentine sociologist, they contribute to building collectives and generate communities and ties of solidarity and friendship. They provide, therefore, a sense of belonging not found in other social spaces, outside of organized groups of supporters and, finally, that they are "power constructions." They are, therefore, an exercise of demonstration of strength.

According to Alabarces (2012), it is precisely because these conflicts have a rationality that they can be explained and avoided. It is interesting to note, however, that the idea of irrationality often encompasses the entire fan mass. Not surprisingly, football and public authorities increasingly create obstacles to its formation—for instance, sectoring and chaining the bleachers. The idea that the supporter mass is irrational and potentially violent is quite widespread in the press and authorities and has three consequences. First, the denial of the guilt of its members (supporters and/or police officers) in a violent action, for if irrationality is a natural characteristic of mass behavior, then we cannot hold it responsible for it and second, the denial of its voice. After all, for the same reason, the mass would have nothing relevant to say. Third, the legitimization of measures aimed at increasing control over it. After all, if supporters, in the mass, act irrationally, then they need to be rigorously controlled and watched (Lopes & Cordeiro, 2015).

The process of pathologizing the (so-called) violent supporter, which positions him as irrational, as we have just seen, constitutes a way of stigmatizing him. According to Goffman (1988), the notion of stigma refers to the reduction of a person (or social group) to some physical, moral, or social "disadvantage" ascribed to him/her. The stigmatized person is therefore reduced to a spoiled or diminished person. The main effect of this process is that it undermines any credit given to the stigmatized person. This is someone who should not have a voice, not be taken seriously. Not surprisingly, the defense of penal stigmatization is practically hegemonic. Apart from the exception of the academic field and entities representing organized groups of supporters, such as the *Associação Nacional das Torcidas Organizadas do Brasil*—ANATORG (Brazilian National Association of Organized Groups of Supporters), there are almost no proposals for dialog and inclusion of fan groups considered "problematic" in the development of violence prevention policies, as can be seen in Germany, Belgium, and Colombia, for example (Teixeira & Lopes, 2018). On the contrary, there are many calls to ban the "troublemakers" forever from the stadiums, as if they were irredeemable and unassimilable by society, a theme that will be deepened in the next section.

Dehumanization, Exclusion, and Social Control: Stigmatized Fans and the Effects of Stigma

The stigma of violence implies, as I have already suggested, a separation, clearly Manichean, between an "us," civilized, and a "them," "barbarians." But who is the "them"? Internationally, fans (labeled as) violent are the members of the ultra's groups, the *barra bravas* and, mainly, the *hooligan* "firms," which lived their peak in the 1980s, in England. The association of these latter groups with the issue of violence is so strong that football confrontations are often referred to as hooliganism. In Brazil, this label falls mainly on members of organized groups of supporters. These associations emerged in the late 1960s and early 1970s, claiming autonomy vis-à-vis the clubs and adopting a new style of cheering, simply to set themselves aside from the previous organized groupings (Teixeira, 2003).

Nowadays, the universe of organized groups of supporters constitutes a microcosm within the macrocosm of football—a social field, to employ the concept coined by Bourdieu (1993). As in any social field, this universe is relatively autonomous because it depicts, rather than reflects, external pressures and demands, which are retranslated under a specific form. In other words, it is a universe endowed with its own laws and tropes. For example, stealing materials from rival groups, such as flags, tends to confer prestige. And the group that has its material stolen, in the quest to recover their lost prestige, must recover this material or steal something from the group that stole it. In this sense, it can be said that organized supporters follow, to some extent, their own rules of conduct, and not those of the society in general, which, in this case, would "demand" a police report (Lopes, 2019).

Within this context, organized fans build their own definitions of violence, which in some cases are in opposition to those conveyed in other social fields, such as sports journalism. These definitions participate, therefore, in the disputes around the demarcation and delimitation of the violence phenomenon. However, as members of such groups tend to occupy a subordinate position in the public debate on football violence—being deemed as discreditable people due to the stigma they carry—these definitions rarely end up prevailing (Lopes, 2013, 2019). The fact that they do not prevail, however, does not exempt us from the responsibility of analyzing them, as they are part of an alternative discourse on the referred violence, which contributes to dismantle some ready-made ideas about it and to illuminate new meanings.

To better understand the positions and viewpoints conveyed in this alternative discourse, it is worth noting that clashes between organized supporters tend to be ritualized, in the same way that the funk dance, the rap "crowd" or even the *chiaraje,* a village where fights are held with a set date in the Andean cultural region (Sodré, 2006). Without losing sight of the specificities of clashes between fans, which cannot be disregarded in a deeper analysis, it can be stated that, following the logic of these rituals, their goal, in principle, is not the elimination of the rival,[3] but to overcome them. Because its permanence is what ensures the continuity of the "competition" between organized groups of supporters. Not surprisingly, the use of firearms and lynching tends to be condemned (at least at a discursive level) even by the groups deemed to be more violent.

At the same time, engaging in bodily clashes tends to be naturalized within these groupings, seen as part of the "rooting" culture. Even those who engage in such clashes and demonstrate ample resilience, stand firm even in the face of the greatest adversities, acquire *status,* essential to climb in their power structure. In this sense, the members of organized groups of supporters tend to displace the meaning of violent supporter from the one who engages in confrontations to one who acts with "cowardice," to use a native expression. For example, hitting the opponent with punches and kicking is not seen as a form of violence, since the "exchange" (of blows) is seen as a legitimate procedure. However, if a group of ten fans surround a rival, who is alone and unprotected, assaulting him with sticks and stones, this action is deemed illegitimate, worthy of condemnation. It is seen as "cowardly."

Organized fans also tend, at different levels, to denounce exclusion and oppression practices as forms of violence. Protests against ticket prices or against repression in the bleachers are not rare, for example. Simply to illustrate this, in 2016, the organized group of supporters Gaviões da Fiel held a series of protests, inside and outside the stands, against the dominant forces of Brazilian football (Rede Globo, the Brazilian Football Confederation-CBF, the São Paulo Football Federation-FPF, the Military

---

[3] This does not mean that, eventually, "excesses" may not occur, resulting in serious bodily injury and death. Nor does it mean that some clashes between organized groups of supporters are not effectively aimed at the elimination of a rival—including internal ones, as happens when there is a dispute for power within the same grouping.

Police-PM and the Public Prosecutor's Office), as well as against the "lunch scandal," related to the diversion of funds for food in public schools in the state of São Paulo. Quite frequently, these protests have led to a violent reaction of the public power against these supporter groups, as occurred in the abovementioned example (Lopes & Hollanda, 2018).

By denouncing these practices, organized groups of supporters become a central actor in the fight against the exclusion of poor fans from the football spectacle. For this reason, I understand that the stigma of violence cast upon them tends to bring negative consequences for the abovementioned fan and not only for their members. I explain discredited, organized supporters are not considered in the policy construction processes for football spectacles. Consequently, their demands tend not to be met.[4] Thus, as part of them are at the service of the poor supporter, the latter ends up being harmed (Lopes, 2019).

At the same time, it is possible to hypothesize that the process of stigmatization of organized groups of supporters is the by-product of a broader stigmatization process: that of poverty. After all, these groups are mostly composed of young men who share, in the relationships established among themselves, a "peripheral" way of life, even if they do not necessarily belong to the working class (Toledo, 2012). Thus, organized groups of supporters would be targeted because they are popular associations. Because their members usually are the ones stigmatized: young, poor, black or, at least, people who share these people's way of life. To make things worse, organized groups of supporters are associations that, as I just noted, often represent the interests of the subordinated classes. In this sense, it is also possible to hypothesize that the attack on their image should be seen through the lenses of a class struggle. A struggle which, it should be remembered, is not unilateral, but involves all sides. It lies both in the protests of subordinate groups against the dominant forces and in the silent oppression that the latter impose on the former (Chauí, 2008).

Another effect of the stigmatization process of organized groups of supporters is that it contaminates the image of all associations and their members. A close look at the universe of these organized groups suggests significant differences between the various existing groupings and their relationship with violence. Although all tend to admit the possibility of a physical clash in extreme situations (when an ambush occurs), there are those groups that tend to reject the deliberate pursuit for this type of clash, and there are those that tend to make the provision for them a "moral obligation" (Teixeira & Lopes, 2018). However, despite these differences, the stigma of violence ends up interconnecting all organized supporters and all associations in a deteriorated collective identity: that of violence.

This process of contagion, however, is not limited to the interior of the organized groups of supporters' universe. On the contrary, it overflows beyond that. After all, stigma has the potential to produce what was called "osmotic contagion," which refers to the fear of contamination by social interaction (Amaral, 1994). Due to the

---

[4] Which does not mean that they are not necessarily attended to. To keep Corinthians' example in mind: due to pressure from the club's organized groups, the Board of Directors decided to remove the seats from the northern sector of the Corinthians Arena, where they are located.

fear of this contamination, it is possible to raise the hypothesis that other actors have avoided supporting these groups (at least publicly) because interaction with their members is seen as harmful. Furthermore, it may be driving away "well-meaning" supporters from the associations. Fans do not want to be deemed as delinquents or become one. At the same time, they may be attracting "ill-intentioned" fans to them. Fans who wish to commit criminal acts or simply be recognized for it (Lopes, 2019). In this sense, we can say that the stigma of violence is not only a violence against the fans themselves, but something that helps turn them into the very thing that society, in general, disapproves of.

Final Considerations

In this chapter, I analyzed some narratives present in the public debate about violence in football, focusing on how the character "violent fan" is constructed discursively. In doing so, I sought to show, among other things, that these narratives are constructed from texts, images, and figures that tend to reify the phenomenon of violence in football. I also sought to show that they disseminate a myth: the one that says that the football universe is structurally peaceful. Finally, I indicated that they stigmatize a specific group of supporters—the organized ones—legitimating the expansion of control over them, as well as their exclusion from the decision-making bodies of professional football.

That said, I reinforce that this debate occurs in an asymmetric space of positions, where some social groups, such as public authorities, have much more chances to assert their positions than others, converting them into laws and public policies. In turn, social groups such as organized groups of supporters are rarely seen as reliable sources of information and reflection. Not surprisingly, they tend to be excluded from legitimate places of speech, such as commissions designed to draft laws (Lopes, 2013, 2019). Indeed, I conclude this chapter by arguing that, to democratize the debate in question, it is necessary to intervene in its very structure, providing all social groups involved in it with the opportunity to participate in its directions, in other words, to participate in the agreements and decisions about the production process of the football spectacle.

References

Alabarces, P. (2012). *Crónicas del aguante: Fútbol, violencia y política.* Capital Intelectual.

Amaral, L. (1994). Mercado de trabalho e deficiência. *Revista Brasileira De Educação Especial, 1*(2), 127–136.

Austin, J. L. (1998). *Cómo hacer cosas con palabras.* Paidós.

Best, J. (2003). Audiences evaluate statistics. In J. Best & D. Loseke (Eds.), *Social problems: Constructionist readings* (pp. 43–50). Walter de Gruyter.

Bourdieu, P. (1993). *Questões de sociologia.* Marco Zero.

Chauí, M. (2006). *Simulacro e poder: Uma análise da mídia*. Perseu Abramo.
Chauí, M. (2008). *O que é ideologia* (2nd ed.). Brasiliense.
Galtung, J. (1985). *Sobre la paz*. Fontamara.
Gergen, K. J., & Gergen, M. (2011). *Reflexiones sobre la construcción social*. Paidós.
Goffman, E. (1988). *Estigma: Notas sobre a manipulação da identidade deteriorada* (4th ed.). Guanabara.
Hollanda, B. B. (2009). *O clube como vontade e representação: O jornalismo esportivo e a formação das torcidas organizadas de futebol no Rio de Janeiro*. Rio de Janeiro: 7 Letras.
Ibáñez, T. (2001). *Municiones para disidentes: Realidad-verdad-política*. Gedisa.
Ibáñez, T. (2005). *Contra la dominación: Variaciones sobre la salvaje exigencia de libertad que brota del relativismo y de las consonancias entre Castoriadis, Foucault, Rorty e Serres*. Gedisa.
Ibáñez, T. (2015). *Anarquismo é movimento: Anarquismo, neoanarquismo e pós-anarquismo*. Intermezzo; Imaginário.
Iñiguez, L. (2002). Construcionismo social. In J. B. Martins, N. Hammouti, & L. Iñiguez (Eds.), *Temas em análise institucional e em construcionismo social* (pp. 99–180). Rima.
Lopes, F. T. P. (2013). Dimensões ideológicas do debate público acerca da violência no futebol brasileiro. *Revista Brasileira de Educação Física e Esporte, 27*(4), 597–612. https://www.scielo. br/pdf/rbefe/v27n4/v27n4a08.pdf
Lopes, F. T. P. (2019). *Violência: ideologia na construção de um problema social*. CRV.
Lopes, F. T. P., & Cordeiro, M. P. (2015). Futebol, massa e poder: Reflexões sobre a "teoria do contágio". *Revista de Psicologia Política, 15*(34), 479–495. http://pepsic.bvsalud.org/pdf/rpp/ v15n34/v15n34a03.pdf
Lopes, F. T. P., & Cordeiro, M. P. (2018). Comunicação, violência e problemas sociais: Uma leitura construcionista. *Organicom, 15*(28), 223–235. https://doi.org/10.11606/issn.2238-2593.organi com.2018.150583
Lopes, F. T. P., & Hollanda, B. B. (2018). "Ódio eterno ao futebol moderno": Poder, dominação e resistência nas arquibancadas dos estádios da cidade de São Paulo. *Movimento, 24*(2), 207–232. https://doi.org/10.1590/TEM-1980-542X2018v240202
Lopes, F. T. P., & Reis, H. H. B. (2017). Ideologia, futebol e violência: Uma análise do relatório "Preservar o espetáculo, garantindo a segurança e o direito à cidadania". *Arquivos Brasileiros de Psicologia, 69*(3), 36–51. http://pepsic.bvsalud.org/pdf/arbp/v69n3/04.pdf
Sodré, M. (2006). *Sociedade, mídia e violência* (2nd ed.). Sulina.
Spink, M. J. (2005). O poder das imagens na naturalização das desigualdades: os crimes no cotidiano da mídia jornalística. In P. Spink, & M. J. Spink (Eds.), *Práticas cotidianas e a naturalização da desigualdade* (pp. 17–41). Cortez.
Spink, P., & Spink, M. J. (2005). Introdução. In P. Spink, & M. J. Spink (Eds.), *Práticas cotidianas e a naturalização da desigualdade* (pp. 7–16). Cortez.
Teixeira, R. C. (2003). *Os perigos da paixão: visitando jovens torcidas cariocas*. Annablume.
Teixeira, R. C., & Lopes, F. T. P. (2018). Reflexões sobre o "Projeto Torcedor" alemão: produzindo subsídios para o debate acerca da prevenção da violência no futebol brasileiro a partir de uma perspectiva sociopedagógica. *Revista de Antropologia, 6*(3), 130–161. https://doi.org/10.11606/ 2179-0892.ra.2018.152037
Thompson, J. B. (1998). *A mídia e a modernidade: Uma teoria social da mídia* (8th ed.). Vozes.
Thompson, J. B. (2000). *Ideologia e cultura moderna: Teoria social e crítica na era dos meios de comunicação de massa* (4th ed.). Vozes.
Toledo, L. H. (2012). Políticas da corporalidade: Sociabilidade torcedora entre 1990–2010. In B. B. Hollanda, J. M. C., L. H. Toledo, & V. A. Melo (Eds.), *A torcida brasileira* (pp. 122–158). Rio de Janeiro: 7 Letras.

Chapter 28
The Experience of Cheering in (So-Called) "Modern Football"

Silvio Ricardo da Silva and Priscila Augusta Ferreira Campos

Football emerges as a practice of modernity,[1] developing new body behaviors and generating new habits (Elias & Dunning, 1992). Throughout its existence, it has been undergoing changes in rules, tactics, legislation, practice sites, athletes and supporters behaviors, and use and exchange value, among others.

Since the 1990s, we have observed a volume of impacting transformations in the Brazilian football scene, as regards the debate on its modernization, having as characteristics the introduction of new managerial guidelines, the revision of sports legislation, the conversion of football into a globalized product, its increasing approximation with the business world, and the physical and symbolic changes in its stadiums (Cruz, 2005; Curi, 2013; Giulianotti, 2002; Mascarenhas, 2013; Proni, 1998).

The football commercialization forced the clubs to create marketing departments, with the purpose of dealing with their image and the image of their athletes as potential brands. Thus, the football experience started to be commercialized in advertising boards, shirts sponsorship, television commercials, competitions costs, and sale of souvenirs with the club's image (Giulianotti, 2002).

Linked to this discussion, another one emerged concerning the need to control violence at football stadiums, particularly in as much as the presence of organized supporters is concerned (Reis & Escher, 2006). Furthermore, the need to improve the infrastructure of Brazilian stadiums—mostly scrapped and poorly managed by the local government—has also been discussed. The lack of stadiums' infrastructure

---

[1] According to Barros (2001, p. 23), we understand modernity in terms of "'modern consciousness', resulting and structuring a new politics, a new aesthetics, a new ethics. more than transformations of the material bases of societies, it is a kind of utopian project in which work, order, time and space, transformed by new knowledge, new technologies and a new normative order, produce modern man."

S. R. da Silva (✉)
Federal University of Minas Gerais, Belo Horizonte, Brazil

P. A. F. Campos
Federal University of Ouro Preto, Ouro Preto, Brazil

in terms of cleaning and equipment such as bars, restrooms, and parking lots and the lack of maintenance of the electrical, hydraulic, and structural systems were factors that contributed to the low presence of supporters (La Corte, 2007).

Having as a prerogative the need to improve sociability standards in public and private spaces of the different sporting practices that congregate a large audience, in 2003, the Fan Defense Statute came into force (Law No. 10,671, May 15, 2003; Law No. 12,299, July 27, 2010). Comprising 45 articles arranged in 12 chapters, the statute has as one of its main objectives to mitigate the "issue of violence." At that time, much was discussed about its effectiveness and efficiency (Campos et al., 2008; Curi et al., 2008; Rigo et al., 2006), since it had as its parameter the *European* supporter ethos, especially as regards the abolition of the space called "general"[2] and the installation of numbered chairs in the stands, so that people could watch the games sitting down and in the appointed place.

The debate on the modernization of Brazilian football took a new turn when Brazil was elected, in 2007, host country for the 2014 FIFA World Cup. What can be observed is that, in the name of this event, a new way of seeing, thinking, and managing Brazilian football was initiated. In the name of comfort and safety, stadiums were transformed into arenas and the supporters, into customers. The justification was that Brazilian football needed to be "modern," with modernity being understood and described "as in Europe" (Curi, 2013).

The choice of Brazil to host the 2014 World Cup gave rise to a series of discussions and controversies in the society at large, especially concerning the choice of host cities and the construction and renovation of stadiums (Campos & Amaral, 2013; Campos, 2016; Damo, 2012). In total, seven stadiums were (re)built, and five more were built. In addition to the high financial investment, there was also an investment in the Brazilian supporter's "procedure," from the way he acquires the ticket to his commuting to the stadium and the behavior he should adopt there, before, during, and after the matches.

A few years after the mega event, we have an important distance that helps us reflect on this planned modernization of Brazilian football and its consequences for the greatest asset of this sport: the supporters.

This chapter aims to report and analyze the experiences of cheering in two distinct contexts: Valencia, in Spain, and Belo Horizonte/MG, in Brazil, more specifically at Ciutat de València and Mineirão stadiums.

In the football globalization conjuncture, we saw the European football discourse as a reference, a way of "becoming" expressed in the speech of the most diverse Brazilian football players. Furthermore, a survey conducted by *Stochos Sports Entertainment,* in 2013,[3] whose objective was to measure the Brazilian supporter's sympathy for clubs abroad, pointed out that, in Brazil, there was a significant increase

---

[2] The "general area" was a space, with no seats, no sectorization and no coverage, located around and at the same level of the field, in which supporters could follow the team's plays. It was usually the cheapest ticket in the stadium.

[3] Research accessed through the *blog* Teoria dos Jogos. Available at <http://globoesporte.globo.com/blogs/special-blog/teoria-dos-jogos/post/sympathy-for-exterior-clubs.html>. Accessed on 14/2/2019.

in the number of these supporters, being Spain the great favorite. It was heard in this survey, a sample of 8345 Brazilians from 16 years old.

Therefore, the choice for these two contexts arose: the proclaimed European football as well as the Brazilian appropriation of this model. That is, we chose to analyze the manifestations of cheering and the procedures adopted at a peripheral stadium within a global football and, on the other hand, by a global stadium within a peripheral football.

Although we understand the diversity that exists in Europe and in each country of that continent, and the different ways of experiencing football established in each region, we acknowledge that there is a hegemonic discourse that associates the concept of Europe and European football, excluding its idiosyncrasies and linking this image to the *ethos of* the Champions League.

To achieve the proposed objectives, we conducted a qualitative research of exploratory-descriptive type. As data collection instruments, we made participant observations, noted in a field notebook, which were subsequently examined in the light of the content analysis technique. Participated in this study men and women, aged over 18 years old, present in the Ciutat de València and Mineirão stadiums, on the days of games that had, respectively, Levante Unión Deportiva and Cruzeiro Esporte Clube teams as hosts. The field research in Ciutat de València stadium occurred during the year 2015 and in Mineirão stadium during the years from 2012 to 2014.

This chapter is organized as follows: First, we will discuss the social meaning of the football stadium not only for the city, but also for the clubs and football itself, and how much it is subject and object of urban transformations. Then, we will discuss the two stadiums studied, and then we will present and analyze the supporters manifestations in these two contexts. Finally, we will weave the final considerations, resuming the reflections about the supporter in face of the studied realities, perhaps implying new researches and positions on other realities.

The Space to Cheer

Stadiums, due to their size and architecture, have great prominence in the urban landscape, being a spatial and symbolic reference. Some authors (Bale, 1993; Bale & Moen, 1995; Gaffney & Bale, 2004; Mascarenhas, 2013) argue that the stadium should be seen, first of all, as a social microcosm. John Bale is a pioneer of this thought when he states that changes in stadiums do not reflect only the sport development, but also the social transformations, since they show how society develops and reveals its preferences (Bale, 1993). In this sense, we can state that the manifestations of cheering are no exception to the rule, being contextualized in a time and space.

From this perspective, the stadiums are loaded with meanings and symbolism. We know that the change of meaning occurs through the appropriation process. According to Lefebvre (1978), the space appropriation is a dialectical process, based on a given sociocultural context, in which the individual relates to himself, to the other and to the space, producing in it physical and/or symbolic transformations, through modifications, additions, deletion, and/or overlapping between what had been previously proposed and what the subjects also propose.

We must take into consideration, however, that the place each stadium occupies within its city and in the imaginary of the population that attends it is different. We understand that the object itself has no life of its own; it is the society in which it is inserted that gives it symbolic meaning. Thus, the place becomes relevant because it modifies the general meaning of the objects, giving them a relative meaning, provisionally true and impossible elsewhere (Santos, 1996).

Based on some studies on the architectural, economic, and social models of evolution of European stadiums, Bale (1993) and Paramio et al. (2008) proposed a classification of stadiums divided into two periods, using England and Spain as parameters: modern stadiums and postmodern stadiums.

According to the authors, modern stadiums would be divided into three generations: (a) late nineteenth century until the early 1920s[4]; (b) early 1920s until the late 1940s[5]; (c) early 1950s until the late 1980s.[6] On the other hand, postmodern stadiums would be part of a fourth generation of stadiums that would have started in the 1990s, continuing until the present day. It is worth noting that (1) these periods are not watertight; (2) there are stadiums of all generations in use until today; (3) some stadiums originally from the third generation operate with the *ethos* of the fourth-generation stadiums. Paramio et al. (2008) mention as an example the Camp Nou—F.C. Barcelona—and Santiago Bernabéu—Real Madrid C.F.) stadiums.

Although there is no academic consensus[7] as to the classification of stadiums as postmodern, and also understanding that the term "postmodernity" requires further studies so as not to fall into the misunderstanding of its frenetic use,[8] Paramio et al. (2008) argue that stadiums of the modern period have gradually witnessed changes, on the part of architects and club owners, in relation to design and management

---

[4] They came with the emergence of the Football Association in 1863 and the passage from fields to stadiums, from where we see the definition of the boundaries between players and supporters. The architecture resembled that of factories and had wood as the main material. As examples: Newcastle United; Hillsborough, 1899, Sheffield Wednesday; Stamford Bridge, 1910, Chelsea F.C.; Old Trafford, 1910 (Bale, 1993; Paramio et al., 2008).

[5] Wars damaged the structure of many stadiums; for the reconstruction, the principle of stadium architecture was developed, with the separation of spectators by social class; there is coverage only in the place intended for the more well-to-do. As examples: Mestalla, 1923, Valencia F. C.; Sarrià, 1923, R.C.D. Espanyol; Barcelona, Les Corts stadium, 1922–1957 (Paramio et al., 2008).

[6] Their architecture is circular/oval, so that those present have a view of the whole; they have space for television broadcasting and reflectors; they enable diversity of use, even though games are their main livelihood. In Spain, this generation of stadiums also arrived through the reformulation of the old ones to host the 1982 World Cup. As examples: Camp Nou, 1957, Barcelona F. C.; Vicente Calderón, 1966, Atletico de Madrid; Ciudad de Valencia, 1969, Levante (Bale, 1993; Paramio et al., 2008).

[7] Some authors call it new stadiums, arenas, non-places (placeness), and stadia. This variation of naming sometimes occurs in the same text.

[8] We agree with Bale (1993) when he argues that there is a trend toward postmodernity in football. Although he acknowledges that the use of this word is emerging (current buzz word), he states that, the way football is developing, it becomes difficult not to use it.

of different types of sports buildings, at the same time that the signs of crisis of the Fordist model of capitalist production, in the 1970s, led to a new economic period (neoliberalism) that brought changes in terms of consumption, aesthetics, architecture, culture, and lifestyle of Western societies, which were also reflected in football and, consequently, in stadiums.

The new stadiums, with emphasis on comfort and safety, were reduced in size and seats started being sold as rare commodities. In addition to increasing the ticket price, clubs opted to reduce its sale at the box office to force supporters to buy the package for the entire season. It increased sectorization of the stadium with the advent of boxes and hospitality areas.[9] The increase in ticket prices and the decrease in stadium capacity caused the popular to be prevented from attending them (Bale, 1993; Cruz, 2005; Giulianotti, 2002; Paramio et al., 2008).

Based on these reflections about the social meaning of football stadiums, we will make a brief presentation of the two stadiums chosen for this study: Ciutat de València and Mineirão.

The Space of the *Granota* Twist[10]

The Ciutat de València Stadium belongs to Levante Unión Deportiva[11] and is located in the Orriols neighborhood (northern area of Valencia), on a 40 thousand square meter site. Although the first plans were made in the 1950s, the final design was not approved until ten years later, when construction began. The stadium was inaugurated on September 9, 1969, with a friendly match against Valencia Football Club (Mínguez, 2010, February 18).

The stadium, originally named Antonio Román, after the club's president at the time, had a capacity of 30,000 supporters; in the 1990s, however, with the insertion of chairs, that number fell to 25,352 supporters (Cortés, 2017, August 21). Later, the stadium was renamed Nou Estadi; however, in order to strengthen the club's bond with the city, it was renamed with its current name.

For almost 20 years, the Ciutat de València stadium remained in an urban void of difficult access, surrounded by gardens and open fields, having only the Monastery of San Miguel de los Reyes as neighbor. Only in the late 1990s and mid-2000s, with the growth of the region, an urbanization process took place, with the opening of access roads and the inauguration of a railway line[12] (Cortés, 2017, August 21; Mínguez, 2010, February 18).

---

[9] Hospitality areas are exclusive spaces (lofts, cabins, restaurants, bar, among others) intended to entertain clients and build relationships in an informal setting.

[10] *Granota* in Valencian is the same as frog. According to the supporters, they were so nicknamed because the club played in the 1930s on a pitch that was in the bed of the Turia River (opposite the San Pio V museum in Valencia), in an area in which there were a large number of frogs and toads.

[11] It should be noted that before the City of Valencia stadium, Levente U. D. played at the Cabañal field and then at the Vallejo stadium, where they played until the current stadium was inaugurated.

[12] Corresponds to a light rail vehicle.

The Ciutat de València stadium was inaugurated in the third generation of stadiums of the modern era. During the 2015–2016 season, Levante announced the renovation of their stadium, planned to take place in stages, thus introducing it into the postmodern era of stadiums[13] (Cortés, 2017, August 21).

The Space to Cheer for the *Raposa*[14]

On September 5, 1965, amidst the dust of the construction works, the gates of Mineirão were opened to the public. In 1959, the project for the construction of the so-called Minas Gerais Stadium had been started, a public stadium, which was now inaugurated, with capacity for 130 thousand supporters, being the second-largest indoor football stadium in the world.[15] It was intended to host the games of the local teams: América Futebol Clube, Clube Atlético Mineiro, and Cruzeiro Esporte Clube. Its construction took place in Pampulha, an area of urban expansion of the city of Belo Horizonte, designed by architects Oscar Niemeyer and Lúcio Costa at the request of the mayor Juscelino Kubitschek, in the 1940s.[16]

The stadium, deemed a grandiose undertaking, of great architectural grandeur and beauty, drew attention to the Minas Gerais people's entrepreneurial capacity. Its main differentials were the covered bleachers, the ease of evacuation and a higher number of drinking fountains and toilets (dos Santos, 2005). The Mineirão was guided by the idea of monumentality and grandeur (for housing a large capacity of people), in a period in which Minas Gerais football needed to establish itself before Brazil, specifically Rio de Janeiro and São Paulo.

In December 2010, 45 years after its opening, the Mineirão was closed for renovation to meet FIFA standards to host World Cup matches. Re-inaugurated as the "New Mineirão," the stadium became part of the public–private partnership, whose administrator is the company Minas Arena. Architecturally, an 80 thousand m^2 esplanade was incorporated into its external part, between the street and the stadium, containing spaces for shops and restaurants. It was designed with two functions: Crowd dispersion and the opening of a leisure area geared toward the consumption of products both on match days and on other days of the year. One should highlight the reduction to 64 thousand seats and the elimination of the general area.

During the renovation period, the clubs from Belo Horizonte signed individual contracts with the company Minas Arena and with the administrators of another stadium in the capital city so that they could hold their matches as the home team

---

[13] For more information, watch the institutional video La nueva cara del Ciutat de València tras la futura remodelación. Available at <www.youtube.com/watch?v=e0DpjznO5gg>. Accessed on 14/2/2019.

[14] *Raposa* (fox) is the Cruzeiro's mascot. The club's two training centers are called "toca da raposa" (fox den) by the *cruzeirense* fans.

[15] At the time, the largest indoor football stadium in the world was Maracanã.

[16] For more details, (see dos Santos, 2005; Campos & Silva, 2013).

and have the right to operate the stadium during matches. In this new configuration, Cruzeiro opted for Mineirão and Atlético opted to play, as a priority, at Independência Stadium. This fact marked a change in football territoriality in the state capital of Minas Gerais.

Two Contexts of Supporters: The Peripheral in Global Football and the Global in Peripheral Football

The stadium is, in many cities, the largest equipment of collective use (public or private), capable of concentrating a crowd. According to Gaffney and Bale (2004), this crowd is recognized by emotions and experiences captured by the sense organs (sight, hearing, taste, touch, smell) and enhanced by some technological artifact, during the uses of the stadium, thus establishing an individual and collective reality, while producing memories and stories. In this way, the experience in the stadium is something very important for the real and symbolic construction of this equipment by the subjects who enjoy it.

Extrapolating the notes of Gaffney and Bale (2004), the factors that influence the experience at the stadium and the forms of appropriation of this space can be considered as follows: (1) gender, age, and social class relations; (2) the stadium itself; (3) the places occupied by supporters in the stadium; (4) the region where the stadium is located (neighborhood, city, state, and country); (5) the subjects involved (spectators, organized supporters, ordinary supporters, visiting supporters, tourists); and (6) the match itself (Campos, 2016).

Gaffney and Bale (2004) point out that the sense of historical continuity, as well as the sense of participation in history, helps build the stadium experience. Thus, not only the classics or the championship final matches are valued, but also the ordinary ones, by the prerogative that each game is unique.

Taking into consideration the issues mentioned above, we shall make a presentation of the fan experiences of *Granotas* and *Cruzeirenses* captured by us, researchers, during the field research. For such purpose, we chose to elect three categories: (1) access, (2) product commercialization, and (3) supporters' manifestations. We understand that such categories greatly influence the sense of appropriation supporters have in relation to the stadium and in each one's cheering.

When dealing with the category access, we will talk about the way we observed and experienced the access to the stadium, the acquisition of tickets, and the search at the entrance. We will not address the issue of accessibility for disabled people, as we did not obtain enough data for that. Regarding the second category, we will present our analysis and our experience about the marketing of products (food, drinks, objects related to the game or to clubs, etc.) inside and around the stadium. As for the third category, we will narrate how we examined the supporter's manifestations before, during, and after the matches. The attempt is to integrate the narrative about these three categories and the two observed realities.

As far as *granota* supporter access to Ciutat de València stadium is concerned, we observed that there is an integration between the stadium and the street. Thus, supporters circulate freely along the sidewalk until accessing the stadium entrance gates. The movement of supporters to the Ciutat de València stadium always seemed smooth to us. As Valencia is a medium-sized city, with around 790 thousand inhabitants, we witnessed that supporters went to the stadium mainly on foot or by tram, although cars, bicycles, or buses were also used as means of transport. Supporters' access to the Mineirão stadium proved to be somewhat different since, after the renovation, it was completely fenced in. Thus, supporters only enter the stadium if the north and south gates are open; otherwise, all remain outside. Fences are justified to provide safety and separate pedestrians and automobiles, clearly delimiting the scope of public and private spaces. On match days, the esplanade gates are usually opened two hours before the time scheduled for the start of the match, exclusively for people who have tickets.[17]

For safety reasons, supporters mostly travel to the field in private cars, even though the Belo Horizonte City Hall has created an exclusive bus line to the stadium, on match days, departing from the city center. What one notices as to accessibility and urban mobility, on the part of supporters from Minas Gerais, is that their demands are much more focused on greater facilities for the use of private transport than on public transport improvements or on the extension of the subway itinerary so as to reach the stadium.

In the Ciutat de València stadium, most supporters do not buy tickets on the day of the match, and there is a culture of buying a ticket at the beginning of the season, that is, buying the right to attend all matches in which the club is home in its stadium. A great campaign is conducted to encourage supporters to become season ticket holders. The pecuniary advantage is significant. The ticket price for a single match in the 2015–2016 season was close to €20, while the campaign to buy the voucher had a minimum value of €120, that is, for those who were vouched, each of the 19 matches played at the Levante U.D. would cost €6.32,[18] with the right to bring, free of charge, children, and grandchildren up to 14 years.[19] These ticket purchase conditions help explain why Levante's home games in the 2015–2016 season have no less than 50% occupancy, even though the team is in the relegation zone and on freezing days.

There is also the figure of the money changer, but, differently from what happens in Brazil, they "sell" the card of the spectator for that particular game in exchange for a payment lower than the value of the ticket for that game. To ensure the return of the card, they enter together with the buyer and the payment is made inside the stadium. A prohibited practice, subject to sanction, but common.

---

[17] Until mid-2013, all people had access to the esplanade on match days, regardless of whether they had a ticket or not. Then, access became restricted to people who carried a ticket. However, at that moment, it is not validated, serving only as a visual control.

[18] The minimum wage in Spain in 2015 was €648.

[19] For more details on encouraging new generations to attend the City of Valencia stadium, we refer to the interview available at <https://blog.uchceu.es/marketing/levante-ud-que-grande-ser-peq ueno/>.

At Mineirão, with the stadium's reduced capacity and the other novelties brought by the stadium's renovation, seats started being sold as a rarity. Concurrently with that, in the years 2012 and 2013, Cruzeiro won the Brazilian Championship twice, which made the club opt for keeping ticket prices at high levels, especially for supporters who chose to buy it at the box office, doing justice to the law of supply and demand. Although the club offered some possibilities of a loyalty program, the one similar to Levante's, that is, the one that gave the right to attend all matches at an advantageous unit value, cost R\$1260. Thus, of the total of 30 matches played by Cruzeiro at the Mineirão, each match would cost R\$42 for the supporter.[20]

We verify that there is a difference in procedure in these two contexts. While in Levante there is an effective desire of its supporter to attend the stadium, investing in the formation of supporters, at Mineirão the sumptuous increase in ticket prices revealed an attempt to keep a very specific audience away from the stadium. We noticed that, in addition to financial exclusion, there was a behavioral one. Thus, it is not enough to have the necessary amount of money to buy a ticket; it is necessary to incorporate the new behavioral habits required in the stadium. Thus, both the popular and the wealthy who have, simultaneously, the resources to go to the stadium and the desired behavior to attend it will be part of the intended audience.

In the Brazilian context, and in view of the football commercialization process, the supporter starts to be seen as a customer of these postmodern stadiums, which brings another configuration to these spaces, since football itself becomes more a commercialized and conveyed product. As Mascarenhas (2013) reminds us, the marketing principle has always been present in football stadiums, since, to access them, it has always been necessary to buy tickets. However, nowadays, what we notice in Brazilian stadiums is an exacerbation of the exchange value in detriment of the use value. Thus, they have been transformed into merchandise, with their appropriation taking place through the logic of the market and consumption.

Before entering the stadium to watch Levante matches, supporters often gather at nearby bars where they consume drinks and have small snacks. In the 2015–2016 season, the consumption of alcoholic beverages was not allowed inside the stadium. In addition, in front of the stadium there is a shopping mall with two floors and many shops. It is common, on match days, for supporters to circulate through this space, including socializing with supporters of visiting teams. We did not notice a change of pace in the city, or even in the neighborhood and in commerce, due to the fact that it is a match day.

The Ciutat de València has an official shop, open to the street, which is open every day of the week. On match days, there is a great demand for *granota* products, especially in the cold season, when the buffets[21] with the match recorders heat up sales. In contrast, the trade of shirts is not so intense in winter. We also did not register a change of uniform of the team at each new competition. Outside the stadium, there

---

[20] The minimum wage in Brazil in 2015 was R\$788.

[21] Analogous to the scarf. On them were written the names of the teams that would face each other and the day of the match.

is informal trade in scarves, caps, and flags with the symbols and colors of Levante. There is also the sale of drinks and food, but without much crowding.

It is part of the *cruzeirense* supporter tradition to arrive at the stadium hours before the match. In that space of time, in front of food and drinks, the subjects exchange impressions about the team, but also discuss about other spheres of life. During the years of field research, we noticed three strategies of supporters to promote these meetings.

The first of these, of a market nature, was the proliferation of bars and restaurants around the stadium, some of which, prior to the renovation, operated as parking lots. The other was an attempt by public authorities to relocate peddlers, permitting the permanence of cars that sell foodstuff around the stadium.[22] Finally, the third strategy perceived came from supporters themselves who, while waiting for the start of the match, take snacks or barbecue in the vicinity of the stadium.

Those who go for the barbecue usually arrive five to seven hours before the start of the match; in matches played during the week and at night, the presence of this practice is reduced. The group that only shows up to drink or enjoy the atmosphere usually arrives approximately two hours before the game time.

It is worth mentioning that the barbecue around Mineirão (and in any public space in Belo Horizonte) was banned, through Decree No. 16,203 of January 11, 2016. And, on the other hand, on March 15, 2016, the convenience fair around Mineirão started, an attempt to rescue the custom of stalls around the stadium, but in a reformulated way. Furthermore, alcoholic beer, which was forbidden until 2015, after the year the World Cup was held, was once again sold inside the stadium (Lei No. 21,737, 2015, August 5), yielding to market pressures.

In Levante stadium, the search of supporters at the entrance of the games is carried out by security employees of a private company, but it occurs differently from what is seen in Brazil. The search takes place in purses, backpacks, and jacket pockets. The only search we suffered more intensely was in the Mestalla Stadium, of Valencia C.F., in a game against Levante[23] in which we attended as members of the visiting supporters, which made us believe that in games with greater rivalry there is a differentiated inspection. It is allowed to enter the stadium with food, as well as with PET bottles of up to 600 ml without caps.

At Mineirão, after entering the access gate to the esplanade, supporters head to the stadium gates. There, when passing through the electronic turnstiles, they are searched by members of a private security company who search the bags and backpacks carried by supporters and also their bodies. Drinks in general and food are forbidden in the stadium. These two procedures demonstrate the difference in the ways supporters are understood by the public security bodies and the clubs.

---

[22] However, throughout the field research, we noticed that, at some moments, this commerce was closer to the stadium and, at others, further away, varying with the determinations of the public authorities for each match. Thus, the location of food carts was not fixed, and their presence was not constant.

[23] Valencia vs Levante, on October 31, 2015. On that occasion, in order to purchase tickets as Levante supporters, we had to provide our name and our Foreigner Identity Number (NIE).

It is a tradition among Levante supporters to carry a bag, purse, or backpack containing a cloth or newspaper to clean their seat,[24] umbrella (for rainy days), and food. Thus, it is common in the intervals of the games to see them enjoying their *bocadillos*[25] and, throughout the duration of the match, eating kites.[26]

In the stadium snack bars, *bocadillos, pipas, chips,* espresso coffee, non-alcoholic beer, soft drinks, and water are sold, but we noticed that the commercialization is small, since most supporters take their food at home, leaving the beverage to buy at the stadium. The impression we had is that these products are made available more in order to make the experience of watching the matches more pleasant and not exactly for the purpose of obtaining profit.

As they are not allowed to enter the stadium with food, *cruzeirenses* who do not consume in its surroundings are restricted to food services offered inside Mineirão. Along the field research, we observed an expansion of this offer; to the "*feijão tropeiro,*" popcorn, soda, water, and non-alcoholic beer were added slices of pizza, cheese bread, *açaí,* and beer with alcohol. These foods usually have abusive prices and a quality that is not always pleasing to people. As an example, we cite the "feijão tropeiro" (cowboy beans). A typical delicacy of Minas Gerais' cuisine and served at Mineirão Stadium since long ago, after the stadium's renovation, it started to be poorly accepted by the public and became the target of criticism and complaints that went beyond the culinary boundaries and challenged the renovation itself. That is because the multinational company that won the bid to manage the Mineirão's bars started producing the "feijão tropeiro" in a smaller version than the one previously sold and without fried egg as one of the ingredients. Supporters then began to question the modernization that the stadium had gone through, as something that represented them so much was removed. The situation was only alleviated when the multinational decided to rent the stadium's bars, individually, hiring some of the former tenants. With the reincorporation of these employees and the reintroduction of something that was representative of the stadium's and of Minas' culture, the situation was circumvented.

Observing the two realities, we see in one respect for tradition, and in the other a policy aligned with the urban renewal process that aims at the elimination of local and popular cultural aspects in detriment of renewed and globalized forms of consumption (Mascarenhas, 2013). Specifically, we see the verticalities and horizontalities that act on the territory.

According to Santos (1996), verticalities are represented by international capital and hegemonic agents that act over territory in a homogenizing and hierarchical process. Sometimes they arrive as vectors of modernization, installing an order for their own benefit, by means of rigid norms. Horizontalities, on the other hand, refer to the existing relations between the phenomena and their incidence on the territory that presents knowledge and group relations.

---

[24] Since the stadium is not covered and the seats are exposed to the weather.

[25] Sandwiches made of baguette with *jamón* (kind of ham), most of the time.

[26] Roasted and salted sunflower seeds.

During Levante's matches, we noticed that the so-called European coldness can be analyzed from another angle. Europeans, in general, are not known for great outbursts of affection and physical contact in their daily social life. Thus, it would not be at the time of cheering that they would practice the *caliente* Latin way of proceeding. However, this does not mean that they do not get emotional during matches. It is common, during the games, to hear individual expressions on controversial shots and missed goals. It is also possible to see enthusiastic celebrations, even if they are restricted to the seating area. The more tense the game, the louder the noise of *kites* being consumed can be heard in the stadium.

Supporters of Spanish clubs are generally organized into *peñas*. These are supporter associations registered with the club, which bring together a group with a varied number of people (friends, relatives, among others) to support the club. In general, they are composed of people of all ages and both genders, although some are exclusively women. The *peñas* Levantistas carry out activities such as trips, lunches, dinners, among other actions. In addition, there is the *peñas* delegation, with voting rights in the club's board and with a room inside the stadium, so its members circulate in it unrestrictedly.

At Mineirão, we noticed a change in the behavior of the *cruzeirense* supporters regarding the manifestation of support to the club. There was a weakening of the organized supporters, who started having difficulties in gathering all their members in the parts of the stadium assigned to them, being forced to convince them to buy supporter packages so that they could concentrate in the same space. During the games, each fan group sings its own chant, thus creating a polyphony inside the stadium. For security and logistic reasons, the organized supporters had to reduce the amount of instruments and flags; due to legislation, sexist and homophobic chants were reduced, being heard only in derby days.

At the Levante stadium, people watch the matches sitting down, only getting up at crucial moments of the match. The exception is the space called the '*Grada de animación'* (cheering section), where supporters of both supporters and *non-Peñistas* who want to show their support gather, made up mostly of young men, who watch the matches standing up, singing, and jumping during the 90 min of the match. The *Grada de Animación* is located behind the south goal, in the upper part of the stadium. At rare moments during the game, the rest of the crowd present in the stadium accompanies their music.

In Mineirão, differently from what was claimed, we observed the existence of a tension related to the way of watching the matches. The renovation of the stadium brought as a novelty the numbering of seats. In general, some of the *cruzeirenses* who started going to the stadium after it was remodeled make a point of sitting in the seat marked on the ticket; those who have the experience of Mineirão before the renovation care little about the seat number. Furthermore, some supporters prefer to watch games standing up, while others are happy to sit in the seats they purchased. These tensions, when they turn into fights and swearing, become more or less visible depending on the sector of the stadium, the audience present, and the importance of the match.

We verify that the use of seats in the stadium is a normative that, on behalf of the supporter comfort, aims at his control, once each seat becomes a small territory that provides safety and individualizes the subject, i.e., he is not hidden in the middle of the crowd. In the Spanish situation, there is an understanding that there are two distinct spaces of cheering for different audiences: those who want to jump and perform choreographies watch the matches standing up, in the space assigned to the *"animación,"* while the others (the majority) watch the matches sitting in chairs, in a process that started in the 1990s. In Brazil, due to the fact that chairs represent a novelty, it will still be necessary to mature its use. Furthermore, no space in the stadium was designed to allow organized supporters to cheer standing up. The Levantista supporters are not used to swearing or booing the team, even in defeat situations. The most recurrent one is to call the referee a donkey[27] in controversial bids against Levante. The loudest protest was against the club's coach after a 4–0 defeat by Real Sociedad.[28] The supporters took out their white scarves and waved them.[29] However, in almost all the games we have attended, the Levante team has been applauded by its supporters, even in defeats.

Levante's main rival is Valencia C.F., located in the same city; their stadiums are 3.5 km apart. The rivalry goes through the economic aspects that separate the two clubs, the position that the teams occupy in the Spanish and European football scene, the form of management of the clubs, the time of media coverage, and the year of foundation.

On derby day[30] at the opponent's home, the *"Granota march"* is held. It is an uprising event in preparation for the match, in which the supporters gather in their stadium, under the stands, for a moment of fraternization, after which they collectively walk to the match. We had the opportunity to follow this ritual, at the invitation of a fan. The game was scheduled for 5 pm. At 11 o'clock, the gathering of supporters began in the Ciutat de València stadium. The atmosphere was very familiar; there were men, women, old people, young people, and children who, for the payment of €5, were entitled to a plate of *paella valenciana*, prepared according to the canons of Spanish cuisine, and a drink. More than the food itself, it was the bonding that drew the crowd together in an atmosphere where most knew and recognized each other for their dedication to the club. In the end, not everyone went out for the march of the fans, young men prevailing.

Through this event, we had the dimension of what the stadium represents to the *Granota* supporter; it synthesizes the sense of belonging that the supporter has in relation to his supporters and his stadium. As a place of this collectivity, we noticed that the Ciutat de València stadium carries signs and symbols that make sense to those

---

[27] We believe that the meaning of "donkey" there is different from ours, since it loads a lot on the letter r, but we cannot figure out what the connotation is.

[28] Levante vs Real Sociedad, October 25, 2015.

[29] Waving the white handkerchiefs is a custom originating from bullfights and gives a farewell tone to football coaches who do not achieve good results with the team. To learn more about the symbolism of the white handkerchief, see Vila Maior (2005, October 18).

[30] Valencia vs Levante, October 31, 2015.

who use it. Sociabilities, rivalries, territorialities, collective memory, and appreciation of local culture could be seen in its uses and appropriations.

Regarding the Mineirão stadium, something that stood out was the amount of supporters who attend it, but do not pay attention to the match; instead, they follow the game through social networks and record in pictures their presence in the stadium, in a process in which it is not enough to go to the game, you need to document and post that you were there. The stadium works as a scenario and football just as another commercialized product. In this sense, Mineirão's business character stands out. As a company, the stadium plays an active role in the search for capital, becoming an economic agent. Thus, in line with clubs, Minas Arena invests in clients that might form its audience, measured by consumption capacity, and image is one of the items to be consumed.

We realize, in this context, how the form change affected the content; in other words, although the two stadiums have emerged at the same time (third generation of stadiums), according to the classification of Paramio et al. (2008), the passage of the Mineirão to the fourth generation (even though not all items have been added) caused the way the supporter was seen to change.

In Levante, we see a supporter who makes a long-term personal and emotional investment in the club, which becomes an extension of his family and the community that surrounds him. The stadium is a meeting place and a place to strengthen the solidarity that exists among these supporters. From this meeting, the special and unique atmosphere that permeates the football stadiums arises. Although there is consumption of goods related to the club, this is not what characterizes and gives legitimacy to this group. These values come from the knowledge and maintenance of traditions and identities that the club has and that are confronted by other clubs. Thus, the supporters are committed to the club cause and fomenters of the rivalries between clubs (Giulianotti, 2012).

At Mineirão, we also see a strong feeling of the Cruzeiro supporter in relation to the club and to the stadium; however, in the way the football economy is conducting the manifestation of cheering, we verify that these supporters have experienced its traditions, its players, its symbols by means of a set of market-based relationships, either in the direct form (purchase of products directly related to the club or financial contribution), or in the indirect form (purchase of television packages about football). Although they have strong identity with Cruzeiro and its manifestations of club belonging, their bonds with the club are transformed into a utilitarian relationship. Thus, if the investment made is not matched, the supporter feels free to migrate to other leisure activities (Giulianotti, 2012).

Final Considerations

The research, carried out in two distinct contexts, enabled us to reflect on how much the supporter relationship with the stadium is fundamental to his bond with the club and with the very act of cheering. We emphasize that there are several spaces and means for the supporters exercise (bar, internet, television, among others), but, undoubtedly, the stadium is the supporter main forming space. It is there that the supporter exercises all his emotion. It is in the stadium that he feels he is a participant of a match.

The stadium is not only the facility in which the football game takes place; it is also a space that enables the reception, memories, belonging, and appropriation. Policies developed in relation to the stadium may fulfill this role or not, bringing to the supporter the feeling of indifference, not belonging and his consequent estrangement.

Levante Unión Deportiva, despite being part of global football, exporter of values all over the world, manages to find itself in what is local, provincial, and unique. It makes, without existential crisis, these characteristics its motto: *"Qué grande ser pequeño"*. We know that the club's stadium is undergoing renovation, influenced by the business world of Spanish and world football. Thus, it is worth the possibility of new investigations to know whether, from this reform that will place it in the fourth generation of stadiums, it will succumb or not to the dictates of postmodernity that pasteurize, alienate, and depersonalize, turning supporters into mere consumers.

Cruzeiro Esporte Clube, on its turn, became associated with a new logic, coined in a political, economic, and social conjuncture, bringing new implications in the relationship with its supporters. For those present at the stadium, comfort, magnificence, distinction, and safety were alluded values. For those who cannot pay, the only thing left is the removal of the daily conviviality with the matches and the team. It became evident in this research that the forms of appropriation of Mineirão are under dispute, exemplified by the resistance in face of the first policies imposed after the stadium's renovation. In football, which is now peripheral, the values of globalization, of the modern, have imposed themselves.

Although recently, the reform of Mineirão and all the changes imposed by it have already become object of reflection of the players of the Minas Gerais and also Brazilian football universe, assessing what went right or not. The modern and global discourse is imperative, but has little support in the face of the greatest risk that football can run: the removal of the supporter of yesterday and today and the consequent loss of the supporter of tomorrow.

References

Bale, J. (1993). *Sport, space and the city*. The Blackburn Press.
Bale, J., & Moen, O. (1995). *The stadium and the city*. Edinburgh University Press.
Barros, J. M. (2001). Cidade e identidade: a avenida do contorno em Belo Horizonte. In R. Medeiros (Org.), *Permanências e mudanças em Belo Horizonte*. Belo Horizonte: Editora Puc Minas; Autêntica.
Campos, P. A. F. (2016). *As formas de uso e apropriação do estádio Mineirão após a reforma.* (Doctoral Thesis in Physical Education), Unicamp, Campinas, Brazil. http://repositorio.unicamp. br/bitstream/REPOSIP/304707/1/Campos_PriscilaAugustaFerreira_D.pdf.

Campos, P. A. F., & Amaral, S. C. F. (2013). A copa do mundo de futebol de 2014 e o (novo) Mineirão. *RUA*, *1*(19), 40–55. https://www.labeurb.unicamp.br/rua/anteriores/pages/home/capaArtigo.rua?id=142

Campos, P. A. F., Melo, M. A., Abrahão, B. O. L., & Silva, S. R. (2008). As determinações do estatuto de Defesa do Torcedor sobre a questão da violência: a segurança do torcedor de futebol na apreciação do espetáculo futebolístico. *Revista Brasileira de Ciências do Esporte*, *30*(1), 9–24. http://revista.cbce.org.br/index.php/RBCE/article/view/188/195

Campos, P. A. F., & Silva, S. R. (2013, novembro). O futebol como instrumento para as transformações urbanas em Belo Horizonte/MG. *Anais do Simpósio de Geografia Urbana*, 13, Rio de Janeiro, Brasil.

Cortés, N. (2017, August 21). De Antonio Román a Ciutat de València, pasando por el Nou Estadi, quien te ha visto y quien te ve. *Som Granotes*. https://somgranotes.wordpress.com/2017/08/21/de-antonio-roman-a-ciutat-de-valencia-pasando-por-el-nou-estadi-quien-te-ha-visto-y-quien-te-ve/

Cruz, A. H. (2005). *A nova economia do futebol: Uma análise do processo de modernização de alguns estádios brasileiros*. (Master's thesis in Social Anthropology), Museu Nacional, UFRJ, Rio de Janeiro, Brazil. https://www.academia.edu/18279878/A_Nova_Economia_do_Futebol_Uma_An%C3%A1lise_do_Processo_de_Moderniza%C3%A7%C3%A3o_de_alguns_Est%C3%A1dios_Brasileiros

Curi, M. et al. (2008). Observatório do torcedor: O estatuto. *Revista Brasileira de Ciências do Esporte*, *30*(1), 25–40. http://www.revista.cbce.org.br/index.php/RBCE/article/view/189

Curi, M. (2013). O estádio Engenhão no Rio de Janeiro: Espaço dos torcedores? In C. H. Biscardi, L. Costa, & M. Curi, (Orgs.), *Enquanto a Copa não vem: Memórias e narrativas sobre futebol*. EDUFF.

Damo, A. S. (2012). O desejo, o direito e o dever: A trama que trouxe a Copa ao Brasil. *Movimento*, *18*(2), 41–81. https://doi.org/10.22456/1982-8918.29910

Decreto No. 16,203, de 11 de janeiro de 2016. Belo Horizonte. https://www.normasbrasil.com.br/norma/decreto-16203-2016-belo-horizonte_315258.html

dos Santos, A. C. (2005). Estádio Mineirão: Orgulho e redenção do futebol mineiro. *EFDeportes.com*, *10*(87). https://www.efdeportes.com/efd87/minerao.htm

Elias, N., & Dunning, E. (1992). *A busca da excitação*. Difel.

Gaffney, C., & Bale, J. (2004). Sensing the stadium. In: P. Vertinsky, C. Gaffney, & J. Bale (Orgs.), *Sites of sports: Space, place, experience*. Routledge.

Giulianotti, R. (2002). *Sociologia do futebol*. Nova Alexandria.

Giulianotti, R. (2012). Fanáticos, seguidores, fãs e flâneurs: uma taxonomia de identidades do torcedor no futebol. *Recorde: Revista de História do Esporte*, *5*(1), 1–35. https://revistas.ufrj.br/index.php/Recorde/article/view/703

La Corte, C. de. (2007). *Estádios brasileiros de futebol: Uma análise de desempenho técnico, funcional e de gestão*. (PhD Thesis in Architecture), Universidade de São Paulo, São Paulo, Brasil. https://repositorio.usp.br/item/001655204

Lefebvre, H. (1978). *De lo rural a lo urbano* (4th ed.). Península.

Lei No. 12, 299, de 27 de julho de. (2010). Dispõe sobre medidas de prevenção e repressão aos fenômenos de violência por ocasião de competições esportivas; altera a Lei No. 10,671, de 15 de maio de 2003; e dá outras providências. Brasília. http://www.planalto.gov.br/ccivil_03/_ato2007-2010/2010/lei/L12299.htm#:~:text=Disp%C3%B5e%20sobre%20medidas%20de%20preven%C3%A7%C3%A3o,2003%3B%20e%20d%C3%A1%20outras%20provid%C3%AAncias

Lei No. 21,737, de 5 de agosto de 2015. Dispõe sobre a comercialização e o consumo de bebida alcoólica nos estádios de futebol localizados no Estado de Minas Gerais e dá outras providências. www.almg.gov.br/consulte/legislacao/completa/completa.html?tipo=lei&num=21737&ano=2015

Mascarenhas, G. (2013). Um jogo decisivo, mas que não termina: a disputa pelo sentido da cidade nos estádios de futebol. *Cidades*, *10*(17), 142–170. https://revista.fct.unesp.br/index.php/revistacidades/article/view/3238

Mínguez, J. (2010, February 18). 9-9-1969: Se inaugura el estadio Antonio Román. *As*. https://as.com/futbol/2010/02/18/mas_futbol/1266478061_850215.html

Paramio, J. L., Buraimo, B., & Campos, C. (2008). From modern to postmodern: The development of football stadia in Europe. *Sport in Society: Cultures, Commerce, Media, Politics, 11*(5), 517–534. https://doi.org/10.1080/17430430802196520

Proni, M. (1998). *Esporte-espetáculo e futebol-empresa*. (Doctoral Thesis in Physical Education), Unicamp, Campinas, Brazil. http://repositorio.unicamp.br/jspui/handle/REPOSIP/275330

Reis, H. H. B., & Escher, T. A. (2006). *Futebol e sociedade*. Liber Livros.

Rigo, L. C., Knuth, A. G., Jahnecka, L., & Tavares, R. P. (2006). Estatuto de Defesa do Torcedor: um diálogo com o futebol pelotense. *Movimento, 12*(2), 223–239. https://doi.org/10.22456/1982-8918.2902

Santos, M. (1996). *A natureza do espaço*. Hucitec.

Vila Maior, P. (2005, October 18). A pedagogia do lenço branco. *O Felino*. https://ofelino.blogspot.com/2005/10/pedagogia-do-leno-branco.html

Chapter 29
Brazilian Racism in Football

Bruno Otávio de Lacerda Abrahão and Antonio Jorge Gonçalves Soares

The term "race" emerged during the sixteenth century in the wake of the discovery that men were different from each other. In the eighteenth century, theories were created to give intelligibility and support to domination among peoples (Schwarcz, 2003). Guided by the paradigm of this period, these theories began to think of race as the characteristics imagined to distinguish different human groups. Its point of departure—and of finalization—would be physical appearance raised to the condition of a determining element in the distinction of culture and civilization of peoples (Seyferth, 2002).

Indeed, race was one of the concepts that served to analyze, differentiate, and rank groups within a nation-state (Malik, 1996) and between nation-states, establishing biological inequality between groups as well as that of civilization (Elias, 1993). The growing interest in the concept of race in the nineteenth century stemmed from the constraint of egalitarianism and the need to explain inequality. According to Malik (1996, p. 39), it would not be the "denial of equality, but the social constraints placed on the scope of equality that [would] lead to the racial categorization of humanity."

Indeed, notions of race have been used differently to classify and hierarchically order socially disqualified individuals and groups in the light of historically engendered power relations. According to Telles (2003, p. 301, our translation), "race is an idea, not a social fact." Although the theories of the supposed superiority of the white race have been discredited in the field of scientific debate, their conceptions remain firmly rooted in social thought, their idea is widely understood, and the effects of this imagined concept have real consequences. In this case, the meaning attributed to phenotype is dependent on the social context in which it is embedded. The central question is how phenotype is transformed from descriptive language into moral evaluation about individuals and groups based on physical appearance. As Jessé de Souza

B. O. de Lacerda Abrahão (✉)
Federal University of Bahia, Salvador, Brazil

A. J. G. Soares
Federal University of Rio de Janeiro, Rio de Janeiro, Brazil

(2017) predicts in his re-reading of Brazilian society and social thought, the definition of social relations in Brazil is the persistence of the slave mentality in our culture.

"Brazilian racism" (DaMatta, 1981; Schwarcz, 2003; Telles, 2003) is the most commonly used expression to describe the type of racial prejudice developed in the country, in which two contradictory movements coexist: inclusion and exclusion. How does this ambiguous character, regarding racial relations, reveal itself in football—one of the spaces in which Brazilian culture most expresses its values and meanings? Observing this dilemma based on this sport is justified because we believe that this modality reflects, with its specificities, this dubious role of racial relations in Brazilian culture.

On the one hand, it seems to be a consensus that, in Brazil, football, as a place for the expression of physical skills, was configured as a liberal space with regard to the absorption or integration of the black, mestizo, and poor white population during the first decades of the Republic and of the development of capitalism in the country. On the other hand, this same universe still resents or retains residues of prejudice rooted in Brazilian culture, inherited from the slave mentality about the black race and manifested in moments of conflict in football.

In the limit, Brazilian football could be thought of as a space that reproduces the ambivalence of socially constructed representations of the black race and the ambiguity of racism in Brazil. Whether praised or neglected, we can risk that the presence of blacks on the football field dramatizes the paradoxical tension of "Brazilian racism" (Telles, 2003, p. 19, our translation), that is: "How can inclusion coexist with exclusion?" Thus, we can have it as a privileged *locus* of investigation of both the ambiguity of socially constructed representations of the black race and the ambivalent character of racism in Brazilian culture.

Thus, football is configured as a space that allows us to analyze some of the recurring ways in which the black race was and has been represented in the symbolic universe of Brazilian culture and, in this sense, serves as a stage to bring elements to assist in understanding racism in the country. The point is not to discuss whether or not there is racism in football, but to problematize it: How does this sport mirror the specificity of racism that developed in Brazil?

Answering this question would help us better understand the subtleties of the discriminatory practices that were, and still are, present in the lives of those who were, and are, recognized as black in Brazilian society. We believe that a specific investigation of racism through football would shed light on racial issues that still persist in the dynamics of Brazilian culture, and that emerge in a unique, *sui generis* way through sports. As Santos (1984, p. 1, our translation) predicted: "the racial prejudice, jealously guarded, comes to the surface, almost always, in a moment of competition.

Taking the perspective of the social anthropology of DaMatta (1982, p. 23, our translation), which suggests that "sport is in society and society is in sport", the objective of this chapter is to analyze the specificities of racism in Brazil, taking football as a horizon in the first 50 years of the twentieth century. We make the proviso, however, that we are not propagating the argumentative fallacy according to which "if it is in the whole, it is in the part," nor much less insinuating that football is a simple reflection of society.

We take as reference the conclusions of two of our articles (Abrahão & Soares, 2009a, b) that analyze the relationship of Brazilian racism in football. Both aimed to illuminate the ambiguous signs of the Brazilian racial language in which the black is sometimes praised and integrated into the nation—even if with a defined space—and sometimes discriminated against and/or reviled, revealing the segregation mechanisms in force in a legal context that defines itself as egalitarian and liberal.

This chapter is divided into three moments: The first presents a synthesis of the historical construction of Brazilian racism; the second illuminates the face of inclusion of this ambiguous racism by analyzing the presence of racial debate in the Brazilian football space and the ambiguous effect of the praise for Afro-Brazilians in this universe; finally, the third exposes the face of exclusion of Brazilian racism as it investigates the blame attributed to goalkeeper Barbosa for Brazil's defeat in the 1950 World Cup. Because of this construction, Barbosa became, for social science in the 1990s and for supposedly critical journalism, one of the emblems of the denunciation of racism in football and, by extension, of racism in Brazil.

"Racism in Brazil"

I went to see blacks in the city
who wanted to rent themselves out.
I spoke with this humility:
- Blacks, do you want to work?
They looked at me sidelong,
and one of them, ugly, gloomy,
answered, puffing out his chest:
-Blacks, there are no more.
We are all citizens nowadays.
Let the white man go to the farm.
(Author unknown, our translation)

The verses in this epigraph, originally published in the newspaper *O Monitor Campista* on March 28, 1888 (as cited in Mattos, 2005, May, p. 16), reveal how social hierarchies were beginning to crumble on the eve of the official abolition of slavery, and it is in the context of the end of the nineteenth century that racism emerged in Brazil (Schwarcz, 2001). With the collapse of the slave system and the consequent passage of blacks from the condition of slaves to that of free men, the established group, in full communication with the scientific theories of Europe, was faced with the need to redefine and demarcate hierarchies and positions among the members of society in the Brazilian context.

In the slaveholding order, there was no reason to do so, since blacks were not seen as citizens, but as subspecies (Santos, 1984). Now, if the asymmetry is explicit and internalized by both the dominant and the dominated groups, segregation becomes naturalized in social life, in law, and in mentalities. Indeed, it is difficult to think of segregation in a society whose domination or hierarchy is naturalized. We can even say that segregation can only be thought of as an argument of denunciation, when there is a struggle for recognition, for equalization, in societies in which hierarchies are denounced (Fraser, 2007; Honneth, 2003).

The justification for placing blacks in the inferior scale of races was based, among others, on the prevailing conception that the backwardness of the African continent would be inherited and assimilated by African descendants as innate characteristics from an essentialist perspective of identity. Essentialism suggests that the character-istics of a group are a crystalline and authentic set for all inhabitants of that group; it relies on history and biology for the affirmation of the identity of a given group, appealing to the "truth" of a shared past of biological "truths."

In this sense, biology would provide one source of group solidarity; the universal, transhistorical search for cultural roots and ties would provide the other (Woodward, 2000). In a way, this assumption helped justify domination and the perception of blacks as inferior beings, even in a society that was moving toward structuring a liberal order. Even today, there are still expressions of racism in Brazilian society, despite Law No. 7,716/1989, known as the "Caó Law," which makes acts of this nature a non-bailable crime in the country.

By transforming the African into a slave, Brazilian society delimited the space for blacks, defining hierarchies, ways of treating and being treated, patterns of interaction with whites, etc. and instituted the parallelism between black color and inferior social position, which, in the prevailing social order, corresponded to the condition of precariousness in the face of social existence (Butler, 2018).

In that society, to be a citizen was to be white or whitened (Nogueira, 1998); thus, respectable positions and jobs were seen by the register of "white services." By opposition, the "black services" corresponded to inferior and manual (bodily) services, both in terms of importance and quality, as Neusa Santos Souza (1983) states. In certain social spaces, black bodies were excluded; if they appeared, it was only to serve subordinately the white elite. To be black was, and still is, to represent the precarious condition in society (Butler, 2018).

At the beginning of the twentieth century, Brazil exhibited a racial classification system of a complex, pluralistic, and multiracial nature. Skin color, hair texture, and facial features, among others, determined the racial category in which a person was recognized by others. The limits of the social mobility of the mulatto depended on his appearance (the more black, the lower the possibility of mobility) and on the degree of cultural whiteness (education, manners, wealth) he would be able to accumulate (Skidmore, 1976, 1994).

The European and North American racism arrived in Brazil and found a hierar-chical and anti-equalitarian scenario, based on the logic of "a place for each thing and each thing for its place" (DaMatta, 1981, p. 83). Although the same DaMatta attributes this to the Portuguese heritage, today and yesterday, we prefer to share the view of Jessé de Souza (2017), who indicates here the permanence of the slave mentality, since Portugal would not have operated with this system in their own country. Moreover, slavery as a mode of production, through the great navigations, was not restricted to the Iberian world. However, it is not incorrect to say that Brazilian racism was oriented toward the interior of the local system, in which many intermediate categories live and coexist, making up a triangular society mediated by the slave mentality: whites, in the upper vertex; black/mulattoes, Indians, and women in the lower vertices.

The color prejudice has a long history among us, having been denied, but also, in blatant contradiction, object of the law that sought to curb it. Race and color were words that were part of a historical journey of reversal of meaning. Initially used by Europeans to designate people and peoples of a darker color, the word *"negro"* became the designation of people and peoples of a social status or biological constitution seen as supposedly inferior, of slaves or peoples in a condition of forced submission; in a third moment, it served as a self-designation of these same peoples in their movements of colonial liberation and recovery of self-esteem (Guimarães, 2004).

The phenotypic characteristics of the black race became the object of classification, generating new forms of representation of difference. Serving as mechanisms of production of inequality and hierarchization, classificatory systems imprint meanings and mark distinctions in the social sphere, which means that the differentiations are not contained in the nature of things or beings. Nature is only the ground on which differences are taken to construct, through binary oppositions, fundamental social distinctions. In this way, each society can be understood as the result or mark of its classificatory choices. Every classificatory system has its internal logic, and each society is, at the same time, slave and mistress of the classificatory system that presides over its existence, although, since the social is always a process of construction, classification cannot be given as an essence.

To discuss racial prejudice in Brazil, we must turn to an important study on race relations by Professor Oracy Nogueira (1917–1996). Against the backdrop of manifestations of prejudice and racial discrimination in Brazil and the US, Nogueira's work reveals the symbolic and practical ways in which racial prejudice against blacks is formed and exercised in our country.

The central point of his reflection is the permanence, development, and specificity of racial prejudice in Brazil, which he calls "color prejudice" or "brand prejudice." The author theorizes about the complex constellation of prejudices based on marks, away from geographic or cultural origins, safeguarded by assimilationist ideologies, which hinder the cultivation of identity differences by the discriminated (Guimarães, 2004).

> Racial brand prejudice is a form of discrimination—as harmful as any other—that operates rather by prejudice than by exclusion. It is ambivalent, since the phenotype is mixed with other classificatory principles, such as class belonging and social distance; however, unlike the prejudice of origin, it does not generate antagonism or deep racial hatred. (Cavalcanti, 1998, p. 17, our translation)

Oracy Nogueira related the logic and functioning of racial prejudice to distinct criteria of social classification. In the US, prejudice occurs by descent, or rather, by hypodescent—a drop of black blood makes you black beyond the expressed phenotype (Skidmore, 1994). In Brazil, the black color of the skin, associated with the complex and assimilable marks and characteristics of the dominant class, the white man, can redefine, to some extent, the racial and social perceptions of those who would be, in other contexts, classified as black. These factors would depend on the *ethos* of each cultural system considered. Nogueira perceived very clearly, anticipating the contemporary anthropological perspective, that "race relations are a fully social construction. Racial prejudice is a matter of meaning, which integrates, as such, systems of social classification. It is, therefore, culturally variable and universally comparable" (Cavalcanti, 1998, p. 18, our translation).

Oracy nogueira indicated that the "brand prejudice" would be the predominant prejudice in Brazilian culture, in which the chromatic nuances of the skin, combined with the marks elected by this society to express positive symbols of the dominant culture, would contribute to a more or less promising future for a black person in the molds of a competitive and excluding economic order. This discriminatory practice occurs through a narrative game in which language occupies a decisive place, since it is through language that the censuses and their ordering categories are perceived as elements of a wider cultural system. Classification and discrimination go together; the first is the system of the peculiar and Brazilian form of racism that the author unveils: the "branded racial prejudice" (Cavalcanti, 1998, p. 18). The second is related to the symbols elected by that society to denote superiority or inferiority.

Nogueira (1998) hesitates to attribute the expression "racial prejudice," used to describe what happens in the US , to the Brazilian reality, since the facts occurring in our country are not, according to the author, of the same nature. For him, in the US and in South Africa (at the time, the South African Union), prejudice would subsist even when the individual did not present, phenotypically, any characteristic of the black race, considered inferior. In Brazil, according to Nogueira (1998), prejudice, different from race prejudice and irreducible to class prejudice, would vary according to the phenotypic characteristics presented by the color of a person's body and also according to the proximity or distance of the *ethos* of the white elite. This type of prejudice varies in intensity according to the shade of blackness: the darker the color of a person's skin, the more he or she suffers the consequences of color prejudice. In Brazil, says Nogueira (1998, p. 199, our translation):

> Prejudice tends, rather, to situate individuals, one in relation to the other, along a *continuum* that goes from extremely "black" on one side, to complementarily "Caucasoid," on the other. [...] [In other words,] individuals are classified and classify themselves as white, brown, or light mulatto, brown or dark mulatto, and black—varying to some extent the recognized types and respective designations from one region of the country to another— taking into consideration, in each case, the absence or concentration of blacks traits (density of pigmentation, contexture and color of hair, shape of nose and lips, etc.), that is, the appearance resulting from the combination or fusion of European and African traits.

In social life, the traits associated with blacks "imply in the bearer's preterition when in competition, in equal conditions, with white or less black-looking individuals" (Nogueira, 1998, p. 200, our translation), consequently, the status or success of the black individual depends largely on the compensation and neutralization of his traits—or their aggravation—"by association with other conditions, innate, or acquired, socially considered of positive or negative value—level of education, occupation, esthetic aspect, personal treatment, artistic gift, character traits, etc." (Nogueira, 1998, p. 200, our translation).

Oracy Nogueira operated with the distinction between racial origins and phenotypic marks associated with various social attributes that would tend to relativize physical characters. The analysis of racial prejudice in Brazil does not consider color subsumed to class; thus, the author concludes that color has a relative weight as an indicator of social status. In his words, "the white color facilitates social ascension but does not guarantee it by itself; on the other hand, the dark color implies social exclusion rather than unconditional exclusion of its bearer" (Nogueira, 1998, p. 177, our translation).

For Maio (2008, p. 9, our translation), the Brazilian ideology of social relations is characterized by a contradiction:

> On one hand, it is "miscegenationist and egalitarian"; on the other hand, it encourages whitening and selectivity of people based on phenotype, "a subtle and surreptitious type of prejudice" (Nogueira, 1998, p. 196). Oracy highlights the fact that the status *of* the individual is not given only by color. Although the physical characters identified as brown and black compete in a situation of inequality with whites, i.e., they are recurrently overlooked, there is a series of psychological, social, and cultural attributes that, associated with color, can overcome the barrier of prejudice, such as: level of education, occupation, esthetic appearance, personal treatment, artistic gift, and character traits. Furthermore, the social position of whites and non-whites interferes with the type of interaction that is established between individuals. The closer to the top of the social structure whites are, the less willing they are to interact with people of color. Among subordinate social segments, one finds greater fraternization and less resistance to intermarriage or permanent union between people of contrasting racial traits.

In the symbolic and practical planes, the manifestation and intensity of this ideology are conditioned to the visibility of physical features, and, therefore, to the racial or phenotypic appearances of the individual. The racial prejudice of mark, different from the racial prejudice of origin, would act in the sense of preterition and not of total segregation or exclusion. Even revealing its perversity, brand prejudice establishes a series of classificatory combinations (class, instruction, habits) that tend to relativize the importance of color, thus hindering the occurrence of insoluble conflict situations or stalemate attitudes due to racial tensions in various fields. Football is one of them.

An activity that emerged in Brazil in the late nineteenth century committed to the values of the economically well-off classes, football succumbed to the participation of the popular. This process occurred soaked in tensions, among which the debate around racism in Brazil, and the stereotypes that populate the imaginary about the black man deserve special attention.

The Ambivalent Effect of Socially Constructed Representations of the "Black Race": The Inclusion of "Brazilian Racism"

The trajectory of football in Brazil, which, from the beginning of the twentieth century onward, became the most popular sport in the context of industrial, urban development, and working-class involvement, represented (and has represented), mainly for the black population, an important means of social ascension, of visibility, and of affirmation of competence (Bruni, 1994). Football was still in the process of structuring in Brazil when, in 1933, it converted from amateur to professional.

In that context, Brazil, the last country in the Americas to abolish slavery, was experiencing the solidification of free labor arising from the consolidation of post-slavery capitalism, whose implementation generated competition among Brazilian citizens. Living the post-abolition period and the First Republic (1889–1930), the right to equality from a legal point of view became one of the elements of the social conjuncture, even though, from a cultural point of view, the hierarchies and even the invisibility of the precarious (black and/or poor) represented the norm that guided relationships in everyday life (Butler, 2018). From that moment on, blacks began to be recognized as equals before the law, which required a reorganization of power relations.

The end of slavery and the advent of the Republic brought about reactive attitudes, based on prejudice, on the part of dominant social sectors, threatened with losing their social positions or their supposed racial purity. Capitalist development would have generated a scenario of growing social tensions and led to the creation of racial barriers due to the possibility of social mobility of the colored population, generating situations of competition among Brazilian citizens. Thus, the explanatory source of discriminatory practices against blacks must be sought in the slave mentality that endures from when the system was replaced by another economic and political order.

In this perspective, there would have been a mismatch "between the traditional racial ideology and the new racial situation" (Costa Pinto, 1998[1953], p. 30, our translation); in other words, how could the right to formal equality of the colored man in society subsists when the cultural practices were hierarchized from the color line and the precariousness in which this population lived its daily life? The results of abolition, which generated a reorganization that was consolidated in the First Republic, were felt throughout the first three decades of the twentieth century.

Prejudice and discrimination acted fundamentally to situate the black the place he had historically occupied in the system of social relations. Thus, stereotyped criteria, values, and judgments are inferred from this framework whose function would be to preserve the black in "his place," namely: an inferior—peripheral—place that he historically occupied (and still occupies) in society; not only to indicate the place that this colored contingent should occupy but also to make these people invisible in the spaces of conviviality of the "good society."

Football, which had spread among young people from the higher and more educated social strata and the technicians of the English companies operating in

Brazil, was quickly disseminated among the popular strata (Pereira, 2000). This rapid and growing popular interest in the sport provoked adverse reactions related both to its practice by intellectuals and to the incorporation of popular clubs or the acceptance of people from the popular classes into elite clubs.

One of these reactions was that of the nationalist writer Lima Barreto, who, concerned with defending Brazilian traditions, positioned himself radically against football. Antunes (2004) observed that, for the writer, football was a "foreignism that expressed little of the authentic national values" (Antunes, 2004, p. 22, our translation) and an "activity of half-naked men who were ready to kick, swear, and get involved in fights" (Antunes, 2004, p. 23). Graciliano Ramos, in the same direction, thought that football would be a passing fad, "fogo de palha" (flash in the pan), in his own words, whose feeling would be that it would cause a short excitement and nothing more (Soares & Lovisolo, 2001). The debate about the authentic in national culture goes back to the dialogs between cosmopolitanism and regionalism and romanticism and enlightenment and seems to be a frequent polarization in the cultural field.

However, as the sport became part of everyday life in the cities, its acceptance became progressively greater, despite occasional criticisms (Pereira, 2000). Football, as an exogenous cultural asset, began to have a renewed significance in national culture, and modernist writers recognized it as part of Brazilian culture. New nationalist discussions emerged that envisioned and defined the character and behavior of the Brazilian people based on football and other cultural expressions, such as music and religiosity. Some of these discussions pointed it as a positive and unifying element of a miscegenated country, whose elaborations were still under construction during the diffusion process (Antunes, 2004, p. 26).

The 1920s and 1930s were taken as times of appropriation of the English sport as a symbol of Brazilian identity (Franzini, 2003, p. 11). The ideology of miscegenation valued the fusion of races and cultures that gave rise to the Brazilian people, and it was in this period, for example, that Gilberto Freyre elaborated an optimistic reinterpretation of the national character, overcoming the pessimism and attributing a positive sense to the debate about miscegenation in Brazil (Skidmore, 1976, 1994), a reinterpretation that extended to football, as stated by Mário Rodrigues Filho in the preface of his book *O negro no futebol brasileiro* (Soares, 1998).

The idea of cultural synthesis led to the definition of a national identity or of personality traits that would express the national character through football. Attributes such as *"brejeirice"* (fun football), *"ginga,"* astuteness, simplicity, and others were recognized in the Brazilian way or style of playing football (Antunes, 2004; Soares, 1994, 1998, 2003, 2014; Soares & Lovisolo, 2003).

In the same way as the Brazilian nation, football was thought of as resulting from the mixture of races, that is, if Brazil was identified as a mestizo nation, so was our football. The idea of a racial democracy was present in this construction through the performance of the Brazilian national team of the 1930s and constituted an encouragement not only for the affirmation of mestizaje, but also for the construction of a narrative that identified the style of play as an effective product of the meeting of races.

Football progressively became an element of strong identity trait of the Brazilian nation, through the performance of national teams and clubs. In the context of nation-states, sports, and other manifestations of culture (science, art, music, etc.) became, throughout the twentieth century, privileged spaces for the construction of metaphors and analogies about the quality or character of the people who inhabit the market of nations. In Brazil, football was one of these elements used to build the identity of this sport and of the nation.

The national literature is unanimous in affirming that football was one of the social spaces in which blacks obtained the most success and visibility after the abolition of slavery. If, on the one hand, visibility can indicate a prominent presence for those who are precarious in their daily social relations, on the other hand, it does not mean that this recognition of competence transfers directly to other spaces of sociability. The prominence given to the performance of African descendants in the universe of football ended up legitimizing a discourse on the bodily qualities of the race— qualities also praised by positivists, who saw blacks as skilled artists because of their emotional characteristics, like women (Soares, 1998).

Abrahão and Soares (2009a) call attention to the fact that the perverse effect of the praise to the black in the sports field was the naturalization of the understanding that the aptitude and inclination of African descendants for bodily and artistic activities came at the expense of their aptitude and inclination for intellectual activities. Let us note that the discourse on the potentiality of the use of the black body can be read as a kind of "racism in reverse" that places it in the feminine condition, in the condition of recognized and at the same time precarious (Butler, 2018; Soares, 1998).

An important issue for the elite of that context was to include Afro-Brazilians in the period after slavery while maintaining the hierarchies of the time. Therefore, we can think that the praise for Afro-Brazilians in the football space aspired to the integration of the black in a delimited space. In the view of Neusa Santos Souza (1983), the corporal qualifiers privileged in black identity oppose the idea of the rationality of the white race. The supposed superiority revealed by the blacks for the corporal arts, by the white discourse, perversely indicates the place they should occupy in society. Such representations, which, at first sight, would seem to favor a positive signification, end up having a malefic effect and scrutinizing the visibility and social performance of the black in Brazil.

With the hierarchy maintained, we would have the continuity of the mentality characteristic of the transition period from the nineteenth to the twentieth century, which, by hierarchizing the races, placed the blacks as a group endowed with aptitude for sports and dances and activities that depend especially on emotion and/or body skills (Soares, 1998); i.e., we would maintain, according to Jessé de Souza (2017), the slave mentality in a new social order. Thus, the social place that these representations assigned to the black is distinct from the one considered superior or rational.

In short, the supposed physical superiority of blacks for activities requiring the use of the body indicates one of the ways in which African descendants are integrated into Brazilian society. At the same time, the praise has the effect of indicating social spaces that are distant from the superior activities of reason, namely: the lawns and the samba and capoeira circles. Therein lies, according to our reading, the face of inclusion/exclusion, the spaces defined as belonging to race, of Brazilian racism (Abrahão & Soares, 2009). Even the space of inclusion manages, at times of conflict and dissonance, to construct the face of exclusion, as personified in the biography of former goalkeeper Barbosa, blamed for the defeat in the 1950 World Cup final, as reported by Mário Rodrigues Filho (2003), precisely because of the emotional instability attributed to race.

Barbosa and the Personification of the Exclusion of Racism in Brazil

Brazilian racism would have a specificity (Schwarcz, 2003, p. 202) embodied in Florestan Fernandes who states the existence in Brazil of "a prejudice of not having prejudice," that is, "the Brazilian tendency would be to continue discriminating, despite considering such attitude outrageous (for those who suffer) and degrading (for those who practice it)" (Schwarcz, 2003, p. 202, our translation). In everyday practices, Brazilian racism would be committed in a subtler way than that evidenced in the episode of Barbosa's life.

Abrahão and Soares (2009b) analyzed, in the light of the debate on race and racism in Brazil, the consequences of the blame attributed to goalkeeper Barbosa for the defeat of the national team in the 1950 World Cup. The rescue of this text is justified to the extent that Barbosa personifies the face of *exclusion* promoted by Brazilian racism, even in a space that gave visibility to blacks. Brazil's defeat to Uruguay, in the recently inaugurated Maracanã stadium, is constantly remembered by sports chroniclers and writers who elect football as the focus of their analyses, and such remembrance occurs, above all, because the explanations for the failure would have dramatized the racial debate, metonymized, at that moment, by the blacks in the team, especially by goalkeeper Barbosa.

The justifications elaborated for the defeat are similar to those used to explain Brazil's backwardness. Gordon (1996) denounces that the representations about the 1950 World Cup are aligned with nineteenth century theories, which viewed Brazil's future with pessimism arising from the presence of blacks among the races that composed its people:

> [...] as long as we depend on the black, it will be like this... [...] "this racially impure society could not really get anywhere [...] for the big decisions, it was not possible to count on the blacks and mestizos. They cowered, they all shit themselves. Just like Barbosa, when he debuted in the Brazilian team. (Gordon, 1996, p. 72, our translation)

From the symbolic point of view, Gordon's analysis is impeccable; however, from the historiographical point of view, it presents problems (Soares, 1999). The accusation of increased racism against black players, especially Barbosa, after the 1950 World Cup, became an argument and object of various analyses in academic and journalistic texts (DaMatta, 1982; Gordon, 1996; Perdigão, 2000). Different authors point out, with all due differences, that the guilt that fell upon these black players revived, in the context of the time, the theories about Brazilian racial inferiority, constituted by miscegenation with inferior races. According to social analysts, the racist feelings aroused by the 1950 defeat were empirical proof of the persistence of the argument that the destiny of Brazilian society was doomed to failure due to its racial makeup.

Soares (1998) observed that, from the point of view of social history, Barbosa's denunciation of racism is not supported by the evidence presented. However, the remembrance of this narrative from a cultural point of view indicates the tension between meanings and representations about racism and race relations in our society, since such remembrance becomes a pedagogy or denunciation against the prejudice of not having prejudice (Schwarcz, 2003).

It is worth remembering that the possible technical failure of the goalkeeper generated accusations in racial/psychological terms, both in the narrative of Mário Rodrigues Filho (2003) and in the academic and journalistic memory. Such representations associate the black race with the body, emotion, and impulsiveness.

As previously discussed, the hideous effect of these compliments is that they end up distancing blacks from rational activities. So much so that the discourse that denounces the racism suffered by Barbosa indicates that the goalkeeper did not have the psychological balance necessary to act in a situation of pressure and decision. The question that interests us is to think about the meaning of the constant remembrance of Barbosa's failure and the subsequent denunciation of racism in academic texts that dealt with this episode.

In Uruguay's second and decisive goal, the ball would have passed under the body of our goalkeeper. If we took the decisive goal from the level of analysis of the game, we could think that it was the result of an individual failure, regardless of whether Barbosa was black or not. On a symbolic level, that technical failure of the black goalkeeper amplifies and generalizes socially constructed representations about the black race to justify the Brazilian defeat. In this case, we must remember that representations about the black race preexist the alleged failure of the goalkeeper in 1950.

In fact, according to social analysts and journalists, Barbosa became one of the emblems necessary to denounce the racist representations of our society—representations that indicate that emotional instability, lack of rationality, and even lack of character, honesty, and fidelity are associated with blacks; therefore, the black goalkeeper is always under suspicion. It has been speculated that the blame attributed to Barbosa for the 1950 defeat reignited the prejudice that "blacks can not be goalkeepers."

If, for some, the second Uruguayan goal was seen at the time as an individual fault, for historiography, the individual guilt of a black goalkeeper represented one more face of racism in Brazil, based on the legacy of the representations built by nineteenth-century science, which, by hierarchizing the races, suspected the rational, moral, and psychological capacity of blacks (Schwarcz, 2001, 2002). These representations were diachronically constructed and generated within national culture; their meanings are important for understanding the terrain on which the contradictory Brazilian racial debate rests.

We must understand that two universes coexist in the collective memory about the defeat of 1950: the one of the drama, which is revealed in the symbolic plane of the culture that denounces the existence of racism in Brazilian society and the other of the "temporality of the event"—borrowing the terms of Damo (2002, p. 56)—in both of which the aspects of the football clash are highlighted, in which the justifications of the defeat are restricted to the disjunctive sphere of the game and are explained in the failures of other players, not only the goalkeeper.

We know that the press functions as one of the guardians of collective memory, and that the articles published even today partially follow the interpretations of the past divulged by Mário Rodrigues Filho and reiterated by scholars in the 1990s (Soares, 1999). Recalling the figure of Barbosa may reveal the permanence of these wounds in the collective memory, while representing a way to denounce racism in a miscegenated society, in which the debts of the past still emerge in the present. The fact that Barbosa's flaw is not erased reveals that the racial issue associated with what "is the character of the Brazilian" constitutes a permanent identity dilemma. If not, what would the constant remembrance of the 1950 setback and the permanent criticism of the attribution of blame for the defeat to the blacks of the national team mean?

Even with the abolition, discrimination and the slave mentality did not disappear from Brazil's social history, as Jessé de Souza (2017) states. The absence of laws that mentioned segregation meant that, in our society, discrimination was exercised in a subtler way, in non-formalized spaces (Schwarcz, 2003). In our analysis, we point out that Barbosa and the remembrance of 1950 show the face of the inclusion of blacks in the social space, while confirming the Brazilian racism and its recurrent forms of actualization: of complex identification and proof, but felt by many in everyday life.

We can follow Ortiz's (1985, p. 133) argument that "representations only have meanings when they are embodied in the discourse of social actors." Thus, from the academic and journalistic memory, Barbosa means the recognition of a racist ideology present in the Brazilian society and, at the same time, the repudiation of this ideology. The constant remembrance of Barbosa in the 1950 World Cup suggests that we remember that the country of "racial democracy" has in the bowels of its culture an unacknowledged racism. As Jessé de Souza (2017) emphasizes, we were all socialized in a society with a slavery and hierarchical mentality; the difference is that some are aware of this and fight against this feeling ingrained in social relations, while others reiterate the "prejudice of not having prejudice."

Conclusion

One of the dramas interpreted by Oracy Nogueira (1998) is the contradictory character of Brazilian racism, at the same time miscegenationist and egalitarian, which covers up a subtle and disguised type of prejudice, in the form of encouragement to whitening and the ranking of individuals according to their racial appearance. In the same direction, recalling the questioning of Telles (2003, p. 19) about the peculiarity of Brazilian racism, that is, "how inclusion coexists with exclusion", we observe that Brazilian football, in turn, dramatizes the ambiguity and complexity of its racial system.

Historical and sociological literature presents us with the way in which positive representations about the black race were incorporated into the construction of Brazilian identity through football. Therein lies the face of the inclusion of racism in the Brazilian way. It was not enough, however, to integrate; it was necessary to locate the place of action of the black in its anti-equality and hierarchical structure. In this way, the praise coming from socially constructed representations of the black man in the space of football—representations that, in turn, facilitated his integration—had as a cruel consequence the delimitation of the social space reserved for the black race, and, even in this space, when a black man is not successful, his race would explain the failure.

The exclusionary face of racism in Brazil was exemplified by the case of the former goalkeeper Barbosa. At the symbolic level, of the meanings of culture in the sense of Geertz (1973), Barbosa became one of the emblems necessary to denounce the existence of racism in the country of "racial democracy," initially in journalism, then in academic literature (Soares, 1998). The remembrance of the hypothetical failure of the goalkeeper, beyond the technical discussions of the game, reveals the level of drama in which racism still persists as a political, ideological, and cultural dilemma of Brazilian society.

Whether or not Barbosa suffered discrimination after the defeat is not one of the concerns of this chapter. What is at stake in the academic and journalistic remembrances is the permanent construction of the pedagogy of antiracism in a society that has been rereading its past and present ethnic relations and that has not yet recognized that places the black as a precarious being, along with other minorities, in the public space, as Butler (2018) refers. As an effect, we can observe that football dramatizes the coexistence of a present racism, but not assumed, such as the one that blamed the goalkeeper, and a miscegenationist antiracism, coined in the terms of "racial democracy," which takes football as a positive model to think ethnic-racial relations in Brazilian society.

Perhaps because of that, manifestations of racism in the football space, in which players recognized by their opponents as black or mixed race have been attacked through sounds, symbols, and onomatopoeia referring to "monkeys," are received with so much repudiation (Abrahão, 2009). Not only because they draw on the old hierarchizations between countries, peoples, and ethnicities built throughout the twentieth century, but, above all, because they attack the demands for the consolidation of equality values in the west in the forms of recognition (social esteem) and objective distribution to provide dignified lives for the precarious (Butler, 2018; Fraser, 2007; Honneth, 2003).

This relationship of inclusion and exclusion engenders a perverse mode that is inscribed in Brazilian social relations. Here, racism and discrimination are established through informal means and intensified to the extent that skin color and its nuances—which may be attenuated or reinforced by the assimilation or not of the marks of a dominant culture—coexist with the nationalist discourse that praises the mestizaje and the harmonic relationship that would have existed between the different ethnicities that composed our society.

In Brazil, contradictorily coexists, on the one hand, an evident racism, but not assumed, and on the other hand, a declared anti-racism. Racism, here, is always in the other, and there is also a chorus that preaches its non-existence, and when it appears in any form, it is widely repudiated. The cultural message sent by Brazilian society through football is that we do not admit racism, even though its effects persist in the private lives of many of those identified as black.

Do socially constructed representations of the black race contribute to the limited access of black and brown people to prestigious positions? To what extent can stereotypes embedded in culture and reflected in football be used to explain the difference between citizens in an order that claims to be liberal? Inheritance of a slavocratic past, the meanings attributed to the black race tension the members of a competitive society that, even constrained by the supposed principles of a liberal and egalitarian order, structures, in one way or another, strategies, conscious or not, to maintain the hierarchies, the unequal relationships and the inferiority of those placed in precariousness and lack of social recognition. In our reading, football, with its specificities, mirrors part of the dilemmas of the integration of the "black race" in Brazil.

References

Abrahão, B. O. L., & Soares, A. J. G. (2009a). O elogio ao negro no espaço do futebol: entre a integração pós-escravidão e a manutenção das hierarquias sociais. *Revista Brasileira de Ciências do Esporte, 30*(2), 9–23. https://www.redalyc.org/pdf/4013/401338537002.pdf

Abrahão, B. O. L., & Soares, A. J. (2009b). O que o brasileiro não esquece nem a tiro é o chamado frango de Barbosa: Questões sobre o racismo no futebol brasileiro. *Movimento, 15*(2), 13–31. https://www.redalyc.org/pdf/1153/115315433002.pdf

Antunes, F. M. R. F. (2004). *"Com brasileiros, não há quem possa!" Futebol e identidade nacional em José Lins do Rego, Mário Filho e Nelson Rodrigues.* São Paulo: Editora Unesp.

Bruni, J. C. (1994). Apresentação. *Revista USP,* 22.

Butler, J. (2018). *Corpos em aliança e a política das ruas: Notas para uma teoria performativa de assembléia.* Tradução de Fernanda S. Miguens. Rio de Janeiro: Civilização Brasileira.

Cavalcanti, M. L. V. C. (1998). Apresentação. In O. Nogueira, *Preconceito de marca: As relações raciais em Itapetininga.* São Paulo: Edusp.

Costa Pinto, L. D. A. (1998). *O negro no Rio de Janeiro: Relações de raças numa sociedade em mudança* (2nd ed.). Rio de Janeiro: Editora UFRJ. (Original work published 1953)

DaMatta, R. (1981). *Relativizando: Uma introdução à antropologia estrutural.* Petrópolis: Vozes.

DaMatta, R. (1982). Esporte na sociedade: Um ensaio sobre o futebol brasileiro. In R. DaMatta (Ed.), *Universo do futebol: esporte e sociedade brasileira* (pp. 19–42). Rio de Janeiro: Pinakotheke.

Damo, A. S. (2002). *Futebol e identidade social: Uma leitura antropológica das rivalidades entre torcedores e clubes.* Porto Alegre: Ed. Universidade UFRGS.

Elias, N. (1993). *O processo civilizador* (R. Jugmann, Trans.). Rio de Janeiro: Jorge Zahar.

Franzini, F. (2003). *Corações na ponta da chuteira: Capítulos iniciais da história do futebol brasileiro (1919–1938).* Rio de Janeiro: DP&A Editora.

Fraser, N. (2007). Reconhecimento sem ética? *Lua Nova: Revista De Cultura e Política, 70,* 101–138. https://doi.org/10.1590/S0102-64452007000100006

Geertz, C. (1973). *A interpretação das culturas.* Rio de Janeiro: Zahar Editores.

Gordon Jr., C. (1996). Eu já fui preto e sei o que é isso: história social dos negros no futebol brasileiro: segundo tempo. *Pesquisa de Campo*, (3/4), 65–78. https://ludopedio.org.br/biblioteca/eu-ja-fui-preto-e-sei-o-que-e-isso-historia-social-dos-negros-no-futebol-brasileiro-segundo-tempo/

Guimarães, A. S. A. (2004). Preconceito de cor e racismo no Brasil. *Revista De Antropologia, 47*(1), 9–43. https://doi.org/10.1590/S0034-77012004000100001

Honneth, A. (2003). *Luta por reconhecimento: A gramática moral dos conflitos sociais*. São Paulo: Editora 34.

Lei no 7.716, de 5 de janeiro de. (1989). (Define os crimes resultantes de preconceito de raça ou de cor). Presidência da República, Casa Civil. Brasília. http://www.planalto.gov.br/ccivil_03/leis/l7716.htm

Maio, M. C. (2008). O racismo no microscópio: Oracy Nogueira e o projeto UNESCO. *Estudios Interdisciplinarios de America Latina y el Caribe, 19*(1), 35–52. http://eial.tau.ac.il/index.php/eial/article/view/469

Malik, K. (1996). *The meaning of race: Race, history and culture in Western society*. Londres: Macmillan International Higher Education.

Mattos, H. M. (2005, May). A face negra da abolição. *Revista Nossa História, 2*(19), 16–20. Republished on the Anjovida website: http://act14-anjovida.blogspot.com/2016/03/a-face-negra-da-abolicao.html

Nogueira, O. (1998). *Preconceito de marca: As relações raciais em Itapetininga*. São Paulo: Edusp.

Ortiz, R. (1985). *Cultura brasileira e identidade nacional* (Vol. 3). São Paulo: Brasiliense.

Perdigão, P. (2000). *Anatomia de uma derrota*. São Paulo: L&PM Editores.

Pereira, L. A. D. M. (2000). *Footballmania: uma história social do futebol no Rio de Janeiro (1902–1938)*. Rio de Janeiro: Nova Fronteira.

Rodrigues Filho, M. (2003). *O negro no futebol brasileiro* (4th ed.). Rio de Janeiro: Mauad Editora.

Santos, J. R. (1984). *O que é racismo*. São Paulo: Brasiliense.

Schwarcz, L. M. (2001). *Retrato em branco e negro: Jornais, escravos e cidadãos em São Paulo no final do século XIX*. São Paulo: Companhia das Letras.

Schwarcz, L. M. (2002). *O espetáculo das raças*. São Paulo: Companhia das Letras.

Schwarcz, L. M. (2003). Nem preto nem branco, muito pelo contrário: Cor e raça na sociabilidade brasileira. In F. A. Novaes, & L. M. Schwarcz (Eds.), *História da vida privada no Brasil* (Vol. 4) (pp. 173 -245). São Paulo: Companhia das Letras.

Seyferth, G. (2002). O beneplácito da desigualdade: Breve digressão sobre racismo. In G. Seyferth et al. (Orgs.), *Racismo no Brasil* (pp. 17–43). São Paulo: Peirópolis; ABONG.

Skidmore, T. E. (1976). *Preto no branco: Raça e nacionalidade no pensamento brasileiro* (Vol. 9). Rio de Janeiro: Paz e Terra.

Skidmore, T. E. (1994). *O Brasil visto de fora*. Rio de Janeiro: Paz e Terra.

Soares, A. J. G. (1994). *Futebol, malandragem e identidade* (Vol. 20). Vitória: Secretaria de Produção e Difusão Cultural da UFES.

Soares, A. J. G. (1998). *Futebol, raça e nacionalidade: Releitura da história oficial*. (Doctoral Thesis in Physical Education), University Gama Filho, Rio de Janeiro, Brazil. https://ludopedio.org.br/biblioteca/futebol-raca-e-nacionalidade-no-brasil-releitura-da-historia-oficial/

Soares, A. J. (1999). História e a invenção das tradições. *Revista Estudos Históricos, 13*(23), 119–146. http://bibliotecadigital.fgv.br/ojs/index.php/reh/article/view/2087/1226

Soares, A. J. (2003). Futebol brasileiro e sociedade: a interpretação culturalista de Gilberto Freyre. *Futbologías. Fútbal, identidad y violencia en América Latina. Buenos Aires: Clacso*, 145–162. http://biblioteca.clacso.edu.ar/gsdl/collect/clacso/index/assoc/D2304.dir/9PII-Soares.pdf

Soares, A. J. G. (2014). Futebol: um estilo de jogo brasileiro. In V. M. Andrade, & F. P. Faria (Eds.), *Esporte, cultura, nação, estado: Brasil e Portugal* (pp. 218–232). Rio de Janeiro: 7 Letras.

Soares, J., & Lovisolo, H. (2001). Futebol é fogo de palha, a profecia de Graciliano Ramos. In R. Helal, A. J. Soares, & H. Lovisolo (Eds.), *A invenção do país do futebol: mídia, raça e idolatria* (pp. 123–134). Rio de Janeiro: Mauad.

Soares, A. J., & Lovisolo, H. R. (2003). Futebol: A construção histórica do estilo nacional. *Revista Brasileira de Ciências do Esporte, 25*(1). http://revista.cbce.org.br/index.php/RBCE/article/vie w/180

Souza, J. (2017). *A elite do atraso: Da escravidão à Lava Jato.* Rio de Janeiro: Leya.

Souza, N. S. (1983). *Tornar-se negro.* Rio de Janeiro: Graal.

Telles, E. (2003). *Racismo à brasileira: Uma nova perspectiva sociológica* (p. 2003). Rio de Janeiro: Relume-Dumará.

Woodward, K. (2000). Identidade e diferença: uma introdução teórica e conceitual. In T. T. Silva (Ed), *Identidade e diferença: A perspectiva dos estudos culturais* (pp. 7–72). Petrópolis: Vozes.

Chapter 30
"This is a Reality": The Racism Narrated by Black Characters in Brazilian Football

Marcel Diego Tonini

"This is a reality" was the phrase said by Lula Pereira, a late black coach, about racism in Brazilian football. Using it as the title of this chapter, I will summarize the debates developed in my master's thesis (Tonini, 2010). The objective is to reflect on racism in Brazilian football beyond the field, that is, considering other areas of action than that of the professional athlete, such as coaches, referees, sporting directors, and journalists. More than that, it is to think about the present time based on the experiences of professionals in this universe. To do so, I will use excerpts from oral history interviews I conducted with blacks and whites throughout that investigation. In the end, I will assess the research, which completed ten years of completion in 2020, indicating its main considerations and the paths pointed out by it.

"Football and race relations" figure as one of the most consolidated themes since the human sciences in Brazil took this sport as an object of study, in the late 1970s (Toledo, 2001).[1] In the initial kickoff of my research, it was essential that I surveyed, read, and took stock of the bibliography that dealt with this theme. Not only to present it and show its historical and social relevance but, above all, to list important aspects to be considered throughout the research, especially in the interviews. In short, I sought to better understand the problem that I had chosen and to delimit my research object. Basically, I worked with memory books, sports chronicles, and academic papers published from 1930 to 2010. To synthesize the analysis of the consulted bibliography and not to make this introduction too long, I will highlight the points that I consider the main ones in the debate about the racial issue in Brazilian football:

---

[1] The cited author, by the way, makes a detailed analysis of the Brazilian scientific production regarding football between the beginning of the 1980s and the beginning of the third millennium.

M. D. Tonini (✉)
Campinas, Brazil

© The Author(s), under exclusive license to Springer Nature Switzerland AG 2021   507
S. S. Giglio and M. W. Proni (eds.), *Football and Social Sciences in Brazil*,
https://doi.org/10.1007/978-3-030-84686-2_30

1.   In the social imaginary, football is seen as a racially democratic space in its entirety, something that is not only shared but also reproduced by several intellectuals in the field (Filho, 2003; Freyre, 2003; Lyra Filho, 1973; Rego, 1943; Rosenfeld, 1993, among others). In fact, the gradual acceptance of blacks as players during the first decades of this sport in Brazil plays an important role in the consolidation of this imaginary.

2.   Another belief similarly shared by some of these scholars (Gordon Júnior, 1996; Levine, 1982; Lopes, 2004; Murad, 1996; Santos, 1981; Wisnik, 2008) is that blacks have a "natural" gift for sports, particularly football, and that they are associated with the Brazilian style of playing football, which is called "futebol-arte" or "the beautiful game".

3.   In general, the academic literature (Filho, 2003; Gordon Júnior, 1996; Lopes, 2004; Murad, 1996; Souza, 1996; Vogel, 1982) points to a more apparent existence of racism in the football practiced here until the first Brazilian victory in World Cups (1958), and also to the symbolic importance of the third world championship (1970), which had Pelé as the greatest world idol.[2]

4.   The period addressed by the vast majority of research[3] that emphasizes or, at least, goes through the trajectory of blacks in Brazilian football goes from the official introduction of football in Brazil (1894) until the mid-1970s, marking: the elitist beginnings and blatant discrimination against blacks and the poor; popularization in the transition from the 1910s to the 1920s; the institutional crisis that this gave rise to; the professionalization of football players in the 1930s; the social ascension and integration of blacks into the big clubs and the Brazilian national team throughout the 1930s and 1940s; participation in the first World Cups; defeat at home in the 1950 World Cup and the resurgence of racism; the inversion of social stigmas with Brazil's victories in world championships and the mythification of Pelé.

5.   To undertake such analyses, scholars basically made use of written sources. The exception was Mario Filho who, even without methodological rigor, also used oral sources, which were reproduced in many of his later investigations.

6.   In the analysis of the presence and performance of blacks in Brazilian football, the vast majority of studies take as reference only the profession of the football player.[4]

In summary, the bibliography evidenced three gaps in historiography: There was no consistent production on the racial issue in Brazilian football at present, in the various sectors of performance in professional football, and the light of oral sources

---

[2] The critical view of Santos (1981, 2005) about racism in football and Brazil influenced me a lot to reflect on the problem.

[3] Two exceptions were the works of Silva and Votre (2006) and Abrahão and Soares (2007). Abrahão, at the time, was developing his doctoral research on Brazilian racism in football.

[4] It is worth mentioning four exceptions: Santos (2005), Corrêa (1985), Vieira (2003), and Damo (2010).

(even less based on the discourses of blacks themselves).[5] After all, what do the subjects of this historical process themselves have to tell us about their current situation in Brazilian football? How do Blacks see racism in Brazil and in our football? What are their lived experiences, remembered memories, and the discourses they construct? Based on that, how can we analyze other areas of action in the universe of football and characterize racism in this sport?

Taking these questions as a guide, I developed my master's research, whose object of study was the blacks in professional Brazilian football between 1970 and 2010. The goal was to propose an overview of the current situation of African descendants in this sport. Inspired by the works of Toledo (2002) and Damo (2007), I formed several networks in order to interview not only players but also coaches, referees, sporting directors, fans, journalists and intellectuals, in an attempt to broaden as much as possible the subjects of this historical process and their discourses. Instead of consulting existing sources (especially written ones), the proposal, however, was to constitute my own source, adopting for that purpose the methodological procedures of oral history, particularly those referring to life stories.[6]

Thus, I recorded unpublished narratives of autobiographical nature, which were more interested in the experiences of the interviewees than in the exact chronology of their life and professional trajectories, let alone in objective data. The narrative freedom facilitated access to subjective aspects, such as values, worldviews, dreams, selections, silences, omissions, distortions, lies. If with the adoption of this genre of oral history, the protagonism and memory of individuals are valued, it is in their collective that I intended to give unity to the set of narrators and recognize common identities. In all, I conducted 20 interviews, 14 with blacks and 6 with whites.[7]

Before presenting some excerpts that specifically address how situations of racial discrimination were experienced, narrated, and thought about by some blacks who played in the universe of Brazilian football, it is worth presenting an overview of the life trajectories of the interviewees. Twelve of the fourteen blacks interviewed had a trajectory very similar to that of the majority of the black population in Brazil, that is, full of setbacks. This translates into large families, poverty, incomplete schooling, work since childhood, absence of a close family member (especially the father figure), characteristics that, taken together, in most cases did not indicate great prospects for life, quite the contrary. Given the clumsy family background, the lack of studies, and the difficulty in breaking with the racist structure prevailing in the Brazilian labor market (Hasenbalg, 2005), football appeared as a better, if not the only, opportunity to integrate and ascend socially.

---

[5] Some exceptions were registered by Maurício Murad (1999) and filed at the Núcleo de Sociologia do Futebol (UERJ).

[6] Without disregarding the contributions of other lines of research, I based myself on the perspective adopted by the Center for Oral History Studies (USP), coordinated by Professor José Carlos Sebe Bom Meihy, whose following works are references: Meihy (2005), Meihy and Holanda (2007), and Meihy and Ribeiro (2011).

[7] Racial classification in Brazil is based both on biological scientism and on phenotypic characteristics and subjective, ideological, and social *status* criteria. About this, see Andrews (1998), D'Adesky (2001), and Schwarcz (2001).

I present below excerpts of some narratives that, more than revealing personal situations of discrimination experienced by the blacks interviewed, help us understand how racism operates in the various areas of performance in professional football, as well as allow us to trace its specificities.

Players' Network

Junior[8]

> I, particularly, did not experience any situation of discrimination, but I saw colleagues... Why does it happen? I think that the problem of blacks in Brazil is a much more social issue than what we see, I don't know, in the United States, for example, right? I mean, the black person is seen in a different way. Here in Brazil, if the black person has a good social situation, a good financial situation, he practically goes unnoticed. There are those people, of course, who say "nigga", speaking in a tone of voice that you feel has a prejudice side! But, as for me... I mean, my paternal grandfather was darker than me, he was a real jambo [mixed race, mulatto]! On my mother's side, it was all white. So... I spent a lot of time with people from the slums. Come on! I have black friends. When you live together for a long time you don't feel it, but when you see it, you do. Especially with other people about black people. When someone says:
>
> - This here is Toninho who plays for Flamengo.
>
> Then things change. While the person doesn't identify... If it was only Toninho, he'd be a black man! But if it's Toninho who plays for Flamengo, then... Do you understand? Here, we have a lot of that... This is less common in today's football, but I think there was a lot more of it in the past. I'm not talking about inside the match because, in the heat of the moment, someone might say something:
>
> - Fuck! You fucking monkey!
>
> That happens... That case of Antônio Carlos: those who know him know that he would never... He did that because he was pissed off with the guy! Instead of calling him:
>
> - Oh, Sergio, fuck you...
>
> He said:
>
> - Monkey!
>
> Do you know? But not that he was prejudiced... I think it is difficult that, within football, there is a guy who has this prejudice because we spent a lot of time together! Unless it comes from the player's blood, or from his family, I don't know... Do you understand? But, inside the match? Day by day? Come on! In the South, there are a lot of black people! In the Northeast, too... It's not that we don't have it [racism]. I've seen it! Well, in the football work environment, I witnessed only this: the guy gets pissed off and gets to talk, but not that it's something to humiliate, to degrade ...

Of the five players interviewed, Junior was the most successful in his professional career, being one of the great idols in the history of C.R. Flamengo, playing in Italian football exactly in the period when it was seen as the best national league in the world, and playing for the Brazilian national team in two World Cups, especially in

---

[8] Leovegildo Lins da Gama Junior, born in 1954. Interview conducted on July 7, 2008, Rio de Janeiro.

1982, whose performance enchanted despite not being victorious. It was not for this reason, however, that I chose an excerpt from his narrative, but rather for the fact that its content raises important points about the network of interviewees in question.

At first, the former defender said he had not experienced "any situation of discrimination", although he had seen teammates go through it.[9] Then, he argued that "the problem of blacks in Brazil is a much more social issue" than a racial one. The academic literature dealing with this issue is abundant on this subject and critical of this type of vision that ignores certain particularities in the social construction of poverty. Instead of coinciding or superimposing, what would be worse, poverty to "skin color" in Brazil, one should investigate the constitutive role of the latter on the former, that is, "other determinations that are not subsumed to the concept of social class" (Guimarães, 2002).

Developing his point of view, Junior compared Brazilian racism with that of the North American, suggesting that in the USA the problem is more serious than in Brazil. It is convenient, therefore, to resume the classic thesis of Nogueira (1985), who distinguishes exactly these two types of "prejudice": one of brand and the other of origin. The first, observed in Brazil, is characterized by being unsystematic and dissimulated, victimizing individuals who physically appear to be black. The second, present in the USA, is systematic and explicit, victimizing any individual whose ancestry is black. In the South American country, the ideology is assimilationist and miscegenationist; in the North American country, it is segregationist and racist.

Some of these characteristics pointed out by Nogueira are perceptible when Junior, among other moments, reported that "in Brazil, if the black person has a good social situation, a good financial situation, he practically goes unnoticed", or when he stated that "When you live together for a long time you don't feel it." His speech corroborates the idea that the economic ascension of the black is followed by social ascension, which in turn leads to whitening, something present in the popular saying "money whitens". The presence, however, of the adverb "practically" allows us to say that somehow, whether rich or poor, the black man will be noticed by his "skin color", which does not let him go "unnoticed". Proof of this is the people who insult African descendants by calling them "nigga", as the former athlete recalls. In his opinion, the long coexistence in the same workspace between whites and blacks makes racial discrimination difficult. Obviously, this does not mean that the former are not prejudiced against the latter. Something that becomes transparent in an observable attitude: "when you see it", according to the former defender's own words.

In order to sustain his thought, Junior used the distinction of the black man in society: "Toninho who plays for Flamengo". This is a crucial point in the debate since it refers to the precise identification of the blacks he is talking about: "Zé Carlos from São Paulo", "Jairo from Caxias", "Badeco from América", "Bizi from Juventus", and in his narrative, "Toninho who plays for Flamengo". Without the

---

[9] It is worth mentioning that, later on, Junior would reveal a personal episode that occurred in the Turin derby, in 1984. The way he narrated this event was fundamental to prepare my doctoral research project (Tonini, 2016).

adjuncts, blacks would just be common people, like so many Zé Carlos, Toninhos, and so on. According to the argument of the former fullback, what is more serious is that, without the mention of the football club, a factor that ensures a person a certain social status, his blackness—implied as a stigma—is placed as a visible characteristic. However, if there is the reference, the black person is socially distinguished and can enjoy white privileges, such as circulating in hotels, restaurants, distinguished clubs, and designer stores, as quoted in several narratives.

If during the career the blackness was unnoticed, the same cannot be said in post-athlete life. On the contrary, from the moment they lost notoriety and a financial condition that maintained a different standard of living, there was a reversal in their trajectories, expressed mainly by the divorce faced by four of the five players interviewed before the white women they had married—in this case, Junior was the exception. Knowing that this type of discourse was repeated in all interviews, we can analyze football as an instrument of concealment of racism in Brazil, in the opposite direction of the social imaginary.

The former defender pointed out that discriminatory acts have decreased over time, but have not ceased. He does not refer, however, to what happens "inside the match", when, in his opinion, racial slurs such as "Fuck! You fucking monkey!" In his view, it is not a matter of "humiliation" or "degradation", it is just a sudden reaction. Therefore, he absolved the former white defender Antônio Carlos (E.C. Juventude) who offended the black former midfielder Jeovânio (Grêmio F.B.P.A.) in Caxias do Sul in 2006 (Gerchmann, 2006, March 6). On that occasion, however, this player not only uttered such an indecorous insult but also, on leaving the field after being expelled, rubbed his fingers on his forearm, in a clear allusion to the opponent's skin color. Because of so many events throughout his career, the interviewees showed to face such insults with certain normality, given the use of the terms "match situation", "normal", "natural", "common", "provocation".

I argue, thus, that black players are discouraged to fight racism in football due to repetition, lack of support, and the "football culture". Throughout their careers, they go through several "small" situations (pranks, racist jokes, and derogatory nicknames) that often lead them not to face explicit or verbalized cases of racial discrimination. To a great extent, even in the face of these episodes, they do not find a voice of support for the denunciation and confrontation, whether by the sporting directors, the coach, the professional[10] colleagues, or even their own football agent, press officer, or family members, who believe that the fight against racism may harm the continuation of the professional career. Appropriating the argument of Schwarcz (2001) about racism in Brazil, "everything seems an invitation to 'leave aside'", due to different allegations of those involved in such an episode; lack of seriousness of the sports, police, and legal authorities in dealing with the issue, even in the face of the flagrant; and application of derisory penalties. Thus, I understand that a "culture"

---

[10] On the contrary, many of them in reference to these situations not only reproduce the discourse that "this is part of football" but also ridicule the black player who publicly reveals and combats such events, either through ironies (calling them "white") or through provocations ("don't say that this nigger is nigger" or "monkey is monkey"), which, as can be seen, entails new discriminatory acts.

has been built in football, specifically in Brazil, in which "everything that happens on the field should stay on the field", as if during that space–time (field-90 min) other social norms were in force, in which discriminatory acts were permitted, tolerated or, at least, should not be taken seriously.

Coaches' Network

Lula Pereira[11]

Even I, who don't participate in any movement, have suffered several times! I had businessmen who said that to me:

- Look, the club president said you're the man, but unfortunately you're black.

It didn't cause me any... remorse or trauma. I even thought it was cool because they were objective and direct. It's worse when they're not! That's our big problem. Nobody has "I like black people" or "I don't like black people" on their foreheads. If we did, we would avoid the annoyance, the embarrassment... It's logical that, inside my heart, we say:

- Well, it wasn't supposed to be like this.

Men should have the opportunities for their competence, regardless of skin color... But what we see in Brazil...

So, we have some problems and I hope that one day this will pass so that we can have blacks, whites, Indians, poor, rich, that is, society, in general, living in peace and with the same opportunities. Because, in a certain way, we live in peace, the white having the best conditions and opportunities. The black people, no...

What I was telling you is true. When I played football, I didn't have so many problems, no... What we have now, when a guy tries to offend, calling blacks a monkey, this or that, it is a problem, but it is not one of the worst... It hurts, it triggers, but there are other, stronger offenses...

One of the things I say is that the black man, when he is subordinate, is well accepted... Even because he works hard to do everything better than the white man and deserves the opportunity... But to get to the command level, it gets tough. Then it's very serious!

[...] Now, there is a fact that is difficult to be diluted: how is it that we, with so many black players, don't have black coaches? In the youth academies, we even have one or two, but not at the professional level... This is a reality. If you do a survey today, in Serie B and Serie A there aren't any black people working! When I say 'black' I mean the same as me or a little bit more. After all, there are a lot of mulattos out there. For example, is Luxemburgo black? He's not black. Is Joel Santana black? He's not black. Is Celso Roth black? He isn't. And Serrão? He's not black either. Black is me, Lula Pereira.

So, I ask you: where's another one? Even to give you a base. Where's another one? We do not have one! We have them in the youth divisions, but not at the professional level. In the A and B Series, we have 40 clubs! And even so, we do not have any black coaches. I could have been working if I had accepted Campinense's offer. And if you go to the C Series, you do not have one either! That's why I talk about the subtle process of elimination. Do we not have in a country so large some three black athletes with the ability to be a coach? Logically, it is not because you played football or because you are black that you have to be a coach. No, you have to be a competent coach. That's why I always tell them and everyone else:

---

[11] Lula Pereira, deceased in 2021 at the age of 64. Interview conducted on July 15, 2009, Fortaleza.

- Brace yourself!

I prepared myself to be a coach! I took several courses!

[...] I like to do this, but I don't see black people as coaches... So, something's wrong, right?!
I'll say it again: nobody wants to touch this... Nobody goes deeper into this issue.

First of all, the lucidity and frankness of Lula Pereira stand out. That is why his report was chosen. Among the five former black players interviewed, he was one of four who took the risk of becoming a coach. The only one who did not challenge the job market, the former goalkeeper Jairo do Nascimento, apparently realized throughout his career, given the absence of blacks in higher positions in the hierarchy of professional football, what was "his place" (Fernandes, 2008): at most, goalkeeping coach. Discouraged to invest in this career and introjecting racism, many in post-athlete life opt to "drop out of football" and start new professional paths.

Except for Junior, who given his extremely successful career only held such a position in big clubs (C.R. Flamengo and S.C. Corinthians P.),[12] the other three,[13] just like the very few black men who enter this profession, started at the bottom, as coaches in youth categories over the years. Two of them reached the professional, even so in times of crisis and in the condition of "interim", i.e., that person who occupies temporarily the function until a professional of confidence of the direction of the clubs is hired. Among other difficulties pointed out, which generally involved the technical (lack of qualified players), financial (shortage of money to hire athletes and investments in the club) and political (pressure, lack of support, and false promises from leaders), racial discrimination, which at some point explicitly manifested itself as a barrier limiting career development, gained prominence.

In the case of Lula Pereira, he revealed that there were businessmen who shamelessly said: "Look, the president of the club said you're the man, but unfortunately you're black." In other words, they recognized that he had the technical qualities to occupy the position, but his ethnic identity was an impediment to doing so. He thus made public the racial discrimination suffered "several times" throughout his career. At first, he said that such talk from businessmen "did not cause me any... remorse or trauma", at least "they were objective and direct", in an attitude that goes against the "cordiality" (Holanda, 1995; Turra and Venturi, 1998) so preached to Brazilians or even to our racism. Shortly after, he acknowledged: "It wasn't supposed to be like that", since anyone "should have the opportunities for their competence, regardless of skin color..."

It is worth mentioning that Lula Pereira prepared himself and invested in this career. He took courses in Brazil and did internships in Europe (Barcelona, Bayern Munich, Ajax, and Milan), which brought him technical, tactical, and physiological knowledge, besides increasing his network of contacts. He developed excellent works in different Brazilian states, winning championships in Santa Catarina, Ceará, Minas Gerais, Distrito Federal, and São Paulo—champion of the interior four times—, besides a title of the Brazilian Championship B Series. It also revealed players of

---

[12] Junior was only in charge of Corinthians for ten days. In this case, despite his triumphant career as a professional athlete, he did not have longevity as a coach.

[13] Namely: Carlos Roberto Bento (Bizi), Jairo do Nascimento, and José Carlos Serrão.

international level, such as Doni, Cicinho, Ricardo Oliveira, Liédson, Felipe Melo and André Dias. Despite this, he had only one opportunity in his career to manage a big club, C. R. Flamengo, in 2002. The "dream", however, was short-lived: "five months and twenty-three days...", he recounted the days, lamenting, in another moment of his narrative.

Next, Lula Pereira argued that social "peace" is guaranteed as long as whites maintain their privileges. That is why he said, in another passage, that the "racial quotas" were causing a "stir" and "dissatisfaction", precisely because they provide blacks "with a way to truly have conditions to study and to be somebody". It was for this reason that the interviewee said he considered a racial insult, such as "calling blacks a monkey", a minor problem in relation to the racist social structure, in which black people are "accepted" only if they maintain their "subordinate" condition. The key point, therefore, is to cross the "color line", to "reach the command level", demonstrating an awareness that is very rare to find in the football universe.

Shortly afterward, Lula Pereira said it was difficult to understand the lack of black coaches in Brazil, given a large number of athletes of African descent. It is notorious that the recruiting base for coaches is formed by former players. Knowing that the vast majority of this group is composed of blacks, Lula's questioning makes even more sense. To back up his argument, he compared the amateur and professional categories, suggesting that the few black coaches in the youth ranks are unable to rise to the top of the match. Hence the phrase that gives this chapter its title: "This is a reality".

Indignant at the absence of black coaches in Brazilian football, even shouting during this passage, he demonstrated his belief in the existence of a "subtle process of elimination of the black race". In the end, Lula ironically used the stigma of the supposed incapacity of blacks to question the lack of opportunities for black players who aim to start a coaching career in Brazilian football. The discourse of competence *versus* opportunity is used by many intellectuals to overthrow the myth of racial democracy and to expose discrimination in the Brazilian labor market (Hasenbalg, 2005).

Thus, we get to the edges of racism in Brazilian football, not allowing denying its reality. Considering our slave-owning past, Damo (2010, p. 168, our translation) was, in my opinion, precise when trying to answer this question:

> The position of coach is considered to be held by those naturally inclined to boss others around, which is why blacks are excluded from competing for the job. From the perspective of the *status quo*, obedience is theirs, and that does not match the demands on a coach, a man who makes himself respected by other men.

These are, then, the symbolic parameters that continue to distance Afro-Brazilians from positions of command, while at the same time condemning them to subordinate position, to activities that demand few intellectual skills. In agreement with this analysis, Vieira (2003) warns that the function of a football coach is associated with characteristics such as leadership, tactical insight, power of abstraction, and intellectual capacity. Counting on his fingers the number of Afro-Brazilians who have had such an opportunity in this market, he concludes that "in Brazilian football, Afro-Brazilians are more suited for a tough defender than for a strategist coach".

Referees' Network

Luiz Flavio de Oliveira[14]

This is quite common in amateur football. In professional football, it's more difficult. Could it have happened? Of course, but not that I've noticed. It even happened to me, but I prefer not to name the club or the place. It happened at the same time as the problem with Grafite. There was one isolated incident during the match: a penalty was taken and then a chorus of fans calling me a monkey. They thought that was better than calling me a 'thief referee'. The players came over and asked them to stop, the opposing team wanted me to suspend the match and the assistants also asked me if I would take any action after the match. But I said I would not let myself get down or get on that fad. After all, everything in football is a fad. If something happens here, it starts everywhere else. Sometimes they even take advantage of it to try and show off...

I didn't want to create more controversy. Even more so because the media was all over the issue! So much so that I gave an interview before the match about racism and then a situation like this arose during the match... I didn't file a police report for the same reason. It could even hurt my career, as there would be many interviews and I'd be in the spotlight, right? Was I hurt at first? Yes, but whatever happened, happened. I didn't worry that much. There are so many more important things to worry about in the 90 minutes. I can't let myself get carried away with a comment that comes mainly from fans, not least because I know that we stir up more emotion than their own reason...

I just put in the summary that the behavior of the crowd had been irregular. I'm not sure, but I think the Federation [São Paulo State Football Federation] punished the team with a fine and a stadium ban, making them play in another stadium and without fans. But I am sure that if I took sides and made an occurrence, the Federation would support me in relation to this and the club could even be punished in another way. I filed a report, it was over and that was that.

In the eyes of others, it may look like an omission, but it was not. I just didn't want to continue with the situation that was quickly resolved. If I had gone into detail, it would have inflamed it even more. I'm kind of used to hearing it indirectly. So I didn't let that direct comment get in the way of my concentration during the match. It just slipped by. I'd rather be well-liked as a referee than appear that way, which would be negative for me. That's not my interest in refereeing.

It was not easy to find and interview black referees. At first, I sought to record the accounts of two brothers, Luiz Flávio and Paulo César de Oliveira, who had been active at the time, since the second half of the 1990s. Later on, I contacted another former referee from São Paulo, João Paulo Araújo, who worked from 1980 to 1997. The three of them started working in amateur football as a way of increasing the family income since they all had other activities and the livelihood of their families, of humble origins, depended on them. Throughout their careers, they were members of

---

[14] Luiz Flávio de Oliveira, born in 1977. Interviews carried out on October 9, 2008, and November 13, 2008, São Paulo.

the São Paulo State Football Federation (FPF), the Brazilian Football Confederation (CBF), and the International Football Federation (FIFA).

The non-recognition of Brazilian arbitration as a profession was an issue mentioned spontaneously by all three interviewees. All argued that the lack of professionalization obstructs the improvement in the quality of national arbitration. According to João Paulo, in his time, to referee it was necessary to have a signed contract, which prevented many, especially blacks, from pursuing this activity, including the need to travel all the time. How could they keep their jobs in their hometowns? As a result, he was not surprised by the low number of blacks in national arbitration. The two brothers, in turn, expressed different opinions. Paulo César revealed too much pride and blamed the blacks themselves for their social situation and the lack of opportunities, in almost total assimilation of the "white ideology", as Ianni (2004) theorized. Luiz Flávio, on the other hand, when reflecting on this, noted the low presence of blacks in the FPF, not remembering any other referee besides himself and his brother at that time, and in CBF, where he estimated a maximum of 20% of black referees, far below, as he himself said, the percentage of blacks in the Brazilian population.

Regarding racial discrimination, all three revealed having suffered it. João Paulo, exactly because he no longer exercises such activity and does not maintain any relationship with football entities, told in detail certain situations that he experienced and made heavy criticism of the FPF. He said there is politicking and relationships between referees and sporting directors, which, according to him, undermines the fairness in the exercise of this activity. This would be one of the reasons that would have prevented him from refereeing even a single final of the State Championship, although always maintained a high level of performance. Another reason, according to him, was racial: "Any mistake I made was bigger than the others, right? Because I am black, no doubt about it..." He said he had been supported in the international arena by the refereeing director of CBF, not by the support of the São Paulo state officials. Worse than that, he suffered discrimination by his own colleagues, by "people who were going to flag the match for us!" White "judges", in his words, blatantly alluded to the "black race" through the characteristic gesture of rubbing their hands on their arms to subdue and ridicule them in public and in front of other referees, a fact that directly interfered with working relationships and their performance on the field.

Paulo César, in turn, preferred not to give details of personal cases, minimizing the insults uttered by fans. His brother, on the other hand, said racism is "quite common in amateur football", being "more difficult" in professional football. After a moment of hesitation, he revealed having been a victim of racism some 15 days after the "Grafite-Desábato case" (Tonini, 2012): "There was an isolated event during the match: a penalty kick and then a chorus of fans calling me 'monkey'." Instead of calling him a "thief judge", they decided to racially insult him, through animalization, removing his human condition. When pressured to take some action, both by the opposing players and by the assistant referees, he said that he would not "let himself be discouraged or get on that fad", implying that the cause of the offense was more a matter of "fad" than a reproduction of the racist reality of Brazilian society. In the sequence, it became evident the real reason for not registering the case in the police: "It could even harm my career." Although he was "hurt" by the fact, he ignored his own feelings: "whatever happened, happened." For him, fighting for his rights would "create more controversy". Thus, he looked for arguments that would comfort his choice, such as saying that "there are so many more important things for us to worry about during the 90 min…", or not being able to "get carried away by a comment that comes mainly from fans", or hinder his "concentration during the match".

In the following sentence, there is an indication that perhaps he himself found his attitude insufficient: "I *only* put in the summary sheet that the behavior of the fans had been *irregular*", instead of using the word *racist*. He also showed some indifference to the exact punishment defined by the FPF. Apparently, he deceived himself when he said that he was "sure" that the Federation would support him if he "took sides and made an occurrence". In a free narrative, he himself expressed that his decision could "even seem like omission", although he denied it. It is understood that his "interest in refereeing" is "to be well seen refereeing", not "appearing in this way, which, for me, would be negative." In my analysis, his account offers several signs that the FPF imposes a standard of behavior on referees, persuading them, putting psychological pressure on them, weakening their personality, and making them renounce their convictions.

Sporting Directors' Network

Sergio Grillo[15]

> Colored people must seek their space! When his time as an athlete is over, he has to prepare himself to live in society, whether as a fitness coach, as a head coach, or as an executive in the world of football. For that, you have to leave your girlfriend, the soap opera, the game, the canasta or the bingo with friends. Go to school and get ready. You have to train yourself! Because it is not enough, because he is colored, to ask for an opportunity. Otherwise, no one will give you an opportunity, whether you are white or dark-skinned…
>
> We live in times of competence in everything, including football, which is now managed, thank God, by concepts of business management. This is a great idea in my view because, if not, the clubs will disappear… What will remain will be those who practice these concepts…
>
> […] I think the job market in football has not expanded more strongly for colored people because they have not sought their space. Dark-skinned people go strongly to the athlete. And after that? How many dark-colored head coaches do we have? How many fitness coaches? Do you understand?
>
> In management positions, there's no need to talk about it. Not because one doesn't want to, but it is necessary to look at the family origins of these people, the type of education and training they received. Usually, they are humble families that do not have a structure. This is the truth.
>
> I tell you that, in the private sector, although there are one or two examples of colored people occupying positions in the intermediary structures of companies, the situation is much stronger than in football. Why is that? So, I blame dark-skinned people for omission

---

[15] Sérgio Grillo, 76 years old. Interview conducted on September 16, 2009, Caxias do Sul.

and for not looking their space than the entities for receiving them and allowing them to occupy those positions. I say this to you with absolute conviction! If we consult ten people, certainly seven or eight will have the same opinion... We have to try to improve on this. When I say "we have", I mean the colored people and the entities.

How to insert them? It is not enough that they want to. They have to seek training. For me to give or not space in my company to a colored person, I will see his competence. It is not enough to be a friend of the president of the club or a friend of the football assessor. He can be a friend, but he has to be, first of all, competent. After all, we live in times of competence!

According to the structure of football, political power, strategic because of the social status that it confers and because it controls the finances of clubs and federations, is the most closely watched, remaining always in the hands of the white elite. One of the mechanisms, if not the most effective one, to ensure this control is the maintenance of managerial positions without remuneration, preventing the participation of the popular layers, who depend on the income derived from their jobs. It is not without reason that football's managerial class is generally formed by businessmen, politicians, and liberal professionals, whose performance comes from generation to generation. One may state, therefore, that there is a social and racial criterion in the recruitment base of sporting directors in Brazil.

Three of them were interviewed, all white: Sérgio Grillo (E.C. Juventude), Luiz Onofre Meira (Grêmio F.B.P.A.), and Benecy Queiroz (Cruzeiro E.C.). The trio fits the described characteristics: They all come from wealthy families, have completed their studies up to university level, own businesses outside football, became partners and board members of the aforementioned clubs in the 1970s and 1980s, and have acted as sporting directors for several years since then, fully dedicating themselves to such activity, without any remuneration. The excerpt chosen is in the narrative of Sérgio Grillo, whose reason is obvious. He was indicated to me by the club itself, after requesting an interview with any of the directors of this Brazilian club, which is one of the most involved in cases of racism in football.[16]

In his speech, Sérgio Grillo, then administrative and financial vice-president, transported his business/capitalist vision to football, seeing the player as a "product" and the club as a "factory". He proved to be not only a reproducer but also a defender of the meritocracy discourse: "To give or not space in my company to a colored person, I will check his competence." He projected onto the blacks themselves the responsibility for the fact that they do not have many opportunities—not only in football but in life as a whole—due to their socioeconomic situation and for suffering racism. In his view, they themselves are to blame for their fate. This "color complex", to use the terms of Santos (2005), is a recurring argument in the racist ideology of Brazilian society.

Grillo's speech is so loaded with prejudices that almost none of his sentences is free of stigmas imputed to blacks. From both the interdicts and the unspoken, we can affirm without fear of error that he sees black people as uncivilized ("has

---

[16] Cases of racism reported by the press: Tinga (Internacional), fans of Juventude, Caxias do Sul-RS, October 22, 2005; Jeovânio (Grêmio), Antônio Carlos (Juventude), Caxias do Sul-RS, March 5, 2006; Júlio César (Juventude), fans of Juventude, Caxias do Sul-RS, August 5, 2007; Felipe (Corinthians), fans of Juventude, Caxias do Sul-RS, November 12, 2008.

to prepare to live together later in society"), addicted ("has to leave [...] the game, the canasta or the bingo with friends"), flirtatious ("has to leave the girlfriend"), tramp/lazy ("has to leave [...] the soap opera"), incapable ("one has to train oneself!"), profiteer/opportunist ("it is not enough, for being colored, to ask for an opportunity"), incompetent ("we live in times of competence in everything, including football"), negligent ("they did not look for their space"), without schooling ("go to school and prepare yourself"), and without family education ("it is necessary to look at the family origins of these people, the type of education, and training they received"). I confess that it was shocking to hear and be in front of someone who had no shame in verbalizing such prejudices.

If that wasn't enough, the sporting director also gave the message that the black man has the ability to use his body for physical activities, but not to think: "dark-skinned people go strongly to the athlete and after that? How many dark-colored coaches do we have? How many physical trainers?" he inquired, trying to seduce me with his speech. It is also irrefutable to the use of a vocabulary that is not only conservative but racist and retrograde: "niggers", "colored people", "dark-skinned people", and so on.

Journalists' Network

Valmir Jorge[17]

In my case, as I was a reporter, there was only me. Then the guys:

- Man, that cheeky nigga! He arrived yesterday and already... You gotta talk like that! It's the Bandeirantes standard.

But I used to do it the other way. And the guys started to get mad at me...

Getting back, one of those three confusions was like this: once, they were playing São Paulo and Palmeiras, and Roni Silva, who is also from Campinas, was the Bandeirantes operator at the time. We started arguing about the equipment. He was pulling a wire and I said:

- If you pull that wire, I'm gonna punch you right here in the middle of everybody.

- Ahhh... - he debauched - Are you going to do that? I doubt it!

I mean, the guy didn't believe I was going to pick a fight inside the São Paulo match, behind Zetti's goal. Then, the guy pulled it and I hit him in the face... By the way, Paulo Pinto, who is a very famous reporter, a tiny little guy, who was at *Diario de Sao Paulo at* the time, took a sequence of photos. Me and Roni Silva rolled on the floor, we ended up at the police, it was shit!

There's a book that some guys did, *My Unforgettable Match*, and they got testimonials from a lot of people. And there's one of mine in it, which is exactly this one. So, Fiori Gigliotti was narrating like this:

- Forty-five minutes. Jesus Christ! Brazilian fans, there's something strange behind Zetti's goal. The match is stopped. Valmir Jorge, the reporter from RB 840, tells us what's happening! Shhh... Cassio Ricardo, the other reporter. Nothing gets away from Bandeirantes, people!

---

[17] Valmir Jorge, born in 1961. Interview conducted on September 12, 2009, Londrina.

Shhh... It's not possible! Azevedo Marques, the loose reporter from Bandeirantes, what's going on, Azevedo? Shhh...

Then, Dalmo Pessoa:

- Yes, Fiori, it seems that there is some trouble there and our colleagues are helping to separate it. There's a fight there, Fiori!

It was Valmir Jorge and Roni Silva rolling on the ground, fighting, and Azevedo trying to separate us... The ball went through the goal line, and Zetti:

- Guys, stop, stop, stop!

It was shit, man. I was dismissed. The next day, João Zanforlin, a great lawyer, went there and defended me to the company's management. He explained the reason for the fight, right?! Then, the guys saw that there was racism and a lot of things in the conflict. Zanforlin defended me:

- Look, Samir, the kid came from the countryside, humble, he's growing up and the guys keep calling him a "nigger", a "monkey"... Then he lost his mind.

- All right.

Well, they gave me a week to cool off. I went to the beach, came back, and continued, among other troubles that I arranged.

[...] Well, then, they started to call me Pretão (the big black one)... All right. But when they called me:

- Oh, nigger...

- Nigger, no! There's a lot of niggers out there. Pretão! There's only me. I'm the only one.

Because the black man gets fucked up a lot! The story of the nigga on the radio is fucked up, man!... Nowadays, it's opened up a lot more. In the old days, I either fought back or I was left behind... Today I am registered as a journalist since the Ministry of Labor accepted for length of service after they checked my contribution to our union. After all, I only went to the fifth grade. I did not go to college, I did not graduate in journalism...

I interviewed four journalists: two white (Juca Kfouri and Celso Unzelte) and two black (Valmir Jorge and Abel Neto). Those were among my first interviewees and helped me a lot with their knowledge and precious indications of names. These were difficult to contact, but there lived and narrated experiences contributed a lot to the research. Of the four, I chose a passage from the narrative of Valmir Jorge, in which he reveals having been discriminated against more than once in his place of work.

Valmir, the only one of humble origin, became a radio broadcaster not only because he always liked music, "especially English music", but also because he was "Taurus" and thus "very stubborn and headstrong". Working as a bricklayer's helper with his older brother, on November 30, 1980, while correcting the pronunciation of English band names for the umpteenth time, his sister challenged him to be a radio broadcaster. He learned the language by self-taught, listening, and saving music lyrics. That same day, he went to ask for a job at Radio Nova Dracena and got a position as a copywriter, even without knowing how to type. According to him, "in about four or six months, I was already running a program from 2 to 5 p.m., which was the best time for us." This way, he was gaining positions in the radio until, in 1984, he was invited to be on duty on Sundays during Dracena F.C. matches, when he started working with sports.

A few years later he went to work at Rádio Bandeirantes. He said he was involved in three conflicts because he was called a "nigger". Being black and from the countryside, he was discriminated against by some of his colleagues: "Man, this cheeky nigger! He arrived yesterday and already... You gotta talk like that! It's the Bandeirantes standard." Once, during a match between São Paulo and Palmeiras, at Morumbi Stadium, he and a radio operator disagreed "because of some equipment". The latter didn't believe that Valmir Jorge could "pick a fight in the middle of São Paulo's match, behind Zetti's goal", and so they got into a fight. The episode was photographed, published in *Diário de São Paulo* newspaper the next day, and was even told in a book.

With his beautiful voice and jocular manner, Valmir Jorge imitated Fiori Gigliotti narrating the dispute. Result: The case was registered at the police station and he was dismissed. The next day, a renowned lawyer defended him to the company's management, explaining the racist content: "Look, Samir, the kid came from the countryside, humble, he is growing up and the guys keep calling him a 'nigger', a 'cheeky monkey'... Then he lost his head." He was rehired.

The broadcaster also reported that several times he argued with colleagues because of his supposedly "unique" nickname: Pretão. Then, he said with regret: "Because the black man gets fucked up a lot! The story of the nigga on the radio is fucked up, man!" Although in another excerpt he couldn't remember more than three black colleagues, he said that "nowadays, it has opened up a lot more", justifying his violent reaction: "In the old days, I either fought back or stayed behind..." At the end, he revealed that he had not "graduated in journalism..." even though the Ministry of Labor had accepted his "length of service". This is a story of struggle, resistance, and victory. A very rare exception in a racist job market.

Final Considerations

While the phrase "This is a reality" concerning the racism in Brazilian football may seem obvious today, approximately ten years ago such a statement carried a different weight. To affirm such a phenomenon in the most popular sport in Brazil meant, on the one hand, reversing a whole imaginary built about blacks in football and, on the other, giving up one's own career. Indeed, wouldn't that still be the case today? It is not without reason that in 2005, when the "Grafite-Desábato case"[18] occurred, there was an outcry in the press about the way that episode happened. Not a few

---

[18] On April 13, 2005, São Paulo F.C. played the second match against Quilmes, from Argentina, in the first phase of Copa Libertadores da América, at Morumbi Stadium. After a ball dispute at the end of the first half, Brazilian striker Grafite (Edinaldo Batista Libânio) and Argentinean defender Leandro Desábato got into an argument that led to the expulsion of the Brazilian athlete and another Argentinean player. During the intermission of the match, the game was rebroadcast several times by Rede Globo; apparently one could read lips indicating a racial slur by Desábato. Some authorities sought Grafite to know what had happened, still during the match. At the end of the match, a police officer entered the field and arrested Desábato on charges of racially aggravated harassment. The case gained international repercussions and generated anger, especially among Argentinean players and the press. See Abrahão and Soares (2007) and Tonini (2012).

columnists claimed that "it was part of football practice" (Tonini, 2012). Recently, the coach Cristóvão Borges (Cristóvão… 2015, August 10), for example, by timidly raising this flag, fell into ostracism.

The narratives recorded throughout the research allow for some findings followed by conclusions:

1. Discriminatory acts were reported in all sectors;
2. Two attitudes toward racism in football were noted, one of denunciation, on the part of most of the blacks interviewed from the most varied areas of activity, another of dissimulation, present in particular in the speeches of white sporting directors;
3. Blackness posed as a barrier to professional advancement, especially for coaches;
4. The universe of professional football, therefore, also reproduces the racist structure existing in the Brazilian labor market, which manifests itself mainly as one moves up the hierarchy;
5. The possibility for blacks, therefore, only occurs in an individual and not collective terms, whose rare exceptions only confirm the rule;
6. The analysis of football as a "soft" or "light" area[19] (Helal & Gordon Júnior, 1999) of race relations in Brazil finally proves to be wrong, since such an assumption is anchored only on the presence of numerous black football players (as if quantity meant the absence of racism), disregarding other areas of action, as well as the discriminatory practices existing within each of them.

By including speeches not contemplated by historiography, this research revealed memories and experiences of blacks in football, both aiming that their history in this sport was told by the group itself and raising the development of new investigations, which can deepen the discussions elaborated in each of the interviewees' networks.

References

Abrahão, B. O. L., & Soares, A. J. (2007). Uma análise sobre o caso "Grafite x Desábato" à luz do "racismo à brasileira". *Esporte e Sociedade*, 2(5), 1–17. https://periodicos.uff.br/esportesocie dade/article/view/48017

Andrews, G. R. (1998). *Negros e brancos em São Paulo (1888-1988)*. Edusc.

Corrêa, L. H. (1985). Racismo no futebol brasileiro. In G. K. Dieguez (Ed.), *Esporte e poder*. Vozes.

Cristóvão Borges revela racismo em crítica ao seu trabalho no Fla (2015, August 10). *O Estado de S. Paulo*. https://esportes.estadao.com.br/noticias/futebol,cristovao-borges-revela-rac ismo-em-criticas-ao-seu-trabalho,1741603

---

[19] The "soft" or "light" areas, generally linked to leisure and religious practice, are those spaces in which being black is no obstacle and where blacks and non-blacks coexist in a climate relatively free of racial tensions. On certain occasions, even being Afro-descendant can bring prestige, as, for example, in candomblé, in capoeira, and in Afro blocks. Even for this reason, these spaces are often labelled as "black culture". The "hard" or "heavy" areas, on the other hand, would be those of work, particularly the search for a job, marriage and dating, and interactions with the police. See, in this sense, the research of Sansone (2007).

D'Adesky, J. (2001). *Pluralismo étnico e multiculturalismo*. Pallas.

Damo, A. S. (2007). *Do dom à profissão: Formação de futebolistas no Brasil e na França*. Hucitec/Anpocs.

Damo, A. S. (2010). Os racismos no esporte. In A. C. S. Mandarino & E. Gomberg (Eds.), *Racismos: Olhares plurais* (pp. 155–178). Edufba.

Fernandes, F. (2008). *A integração do negro na sociedade de classes* (Vol. 2). Globo.

Filho, M. (2003). *O negro no futebol brasileiro* (4th ed.). Mauad.

Freyre, G. (2003). Prefácio à 1ª edição. In M. Filho, *O negro no futebol brasileiro* (4th ed., pp. 24–26). Mauad.

Gerchmann, L. (2006, March 6) Ex-zagueiro da seleção é acusado de ato racista. *Folha de S. Paulo*, p. D5. https://www1.folha.uol.com.br/esporte/2021/05/ex-goleiro-alemao-jens-lehmann-e-demitido-do-hertha-por-mensagem-racista.shtml

Gordon Júnior, C. (1996). "Eu já fui preto e sei o que é isso": História social dos negros no futebol brasileiro. *Pesquisa de Campo*, (3–4), 65–78. https://ludopedio.org.br/biblioteca/eu-ja-fui-preto-e-sei-o-que-e-isso-historia-social-dos-negros-no-futebol-brasileiro-segundo-tempo/

Guimarães, A. S. A. (2002). *Classes, raças e democracia*. Editora 34.

Hasenbalg, C. (2005). *Discriminação e desigualdades raciais no Brasil* (2nd ed.). Editora da UFMG/IUPERJ.

Helal, R., & Gordon Júnior, C. (1999). Sociologia, história e romance na construção da identidade nacional através do futebol. *Estudos Históricos*, *13*(23), 147–165. http://bibliotecadigital.fgv.br/ojs/index.php/reh/article/view/2092

Holanda, S. B. (1995). *Raízes do Brasil* (26th ed.). Companhia das Letras. (Original work published 1936).

Ianni, O. (2004). *Raças e classes sociais no Brasil* (3rd ed.). Brasiliense.

Levine, R. (1982). Esporte e sociedade: O caso do futebol brasileiro. In J. C. S. Meihy, & J. S. Witter (Orgs.), *Futebol e cultura: Coletânea de estudos* (pp. 21–44). Imesp/Daesp.

Lopes, J. S. L., et al. (2004). Classe, etnicidade e cor na formação do futebol brasileiro. In C. H. M. Batalha (Ed.), *Culturas de classe* (pp. 121–166). Editora da Unicamp.

Lyra Filho, J. (1973). *Introdução à sociologia dos desportos*. Bloch/INL.

Meihy, J. C. S. B. (2005). *Manual de história oral* (5th ed.). Loyola.

Meihy, J. C. S. B., & Holanda, F. (2007). *História oral: Como fazer, como pensar*. Contexto.

Meihy, J. C. S. B., & Ribeiro, S. L. S. (2011). *Guia prático de história oral: Para empresas, universidades, comunidades, famílias*. Contexto.

Murad, M. (1996). *Dos pés à cabeça: Elementos básicos de sociologia do futebol*. Irradiação Cultural.

Murad, M. (1999). Considerações possíveis de uma resposta necessária. *Estudos Históricos*, *13*(24), 431–446. https://bibliotecadigital.fgv.br/ojs/index.php/reh/article/view/2094

Nogueira, O. (1985). *Tanto preto quanto branco: Estudos de relações raciais*. T. A. Queiroz.

Rego, J. L. (1943). Biografia de uma vitória. In M. Filho, *Copa do Rio Branco, 32* (pp. 7–8). Irmãos Pongetti.

Rosenfeld, A. (1993). *Negro, macumba e futebol*. Perspectiva.

Sansone, L. (2007). *Negritude sem etnicidade: O local e o global nas relações raciais e na produção cultural negra do Brasil*. Edufba/Pallas.

Santos, J. R. (1981). *História política do futebol brasileiro*. Brasiliense.

Santos, J. R. (2005). *O que é racismo* (15th ed.). Brasiliense.

Schwarcz, L. M. (2001). *Racismo no Brasil*. PubliFolha.

Silva, C. A. F.; & Votre, S. J. (2006). *Racismo no futebol*. HP Comunicação.

Souza, M. A. (1996). Gênero e raça: a nação construída pelo futebol brasileiro. *Cadernos Pagu*, (6–7), 109–152. https://periodicos.sbu.unicamp.br/ojs/index.php/cadpagu/article/view/1864

Toledo, L. H. (2001). Futebol e teoria social: Aspectos da produção científica brasileira (1982–2002). *Boletim Informativo e Bibliográfico de Ciências Sociais*, (52), 133–165. https://ludopedio.org.br/biblioteca/futebol-e-teoria-social-aspectos-da-producao-cientifica-brasileira-1982-2002/

Toledo, L. H. (2002). *Lógicas no futebol*. Hucitec/Fapesp.

Tonini, M. D. (2010). *Além dos gramados: História oral de vida de negros no futebol brasileiro (1970-2010)*. (Master's Dissertation in Social History), USP, São Paulo, Brazil. https://www.teses.usp.br/teses/disponiveis/8/8138/tde-06062011-173422/pt-br.php

Tonini, M. D. (2012). Racismo no futebol brasileiro: Revisitando o caso Grafite/Desábato. *Revista De História Regional, 17*(2), 438–468. https://doi.org/10.5212/Rev.Hist.Reg.vol17i2.0004

Tonini, M. D. (2016). *Dentro e fora de outros gramados: Histórias orais de vida de futebolistas brasileiros negros no continente europeu*. (Doctoral Thesis in Social History), USP, São Paulo, Brazil. https://www.teses.usp.br/teses/disponiveis/8/8138/tde-13102016-152144/pt-br.php

Turra, C., & Venturi, G. (Orgs.) (1998). *Racismo cordial* (2nd ed.). Ática.

Vieira, J. J. (2003). Considerações sobre preconceito e discriminação racial no futebol brasileiro. *Teoria e Pesquisa*, (42–43), 221–244. http://www.teoriaepesquisa.ufscar.br/index.php/tp/article/viewFile/62/52

Vogel, A. (1982). O momento feliz. In R. Damatta (Org.), *Universo do futebol*. Pinakotheke.

Wisnik, J. M. (2008). *Veneno remédio*. Companhia das Letras.

Index

A

Anthropology, 205, 206, 208, 210, 212, 215–218, 220, 222, 223, 227–235, 238–240, 246, 282–284
Anthropology of sports, 52

B

Biography, 419
Blacks, 507–515, 517, 519, 522, 523
Brand, 149–151, 153–156, 158, 159, 161, 162, 166, 167, 169
Brazil, 1–8, 133–138, 141–145, 173–177, 179–181, 183–189, 205–209, 211, 213–223, 413–415, 417, 418, 420–424, 426, 507–515, 519, 522, 523
Brazilian football, 50, 52, 54, 55, 57, 58, 60, 61, 100, 335–337, 346, 350–352, 357, 363, 365, 367, 374, 376, 386–388, 390, 429, 507–509, 515, 516, 522
Brazilian national team, 76
Brazilian political history, 127
Brazilian press, 293, 295, 297, 300, 303
Brazilian stadiums, 309, 310, 313
Brazilian urbanization, 309, 318
BRICS, 193–195, 197, 198, 200–202

C

Career, 415–421
Cheering experience, 472
Communication, 281–288
Culture, 205, 216, 217, 223

D

DaMatta, Roberto, 133–146
Democracy, 443, 444, 450–453
Dictatorship, 65, 67, 74, 80, 83

E

Ethnography, 231, 232, 239, 240, 284, 285
Exclusion, 458, 462, 463, 466–468

F

Fair play, 373, 374, 388, 389, 391
Fan-consumer, 321, 322, 328
Fans, 446–450
FIFA, 193–195, 197–202
Football, 1–8, 13, 14, 16–28, 66–72, 74–83, 133–146, 149–153, 156–158, 160, 161, 165–169, 205–223, 227–240, 264–266, 268–270, 275, 281–288, 291–304, 307–319, 443–448, 450–453, 457–468, 490, 491, 495–499, 501–503
Football business, 340, 345, 350
Football clubs, 475
Football historiography, 85–91, 93–95
Football industry, 335, 337, 341, 343, 345, 346, 355, 361, 363, 365–368

G

Garrincha, 102–109, 245–247, 256–258
Gender, 403, 407, 429–433, 436–440

H

Historical research, 85–93, 95

Historical sources, 87
History, 27, 28

I
Identity, 206, 210–213, 220
Idol, 423, 426
Individual action, 266

L
Legacy, 263, 264, 277
Leonidas da Silva, 99–102
LGBTIQ sports, 434, 435
Life projects, 397, 398, 401, 406, 412

M
Maradona, 243, 245–247, 252–256
Media, 291, 293, 294, 297–300, 303, 304
Mega-sports events, 194–196, 199
Memory, 80
Methodology of history, 85, 91
Military dictatorship, 31, 32, 37, 38, 40, 41,
    43, 44
Military regime, 50
Modernity, 135, 142–144

N
National identity, 98, 99, 102, 109, 110
Neoliberalism, 166
Neymar, 149, 151, 159–163, 165–169
1950 World cup, 309, 314–316, 318, 319

O
Olympic football, 32, 33, 39, 40, 43, 45
Oral history, 507, 509
Organized supporters, 465–467

P
Pelé, 102–109, 243, 245–247, 250–253, 255
Politics, 13–16, 18–20, 22, 27, 28, 36–39, 45
Popular football, 326
Popular myths, 99, 104, 106, 108, 109

Power, 14–16, 18, 19, 21, 27, 28

R
Race relations, 507, 523
Racial hierarchies, 489, 498, 500
Racism, 507–512, 514–517, 519, 521–523
Racism in Brazil, 490, 491, 495, 499, 500,
    502
Research methodology, 239

S
Sacred, 243, 245, 248–251, 253, 255, 257–
    259
Selective modernization, 174
Sexual identities, 431
Soccer, 184
Social control, 465
Social sciences, 2–4, 8
Soft power, 193–197, 199, 201
Sports, 228–239, 291–304
Sports geography, 321, 332
Sports media, 282, 285, 288
Sports press, 114, 120, 121, 126
Stadiums, 471–485
Stadiums and arenas, 321, 324, 328, 331, 332
Stadiums and cities, 321, 332
State, 14–16, 19–22, 25, 28
Stigma, 465–468

T
Tradium, 322, 324, 328, 330

V
Video Assistant Referee (VAR), 373, 376,
    379, 388
Violence, 457–468

W
Women's football, 397, 399, 401, 402, 404,
    405, 407, 409, 411
World cup, 65–67, 69–78, 80–83, 263, 264,
    267–277

CPSIA information can be obtained
at www.ICGtesting.com
Printed in the USA
LVHW081640091122
732673LV00005B/210